GREAT BOOKS OF THE WESTERN WORLD

28. GILBERT
    GALILEO
    HARVEY

29. CERVANTES

30. FRANCIS BACON

31. DESCARTES
    SPINOZA

32. MILTON

33. PASCAL

34. NEWTON
    HUYGENS

35. LOCKE
    BERKELEY
    HUME

36. SWIFT
    STERNE

37. FIELDING

38. MONTESQUIEU
    ROUSSEAU

39. ADAM SMITH

40. GIBBON I

41. GIBBON II

42. KANT

43. AMERICAN STATE
    PAPERS
    THE FEDERALIST
    J. S. MILL

44. BOSWELL

45. LAVOISIER
    FOURIER
    FARADAY

46. HEGEL

47. GOETHE

48. MELVILLE

49. DARWIN

50. MARX
    ENGELS

51. TOLSTOY

52. DOSTOEVSKY

53. WILLIAM JAMES

54. FREUD

GREAT BOOKS
OF THE WESTERN WORLD

ROBERT MAYNARD HUTCHINS, *EDITOR IN CHIEF*

12.

LUCRETIUS

EPICTETUS

MARCUS AURELIUS

LUCRETIUS:
ON THE NATURE OF THINGS
Translated by H. A. J. Munro

THE DISCOURSES OF EPICTETUS
Translated by George Long

THE MEDITATIONS
OF MARCUS AURELIUS
Translated by George Long

William Benton, *Publisher*

ENCYCLOPÆDIA BRITANNICA, INC.

CHICAGO · LONDON · TORONTO

THE UNIVERSITY OF CHICAGO

The Great Books
is published with the editorial advice of the faculties
of The University of Chicago

GENERAL CONTENTS

Lucretius: On the Nature of Things, Page 1
Translated by H. A. J. MUNRO

The Discourses of Epictetus, Page 105
Translated by GEORGE LONG

The Meditations of Marcus Aurelius, Page 253
Translated by GEORGE LONG

LUCRETIUS
ON THE NATURE OF THINGS

BIOGRAPHICAL NOTE

LUCRETIUS, c.98–c.55 B.C.

TITUS LUCRETIUS CARUS was born somewhere between 99 and 95 B.C., probably at Rome. The Lucretian *gens* to which he belonged was one of the oldest of the great Roman houses, and it is likely that he was a member of either a senatorial or an equestrian family. In his poem he speaks to the aristocratic Gaius Memmius, to whom he dedicated his work, as to an equal.

Nothing is known of the poet's education except what might be inferred from the presence in Rome during his youth of eminent Greek teachers of the Epicurean sect who lived on terms of intimacy with members of the governing class. Lucretius' reading is evident from his poem. In addition to the works of his master, Epicurus, he shows knowledge of the philosophical poem of Empedocles and at least an acquaintance with the works of Democritus, Anaxagoras, Heraclitus, Plato, and the Stoics. Of the other Greek prose writers he knew Thucydides and Hippocrates. Among the poets he expresses highest admiration for Homer, frequently reproduces Euripides, and shows a close study of Ennius.

The only account of Lucretius' life is a short note by St. Jerome written more than four centuries after the poet's death. St. Jerome in his *Chronicle* under the year 94 B.C. has the entry: "Titus Lucretius the poet is born. He was rendered insane by a love-philtre and, after writing during intervals of lucidity, some books, which Cicero emended, he died by his own hand in the forty-third year of his life."

The account of St. Jerome, though perhaps based on a lost work of Suetonius, has not been traced to any earlier source and has been found incapable of either proof or disproof. Historians have pointed out that love potions, which occasionally caused madness, were sufficiently common at the time of Lucretius to necessitate a legal penalty against their use. Some critics have argued that the supposed mental ailment is compatible with the impression the poem makes and have pointed to the evidence of its not having received a final revision. Other critics have inferred that the whole story is a fiction invented by the enemies of Epicureanism to discredit the work of its greatest expositor.

Cicero's relation to the poem as emender or editor rests on no other authority than that of St. Jerome. A letter of Cicero's to his brother does reveal that the poem, probably published posthumously, was being read in 54 B.C.

Donatus, in his *Life of Virgil,* states that Lucretius died on the same day in 55 B.C. that Virgil assumed the *toga virilis.*

CONTENTS

Biographical Note, p. ix

Book I, p. 1   Book II, p. 15   Book III, p. 30

Book IV, p. 44   Book V, p. 61   Book VI, p. 80

LUCRETIUS

ON THE NATURE OF THINGS

·BOOK ONE·

MOTHER of the Aeneadae, darling of men and gods, increase-giving Venus, who beneath the gliding signs of heaven fillest with thy presence the ship-carrying sea, the corn-bearing lands, since through thee every kind of living things is conceived, rises up and beholds the light of the sun. Before thee, goddess, flee the winds, the clouds of heaven; before thee and thy advent; for thee earth manifold in works puts forth sweet-smelling flowers; for thee the levels of the sea do laugh and heaven propitiated shines with outspread light. For soon as the vernal aspect of day is disclosed, and the birth-favouring breeze of Favonius unbarred is blowing fresh, first the fowls of the air, O lady, show signs of thee and thy entering in, thoroughly smitten in heart by thy power. Next the wild herds bound over the glad pastures and swim the rapid rivers: in such wise each made prisoner by thy charms follows thee with desire, whither thou goest to lead it on. Yes, throughout seas and mountains and sweeping rivers and leafy homes of birds and grassy plains, striking fond love into the breasts of all thou constrainest them each after its kind to continue their races with desire. Since thou then art sole mistress of the nature of things and without thee nothing rises up into the divine borders of light, nothing grows to be glad or lovely, fain would I have thee for a helpmate in writing the verses which I essay to pen on the nature of things for our own son of the Memmii, whom thou, goddess, hast willed to have no peer, rich as he ever is in every grace. Wherefore all the more, O lady, lend my lays an everliving charm. Cause meanwhile the savage works of war to be lulled to rest throughout all seas and lands; for thou alone canst bless mankind with calm peace, seeing that Mavors lord of battle controls the savage works of war, Mavors who often flings himself into thy lap quite vanquished by the never-healing wound of love; and then with upturned face and shapely neck thrown back feeds with love his greedy sight gazing, goddess, open-mouthed on thee; and as backward he reclines, his breath stays hanging on thy lips. While then, lady, he is reposing on thy holy body, shed thyself about him and above, and pour from thy lips sweet discourse, asking, glorious dame, gentle peace for the Romans. For neither can we in our country's day of trouble with untroubled mind think only of our work, nor can the illustrious offset of Memmius in times like these be wanting to the general weal. . . . for what remains to tell, apply to true reason unbusied ears and a keen mind withdrawn from cares, lest my gifts set out for you with steadfast zeal you abandon with disdain, before they are understood. For I will essay to discourse to you of the most high system of heaven and the gods and will open up the first beginnings of things, out of which nature gives birth to all things and increase and nourishment, and into which nature likewise dissolves them back after their destruction. These we are accustomed in explaining their reason to call matter and begetting bodies of things and to name seeds of things and also to term first bodies, because from them as first elements all things are.

62] When human life to view lay foully prostrate upon earth crushed down under the weight of religion, who showed her head from the quarters of heaven with hideous aspect lowering upon mortals, a man of Greece[1] ventured first to lift up his mortal eyes to her face and first to withstand her to her face. Him

[1] Epicurus.

I

neither story of gods nor thunderbolts nor heaven with threatening roar could quell: they only chafed the more the eager courage of his soul, filling him with desire to be the first to burst the fast bars of nature's portals. Therefore the living force of his soul gained the day: on he passed far beyond the flaming walls of the world and traversed throughout in mind and spirit the immeasurable universe; whence he returns a conqueror to tell us what can, what cannot come into being; in short on what principle each thing has its powers defined, its deepset boundary mark. Therefore religion is put under foot and trampled upon in turn; us his victory brings level with heaven.

80] This is what I fear herein, lest haply you should fancy that you are entering on unholy grounds of reason and treading the path of sin; whereas on the contrary often and often that very religion has given birth to sinful and unholy deeds. Thus in Aulis the chosen chieftains of the Danaï, foremost of men, foully polluted with Iphianassa's[1] blood the altar of the Trivian maid. Soon as the fillet encircling her maiden tresses shed itself in equal lengths adown each cheek, and soon as she saw her father standing sorrowful before the altars and beside him the ministering priests hiding the knife and her countrymen at sight of her shedding tears, speechless in terror she dropped down on her knees and sank to the ground. Nor aught in such a moment could it avail the luckless girl that she had first bestowed the name of father on the king. For lifted up in the hands of the men she was carried shivering to the altars, not after due performance of the customary rites to be escorted by the clear-ringing bridal song, but in the very season of marriage, stainless maid mid the stain of blood, to fall a sad victim by the sacrificing stroke of a father, that thus a happy and prosperous departure might be granted to the fleet. So great the evils to which religion could prompt!

102] You yourself some time or other overcome by the terror-speaking tales of the seers will seek to fall away from us. Ay indeed for how many dreams may they now imagine for you, enough to upset the calculations of life and trouble all your fortunes with fear! And with good cause; for if men saw that there was

[1] Iphigenia.

a fixed limit to their woes, they would be able in some way to withstand the religious scruples and threatenings of the seers. As it is, there is no way, no means of resisting, since they must fear after death everlasting pains. For they cannot tell what is the nature of the soul, whether it be born or on the contrary find its way into men at their birth, and whether it perish together with us when severed from us by death or visit the gloom of Orcus and wasteful pools or by divine decree find its way into brutes in our stead, as sang our Ennius who first brought down from delightful Helicon a crown of unfading leaf, destined to bright renown throughout Italian clans of men. And yet with all this Ennius sets forth that there are Acherusian quarters, publishing it in immortal verses; though in our passage thither neither our souls nor bodies hold together, but only certain idols pale in wondrous wise. From these places he tells us the ghost of everliving Homer uprose unfold in words the nature of things. Wherebefore him and began to shed salt tears and to fore we must well grasp the principle of things above, the principle by which the courses of the sun and moon go on, the force by which every thing on earth proceeds, but above all we must find out by keen reason what the soul and the nature of the mind consist of, and what thing it is which meets us when awake and frightens our minds, if we are under the influence of disease; meets and frightens us too when we are buried in sleep; so that we seem to see and hear speaking to us face to face them who are dead, whose bones earth holds in its embrace.

136] Nor does my mind fail to perceive how hard it is to make clear in Latin verses the dark discoveries of the Greeks, especially as many points must be dealt with in new terms on account of the poverty of the language and the novelty of the questions. But yet your worth and the looked-for pleasure of sweet friendship prompt me to undergo any labour and lead me on to watch the clear nights through, seeking by what words and in what verse I may be able in the end to shed on your mind so clear a light that you can thoroughly scan hidden things.

146] This terror then and darkness of mind must be dispelled not by the rays of the sun and glittering shafts of day, but by the aspect and the law of nature; the warp of whose design we shall begin with this first principle, nothing is ever gotten out of nothing by divine power. Fear in sooth holds so in check all mortals, because they see many operations go on in earth and heaven, the causes of which they can in no way understand, believing them therefore to be done by power divine. For these reasons when we shall have seen that nothing can be produced from nothing, we shall then more correctly ascertain that which we are seeking, both the elements out of which every thing can be produced and the manner in which all things are done without the hand of the gods.

159] If things came from nothing, any kind might be born of any thing, nothing would require seed. Men for instance might rise out of the sea, the scaly race out of the earth, and birds might burst out of the sky; horned and other herds, every kind of wild beasts would haunt with changing brood tilth and wilderness alike. Nor would the same fruits keep constant to trees, but would change; any tree might bear any fruit. For if there were not begetting bodies for each, how could things have a fixed unvarying mother? But in fact because things are all produced from fixed seeds, each thing is born and goes forth into the borders of light out of that in which resides its matter and first bodies; and for this reason all things cannot be gotten out of all things, because in particular things resides a distinct power. Again why do we see the rose put forth in spring, corn in the season of heat, vines yielding at the call of autumn, if not because, when the fixed seeds of things have streamed together at the proper time, whatever is born discloses itself, while the due seasons are there and the quickened earth brings its weakly products in safety forth into the borders of light? But if they came from nothing, they would rise up suddenly at uncertain periods and unsuitable times of year, inasmuch as there would be no first-beginnings to be kept from a begetting union by the unpropitious season. No nor would time be required for the growth of things after the meeting of the seed, if they could increase out of nothing. Little babies would at once grow into men and trees in a moment would rise and spring out of the ground. But none of these events it is plain ever comes to pass, since all things grow step by step at a fixed time, as is

natural, since they all grow from a fixed seed and in growing preserve their kind; so that you may be sure that all things increase in size and are fed out of their own matter. Furthermore without fixed seasons of rain the earth is unable to put forth its gladdening produce, nor again if kept from food could the nature of living things continue its kind and sustain life; so that you may hold with greater truth that many bodies are common to many things, as we see letters common to different words, than that any thing could come into being without first-beginnings. Again why could not nature have produced men of such a size and strength as to be able to wade on foot across the sea and rend great mountains with their hands and outlive many generations of living men, if not because an unchanging matter has been assigned for begetting things and what can arise out of this matter is fixed? We must admit therefore that nothing can come from nothing, since things require seed before they can severally be born and be brought out into the buxom fields of air. Lastly since we see that tilled grounds surpass untilled and yield a better produce by the labour of hands, we may infer that there are in the earth first-beginnings of things which by turning up the fruitful clods with the share and labouring the soil of the earth we stimulate to rise. But if there were not such, you would see all things without any labour of ours spontaneously come forth in much greater perfection.

215] Moreover nature dissolves every thing back into its first bodies and does not annihilate things. For if aught were mortal in all its parts alike, the thing in a moment would be snatched away to destruction from before our eyes; since no force would be needed to produce disruption among its parts and undo their fastenings. Whereas in fact, as all things consist of an imperishable seed, nature suffers the destruction of nothing to be seen, until a force has encountered it sufficient to dash things to pieces by a blow or to pierce through the void places within them and break them up. Again if time, whenever it makes away with things through age, utterly destroys them eating up all their matter, out of what does Venus bring back into the light of life the race of living things each after its kind, or, when they are brought back, out of what does earth manifold in works give them nourishment and increase, furnishing them with food each after its kind? Out of what do its own native fountains and extraneous rivers from far and wide keep full the sea? Out of what does ether feed the stars? For infinite time gone by and lapse of days must have eaten up all things which are of mortal body. Now if in that period of time gone by those things have existed, of which this sum of things is composed and recruited, they are possessed no doubt of an imperishable body, and cannot therefore any of them return to nothing. Again the same force and cause would destroy all things without distinction, unless everlasting matter held them together, matter more or less closely linked in mutual entanglement: a touch in sooth would be sufficient cause of death, inasmuch as any amount of force must of course undo the texture of things in which no parts at all were of an everlasting body. But in fact, because the fastenings of first-beginnings one with the other are unlike and matter is everlasting, things continue with body uninjured, until a force is found to encounter them strong enough to overpower the texture of each. A thing therefore never returns to nothing, but all things after disruption go back into the first bodies of matter. Lastly rains die, when father ether has tumbled them into the lap of mother earth; but then goodly crops spring up and boughs are green with leaves upon the trees, trees themselves grow and are laden with fruit; by them in turn our race and the race of wild beasts are fed, by them we see glad towns teem with children and the leafy forests ring on all sides with the song of new birds; through them cattle wearied with their load of fat lay their bodies down about the glad pastures and the white milky stream pours from the distended udders; through them a new brood with weakly limbs frisks and gambols over the soft grass, rapt in their young hearts with the pure new milk. None of the things therefore which seem to be lost is utterly lost, since nature replenishes one thing out of another and does not suffer any thing to be begotten, before she has been recruited by the death of some other.

265] Now mark me: since I have taught that things cannot be born from nothing, cannot when begotten be brought back to nothing, that you may not haply yet begin in any shape to mistrust my words, because the first-beginnings of things cannot be seen by the eyes, take moreover this list of bodies which you must yourself admit are in the number of things and cannot be seen. First of all the force of the wind when aroused beats on the harbours and whelms huge ships and scatters clouds; sometimes in swift whirling eddy it scours the plains and straws them with large trees and scourges the mountain summits with forest-rending blasts: so fiercely does the wind rave with a shrill howling and rage with threatening roar. Winds therefore sure enough are unseen bodies which sweep the seas, the lands, ay and the clouds of heaven, tormenting them and catching them up in sudden whirls. On they stream and spread destruction abroad in just the same way as the soft liquid nature of water, when all at once it is borne along in an overflowing stream, and a great downfall of water from the high hills augments it with copious rains, flinging together fragments of forests and entire trees; nor can the strong bridges sustain the sudden force of coming water: in such wise turbid with much rain the river dashes upon the piers with mighty force: makes havoc with loud noise and rolls under its eddies huge stones: wherever aught opposes its waves, down it dashes it. In this way then must the blasts of wind as well move on, and when they like a mighty stream have borne down in any direction, they push things before them and throw them down with repeated assaults, sometimes catch them up in curling eddy and carry them away in swift-circling whirl. Wherefore once and again I say winds are unseen bodies, since in their works and ways they are found to rival great rivers which are of a visible body. Then again we perceive the different smells of things, yet never see them coming to our nostrils; nor do we behold heats nor can we observe cold with the eyes nor are we used to see voices. Yet all these things must consist of a bodily nature, since they are able to move the senses; for nothing but body can touch and be touched. Again clothes hung up on a shore which waves break upon become moist, and then get dry if spread out in the sun. Yet it has not been seen in what way the moisture of water has sunk into them nor again in what way this has been dispelled by heat. The moisture therefore is dispersed into small particles which the eyes are quite unable to see. Again after the revolution of many of the sun's years a ring on the finger is thinned on the underside by wearing, the dripping from the eaves hollows a stone, the bent plough-share of iron imperceptibly decreases in the fields, and we behold the stone-paved streets worn down by the feet of the multitude; the brass statues too at the gates show their right hands to be wasted by the touch of the numerous passers by who greet them. These things then we see are lessened, since they have been thus worn down; but what bodies depart at any given time the nature of vision has jealously shut out our seeing. Lastly the bodies which time and nature add to things by little and little, constraining them to grow in due measure, no exertion of the eyesight can behold; and so too wherever things grow old by age and decay, and when rocks hanging over the sea are eaten away by the gnawing salt spray, you cannot see what they lose at any given moment. Nature therefore works by unseen bodies.

329] And yet all things are not on all sides jammed together and kept in by body: there is also void in things. To have learned this will be good for you on many accounts; it will not suffer you to wander in doubt and be to seek in the sum of things and distrustful of our words. If there were not void, things could not move at all; for that which is the property of body, to let and hinder, would be present to all things at all times; nothing therefore could go on, since no other thing would be the first to give way. But in fact throughout seas and lands and the heights of heaven we see before our eyes many things move in many ways for various reasons, which things, if there were no void, I need not say would lack and want restless motion: they never would have been begotten at all since matter jammed on all sides would have been at rest. Again however solid things are thought to be, you may yet learn from this that they are of rare body: in rocks and caverns the moisture of water oozes through and all things weep with abundant drops; food distributes itself through the whole body of living things; trees grow and yield fruit in season, because food is diffused through the whole from the very roots over the stem and all the boughs.

Voices pass through walls and fly through houses shut, stiffening frost pierces to the bones. Now if there are no void parts, by what way can the bodies severally pass? You would see it to be quite impossible. Once more, why do we see one thing surpass another in weight though not larger in size? For if there is just as much body in a ball of wool as there is in a lump of lead, it is natural it should weigh the same, since the property of body is to weigh all things downwards, while on the contrary the nature of void is ever without weight. Therefore when a thing is just as large, yet is found to be lighter, it proves sure enough that it has more of void in it; while on the other hand that which is heavier shows that there is in it more of body and that it contains within it much less of void. Therefore that which we are seeking with keen reason exists sure enough, mixed up in things; and we call it void.

370] And herein I am obliged to forestall this point which some raise, lest it draw you away from the truth. The waters they say make way for the scaly creatures as they press on, and open liquid paths, because the fish leave room behind them, into which the yielding waters may stream; thus other things too may move and change place among themselves, although the whole sum be full. This you are to know has been taken up on grounds wholly false. For on what side I ask can the scaly creatures move forwards, unless the waters have first made room? again on what side can the waters give place, so long as the fish are unable to go on? Therefore you must either strip all bodies of motion or admit that in things void is mixed up from which every thing gets its first start in moving. Lastly if two broad bodies after contact quickly spring asunder, the air must surely fill all the void which is formed between the bodies. Well, however rapidly it stream together with swift-circling currents, yet the whole space will not be able to be filled up in one moment; for it must occupy first one spot and then another, until the whole is taken up. But if haply any one supposes that, when the bodies have started asunder, that result follows because the air condenses, he is mistaken; for a void is then formed which was not before, and a void also is filled which existed before; nor can the air condense in such a way, nor supposing it could, could it methinks without void draw into itself and bring its parts together.

398] Wherefore, however long you hold out by urging many objections, you must needs in the end admit that there is a void in things. And many more arguments I may state to you in order to accumulate proof on my words; but these slight footprints are enough for a keen-searching mind to enable you by yourself to find out all the rest. For as dogs often discover by smell the lair of a mountain-ranging wild beast though covered over with leaves, when once they have got on the sure tracks, thus you in cases like this will be able by yourself alone to see one thing after another and find your way into all dark corners and draw forth the truth. But if you lag or swerve a jot from the reality, this I can promise you, Memmius, without more ado: such plenteous draughts from abundant wellsprings my sweet tongue shall pour from my richly furnished breast, that I fear slow age will steal over our limbs and break open in us the fastnesses of life, ere the whole store of reasons on any one question has by my verses been dropped into your ears.

418] But now to resume the thread of the design which I am weaving in verse: all nature then, as it exists by itself, is founded on two things: there are bodies and there is void in which these bodies are placed and through which they move about. For that body exists by itself the general feeling of mankind declares; and unless at the very first belief in this be firmly grounded, there will be nothing to which we can appeal on hidden things in order to prove anything by reasoning of mind. Then again, if room and space which we call void did not exist, bodies could not be placed anywhere nor move about at all to any side; as we have demonstrated to you a little before. Moreover there is nothing which you can affirm to be at once separate from all body and quite distinct from void, which would so to say count as the discovery of a third nature. For whatever shall exist, this of itself must be something or other. Now if it shall admit of touch in however slight and small a measure, it will, be it with a large or be it with a little addition, provided it do exist, increase the amount of body and join the sum. But if it shall be intangible and unable to hinder any thing from passing through it on any side, this you are to know will be that which we call empty void. Again whatever shall exist by itself, will either do something or will itself suffer by the action of other things, or will be of such a nature as things are able to exist and go on in. But no thing can do and suffer without body, nor aught furnish room except void and vacancy. Therefore beside void and bodies no third nature taken by itself can be left in the number of things, either such as to fall at any time under the ken of our senses or such as any one can grasp by the reason of his mind.

449] For whatever things are named, you will either find to be properties linked to these two things or you will see to be accidents of these things. That is a property which can in no case be disjoined and separated without utter destruction accompanying the severance, such as the weight of a stone, the heat of fire, the fluidity of water. Slavery on the other hand, poverty and riches, liberty, war, concord, and all other things which may come and go while the nature of the thing remains unharmed, these we are wont, as it is right we should, to call accidents. Time also exists not by itself, but simply from the things which happen the sense apprehends what has been done in time past, as well as what is present and what is to follow after. And we must admit that no one feels time by itself abstracted from the motion and calm rest of things. So when they say that the daughter of Tyndarus was ravished and the Trojan nations were subdued in war, we must mind that they do not force us to admit that these things are by themselves, since those generations of men, of whom these things were accidents, time now gone by has irrevocably swept away. For whatever shall have been done may be termed an accident in one case of the Teucran people, in another of the countries simply. Yes for if there had been no matter of things and no room and space in which things severally go on, never had the fire, kindled by love of the beauty of Tyndarus' daughter, blazed beneath the Phrygian breast of Alexander and lighted up the famous struggles of cruel war, nor had the timber horse unknown to the Trojans wrapt Pergama in flames by its night issuing brood of sons of the Greeks; so that you may clearly perceive that all actions from first to last exist not by themselves and are not by themselves in the way that body is, nor are terms of the same kind as void is, but are rather of such a kind that you may fairly call them accidents of body and of the room in which they severally go on.

483] Bodies again are partly first-beginnings of things, partly those which are formed of a union of first-beginnings. But those which are first-beginnings of things no force can quench: they are sure to have the better by their solid body. Although it seems difficult to believe that aught can be found among things with a solid body. For the lightning of heaven passes through the walls of houses, as well as noise and voices; iron grows red-hot in the fire and stones burn with fierce heat and burst asunder; the hardness of gold is broken up and dissolved by heat; the ice of brass melts vanquished by the flame; warmth and piercing cold ooze through silver, since we have felt both, as we held cups with the hand in due fashion and the water was poured down into them. So universally there is found to be nothing solid in things. But yet because true reason and the nature of things constrains, attend until we make clear in a few verses that there are such things as consist of solid and everlasting body, which we teach are seeds of things and first-beginnings, out of which the whole sum of things which now exists has been produced.

503] First of all then since there has been found to exist a two-fold and widely dissimilar nature of two things, that is to say of body and of place in which things severally go on, each of the two must exist for and by itself and quite unmixed. For wherever there is empty space which we call void, there body is not; wherever again body maintains itself, there empty void no wise exists. First bodies therefore are solid and without void. Again since there is void in things begotten, solid matter must exist about this void, and no thing can be proved by true reason to conceal in its body and have within it void, unless you choose to allow that that which holds it in is solid. Again that can be nothing but a union of matter which can keep in the void of things. Matter therefore, which consists of a solid body, may be everlasting, though all things else are dissolved. Moreover if there

were no empty void, the universe would be solid; unless on the other hand there were certain bodies to fill up whatever places they occupied, the existing universe would be empty and void space. Therefore sure enough body and void are marked off in alternate layers, since the universe is neither of a perfect fullness nor a perfect void. There are therefore certain bodies which can vary void space with full. These can neither be broken in pieces by the stroke of blows from without nor have their texture undone by aught piercing to their core nor give way before any other kind of assault; as we have proved to you a little before. For without void nothing seems to admit of being crushed in or broken up or split in two by cutting, or of taking in wet or permeating cold or penetrating fire, by which all things are destroyed. And the more anything contains within it of void, the more thoroughly it gives way to the assault of these things. Therefore if first bodies are as I have shown solid and without void, they must be everlasting. Again unless matter had been eternal, all things before this would have utterly returned to nothing and whatever things we see would have been born anew from nothing. But since I have proved above that nothing can be produced from nothing, and that what is begotten cannot be recalled to nothing, first-beginnings must be of an imperishable body into which all things can be dissolved at their last hour, that there may be a supply of matter for the reproduction of things. Therefore first-beginnings are of solid singleness, and in no other way can they have been preserved through ages during infinite time past in order to reproduce things.

551] Again if nature had set no limit to the breaking of things, by this time the bodies of matter would have been so far reduced by the breaking of past ages that nothing could within a fixed time be conceived out of them and reach its utmost growth of being. For we see that anything is more quickly destroyed than again renewed; and therefore that which the long, the infinite duration of all bygone time had broken up, demolished and destroyed, could never be reproduced in all remaining time. But now sure enough a fixed limit to their breaking has been set, since we see each thing renewed, and at the same time definite periods fixed for things each after its kind to reach the flower of their age. Moreover while the bodies of matter are most solid, it may yet be explained in what way all things which are formed soft, as air, water, earth, fires, are so formed and by what force they severally go on, since once for all there is void mixed up in things. But on the other hand if the first-beginnings of things be soft, it cannot be explained out of what enduring basalt and iron can be produced; for their whole nature will utterly lack a first foundation to begin with. First-beginnings therefore are strong in solid singleness, and by a denser combination of these all things can be closely packed and exhibit enduring strength.

577] Again if no limit has been set to the breaking of bodies, nevertheless the several bodies which go to things must survive from eternity up to the present time, not yet assailed by any danger. But since they are possessed of a frail nature, it is not consistent with this that they could have continued through eternity harassed through ages by countless blows. Again too since a limit of growing and sustaining life has been assigned to things each after its kind, and since by the laws of nature it stands decreed what they can each do and what they cannot do, and since nothing is changed, but all things are so constant that the different birds all in succession exhibit in their body the distinctive marks of their kind, they must sure enough have a body of unchangeable matter also. For if the first-beginnings of things could in any way be vanquished and changed, it would then be uncertain too what could and what could not rise into being, in short on what principle each thing has its powers defined, its deepset boundary mark; nor could the generations reproduce so often each after its kind the nature habits, way of life and motions of the parents.

599] Then again since there is ever a bounding point to bodies, which appears to us to be a least, there ought in the same way to be a bounding point the least conceivable to that first body which already is beyond what our senses can perceive: that point sure enough is without parts and consists of a least nature and never has existed apart by itself and will not be able in future so to exist, since it is in itself

a part of that other; and so a first and single part and then other and other similar parts in succession fill up in close serried mass the nature of the first body; and since these cannot exist by themselves, they must cleave to that from which they cannot in any way be torn. First-beginnings therefore are of solid singleness, massed together and cohering closely by means of least parts, not compounded out of a union of those parts, but, rather, strong in everlasting singleness. From them nature allows nothing to be torn, nothing further to be worn away, reserving them as seeds for things. Again unless there shall be a least, the very smallest bodies will consist of infinite parts, inasmuch as the half of the half will always have a half and nothing will set bounds to the division. Therefore between the sum of things and the least of things what difference will there be? There will be no distinction at all; for how absolutely infinite soever the whole sum is, yet the things which are smallest will equally consist of infinite parts. Now since on this head true reason protests and denies that the mind can believe it, you must yield and admit that there exist such things as are possessed of no parts and are of a least nature. And since these exist, those first bodies also you must admit to be solid and everlasting. Once more, if nature creatress of things had been wont to compel all things to be broken up into least parts, then too she would be unable to reproduce anything out of those parts, because those things which are enriched with no parts cannot have the properties which begetting matter ought to have, I mean the various entanglements, weights, blows, clashings, motions, by means of which things severally go on.

635] For which reasons they who have held fire to be the matter of things and the sum to be formed out of fire alone, are seen to have strayed most widely from true reason. At the head of whom enters Heraclitus to do battle, famous for obscurity more among the frivolous than the earnest Greeks who seek the truth. For fools admire and like all things the more which they perceive to be concealed under involved language, and determine things to be true which can prettily tickle the ears and are varnished over with finely sounding phrase.

645] For I want to know how things can be

so various, if they are formed out of fire one and unmixed: it would avail nothing for hot fire to be condensed or rarefied, if the same nature which the whole fire has, belonged to the parts of fire as well. The heat would be more intense by compression of parts, more faint by their severance and dispersion. More than this you cannot think it in the power of such causes to effect, far less could so great a diversity of things come from mere density and rarity of fires. Observe also, if they suppose void to be mixed up in things, fire may then be condensed and left rare; but because they see many things rise up in contradiction to them and shrink from leaving unmixed void in things, fearing the steep, they lose the true road, and do not perceive on the other hand that if void is taken from things, all things are condensed and out of all things is formed one single body, which cannot briskly radiate anything from it, in the way heat-giving fire emits light and warmth, letting you see that it is not of closely compressed parts. But if they haply think that in some other way fires may be quenched in the union and change their body, you are to know that if they shall scruple on no side to do this, all heat sure enough will be utterly brought to nothing, and all things that are produced will be formed out of nothing. For whenever a thing changes and quits its proper limits, at once this change of state is the death of that which was before. Therefore something or other must needs be left to those fires of theirs undestroyed, that you may not have all things absolutely returning to nothing, and the whole store of things born anew and flourishing out of nothing. Since then in fact there are some most unquestionable bodies which always preserve the same nature, on whose going or coming and change of order things change their nature and bodies are transformed, you are to know that these first bodies of things are not of fire. For it would matter nothing that some should withdraw and go away and others should be added on and some should have their order changed, if one and all they yet retained the nature of heat; for whatever they produced would be altogether fire. But thus methinks it is: there are certain bodies whose clashings, motions, order, position, and shapes produce fires, and which by a change of order change the nature of the things and do not resemble fire nor anything else which has the power of sending bodies to our senses and touching by its contact our sense of touch.

690] Again to say that all things are fire and that no real thing except fire exists in the number of things, as this same man does, appears to be sheer dotage. For he himself takes his stand on the side of the senses to fight against the senses and shakes their authority, on which rests all our belief, ay from which this fire as he calls it is known to himself; for he believes that the senses can truly perceive fire, he does not believe they can perceive all other things which are not a whit less clear. Now this appears to me to be as false as it is foolish; for to what shall we appeal? what surer test can we have than the senses, whereby to note truth and falsehood? Again why should any one rather abolish all things and choose to leave the single nature of heat, than deny that fires exist, while he allows anything else to be? it seems to be equal madness to affirm either this or that.

705] For these reasons they who have held that fire is the matter of things and that the sum can be formed out of fire, and they who have determined air to be the first-beginning in begetting things, and all who have held that water by itself alone forms things, or that earth produces all things and changes into all the different natures of things, appear to have strayed exceedingly wide of the truth; as well as they who make the first-beginnings of things twofold coupling air with fire and earth with water, and they who believe that all things grow out of four things, fire, earth and air and water. Chief of whom is Agrigentine Empedocles: him within the three-cornered shores of its lands that island bore, about which the Ionian sea flows in large cranklings, and splashes up brine from its green waves. Here the sea racing in its straitened frith divides by its waters the shores of Italy's lands from the other's coasts; here is wasteful Charybdis and here the rumblings of Aetna threaten anew to gather up such fury of flames, as again with force to belch forth the fires bursting from its throat and carry up to heaven once more the lightnings of flame. Now though this great country is seen to deserve in many ways the wonder of mankind and is held to be well worth visiting, rich in all good things, guarded by large force of men, yet seems it to have held within it nothing more glorious than this man, nothing more holy, marvellous and dear. The verses too of his godlike genius cry with a loud voice and set forth in such wise his glorious discoveries that he hardly seems born of a mortal stock.

734] Yet he and those whom we have mentioned above immeasurably inferior and far beneath him, although, the authors of many excellent and godlike discoveries, they have given responses from so to say their hearts' holy of holies with more sanctity and on much more unerring grounds than the Pythia who speaks out from the tripod and laurel of Phoebus, have yet gone to ruin in the first-beginnings of things: it is there they have fallen, and, great themselves, great and heavy has been that fall; first because they have banished void from things and yet assign to them motions, and allow things soft and rare, air, sun, fire, earth, living things and corn, and yet mix not up void in their body; next because they suppose that there is no limit to the division of bodies and no stop set to their breaking and that there exists no least at all in things; though we see that that is the bounding point of any thing which seems to be least to our senses, so that from this you may infer that because the things which you do not see have a bounding point, there is a least in them. Moreover since they assign soft first-beginnings of things, which we see to have birth and to be of a body altogether mortal, the sum of things must in that case revert to nothing and the store of things be born anew and flourish out of nothing: how wide now of the truth both these doctrines are you will already comprehend. In the next place these bodies are in many ways mutually hostile and poisonous; and therefore they will either perish when they have met, or will fly asunder just as we see, when a storm has gathered, lightnings and rains and winds fly asunder.

763] Again if all things are produced from four things and all again broken up into those things, how can they be called first-beginnings of things any more than things be called their first-beginnings, the supposition being reversed? For they are begotten time about and interchange colour and their whole nature without ceasing. But if haply you suppose that the body of fire and of earth and air and the moisture of water meet in such a way that none of them in the union changes its nature, no thing I tell you can be then produced out of them, neither living thing nor thing with inanimate body, as a tree; in fact each thing amid the medley of this discordant mass will display its own nature and air will be seen to be mixed up with earth and heat to remain in union with moisture. But first-beginnings ought in begetting things to bring with them a latent and unseen nature in order that no thing stand out, to be in the way and prevent whatever is produced from having its own proper being.

782] Moreover they go back to heaven and its fires for a beginning, and first suppose that fire changes into air, next that from air water is begotten and earth is produced out of water, and that all in reverse order come back from earth, water first, next air, then heat, and that these cease not to interchange, to pass from heaven to earth, from earth to the stars of ether. All which first-beginnings must on no account do; since something unchangeable must needs remain over, that things may not utterly be brought back to nothing. For whenever a thing changes and quits its proper limits, at once this change of state is the death of that which was before. Wherefore since those things which we have mentioned a little before pass into a state of change, they must be formed out of others which cannot in any case be transformed, that you may not have things returning altogether to nothing. Why not rather hold that there are certain bodies possessed of such a nature, that, if they have haply produced fire, the same may, after a few have been taken away and a few added on and the order and motion changed, produce air; and that all other things may in the same way interchange with one another?

803] "But plain matter of fact clearly proves" you say "that all things grow up into the air and are fed out of the earth; and unless the season at the propitious period send such abundant showers that the trees reel beneath the soaking storms of rain, and unless the sun on its part foster them and supply heat, corn, trees, and living things could not grow." Quite true, and unless solid food and soft water should recruit us, our substance would waste away and life break wholly up out of all the sinews and bones; for we beyond doubt are recruited and fed by certain things, this and that other thing by certain other things. Because many first-beginnings common to many things in many ways are mixed up in things, therefore sure enough different things are fed by different things. And it often makes a great difference with what things and in what position the same first-beginnings are held in union and what motions they mutually impart and receive; for the same make up heaven, sea, lands, rivers, sun, the same make up corn, trees, and living things; but they are mixed up with different things and in different ways as they move. Nay you see throughout even in these verses of ours many elements common to many words, though you must needs admit that the lines and words differ one from the other both in meaning and in sound wherewith they sound. So much can elements effect by a mere change of order; but those elements which are the first-beginnings of things can bring with them more combinations out of which different things can severally be produced.

830] Let us now also examine the homoeo-meria of Anaxagoras as the Greeks term it, which the poverty of our native speech does not allow us to name in our own tongue; though it is easy enough to set forth in words the thing itself. First of all then, when he speaks of the homoeomeria of things, you must know he supposes bones to be formed out of very small and minute bones and flesh of very small and minute fleshes and blood by the coming together of many drops of blood, and gold he thinks can be composed of grains of gold and earth be a concretion of small earths, and fires can come from fires and water from waters, and everything else he fancies and supposes to be produced on a like principle. And yet at the same time he does not allow that void exists anywhere in things, or that there is a limit to the division of things. Wherefore he appears to me on both these grounds to be as much mistaken as those whom we have already spoken of above. Moreover the first-beginnings which he supposes are too frail; if first-beginnings they be which are possessed of a nature like to the things themselves and are just as liable to suffering and death, and which nothing reins back from destruction. For which of them will

hold out, so as to escape death, beneath so strong a pressure within the very jaws of destruction? fire or water or air? which of these? blood or bones? Not one methinks, where everything will be just as essentially mortal as those things which we see with the senses perish before our eyes vanquished by some force. But I appeal to facts demonstrated above for proof that things cannot fall away to nothing nor on the other hand grow from nothing. Again since food gives increase and nourishment to the body, you are to know that our veins and blood and bones and the like are formed of things foreign to them in kind; or if they shall say that all foods are of a mixed body and contain in them small bodies of sinews and bones and veins as well and particles of blood, it will follow that all food, solid as well as liquid, must be held to be composed of things foreign to them in kind, of bones that is and sinews and matter and blood mixed up. Again if all the bodies which grow out of the earth, are in the earths, the earth must be composed of things foreign to it in kind which grow out of these earths. Apply again this reasoning to other things, and you may use just the same words. If flame and smoke and ash are latent in woods, woods must necessarily be composed of things foreign to them in kind. Again all those bodies, to which the earth gives food, it increases out of things foreign to them in kind which rise out of the earth: thus too the bodies of flame which issue from the woods, are fed out of things foreign to them in kind which rise out of these woods.

875] Here some slight opening is left for evasion, which Anaxagoras avails himself of, choosing to suppose that all things though latent are mixed up in things, and that is alone visible of which there are the largest number of bodies in the mixture and these more ready to hand and stationed in the first rank. This however is far banished from true reason. For then it were natural that corn too should often, when crushed by the formidable force of the stone, show some mark of blood or some other of the things which have their nourishment in our body. For like reasons it were fitting that from grasses too, when we rub them between two stones, blood should ooze out; that waters should yield sweet drops, in flavour like to the udder of milk in sheep; yes and that often, when clods of earth have been crumbled, kinds of grasses and corn and leaves should be found to lurk distributed among the earth in minute quantities; and lastly that ash and smoke and minute fires should be found latent in woods, when they were broken off. Now since plain matter of fact teaches that none of these results follows, you are to know that things are not so mixed up in things; but rather seeds common to many things must in many ways be mixed up and latent in things.

897] "But it often comes to pass on high mountains", you say, "that contiguous tops of tall trees rub together, the strong southwinds constraining them so to do, until the flower of flame has broken out and they have burst into a blaze." Quite true and yet fire is not innate in woods; but there are many seeds of heat, and when they by rubbing have streamed together, they produce conflagrations in the forests. But if the flame was stored up ready made in the forests, the fire could not be concealed for any length of time, but would destroy forests, burn up trees indiscriminately. Do you now see, as we said a little before, that it often makes a very great difference with what things and in what position the same first-beginnings are held in union and what motions they mutually impart and receive, and that the same may when a little changed in arrangement produce say fires and a fir? just as the words too consist of elements only a little changed in arrangement, though we denote firs and fires with two quite distinct names. Once again, if you suppose that whatever you perceive among visible things cannot be produced without imagining bodies of matter possessed of a like nature, in this way, you will find, the first-beginnings of things are destroyed: it will come to this that they will be shaken by loud fits of convulsive laughter and will bedew with salt tears face and cheeks.

921] Now mark and learn what remains to be known and hear it more distinctly. Nor does my mind fail to perceive how dark the things are; but the great hope of praise has smitten my heart with sharp thyrsus, and at the same time has struck into my breast sweet love of the Muses, with which now inspired I traverse in blooming thought the pathless haunts of the Pierides never yet trodden by sole of man. I love to approach the untasted springs and to quaff, I love to cull fresh flowers and gather for my head a distinguished crown from spots whence the Muses have yet veiled the brows of none; first because I teach of great things and essay to release the mind from the fast bonds of religious scruples, and next because on a dark subject I pen such lucid verses o'erlaying all with the Muses' charm. For that too would seem to be not without good grounds: just as physicians when they purpose to give nauseous wormwood to children, first smear the rim round the bowl with the sweet yellow juice of honey, that the unthinking age of children may be fooled as far as the lips, and meanwhile drink up the bitter draught of wormwood and though beguiled yet not be betrayed, but rather by such means recover health and strength; so I now, since this doctrine seems generally somewhat bitter to those by whom it has not been handled, and the multitude shrinks back from it in dismay, have resolved to set forth to you our doctrine in sweet-toned Pierian verse and o'erlay it as it were with the pleasant honey of the Muses, if haply by such means I might engage your mind on my verses, till you clearly perceive the whole nature of things, its shape and frame.

951] But since I have taught that most solid bodies of matter fly about for ever unvanquished through all time, mark now, let us unfold whether there is or is not any limit to their sum; likewise let us clearly see whether that which has been found to be void, or room and space, in which things severally go on, is all of it altogether finite or stretches without limits and to an unfathomable depth.

958] Well then the existing universe is bounded in none of its dimensions; for then it must have had an outside. Again it is seen that there can be an outside of nothing, unless there be something beyond to bound it, so that that is seen, farther than which the nature of this our sense does not follow the thing. Now since we must admit that there is nothing outside the sum, it has no outside, and therefore is without end and limit. And it matters not in which of its regions you take your stand; so invariably, whatever position any one has taken up, he leaves the universe just as infinite as before in all directions. Again if for the moment all existing space be held to be bounded, supposing a man runs forward to its outside borders, and stands on the utmost verge and then throws a winged javelin, do you choose that when hurled with vigorous force it shall advance to the point to which it has been sent and fly to a distance, or do you decide that something can get in its way and stop it? for you must admit and adopt one of the two suppositions; either of which shuts you out from all escape and compels you to grant that the universe stretches without end. For whether there is something to get in its way and prevent its coming whither it was sent and placing itself in the point intended, or whether it is carried forward, in either case it has not started from the end. In this way I will go on and, wherever you have placed the outside borders, I will ask what then becomes of the javelin. The result will be that an end can nowhere be fixed, and that the room given for flight will still prolong the power of flight. Lastly one thing is by the eyes to end another thing; air bounds off hills, and mountains air, earth limits sea and sea again all lands; the universe however there is nothing outside to end.

988] Again if all the space of the whole sum were enclosed within fixed borders and were bounded, in that case the store of matter by its solid weights would have streamed together from all sides to the lowest point nor could anything have gone on under the canopy of heaven, no nor would there have been a heaven nor sunlight at all, inasmuch as all matter, settling down through infinite time past, would lie together in a heap. But as it is, sure enough no rest is given to the bodies of the first-beginnings, because there is no lowest point at all, to which they might stream together as it were, and where they might take up their positions. All things are ever going on in ceaseless motion on all sides and bodies of matter stirred to action are supplied from beneath out of infinite space. Therefore the nature of room and the space of the unfathomable void are such as bright thunderbolts cannot race through in their course though gliding on through endless tract of time, no nor lessen one jot the journey that remains to go by all their travel: so huge a room is spread out on all sides for things without any bounds in all directions round.

1008] Again nature keeps the sum of things from setting any limit to itself, since she compels body to be ended by void and void in turn by body, so that either she thus renders the universe infinite by this alternation of the two, or else the one of the two, in case the other does not bound it, with its single nature stretches nevertheless immeasurably. But void I have already proved to be infinite; therefore matter must be infinite: for if void were infinite, and matter finite neither sea nor earth nor the glittering quarters of heaven nor mortal kind nor the holy bodies of the gods could hold their ground one brief passing hour; since forced asunder from its union the store of matter would be dissolved and borne along the mighty void, or rather I should say would never have combined to produce any thing, since scattered abroad it could never have been brought together. For verily not by design did the first-beginnings of things station themselves each in its right place guided by keen intelligence, nor did they bargain sooth to say what motions each should assume, but because many in number and shifting about in many ways throughout the universe they are driven and tormented by blows during infinite time past, after trying motions and unions of every kind at length they fall into arrangements such as those out of which this our sum of things has been formed, and by which too it is preserved through many great years when once it has been thrown into the appropriate motions, and causes the streams to replenish the greedy sea with copious river waters and the earth, fostered by the heat of the sun, to renew its produce, and the race of living things to come up and flourish, and the gliding fires of ether to live: all which these several things could in no wise bring to pass, unless a store of matter could rise up from infinite space, out of which store they are wont to make up in due season whatever has been lost. For as the nature of living things when robbed of food loses its substance and wastes away, thus all things must be broken up, as soon as matter has ceased to be supplied, diverted in any way from its proper course. Nor can blows from without hold together all the sum which has been brought into union. They can, it is true, frequently strike upon and stay a part, until others come and the sum can be completed. At times however they are compelled to rebound and in so doing grant to the first-beginnings of things room and time for flight, to enable them to get clear away from the mass in union. Wherefore again and again I repeat many bodies must rise up; nay for the blows themselves not to fail, there is need of an infinite supply of matter on all sides.

1052] And herein, Memmius, be far from believing this, that all things as they say press to the centre of the sum, and that for this reason the nature of the world stands fast without any strokes from the outside and the uppermost and lowest parts cannot part asunder in any direction, because all things have been always pressing towards the centre (if you can believe that anything can rest upon itself); or that the heavy bodies which are beneath the earth all press upwards and are at rest on the earth, turned topsy-turvy, just like the images of things we see before us in the waters. In the same way they maintain that living things walk head downwards and cannot tumble out of earth into the parts of heaven lying below them any more than our bodies can spontaneously fly into the quarters of heaven; that when those see the sun, we behold the stars of night; and that they share with us time about the seasons of heaven and pass nights equal in length to our days. But groundless error has devised such dreams for fools, because they have embraced false principles of reason. For there can be no centre where the universe is infinite; no nor, even if there were a centre, could anything take up a position there any more on that account than for some quite different reason be driven away. For all room and space, which we term void, must through centre, through no-centre alike give place to heavy bodies, in whatever directions their motions tend. Nor is there any spot of such a sort that when bodies have reached it, they can lose their force of gravity and stand upon void; and that again which is void must not serve to support anything, but must, as its nature craves, continually give place. Things cannot therefore in such a way be held in union, o'ermas-

tered by love of a centre.

1083] Again since they do not suppose that all bodies press to the centre, but only those of earth, and those of water, both such as descend to the earth in rain and those which are held in by the earth's body, so to say, the fluid of the sea and great waters from the mountains; while on the other hand they teach that the subtle element of air and hot fires at the same time are carried away from the centre and that for this reason the whole ether round bickers with signs and the sun's flame is fed throughout the blue of heaven, because heat flying from the centre all gathers together there, and that the topmost boughs of trees could not put forth leaves at all, unless from time to time nature supplied food from the earth to each throughout both stem and boughs, their reasons are not only false, but they contradict each other. Space I have already proved to be infinite; and space being infinite matter as I have said must also be infinite lest after the winged fashion of flames the walls of the world should suddenly break up and fly abroad along the mighty void, and all other things follow for like reasons and the innermost quarters of heaven tumble in from above and the earth in an instant withdraw from beneath our feet and amid the commingled ruins of things in it and of heaven, ruins unloosing the first bodies, should wholly pass away along the unfathomable void, so that in a moment of time not a wrack should be left behind, nothing save untenanted space and viewless first-beginnings. For on whatever side you shall first determine first bodies to be wanting, this side will be the gate of death for things, through this the whole crowd of matter will fling itself abroad.

1114] If you will thoroughly con these things, then carried to the end with slight trouble you will be able by yourself to understand all the rest. For one thing after another will grow clear and dark night will not rob you of the road and keep you from surveying the utmost ends of nature: in such wise things will light the torch for other things.

IT IS sweet, when on the great sea the winds trouble its waters, to behold from land another's deep distress; not that it is a pleasure and delight that any should be afflicted, but because it is sweet to see from what evils you are yourself exempt. It is sweet also to look upon the mighty struggles of war arrayed along the plains without sharing yourself in the danger. But nothing is more welcome than to hold the lofty and serene positions well fortified by the learning of the wise, from which you may look down upon others and see them wandering all abroad and going astray in their search for the path of life, see the contest among them of intellect, the rivalry of birth, the striving night and day with surpassing effort to struggle up to the summit of power and be masters of the world.

14] O miserable minds of men! O blinded breasts! in what darkness of life and in how great dangers is passed this term of life whatever its duration! not choose to see that nature craves for herself no more than this, that pain hold aloof from the body, and she in mind enjoy a feeling of pleasure exempt from care and fear? Therefore we see that for the body's nature few things are needed at all, such and such only as take away pain. Nay, though more gratefully at times they can minister to us many choice delights, nature for her part wants them not, when there are no golden images of youths through the house holding in their right hands flaming lamps for supply of light to the nightly banquet, when the house shines not with silver nor glitters with gold nor do the panelled and gilded roofs re-echo to the harp, what time, though these things be wanting, they spread themselves in groups on the soft grass beside a stream of water under the boughs of a high tree and at no great cost pleasantly refresh their bodies, above all when the weather smiles and the seasons of the year besprinkle the green grass with flowers. Nor do hot fevers sooner quit the body, if you toss about on pictured tapestry and blushing purple, than if you must lie under a poor man's blanket. Wherefore since treasures avail nothing in respect of our body nor birth nor the glory of kingly power, advancing farther you must hold that they are of no service to the mind as well; unless may be when you see your legions swarm over the ground of the campus waging the mimicry of war, strengthened flank and rear by powerful reserves and great force of cavalry, and you marshall them equipped in arms and animated with one spirit, thereupon you find that religious scruples scared by these things fly panic-stricken from the mind; and that then fears of death leave the breast unembarrassed and free from care, when you see your fleet swarm forth and spread itself far and wide. But if we see that these things are food for laughter and mere mockeries, and in good truth the fears of men and dogging cares dread not the clash of arms and cruel weapons, if unabashed they mix among kings and kesars and stand not in awe of the glitter from gold nor the brilliant sheen of the purple robe, how can you doubt that this is wholly the prerogative of reason, when the whole of life withal is a struggle in the dark? For even as children are flurried and dread all things in the thick darkness, thus we in the daylight fear at times things not a whit more to be dreaded than those which children shudder at in the dark and fancy sure to be. This terror therefore and darkness of mind must be dispelled not by the rays of the sun and glittering shafts of day, but by the aspect and law of nature.

62] Now mark and I will explain by what motion the begetting bodies of matter do beget different things and after they are begotten again break them up, and by what force they are compelled so to do and what velocity is given to them for travelling through the great void: do you mind to give heed to my words.

66] For verily matter does not cohere inseparably massed together, since we see that everything wanes and perceive that all things ebb as it were by length of time and that age withdraws them from our sight, though yet the sum is seen to remain unimpaired by reason that the bodies which quit each thing, lessen the things from which they go, gift with increase those to which they have come, compel the former to grow old, the latter to come to their prime, and yet abide not with these. Thus the sum of things is ever renewed and mortals live by a reciprocal dependency. Some nations wax, others wane, and in a brief space the races of living things are changed and like runners hand over the lamp of life.

80] If you think that first-beginnings of things can lag and by lagging give birth to new motions of things, you wander far astray from the path of true reason: since they travel about through void, the first-beginnings of things must all move on either by their own weight or haply by the stroke of another. For when during motion they have, as often happens, met and clashed, the result is a sudden rebounding in an opposite direction; and no wonder, since they are most hard and of weight proportioned to their solidity and nothing behind gets in their way. And that you may more clearly see that all bodies of matter are in restless movement, remember that there is no lowest point in the sum of the universe, and that first bodies have not where to take their stand, since space is without end and limit and extends immeasurably in all directions round, as I have shown in many words and as has been proved by sure reason. Since this then is a certain truth, sure enough no rest is given to first bodies throughout the unfathomable void, but driven on rather in ceaseless and varied motion they partly, after they have pressed together, rebound leaving great spaces between, while in part they are so dashed away after the stroke as to leave but small spaces between. And all that form a denser aggregation when brought together and rebound leaving trifling spaces between, held fast by their own close-tangled shapes, these form enduring bases of stone and unyielding bodies of iron and the rest of their class, few in number, which travel onward along the great void. All the others spring far off and rebound far leaving great spaces between: these furnish us with thin air and bright sunlight. And many more travel along the great void, which have been thrown off from the unions of things or

though admitted have yet in no case been able likewise to assimilate their motions. Of this truth, which I am telling, we have a representation and picture always going on before our eyes and present to us: observe whenever the rays are let in and pour the sunlight through the dark chambers of houses: you will see many minute bodies in many ways through the apparent void mingle in the midst of the light of the rays, and as in never-ending conflict skirmish and give battle combating in troops and never halting, driven about in frequent meetings and partings; so that you may guess from this, what it is for first-beginnings of things to be ever tossing about in the great void. So far as it goes, a small thing may give an illustration of great things and put you on the track of knowledge. And for this reason too it is meet that you should give greater heed to these bodies which are seen to tumble about in the sun's rays, because such tumblings imply that motions also of matter latent and unseen are at the bottom. For you will observe many things were impelled by unseen blows to change their course and driven back to return the way they came now this way now that way in all directions round. All you are to know derive this restlessness from the first-beginnings. For the first-beginnings of things move first of themselves; next those bodies which form a small aggregate and come nearest so to say to the powers of the first-beginnings, are impelled and set in movement by the unseen strokes of those first bodies, and they next in turn stir up bodies which are a little larger. Thus motion mounts up from the first-beginnings and step by step issues forth to our senses, so that those bodies also move, which we can discern in the sunlight, though it is not clearly seen by what blows they so act.

142] Now what velocity is given to bodies of matter, you may apprehend, Memmius, in few words from this: when morning first sprinkles the earth with fresh light and the different birds flitting about the pathless woods through the buxom air fill all places with their clear notes, we see it to be plain and evident to all how suddenly the sun after rising is wont at such a time to overspread all things and clothe them with his light. But that heat which the sun emits and that bright light pass not through empty void; and therefore they are forced to travel more slowly, until they cleave through the waves so to speak of air. Nor do the several minute bodies of heat pass on one by one, but closely entangled and massed together; whereby at one and the same time they are pulled back by one another and are impeded from without, so that they are forced to travel more slowly. But the first-beginnings which are of solid singleness, when they pass through empty void and nothing delays them from without and they themselves, single from the nature of their parts, are borne with headlong endeavour towards the one single spot to which their efforts tend, must sure enough surpass in velocity and be carried along much more swiftly than the light of the sun, and race through many times the extent of space in the same time in which the beams of the sun fill the heaven throughout. . . . nor follow up the several first-beginnings to see by what law each thing goes on.

167] But some in opposition to this, ignorant of matter, believe that nature cannot without the providence of the gods in such nice conformity to the ways of men vary the seasons of the year and bring forth crops, ay and all the other things, which divine pleasure the guide of life prompts men to approach, escorting them in person and enticing them by her fondlings to continue their races through the arts of Venus, that mankind may not come to an end. Now when they suppose that the gods designed all things for the sake of men, they seem to me in all respects to have strayed most widely from true reason. For even if I did not know what first-beginnings are, yet this, judging by the very arrangements of heaven, I would venture to affirm, and led by many other circumstances to maintain, that the nature of the world has by no means been made for us by divine power: so great are the defects with which it stands encumbered. All which, Memmius, we will hereafter make clear to you: we will now go on to explain what remains to be told of motions.

184] Now methinks is the place, herein to prove this point also that no bodily thing can by its own power be borne upwards and travel upwards; that the bodies of flames may not in this manner lead you into error. For they are begotten with an upward tendency, and in the same direction receive increase, and goodly crops and trees grow upwards, though their weights, so far as in them is, all tend downwards. And when fires leap to the roofs of houses and with swift flame lick up rafters and beams, we are not to suppose that they do so spontaneously without a force pushing them up. Even thus blood discharged from our body spirts out and springs up on high and scatters gore about. See you not too with what force the liquid of water spits out logs and beams? The more deeply we have pushed them sheer down and have pressed them in, many of us together, with all our might and much painful effort, with the greater avidity it vomits them up and casts them forth, so that they rise and start out more than half their length. And yet methinks we doubt not that these, so far as in them is, are all borne downwards through the empty void. In the same way flames also ought to be able, when squeezed out, to mount upward through the air, although their weights, so far as in them is, strive to draw them down. See you not too that the nightly meteors of heaven as they fly aloft draw after them long trails of flames in whatever direction nature has given them a passage? Do you not perceive stars and constellations fall to the earth? The sun also from the height of heaven sheds its heat on all sides and sows the fields with light; to the earth therefore as well the sun's heat tends. Lightnings also you see fly athwart the rains: now from this side now from that fires burst from the clouds and rush about; the force of flame falls to the earth all round.

216] This point too herein we wish you to apprehend: when bodies are borne downwards sheer through void by their own weights, at quite uncertain times and uncertain spots they push themselves a little from their course: you just and only just can call it a change of inclination. If they were not used to swerve, they would all fall down, like drops of rain, through the deep void, and no clashing would have been begotten nor blow produced among the first-beginnings: thus nature never would have produced aught.

225] But if haply any one believes that heavier bodies, as they are carried more quickly sheer through space, can fall from above on the lighter and so beget blows able to produce begetting motions, he goes most widely astray from true reason. For whenever bodies fall through water and thin air, they must quicken their descents in proportion to their weights, because the body of water and subtle nature of air cannot retard everything in equal degree, but more readily give way, overpowered by the heavier: on the other hand empty void cannot offer resistance to anything in any direction at any time, but must, as its nature craves, continually give way; and for this reason all things must be moved and borne along with equal velocity though of unequal weights through the unresisting void. Therefore heavier things will never be able to fall from above on lighter nor of themselves to beget blows sufficient to produce the varied motions by which nature carries on things. Wherefore again and again I say bodies must swerve a little; and yet not more than the least possible; lest we be found to be imagining oblique motions and this the reality should refute. For this we see to be plain and evident, that weights, so far as in them is, cannot travel obliquely, when they fall from above, at least so far as you can perceive; but that nothing swerves in any case from the straight course, who is there that can perceive?

251] Again if all motion is ever linked together and a new motion ever springs from another in a fixed order and first-beginnings do not by swerving make some commencement of motion to break through the decrees of fate, that cause follow not cause from everlasting, whence have all living creatures here on earth, whence, I ask, has been wrested from the fates the power by which we go forward whither the will leads each, by which likewise we change the direction of our motions neither at a fixed time nor fixed place; but when and where the mind itself has prompted? For beyond a doubt in these things his own will makes for each a beginning and from this beginning motions are welled through the limbs. See you not too, when the barriers are thrown open at a given moment, that yet the eager powers of the horses cannot start forward so instantaneously as the mind itself desires? the whole store of matter through the whole body must be sought out, in order that stirred up

through all the frame it may follow with undivided effort the bent of the mind; so that you see the beginning of motion is born from the heart, and the action first commences in the will of the mind and next is transmitted through the whole body and frame. Quite different is the case when we move on propelled by a stroke inflicted by the strong might and strong compulsion of another; for then it is quite clear that all the matter of the whole body moves and is hurried on against our inclination, until the will has reined it in throughout the limbs. Do you see then in this case that, though an outward force often pushes men on and compels them frequently to advance against their will and to be hurried headlong on, there yet is something in our breast sufficient to struggle against and resist it? And when too this something chooses, the store of matter is compelled sometimes to change its course through the limbs and frame, and after it has been forced forward, is reined in and settles back into its place. Wherefore in seeds too you must admit the same, admit that besides blows and weights there is another cause of motions, from which this power of free action has been begotten in us, since we see that nothing can come from nothing. For weight forbids that all things be done by blows through as it were an outward force; but that the mind itself does not feel an internal necessity in all its actions and is not as it were overmastered and compelled to bear and put up with this, is caused by a minute swerving of first-beginnings at no fixed part of space and no fixed time.

294] Nor was the store of matter ever more closely massed nor held apart by larger spaces between; for nothing is either added to its bulk or lost to it. Wherefore the bodies of the first-beginnings in time gone by moved in the same way in which now they move, and will ever hereafter be borne along in like manner, and the things which have been wont to be begotten will be begotten after the same law and will be and will grow and will wax in strength so far as is given to each by the decrees of nature. And no force can change the sum of things; for there is nothing outside, either into which any kind of matter can escape out of the universe or out of which a new supply can arise and burst into the universe and change all the nature of things and alter their motions.

308] And herein you need not wonder at this, that though the first-beginnings of things are all in motion, yet the sum is seen to rest in supreme repose, unless where a thing exhibits motions with its individual body. For all the nature of first things lies far away from our senses beneath their ken; and therefore since they are themselves beyond what you can see, they must withdraw from sight their motion as well; and the more so that the things which we can see, do yet often conceal their motions when a great distance off. Thus often the woolly flocks as they crop the glad pastures on a hill, creep on whither the grass jewelled with fresh dew summons and invites each, and the lambs fed to the full gambol and playfully butt; all which objects appear to us from a distance to be blended together and to rest like a white spot on a green hill. Again when mighty legions fill with their movements all parts of the plains waging the mimicry of war, the glitter then lifts itself up to the sky and the whole earth round gleams with brass and beneath a noise is raised by the mighty trampling of men and the mountains stricken by the shouting re-echo the voices to the stars of heaven, and horsemen fly about and suddenly wheeling scour across the middle of the plains, shaking them with the vehemence of their charge. And yet there is some spot on the high hills, seen from which they appear to stand still and to rest on the plains as a bright spot.

333] Now mark and next in order apprehend of what kind and how widely differing in their forms are the beginnings of all things, how varied by manifold diversities of shape; not that a scanty number are possessed of a like form, but because as a rule they do not all resemble one the other. And no wonder; for since there is so great a store of them that, as I have shown, there is no end or sum, they must sure enough not one and all be marked by an equal bulk and like shape, one with another. Let the race of man pass before you in review, and the mute swimming shoals of the scaly tribes and the blithe herds and wild beasts and the different birds which haunt the gladdening watering spots about river-banks and springs and pools, and those which flit about and throng the pathless woods: then go and take any one you like in any one kind, and you will yet find that they differ in their shapes, every one from every other. And in no other way could child recognise mother or mother child; and this we see that they all can do, and that they are just as well known to one another as human beings are. Thus often in front of the beauteous shrines of the gods a calf falls sacrificed beside the incense-burning altars, and spirts from its breast a warm stream of blood; but the bereaved mother as she ranges over the green lawns knows the footprints stamped on the ground by the cloven hoofs, scanning with her eyes every spot to see if she can anywhere behold her lost youngling: then she fills with her moanings the leafy wood each time she desists from her search and again and again goes back to the stall pierced to the heart by the loss of her calf; nor can the soft willows and grass quickened with dew and yon rivers gliding level with their banks comfort her mind and put away the care that has entered into her, nor can other forms of calves throughout the glad pastures divert her mind and ease it of its care: so persistently she seeks something special and known. Again the tender kids with their shaking voices know their horned dams and the butting lambs the flocks of bleating sheep; thus they run, as nature craves, each without fail to its own udder of milk. Lastly in the case of any kind of corn you like you will yet find that any one grain is not so similar to any other in the same kind, but that there runs through them some difference to distinguish the forms. On a like principle of difference we see the class of shells paint the lap of earth, where the sea with gentle waves beats on the thirsty sand of the winding shore. Therefore again and again I say it is necessary for like reasons that first-beginnings of things, since they exist by nature and are not made by hand after the exact model of one, should fly about with shapes in some cases differing one from the other.

381] It is right easy for us on such a principle to explain why the fire of lightning has much more power to pierce than ours which is born of earthly pinewood: you may say that the heavenly fire of lightning subtle as it is is formed of smaller shapes and therefore passes through openings which this our fire cannot pass born as it is of woods and sprung from pine. Again light passes through horn, but rain is thrown off. Why? but that those first bodies of light are smaller than those of which the nurturing liquid of water is made. And quickly as we see wines flow through a strainer, sluggish oil on the other hand is slow to do so, because sure enough it consists of elements either larger in size or more hooked and tangled in one another, and therefore it is that the first-beginnings of things cannot so readily be separated from each other and severally stream through the several openings of any thing.

398] Moreover the liquids honey and milk excite a pleasant sensation of tongue when held in the mouth; but on the other hand the nauseous nature of wormwood and of harsh centaury writhes the mouth with a noisome flavour; so that you may easily see that the things which are able to affect the senses pleasantly, consist of smooth and round elements; while all those on the other hand which are found to be bitter and harsh, are held in connexion by particles that are more hooked and for this reason are wont to tear open passages into our senses and in entering in to break through the body.

408] All things in short which are agreeable to the senses and all which are unpleasant to the feeling are mutually repugnant, formed as they are out of an unlike first shape; lest haply you suppose that the harsh grating of the creaking saw consists of elements as smooth as those of tuneful melodies which musicians wake into life with nimble fingers and give shape to on strings; or suppose that the first-beginnings are of like shape which pass into the nostrils of men, when noisome carcases are burning, and when the stage is fresh sprinkled with Cilician saffron, while the altar close by exhales Panchaean odours; or decide that the pleasant colours of things which are able to feast the eyes are formed of a seed like to the seed of those which make the pupil smart and force it to shed tears or from their disgusting aspect look hideous and foul. For every shape which gratifies the senses has been formed not without a smoothness in its elements; but on the other hand whatever is painful and harsh, has been produced not without some roughness of matter. There are too some elements which are

with justice thought to be neither smooth nor altogether hooked with barbed points, but rather to have minute angles slightly projecting, so that they can tickle rather than hurt the senses; of which class tartar of wine is formed and the flavours of elecampane. Again that hot fires and cold frost have fangs of a dissimilar kind wherewith to pierce the senses, is proved to us by the touch of each. For touch, touch, ye holy divinities of the gods, the body's feeling is, either when an extraneous thing makes its way in, or when a thing which is born in the body hurts it, or gives pleasure as it issues forth by the birth-bestowing ways of Venus, or when from some collision the seeds are disordered within the body and distract the feeling by their mutual disturbance; as if haply you were yourself to strike with the hand any part of the body you please and so make trial. Wherefore the shapes of the first-beginnings must differ widely, since they are able to give birth to different feelings.

444] Again things which look to us hard and dense must consist of particles more hooked together, and be held in union because welded all through with branch-like elements. In this class first of all diamond stones stand in foremost line inured to despise blows, and stout blocks of basalt and the strength of hard iron and brass bolts which scream out as they hold fast to their staples. Those things which are liquid and of fluid body ought to consist more of smooth and round elements; for the several drops have no mutual cohesion and their onward course too has a ready flow downwards. All things lastly which you see disperse themselves in an instant, as smoke mists and flames, if they do not consist entirely of smooth and round, must yet not be held fast by closely tangled elements, so that they may be able to pierce the body and enter it with biting power, yet not stick together: thus you may easily know, that whatever we see the senses have been able to allay, consists not of tangled but of pointed elements. Do not however hold it to be wonderful that some things which are fluid you see to be likewise bitter, for instance the sea's moisture: because it is fluid, it consists of smooth and round particles, and many rough bodies mixed up with these produce pains; and yet they must not be hooked so as to hold together: you are to know that though rough, they are yet spherical, so that while they roll freely on, they may at the same time hurt the senses. And that you may more readily believe that with smooth are mixed rough first-beginnings from which Neptune's body is made bitter, there is a way of separating these, and of seeing how the fresh water, when it is often filtered through the earth, flows by itself into a trench and sweetens; for it leaves above the first-beginnings of the nauseous saltness, inasmuch as the rough particles can more readily stay behind in the earth.

478] And now that I have shown this, I will go on to link to it a truth which depends on this and from this draws its proof: the first-beginnings of things have different shapes, but the number of shapes is finite. If this were not so, then once more it would follow that some seeds must be of infinite bulk of body. For in the same seed, in the single small size of any first body you like the shapes cannot vary much from one another: say for instance that first bodies consist of three least parts, or augment them by a few more; when to wit in all possible ways, by placing each in turn at the top and at the bottom, by making the right change places with the left, you shall have tried all those parts of one first body and found what manner of shape each different arrangement gives to the whole of that body, if after all this haply you shall wish still to vary the shapes, you will have to add other parts; it will next follow that for like reasons the arrangement will require other parts, if haply you shall wish still again to vary the shapes. From all this it results that increase of bulk in the body follows upon newness of the shapes. Wherefore you cannot possibly believe that seeds have an infinite variety of forms, lest you force some to be of a monstrous hugeness, which as I have above shown cannot be proved. Moreover I tell you barbaric robes and radiant Meliboean purple dipped in Thessalian dye of shells and the hues which are displayed by the golden brood of peacocks steeped in laughing beauty would all be thrown aside surpassed by some new colour of things; the smell of myrrh would be despised and the flavours of honey, and the melodies of the swan and Phoebean tunes set off by the varied play of strings would

in like sort be suppressed and silenced; for something ever would arise more surpassing than the rest. All things likewise might fall back into worse states, even as we have said they might advance to better; for reversely too one thing would be more noisome than all other things to nostril, ear and eye and taste. Now since these things are not so, but a fixed limit has been assigned to things which bounds their sum on each side, you must admit that matter also has a finite number of different shapes. Once more from summer fires to chill frosts a definite path is traced out and in like manner is again travelled back; for every degree of cold and heat and intermediate warmths lie between those extremes, filling up in succession the sum. Therefore the things produced differ by finite degrees, since at both ends they are marked off by points, one at one, another at the other, molested on the one hand by flames, on the other by stiffening frosts.

522] And now that I have shown this, I will go on to link to it a truth which depends on this and from this draws its proof: the first-beginnings of things which have a like shape one with the other, are infinite in number. For since the difference of forms is finite, those which are like must be infinite or the sum of matter will be finite, which I proved not to be the case, when I showed in my verses that the minute bodies of matter from everlasting continually uphold the sum of things through an uninterrupted succession of blows on all sides. For though you see that some animals are rarer than others and discern a less fruitful nature in them, yet in another quarter and spot and in distant lands there may be many of that kind and the full tale may be made up; just as we see that in the class of four-footed beasts snake-handed elephants are elsewhere especially numerous; for India is so fenced about with an ivory rampart made out of many thousands of these, that its inner parts cannot be reached, so great is the quantity of brutes, of which we see but very few samples. But yet though I should grant this point too: be there even as you will some one thing sole in its kind existing alone with a body that had birth, and let no other thing resemble it in the whole world; yet unless there shall be an infinite supply of matter out of which it may be conceived and brought into being, it cannot be produced, and, more than this, it cannot have growth and food. For though I should assume this point also that birth-giving bodies of some one thing are tossed about in finite quantity throughout the universe, whence, where, by what force and in what way shall they meet together and combine in so vast a sea, such an alien medley of matter? They have methinks no way of uniting; but even as when great and numerous shipwrecks have occurred, the great sea is wont to tumble about banks, rudders, yards, prow, masts and swimming oars, so that poop-fittings are seen floating about along every shore and utter to mortals a warning to try to shun the snares and violence and guile of the faithless sea, and never at any time to trust to it, when the winning face of calm ocean laughs treacherously; thus too if you shall once decide that certain first-beginnings are finite, different currents of matter must scatter and tumble them about through all time, so that they can never be brought into union and combine, nor abide in any union nor grow up and increase. But plain matter of fact shows that each of these results manifestly does take place, that things can be brought into being and when begotten advance in growth. It is clear then that in any class you like the first-beginnings of things are infinite, out of which all supplies are furnished.

569] Thus neither can death-dealing motions keep the mastery always nor entomb existence for evermore, nor on the other hand can the birth and increase giving motions of things preserve them always after they are born. Thus the war of first-beginnings waged from eternity is carried on with dubious issue: now here now there the life-bringing elements of things get the mastery and are o'ermastered in turn: with the funeral wail blends the cry which babies raise when they enter the borders of light; and no night ever followed day nor morning night that heard not mingling with the sickly infant's cries wailings the attendants on death and black funeral.

581] And herein it is proper you should keep under seal, and guard, there consigned, in faithful memory this truth, that there is nothing whose nature is apparent to sense, which consists of one kind of first-beginnings; nothing which is not formed by a mixing of seed. And whenever a thing possesses in itself in larger measure many powers and properties, in that measure it shows that there are in it the greatest number of different kinds and varied shapes of first-beginnings. First of all the earth has in her first bodies out of which springs rolling coolness along replenish without fail the boundless sea, she has bodies out of which fires rise up; for in many spots the earth's crust is on fire and burns, though headstrong Aetna rages with fire of surpassing force. Then too she has bodies out of which she can raise for mankind goodly crops and joyous trees, out of which too she can supply to the mountain-ranging race of wild beasts rivers, leaves, and glad pastures. Wherefore she has alone been named great mother of gods and mother of beasts and parent of our body.

600] Of her the old and learned poets of the Greeks have sung, that borne aloft on high raised seat in a chariot she drives a pair of lions, teaching that the great earth hangs in the expanse of air and that earth cannot rest on earth. To her chariot they have yoked wild beasts, because a brood however savage ought to be tamed and softened by the kind offices of parents. They have encircled the top of her head with a mural crown, because fortified in choice positions she sustains towns; adorned with which emblem the image of the divine mother is carried now-a-days through wide lands in awe-inspiring state. Her different nations after old-established ritual term Idaean mother, and give for escort Phrygian bands, because they tell that from those lands corn first began to be produced throughout the world. They assign her Galli,[1] because they would show by this type that they who have done violence to the divinity of the mother and have proved ungrateful to their parents, are to be deemed unworthy to bring a living off-spring into the borders of light. Tight-stretched tambourines and hollow cymbals resound all round to the stroke of their open hands, and horns menace with hoarse-sounding music, and the hollow pipe stirs their minds in Phrygian mood. They carry weapons before them, emblems of furious rage, meet to fill the thankless souls and godless breasts of the rabble with

[1]The eunuch priests of the cult of Cybele.

terror for the divinity of the goddess. Therefore when first borne in procession through great cities she mutely enriches mortals with a blessing not expressed in words, they strew all her path with brass and silver presenting her with bounteous alms, and scatter over her a snow-shower of roses, o'ershadowing the mother and her troops of attendants. Here an armed band to which the Greeks give the name of Phrygian Curetes, in that it haply joins in the game of arms and springs up in measure all dripping with blood, shaking with its nodding the frightful crests upon the head, represents the Dictaean Curetes who, as the story is, erst drowned in Crete that infant cry of Jove, when the young band about the young babe in rapid dance arms in hand to measured tread beat brass on brass, that Saturn might not get him to consign to his devouring jaws and stab the mother to the heart with a never-healing wound. For these reasons they escort in arms the Great Mother, or else because they mean by this sign that the goddess preaches to men to be willing with arms and valour to defend their country and be ready to be a safeguard and an ornament to their parents.

644] All which, well and beautifully as it is set forth and told, is yet widely removed from true reason. For the nature of gods must ever in itself of necessity enjoy immortality together with supreme of repose, far removed and withdrawn from our concerns; since exempt from every pain, exempt from all dangers, strong in its own resources, not wanting aught of us, it is neither gained by favours nor moved by anger. And here if any one thinks proper to call the sea Neptune and corn Ceres and chooses rather to misuse the name of Bacchus than to utter the term that belongs to that liquor, let us allow him to declare that the earth is mother of the gods, if he only forbear in earnest to stain his mind with foul religion. The earth however is at all time without feeling, and because it receives into it the first-beginnings of many things, it brings them forth in many ways into the light of the sun.

661] And so the woolly flocks and the martial breed of horses and horned herds, though often cropping the grass from one field beneath the same canopy of heaven and slaking their thirst from one stream of water, yet have all their life a dissimilar appearance and retain the nature of their parents and severally imitate their ways each after its kind: so great is the diversity of matter in any kind of herbage, so great in every river. And hence too any one you please out of the whole number of living creatures is made up of bones, blood, veins, heat, moisture, flesh, sinews; and these things again differ widely from one another and are composed of first-beginnings of unlike shape. Furthermore whatever things are set on fire and burned, store up in their body, if nothing else, at least those particles, out of which they may radiate fire and send out light and make sparks fly and scatter embers all about. If you will go over all other things by a like process of reasoning, you will thus find that they conceal in their body the seeds of many things and contain elements of various shapes. Again you see many things to which are given at once both colour and taste together with smell; especially those many offerings which are burned on the altars. These must therefore be made up of elements of different shapes; for smell enters in where colour passes not into the frame, colour too in one way, taste in another makes its entrance into the senses; so that you know they differ in the shapes of their first elements. Therefore unlike forms unite into one mass and things are made up of a mixture of seed. Throughout moreover these very verses of ours you see many elements common to many words, though yet you must admit that the verses and words one with another are different and composed of different elements; not that but few letters which are in common run through them or that no two words or verses one with another are made up entirely of the same, but because as a rule they do not all resemble one the other. Thus also though in other things there are many first-beginnings common to many things, yet they can make up one with the other a quite dissimilar whole; so that men and corn and joyous trees may fairly be said to consist of different elements.

700] And yet we are not to suppose that all things can be joined together in all ways; for then you would see prodigies produced on all hands, forms springing up half man half beast and sometimes tall boughs sprouting from the living body, and many limbs of land-creatures joined with those of sea-animals, nature too throughout the all-bearing lands feeding chimeras which breathed flames from noisome mouth. It is plain however that nothing of the sort is done, since we see that all things produced from fixed seeds and a fixed mother can in growing preserve the marks of their kind. This you are to know must take place after a fixed law. For the particles suitable for each thing from all kinds of food when inside the body pass into the frame and joining on produce the appropriate motions; but on the other hand we see nature throw out on the earth those that are alien, and many things with their unseen bodies fly out of the body impelled by blows: those I mean which have not been able to join on to any part nor when inside to feel in unison with and adopt the vital motions. But lest you haply suppose that living things alone are bound by these conditions, such a law keeps all things within their limits. For even as things begotten are in their whole nature all unlike one the other, thus each must consist of first-beginnings of unlike shape; not that a scanty number are possessed of a like form, but because as a rule they do not all resemble one the other. Again since the seeds differ, there must be a difference in the spaces between, the passages, the connexions, the weights, the blows, the clashings, the motions; all which not only disjoin living bodies, but hold apart the lands and the whole sea, and keep all heaven away from the earth.

730] Now mark, and apprehend precepts amassed by my welcome toil, lest haply you deem that those things which you see with your eyes to be bright, because white are formed of white principles, or that the things which are black are born from black seed; or that things which are steeped in any other colour, bear that colour because the bodies of matter are dyed with a colour like to it. For the bodies of matter have no colour at all either like to the things or unlike. But if haply it seems to you that no impression of the mind can throw itself into these bodies, you wander far astray. For since men born blind who have never beheld the light of the sun, yet recognise bodies by touch, though linked with no colour for them from their first birth, you are to know that bodies can fall under the ken of our mind too, though stained with no colour. Again whatever things we ourselves touch in the thick darkness, we do not perceive to be dyed with any colour. And since I prove that this is the case, I will now show that there are things which are possessed of no colour. Well, any colour without any exception changes into any other; and this first-beginnings ought in no wise to do: something unchangeable must remain over, that all things be not utterly reduced to nothing. For whenever a thing changes and quits its proper limits, at once this change of state is the death of that which was before. Therefore mind not to dye with colour the seeds of things, that you may not have all things altogether returning to nothing.

757] Moreover if no quality of colour is assigned to first-beginnings and they are yet possessed of varied shapes out of which they beget colours of every kind and change them about by reason that it makes a great difference with what other seeds and in what position the seeds are severally held in union and what motions they mutually impart and receive, you can explain at once with the greatest ease why those things which just before were of a black colour, may become all at once of marble whiteness; as the sea, when mighty winds have stirred up its waters, is changed into white waves of the brightness of marble: you may say that when the matter of that which we often see to be black, has been mixed up anew and the arrangement of its first-beginnings has been changed and some have been added and some been taken away, the immediate result is that it appears bright and white. But if the waters of the sea consisted of azure seeds, they could in no wise become white; for however much you jumble together seeds which are azure, they can never pass into a marble colour. But if the seeds which make up the one unmixed brightness of the sea are dyed some with one, some with other colours, just as often out of different forms and varied shapes something square and of a uniform figure is made up, in that case it were natural that as we see unlike forms contained in the square, so we should see in the water of the sea or in any other one and unmixed brightness colours widely unlike and different to one another. Moreover the unlike figures do not in the least hinder or prevent the whole figure from being a square on the outside; but the various colours of things are a let and hindrance to the whole things being of a uniform brightness.

788] Then too the reason which leads and draws us on sometimes to assign colours to the first-beginnings of things, falls to the ground, since white things are not produced from white, nor those which are black from black, but out of things of various colours. For white things will much more readily rise up and be born from no colour than from a black or any other colour which thwarts and opposes it.

795] Moreover since colours cannot exist without light and first-beginnings of things do not come out into the light, you may be sure they are clothed with no colour. For what colour can there be in total darkness? nay it changes in the light itself according as its brightness comes from a straight or slanting stroke of light. After this fashion the down which encircles and crowns the nape and throat of doves shows itself in the sun: at one time it is ruddy with the hue of bright pyropus; at another it appears by a certain way of looking at it to blend with coral-red green emeralds. The tail of the peacock when it is saturated with abundant light, changes in like fashion its colours as it turns about. And since these colours are begotten by a certain stroke of light, sure enough you must believe that they cannot be produced without it. And since the pupil receives into it a kind of blow, when it is said to perceive a white colour, and then another, when it perceives black or any other colour, and since it is of no moment with what colour the things which you touch are provided, but rather with what sort of shape they are furnished, you are to know that first-beginnings have no need of colours, but produce sensations of touch varying according to their various shapes.

817] Moreover since no particular kind of colour is assigned to particular shapes and every configuration of first-beginnings can exist in any colour, why on a like principle are not the things which are formed out of them in every kind o'erlaid with colours of every kind? For then it were natural that crows too in flying should often display a white colour

from white wings and that swans should come to be black from a black seed, or of any other different colour you please.

826] Again the more minute the parts are into which any thing is rent, the more you may perceive the colour fade away by little and little and become extinct; as for instance if a piece of purple is torn into small shreds: when it has been plucked into separate threads, the purple, and the scarlet far the most brilliant of colours, are quite effaced; from which you may infer that the shreds part with all their colour before they come back to the seeds of things.

834] Lastly since you admit that all bodies do not utter a voice nor emit a smell, for this reason you do not assign to all sounds and smells. So also since we cannot perceive all things with the eyes, you are to know that some things are as much denuded of colour as others are without smell and devoid of sound, and that the keen-discerning mind can just as well apprehend these things as it can take note of things which are destitute of other qualities.

842] But lest haply you suppose that first bodies remain stripped of colour alone, they are also wholly devoid of warmth and cold and violent heat, and are judged to be barren of sound and drained of moisture, and emit from their body no scent of their own. Just as when you set about preparing the balmy liquid of sweet marjoram and myrrh and the flower of spikenard which gives forth to the nostrils a scent like nectar, before all you should seek, so far as you may and can find it, the substance of scentless oil, such as gives out no perfume to the nostrils, that it may as little as possible meddle with and destroy by its own pungency the odours mixed in its body and boiled up with it; for the same reason the first-beginnings of things must not bring to the begetting of things a smell or sound of their own, since they cannot discharge anything from themselves, and for the same reason no taste either nor cold nor any heat moderate or violent, and the like. For as these things, be they what they may, are still such as to be liable to death, whether pliant with a soft, brittle with a crumbling, or hollow with a porous body, they must all be withdrawn from the first-beginnings, if we wish to assign to things imperishable foundations for the whole

sum of existence to rest upon: that you may
not have things returning altogether to nothing.

865] To come to another point, whatever
things we perceive to have sense, you must yet
admit to be all composed of senseless first-beginnings: manifest tokens which are open to
all to apprehend, so far from refuting or con-
tradicting this, do rather themselves take us
by the hand and constrain us to believe that, as
I say, living things are begotten from senseless
things. We may see in fact living worms spring
out of stinking dung, when the soaked earth
has gotten putridity after excessive rains; and
all things besides change in the same way:
rivers, leaves, and glad pastures change into
cattle, cattle change their substance into our
bodies, and often out of these the powers of
wild beasts and the bodies of the strong of
wing are increased. Therefore nature changes
all foods into living bodies and engenders out
of them all the senses of living creatures, much
in the same way as she dissolves dry woods
into flames and converts all things into fires.
Now do you see that it is of great moment in
what sort of arrangement the first-beginnings
of things are severally placed and with what
others they are mixed up, when they impart
and receive motions?

886] Then again what is that which strikes
your mind, affects that mind and constrains
it to give utterance to many different thoughts,
to save you from believing that the sensible
is begotten out of senseless things? Sure
enough it is because stones and wood and
earth however mixed together are yet unable
to produce vital sense. This therefore it will be
well to remember herein, that I do not assert
that the sensible and sensations are forthwith
begotten out of all elements without exception
which produce things; but that it is of great
moment first how minute the particles are
which make up the sensible thing and then
what shape they possess and what in short
they are in their motions, arrangements and
positions. None of which conditions we find in
woods and clods; and yet even these when they
have so to speak become rotten through the
rains, bring forth worms, because bodies of
matter driven from their ancient arrangements
by a new condition are combined in the manner needed for the begetting of living creatures. Next they who hold that the sensible
can be produced out of sensible elements, accustomed thus to derive their own sense from
elements which are sensible in their turn, do
thus render their own seeds mortal, when
they make them soft; for all sense is bound up
with flesh, sinews and veins; which in everything we see to be soft and formed of a mortal
body. But even suppose that these things can
remain eternal: they must yet I presume either
have the sense of some part or else be deemed
to possess a sense similar to the entire living
creatures. But the parts cannot possibly have
sense by themselves alone; for all sense of the
different members has reference to something
else; nor can the hand when severed from us
nor any other part of the body whatever by
itself maintain sensation. It remains to assume
that they resemble the entire living creatures.
In this case it is necessary that they should feel
the things which we feel in the same way as
we do, in order that they may be able in all
points to work in concert with the vital sense.
How then can they be called first-beginnings
of things and shun the paths of death, seeing
that they are living things, and that living
things are one and the same with mortal
things? Nay granting they could do this, yet
by their meeting and union they will make
nothing but a jumble and medley of living
things; just, you are to know, as men, cattle,
and wild beasts would be unable to beget any
other thing by all their mixing with one another. But if haply they lose from their body
their own sense and adopt another, what use
was it to assign what is again withdrawn?
moreover, the instance to which we had before
recourse, inasmuch as we see the eggs of fowls
change into living chicks and worms burst
forth, when putridity has seized on the earth
after excessive rains, you are to know that sensations can be begotten out of no-sensations.

931] But if haply any one shall say that sense
so far may arise from no-sensation by a process
of change, or because it is brought forth by a
kind of birth, it will be enough to make plain
and to prove to him that no birth takes place
until a union of elements has first been effected, and that nothing changes without their
having been united. Above all senses cannot

exist in any body before the nature itself of the living thing has been begotten, because sure enough the matter remains scattered about in air, rivers, earth, and things produced from earth, and has not met together and combined in appropriate fashion the vital motions by which the all-discerning senses are kindled into action in each living thing.

944] Again a blow more severe than its nature can endure, prostrates at once any living thing and goes on to stun all the senses of body and mind. For the positions of the first-beginnings are broken up and the vital motions entirely stopped, until the matter, disordered by the shock through the whole frame, unties from the body the vital fastenings of the soul and scatters it abroad and forces it out through all the pores. For what more can we suppose the infliction of a blow can do, than shake from their place and break up the union of the several elements? Often too when the blow is inflicted with less violence, the remaining vital motions are wont to prevail, ay, prevail and still the huge disorders caused by the blow and recall each part into its proper channels and shake off the motion of death now reigning as it were paramount in the body and kindle afresh the almost lost senses. For in what other way should the thing be able to gather together its powers of mind and come back to life from the very threshold of death, rather than pass on to the goal to which it had almost run and so pass away?

963] Again since there is pain when the bodies of matter are disordered by any force throughout the living flesh and frame and quake in their seats within, and as when they travel back into their place, a soothing pleasure ensues, you are to know that first-beginnings can be assailed by no pain and can derive no pleasure from themselves; since they are not formed of any bodies of first-beginnings, so as to be distressed by any novelty in their motion or derive from it any fruit of fostering delight; and therefore they must not be possessed of any sense.

973] Again if in order that living creatures may severally have sense, sense is to be assigned to their first-beginnings as well, what are we to say of those of which mankind is specifically made? Sure enough they burst into fits of shaking laughter and sprinkle with dewy tears face and cheeks and have the cunning to say much about the composition of things and to enquire next what their own first-beginnings are; since like in their natures to the entire mortals they must in their turn be formed out of other elements, then those others out of others, so that you can venture nowhere to come to a stop: yes, whatever you shall say speaks and laughs and thinks, I will press you with the argument that it is formed of other things performing these same acts. But if we see these notions to be sheer folly and madness, and a man may laugh though not made of laughing things, and think and reason in learned language though not formed of thoughtful and eloquent seeds, why cannot the things which we see to have sense, just as well be made up of a mixture of things altogether devoid of sense?

991] Again we are all sprung from a heavenly seed, all have that same father, by whom mother earth the giver of increase, when she has taken in from him liquid drops of moisture, conceives and bears goodly crops and joyous trees and the race of man, bears all kinds of brute beasts, in that she supplies food with which all feed their bodies and lead a pleasant life and continue their race; wherefore with good cause she has gotten the name of mother. That also which before was from the earth, passes back into the earth, and that which was sent from the borders of ether, is carried back and taken in again by the quarters of heaven. Death does not extinguish things in such a way as to destroy the bodies of matter, but only breaks up the union amongst them, and then joins anew the different elements with others; and thus it comes to pass that all things change their shapes and alter their colours and receive sensations and in a moment yield them up; so that from all this you may know it matters much with what others and in what position the same first-beginnings of things are held in union and what motions they do mutually impart and receive, and you must not suppose that that which we see floating about on the surface of things and now born, then at once perishing, can be a property inherent in everlasting first bodies. Nay in our verses themselves it matters much with what other elements and in what kind of order the several elements are placed. If not all, yet by far the greatest number are alike; but the totals composed of them are made to differ by the position of these elements. Thus in actual things as well when the clashings, motions, arrangement, position, and shapes of matter change about, the things must also change.

1023] Apply now, we entreat, your mind to true reason. For a new question struggles earnestly to gain your ears, a new aspect of things to display itself. But there is nothing so easy as not to be at first more difficult to believe than afterwards; and nothing too so great, so marvellous, that all do not gradually abate their admiration of it. Look up at the bright and unsullied hue of heaven and the stars which it holds within it, wandering all about, and the moon and the sun's light of dazzling brilliancy: if all these things were now for the first time, if I say they were now suddenly presented to mortals beyond all expectation, what could have been named that would be more marvellous than these things, or that nations beforehand would less venture to believe could be? Nothing, methinks: so wondrous strange had been this sight. Yet how little, you know, wearied as all are to satiety with seeing, any one now cares to look up into heaven's glittering quarters! Cease therefore to be dismayed by the mere novelty and so to reject reason from your mind with loathing: weigh the questions rather with keen judgement and if they seem to you to be true, surrender, or if they are a falsehood, gird yourself to the encounter. For since the sum of space is unlimited outside beyond these walls of the world, the mind seeks to apprehend what there is yonder there, to which the spirit ever yearns to look forward, and to which the mind's immission reaches in free and unembarrassed flight.

1048] In the first place we see that round in all directions, about, above, and underneath, throughout the universe there is no bound, as I have shown and as the thing of itself proclaims with loud voice and as clearly shines out in the nature of bottomless space. In no wise then can it be deemed probable, when space yawns illimitable towards all points and

seeds in number numberless and sum unfathomable fly about in manifold ways driven on in ceaseless motion, that this single earth and heaven have been brought into being, that those bodies of matter so many in number do nothing outside them; the more so that this world has been made by nature, just as the seeds of things have chanced spontaneously to clash, after being brought together in manifold wise without purpose, without foresight, without result, and at last have filtered through such seeds as, suddenly thrown together, were fitted to become on each occasion the rudiments of great things, of earth, sea, and heaven and the race of living things. Wherefore again and again I say you must admit that there are elsewhere other combinations of matter like to this which ether holds in its greedy grasp.

1067] Again when much matter is at hand, when room is there and there is no thing, no cause to hinder, things sure enough must go on and be completed. Well then if on the one hand there is so great a store of seeds as the whole life of living creatures cannot reckon up, and if the same force and nature abide in them and have the power to throw the seeds of things together into their several places in the same way as they are thrown together into our world, you must admit that in other parts of space there are other earths and various races of men and kinds of wild beasts.

1077] Moreover in the sum of all there is no one thing which is begotten single in its kind and grows up single and sole of its kind; but a thing always belongs to some class and there are many other things in the same kind. First in the case of living things, most noble Memmius, you will find that in this sort has been begotten the mountain-ranging race of wild beasts, in this sort the breed of men, in this sort too the mute shoals of scaly creatures and all bodies of fowls. Wherefore on a like principle you must admit that earth and sun, moon, sea, and all things else that are, are not single in their kind, but rather in number past numbering; since the deep-set boundary-mark of life just as much awaits these and they are just as much of a body that had birth, as any class of things which here on earth abounds in samples of its kind.

1090] If you well apprehend and keep in mind these things, nature free at once and rid of her haughty lords is seen to do all things spontaneously of herself without the meddling of the gods. For I appeal to the holy breasts of the gods who in tranquil peace pass a calm time and an unruffled existence, who can rule the sum, who hold in his hand with controlling force the strong reins, of the immeasurable deep? who can at once make all the different heavens to roll and warm with ethereal fires all the fruitful earths, or be present in all places at all times, to bring darkness with clouds and shake with noise the heaven's serene expanse, to hurl lightnings and often throw down his own temples, and withdrawing into the deserts there to spend his rage in practising his bolt which often passes the guilty by and strikes dead the innocent and unoffending?

1105] And since the birth-time of the world and first day of being to sea and earth and the formation of the sun many bodies have been added from without, many seeds added all round, which the great universe in tossing to and fro has contributed; that from them the sea and lands might increase and from them heaven's mansion might enlarge its expanse and raise its high vaults far above earth, and that air might rise up around. For all bodies from all quarters are assigned by blows each to its appropriate thing and all withdraw to their proper classes; moisture passes to moisture, from an earthy body earth increases and fires forge fires and ether ether, until nature, parent of things, with finishing hand has brought all things on to their utmost limit of growth. And this comes to pass when that which is infused into the life-arteries is no more than that which ebbs from them and withdraws: at this point the life-growth in all things must stop, at this point nature by her powers checks further increase. For whatever things you see grow in size with joyous increase and mount by successive steps to mature age, take to themselves more bodies than they discharge from themselves, while food is readily infused into all the arteries and the things are not so widely spread out as to throw off many particles and occasion more waste than their age can take in as nourishment.

For no doubt it must be conceded that many bodies ebb away and withdraw from things; but still more must join them, until they have touched the utmost point of growth. Then piece by piece age breaks their powers and matured strength and wastes away on the side of decay. For the larger a thing is and the wider, as soon as its growth is stopped, at once it sheds abroad and discharges from it more bodies in all directions round; and its food is not readily transmitted into all its arteries and is not enough, in proportion to the copious exhalations which the thing throws off, to enable a like amount to rise up and be supplied. For food must keep all things entire by renewing them, food must uphold, food sustain all things: all in vain, since the arteries refuse to hold what is sufficient, and nature does not furnish the needful amount. With good reason therefore all things perish, when they have been rarefied by the ebb of particles and succumb to blows from without, since food sooner or later fails advanced age, and bodies never cease to destroy a thing by thumping it from without and to overpower it by aggressive blows.

1148] In this way then the walls too of the great world around shall be stormed and fall to decay and crumbling ruin. Yes and even now the age is enfeebled and the earth exhausted by bearing scarce produces little living creatures, she who produced all races and gave birth to the huge bodies of wild beasts. For methinks no golden chain let down to earth from heaven above the races of mortal beings, nor did the sea and waves which lash the rocks produce them, but the same earth bare them which now feeds them out of herself. Moreover she first spontaneously of herself produced for mortals goodly corn-crops and joyous vineyards; of herself gave sweet fruits and glad pastures; which now-a-days scarce attain any size when furthered by our labour: we exhaust the oxen and the strength of the husband-men; we wear out our iron, scarcely fed after all by the tilled fields; so niggardly are they of their produce and after so much labour do they let it grow. And now the aged ploughman shakes his head and sighs again and again to think that the labours of his hands have come to nothing; and when he compares present times with times past, he often praises the fortunes of his sire and harps on the theme, how the men of old rich in piety comfortably supported life on a scanty plot of ground, since the allotment of land to each man was far less of yore than now. The sorrowful planter too of the exhausted and shrivelled vine impeaches the march of time and wearies heaven, and comprehends not that all things are gradually wasting away and passing to the grave, quite forspent by age and length of days.

· BOOK THREE ·

THEE, who first wast able amid such thick darkness to raise on high so bright a beacon and shed a light on the true interests of life, thee I follow, glory of the Greek race, and plant now my footsteps firmly fixed in thy imprinted marks, not so much from a desire to rival thee as that from the love I bear thee I yearn to imitate thee; for why need the swallow contend with swans, or what likeness is there between the feats of racing performed by kids with tottering limbs and by the powerful strength of the horse? Thou, father, art discoverer of things, thou furnishest us with fatherly precepts, and like as bees sip of all things in the flowery lawns, we, O glorious being, in like manner feed from out thy pages upon all the golden maxims, golden I say, most worthy ever of endless life. For soon as thy philosophy issuing from a godlike intellect has begun with loud voice to proclaim the nature of things, the terrors of the mind are dispelled, the walls of the world part asunder, I see things in operation throughout the whole void: the divinity of the gods is revealed and their tranquil abodes which neither winds do shake nor clouds drench with rains nor snow congealed by sharp frosts harms with hoary fall: an ever cloudless ether o'ercanopies them, and they laugh with light shed largely round. Nature too supplies all their wants and nothing ever impairs their peace of mind. But on the other hand the Acherusian quarters are nowhere to be seen, though earth is no bar to all things being described, which are in operation underneath our feet throughout the void. At all this a kind of godlike delight mixed with shuddering awe comes over me to think that nature by thy power is laid thus visibly open, is thus unveiled on every side.

31] And now since I have shown what-like the beginnings of all things are and how diverse with varied shapes as they fly spontaneously driven on in everlasting motion, and how all things can be severally produced out of these, next after these questions the nature of the mind and soul should methinks be cleared up by my verses and that dread of Acheron be driven headlong forth, troubling as it does the life of man from its inmost depths and overspreading all things with the blackness of death, allowing no pleasure to be pure and unalloyed. For as to what men often give out that diseases and a life of shame are more to be feared than Tartarus, place of death, and that they know the soul to be of blood or it may be of wind, if haply their choice so direct, and that they have no need at all of our philosophy, you may perceive for the following reasons that all these boasts are thrown out more for glory's sake than because the thing is really believed. These very men, exiles from their country and banished far from the sight of men, live degraded by foul charge of guilt, sunk in a word in every kind of misery, and whithersoever the poor wretches are come, they yet do offer sacrifices to the dead and slaughter black sheep and make libations to the gods Manes and in times of distress turn their thoughts to religion much more earnestly. Wherefore you can better test the man in doubts and dangers and mid adversity learn who he is; for then and not till then the words of truth are forced out from the bottom of his heart: the mask is torn off, the reality is left. Avarice again and blind lust of honours which constrain unhappy men to overstep the bounds of right and sometimes as partners and agents of crimes to strive night and day with surpassing effort to struggle up to the summit of power—these sores of life are in no small measure fostered by the dread of death. For foul scorn and pinching want in every case are seen to be far removed from a life of pleasure and security and to be a loitering so to say before the gates of death. And while men driven on by an unreal dread wish to escape far away from these and keep them far from them, they amass wealth by civil bloodshed and greedily double their riches piling up murder on murder; cruelly triumph in the sad death of a brother and hate and fear the tables of kinsfolk. Often likewise from the same fear envy causes them to pine: they make moan that before their very eyes he is powerful, he attracts attention, who walks arrayed in gorgeous dignity, while they are wallowing in darkness and dirt. Some wear themselves to death for the sake of statues and a name. And often to such a degree through dread of death does hate of life and of the sight of daylight seize upon mortals, that they commit self-murder with a sorrowing heart, quite forgetting that this fear is the source of their cares, this fear which urges men to every sin, prompts this one to put all shame to rout, another to burst asunder the bonds of friendship, and in fine to overturn duty from its very base; since often ere now men have betrayed country and dear parents in seeking to shun the Acherusian quarters. For even as children are flurried and dread all things in the thick darkness, thus we in the daylight fear at times things not a whit more to be dreaded than what children shudder at in the dark and fancy sure to be. This terror therefore and darkness of mind must be dispelled not by the rays of the sun and glittering shafts of day, but by the aspect and law of nature.

94] First then I say that the mind which we often call the understanding, in which dwells the directing and governing principle of life, is no less part of the man, than hand and foot and eyes are parts of the whole living creature. Some however affirm that the sense of the mind does not dwell in a distinct part, but is a certain vital state of the body, which the Greeks call harmonia, because by it, they say, we live with sense, though the understanding is in no one part; just as when good health is said to belong to the body, though yet it is not any one part of the man in health. In this way they do not assign a distinct part to the sense of the mind; in all which they appear to me to be grievously at fault in more ways than one. Oftentimes the body which is visible to sight, is sick, while yet we have pleasure in another hidden part; and oftentimes the case is the very reverse, the man who is unhappy in mind feeling pleasure in his whole body; just as if, while a sick man's foot is pained, the head meanwhile should be in no pain at all. Moreover when the limbs are consigned to soft sleep and the burdened body lies diffused without sense, there is yet a something else in us which during that time is moved in many ways and admits into it all the motions of joy and unreal cares of the heart. Now that you may know that the soul as well is in the limbs and that the body is not wont to have sense by any harmony, this is a main proof: when much of the body has been taken away, still life often stays in the limbs; and yet the same life, when a few bodies of heat have been dispersed abroad and some air has been forced out through the mouth, abandons at once the veins and quits the bones: by this you may perceive that all bodies have not functions of like importance nor alike uphold existence, but rather that those seeds which constitute wind and heat, cause life to stay in the limbs. Therefore vital heat and wind are within the body and abandon our frame at death. Since then the nature of the mind and that of the soul have been proved to be a part as it were of the man, surrender the name of harmony, whether brought down to musicians from high Helicon, or whether rather they have themselves taken it from something else and transferred it to that thing which then was in need of a distinctive name; whatever it be, let them keep it: do you take in the rest of my precepts.

136] Now I assert that the mind and the soul are kept together in close union and make up a single nature, but that the directing principle which we call mind and understanding, is the head so to speak and reigns paramount in the whole body. It has a fixed seat in the middle region of the breast: here throb fear and apprehension, about these spots dwell soothing joys; therefore here is the understanding or mind. All the rest of the soul disseminated through the whole body obeys and moves at the will and inclination of the mind. It by itself alone knows for itself, rejoices for itself, at times when the impression does not move either soul or body together with it. And as when some part of us, the head or the eye, suffers from an attack of pain, we do not feel the anguish at the same time over the whole body, thus the mind sometimes suffers pain by itself or is inspirited with joy, when all the rest of the soul throughout the limbs and frame is stirred by no novel sensation. But when the mind is excited by some more vehement apprehension, we see the whole soul feel in unison through all the limbs, sweats and paleness spread over the whole body, the tongue falter, the voice die away, a mist cover the eyes, the ears ring, the limbs sink under one; in short we often see men drop down from terror of mind; so that anybody may easily perceive from this that the soul is closely united with the mind, and, when it has been smitten by the influence of the mind, forthwith pushes and strikes the body.

161] This same principle teaches that the nature of the mind and soul is bodily; for when it is seen to push the limbs, rouse the body from sleep, and alter the countenance and guide and turn about the whole man, and when we see that none of these effects can take place without touch nor touch without body, must we not admit that the mind and the soul are of a bodily nature? Again you perceive that our mind in our body suffers together with the body and feels in unison with it. When a weapon with a shudder-causing force has been driven in and has laid bare bones and sinews within the body, if it does not take life, yet there ensues a faintness and a lazy sinking to the ground and on the ground the turmoil of mind which arises, and sometimes a kind of undecided inclination to get up. Therefore the nature of mind must be bodily, since it suffers from bodily weapons and blows.

177] I will now go on to explain in my verses of what kind of body the mind consists and out of what it is formed. First of all I say that it is extremely fine and formed of exceedingly minute bodies. That this is so you may, if you please to attend, clearly perceive from what follows: nothing that is seen takes place with

a velocity equal to that of the mind when it starts some suggestion and actually sets it agoing; the mind therefore is stirred with greater rapidity than any of the things whose nature stands out visible to sight. But that which is so passing nimble, must consist of seeds exceedingly round and exceedingly minute, in order to be stirred and set in motion by a small moving power. Thus water is moved and heaves by ever so small a force, formed as it is of small particles apt to roll. But on the other hand the nature of honey is more sticky, its liquid more sluggish and its movement more dilatory; for the whole mass of matter coheres more closely, because sure enough it is made of bodies not so smooth, fine, and round. A breeze however gentle and light can force, as you may see, a high heap of poppy seed to be blown away from the top downwards; but on the other hand Eurus itself cannot move a heap of stones. Therefore bodies possess a power of moving in proportion to their smallness and smoothness; and on the other hand the greater weight and roughness bodies prove to have, the more stable they are. Since then the nature of the mind has been found to be eminently easy to move, it must consist of bodies exceedingly small, smooth, and round. The knowledge of which fact, my good friend, will on many accounts prove useful and be serviceable to you. The following fact too likewise demonstrates how fine the texture is of which its nature is composed, and how small the room is in which it can be contained, could it only be collected into one mass: soon as the untroubled sleep of death has gotten hold of a man and the nature of the mind and soul has withdrawn, you can perceive then no diminution of the entire body either in appearance or weight: death makes all good save the vital sense and heat. Therefore the whole soul must consist of very small seeds and be inwoven through veins and flesh and sinews; inasmuch as, after it has all withdrawn from the whole body, the exterior contour of the limbs preserves itself entire and not a tittle of the weight is lost. Just in the same way when the flavour of wine is gone or when the delicious aroma of a perfume has been dispersed into the air or when the savour has left some body, yet the thing itself does not therefore look smaller to the eye, nor does aught seem to have been taken from the weight, because sure enough many minute seeds make up the savours and the odour in the whole body of the several things. Therefore, again and again I say, you are to know that the nature of the mind and the soul has been formed of exceedingly minute seeds, since at its departure it takes away none of the weight.

231] We are not however to suppose that this nature is single. For a certain subtle spirit mixed with heat quits men at death, and then the heat draws air along with it; there being no heat which has not air too mixed with it: for since its nature is rare, many first-beginnings of air must move about through it. Thus the nature of the mind is proved to be threefold; and yet these things all together are not sufficient to produce sense; since the fact of the case does not admit that any of these can produce sense-giving motions and the thoughts which a man turns over in mind. Thus some fourth nature too must be added to these: it is altogether without name; than it nothing exists more nimble or more fine, or of smaller or smoother elements: it first transmits the sense-giving motions through the frame; for it is first stirred, made up as it is of small particles; next the heat and the unseen force of the spirit receive the motions, then the air; then all things are set in action, the blood is stirred, every part of the flesh is filled with sensation; last of all the feeling is transmitted to the bones and marrow, whether it be one of pleasure or an opposite excitement. No pain however can lightly pierce thus far nor any sharp malady make its way in, without all things being so thoroughly disordered that no room is left for life and the parts of the soul fly abroad through all the pores of the body. But commonly a stop is put to these motions on the surface as it were of the body: for this reason we are able to retain life.

258] Now though I would fain explain in what way these are mixed up together, by what means united, when they exert their powers, the poverty of my native speech deters me sorely against my will: yet will I touch upon them and in summary fashion to the best of my ability: the first-beginnings by their mutual motions are interlaced in such a way that none of them can be separated by itself, nor can the function of any go on divided from the rest by any interval; but they are so to say the several powers of one body. Even so in any flesh of living creature you please without exception there is smell and some colour and a savour, and yet out of all these is made up one single bulk of body. Thus the heat and the air and the unseen power of the spirit mixed together produce a single nature, together with that nimble force which transmits to them from itself the origin of motion; by which means sense-giving motion first takes its rise through the fleshly frame. For this nature lurks secreted in its inmost depths, and nothing in our body is farther beneath all ken than it, and more than this it is the very soul of the whole soul. Just in the same way as the power of the mind and the function of the soul are latent in our limbs and throughout our body, because they are each formed of small and few bodies: even so, you are to know, this nameless power made of minute bodies is concealed and is moreover the very soul so to say of the whole soul, and reigns supreme in the whole body. On a like principle the spirit and air and heat must, as they exert their powers, be mixed up together through the frame, and one must ever be more out of view or more prominent than another, that a single substance may be seen to be formed from the union of all, lest the heat and spirit apart by themselves and the power of the air apart by itself should destroy sense and dissipate it by their disunion.

288] Thus the mind possesses that heat which it displays when it boils up in anger and fire flashes from the keen eyes; there is too much cold spirit comrade of fear, which spreads a shivering over the limbs and stirs the whole frame; yes and there is also that condition of still air which has place when the breast is calm and the looks cheerful. But they have more of the hot whose keen heart and passionate mind lightly boil up in anger. Foremost in this class comes the fierce violence of lions who often as they chafe break their hearts with their roaring and cannot contain within their breast the billows of their rage. Then the chilly mind of stags is fuller of the spirit and more quickly rouses through all the flesh its icy currents which cause a shivering motion to pass over the limbs. But the nature of oxen has its life rather from the still air, and never does the smoky torch of anger applied to it stimulate it too much, shedding over it the shadow of murky gloom, nor is it transfixed and stiffened by the icy shafts of fear: it lies between the other two, stags and cruel lions. And thus it is with mankind: however much teaching renders some equally refined, it yet leaves behind those earliest traces of the nature of each mind; and we are not to suppose that evil habits can be so thoroughly plucked up by the roots, that one man shall not be more prone than another to keen anger, a second shall not be somewhat more quickly assailed by fear, a third shall not take some things more meekly than is right. In many other points there must be differences between the varied natures of men and the tempers which follow upon these; though at present I am unable to set forth the hidden causes of these or to find names enough for the different shapes which belongs to the first-beginnings, from which shapes arises this diversity of things. What herein I think I may affirm is this: traces of the different natures left behind, which reason is unable to expel from us, are so exceedingly slight that there is nothing to hinder us from living a life worthy of gods.

323] Well this nature is contained by the whole body and is in turn the body's guardian and the cause of its existence; for the two adhere together with common roots and cannot it is plain be riven asunder without destruction. Even as it is not easy to pluck the perfume out of lumps of frankincense without quite destroying its nature as well; so it is not easy to withdraw from the whole body the nature of the mind and soul without dissolving all alike. With first-beginnings so interlaced from their earliest birth are they formed and gifted with a life of joint partnership, and it is plain that that faculty of the body and of the mind cannot feel separately, each alone without the other's power, but sense is kindled throughout our flesh and blown into flame between the two by the joint motions on the part of both. Moreover the body by itself is never either begotten or grows or, it is plain, continues to exist after death. For not in the way that the liquid of water often loses the heat which has been given to it, yet is not for that reason itself riven in pieces, but remains unimpaired—not in this way, I say, can the abandoned frame endure the separation of the soul, but riven in pieces it utterly perishes and rots away. Thus the mutual connexions of body and soul from the first moment of their existence learn the vital motions even while hid in the body and womb of the mother, so that no separation can take place without mischief and ruin. Thus you may see that, since the cause of existence lies in their joint action, their nature too must be a joint nature.

350] Furthermore if any one tries to disprove that the body feels and believes that the soul mixed through the whole body takes upon it this motion which we name sense, he combats even manifest and undoubted facts. For who will ever bring forward any explanation of what the body's feeling is, except that which the plain fact of the case has itself given and taught to us? But when the soul it is said has departed, the body throughout is without sense; yes, for it loses what was not its own peculiar property in life; ay and much else it loses, before that soul is driven out of it.

359] Again to say that the eyes can see no object, but that the soul discerns through them as through an open door, is far from easy, since their sense contradicts this; for this sense e'en draws it and forces it out to the pupil: nay often we are unable to perceive shining things, because our eyes are embarrassed by the lights. But this is not the case with doors; for, because we ourselves see, the open doors do not therefore undergo any fatigue. Again if our eyes are in the place of doors, in that case when the eyes are removed the mind ought it would seem to have more power of seeing things, after doors, jambs and all, have been taken out of the way.

370] And herein you must by no means adopt the opinion which the revered judgement of the worthy man Democritus lays down, that the first-beginnings of body and mind placed together in successive layers come in alternate order and so weave the tissue of our limbs. For not only are the elements of the soul much smaller than those of which our body and flesh are formed, but they are also much fewer in number and are disseminated merely in scanty number through the frame, so that you can warrant no more than this: the first-beginnings of the soul keep spaces between them at least as great as are the smallest bodies which, if thrown upon it, are first able to excite in our body the sense-giving motions. Thus at times we do not feel the adhesion of dust when it settles on our body, nor the impact of chalk when it rests on our limbs, nor do we feel a mist at night or a spider's slender threads as they come against us, when we are caught in its meshes in moving along, nor the same insect's flimsy web when it has fallen on our head, nor the feathers of birds and down of plants as it flies about, which commonly from exceeding lightness does not lightly fall, nor do we feel the tread of every creeping creature whatsoever nor each particular foot-print which gnats and the like stamp on our body. So very many first-beginnings must be stirred in us, before the seeds of the soul mixed up in our bodies feel that these have been disturbed, and by thumping with such spaces between can clash, unite, and in turn recoil.

396] The mind has more to do with holding the fastnesses of life and has more sovereign sway over it than the power of the soul. For without the understanding and the mind no part of the soul can maintain itself in the frame the smallest fraction of time, but follows at once in the other's train and passes away into the air and leaves the cold limbs in the chill of death. But he abides in life whose mind and understanding continue to stay with him: though the trunk is mangled with its limbs shorn all round about it, after the soul has been taken away on all sides and been severed from the limbs, the trunk yet lives and inhales the ethereal airs of life. When robbed, if not of the whole, yet of a large portion of the soul, it still lingers in and cleaves to life; just as, after the eye has been lacerated all round if the pupil has continued uninjured, the living power of sight remains, provided always you do not destroy the whole ball of the eye and pare close round the pupil and leave only it; for that will not be done even to the ball without the entire destruction of the eye. But if that middle portion of the eye, small as it is, is eaten into, the sight is gone at once and darkness ensues, though a man have the bright ball quite unim-

paired. On such terms of union soul and mind are ever bound to each other.

417] Now mark me: that you may know that the minds and light souls of living creatures have birth and are mortal, I will go on to set forth verses worthy of your attention, got together by long study and invented with welcome effort. Do you mind to link to one name both of them alike, and when for instance I shall choose to speak of the soul, showing it to be mortal, believe that I speak of the mind as well, inasmuch as both make up one thing and are one united substance. First of all then since I have shown the soul to be fine and to be formed of minute bodies and made up of much smaller first-beginnings than is the liquid of water or mist or smoke:—for it far surpasses these in nimbleness and is moved, when struck by a far slenderer cause; inasmuch as it is moved by images of smoke and mist; as when for instance sunk in sleep we see altars steam forth their heat and send up their smoke on high; for beyond a doubt images are begotten for us from these things:—well then since you see on the vessels being shattered the water flow away on all sides, and since mist and smoke pass away into air, believe that the soul too is shed abroad and perishes much more quickly and dissolves sooner into its first bodies, when once it has been taken out of the limbs of a man and has withdrawn. For, when the body that serves for its vessel cannot hold it, if shattered from any cause and rarefied by the withdrawal of blood from the veins, how can you believe that this soul can be held by any air? How can that air which is rarer than our body hold it in?

445] Again we perceive that the mind is begotten along with the body and grows up together with it and becomes old along with it. For even as children go about with a tottering and weakly body, so slender sagacity of mind follows along with it; then when their life has reached the maturity of confirmed strength, the judgement too is greater and the power of the mind more developed. Afterwards when the body has been shattered by the mastering might of time and the frame has drooped with its forces dulled, then the intellect halts, the tongue dotes, the mind gives way, all faculties fail and are found wanting at the same time.

It naturally follows then that the whole nature of the soul is dissolved, like smoke, into the high air; since we see it is begotten along with the body and grows up along with it and, as I have shown, breaks down at the same time worn out with age.

459] Moreover we see that even as the body is liable to violent diseases and severe pain, so is the mind to sharp cares and grief and fear; it naturally follows therefore that it is its partner in death as well. Again in diseases of the body the mind often wanders and goes astray; for it loses its reason and drivels in its speech and often in a profound lethargy is carried into deep and never-ending sleep with drooping eyes and head; out of which it neither hears the voices nor can recognise the faces of those who stand round calling it back to life and bedewing with tears, face and cheeks. Therefore you must admit that the mind too dissolves, since the infection of disease reaches to it; for pain and disease are both forgers of death: a truth we have fully learned ere now by the death of many. Again, when the pungent strength of wine has entered into a man and its spirit has been infused into and transmitted through his veins, why is it that a heaviness of the limbs follows along with this, his legs are hampered as he reels about, his tongue falters, his mind is besotted, his eyes swim, shouting, hiccuping, wranglings are rife, together with all the other usual concomitants, why is all this, if not because the overpowering violence of the wine is wont to disorder the soul within the body? But whenever things can be disordered and hampered, they give token that if a somewhat more potent cause gained an entrance, they would perish and be robbed of all further existence.

487] Moreover it often happens that some one constrained by the violence of disease suddenly drops down before our eyes, as by a stroke of lightning, and foams at the mouth, moans and shivers through his frame, loses his reason, stiffens his muscles, is racked, gasps for breath fitfully, and wearies his limbs with tossing. Sure enough, because the violence of the disease spreads itself through his frame and disorders him, he foams as he tries to eject his soul, just as in the salt sea the waters boil with the mastering might of the winds. A moan too

is forced out, because the limbs are seized with pain, and mainly because seeds of voice are driven forth and are carried in a close mass out by the mouth, the road which they are accustomed to take and where they have a well-paved way. Loss of reason follows, because the powers of the mind and soul are disordered and, as I have shown, are riven and forced asunder, torn to pieces by the same baneful malady. Then after the cause of the disease has bent its course back and the acrid humours of the distempered body return to their hiding-places, then he first gets up like one reeling, and by little and little comes back into full possession of his senses and regains his soul. Since therefore even within the body mind and soul are harassed by such violent distempers and so miserably racked by sufferings, why believe that they without the body in the open air can continue existence battling with fierce winds? And since we perceive that the mind is healed like the sick body, and we see that it can be altered by medicine, this too gives warning that the mind has a mortal existence. For it is natural that whosoever essays and attempts to change the mind or seeks to alter any other nature you like, should add new parts or change the arrangement of the present, or withdraw in short some tittle from the sum. But that which is immortal wills not to have its parts transposed nor any addition to be made nor one tittle to ebb away; for whenever a thing changes and quits its proper limits, this change is at once the death of that which was before. Therefore the mind, whether it is sick or whether it is altered by medicine, alike, as I have shown, gives forth mortal symptoms. So invariably is truth found to make head against false reason and to cut off all retreat from the assailant and by a twofold refutation to put falsehood to rout.

526] Again we often see a man pass gradually away and limb by limb lose vital sense; first the toes of his feet and the nails turn livid, then the feet and shanks die, then next the steps of chilly death creep with slow pace over the other members. Therefore since the nature of the soul is rent and passes away and does not at one time stand forth in its entireness, it must be reckoned mortal. But if haply you suppose that it can draw itself in through the whole frame and mass its parts together and in this way withdraw sense from all the limbs, yet then that spot into which so great a store of soul is gathered, ought to show itself in possession of a greater amount of sense. But as this is nowhere found, sure enough as we said before, it is torn in pieces and scattered abroad, and therefore dies. Moreover if I were pleased for the moment to grant what is false and admit that the soul might be collected in one mass in the body of those who leave the light dying piecemeal, even then you must admit the soul to be mortal; and it makes no difference whether it perish dispersed in air, or gathered into one lump out of all its parts lose all feeling, since sense ever more and more fails the whole man throughout and less and less of life remains throughout.

548] And since the mind is one part of a man which remains fixed in a particular spot, just as are the ears and eyes and the other senses which guide and direct life; and just as the hand or eye or nose when separated from us cannot feel and exist apart, but in however short a time wastes away in putrefaction, thus the mind cannot exist by itself without the body and the man's self which as you see serves for the mind's vessel or any thing else you choose to imagine which implies a yet closer union with it, since the body is attached to it by the nearest ties.

558] Again the quickened powers of body and mind by their joint partnership enjoy health and life; for the nature of the mind cannot by itself alone without the body give forth vital motions nor can the body again bereft of the soul continue to exist and make use of its senses: just, you are to know, as the eye itself torn away from its roots cannot see anything when apart from the whole body, thus the soul and mind cannot it is plain do anything by themselves. Sure enough, because mixed up through veins and flesh, sinews and bones, their first-beginnings are confined by all the body and are not free to bound away leaving great spaces between, therefore thus shut in they make those sense-giving motions which they cannot make after death when forced out of the body into the air by reason that they are not then confined in a like manner; for the air will be a body and a living thing, if the soul

shall be able to keep itself together and to enclose in it those motions which it used before to perform in the sinews and within the body. Moreover even while it yet moves within the confines of life, often the soul shaken from some cause or other is seen to wish to pass out and be loosed from the whole body, the features are seen to droop as at the last hour and all the limbs to sink flaccid over the bloodless trunk: just as happens, when the phrase is used, the mind is in a bad way, or the soul is quite gone; when all is hurry and every one is anxious to keep from parting the last tie of life; for then the mind and the power of the soul are shaken throughout and both are quite loosened together with the body; so that a cause somewhat more powerful can quite break them up. Why doubt I would ask that the soul when driven forth out of the body, when in the open air, feeble as it is, stript of its covering, not only cannot continue through eternity, but is unable to hold together the smallest fraction of time? Therefore, again and again I say, when the enveloping body has been all broken up and the vital airs have been forced out, you must admit that the senses of the mind and the soul are dissolved, since the cause of destruction is one and inseparable for both body and soul.

595] Again since the body is unable to bear the separation of the soul without rotting away in a noisome stench, why doubt that the power of the soul gathering itself up from the inmost depths of body has oozed out and dispersed like smoke, and that the crumbling body has changed and tumbled in with so total a ruin for this reason because its foundations throughout are stirred from their places, the soul oozing out abroad through the frame, through all the winding passages which are in the body, and all openings? So that in ways manifold you may learn that the nature of the soul has been divided piecemeal and gone forth throughout the frame, and that it has been torn to shreds within the body, ere it glided forth and swam out into the air. For no one when dying appears to feel the soul go forth entire from his whole body or first mount up to the throat and gullet, but all feel it fail in that part which lies in a particular quarter; just as they know that the senses as well suffer dissolution each in its own place. But if our mind were immortal, it would not when dying complain so much of its dissolution, as of passing abroad and quitting its vesture, like a snake.

615] Again why are the mind's understanding and judgement never begotten in the head or feet or hands, but cling in all alike to one spot and fixed quarter, if it be not that particular places are assigned for the birth of everything, and nature has determined where each is to continue to exist after it is born? Our body then must follow the same law and have such a manifold organisation of parts, that no perverted arrangement of its members shall ever show itself: so invariably effect follows cause, nor is flame wont to be born in rivers nor cold in fire.

624] Again if the nature of the soul is immortal and can feel when separated from our body, methinks we must suppose it to be provided with five senses; and in no other way can we picture to ourselves souls below flitting about Acheron. Painters therefore and former generations of writers have thus represented souls provided with senses. But neither eyes nor nose nor hand can exist for the soul apart from the body nor can tongue, nor can ears perceive by the sense of hearing or exist for the soul by themselves apart from the body.

634] And since we perceive that vital sense is in the whole body and we see that it is all endowed with life, if on a sudden any force with swift blow shall have cut it in twain so as quite to dissever the two halves, the power of the soul will without doubt at the same time be cleft and cut asunder and dashed in twain together with the body. But that which is cut and divides into any parts, you are to know disclaims for itself an everlasting nature. Stories are told how scythed chariots reeking with indiscriminate slaughter often lop off limbs so instantaneously that that which has fallen down lopped off from the frame is seen to quiver on the ground, while yet the mind and faculty of the man from the suddenness of the mischief cannot feel the pain; and because his mind once for all is wholly given to the business of fighting, with what remains of his body he mingles in the fray and carnage, and often perceives not that the wheels and de-

vouring scythes have carried off among the horses' feet his left arm shield and all; another sees not that his right arm has dropped from him, while he mounts and presses forward. Another tries to get up after he has lost his leg, while the dying foot quivers with its toes on the ground close by. The head too when cut off from the warm and living trunk retains on the ground the expression of life and open eyes, until it has yielded up all the remnants of soul. To take another case, if, as a serpent's tongue is quivering, as its tail is darting out from its long body, you choose to chop with an axe into many pieces both tail and body, you will see all the separate portions thus cut off writhing under the fresh wound and bespattering the earth with gore, the fore part with the mouth making for its own hinder part, to allay with burning bite the pain of the wound with which it has been smitten. Shall we say then that there are entire souls in all those pieces? why from that argument it will follow that one living creature had many souls in its body; and this being absurd, therefore the soul which was one has been divided together with the body; therefore each alike must be reckoned mortal, since each is alike chopped up into many pieces.

670] Again if the nature of the soul is immortal and makes its way into our body at the time of birth, why are we unable to remember besides the time already gone, and why do we retain no traces of past actions? If the power of the mind has been so completely changed, that all remembrance of past things is lost, that methinks differs not widely from death; therefore you must admit that the soul which was before has perished and that which now is has now been formed.

679] Again if the quickened power of the mind is wont to be put into us after our body is fully formed, at the instant of our birth and our crossing the threshold of life, it ought agreeably to this to live not in such a way as to seem to have grown with the body and together with its members within the blood, but as in a den apart by and to itself: the very contrary to what undoubted fact teaches; for it is so closely united with the body throughout the veins, flesh, sinews, and bones, that the very teeth have a share of sense; as their aching proves and the sharp twinge of cold water and the crunching of a rough stone, when it has got into them out of bread. Wherefore, again and again I say, we must believe souls to be neither without a birth nor exempted from the law of death; for we must not believe that they could have been so completely united with our bodies, if they found their way into them from without, nor, since they are so closely inwoven with them, does it appear that they can get out unharmed and unloose themselves unscathed from all the sinews and bones and joints. But if haply you believe that the soul finds its way in from without and is wont to ooze through all our limbs, so much the more it will perish thus blended with the body; for what oozes through another is dissolved, and therefore dies. As food distributed through all the cavities of the body, while it is transmitted into the limbs and the whole frame, is destroyed and furnishes out of itself the matter of another nature, thus the soul and mind, though they pass entire into a fresh body, yet in oozing through it are dissolved, whilst there are transmitted so to say into the frame through all the cavities those particles of which this nature of mind is formed, which now is sovereign in our body, being born out of that soul which then perished when dispersed through the frame. Wherefore the nature of the soul is seen to be neither without a birthday nor exempt from death.

713] Again are seeds of the soul left in the dead body or not? If they are left and remain in it, the soul cannot fairly be deemed immortal, since it has withdrawn lessened by the loss of some parts; but if when taken away from the yet untainted limbs it has fled so entirely away as to leave in the body no parts of itself, whence do carcases exude worms from the now rank flesh and whence does such a swarm of living things, boneless and bloodless, surge through the heaving frame? But if haply you believe that souls find their way into worms from without and can severally pass each into a body and you make no account of why many thousands of souls meet together in a place from which one has withdrawn, this question at least must, it seems, be raised and brought to a decisive test, whether souls hunt out the several seeds of worms and build for

themselves a place to dwell in, or find their way into bodies fully formed so to say. But why they should on their part make a body or take such trouble, cannot be explained; since being without a body they are not plagued as they flit about with diseases and cold and hunger, the body being more akin to, more troubled by such infirmities, and by its contact with it the mind suffering many ills. Nevertheless be it ever so expedient for them to make a body, when they are going to enter, yet clearly there is no way by which they can do so. Therefore souls do not make for themselves bodies and limbs; no nor can they by any method find their way into bodies after they are fully formed; for they will neither be able to unite themselves with a nice precision nor will any connexion of mutual sensation be formed between them.

741] Again why does untamed fierceness go along with the sullen brood of lions, cunning with foxes and proneness to flight with stags? And to take any other instance of the kind, why are all qualities engendered in the limbs and temper from the very commencement of life, if not because a fixed power of mind derived from its proper seed and breed grows up together with the whole body? If it were immortal and wont to pass into different bodies, living creatures would be of interchangeable dispositions; a dog of Hyrcanian breed would often fly before the attack of an antlered stag, a hawk would cower in mid air as it fled at the approach of a dove, men would be without reason, the savage races of wild beasts would have reason. For the assertion that an immortal soul is altered by a change of body is advanced on a false principle. What is changed is dissolved, and therefore dies: the parts are transposed and quit their former order; therefore they must admit of being dissolved too throughout the frame, in order at last to die one and all together with the body. But if they shall say that souls of men always go into human bodies, I yet will ask how it is a soul can change from wise to foolish, and no child has discretion, and why the mare's foal is not so well trained as the powerful strength of the horse. You may be sure they will fly to the subterfuge that the mind grows weakly in a weakly body. But granting this is so, you must admit the soul to be mortal, since changed so completely throughout the frame it loses its former life and sense. Then too in what way will it be able to grow in strength uniformly with its allotted body and reach the coveted flower of age, unless it shall be its partner at its first beginning? Or what means it by passing out from the limbs when decayed with age? Does it fear to remain shut up in a crumbling body, fear that its tenement, worn out by protracted length of days, bury it in its ruins? Why an immortal being incurs no risks.

776] Again for souls to stand by at the unions of Venus and the birth-throes of beasts seems to be passing absurd, for them the immortals to wait for mortal limbs in number numberless and struggle with one another in forward rivalry, which shall first and by preference have entrance in; unless haply bargains are struck among the souls on these terms, that whichever in its flight shall first come up, shall first have right of entry, and that they shall make no trial at all of each other's strength.[1]

784] Again a tree cannot exist in the ether, nor clouds in the deep sea nor can fishes live in the fields nor blood exist in woods nor sap in stones. Where each thing can grow and abide is fixed and ordained. Thus the nature of the mind cannot come into being alone without the body nor exist far away from the sinews and blood. But if (for this would be much more likely to happen than that) the force itself of the mind might be in the head or shoulders or heels or might be born in any other part of the body, it would after all be wont to abide in one and the same man or vessel. But since in our body even it is fixed and seen to be ordained where the soul and the mind can severally be and grow, it must still more strenuously be denied that it can abide and be born out of the body altogether. Therefore when the body has died, we must admit that the soul has perished, wrenched away throughout the body. To link forsooth a mortal thing with an everlasting and suppose that they can have sense in common and can be reciprocally acted upon, is sheer folly; for what can be conceived more incongruous, more discordant and inconsistent with itself,

[1] Cf. Er's vision: Plato, *Republic*, x.

than a thing which is mortal, linked with an immortal and everlasting thing, trying in such union to weather furious storms?[2]

819] But if haply the soul is to be accounted immortal for this reason rather, because it is kept sheltered from death-bringing things, either because things hostile to its existence do not approach at all, or because those which do approach, in some way or other retreat discomfited before we can feel the harm they do, manifest experience proves that this can not be true. For besides that it sickens in sympathy with the maladies of the body, it is often attacked by that which frets it on the score of the future and keeps it on the rack of suspense and wears it out with cares; and when ill deeds are in the past, remorse for sins yet gnaws: then there is madness peculiar to the mind and forgetfulness of all things; then too it often sinks into the black waters of lethargy.

830] Death therefore to us is nothing, concerns us not a jot, since the nature of the mind is proved to be mortal; and as in time gone by we felt no distress, when the Poeni from all sides came together to do battle, and all things shaken by war's troublous uproar shuddered and quaked beneath high heaven, and mortal men were in doubt which of the two peoples it should be to whose empire all must fall by sea and land alike, thus when we shall be no more, when there shall have been a separation of body and soul, out of both of which we are each formed into a single being, to us, you may be sure, who then shall be no more, nothing whatever can happen to excite sensation, not if earth shall be mingled with sea and sea with heaven. And even supposing the nature of the mind and power of the soul do feel, after they have been severed from our body, yet that is nothing to us who by the binding tie of marriage between body and soul are formed each into one single being. And if time should gather up our matter after our death and put it once more into the position in which it now is, and the light of life be given to us again, this result even would concern us not at all, when the chain of our self-consciousness has once been snapped asunder.

[2] The Munro translation omits lines 806-818, which occur also in v. 351-63, where they seem to be more appropriate.

So now we give ourselves no concern about any self which we have been before, nor do we feel any distress on the score of that self. For when you look back on the whole past course of immeasurable time and think how manifold are the shapes which the motions of matter take, you may easily credit this too, that these very same seeds of which we now are formed, have often before been placed in the same order in which they now are; and yet we cannot recover this in memory: a break in our existence has been interposed, and all the motions have wandered to and fro far astray from the sensations they produced. For he whom evil is to befall, must in his own person exist at the very time it comes, if the misery and suffering are haply to have any place at all; but since death precludes this, and forbids him to be, upon whom the ills can be brought, you may be sure that we have nothing to fear after death, and that he who exists not, cannot become miserable, and that it matters not a whit whether he has been born into life at any other time, when immortal death has taken away his mortal life.

870] Therefore when you see a man bemoaning his hard case, that after death he shall either rot with his body laid in the grave or be devoured by flames or the jaws of wild beasts, you may be sure that his ring betrays a flaw and that there lurks in his heart a secret goad, though he himself declare that he does not believe that any sense will remain to him after death. He does not methinks really grant the conclusion which he professes to grant nor the principle on which he so professes, nor does he take and force himself root and branch out of life, but all unconsciously imagines something of self to survive. For when any one in life suggests to himself that birds and beasts will rend his body after death, he makes moan for himself: he does not separate himself from that self, nor withdraw himself fully from the body so thrown out, and fancies himself that other self and stands by and impregnates it with his own sense. Hence he makes much moan that he has been born mortal, and sees not that after real death there will be no other self to remain in life and lament to self that his own self has met death, and there to stand and grieve that his own self there ly-

ing is mangled or burnt. For if it is an evil after death to be pulled about by the devouring jaws of wild beasts, I cannot see why it should not be a cruel pain to be laid on fires and burn in hot flames, or to be placed in honey and stifled, or to stiffen with cold, stretched on the smooth surface of an icy slab of stone, or to be pressed down and crushed by a load of earth above.

894] "Now no more shall thy house admit thee with glad welcome, nor a most virtuous wife and sweet children run to be the first to snatch kisses and touch thy heart with a silent joy. No more mayst thou be prosperous in thy doings, a safeguard to thine own. One disastrous day has taken from thee luckless man in luckless wise all the many prizes of life." This do men say; but add not thereto "and now no longer does any craving for these things beset thee withal." For if they could rightly perceive this in thought and follow up the thought in words, they would release themselves from great distress and apprehension of mind. "Thou, even as now thou art, sunk in the sleep of death, shalt continue so to be all time to come, freed from all distressful pains; but we with a sorrow that would not be sated wept for thee, when close by thou didst turn to an ashen hue on thy appalling funeral pile, and no length of days shall pluck from our hearts our ever-during grief." This question therefore should be asked of this speaker, what there is in it so passing bitter, if it come in the end to sleep and rest, that any one should pine in never-ending sorrow.

912] This too men often, when they have reclined at table cup in hand and shade their brows with crowns, love to say from the heart, "short is this enjoyment for poor weak men; presently it will have been and never after may it be called back." As if after their death it is to be one of their chiefest afflictions that thirst and parching drought is to burn them up hapless wretches, or a craving for any thing else is to beset them. What folly! no one feels the want of himself and life at the time when mind and body are together sunk in sleep; for all we care this sleep might be everlasting, no craving whatever for ourselves then moves us. And yet by no means do those first-beginnings throughout our frame wander at that time far away from their sense-producing motions, at the moment when a man starts up from sleep and collects himself. Death therefore must be thought to concern us much less, if less there can be than what we see to be nothing; for a greater dispersion of the mass of matter follows after death, and no one wakes up, upon whom the chill cessation of life has once come.

931] Once more, if the nature of things could suddenly utter a voice and in person could rally any of us in such words as these, "What hast thou, O mortal, so much at heart, that thou goest such lengths in sickly sorrows? Why bemoan and bewail death? For say thy life past and gone has been welcome to thee and thy blessings have not all, as if they were poured into a perforated vessel, run through and been lost without avail: why not then take thy departure like a guest filled with life, and with resignation, thou fool, enter upon untroubled rest? But if all that thou hast enjoyed, has been squandered and lost, and life is a grievance, why seek to make any addition, to be wasted perversely in its turn and lost utterly without avail? Why not rather make an end of life and travail? For there is nothing more which I can contrive and discover for thee to give pleasure: all things are ever the same. Though thy body is not yet decayed with years nor thy frame worn out and exhausted, yet all things remain the same, ay though in length of life thou shouldst outlast all races of things now living, nay even more if thou shouldst never die," what answer have we to make save this, that nature sets up against us a well-founded claim and puts forth in her pleading a true indictment?

952] If however one of greater age and more advanced in years should complain and lament poor wretch his death more than is right, would she not with greater cause raise her voice and rally him in sharp accents, "Away from this time forth with thy tears, rascal; a truce to thy complainings: thou decayest after full enjoyment of all the prizes of life. But because thou ever yearnest for what is not present, and despisest what is, life has slipped from thy grasp unfinished and unsatisfying, and or ever thou thoughtest, death has taken his stand at thy pillow, before thou canst take thy departure sated and filled with good things. Now however resign all things unsuited to thy age, and with a good grace up and greatly go: thou must." With good reason methinks she would bring her charge, with reason rally and reproach; for old things give way and are supplanted by new without fail, and one thing must ever be replenished out of other things; and no one is delivered over to the pit and black Tartarus: matter is needed for after generations to grow; all of which though will follow thee when they have finished their term of life; and thus it is that all these no less than thou have before this come to an end and hereafter will come to an end. Thus one thing will never cease to rise out of another, and life is granted to none in fee-simple, to all in usufruct. Think too how the bygone antiquity of everlasting time before our birth was nothing to us. Nature therefore holds this up to us as a mirror of the time yet to come after our death. Is there aught in this that looks appalling, aught that wears an aspect of gloom? Is it not more untroubled than any sleep?

978] And those things sure enough, which are fabled to be in the deep of Acheron, do all exist for us in this life. No Tantalus, numbed by groundless terror, as the story is, fears poor wretch a huge stone hanging in air; but in life rather a baseless dread of the god vexes mortals: the fall they fear is such fall of luck as chance brings to each. Nor do birds eat a way into Tityos laid in Acheron, nor can they sooth to say find during eternity food to peck under his large breast. However huge the bulk of body he extends, though such as to take up with outspread limbs not nine acres merely, but the whole earth, yet will he not be able to endure everlasting pain and supply food from his own body for ever. But he is for us a Tityos, whom, as he grovels in love, vultures rend and bitter bitter anguish eats up or troubled thoughts from any other passion do rive. In life too we have a Sisyphus before our eyes who is bent on asking from the people the rods and cruel axes, and always retires defeated and disappointed. For to ask for power, which empty as it is is never given, and always in the chase of it to undergo severe toil, this is forcing up-hill with much effort a stone which after all rolls back again from the summit and seeks in headlong haste the levels of the plain. Then to be ever feeding the thankless nature of the mind, and never to fill it full and sate it with good things, as the seasons of the year do for us, when they come round and bring their fruits and varied delights, though after all we are never filled with the enjoyments of life, this methinks is to do what is told of the maidens in the flower of their age, to keep pouring water into a perforated vessel which in spite of all can never be filled full. Moreover Cerberus and the furies and yon privation of light are idle tales, as well as all the rest, Ixion's wheel and black Tartarus belching forth hideous fires from his throat: things which nowhere are nor sooth to say can be. But there is in life a dread of punishment for evil deeds, signal as the deeds are signal, and for atonement of guilt, the prison and the frightful hurling down from the rock, scourgings, executioners, the dungeon of the doomed, the pitch, the metal plate, torches; and even though these are wanting, yet the conscience-stricken mind through boding fears applies to itself goads and frightens itself with whips, and sees not meanwhile what end there can be of ills or what limit at last is to be set to punishments, and fears lest these very evils be enhanced after death. The life of fools at length becomes a hell here on earth.

1024] This too you may sometimes say to yourself, "Even worthy Ancus has quitted the light with his eyes, who was far far better than thou, unconscionable man. And since then many other kings and kesars have been laid low, who lorded it over mighty nations. He[1] too, even he who erst paved a way over the great sea and made a path for his legions to march over the deep and taught them to pass on foot over the salt pools and set at naught the roarings of the sea, trampling on them with his horses, had the light taken from him and shed forth his soul from his dying body. The son of the Scipios, thunderbolt of war, terror of Carthage, yielded his bones to earth just as if he were the lowest menial. Think too of the inventors of all sciences and graceful arts, think of the companions of the Heliconian maids; among whom Homer bore the sceptre without a peer, and he now sleeps the same sleep as

[1] Xerxes.

others. Then there is Democritus, who, when a ripe old age had warned him that the memory-waking motions of his mind were waning, by his own spontaneous act offered up his head to death. Even Epicurus passed away, when his light of life had run its course, he who surpassed in intellect the race of man and quenched the light of all, as the ethereal sun arisen quenches the stars." Wilt thou then hesitate and think it a hardship to die? Thou for whom life is well nigh dead whilst yet thou livest and seest the light, who spendest the greater part of thy time in sleep and snorest wide awake and ceasest not to see visions and hast a mind troubled with groundless terror and canst not discover often what it is that ails thee, when besotted man thou art sore pressed on all sides with full many cares and goest astray tumbling about in the wayward wanderings of thy mind.

1053] If, just as they are seen to feel that a load is on their mind which wears them out with its pressure, men might apprehend from what causes too it is produced and whence such a pile, if I may say so, of ill lies on their breast, they would not spend their life as we see them now for the most part do, not knowing any one of them what he means and wanting ever change of place as though he might lay his burden down. The man who is sick of home often issues forth from his large mansion, and as suddenly comes back to it, finding as he does that he is no better off abroad. He races to his country-house, driving his jennets in headlong haste, as if hurrying to bring help to a house on fire: he yawns the moment he has reached the door of his house, or sinks heavily into sleep and seeks forgetfulness, or even in haste goes back again to town. In this way each man flies from himself (but self from whom, as you may be sure is commonly the case, he cannot escape, clings to him in his own despite), hates too himself, because he is sick and knows not the cause of the malady; for if he could rightly see into this, relinquishing all else each man would study to learn the nature of things, since the point at stake is the condition for eternity, not for one hour, in which mortals have to pass all the time which remains for them to expect after death.

1076] Once more what evil lust of life is this which constrains us with such force to be so mightily troubled in doubts and dangers? A sure term of life is fixed for mortals, and death cannot be shunned, but meet it we must. Moreover we are ever engaged, ever involved in the same pursuits, and no new pleasure is struck out by living on; but whilst what we crave is wanting, it seems to transcend all the rest; then, when it has been gotten, we crave something else, and ever does the same thirst of life possess us, as we gape for it open-mouthed. Quite doubtful it is what fortune the future will carry with it or what chance will bring us or what end is at hand. Nor by prolonging life do we take one tittle from the time past in death nor can we fret anything away, whereby we may haply be a less long time in the condition of the dead. Therefore you may complete as many generations as you please during your life; none the less however will that everlasting death await you; and for no less long a time will he be no more in being, who beginning with to-day has ended his life, than the man who has died many months and years ago.

· BOOK FOUR ·

I TRAVERSE the pathless haunts of the Pierides never yet trodden by sole of man. I love to approach the untasted springs and to quaff, I love to cull fresh flowers and gather for my head a distinguished crown from spots whence the Muses have yet veiled the brows of none; first because I teach of great things and essay to release the mind from the fast bonds of religious scruples, and next because on a dark subject I pen such lucid verses o'erlaying all with the Muses' charm. For that too would seem to be not without good grounds: even as physicians when they propose to give nauseous wormwood to children, first smear the rim round the bowl with the sweet yellow juice of honey, that the unthinking age of children may be fooled as far as the lips, and meanwhile drink up the bitter draught of wormwood and though beguiled yet not be betrayed, but rather by such means recover health and strength: so I now, since this doctrine seems generally somewhat bitter to those by whom it has not been handled, and the multitude shrinks back from it in dismay, have resolved to set forth to you our doctrine in sweet-toned Pierian verse and o'erlay it as it were with the pleasant honey of the Muses, if haply by such means I might engage your mind on my verses, till such time as you apprehend all the nature of things and thoroughly feel what use it has.

26] And now that I have taught what the nature of the mind is and out of what things it is formed into one quickened being with the body, and how it is dissevered and returns into its first-beginnings, I will attempt to lay before you a truth which most nearly concerns these questions, the existence of things which we call idols of things: these, like films peeled off from the surface of things, fly to and fro through the air, and do likewise frighten our minds when they present themselves to us awake as well as in sleep, what time we behold strange shapes and idols of the light-bereaved, which have often startled us in appalling wise as we lay relaxed in sleep: this I will essay, that we may not haply believe that souls break loose from Acheron or that shades fly about among the living or that something of us is left behind after death, when the body and the nature of the mind destroyed together have taken their departure into their several first-beginnings.

42] I say then that pictures of things and thin shapes are emitted from things off their surface,[1] to which an image serves as a kind of film, or name it if you like a rind, because such image bears an appearance and form like to the thing whatever it is from whose body it is shed and wanders forth. This you may learn however dull of apprehension from what follows.

54] First of all since among things open to sight many emit bodies, some in a state of loose diffusion, like smoke which logs of oak, heat

---

[1] Munro drops a few lines that seem to be out of order.

which fires emit; some of a closer and denser texture, like the gossamer coats which at times cicadas doff in summer, and the films which calves at their birth cast from the surface of their body, as well as the vesture which the slippery serpent puts off among the thorns; for often we see the brambles enriched with their flying spoils: since these cases occur, a thin image likewise must be emitted from things off their surface. For why those films should drop off and withdraw from things rather than films which are really thin, not one tittle of proof can be given; especially since there are on the surface of things many minute bodies which may be discharged in the same order they had before and preserve the outline of the shape, and be discharged with far more velocity, inasmuch as they are less liable to get hampered being few in number and stationed in the front rank. For without doubt we see many things discharge and freely give not only from the core and centre, as we said before, but from their surfaces, besides other things colour itself. And this is commonly done by yellow and red and dark-blue awnings, when they are spread over large theatres and flutter and wave as they stretch across their poles and crossbeams; for then they dye the seated assemblage below and all the show of the stage and the richly attired company of the fathers, and compel them to dance about in their colour. And the more these objects are shut in all round by the walls of the theatre the more do all of them within laugh on all hands, o'erlaid with graceful hues, the light of day being, narrowed. Therefore since sheets of canvas emit colour from their surface, all things will naturally emit thin pictures too, since in each case alike they discharge from the surface. There are therefore as now shown sure outlines of shapes, which fly all about possessed of an exquisitely small thickness and cannot when separate be seen one at a time. Again all smell, smoke, heat, and other such-like things stream off things in a state of diffusion, because while they are coming from the depths of the body having arisen within it, they are torn in their winding passage, and there are no straight orifices to the paths, for them to make their way out by in a mass. But on the other hand

when a thin film of surface colour is discharged, there is nothing to rend it, since it is ready to hand stationed in front rank. Lastly in the case of all idols which show themselves to us in mirrors, in water or any other shining object, since their outsides are possessed of an appearance like to the things they represent, they must be formed of emitted images of things. There are therefore thin shapes and pictures like to the things, which, though no one can see them one at a time, yet when thrown off by constant and repeated reflexion give back a visible image from the surface of mirrors; and in no other way it would seem can they be kept so entire that shapes are given back so exceedingly like each object.

110] Now mark, and learn how thin the nature of an image is. And first of all, since the first-beginnings are so far below the ken of our senses and much smaller than the things which our eyes first begin to be unable to see, to strengthen yet more the proof of this also, learn in a few words how minutely fine are the beginnings of all things. First, living things are in some cases so very little, that their third part cannot be seen at all. Of what size are we to suppose any gut of such creatures to be? Or the ball of the heart or the eyes? the limbs? Or any part of the frame? How small they must be! And then further the several first-beginnings of which their soul and the nature of their mind must be formed? Do you not perceive how fine, how minute they are? Again in the case of all things which exhale from their body a pungent smell, all-heal, nauseous wormwood, strong-scented southernwood and the bitter centauries, any one of which, if you happen to feel it lightly between two fingers, will impregnate them with a strong smell. . . . but rather you are to know that idols of things wander about many in number in many ways, of no force, powerless to excite sense.

129] But lest haply you suppose that only those idols of things which go off from things and no others wander about, there are likewise those which are spontaneously begotten and are formed by themselves in this lower heaven which is called air: these fashioned in many ways are borne along on high and being in a fluid state cease not to alter their appearance and change it into the outline of shapes of every possible kind; as we see clouds sometimes gather into masses on high and blot the calm clear face of heaven, fanning the air with their motion. Thus often the faces of giants are seen to fly along and draw after them a far-spreading shadow; sometimes great mountains and rocks torn from the mountains are seen to go in advance and pass across the sun; and then some huge beast is observed to draw with it and bring on the other stormclouds.

143] Now I will proceed to show with what ease and celerity they are begotten and how incessantly they flow and fall away from things. The outermost surface is ever streaming off from things and admits of being discharged: when this reaches some things, it passes through them, glass especially. But when it reaches rough stones or the matter of wood, it is then so torn that it cannot give back any idol. But when objects at once shining and dense have been put in its way, a mirror especially, none of these results has place: it can neither pass through it, like glass, nor can it be torn either; such perfect safety the polished surface minds to ensure. In consequence of this idols stream back to us from such objects; and however suddenly at any moment you place any thing opposite a mirror, an image shows itself: hence you may be sure that thin textures and thin shapes of things incessantly stream from their surface. Therefore many idols are begotten in a short time, so that the birth of such things is with good reason named a rapid one. And as the sun must send forth many rays of light in a short time in order that all things may be continually filled with it, so also for a like reason there must be carried away from things in a moment of time idols of things, many in number, in many ways, in all directions round; since to whatever part of them we present a mirror before their surfaces, other things correspond to these in the mirror of a like shape and like colour. Moreover though the state of heaven has just before been of unsullied purity, with exceeding suddenness it becomes so hideously overcast, that you might imagine all its darkness had abandoned Acheron through-

out and filled up the great vaults of heaven: in such numbers do faces of black horror rise up from amid the frightful night of stormclouds and hang over us on high. Now there is no one who can tell how small a fraction of these an image is, or express that sum in language.

176] Now mark: how swift the motion is with which idols are borne along, and what velocity is assigned to them as they glide through the air, so that but a short hour is spent on a journey through long space, whatever the spot towards which they go with a movement of varied tendency, all this I will tell in sweetly worded rather than in many verses; as the short song of the swan is better than the loud noise of cranes scattered abroad amid the ethereal clouds of the south. First of all we may very often observe that things which are light and made of minute bodies are swift. Of this kind are the light of the sun and its heat, because they are made of minute first things which are knocked forward so to speak and do not hesitate to pass through the space of air between, ever driven on by a blow following behind; for light on the instant is supplied by fresh light and brightness goaded to show its brightness in what you might call an ever on-moving team. Therefore in like manner idols must be able to scour in a moment of time through space unspeakable, first because they are exceedingly small and there is a cause at their back to carry and impel them far forward; where moreover they move on with such winged lightness; next because when emitted they are possessed of so rare a texture, that they can readily pass through any things and stream as it were through the space of air between. Again if those minute bodies of things which are given out from the inmost depths of these things, as the light and heat of the sun, are seen in a moment of time to glide and spread themselves through the length and breadth of heaven, fly over sea and lands and flood the heaven, what then of those which stand ready posted in front rank, when they are discharged and nothing obstructs their egress? How much faster, you see, and farther must they travel, scouring through many times the same amount of space in the same time that the sunlight takes to spread over heaven! This too appears to be an eminently true proof of the velocity with which idols of things are borne along: as soon as ever the brightness of water is set down in the open air, if the heaven is starry, in a moment the clear radiant constellations of ether imaged in the water correspond to those in the heaven. Now do you see in what a moment of time an image drops down from the borders of heaven to the borders of earth? Therefore again and again I repeat you must admit that bodies capable of striking the eyes and of provoking vision constantly travel with a marvellous velocity. Smells too incessantly stream from certain things; as does cold from rivers, heat from the sun, spray from the waves of the sea, that enter into walls near the shore. Various sounds also cease not to fly through the air. Then too a moist salt flavour often comes into the mouth, when we are moving about beside the sea; and when we look on at the mixing of a decoction of wormwood, its bitterness affects us. In such a constant stream from all things the several qualities are carried and are transmitted in all directions round, and no delay, no respite in the flow is ever granted, since we constantly have feeling, and may at any time see, smell, and hear the sound of anything.

230] Again since a particular figure felt by the hands in the dark is known to be the same which is seen in the bright light of day, touch and sight must be excited by a quite similar cause. Well then if we handle a square thing and it excites our attention in the dark, in the daylight what square thing will be able to fall on our sight, except the image of that thing? Therefore the cause of seeing, it is plain, lies in images and no thing can be perceived without them.

239] Well the idols of things I speak of are borne along all round and are discharged and transmitted in all directions; but because we can see with the eyes alone, the consequence is that, to whatever point we turn our sight, there all the several things meet and strike it with their shape and colour. And the image gives the power to see and the means to distinguish how far each thing is distant from us; for as soon as ever it is discharged, it pushes

before it and impels all the air which lies between it and the eyes; and thus that air all streams through our eyes and brushes so to say the pupils and so passes through. The consequence is that we see how far distant each thing is. And the greater the quantity of air which is driven on before it and the larger the current which brushes our eyes, the more distant each different thing is seen to be. You must know these processes go on with extreme rapidity, so that at one and the same moment we see what like a thing is and how far distant it is. And this must by no means be deemed strange herein that, while the idols which strike the eyes cannot be seen one at a time, the things themselves are seen. For thus when the wind too beats us with successive strokes and when piercing cold streams, we are not wont to feel each single particle of that wind and cold, but rather the whole result; and then we perceive blows take effect on our body just as if something or other were beating it and giving us a sensation of its body outside. Again when we thump a stone with a finger, we touch merely the outermost colour on the surface of the stone, and yet we do not feel that colour by our touch, but rather we feel the very hardness of the stone seated in its inmost depths.

269] Now mark, and learn why the image is seen beyond the mirror; for without doubt it is seen withdrawn far within. The case is just the same as with things which are viewed in their reality beyond a door, when it offers through it an unobstructed prospect and lets many things outside be seen from a house. That vision too is effected by two separate airs: first there is an air seen in such a case inside the doorway; next come the leaves of the door right and left; next a light outside brushes the eyes, then a second air, then those things outside which are viewed in their reality. Thus when the image of the mirror has first discharged itself, in coming to our sight it pushes forward and impels all the air which lies between it and the eyes, and enables us to see the whole of it before the mirror. But when we have perceived the mirror as well, at once the image which is conveyed from us reaches the mirror and then is reflected and comes back to our eyes, and drives on and rolls in front of it a second air and lets us see this before itself, and for this reason it looks so far withdrawn from the mirror. Wherefore again and again I repeat there is no cause at all to wonder why the images give back the reflexion from the surface of mirrors in the spot they do, since in both the given cases the result is produced by two airs. To proceed, the right side of our body is seen in mirrors to be on the left, because when the image comes and strikes on the plane of the mirror, it is not turned back unaltered, but is beaten out in a right line backwards, just as if you were to take a plaster mask before it is dry and dash it on a pillar or beam, and it forthwith were to preserve the lines of its features undistorted in front and were to strike out an exact copy of itself straight backwards. The result will be that the eye which was right will now be left; and conversely the left become the right. An image may also be so transmitted from one mirror to another that five or six idols are often produced. And thus all the things which lurk in the inmost corners of a house, however far they are withdrawn into tortuous recesses, may yet be all brought out through winding passages by the aid of a number of mirrors and be seen to be in the house. So unfailingly does the image reflect itself from mirror to mirror; and when the left side is presented, it becomes the right in the new image; then it is changed back again and turns round to what it was. Moreover all little sides of mirrors which possess a curvature resembling our side, send back to us idols with their right corresponding to our right either for this reason, because the image is transmitted from one mirror to another, and then after it has been twice struck out flies to us, or else because the image, when it has come to the mirror, wheels about, because the curved shape of the mirror teaches it to turn round and face us. Again you would think that idols step out and put down their foot at the same time with us and mimic our action, because from before whatever part of a mirror you move away, from that part forthwith no idols can be reflected; since nature constrains all things, when they are carried back and recoil from things, to be given back at angles equal to those at which they impinged.

324] Bright things again the eyes eschew and shun to look upon: the sun even blinds them, if you persist in turning them towards it, because its power is great and idols are borne through the clear air with great downward force from on high, and strike the eyes and disorder their fastenings. Moreover any vivid brightness often burns the eyes, because it contains many seeds of fire which make a way in and beget pain in the eyes. Again whatever the jaundiced look at, becomes a greenish-yellow, because many seeds of greenish-yellow stream from their body and meet the idols of things, and many too are mixed up in their eyes, and these by their infection tinge all things with sallow hues.

337] Again we see out of the dark things which are in the light for this reason: when the black air of darkness being the nearer has first entered and taken possession of the open eyes, the bright white air follows straightway after and cleanses them so to say and dispels the black shadows of the other air; for this is a great deal more nimble, a great deal more subtle and more efficacious. As soon as it has filled with light and opened up the passages of the eyes which the black air had before blocked up, forthwith the idols of things which are situated in the light follow and excite them so that we see. This we cannot do conversely in the dark out of the light, because the grosser air of darkness follows behind and quite fills all the openings and blocks up the passages of the eyes, not letting the idols of any things at all be thrown into the eyes to move them.

353] Again when we descry far off the square towers of a town, they often appear to be round for this reason: all the angles are seen from a distance to look obtuse, or rather are not seen at all, and their blow is lost and their stroke never makes its way to our sight, because while the idols are borne on through much air, the air by repeated collisions blunts the stroke perforce. When in this way all the angles have together eluded the sense, the stone structures are rounded off as if by the lathe; yet they do not look like the things which are close before us and really round, but somewhat resembling them as in shadowy outline.

364] Our shadow likewise seems to move in

the sunshine and to follow our steps and mimic our action; if you think forsooth that air deprived of life can step, imitating the motions and the actions of men; for that which we are wont to term shadow can be nothing but air devoid of light. Sure enough because the earth in certain spots successively is deprived of light wherever we intercept it in moving about, while that part of it which we have quitted is filled with light, therefore that which was the shadow of our body, seems to have always followed us unchanged in a direct line with us. For new rays of light ever pour in and the old are lost, just as if wool were drawn into the fire. Therefore the earth is readily stripped of light, and again filled, and cleanses itself from black shadows.

379] And yet in all this we do not admit that the eyes are cheated one whit. For it is their province to observe in what spot soever light and shade are; but whether the lights are still the same or not, and whether it is the same shadow which was in this spot that is now passing to that, or whether what we said a little before is not rather the fact, this the reason of the mind, and only it, has to determine; nor can the eyes know the nature of things. Do not then fasten upon the eyes this frailty of the mind.

387] The ship in which we are sailing, moves on while seeming to stand still; that one which remains at its moorings, is believed to be passing by. The hills and fields seem to be dropping astern, past which we are driving our ship and flying under sail. The stars all seem to be at rest fast fixed to the ethereal vaults, and yet are all in constant motion, since they rise and then go back to their far-off places of setting, after they have traversed the length of heaven with their bright bodies. In like manner sun and moon seem to stay in one place, bodies which simple fact proves are carried on. And though between mountains rising up afar off from amid the waters there opens out for fleets a free passage of wide extent, yet a single island seems to be formed out of them united into one. When children have stopped turning round themselves, the halls appear to them to whirl about and the pillars to course round to such a degree, that they can scarce believe that the whole roof is

not threatening to tumble down upon them.

404] Again when nature begins to raise on high the sun's beam ruddy with bickering fires and to lift it up above the mountains, those hills above which the sun then seems to you to be, as blazing close at hand he dyes them with his own fire, are distant from us scarce two thousand arrow-flights, yea often scarce five hundred casts of a javelin; and yet between them and the sun lie immense levels of sea, spread out below the huge borders of ether, and many thousands of lands are between, held by divers peoples and races of wild beasts. Then a puddle of water not more than a finger-breadth deep, which stands between the stones in the streets, offers a prospect beneath the earth of a reach as vast, as that with which the high yawning maw of heaven opens out above the earth; so that you seem to discern clouds and see the bodies of birds far withdrawn into that wondrous sky beneath the earth. Again when our stout horse has stuck in the middle of a river and we have looked down on the swift waters of the stream, some force seems to carry athwart the current the body of the horse which is standing still and to force it rapidly up the stream; and to whatever point we cast our eyes about all things seem to be carried on and to be flowing in the same way as we are. Again although a portico runs in parallel lines from one end to the other and stands supported by equal columns along its whole extent, yet when from the top of it it is seen in its entire length, it gradually forms the contracted top of a narrowing cone, until uniting roof with floor and all the right side with the left it has brought them together into the vanishing point of a cone.

432] To sailors on the sea the sun appears to rise out of the waters and in the waters to set and bury his light; just because they behold nothing but water and sky; that you may not lightly suppose the credit of the senses to be shaken on all hands. Then to people unacquainted with the sea, ships in harbour seem to be all askew and with poop-fittings broken to be pressing up against the water. For whatever part of the oars is raised above the salt water, is straight, and the rudders in their upper half are straight: the parts which are sunk below the water-level, appear to be broken and bent round and to slope up and turn back towards the surface and to be so much twisted back as well-nigh to float on the top of the water. And when the winds carry the thinly scattered clouds across heaven in the night-time, then do the glittering signs appear to glide athwart the rack and to be travelling on high in a direction quite different to their real course. Then if our hand chance to be placed beneath one eye and press it below, through a certain sensation all things which we look at appear then to become double as we look; the light of lamps brilliant with flames to be double, double too the furniture through the whole house, double men's faces and men's bodies. Again when sleep has chained down our limbs in sweet slumber and the whole body is sunk in profound repose, yet then we seem to ourselves to be awake and to be moving our limbs, and mid the thick darkness of night we think we see the sun and the daylight; and though in a confined room, we seem to be passing to new climates, seas, rivers, and mountains, and to be crossing plains on foot and to hear noises, though the austere silence of night prevails all round, and to be uttering speech though quite silent.

462] Many are the other marvels of this sort we see, which all seek to shake as it were the credit of the senses: quite in vain, since the greatest part of these cases cheats us on account of the mental suppositions which we add of ourselves, taking those things as seen which have not been seen by the senses. For nothing is harder than to separate manifest facts from doubtful which straightway the mind adds on of itself.

469] Again if a man believe that nothing is known, he knows not whether this even can be known, since he admits he knows nothing. I will therefore decline to argue the case against him who places himself with head where his feet should be. And yet granting that he knows this, I would still put this question, since he has never yet seen any truth in things, whence he knows what knowing and not knowing severally are, and what it is that has produced the knowledge of the true and the false and what has proved the doubtful to differ from the certain. You will find that from the senses first has proceeded the knowledge of the true and that the senses cannot be refuted. For that which is of itself to be able to refute things false by true things must from the nature of the case be proved to have the higher certainty. Well then what must fairly be accounted of higher certainty than sense? Shall reason founded on false sense be able to contradict them, wholly founded as it is on the senses? And if they are not true, then all reason as well is rendered false. Or shall the ears be able to take the eyes to task, or the touch the ears? Again shall the taste call·in question this touch, or the nostrils refute or the eyes controvert it? Not so, I guess; for each apart has its own distinct office, each its own power; and therefore we must perceive what is soft and cold or hot by one distinct faculty, by another perceive the different colours of things and thus see all objects which are conjoined with colour. Taste too has its faculty apart; smells spring from one source, sounds from another. It must follow therefore that any one sense cannot confute any other. No nor can any sense take itself to task, since equal credit must be assigned to it at all times. What therefore has at any time appeared true to each sense, is true. And if reason shall be unable to explain away the cause why things which close at hand were square, at a distance looked round, it yet is better, if you are at a loss for the reason, to state erroneously the causes of each shape, than to let slip from your grasp on any side things manifest and ruin the groundwork of belief and wrench up all the foundations on which rest life and existence. For not only would all reason give way, life itself would at once fall to the ground, unless you choose to trust the senses and shun precipices and all things else of this sort that are to be avoided, and to pursue the opposite things. All that host of words then be sure is quite unmeaning, which has been drawn out in array against the senses.

513] Once more, as in a building, if the rule first applied is wry, and the square is untrue and swerves from its straight lines, and if there is the slightest hitch in any part of the level, all the construction must be faulty, all must be wry, crooked, sloping, leaning forwards, leaning backwards, without symmetry, so that some parts seem ready to fall, others do fall, ruined all by the first erroneous measurements; so too all reason of things must needs prove to you distorted and false, which is founded on false senses.

522] And now to explain in what way the other senses do each perceive their several objects, is the nowise arduous task which is still left.

524] In the first place all sound and voice is heard when they have made their way into the ears and have struck with their body the sense of hearing. For voice too and sound you must admit to be bodily, since they are able to act upon the senses. Again voice often abrades the throat, and shouting in passing forth makes the windpipe more rough: when to wit the first-beginnings of voices have risen up in larger mass and commenced to pass abroad through their strait passage, you are to know the door of the mouth now crammed itself is abraded. There is no doubt then that voices and words consist of bodily first-beginnings, with the power to hurt; nor can you fail to know how much of body is taken away and how much is withdrawn from men's very sinews and strength by a speech continued without interruption from the dawning brightness of morning to the shadow of black night, above all if it has been poured forth with much loud shouting. Voice therefore must be bodily, since a man by much speaking loses a portion from his body. Next roughness of voice comes from roughness of first-beginnings, as smoothness is produced from smoothness. Nor are the first-beginnings of like shape which pierce the ears in these two cases: when the trumpet brays dully in deep low tones, the barbarian country roused echoing back the hoarse hollow sound, and when swans from the headstrong torrents of Helicon raise their clear-toned dirge with plaintive voice.

549] When therefore we force these voices forth from the depths of our body and discharge them straight out at the mouth, the pliant tongue deft fashioner of words gives them articulate utterance and the structure of the lips does its part in shaping them. Therefore when the distance is not long between the point from which each several voice has started and that at which it arrives, the very words too must be plainly heard and distinguished syllable by syllable; for each voice retains its structure and retains its shape. But if the space between be more than is suitable, the words must be huddled together in passing through much air and the voice be disorganised in its flight through the same. Therefore it is that you can hear a sound, yet cannot distinguish what the meaning of the words is: so huddled and hampered is the voice when it comes. Again a single word often stirs the ears of a whole assembly of people, when uttered by the crier's mouth. One voice therefore in a moment starts asunder into many voices, since it distributes itself separately into all the ears, stamping upon them the form and distinct sound of the word. But such of the voices as do not fall directly on the ears, are carried past and lost, fruitlessly dispersed in air: some striking upon solid spots are thrown back and give back a sound and sometimes mock by an echo of the word.

572] When you fully perceive all this, you may explain to yourself and others how it is that in lonely spots rocks give back in regular succession forms of words like to those sent forth, as we seek our comrades straying about among the darkened hills and with loud voice call upon them scattered abroad. I have seen places give back as many as six or seven voices, when you sent forth one: in such wise did the very hills dash back on hills and repeat the words thus trained to come back. These spots the people round fancy that the goat-footed satyrs and nymphs inhabit, and tell that they are the fauns by whose night-pervading noise and sportive play as they declare the still silence is broken and sounds produced of stringed instruments and sweet plaintive melodies, such as the pipe pours forth when beaten by the fingers of the players, the country-people hearing far and wide, what time Pan nodding the piny covering of his head half a beast's oft runs over the gaping reeds with curved lip, making the pipe without ceasing to pour forth its woodland song. Other such like prodigies and marvels they tell of, that they may not haply be thought to inhabit lonely places, abandoned even by the gods. On this account they vaunt such wonders in their stories or are led on by some other reason; inasmuch as the whole race of man is all too greedy after listening ears.

595] To proceed, you need not wonder how it is that through places, through which the eyes cannot see plain things, voices come and strike the ears. We often see a conversation go on even through closed doors, sure enough because the voice can pass uninjured through the winding openings of things, while idols refuse to pass: they are torn to shreds, if the openings through which they glide are not straight, like those of glass, through which every image passes. Again a voice distributes itself in all directions, since voices are begotten one out of another, when a single voice has once gone forth and sprung into many, as a spark of fire is often wont to distribute itself into its constituent fires. Therefore places are filled with voices, which though far withdrawn out of view yet are all in commotion and stirred by sound. But idols all proceed in straight courses as soon as they have been discharged; and therefore you can never see beyond a wall, but you may hear voices outside it. And yet this very voice even in passing through the walls of houses is blunted and enters the ears in a huddled state, and we seem to hear the sound rather than the actual words.

615] The tongue and palate whereby we perceive flavour, have not in them anything that calls for longer explanation or offers more difficulty. In the first place we perceive flavour in the mouth when we press it out in chewing our food, in the same way as when one haply begins to squeeze with his hand and dry a sponge full of water. Next the whole of what we press out distributes itself through the cavities of the palate and the intricate openings of the porous tongue. Therefore when the bodies of oozing flavour are smooth, they pleasantly touch and pleasantly feel all the parts about the moist exuding quarters of the palate. But on the other hand when they rise in a mass they puncture and tear the sense according to the degree in which they are pervaded by roughness. Next the pleasure from the flavour reaches as far as the palate; when however it has passed down through the throat, there is no pleasure while it is all

distributing itself into the frame. And it makes no matter what the food is with which the body is nurtured, provided you can digest what you take and transmit it into the frame and keep the stomach in an equable condition of moistness.

633] I will now explain how it is that different food is pleasant and nutritious for different creatures; also why that which to some is nauseous and bitter, may yet to others seem passing sweet; and why in these matters the difference and discrepancy is so great that what to one man is food, to another is rank poison; and there is actually a serpent which on being touched by a man's spittle wastes away and destroys itself by gnawing its body. Again hellebore for us is rank poison, but helps to fatten goats and quails. That you may know how this comes to pass, first of all you must remember what we have said before, that the seeds which are contained in things are mixed up in manifold ways. Again all living creatures soever which take food, even as they are unlike on the outside, and, differing in each after its kind, an exterior contour of limbs bounds them, so likewise are they formed of seeds of varying shape. Again since the seeds differ, there must be a discrepancy in the spaces between and the passages, which we name openings, in all the limbs and mouth and palate as well. Some openings therefore must be smaller, some larger; some things must have them three-cornered, others square; many must be round, some many-angled after many fashions. For as the relation between the shapes of seeds and their motions require, the openings also must differ accordingly in their shapes; and the passages must vary, as varies the texture formed by the seeds which bound them. For this reason when that which is sweet to some becomes bitter to others, for that creature to whom it is sweet the smoothest bodies must enter the cavities of the palate with power to feel them all over; but on the other hand in the case of those to whom the same thing is bitter within, rough and barbed seeds sure enough pass down the throat. It is easy now from these principles to understand all particular cases: thus when a fever has attacked anyone from too great a flow of bile, or a violent disease has been excited in any other way, thereupon the whole body is disordered and all the arrangements of particles then and there changed; the consequence of which is that the bodies which before were suited to excite sensation, suit no more; and those fit it better, which are able to make their way in and beget a bitter sense. Both kinds for instance are mixed up in the flavour of honey: a point we have often proved before.

673] Now mark me, and I will discuss the way in which the contact of smell affects the nostrils: and first there must be many things from which a varied flow of smells streams and rolls on; and we must suppose that they thus stream and discharge and disperse themselves among all things alike; but one smell fits itself better to one creature, another to another on account of their unlike shapes; and therefore bees are drawn on by the smell of honey through the air to a very great distance, and so are vultures by carcases. Also the onward-reaching power of scent in dogs leads them withersoever the cloven hoof of wild beasts has carried them in their course; and the smell of man is felt far away by the saviour of the Roman's citadel, the bright white goose.[1] Thus different scents assigned to different creatures lead each to its appropriate food and constrain them to recoil from nauseous poison, and in this way the races of beasts are preserved.

687] Of all these different smells then which strike the nostrils one may reach to a much greater distance than another; though none of them is carried so far as sound, as voice, to say nothing of things which strike the eyesight and provoke vision. For in its mazy course each comes slowly on and is sooner lost, being gradually dispersed into the readily receiving expanse of air; first because coming out of its depths it with difficulty discharges itself from the thing: for the fact that all things are found to have a stronger smell when crushed, when pounded, when broken up by fire, shows that odours stream and withdraw from the inner parts of things: next you may see that smell is formed of larger first-beginnings than voice, since it does not pass through stone walls, through which voice and sound are borne

[1] Having heard the Gauls, the white geese cackled and roused the guards of the Capitol (387 B. C.).

without fail. For this reason also you will find that it is not so easy to trace out in what quarter a thing which smells is situated; for the blow cools down as it loiters through the air, and the courier particles of things are no longer hot when they finish their race to sense; for which reason dogs are often at fault and lose the scent.

706] But what I have said is not found in smells and in the class of flavours only, but also the forms and colours of things are not all so well suited to the senses of all, but that some will be more distressing to the sight than others. Moreover ravenous lions cannot face and bear to gaze upon a cock with flapping wings putting night to rout and wont to summon morning with shrill voice: in such wise they at once bethink themselves of flight, because sure enough in the body of cocks are certain seeds, and these, when they have been discharged into the eyes of lions, bore into the pupils and cause such sharp pain that courageous though they be, they cannot continue to face them; while at the same time these things cannot hurt at all our sight either because they do not enter in or because the moment they enter, a free passage out of the eyes is granted them, so that they cannot by staying behind hurt the eyes in any part.

722] Now mark, and hear what things move the mind, and learn in a few words whence the things which come into it do come. I say first of all that idols of things wander about many in number, in many ways, in all directions round, extremely thin; and these when they meet, readily unite, like a cobweb or piece of gold-leaf. For these idols are far thinner in texture than those which take possession of the eyes and provoke vision; since these enter in through the porous parts of the body and stir the fine nature of the mind within and provoke sensation. Therefore we see Centaurs and limbs of Scyllas and Cerberus-like faces of dogs and idols of those who are dead whose bones earth holds in its embrace; since idols of every kind are everywhere borne about, partly those which are spontaneously produced within the air, partly all those which withdraw from various things and those which are formed by compounding the shapes of these. For assuredly no image of

Centaur is formed out of a live one, since no such nature of living creature ever existed; but when images of a horse and a man have by chance come together, they readily adhere at once, as we said before, on account of their fine nature and thin texture. All other things of the kind are produced in like fashion. And when these from extreme lightness are borne on with velocity, as I showed before, any one subtle composite image you like readily moves the mind by a single stroke; for the mind is fine and is itself wondrously nimble.

749] That all this is done as I relate you may easily learn from what follows. So far as the one is like the other, seeing with the mind and seeing with the eyes must be produced in a like way. Well then since I have shown that I perceive for instance a lion by means of idols which provoke the eyes, you may be sure that the mind is moved in a like way, which by means of idols sees a lion or anything else just as well as the eyes, with this difference that it perceives much thinner idols.

757] And when sleep has prostrated the body, for no other reason does the mind's intelligence wake, except because the very same idols provoke our minds which provoke them when we are awake, and to such a degree that we seem without a doubt to perceive him whom life has left and death and earth gotten hold of. This nature constrains to come to pass because all the senses of the body are then hampered and at rest throughout the limbs and cannot refute the unreal by real things. Moreover memory is prostrate and relaxed in sleep and protests not that he has long been in the grasp of death and destruction whom the mind believes it sees alive.

768] Furthermore it is not strange that idols move and throw about their arms and other limbs in regular measure: for sometimes in sleep an image is seen to do this: when the first to wit has gone and a second then been born in another posture, that former one seems to have altered its attitude. This remember you must assume to take place with exceeding celerity: so great is the velocity, so great the store of things; so great in any one unit of time that sense can seize is the store of particles, out of which the supply may go on.

777] And here many questions present

themselves and many points must be cleared up by us, if we desire to give a plain exposition of things. The first question is why, when the wish has occurred to any one to think of a thing, his mind on the instant thinks of that very thing. Do idols observe our will, and so soon as we will does an image present itself to us, if sea, if earth, ay or heaven is what we wish? Assemblies of men, a procession, feasts, battles, everything in short does nature at command produce and provide? And though to increase the marvel the mind of others in the same spot and room is thinking of things all quite different. What again are we to say, when we see in sleep idols advance in measured tread and move their pliant limbs, when in nimble wise they put out each pliant arm in turn and represent to the eyes over and over again an action with foot that moves in time? Idols to wit are imbued with art and move about well-trained, to be able in the night-time to exhibit such plays. Or will this rather be the truth? Because in one unit of time, when we can perceive it by sense and while one single word is uttered, many latent times are contained which reason finds to exist, therefore in any time you please all the several idols are at hand ready prepared in each several place. And because they are so thin, the mind can see distinctly only those which it strains itself to see; therefore all that there are besides are lost, save only those for which it has made itself ready. Moreover it makes itself ready and hopes to see that which follows upon each thing; therefore the result does follow. Do you not see that the eyes also, when they essay to discern things which are thin and fine, strain themselves and make themselves ready, and without that we cannot see distinctly? And yet you may observe even in things which are plain before us, that if you do not attend, it is just as if the thing were all the time away and far distant. What wonder then, if the mind loses all other things save those with which it is itself earnestly occupied? Then too from small indications we draw the widest inferences and by our own fault entangle ourselves in the meshes of self-delusion.

818] Sometimes it happens too that an image of the same kind is not supplied, but what before was a woman, turns out in our hands to have changed into a man; or a different face and age succeed to the first. But sleep and forgetfulness prevent us from feeling surprise at this.

823] And herein you should desire with all your might to shun the weakness, with a lively apprehension to avoid the mistake of supposing that the bright lights of the eyes were made in order that we might see; and that the tapering ends of the shanks and hams are attached to the feet as a base in order to enable us to step out with long strides; or again that the forearms were slung to the stout upper arms and ministering hands given us on each side, that we might be able to discharge the needful duties of life. Other explanations of like sort which men give, one and all put effect for cause through wrongheaded reasoning; since nothing was born in the body that we might use it, but that which is born begets for itself a use: thus seeing did not exist before the eyes were born, nor the employment of speech ere the tongue was made; but rather the birth of the tongue was long anterior to language and the ears were made long before sound was heard, and all the limbs, I trow, existed before there was any employment for them: they could not therefore have grown for the purpose of being used. But on the other hand engaging in the strife of battle and mangling the body and staining the limbs with gore were in vogue long before glittering darts ever flew; and nature prompted to shun a wound or ever the left arm by the help of art held up before the person the defence of a shield. Yes and consigning the tired body to rest is much older than a soft-cushioned bed, and the slaking of thirst had birth before cups. These things therefore which have been invented in accordance with the uses and wants of life, may well be believed to have been discovered for the purpose of being used. Far otherwise is it with all those things which first were born, then afterwards made known the purposes to which they might be put; at the head of which class we see the senses and the limbs. Wherefore again and again I repeat, it is quite impossible to believe that they could have been made for the duties which they discharge.

858] It ought likewise to cause no wonder

that the nature of the body of each living creature absolutely requires food. I have shown that bodies ebb away and withdraw from things, many in number in many ways; but most numerous must be those which withdraw from living things; for because these are tried by active motion, and many particles are pressed out from the depths of the frame and carried off by sweating, many breathed out through the mouth, when they pant from exhaustion, from such causes the body becomes rarefied and the whole nature undermined; and this state is attended by pain. Food therefore is taken in order to give support to the frame and recruit the strength by its infusion, and to close up the open-mouthed craving for meat throughout limbs and veins. The moisture too passes into all the parts which call for moisture; and many accumulated bodies of heat which cause a burning in our stomach, the approach of liquid scatters and quenches as if they were fire, so that dry heat can no longer parch the frame. In this way then you see gasping thirst is drenched out of our body, in this way the hungry craving is satisfied.

877] Now how it comes to pass that we are able to step out when we please, and how it is given us to move about our limbs, and what cause is wont to push forward the great load of this our body I will tell: do you take in my words. I say that idols of walking first present themselves to our mind and strike on the mind, as we said before: then the will arises; for no one begins to do anything, until his mind has first determined what it wills. From the very fact that it determines such thing, there is an image of that thing. When therefore the mind bestirs itself in such a way as to will to walk and step out, it strikes at the same moment the force of the soul which is spread over the whole body throughout the limbs and frame; and this is easily done, since the whole is held in close union with the mind. Next the soul in its turn strikes the body, and thus the whole mass by degrees is pushed on and set in motion. Then again the body becomes also rarefied, and the air, as you see its nature is, being always so nimble in moving, comes and passes in great quantity through the opened pores and is thus distributed into the most minute parts of the body. In this way then by these two causes acting in two ways the body like a ship is carried on by sails and wind. And herein it need not excite any surprise that such very minute bodies can steer so great a body and turn about the whole of this our load; for wind though fine with subtle body drives and pushes on a large ship of large moving mass and one hand directs it however great the speed at which it is going and one rudder steers it to any point you like; and by means of blocks of pulleys and tread-wheels a machine stirs many things of great weight and raises them up with slight effort.

907] Now by what means yon sleep lets a stream of repose over the limbs and dispels from the breast the cares of the mind, I will tell in sweetly worded rather than in many verses; as the short song of the swan is better than the loud noise of cranes scattered abroad amid the ethereal clouds of the south. Do you lend me a nice ear and a keen mind, that you may not deny what I say to be possible and secede with breast disdainfully rejecting the words of truth, you yourself being in fault the while and unable to discern. Sleep mainly takes place when the force of the soul has been scattered about through the frame, and in part has been forced abroad and taken its departure, and in part has been thrust back and has withdrawn into the depths of the body: after that the limbs are relaxed and droop. For there is no doubt that this sense exists in us by the agency of the soul; and when sleep obstructs the action of this sense, then we must assume that our soul has been disordered and forced abroad; not indeed all; for then the body would lie steeped in the everlasting chill of death. Where no part of the soul remained behind concealed in the limbs, as fire remains concealed when buried under much ash, whence could sense be suddenly rekindled through the limbs, as flame can spring up from hidden fire?

929] But by what means this change of condition is accomplished and from what the soul can be disordered and the body grow faint, I will explain: do you mind that I waste not my words on the wind. In the first place the body in its outer side, since it is next to and is touched by the air, must be thumped and beaten by its repeated blows; and for this reason all things as a rule are covered either by a hide or else by shells or by a callous skin or by bark. When creatures breathe, this air at the same time buffets the inner side also, as it is inhaled and exhaled. Therefore since the body is beaten on both sides alike and blows arrive by means of the small apertures at the primal parts and primal elements of our body, there gradually ensues a sort of breaking up throughout our limbs, the arrangements of the first-beginnings of body and mind getting disordered. Then next a part of the soul is forced out and a part withdraws into the inner recesses; a part too scattered about through the frame cannot get united together and so act and be acted upon by motion; for nature intercepts all communication and blocks up all the passages; and therefore sense retires deep into the frame as the motions are all altered. And since there is nothing as it were to lend support to the frame, the body becomes weak and all the limbs are faint, the arms and eyelids droop and the hams even in bed often give way under you and relax their powers. Then sleep follows on food, because food produces just the same effects as air, while it is distributed into all the veins; and that sleep is much the heaviest which you take when full or tired, because then the greatest number of bodies fall into disorder, bruised by much exertion. On the same principle the soul comes in part to be forced more deeply into the frame, and there is also a more copious emission of it abroad, and at the same time it is more divided and scattered in itself within you.

962] And generally to whatever pursuit a man is closely tied down and strongly attached, on whatever subject we have previously much dwelt, the mind having been put to a more than usual strain in it, during sleep we for the most part fancy that we are engaged in the same; lawyers think they plead causes and draw up covenants of sale, generals that they fight and engage in battle, sailors that they wage and carry on war with the winds, we think we pursue our task and investigate the nature of things constantly and consign it when discovered to writings in our native tongue. So all other pursuits and arts are seen for the most part during sleep to occupy and mock the minds of men. And whenever men have given during many days in succession undivided attention to games, we generally see that after they have ceased to perceive these with their senses, there yet remain passages open in the mind through which the same idols of things may enter. Thus for many days those same objects present themselves to the eyes, so that even when awake they see dancers as they think moving their pliant limbs, and receive into the ears the clear music of the harp and speaking strings, and behold the same spectators and at the same time the varied decorations of the stage in all their brilliancy.

984] So great is the influence of zeal and inclination, so great is the influence of the things in which men have been habitually engaged, and not men only but all living creatures. Thus you will see stout horses, even when their bodies are lying down, yet in their sleep sweat and pant without ceasing and strain their powers to the utmost as if for the prize, or as if the barriers were thrown open. And often during soft repose the dogs of hunters do yet all at once throw about their legs and suddenly utter cries and repeatedly snuff the air with their nostrils, as though they had found and were on the tracks of wild beasts; and after they are awake often chase the shadowy idols of stags, as though they saw them in full flight, until they have shaken off their delusions and come to themselves again. And the fawning brood of dogs brought up tame in the house haste to shake their body and raise it up from the ground, as if they beheld unknown faces and features. And the fiercer the different breeds are, the greater rage they must display in sleep. But the various kinds of birds flee and suddenly in the night-time trouble with their wings the groves of the gods, when in gentle sleep hawks and pursuing birds have appeared to show fight and offer battle.

1011] Again the minds of men which pursue great aims under great emotions, often during sleep pursue and carry on the same in like manner; kings take by storm, are taken, join battle, raise a loud cry as if stabbed on the spot. Many struggle hard and utter groans in pain, and as if gnawed by the bite of panther or cruel lion fill all the place with loud cries. Many during sleep speak of important affairs and have often and often disclosed their own guilt. Many meet death; many as if tumbling down from high precipices to the ground with their whole body, are scared with terror and after sleep as if out of their judgement scarce come to themselves again, quite disordered by their body's turmoil. Again a thirsty man sits down beside a river or a pleasant spring and gulps down wellnigh all the stream. Cleanly people often, when sound asleep, believing that they are lifting their dress beside a urinal or the public vessels, pour forth the filtered liquid of their whole body, and the Babylonian coverlets of surpassing brilliancy are drenched. Then too those, into the boiling currents of whose age seed is for the first time passing, when the ripe fulness of days has produced it in their limbs, idols encounter from without from what body soever, harbingers of a glorious face and a beautiful bloom, which stir and excite the frame.

1037] That seed we have spoken of before is stirred up in us, as soon as ripe age fortifies the frame. For as different causes set in motion and excite different things, so from man the sole influence of man draws forth human seed. As soon then as it has been forced out from and quits its proper seats throughout the limbs and frame, it withdraws itself from the whole body and meets together in appropriate places and rouses forthwith the appropriate parts of the body. The places are excited and swell with seed, and the inclination arises to emit the seed towards that to which the fell desire all tends, and the body seeks that object from which the mind is wounded by love; for all as a rule fall towards their wound and the blood spirts out in that direction whence comes the stroke by which we are struck; and if he is at close quarters, the red stream covers the foe. Thus then he who gets a hurt from the weapons of Venus, whatever be the object that hits him, inclines to the quarter whence he is wounded, and yearns to unite with it and join body with body; for a mute desire gives a presage of the pleasure.

1058] This pleasure is for us Venus; from

that desire is the Latin name of love, from that desire has first trickled into the heart yon drop of Venus' honeyed joy, succeeded soon by chilly care; for though that which you love is away, yet idols of it are at hand and its sweet name is present to the ears. But it is meet to fly idols and scare away all that feeds love and turn your mind on another object, distract your passion elsewhere and not keep it, with your thoughts once set on one object by love of it, and so lay up for yourself care and un-failing pain. For the sore gathers strength and becomes inveterate by feeding, and every day the madness grows in violence and the misery becomes aggravated, unless you erase the first wounds by new blows and first heal them when yet fresh, roaming abroad after Venus the pandemian, or transfer to something else the emotions of your mind.

1073] Nor is he who shuns love without the fruits of Venus, but rather enjoys those bless-ings which are without any pain: doubtless the pleasure from such things is more unal-loyed for the healthy-minded than for the love-sick; for in the very moment of enjoying the burning desire of lovers wavers and wanders undecided, and they cannot tell what first to enjoy with eyes and hands. What they have sought, they tightly squeeze and cause pain of body and often imprint their teeth on the lips and clash mouth to mouth in kissing, because the pleasure is not pure and there are hidden stings which stimulate to hurt even that what-ever it is from which spring those germs of frenzy. But Venus with light hand breaks the force of these pains during love, and the fond pleasure mingled therein reins in the bites. For in this there is hope, that from the same body whence springs their burning desire, their flame may likewise be quenched; though nature protests that the very opposite is the truth; and this is the one thing of all, in which, when we have most of it, then all the more the breast burns with fell desire. Meat and drink are taken into the body; and as they can fill up certain fixed parts, in this way the craving for drink and bread is easily satisfied; but from the face and beautiful bloom of man nothing is given into the body to enjoy save flimsy idols; a sorry hope which is often snatched off by the wind.

1097] As when in sleep a thirsty man seeks to drink and water is not given to quench the burning in his frame, but he seeks the idols of waters and toils in vain and thirsts as he drinks in the midst of the torrent stream, thus in love Venus mocks lovers with idols, nor can bodies satisfy them by all their gazing upon them nor can they with their hands rub aught off the soft limbs, wandering undecided over the whole body. At last when they have united and enjoy the flower of age, when the body now has a presage of delights and Venus is in the mood to sow the fields of woman, they greedily clasp each other's body and suck each other's lips and breathe in, pressing meanwhile teeth on each other's mouth; all in vain, since they can rub nothing off nor enter and pass each with his whole body into the other's body; for so sometimes they seem to will and strive to do: so greedily are they held in the chains of Venus, while their limbs melt overpowered by the might of the pleasure. At length when the gathered desire has gone forth, there ensues for a brief while a short pause in the burning passion; and then re-turns the same frenzy, then comes back the old madness, when they are at a loss to know what they really desire to get, and cannot find what device is to conquer that mischief; in such utter uncertainty they pine away by a hidden wound.

1121] Then too they waste their strength and ruin themselves by the labour, then too their life is passed at the beck of another. Mean-while their estate runs away and is turned into Babylonian coverlets; duties are neglected and their good name staggers and sickens. On her feet laugh elastic and beautiful Sicyonian shoes, yes, and large emeralds with green light are set in gold and the sea-coloured dress is worn constantly and much used drinks in the sweat. The noble earnings of their fathers are turned into hair-bands, head-dresses; some-times are changed into a sweeping robe and Alidensian and Cean dresses. Feasts set out with rich coverlets and viands, games, numer-ous cups, perfumes, crowns, and garlands are prepared; all in vain, since out of the very well-spring of delights rises up something of bitter, to pain amid the very flowers; either when the conscience-stricken mind haply gnaws itself with remorse to think that it is passing a life of sloth and ruining itself in brothels, or because she has launched forth some word and left its meaning in doubt and it cleaves to the love-sick heart and burns like living fire, or because it fancies she casts her eyes too freely about or looks on another, and it sees in her face traces of a smile.

1141] And these evils are found in love that is lasting and highly prosperous; but in crossed and hopeless love are ills such as you may seize with closed eyes, past numbering; so that it is better to watch beforehand in the manner I have prescribed, and be on your guard not to be drawn in. For to avoid falling into the toils of love is not so hard as, after you are caught, to get out of the nets you are in and to break through the strong meshes of Venus. And yet even when you are entangled and held fast you may escape the mischief, unless you stand in your own way and begin by overlooking all the defects of her mind or those of her body, whoever it is whom you court and woo. For this men usually do, blinded by passion, and attribute to the beloved those advantages which are not really theirs. We therefore see women in ways manifold deformed and ugly to be objects of endearment and held in the highest admiration. And one lover jeers at others and advises them to propitiate Venus, since they are troubled by a disgraceful passion, and often, poor wretch, gives no thought to his own ills greatest of all.

1160] The black is a brune, the filthy and rank has not the love of order; the cat-eyed is a miniature Pallas, the stringy and wizened a gazelle; the dumpy and dwarfish is one of the Graces, from top to toe all grace; the big and overgrown is awe-inspiring and full of dignity. She is tongue-tied, cannot speak, then she has a lisp; the dumb is bashful; then the firespit, the teasing, the gossiping turns to a shining lamp. One becomes a slim darling then when she cannot live from want of flesh; and she is only spare, who is half-dead with cough. Then the fat and big-breasted is a Ceres' self big-breasted from Iacchus; the pug-nosed is a she Silenus and a satyress; the thick-lipped a very kiss. It were tedious to attempt to report other things of the kind. Let her however be of ever so great dignity of appearance; such

that the power of Venus goes forth from all her limbs; yet there are others too; yet have we lived without her before; yet does she do, and we know that she does, in all things the same as the ugly woman; and fumigates herself, poor wretch, with nauseous perfumes, her very maids running from her and giggling behind her back. But the lover, when shut out, often in tears covers the threshold with flowers and wreaths, and anoints the haughty doorposts with oil of marjoram and imprints kisses, poor wretch, on the doors. When however he has been admitted, if on his approach but one single breath should come in his way, he would seek specious reasons for departing, and the long-conned deep-drawn complaint would fall to the ground; and then he would blame his folly, on seeing that he had attributed to her more than it is right to concede to a mortal. Nor is this unknown to our Venuses; wherefore all the more they themselves hide with the utmost pains all that goes on behind the scenes of life from those whom they wish to retain in the chains of love; but in vain, since you may yet draw forth from her mind into the light all these things and search into all her smiles; and if she is of a fair mind and not troublesome, overlook them in your turn and make allowance for human failings.

1192] Nor does the woman sigh always with feigned passion, when she locks in her embrace and joins with her body the man's body and holds it, sucking his lips into her lips and drinking in his kisses. Often she does it from the heart, and seeking mutual joys courts him to run the complete race of love. And in no other way could birds, cattle, wild beasts, sheep, and mares submit to bear the males, except because the very exuberance of nature in the females is in heat and burns and joyously draws in the Venus of the covering males. See you not too how those whom mutual pleasure has chained are often tortured in their common chains? How often in the highways do dogs, desiring to separate, eagerly pull different ways with all their might, while all the time they are held fast in the strong fetters of Venus! This they would never do, unless they experienced mutual joys, strong enough to force them into the snare and hold them in its meshes. Wherefore again and again

I repeat there is a common pleasure.

1209] And when haply in mixing her seed with the man's the woman by sudden force has overpowered and seized for herself his force, then children are formed from the mothers' seed like to the mothers, as from the fathers' seed like to the fathers. But those whom you see with a share of both forms, blending equally the features of the parents, grow from the union of the father's body and the mother's blood, when the mutual ardour of desire working in concert has brought and clashed together the seeds roused throughout the frame by the goads of Venus; and neither of the two has gotten the mastery nor has been mastered. Sometimes too the children may spring up like their grandfathers and often resemble the forms of their grandfathers' fathers, because the parents often keep concealed in their bodies many first-beginnings mixed in many ways, which first proceeding from the original stock one father hands down to the next father; and then from these Venus produces forms after a manifold chance and repeats not only the features, but the voices and hair of their forefathers. And the female sex equally springs from the father's seed and males go forth equally formed from the mother's body; since these distinctions no more proceed from the fixed seed of one or other parent than our faces and bodies and limbs: the birth is always formed out of the two seeds; and whichever parent that which is produced more resembles, of that parent it has more than an equal share; as you may equally observe, whether it is a male child or a female birth.

1233] Nor do the divine powers debar anybody from the power of begetting, forbidding him ever to receive the name of father from sweet children and forcing him to pass his life in a barren wedlock; as men commonly fancy when in sorrow they drench the altars with much blood and pile the raised altars with offerings, to make their wives pregnant with abundant seed. In vain they weary the divinity of the gods and the sacred lots. They are barren sometimes from the too great thickness of the seed, sometimes from its undue fluidity and thinness: because the thin is unable to get a firm hold on the right spots, it at

once passes away and is repelled and withdrawn abortively: since by others again a too thick seed is discharged in a state more solid than is suitable, it either does not fly forth with so prolonged a stroke or cannot equally pass into the proper spots or when it has passed in with difficulty mixes with the woman's seed. For well-assorted matches are found to be of great importance; and some males impregnate some females more readily than others, and other females conceive and become pregnant more readily from other males. And many women have hitherto been barren during several marriages and have yet in the end found mates from whom they could conceive children and be enriched with a sweet offspring. And often even for those, to whom hitherto wives however fruitful had been unable in their house to bear, has been found a compatible nature, enabling them to fortify their age with sons. Of such great importance is it, in order that seeds may agree and blend with seeds in a way to promote birth, whether the thick comes into contact with the fluid and the fluid with the thick. And on this point it matters much on what diet life is supported; for by some foods seed is thickened in the limbs, and by others again is thinned and wasted. And in what modes the intercourse goes on, is likewise of very great moment; for women are commonly thought to conceive more readily after the manner of wild beasts and quadrupeds, because the seeds in this way can find the proper spots in consequence of the position of the body. Nor have wives the least use for effeminate motions: a woman hinders and stands in the way of her own conceiving, when thus she acts; for she drives the furrow out of the direct course and path of the share and turns away from the proper spots the stroke of the seed. And thus for their own ends harlots are wont to move, in order not to conceive and lie in child-bed frequently, and at the same time to render Venus more attractive to men. This our wives have surely no need of.

1278] Sometimes too by no divine grace and arrows of Venus a sorry woman of inferior beauty comes to be loved; for the wife sometimes by her own acts and accommodating manners and by elegant neatness of person readily habituates you to pass your life with her. Moreover custom renders love attractive; for that which is struck by oft-repeated blows however lightly, yet after long course of time is overpowered and gives way. See you not too that drops of water falling on stones after long course of time scoop a hole through these stones?

· BOOK FIVE ·

Who is able with powerful genius to frame a poem worthy of the grandeur of the things and these discoveries? Or who is so great a master of words as to be able to devise praises equal to the deserts of him who left to us such prizes won and earned by his own genius? None methinks who is formed of mortal body. For if we must speak as the acknowledged grandeur of the things itself demands, a god he was, a god, most noble Memmius, who first found out that plan of life which is now termed wisdom, and who by trained skill rescued life from such great billows and such thick darkness and moored it in so perfect a calm and in so brilliant a light. Compare the godlike discoveries of others in old times: Ceres is famed to have pointed out to mortals corn, and Liber the vine-born juice of the grape; though life might well have subsisted without these things, as we are told some nations even now live without them. But a happy life was not possible without a clean breast; wherefore with more reason this man is deemed by us a god, from whom come those sweet solaces of existence which even now are distributed over great nations and gently soothe men's minds. Then if you shall suppose that the deeds of Hercules surpass his, you will be carried still farther away from true reason. For what would yon great gaping maw of Nemean lion now harm us and the bristled Arcadian boar? Ay or what could the bull of Crete do and the hydra plague of Lerna, fenced round with its envenomed snakes? Or how could the triple-breasted might of threefold Geryon, how could the birds with brazen arrowy feathers that dwelt in the Stymphalian swamps do us such mighty injury, and the horses of Thracian Diomede breathing fire from their nostrils along the Bistonian borders and Ismara? And the serpent which guards the bright golden apples of the Hesperides, fierce, dangerous of aspect, girding the tree's stem with his enormous body, what harm pray could he do us beside the Atlantic shore and its sounding main, which none of us goes near and no barbarian ventures to approach? And all other monsters of the kind which have been destroyed, if they had not been vanquished, what harm could they do, I ask, though now alive? None methinks: the earth even now so abounds to repletion in wild beasts and is filled with troublous terror throughout woods and great mountains and deep forests; places which we have it for the most part in our own power to shun. But unless the breast is cleared, what battles and dangers must then find their way into us in our own despite! What poignant cares inspired by lust then rend the distressful man, and then also what mighty fears! And pride, filthy lust and wantonness? What disasters they occasion, and luxury and all sorts of sloth? He therefore who shall have subdued all these and banished them from the mind by words, not arms, shall he not have a just title to be ranked among the gods? And all the more so that he was wont to deliver many precepts in beautiful and god-like phrase about the immortal gods themselves and to open up by his teachings all the nature of things.

55] While walking in his footsteps I follow out his reasonings and teach by my verses, by what law all things are made, what necessity there is then for them to continue in that law, and how impotent they are to annul the binding statutes of time: foremost in which class of things the nature of the mind has been proved to be formed of a body that had birth and to be unable to endure unscathed through great time, mere idols being wont to mock the mind in sleep, when we seem to see him whom life has abandoned: to continue, the order of my design has now brought me to this point, where I must proceed to show that the world is formed of a mortal body and at the same time had birth; to show too in what way that union of matter founded earth, heaven, sea, stars, sun, and the ball of the moon; also what living creatures sprang out of the earth, as well as those which never at any time were born; in what way too mankind began to use with one another varied speech by the names conferred on things; and also in what ways yon fear of the gods gained an entry into men's breasts, and now throughout the world maintains as holy fanes, lakes, groves, altars, and idols of the gods. Furthermore I shall make clear by what force piloting nature guides the courses of the sun and the wanderings of the moon; lest haply we imagine that these of their own free will between heaven and earth traverse their everlasting orbits, graciously furthering the increase of crops and living creatures, or we think they roll on by any forethought of the gods. For they who have been rightly taught that the gods lead a life without care, if nevertheless they wonder by what plan all things can be carried on, above all in regard to those things which are seen overhead in the ethereal borders, are borne back again into their old religious scruples and take unto themselves hard taskmasters, whom they poor wretches believe to be almighty, not knowing what can, what cannot be, in short by what system each thing has its powers defined, its deep-set boundary mark.

91] Well then not to detain you any longer by mere promises, look before all on seas and lands and heaven: their threefold nature, their three bodies, Memmius, three forms so unlike, three such wondrous textures a single day shall give over to destruction; and the mass and fabric of the world upheld for many years shall tumble to ruin. Nor can I fail to perceive with what a novel and strange effect it falls upon the mind, this destruction of heaven and earth that is to be, and how hard it is for me to produce a full conviction of it by words; as is the case when you bring to the ears a thing hitherto unexampled, and yet you cannot submit it to the eyesight nor put it into the hands; through which the straightest high-

way of belief leads into the human breast and quarters of the mind. But yet I will speak out: it well may be that the reality itself will bring credit to my words and that you will see earthquakes arise and all things grievously shattered to pieces in short time. But this may pilot fortune guide far away from us, and may reason rather than the reality convince that all things may be overpowered and tumble in with a frightful crash.

110] But before I shall begin on this question to pour forth decrees of fate with more sanctity and much more certainty than the Pythia who speaks out from the tripod and laurel of Phoebus, I will clearly set forth to you many comforting topics in learned language; lest held in the yoke of religion you haply suppose that earth and sun and heaven, sea, stars, and moon must last for ever with divine body; and therefore think it right that they after the fashion of the giants should all suffer punishment for their monstrous guilt, who by their reasoning displace the walls of the world and seek to quench the glorious sun of heaven, branding immortal things in mortal speech; though in truth these things are so far from possessing divinity and are so unworthy of being reckoned in the number of gods, that they may be thought to afford a notable instance of what is quite without vital motion and sense. For it is quite impossible to suppose that the nature and judgement of the mind can exist with any body whatever; even as a tree cannot exist in the ether nor clouds in the salt sea, nor can fishes live in the fields nor blood exist in woods nor sap in stones. Where each thing can grow and abide is fixed and ordained. Thus the nature of the mind cannot come into being alone without the body nor exist far away from the sinews and blood. But if (for this would be much more likely to happen than that) the force itself of the mind might be in the head or shoulders or heels or might be born in any other part of the body, it would after all be wont to abide in one and the same man or vessel. But since in our body even it is fixed and seen to be ordained where the soul and the mind can severally be and grow, it must still more strenuously be denied that it can abide out of the body and the living room altogether in crumbling clods of earth or in the fire of the sun or in water or in the high borders of ether. These things therefore are not possessed of divine sense, since they cannot be quickened with the vital feeling.

146] This too you may not possibly believe, that the holy seats of the gods exist in any parts of the world: the fine nature of the gods far withdrawn from our senses is hardly seen by the thought of the mind; and since it has ever eluded the touch and stroke of the hands, it must touch nothing which is tangible for us; for that cannot touch which does not admit of being touched in turn. And therefore their seats as well must be unlike our seats, fine, even as their bodies are fine. All which I will prove to you later in copious argument. To say again that for the sake of men they have willed to set in order the glorious nature of the world and therefore it is meet to praise the work of the gods calling as it does for all praise, and to believe that it will be eternal and immortal, and that it is an unholy thing ever to shake by any force from its fixed seats that which by the forethought of the gods in ancient days has been established on everlasting foundations for mankind, or to assail it by speech and utterly overturn it from top to bottom; and to invent and add other figments of the kind, Memmius, is all sheer folly. For what advantage can our gratitude bestow on immortal and blessed beings, that for our sakes they should take in hand to administer aught? And what novel incident should have induced them hitherto at rest so long after to desire to change their former life?

170] For it seems natural he should rejoice in a new state of things, whom old things annoy; but for him whom no ill has befallen in times gone by, when he passed a pleasant existence, what could have kindled in such a one a love of change? Did life lie grovelling in darkness and sorrow, until the first dawn of the birth-time of things? Or what evil had it been for us never to have been born? Whoever has been born must want to continue in life, so long as fond pleasure shall keep him; but for him who has never tasted the love, never been on the lists, of life, what harm not to have been born? Whence again was first implanted in the gods a pattern for begetting things in general as well as the preconception

of what men are, so that they knew and saw in mind what they wanted to make? And in what way was the power of first-beginnings ever ascertained, and what they could effect by a change in their mutual arrangements, unless nature herself gave the model for making things? For in such-wise the first-beginnings of things many in number in many ways impelled by blows for infinite ages back and kept in motion by their own weights have been wont to be carried along and to unite in all manner of ways and thoroughly test every kind of production possible by their mutual combinations; that it is not strange if they have also fallen into arrangements and have come into courses like to those out of which this sum of things is now carried on by constant renewing.

195] But if I did not know what first-beginnings of things are, yet this judging by the very arrangements of heaven I would venture to affirm, and led by many other facts to maintain, that the nature of things has by no means been made for us by divine power: so great are the defects with which it is encumbered. In the first place of all the space which the vast reach of heaven covers, a portion greedy mountains and forests of wild beasts have occupied, rocks and wasteful pools take up and the sea which holds wide apart the coasts of different lands. Next of nearly two thirds burning heat and the constant fall of frost rob mortals. What is left for tillage, even that nature by its power would overrun with thorns, unless the force of man made head against it, accustomed for the sake of a livelihood to groan beneath the strong hoe and to cut through the earth by pressing down the plough. Unless by turning up the fruitful clods with the share and labouring the soil of the earth we stimulate things to rise, they could not spontaneously come up into the clear air; and even then sometimes when things earned with great toil now put forth their leaves over the lands and are all in blossom, either the ethereal sun burns them up with excessive heats or sudden rains and cold frosts cut them off, and the blasts of the winds waste them by a furious hurricane. Again why does nature give food and increase to the frightful race of wild beasts dangerous to mankind both by sea and land? Why do the seasons of the year bring diseases in their train? Why stalks abroad untimely death? Then too the baby, like to a sailor cast away by the cruel waves, lies naked on the ground, speechless, wanting every furtherance of life, soon as nature by the throes of birth has shed him forth from his mother's womb into the borders of light: he fills the room with a rueful wauling, as well he may whose destiny it is to go through in life so many ills. But the different flocks, herds, and wild beasts grow up; they want no rattles; to none of them need be addressed the fond broken accents of the fostering nurse; they ask not different dresses according to the season; no nor do they want arms or lofty walls, whereby to protect their own, the earth itself and nature manifold in her works producing in plenty all things for all.

235] First of all, since the body of the earth and water and the light breath of air and burning heats, out of which this sum of things is seen to be formed, do all consist of a body that had a birth and is mortal, the whole nature of the world must be reckoned of a like body. For those things whose parts and members we see to be of a body that had a birth and of forms that are mortal, we perceive to be likewise without exception mortal, and at the same time to have had a birth. Since therefore I see that the chiefest members and parts of the world are destroyed and begotten anew, I may be sure that for heaven and earth as well there has been a time of beginning and there will be a time of destruction.

247] And herein that you may not think I have unfairly seized on this point for myself, because I have assumed that earth and fire are mortal and have not doubted that water and air perish, and have said that these are likewise begotten and grow afresh, mark the proofs: first of all some portion of the earth, burnt up by constant suns, trampled by a multitude of feet, sends forth a cloud and flying eddies of dust, which the strong winds disperse over the whole air. Part too of the soil is put under water by rains, and rivers graze against and eat into the banks. Again whatever increases something else, is in its turn replenished; and since beyond a doubt earth the universal mother is found at the same time to

be the general tomb of things, therefore you see she is lessened and increases and grows again.

261] Furthermore, that sea, rivers, fountains always stream over with new moisture and that waters well up without ceasing, it needs no words to prove: the great flow of waters from all sides clearly shows it. But then the water on the surface is always taken off, and thus it is that on the whole there is no overflow, partly because the seas are lessened by the strong winds sweeping over them and by the ethereal sun decomposing them with his rays; partly, because the water is diffused below the surface over all lands; for the salt is strained off and the matter of liquid streams back again to the source and all meets together at the riverheads, and then flows over the lands in a fresh current, where a channel once scooped out has carried down the waters with liquid foot.

273] And next I will speak of the air which is changed over its whole body every hour in countless ways. For whatever ebbs from things, is all borne always into the great sea of air; and unless it in return were to give back bodies to things and to recruit them as they ebb, all things ere now would have been dissolved and changed into air. It therefore ceases not to be begotten from things and to go back into things, since it is a fact that all things constantly ebb.

281] Likewise the abundant source of clear light, the ethereal sun, constantly floods heaven with fresh brightness and supplies the place of light on the instant by new light; for every previous emission of brightness is quite lost to it, wherever it falls. This you may know from the following examples: as soon as ever clouds begin to pass below the sun and to break off so to say the rays of light, forthwith their lower part is wholly lost, and the earth is over-shadowed wherever the clouds pass over; so that you may know that things constantly require new irradiation and that all the preceding emissions of light are lost, and in no other way can things be seen in the sun, unless the fountain head of light itself send a supply. Moreover, you see, nightly lights which belong to earth, such as hanging lamps and torches bright with darting flames, hasten in like fashion amid great darkness with ministering heat to supply new light; are eager to bicker with fires, ay eager; nor is the light ever broken off nor does it quit the spots illuminated: with such suddenness is its destruction concealed by the swift birth of flame from all the fires at once. In the same way then we must believe that sun, moon, and stars emit light from fresh and ever fresh supplies rising up, and always lose every previous discharge of flames; that you may not haply believe that these flourish indestructible.

306] Again see you not that even stones are conquered by time, that high towers fall and rocks moulder away, that shrines and idols of gods are worn out with decay, and that the holy divinity cannot prolong the bounds of fate or struggle against the fixed laws of nature? Then see we not the monuments of men, fallen to ruin, ask for themselves as well whether you'd believe that *they* decay with years? See we not basalt rocks tumble down riven away from high mountains and unable to endure and suffer the strong might of finite age? Surely they would never fall suddenly thus riven away, it for infinite time past they had held out against all the batteries of age without a crash.

318] Again gaze on this, which about and above holds in its embrace all the earth: if it begets all things out of itself, as some say, and takes them back when they are destroyed, then the whole of it has had a birth and is of a mortal body; for whatever gives increase and food but of itself to other things, must be lessened; and must be replenished, when it takes things back.

324] Again if there was no birth-time of earth and heaven and they have been from everlasting, why before the Theban war and the destruction of Troy have not other poets as well sung other themes? Whither have so many deeds of men so often passed away, why live they nowhere embodied in lasting records of fame? The truth methinks is that the sum has but a recent date and the nature of the world is new and has but lately had its commencement. Wherefore even now some arts are receiving their last polish, some are even in course of growth: just now many improvements have been made in ships; only yesterday

musicians have given birth to tuneful melodies; then too this nature or system of things has been discovered lately, and I the very first of all have only now been found able to transfer it into native words. But if haply you believe that before this all things have existed just the same, but that the generations of men have perished by burning heat, or that cities have fallen by some great concussion of the world, or that after constant rains devouring rivers have gone forth over the earth and have whelmed towns, so much the more you must yield and admit that there will be entire destruction too of earth and heaven; for when things were tried by so great distempers and so great dangers, at that time had a more disastrous cause pressed upon them, they would far and wide have gone to destruction and mighty ruin. And in no other way are we proved to be mortals, except because we all alike in turn fall sick of the same diseases which those had whom nature has withdrawn from life.

351] Again whatever things last for ever, must either, because they are of solid body, repel strokes and not suffer aught to pass into them, sufficient to disunite the closely massed parts within: such are the bodies of matter whose nature we have shown before: or they must be able to endure through all time for this reason, because they are exempt from blows, as void is which remains untouched and suffers not a jot from any stroke; or else because there is no extent of room around, into which things so to say may depart and be broken up: in this way the sum of sums is eternal and there is no place outside into which things may spring asunder, nor are there any bodies which can fall upon them and dissolve them by a powerful blow. But the nature of the world, as I have shown, is neither of solid body, since void is mixed up in things, nor is it again like void, no nor is there lack of bodies that may haply rise up in mass out of the infinite and overthrow this sum of things with furious tornado or bring upon them some other perilous disaster; nor further is the nature of room or the space of deep void wanting, into which the walls of the world may be scattered abroad; or they may be assailed and perish by some other force. Therefore the gate of death is not closed against heaven or sun or earth or the deep waters of the sea, but stands open and looks towards them with huge wide-gaping maw. And therefore also you must admit that these things likewise had a birth; for things which are of mortal body could not for an infinite time back up to the present have been able to set at naught the puissant strength of immeasurable age.

380] Again since the chiefest members of the world fight so hotly together, fiercely stirred by no hallowed civil warfare, see you not that some limit may be set to their long struggle? Either when the sun and all heat shall have drunk up all the waters and gotten the mastery: this they are ever striving to do, but as yet are unable to accomplish their endeavours: such abundant supplies the rivers furnish, and threaten to turn aggressors and flood all things with a deluge from the deep gulfs of ocean; all in vain, since the winds sweeping over the seas and the ethereal sun decomposing them with his rays do lessen them, and trust to be able to dry all things up before water can attain the end of its endeavour. Such a war do they breathe out with undecided issue, and strive with each other to determine it for mighty ends; though once by the way fire got the upper hand and once, as the story goes, water reigned paramount in the fields. Fire gained the mastery and licked and burnt up many things, when the headstrong might of the horses of the sun dashed from the course and hurried Phaethon through the whole sky and over all lands. But the almighty father, stirred then to fierce wrath, with a sudden thunderstroke dashed Phaethon down from his horses to earth, and the sun meeting him as he fell caught from him the ever-burning lamp of the world and got in hand the scattered steeds and yoked them shaking all over; then guided them on their proper course and gave fresh life to all things. Thus to wit have the old poets of the Greeks sung; though it is all too widely at variance with true reason. Fire may gain the mastery when more bodies of matter than usual have gathered themselves up out of the infinite; and then its powers decay, vanquished in some way or other, or else things perish burnt up by the torrid air. Water too of yore gathered itself

and began to get the mastery, as the story goes, when it whelmed many cities of men; and then when all that force that had gathered itself up out of the infinite, by some means or other was turned aside and withdrew, the rains were stayed and the rivers abated their fury.

416] But in what ways yon concourse of matter founded earth and heaven and the deeps of the sea, the courses of the sun and moon, I will next in order describe. For verily not by design did the first-beginnings of things station themselves each in its right place by keen intelligence, nor did they bargain sooth to say what motions each should assume, but because the first-beginnings of things many in number in many ways impelled by blows for infinite ages back and kept in motion by their own weights have been wont to be carried along and to unite in all manner of ways and thoroughly to test every kind of production possible by their mutual combinations, therefore it is that spread abroad through great time after trying unions and motions of every kind they at length meet together in those masses which suddenly brought together become often the rudiments of great things, of earth, sea, and heaven and the race of living things.

432] At this time then neither could the sun's disc be discerned flying aloft with its abundant light, nor the stars of great ether, nor sea nor heaven, no nor earth nor air, nor could any thing be seen like to our things, but only a strange stormy crisis and medley, gathered together out of first-beginnings of every kind, whose state of discord joining battle disordered their interspaces, passages, connexions, weights, blows, clashings, and motions, because by reason of their unlike forms and varied shapes they could not all remain thus joined together nor fall into mutually harmonius motions. Then next the several parts began to fly asunder and things to be joined like with like and to mark off the world and portion out its members and arrange its mighty parts, that is to say, to separate high heaven from earth, and let the sea spread itself out apart with its unmixed water, and likewise let the fires of ether spread apart pure and unmixed.

449] For first the several bodies of earth, because they were heavy and closely entangled, met together in the middle and took up all of them the lowest positions; and the more they got entangled and the closer their union, the more they squeezed out those particles which were to make up sea, stars, sun, and moon and the walls of the great world. All these are of smooth and round seeds and of much smaller elements than the earth. Therefore the fire-laden ether first burst out from the different parts of the earth through all the porous openings and lightly bore off with itself many fires; much in the same way as we often see, so soon as the morning light of the beaming sun blushes golden over the grass jewelled with dew, and the pools and the ever-running rivers exhale a mist, and even as the earth itself is sometimes seen to smoke; and when all these are gathered together aloft, then do clouds on high with a now cohering body weave a covering beneath heaven. In this way therefore then the light and expansive ether with its now cohering body swept round and arched itself on all sides and expanding widely in all directions round in this way fenced all other things in with its greedy grasp.

471] After it followed the rudiments of sun and moon, whose spheres turn round in air midway beneath earth and ether: these neither earth has taken unto itself nor greatest ether, because they were neither heavy enough to sink and settle down nor light enough to glide along the uppermost borders; they yet however are so placed between the two as to wheel along their life-like bodies and still to be parts of the whole world; just as in us some members may be at rest, while others at the same time are in motion. These things then being withdrawn, the earth in those parts where the vast azure level of ocean now spreads, in a moment sank in and drenched with salt flood the hollows. At every day the more the heats of ether round and the rays of the sun on all sides compressed the earth into a close mass by oft-repeated blows on all its outer edges, so that thus buffeted it was condensed and drawn together about its centre, ever the more did the salt sweat squeezed out of its body increase by its oozings the sea and floating fields, and ever the more did those many bodies of heat and air

escape and fly abroad and condense far away from earth the high glittering quarters of heaven. The plains sank down, the high hills grew in elevation; for the rocks could not settle down nor all the parts sink to one uniform level.

495] Thus then the ponderous mass of earth was formed with close-cohering body and all the slime of the world so to speak slid down by its weight to the lowest point and settled at the bottom like dregs. Then the sea, then the air, then the fire-laden ether itself, all are left unmixed with their clear bodies; and some are lighter than others, and clearest and lightest of all ether floats upon the airy currents, and blends not its clear body with the troubled airs; it suffers all these things below to be upset with furious hurricanes, suffers them to be troubled by wayward storms; while it carries along its own fires gliding with a changeless onward sweep. For that ether may stream on gently and with one uniform effort the Pontos shows, a sea which streams with a changeless current, ever preserving one uniform gliding course.

509] Let us now sing what causes the motions of the stars. In the first place, if the great sphere of heaven revolves, we must say that an air presses on the pole at each end and confines it on the outside and closes it in at both ends; and then that a third air streams above and moves in the same direction in which roll on as they shine the stars of the eternal world; or else that this third air streams below in order to carry up the sphere in the contrary direction; just as we see rivers turn wheels and water-scoops. It is likewise quite possible too that all the heaven remains at rest, while at the same time the glittering signs are carried on; either because rapid heats of ether are shut in and whirl round while seeking a way out and roll their fires in all directions through heaven's Summanian quarters; or else an air streaming from some part from another source outside drives and whirls the fires; or else they may glide on of themselves going whithersoever the food of each calls and invites them, feeding their flamy bodies everywhere throughout heaven. For which of these causes is in operation in this world, it is not easy to affirm for certain; but what can be and is done throughout the universe in various worlds formed on various plans, this I teach, and I go on to set forth several causes which may exist throughout the universe for the motions of stars; one of which however must in this world also be the cause that imparts lively motion to the signs; but to dictate which of them it is, is by no means the duty of the man who advances step by step.

534] And in order that the earth may rest in the middle of the world, it is proper that its weight should gradually pass away and be lessened, and that it should have another nature underneath it conjoined from the beginning of its existence and formed into one being with the airy portions of the world in which it is embodied and lives. For this reason it is no burden and does not weigh down the air; just as his limbs are of no weight to a man nor is his head a burden to his neck, nor do we feel that the whole weight of the body rests on the feet; but whatever weights come from without and are laid upon us, hurt us though they are often very much smaller: of such great moment it is what function each thing has to perform. Thus then the earth is not an alien body suddenly brought in and forced from some other quarter on air alien to it, but was conceived together with it at the first birth of the world and is a fixed portion of that world, just as our limbs are seen to be to us. Again the earth when suddenly shaken by loud thunder shakes by its motion all the things which are above it; and this it could in no wise do, unless it had been fast bound with the airy portions of the world and with heaven. For the earth and they cohere with one another by common roots, conjoined and formed into a single being from the beginning of their existence. See you not too that great as is the weight of our body, the force of the soul, though of the extremest fineness, supports it, because it is so closely conjoined and formed into a single being with it? Then too what is able to lift the body with a nimble bound save the force of the mind which guides the limbs? Now do you see what power a subtle nature may have, when it is conjoined with a heavy body, as the air is conjoined with the earth and the force of the mind with us?

564] Again the disc of the sun cannot be much larger nor its body of heat much smaller, than they appear to be to our senses. For from whatever distances fires can reach us with their light and breathe on our limbs burning heat, those distances take away nothing by such spaces between from the body of the flames, the fire is not in the least narrowed in appearance. Therefore since the heat of the sun and the light which it sheds reach our senses and stroke the proper places, the form too and size of the sun must be seen from this earth in their real dimensions, so that you may not add anything whatever more or less. And whether the moon as it is borne on illuminates places with a borrowed light, or emits its own light from its own body, whatever that is, the form with which it is thus borne on is not at all larger than the one which it presents to our eyes seems to us to be. For all things which we see at a great distance through much air, look dimmed in appearance before their size is diminished. Therefore since the moon presents a bright aspect and well-defined form, it must be seen on high by us from this earth precisely such as it is in the outline which defines it, and of the size it actually is. Lastly in the case of all those fires of ether which you observe from this earth—since in the case of fires which we see here on earth, so long as their flickering is distinct, so long as their heat is perceived, their size is seen sometimes to change to a very very small extent either way, according to the distance at which they are— you may infer that the fires of ether may be smaller than they look in an extremely minute degree, or larger by a very small and insignificant fraction.

592] This likewise need not excite wonder, how it is that so small a body as yon sun can emit so great a light, enough to flood completely seas and all lands and heaven and to steep all things in its burning heat. It well may be that a single spring for the whole world may open up from this spot and gush out in plenteous stream and shoot forth light, because elements of heat meet together from all sides out of the whole world in such manner and the mass of them thrown together streams to a point in such manner, that this heat wells forth from a single source. See you not too what a breadth of meadowland a small spring of water sometimes floods, streaming out over the fields? It is likewise possible that heat from the sun's flame though not at all great may infect the whole air with fervent fires, if haply the air is in a suitable and susceptible state, so that it can be kindled when struck by small bodies of heat; thus we see sometimes a general conflagration from a single spark catch fields of corn and stubble. Perhaps too the sun as he shines aloft with rosy lamp has round about him much fire with heats that are not visible, and thus the fire may be marked by no radiance, so that fraught with heat it increases to such a degree the stroke of the rays.

614] Nor with regard to the sun is there one single explanation, certain and manifest, of the way in which he passes from his summer positions to the midwinter turning-point of Capricorn and then coming back from thence bends his course to the solstitial goal of Cancer, and how the moon is seen once a month to pass over that space, in traversing which the sun spends the period of a year. No single plain cause, I say, has been assigned for these things. It seems highly probable that that may be the truth which the revered judgement of the worthy man Democritus maintains: the nearer the different constellations are to the earth, the less they can be carried along with the whirl of heaven; for the velocity of its force, he says, passes away and the intensity diminishes in the lower parts, and therefore the sun is gradually left behind with the rearward signs, because he is much lower than the burning signs. And the moon more than the sun: the lower her path is and the more distant she is from heaven and the nearer she approaches to earth, the less she can keep pace with the signs. For the fainter the whirl is in which she is borne along, being as she is lower than the sun, so much the more all the signs around overtake and pass her. Therefore it is that she appears to come back to every sign more quickly, because the signs go more quickly back to her. It is quite possible too that from quarters of the world crossing the sun's path two airs may stream each in its turn at a fixed time; one of which may force the sun away from the summer signs so far as his midwinter turning-point and freezing cold, and the other may force him back

from the freezing shades of cold as far as the heat-laden quarters and burning signs. And in like manner we must suppose that the moon, and the stars which make revolutions of great years in great orbits may pass by means of airs from opposite quarters in turn. See you not too that clouds from contrary winds pass in contrary directions, the upper in a contrary way to the lower? Why may not yon stars just as well be borne on through their great orbits in ether by currents contrary one to the other?

650] But night buries the earth in thick darkness, either when the sun after his long course has struck upon the utmost parts of heaven and now exhausted has blown forth all his fires shaken by their journey and weakened by passing through much air: or else because the same force which has carried on his orb above the earth, compels him to change his course and pass below the earth.

656] At a fixed time too Matuta spreads rosy morning over the borders of ether and opens up her light, either because the same sun, coming back below the earth, seizes heaven before his time trying to kindle it with his rays; or because fires meet together and many seeds of heat are accustomed to stream together at a fixed time, which cause new sunlight to be born every day. Thus they tell that from the high mountains of Ida scattered fires are seen at day-break, that these then unite as it were into a single ball and make up an orb. And herein it ought to cause no surprise that these seeds of fire stream together at a time so surely fixed and reproduce the radiance of the sun. For we see many occurrences which take place at a fixed time in all things. At a fixed time trees blossom and at a fixed time shed their blossoms; and at a time no less surely fixed age bids the teeth be shed and the boy put on the soft dress of puberty and let a soft beard fall down equally from each cheek. Lastly lightnings, snow, rains, clouds, and winds take place at not very irregular seasons of year. For where causes from their very first-beginnings have been in this way and things have thus fallen out from the first birth of the world, in due sequence too they now come round after a fixed order.

680] Likewise days may lengthen and nights wane, and days shorten when the nights receive increase, either because the same sun running his course below the earth and above in curves of unlike length parts the borders of ether and divides his orbit into unequal halves; and as he comes round adds on in the opposite half just as much as he has subtracted from the other of the two halves, until he has arrived at that sign of heaven, where the node of the year makes the shades of night of the same length as the daylight. For when the sun's course lies midway between the blast of the north and of the south, heaven keeps his two goals apart at distances now rendered exactly equal on account of the position of the whole starry circle, in gliding through which the sun takes up the period of a year, lighting with slanting rays earth and heaven; as is clearly shown by the plans of those who have mapped out all the quarters of heaven as they are set off with their array of signs. Or else because the air is denser in certain parts, therefore the quivering beam of fire is retarded below the earth and cannot easily pass through and force its way out to its place of rising: for this reason in wintertime nights linger long, ere the beamy badge of day arrive. Or else, because in the way just mentioned at alternate parts of the year fires are accustomed to stream together more slowly and more quickly, which cause the sun to rise in a certain point, therefore it is that those appear to speak the truth who suppose a fresh sun to be born every day.

705] The moon may shine because struck by the sun's rays, and turn that light every day more and more directly towards our sight, in proportion as she recedes from the sun's orb, until just opposite to him she has shone out with full light and at her rising as she soars aloft has beheld his setting; and then by slow steps reversing as it were her course she must in the same way hide her light, the nearer and nearer she now glides to the sun from a different quarter through the circle of the signs; according to the theory of those who suppose the moon to be like a ball and to hold on her course under the sun. She may also very possibly revolve with her own light and display various phases of brightness; for there may well be another body which is carried on and glides in her company getting before her path

and obstructing her in all manner of ways and yet cannot be seen, because it glides on without light. She may also revolve, like it may be to a spherical ball steeped over one half in shining light, and as she rolls round this sphere she may present changing phases, until she has turned that half which is illuminated full towards our sight and open eyes; then by slow steps she whirls back and withdraws the light-fraught half of the spherical ball; as the Babylonian science of the Chaldees refuting the system of the astronomers essays to prove in opposition to them; just as though that which each party fights for might not be equally true, or there were any reason why you should venture to embrace the one theory less than the other. Again, why a new moon should not be born every day after a regular succession of forms and regular phases, and each day the one which is born perish and another be produced in its room and stead, it is not easy to teach by reasoning or prove by words, since so many things can be born in such a regular succession.

737] Spring and Venus go their way, and the winged harbinger of Venus steps on before; and close on Zephyr's footprints mother Flora strews all the way before them and covers it over with the choicest colours and odours. Next in order follows parching heat, and in its company dusty Ceres and the Etesian blasts of the north winds. Next autumn advances and Euhius Euan steps on together. Then other seasons and winds follow, loud-roaring Volturnus and the south-wind stored with lightning. At last midwinter brings with it snows and gives back benumbing cold; after it follows winter with teeth chattering with cold. It is therefore the less strange that a moon is begotten at a fixed time and at a fixed time is destroyed again, since many things may take place at a time so surely fixed.

751] The eclipses of the sun likewise and the obscurations of the moon you may suppose to take place from many different causes. For why should the moon be able to shut the earth out from the sun's light and on the earthward side put in his way her high-exalted head, placing her dark orb before his burning rays; and yet at the same time it be thought that another body gliding on ever without light cannot do the same? Why too should not the sun be able, quite exhausted, to lose his fires at a fixed time, and again reproduce his light when in his journey through the air he has passed by spots fatal to his flames, which cause his fires to be quenched and to perish? And why should the earth be able in turn to rob the moon of light and moreover herself to keep the sun suppressed, while in her monthly course she glides through the well-defined shadows of the cone; and yet at the same time another body not be able to pass under the moon or glide above the sun's orb, breaking off its rays and the light it sheds forth? Yes and if the moon shines with her own brightness, why should she not be able to grow faint in a certain part of the world, while she is passing through spots hostile to her own light?

772] And now further since I have explained in what way everything might take place throughout the blue of the great heaven; how we might know what force and cause set in motion the varied courses of the sun and wanderings of the moon; and in what way their light might be intercepted and they be lost to us and spread darkness over the earth little expecting it, when so to speak they close their eye of light and opening it again survey all places shining in bright radiance, I now go back to the infancy of the world and the tender age of the fields of earth and show what first in their early essays of production they resolved to raise into the borders of light and give in charge to the wayward winds.

783] In the beginning the earth gave forth all kinds of herbage and verdant sheen about the hills and over all the plains; the flowery meadows glittered with the bright green hue, and next in order to the different trees was given a strong and emulous desire of growing up into the air with full unbridled powers. As feathers and hairs and bristles are first born on the limbs of four-footed beasts and the body of the strong of wing, thus the new earth then first put forth grass and bushes, and next gave birth to the races of mortal creatures springing up many in number in many ways after divers fashions. For no living creatures can have dropped from heaven nor can those belonging to the land have come out of the

salt pools. It follows that with good reason the earth has gotten the name of mother, since all things have been produced out of the earth. And many living creatures even now spring out of the earth taking form by rains and the heat of the sun. It is therefore the less strange if at that time they sprang up more in number and larger in size, having come to maturity in the freshness of earth and ether. First of all the race of fowls and the various birds would leave their eggs, hatched in the springtime, just as now in summer the cicades leave spontaneously their gossamer coats in quest of a living and life. Then you must know did the earth first give forth races of mortal men. For much heat and moisture would then abound in the fields; and therefore wherever a suitable spot offered, wombs would grow attached to the earth by roots; and when the warmth of the infants, flying the wet and craving the air, had opened these in the fulness of time, nature would turn to that spot the pores of the earth and constrain it to yield from its opened veins a liquid most like to milk, even as now-a-days every woman when she has borne, is filled with sweet milk, because all that current of nutriment streams towards the breasts. To the children the earth would furnish food, the heat raiment, the grass a bed rich in abundance of soft down. Then the fresh youth of the world would give forth neither severe colds nor excessive heats nor gales of great violence; for all things grow and acquire strength in a like proportion.

821] Wherefore again and again I say the earth with good title has gotten and keeps the name of mother, since she of herself gave birth to mankind and at a time nearly fixed shed forth every beast that ranges wildly over the great mountains, and at the same time the fowls of the air with all their varied shapes. But because she must have some limit set to her bearing, she ceased like a woman worn out by length of days. For time changes the nature of the whole world and all things must pass on from one condition to another, and nothing continues like to itself: all things quit their bounds, all things nature changes and compels to alter. One thing crumbles away and is worn and enfeebled with age, then another comes unto honour and issues out of its state of contempt. In this way then time changes the nature of the whole world and the earth passes out of one condition into another: what once it could, it can bear no more, in order to be able to bear what before it did not bear.

837] And many monsters too the earth at that time essayed to produce, things coming up with strange face and limbs, the man-woman, a thing between the two and neither the one sex nor the other, widely differing from both; some things deprived of feet, others again destitute of hands, others too proving dumb without mouth, or blind without eyes, and things bound fast by the adhesion of their limbs over all the body, so that they could not do anything nor go anywhere nor avoid the evil nor take what their needs required. Every other monster and portent of this kind she would produce, but all in vain, since nature set a ban on their increase and they could not reach the coveted flower of age nor find food nor be united in marriage. For we see that many conditions must meet together in things in order that they may beget and continue their kinds; first a supply of food, then a way by which the birth-producing seeds throughout the frame may stream from the relaxed limbs; also in order that the woman may be united with the male, the possession of organs whereby they may each interchange mutual joys.

855] And many races of living things must then have died out and been unable to beget and continue their breed. For in the case of all things which you see breathing the breath of life, either craft or courage or else speed has from the beginning of its existence protected and preserved each particular race. And there are many things which, recommended to us by their useful services, continue to exist consigned to our protection. In the first place the fierce breed of lions and the savage races their courage has protected, foxes their craft and stags their proneness to fight. But light-sleeping dogs with faithful heart in breast and every kind which is born of the seed of beasts of burden and at the same time the woolly flocks and the horned herds are all consigned, Memmius, to the protection of man. For they have ever fled with eagerness from wild beasts and have ensued peace and plenty of food obtained without their own labour, as we give it in requital of their useful services. But those to whom nature has granted none of these qualities, so that they could neither live by their own means nor perform for us any useful service in return for which we should suffer their kind to feed and be safe under our protection, those, you are to know, would lie exposed as a prey and booty of others, hampered all in their own death-bringing shackles, until nature brought that kind to utter destruction.

878] But Centaurs never have existed, and at no time can there exist things of twofold nature and double body formed into one frame out of limbs of alien kinds, such that the faculties and powers of this and that portion cannot be sufficiently like. This however dull of understanding you may learn from what follows. To begin, a horse when three years have gone round is in the prime of his vigour, far different the boy: often even at that age he will call in his sleep for the milk of the breast. Afterwards when in advanced age his lusty strength and limbs now faint with ebbing life fail the horse, then and not till then youth in the flower of age commences for that boy and clothes his cheeks in soft down; that you may not haply believe that out of a man and the burden-carrying seed of horses Centaurs can be formed and have being; or that Scyllas with bodies half those of fishes girdled round with raving dogs can exist, and all other things of the kind, whose limbs we see cannot harmonize together; as they neither come to their flower at the same time nor reach the fulness of their bodily strength nor lose it in advanced old age, nor burn with similar passions nor have compatible manners, nor feel the same things give pleasure throughout their frames. Thus we may see bearded goats often fatten on hemlock which for man is rank poison.

901] Since flame moreover is wont to scorch and burn the tawny bodies of lions just as much as any other kind of flesh and blood existing on earth, how could it be that a single chimera with triple body, in front a lion, behind a dragon, in the middle the goat whose name it bears, could breathe out at the mouth fierce flame from its body? Wherefore also he who fables that in the new time of the earth and the fresh youth of heaven such living creatures could have been begotten, resting upon this one futile term new, may babble out many things in like fashion, may say that rivers then ran with gold over all parts of the earth and that trees were wont to blossom with precious stones, or that man was born with such giant force of frame that he could wade on foot across deep seas and whirl the whole heaven about him with his hands. For the fact that there were many seeds of things in the earth what time it first shed forth living creatures, is yet no proof that there could have been produced beasts of different kinds mixed together, and limbs of different living things formed into a single frame, because the kinds of herbage and corn and joyous trees which even now spring in plenty out of the earth yet cannot be produced with the several sorts plaited into one, but each thing goes on after its own fashion, and all preserve their distinctive differences according to a fixed law of nature.

925] But the race of man then in the fields was much hardier, as beseemed it to be, since the hard earth had produced it; and built on a groundwork of larger and more solid bones within, knit with powerful sinews throughout the frame of flesh; not lightly to be disabled by heat or cold or strange kinds of food or any malady of body. And during the revolution of many lustres of the sun through heaven they led a life after the roving fashion of wild beasts. No one then was a sturdy guider of the bent plough or knew how to labour the fields with iron or plant in the ground young saplings or lop with pruning-hooks old boughs from the high trees. What the sun and rains had given, what the earth had produced spontaneously, was guerdon sufficient to content their hearts. Among acorn-bearing oaks they would refresh their bodies for the most part; and the arbute-berries which you now see in the winter-time ripen with a bright scarlet hue, the earth would then bear in greatest plenty and of a larger size; and many coarse kinds of food besides the teeming freshness of the world then bare, more than enough for poor wretched men. But rivers and springs invited to slake thirst, even as now a rush of water down from the great hills summons with clear plash far and wide the thirsty races of wild beasts. Then too as they ranged about they would occupy the well-known woodland haunts of the nymphs, out of which they knew that smooth-gliding streams of water with a copious gush bathed the dripping rocks, the dripping rocks, trickling down over the green moss; and in parts welled and bubbled out over the level plain. And as yet they knew not how to apply fire to their purposes or to make use of skins and clothe their body in the spoils of wild beasts, but they would dwell in woods and mountain-caves and forests and shelter in the brushwood their squalid limbs when driven to shun the buffeting of the winds and the rains. And they were unable to look to the general weal and knew not how to make a common use of any customs or laws. Whatever prize fortune threw in his way, each man would bear off, trained at his own discretion to think of himself and live for himself alone. And Venus would join the bodies of lovers in the woods; for each woman was gained over either by mutual desire or the headstrong violence and vehement lust of the man or a bribe of some acorns and arbute-berries or choice pears. And trusting to the marvellous powers of their hands and feet they would pursue the forest-haunting races of wild beasts with showers of stones and club of ponderous weight; and many they would conquer, a few they would avoid in hiding-places; and like to bristly swine just as they were they would throw their savage limbs all naked on the ground, when overtaken by night, covering themselves up with leaves and boughs. Yet never with loud wailings would they call for the daylight and the sun, wandering terror-stricken over the fields in the shadows of night, but silent and buried in sleep they would wait, till the sun with rosy torch carried light into heaven; for accustomed as they had been from childhood always to see darkness and light begotten time about, never could any wonder come over them, nor any misgiving that never-ending night would cover the earth and the light of the sun be withdrawn for evermore. But what gave them trouble was rather the races of wild beasts which would often render repose fatal to the poor wretches. And driven from their home they would fly from their rocky shelters on the approach of a foaming bear or a strong lion, and in the dead of night they would surrender in terror to their savage guests their sleeping-places strewn with leaves.

988] Nor then much more than now would the races of mortal men leave the sweet light of ebbing life. For then this one or that other one of them would be more likely to be seized, and torn open by their teeth would furnish to the wild beasts a living food, and would fill with his moaning woods and mountains and forests as he looked on his living flesh buried in a living grave. But those whom flight had saved with body eaten into, holding ever after their quivering palms over the noisome sores would summon death with appalling cries, until cruel gripings had rid them of life, forlorn of help, unwitting what wounds wanted. But then a single day gave not over to death many thousands of men marching with banners spread, nor did the stormy waters of the sea dash on the rocks men and ships. At this time the sea would often rise up and rage without aim, without purpose, without result, and just as lightly put off its empty threats; nor could the winning wiles of the calm sea treacherously entice any one to his ruin with laughing waters, when the reckless craft of the skipper had not yet risen into the light. Then too want of food would consign to death their fainting frames, now on the contrary 'tis plenty sinks into ruin. They unwittingly would often pour out poison for themselves; now with nicer skill men give it to their son's wife instead.

1011] Next after they had got themselves huts and skins and fire, and the woman united with the man passed with him into one domicile and the duties of wedlock were learnt by the two, and they saw an offspring born from them, then first mankind began to soften. For fire made their chilled bodies less able now to bear the frost beneath the canopy of heaven, and Venus impaired their strength and children with their caresses soon broke down the haughty temper of parents. Then too neighbours began to join in a league of friendship mutually desiring neither to do nor suffer harm; and asked for indulgence to children and womankind, when with cries and ges-

tures they declared in stammering speech that meet it is for all to have mercy on the weak. And though harmony could not be established without exception, yet a very large portion observed their agreements with good faith, or else the race of man would then have been wholly cut off, nor could breeding have continued their generations to this day.

1028] But nature impelled them to utter the various sounds of the tongue and use struck out the names of things, much in the same way as the inability to speak is seen in its turn to drive children to the use of gestures, when it forces them to point with the finger at the things which are before them. For every one feels how far he can make use of his peculiar powers. Ere the horns of a calf are formed and project from his forehead, he butts with it when angry and pushes out in his rage. Then whelps of panthers and cubs of lions fight with claws and feet and teeth at a time when teeth and claws are hardly yet formed. Again we see every kind of fowl trust to wings and seek from pinions a fluttering succour. Therefore to suppose that some one man at that time apportioned names to things and that men from him learnt their first words, is sheer folly. For why should this particular man be able to denote all things by words and to utter the various sounds of the tongue, and yet at the same time others be supposed not to have been able to do so? Again if others as well as he had not made use of words among themselves, whence was implanted in this man the previous conception of its use and whence was given to him the original faculty, to know and perceive in mind what he wanted to do? Again one man could not constrain and subdue and force many to choose to learn the names of things. It it no easy thing in any way to teach and convince the deaf of what is needful to be done; for they never would suffer nor in any way endure sounds of voice hitherto unheard to continue to be dinned fruitlessly into their ears. Lastly what is there so passing strange in this circumstance, that the race of men whose voice and tongue were in full force, should denote things by different words as different feelings prompted? Since dumb brutes, yes and the races of wild beasts are accustomed to give forth distinct and varied sounds, when they have fear or pain and when joys are rife.

1062] This you may learn from facts plain to sense: when the large spongy open lips of Molossian dogs begin to growl enraged and bare their hard teeth, thus drawn back in rage they threaten in a tone far different from that in which they bark outright and fill with sounds all the places round. Again when they essay fondly to lick their whelps with their tongue or when they toss them with their feet and snapping at them make a feint with lightly closing teeth of swallowing though with gentle forbearance, they caress them with a yelping sound of a sort greatly differing from that which they utter when, left alone in a house, they bay or when they slink away howling from blows with a crouching body. Again is not the neigh too seen to differ, when a young stallion in the flower of age rages among the mares smitten by the goads of winged love, and when with wide-stretched nostrils he snorts out the signal to arms, and when as it chances on any other occasion he neighs with limbs all shaking? Lastly the race of fowls and various birds, hawks and ospreys and gulls seeking their living in the salt water mid the waves of the sea, utter at a different time noises widely different from those they make when they are fighting for food and struggling with their prey. And some of them change together with the weather their harsh croakings, as the long-lived races of crows and flocks of rooks when they are said to be calling for water and rain and sometimes to be summoning winds and gales. Therefore if different sensations compel creatures, dumb though they be, to utter different sounds, how much more natural it is that mortal men in those times should have been able to denote dissimilar things by many different words!

1091] And lest haply on this head you ask in silent thought this question, it was lightning that brought fire down on earth for mortals in the beginning; thence the whole heat of flames is spread abroad. Thus we see many things shine dyed in heavenly flames, when the stroke from heaven has stored them with its heat. Ay and without this when a branching tree sways to and fro and tosses about under the buffeting of the winds, pressing against the boughs of another tree, fire is forced out by the power of the violent friction, and sometimes the burning heat of flame flashes out, the boughs and stems rubbing against each other. Now either of these accidents may have given fire to men. Next the sun taught them to cook food and soften it with the heat of flame, since they would see many things grow mellow, when subdued by the strokes of the rays and by heat throughout the land.

1105] And more and more every day men who excelled in intellect and were of vigorous understanding, would kindly show them how to exchange their former way of living for new methods. Kings began to build towns and lay out a citadel as a place of strength and of refuge for themselves, and divided cattle and lands and gave to each man in proportion to his personal beauty and strength and intellect; for beauty and vigorous strength were much esteemed. Afterwards wealth was discovered and gold found out, which soon robbed of their honours strong and beautiful alike; for men however valiant and beautiful of person generally follow in the train of the richer man. But were a man to order his life by the rules of true reason, a frugal subsistence joined to a contented mind is for him great riches; for never is there any lack of a little. But men desired to be famous and powerful, in order that their fortunes might rest on a firm foundation and they might be able by their wealth to lead a tranquil life; but in vain, since in their struggle to mount up to the highest dignities they rendered their path one full of danger; and even if they reach it, yet envy like a thunderbolt sometimes strikes and dashes men down from the highest point with ignominy into noisome Tartarus; since the highest summits and those elevated above the level of other things are mostly blasted by envy as by a thunderbolt; so that far better it is to obey in peace and quiet than to wish to rule with power supreme and be the master of kingdoms. Therefore let men wear themselves out to no purpose and sweat drops of blood, as they struggle on along the strait road of ambition, since they gather their knowledge from the mouths of others and follow after things from hearsay rather than the dictates of their own feelings; and this prevails not now nor will prevail by and by any more than it has prevailed before.

1136] Kings therefore being slain the old majesty of thrones and proud sceptres were overthrown and laid in the dust, and the glorious badge of the sovereign head bloodstained beneath the feet of the rabble mourned for its high prerogative; for that is greedily trampled on which before was too much dreaded. It would come then in the end to the lees of uttermost disorder, each man seeking for himself empire and sovereignty. Next a portion of them taught men to elect legal officers, and drew up codes, to induce men to obey the laws. For mankind, tired out with a life of brute force, lay exhausted from its feuds; and therefore the more readily it submitted of its own freewill to laws and stringent codes. For as each one moved by anger took measures to avenge himself with more severity than is now permitted by equitable laws, for this reason men grew sick of a life of brute force. Thence fear of punishment mars the prizes of life; for violence and wrong enclose all who commit them in their meshes and do mostly recoil on him from whom they began; and it is not easy for him who by his deeds transgresses the terms of the public peace to pass a tranquil and a peaceful existence. For though he eludes God and man, yet he cannot but feel a misgiving that his secret can be kept for ever; seeing that many by speaking in their dreams or in the wanderings of disease have often we are told betrayed themselves and have disclosed their hidden deeds of evil and their sins.

1161] And now what cause has spread over great nations the worship of the divinities of the gods and filled towns with altars and led to the performance of stated sacred rites, rites now in fashion on solemn occasions and in solemn places, from which even now is implanted in mortals a shuddering awe which raises new temples of the gods over the whole earth and prompts men to crowd them on festive days, all this it is not so difficult to explain in words. Even then in sooth the races of mortal men would see in waking mind glorious forms, would see them in sleep of yet more marvellous size of body. To these then they would attribute sense, because they seemed to move their limbs and to utter lofty words suitable to their glorious aspect and surpassing

powers. And they would give them life everlasting, because their face would ever appear before them and their form abide; yes and yet without all this, because they would not believe that beings possessed of such powers could lightly be overcome by any force. And they would believe them to be pre-eminent in bliss, because none of them was ever troubled with the fear of death, and because at the same time in sleep they would see them perform many miracles, yet feel on their part no fatigue from the effort. Again they would see the system of heaven and the different seasons of the years come round in regular succession, and could not find out by what causes this was done; therefore they would seek a refuge in handing over all things to the gods and supposing all things to be guided by their nod. And they placed in heaven the abodes and realms of the gods, because night and moon are seen to roll through heaven, moon, day, and night and night's austere constellations and night-wandering meteors of the sky and flying bodies of flame, clouds, sun, rains, snow, winds, lightnings, hail, and rapid rumblings and loud threatful thunderclaps.

1194] O hapless race of men, when that they charged the gods with such acts and coupled with them bitter wrath! What groanings did they then beget for themselves, what wounds for us, what tears for our children's children! No act is it of piety to be often seen with veiled head to turn to a stone and approach every altar and fall prostrate on the ground and spread out the palms before the statues of the gods and sprinkle the altars with much blood of beasts and link vow on to vow, but rather to be able to look on all things with a mind at peace. For when we turn our gaze on the heavenly quarters of the great upper world and ether fast above the glittering stars, and direct our thoughts to the courses of the sun and moon, then into our breasts burdened with other ills that fear as well begins to exalt its reawakened head, the fear that we may haply find the power of the gods to be unlimited, able to wheel the bright stars in their varied motion; for lack of power to solve the question troubles the mind with doubts, whether there was ever a birth-time of the world, and whether likewise there is to be any end; how far the walls of the world can endure this strain of restless motion; or whether gifted by the grace of the gods with an everlasting existence they may glide on through a never-ending tract of time and defy the strong powers of immeasurable ages. Again who is there whose mind does not shrink into itself with fear of the gods, whose limbs do not cower in terror, when the parched earth rocks with the appalling thunderstroke and rattlings run through the great heaven? Do not peoples and nations quake, and proud monarchs shrink into themselves smitten with fear of the gods, lest for any foul transgression or overweening word the heavy time of reckoning has arrived at its fulness? When too the utmost fury of the headstrong wind passes over the sea and sweeps over its waters the commander of a fleet together with his mighty legions and elephants, does he not draw near with vows to seek the mercy of the gods and ask in prayer with fear and trembling a lull in the winds and propitious gales; but all in vain, since often caught up in the furious hurricane he is borne none the less to the shoals of death? so constantly does some hidden power trample on human grandeur and is seen to tread under its heel and make sport for itself of the renowned rods and cruel axes. Again when the whole earth rocks under their feet and towns tumble with the shock or doubtfully threaten to fall, what wonder that mortal men abase themselves and make over to the gods in things here on earth high prerogatives and marvelous powers, sufficient to govern all things?

1241] To proceed, copper and gold and iron were discovered and at the same time weighty silver and the substance of lead, when fire with its heat and burnt up vast forests on the great hills, either by a discharge of heaven's lightning, or else because men waging with one another a forest-war had carried fire among the enemy in order to strike terror, or because drawn on by the goodness of the soil they would wish to clear rich fields and bring the country into pasture, or else to destroy wild beasts and enrich themselves with the booty; for hunting with the pitfall and with fire came into use before the practice of enclosing the lawn with toils and stirring it with dogs.

Whatever the fact is, from whatever cause the heat of flame had swallowed up the forests with a frightful crackling from their very roots and had thoroughly baked the earth with fire, there would run from the boiling veins and collect into the hollows of the ground a stream of silver and gold, as well as of copper and lead. And when they saw these afterwards cool into lumps and glitter on the earth with a brilliant gleam, they would lift them up attracted by the bright and polished lustre, and they would see them to be moulded in a shape the same as the outline of the cavities in which each lay. Then it would strike them that these might be melted by heat and cast in any form or shape soever, and might by hammering out be brought to tapering points of any degree of sharpness and fineness, so as to furnish them with tools and enable them to cut the forests and hew timber and plane smooth the planks, and also to drill and pierce and bore. And they would set about these works just as much with silver and gold at first as with the overpowering strength of stout copper, but in vain, since their force would fail and give way and not be able like copper to stand the severe strain. At that time copper was in higher esteem and gold would lie neglected on account of its uselessness, with its dull blunted edge: now copper lies neglected, gold has mounted up to the highest place of honour. Thus time as it goes round changes the seasons of things. That which was in esteem, falls at length into utter disrepute; and then another thing mounts up and issues out of its degraded state and every day is more and more coveted and blossoms forth high in honour when discovered and is in marvellous repute with men.

1281] And now, Memmius, it is easy for you to find out by yourself in what way the nature of iron was discovered. Arms of old were hands, nails, and teeth and stones and boughs broken off from the forests, and flame and fire, as soon as they had become known. Afterwards the force of iron and copper was discovered; and the use of copper was known before that of iron, as its nature is easier to work and it is found in greater quantity. With copper they would labour the soil of the earth, with copper stir up the billows of war and

deal about wide-gaping wounds and seize cattle and lands; for every thing defenceless and
unarmed would readily yield to them with
arms in hand. Then by slow steps the sword
of iron gained ground and the make of the
copper sickle became a by-word; and with iron
they began to plough through the earth's soil,
and the struggles of wavering war were rendered equal. And the custom of mounting in
arms on the back of a horse and guiding him
with reins and showing prowess with the right
hand is older than that of tempting the risks
of war in a two-horsed chariot; and yoking a
pair of horses is older than yoking four or
mounting in arms scythed chariots. Next the
Poeni taught the Lucan kine[1] with towered
body, hideous of aspect, with snake-like hand,
to endure the wounds of war and to disorder
the mighty ranks of Mars. Thus sad discord
begat one thing after another, to affright nations of men under arms, and every day made
some addition to the terrors of war.

1308] They made trial of bulls too in the
service of war and essayed to send savage boars
against the enemy. And some sent before them
valorous lions with armed trainers and courageous keepers to guide them and to hold
them in chains; but in vain, since heated with
promiscuous slaughter they would disorder in
their rage the troops without distinction, shaking all about the frightful crests upon their
heads; and the horsemen were not able to calm
the breasts of the horses scared by the roaring
and turn them with the bridle upon the enemy. The lionesses with a spring would throw
their enraged bodies on all sides and would
attack in the face those who met them, and
others off their guard they would tear down
from behind and twining round them would
bring them to the ground overpowered by the
wound, fastening on them with firm bite and
with hooked claws. The bulls would toss their
own friends and trample them under foot, and
gore with their horns the flanks and bellies of
the horses underneath and turn up the earth
with threatening front. The boars too would
rend their friends with powerful tusks, in
their rage dyeing with their blood the weapons
broken in them, ay dyeing with their blood
the weapons broken in their own bodies; and

[1] Elephants.

would put to promiscuous rout horse and
foot; for the tame beasts would try to avoid by
shying to the side the cruel push of the tusk,
or would rear up and paw the winds, all in
vain, since you might see them tumble down
with their tendons severed and strew the
ground in their heavy fall. Those whom they
believed before to have been sufficiently broken in at home, they would see lash themselves into fury in the heat of action from
wounds and shouting, flight, panic, and uproar; and they could not rally any portion of
them; for all the different kinds of wild beasts
would fly all abroad; just as now the Lucan
kine when cruelly mangled by the steel fly
often all abroad, after inflicting on their
friends many cruel sufferings. But men chose
thus to act not so much in any hope of victory,
as from a wish to give the enemy something to
rue at the cost of their own lives, when they
mistrusted their numbers and were in want of
arms.

1350] A garment tied on the body was in
use before a dress of woven stuff. Woven stuff
comes after iron, because iron is needed for
weaving a web; and in no other way can such
finely polished things be made, as heddles and
spindles, shuttles and ringing yarn-beams.
And nature impelled men to work up the
wool before womankind: for the male sex in
general far excels the other in skill and is
much more ingenious: until the rugged countrymen so upbraided them with it, that they
were glad to give it over into the hands of the
women and take their share in supporting
hard toil, and in such hard work hardened
body and hands.

1361] But nature parent of things was herself the first model of sowing and first gave
rise to grafting, since berries and acorns dropping from the trees would put forth in due
season swarms of young shoots underneath;
and hence also came the fashion of inserting
grafts in their stocks and planting in the
ground young saplings over the fields. Next
they would try another and yet another kind
of tillage for their loved piece of land and
would see the earth better the wild fruits
through genial fostering and kindly cultivation. And they would force the forests to re-
cede every day higher and higher up the hill-

side and yield the ground below to tilth, in order to have on the uplands and plains meadows, tanks, runnels, corn-fields, and glad vineyards, and allow a grey-green strip of olives to
run between and mark the divisions, spread-
ing itself over hillocks and valleys and plains;
just as you now see richly dight with varied
beauty all the ground which they lay out and
plant with rows of sweet fruit-trees and enclose all round with plantations of other goodly trees.

1379] But imitating with the mouth the
clear notes of birds was in use long before men
were able to sing in tune smooth-running
verses and give pleasure to the ear. And the
whistlings of the zephyr through the hollows
of reeds first taught peasants to blow into hollow stalks. Then step by step they learned
sweet plaintive ditties, which the pipe pours
forth pressed by the fingers of the players,
heard through pathless woods and forests and
lawns, through the unfrequented haunts of
shepherds and abodes of unearthly calm.
These things would soothe and gratify their
minds when sated with food; for then all things
of this kind are welcome. Often therefore
stretched in groups on the soft grass beside a
stream of water under the boughs of a high
tree at no great cost they would pleasantly refresh their bodies, above all when the weather
smiled and the seasons of the year painted the
green grass with flowers. Then went round the
jest, the tale, the peals of merry laughter; for
the peasant muse was then in its glory; then
frolic mirth would prompt to entwine head
and shoulders with garlands plaited with flowers and leaves, and to advance in the dance
out of step and move the limbs clumsily and
with clumsy foot beat mother earth; which
would occasion smiles and peals of merry
laughter, because all these things then from
their greater novelty and strangeness were in
high repute. And the wakeful found a solace
for want of sleep in this, in drawing out a
variety of notes and going through tunes and
running over the reeds with curving lip;
whence even at the present day watchmen observe these traditions and have lately learned
to keep the proper tune; and yet for all this
receive not a jot more of enjoyment, than erst
the rugged race of sons of earth received. For

that which we have in our hands, if we have
known before nothing pleasanter, pleases above
all and is thought to be the best; and as a rule
the later discovery of something better spoils
the taste for the former things and changes the
feelings in regard to all that has gone before.
Thus began distaste for the acorn, thus were
abandoned those sleeping-places strewn with
grass and enriched with leaves. The dress too
of wild beasts' skin fell into neglect; though I
can fancy that in those days it was found to
arouse such jealousy that he who first wore it
met his death by an ambuscade, and after all
it was torn in pieces among them and
drenched in blood was utterly destroyed and
could not be turned to any use. In those times
therefore skins, now gold and purple plague
men's lives with cares and wear them out with
war. And in this methinks the greater blame
rests with us; for cold would torture the
naked sons of earth without their skins; but
us it harms not in the least to do without a
robe of purple, spangled with gold and large
figures, if only we have a dress of the people
to protect us. Mankind therefore ever toils
vainly and to no purpose and wastes life in
groundless cares, because sure enough they
have not learnt what is the true end of getting
and up to what point genuine pleasure goes
on increasing: this by slow degrees has carried life out into the deep sea and stirred up
from their lowest depths the mighty billows of
war.

1436] But those watchful guardians, sun
and moon, traversing with their light all
round the great revolving sphere of heaven
taught men that the seasons of the year came
round and that the system was carried on after
a fixed plan and fixed order.

1440] Already they would pass their life
fenced about with strong towers, and the
land, portioned out and marked off by bound-
aries, be tilled; the sea would be filled with
ships scudding under sail; towns have auxil-
iaries and allies as stipulated by treaty, when
poets began to consign the deeds of men to
verse; and letters had not been invented long
before. For this reason our age cannot look
back to what has gone before, save where reason points out any traces.

1448] Ships and tillage, walls, laws, arms,

roads, dress, and all such like things, all the prizes, all the elegancies too of life without exception, poems, pictures, and the chiselling of fine-wrought statues, all these things practiced together with the acquired knowledge of the untiring mind taught men by slow degrees as they advanced on the way step by step. Thus time by degrees brings each several thing forth before men's eyes and reason raises it up into the borders of light; for things must be brought to light one after the other and in due order in the different arts, until these have reached their highest point of development.

· BOOK SIX ·

IN DAYS of yore Athens of famous name first imparted corn-producing crops to suffering mankind, and modelled life anew and passed laws; and first too bestowed sweet solaces of existence, when she gave birth to a man who showed himself gifted with such a genius and poured forth all knowledge of old from his truth-telling mouth; whose glory, even now that he is dead, on account of his godlike discoveries confirmed by length of time is spread abroad among men and reaches high as heaven. For when he saw that the things which their needs imperiously demand for subsistence, had all without exception been already provided for men, and that life, so far as was possible, was placed on a sure footing, that men were great in affluence of riches and honours and glory and swelled with pride in the high reputation of their children, and yet that none of them at home for all that had a heart the less disquieted, and that this heart in despite of the understanding plagued life without any respite and was constrained to rave with distressful complainings, he then perceived that the vessel itself did cause the corruption and that by its corruption all the things that came into it and were gathered from abroad, however salutary were spoilt within it; partly because he saw it to be leaky and full of holes so that it could never by any means be filled full; partly because he perceived that it befouled so to say with a nauseous flavour everything within it, which it had taken in. He therefore cleansed men's breasts with truth-telling precepts and fixed a limit to lust and fear and explained what was the chief good which we all strive to reach, and pointed out the road along which by a short crosstrack we might arrive at it in a straightforward course; he showed too what evils existed in mortal affairs throughout, rising up and manifoldly flying about by a natural—call it chance or force, because nature had so brought it about; and from what gates you must sally out duly to encounter each; and he proved that mankind mostly without cause arouse in their breast the melancholy tumbling billows of cares. For even as children are flurried and dread all things in the thick darkness, thus we in the daylight fear at times things not a whit more to be dreaded than what children shudder at in the dark and fancy sure to be. This terror therefore and darkness of mind must be dispelled not by the rays of the sun and glittering shafts of day, but by the aspect and law of nature. Wherefore the more readily I will go on in my verses to complete the web of my design.

43] And since I have shown that the quarters of ether are mortal and that heaven is formed of a body that had a birth, and since of all the things which go on and must go on in it, I have unravelled most, hear further what remains to be told; since once for all I have willed to mount the illustrious chariot of the Muses, and ascending to heaven to explain the true law of winds and storms, which men foolishly lay to the charge of the gods, telling how, when they are angry, they raise fierce tempests; and, when there is a lull in the fury of the winds, how that anger is appeased, how the omens which have been are again changed, when their fury has thus been appeased: I have willed at the same time to explain all the other things which mortals observe to go on upon earth and in heaven, when often they are in anxious suspense of mind, and which abase their souls with fear of the gods and weigh and press them down to earth, because ignorance of the causes constrains them to submit things to the empire of the gods and to make over to them the kingdom. For they who have been rightly taught that the gods lead a life without care, if nevertheless they wonder on what plan all things can be carried on, above all in regard to those things which are seen overhead in the ethereal borders, are borne back again into their old religious scruples and take unto themselves hard task-masters, whom they poor wretches believe to be almighty, not knowing what can, what cannot be, in short on what principle each thing has its powers defined, its deep-set boundary mark; and therefore they are led all the farther astray by blind reason.

68] Now unless you drive from your mind with loathing all these things, and banish far from you all belief in things degrading to the gods and inconsistent with their peace, then often will the holy deities of the gods, having their majesty lessened by you, do you hurt; not that the supreme power of the gods can be so outraged, that in their wrath they shall resolve to exact sharp vengeance, but because you will fancy to yourself that they, though they enjoy quiet and calm peace, do roll great billows of wrath; nor will you approach the sanctuaries of the gods with a calm breast nor will you be able with tranquil peace of mind to take in those idols which are carried from their holy body into the minds of men, as heralds of their divine form. And what kind of life follows after this, may be conceived. But in order that most veracious reason may drive it far away from us, though much has already gone forth from me, much however still remains and has to be embellished in smooth-polished verses; the law and aspect of heaven have to be grasped; storms and bright lightnings, what they do and from what cause they are borne along, all this has to be sung; that you may not mark out the heaven into quarters and be startled and distracted on seeing from which of them the volant fire has come or to which of the two halves it has betaken itself, in what way it has gained an entrance within walled places, and how after lording it with tyrant sway, it has gotten itself out from these. Do thou, deft muse Calliope, solace of men

and joy of gods, point out the course before me as I race to the white boundary-line of the final goal, that under thy guidance I may win the crown with signal applause.

96] In the first place the blue of heaven is shaken with thunder, because the ethereal clouds clash together as they fly aloft when the winds combat from opposite quarters. For no sound ever comes from a cloudless part of heaven, but wheresoever the clouds are gathered in a denser mass, from that part with greater frequency comes a clap with a loud growl. Again clouds cannot be either of so dense a body as stones and timbers, nor again so fine as mists and flying bodies of smoke; for then they must either fall borne down by their dead weight like stones, or like smoke they would be unable to keep together and hold within frozen snows and hail-showers. They also give forth a sound over the levels of the wide-stretching upper world, just as at times a canvas-awning stretched over large theatres makes a creaking noise, when it tosses about among the poles and beams; sometimes, too, rent by the boisterous gales it madly howls and closely imitates the rasping noise of pieces of paper: for this kind of noise too you may observe in thunder: you may observe again the sound which is heard when the winds whirl about with their blows and buffet through the air either a hanging cloth or flying bits of paper. For sometimes the clouds cannot meet front to front in direct collision, but must rather move from the flank and so with contrary motions graze leisurely along each other's bodies; whence comes that dry sound which brushes the ears and is long drawn out, until they have made their way out of their confined positions.

121] In this way also all things appear to quake often from the shock of heavy thunder, and the mighty walls of the far-stretching ether seem in an instant to have been riven and to have sprung asunder; when a storm of violent wind has suddenly gathered and worked itself into the clouds and, there shut in, with its whirling eddy ever more and more on all sides, forces the cloud to become hollow with a thick surrounding crust of body; afterwards when its force and impetuous onset have split it, then the cloud thus rent gives forth a crash with a frightful hurtling noise. And no wonder, when a small bladder filled with air often emits a hideous sound if suddenly burst.

132] It can also be explained how the winds, when they blow through the clouds, make noises: we see branching and rough clouds often borne along in many ways; thus, you are to know, when the blasts of the northwest blow through a dense forest, the leaves give forth a rustling and the boughs a crashing. Sometimes too the force of the strong wind in rapid motion rends the cloud, breaking through it by an assault right in front: what a blast of wind can do there, is shown by facts plain to sense, when here on earth where it is gentler it yet twists out tall trees and tears them up from their deepest roots. There are also waves among the clouds and they give a kind of roar as they break heavily; just as in deep rivers and on the great sea when the surf breaks. Sometimes too when the burning force of thunder has fallen out of one cloud into another, if haply the latter contains much moisture when it has taken the fire into it, it drowns it at once with a loud noise; just so iron glowing hot from the fiery furnaces sometimes hisses, when we have plunged it quickly into cold water. Again if the cloud which receives the fire is drier, it is set on fire in an instant and burns with a loud noise; just as if a flame should range over the laurel-covered hills through a whirlwind and burn them up with its impetuous assault; and there is not anything that burns in the crackling flame with a more startling sound than the Delphic laurel of Phoebus. Then often too much crashing of ice and tumbling in of hail make a noise in the great clouds on high; for when the wind packs them together into a confined space, the mountains of storm-clouds congealed and mixed with hail break up.

160] It lightens too, when the clouds have struck out by their collision many seeds of fire; just as if a stone were to strike another stone or a piece of iron; for then too light bursts out and fire scatters about bright sparks. But we hear the thunder with our ears after the eyes see the flash of lightning, because things always travel more slowly to the ears than those which excite vision travel to the eyes. This you may perceive from the following instance as well: when you see a man at a distance cutting with a double-edged axe a large tree, you perceive the stroke before the blow carries the sound to the ear: thus we see lightning too before we hear the thunder, which is discharged at the same time as the fire from the same cause, being born indeed from the same collision.

173] Also in the following manner clouds dye places with winged light and the storm flashes out with a rapid quivering movement. When the wind has made its way into a cloud and whirling about in it has, as I have shown above, made the cloud hollow with a dense crust, it becomes hot by its own velocity: thus you see all things thoroughly heated and fired by motion; nay a leaden ball in whirling through a long course even melts. When therefore this wind now on fire has rent the black cloud, it scatters abroad at once seeds of fire pressed out by force so to speak, and these produce the throbbing flashes of flame; then follows a sound which strikes on the ears more slowly than the things which travel to our eyes strike on them. This you are to know takes place when the clouds are dense and at the same time piled up on high one above the other in marvellous accumulation; that you be not led into error, because we see how great their breadth is below, rather than to how great a height they are piled up. Observe, at a time when the winds shall carry clouds like to mountains with a slanting course through the air, or when you shall see them piled on the sides of great mountains one on the top of the other and pressing down from above perfectly at rest, the winds being buried on all sides: you will then be able to observe their great masses and to see caverns as it were built of hanging rocks; and when a storm has gathered and the winds have filled these, they chafe with a loud roaring shut up in the clouds, and bluster in their dens after the fashion of wild beasts: now from this point, now from that the winds send their growlings through the clouds, and seeking a way out whirl about and roll together seeds of fire out of the clouds and then gather many into a mass and make flame rotate in the hollow furnaces within, until they have burst the cloud and shone forth in forked flashes.

204] From this cause again yon golden colour of clear bright fire flies down with velocity to the earth: the clouds must themselves have very many seeds of fire; for when they are without any moisture, they are mostly of a brilliant flame colour. Moreover they must take in many from the sun's light, so that with good cause they are ruddy and shed forth fires. When therefore the wind has driven, thrust, squeezed together, and collected into one spot these clouds, they press out and shed forth seeds which cause the colours of flame to flash out. It also lightens, when the clouds of heaven are rarefied as well. For when the wind lightly unravels them and breaks them up as they move, those seeds which produce the lightning must fall perforce; and then it lightens without a hideous startling noise and without any uproar.

219] Well, to proceed, what kind of nature thunderbolts possess, is shown by their strokes and the traces of their heat which have burnt themselves into things and the marks which exhale the noxious vapours of sulphur: all these are signs of fire, not of wind or rain. Again they often set on fire even the roofs of houses and with swift flame rule resistless within the house. This fire subtle above all fires nature, you are to know, forms of minute and lightly moving bodies, and it is such as nothing whatever can withstand. The mighty thunderbolt passes through the walls of houses, like a shout and voices, passes through stones, through brass, and in a moment of time melts brass and gold; and causes wine too in an instant to disappear, while the vessels are untouched, because sure enough its heat on reaching it readily loosens and rarefies all the earthen material of the vessel on every side and forcing a way within lightly separates and disperses the first-beginnings of the wine. This the sun's heat would be unable to accomplish in an age, though beating on it incessantly with its quivering heat: so much more nimble and overpowering is this other force.

239] And now in what way these are begotten and are formed with a force so resistless as to be able with their stroke to burst asunder towers, throw down houses, wrench away beams and rafters, and cast down and burn up the monuments of men, to strike men dead, prostrate cattle far and near, by what force they can do all this and the like, I will make clear and will not longer detain you with mere professions.

246] Thunderbolts we must suppose to be begotten out of dense clouds piled up high; for they are never sent forth at all when the sky is clear or when the clouds are of a slight density. That this is so beyond all question is proved by facts evident to sense: clouds at such times form so dense a mass over the whole sky that we might imagine all its darkness had abandoned Acheron throughout and filled up the great vaults of heaven: in such numbers, gathering up out of the frightful night of storm-clouds, do faces of black horror hang over us on high; what time the storm begins to forge its thunderbolts. Very often again a black storm-cloud too out at sea, like a stream of pitch sent down from heaven, falls in such wise upon the waters heavily charged with darkness afar off and draws down a black tempest big with lightnings and storms, itself so fraught above all the rest with fires and winds, that even on land men shudder and seek shelter. Thus then we must suppose that the storm above our head reaches high up; for the clouds would never bury the earth in such thick darkness, unless they were built up high heap upon heap, the sunlight totally disappearing; nor could the clouds when they descend drown it with so great a rain, as to make rivers overflow and put fields under water, if they were not piled high up in the sky. In this case then all things are filled with winds and fire; therefore thunderings and lightnings go on all about. For I have shown above that hollow clouds have very many seeds of heat, and they must also take many in from the sun's rays and their heat. On this account when the same wind which happens to collect them into any one place, has forced out many seeds of heat and has mixed itself up with that fire, then the eddy of wind forces a way in and whirls about in the straitened room and points the thunderbolt in the fiery furnaces within; for it is kindled in two ways at once: it is heated by its own velocity and from the contact of fire. After that when the force of the wind has been thoroughly heated and the impetuous power of the fire has entered in, then the thunderbolt fully forged as it were suddenly rends the cloud, and the heat put in motion is carried on traversing all places with flashing lights.

285] Close upon it falls so heavy a clap that it seems to crush down from above the quarters of heaven which have all at once sprung asunder. Then a trembling violently seizes the earth and rumblings run through high heaven; for the whole body of the storm then without exception quakes with the shock and loud roarings are aroused. After this shock follows so heavy and copious a rain that the whole ether seems to be turning into rain and then to be tumbling down and returning to a deluge: so great a flood of it is discharged by the bursting of the cloud and the storm of wind, when the sound flies forth from the burning stroke. At times too the force of the wind set in motion from without falls on a cloud hot with a fully forged thunderbolt; and when it has burst it, forthwith there falls down yon fiery eddying whirl which in our native speech we call a thunderbolt. The same takes place on every other side towards which the force in question has borne down. Sometimes too the power of the wind though discharged without fire, yet catches fire in the course of its long travel, and while it is passing on, it loses on the way some large bodies which cannot like the rest get through the air; and gathers together out of the air itself and carries along with it other bodies of very small size which mix with it and produce fire by their flight; very much in the same way as a leaden ball becomes hot during its course, when it loses many bodies of cold and has taken up fire in the air. Sometimes too the force of the blow itself strikes out fire, when the force of wind discharged in a cold state without fire has struck, because sure enough, when it has smitten with a powerful stroke, the elements of heat are able to stream together out of the wind itself and at the same time out of the thing which then encounters the stroke. Thus, when we strike a stone with iron, fire flies out; and none the less, because

the force of the iron is cold, do its seeds of fiery brightness meet together upon the stroke. Therefore in the same way too a thing ought to be set on fire by the thunderbolt, if it has happened to be in a state suited to receive and susceptible of the flames. At the same time the might of the wind cannot lightly be thought to be absolutely and decidedly cold, seeing that it is discharged with such force from above; but if it is not already set on fire during its course, it yet arrives in a warm state with heat mixed up in it.

323] But the velocity of thunderbolts is great and their stroke powerful, and they run through their course with a rapid descent, because their force when set in motion first in all cases collects itself in the clouds and gathers itself up for a great effort at starting; then when the cloud is no longer able to hold the increased moving power, their force is pressed out and therefore flies with a marvellous moving power, like to that with which missiles are carried when discharged from powerful engines. Then too the thunderbolt consists of small and smooth elements, and such a nature it is not easy for anything to withstand; for it flies between and passes in through the porous passages; therefore it is not checked and delayed by many collisions, and for this reason it glides and flies on with a swift moving power. Next, all weights without exception naturally pressing downward, when to this a blow is added, the velocity is doubled and yon moving power becomes so intense that the thunderbolt dashes aside more impetuously and swiftly whatever gets in its way and tries to hinder it, and pursues its journey. Then too as it advances with a long-continued moving power, it must again and again receive new velocity which ever increases as it goes on and augments its powerful might and gives vigour to its stroke; for it forces all the seeds of the thunder to be borne right onward to one spot so to speak, throwing them all together, as on they roll, into that single line. Perhaps too as it goes on it attracts certain bodies out of the air itself, and these by their blows kindle apace its velocity. It passes too through things without injuring them, and leaves many things quite whole after it has gone through, because the clear bright fire flies through by the pores. And it breaks to pieces many things, when the first bodies of the thunderbolt have fallen exactly on the first bodies of these things, at the points where they are intertwined and held together. Again it easily melts brass and fuses gold in an instant, because its force is formed of bodies minutely small and of smooth elements, which easily make their way in and when they are in, in a moment break up all the knots and untie the bonds of union.

357] And more especially in autumn the mansion of heaven studded with glittering stars and the whole earth are shaken on all sides, and also when the flowery season of spring discloses itself. For during the cold fires are wanting and winds fail during the heat, and the clouds then are not of so dense a body. When therefore the seasons of heaven are between the two extremes, the different causes of thunder and lightning all combine; for the very cross-current of the year mixes up cold and heat, both of which a cloud needs for forging thunderbolts; so that there is great discord in things and the air raving with fires and winds heaves in mighty disorder. The first part of heat and the last of cold is the spring-time; therefore unlike things must battle with one another and be turbulent when mixed together. And when the last heat mixed with the first cold rolls on its course, a time which goes by the name of autumn, then too fierce winters are in conflict with summers. Therefore these seasons are to be called the cross-seas of the year; and it is not wonderful that in that season thunderbolts are most frequent and troublous storms are stirred up in heaven; since both sides then engage in the troublous medley of dubious war, the one armed with flames, the other with winds and water commingled.

379] This is the way to see into the true nature of the thunderbolt and to understand by what force it produces each effect, and not the turning over the scrolls of Tyrrhene charms and vainly searching for tokens of the hidden will of the gods, in order to know from what quarter the volant fire has come or to which of the two halves it has betaken itself, in what way it has gained an entrance within walled places, and how after lording it with tyrant sway it has gotten itself out from these; also what harm the thunderstroke from heaven can do. But if Jupiter and other gods shake with an appalling crash the glittering quarters of heaven, and hurl their fire whither each is so minded, why strike they not those whoever they be who have recked not of committing some abominable sin and make them give forth the flames of lightning from breast pierced through and through, a sharp lesson to men? and why rather is he whose conscience is burdened with no foul offence, innocent though he be, wrapped and enveloped in the flames, in a moment caught up by the whirlwind and fire of heaven? Why too aim they at solitary spots and spend their labour in vain? Or are they then practising their arms and strengthening their sinews? And why do they suffer the father's bolt to be blunted on the earth? Why does he allow it himself, and not spare it for his enemies? Why again, when heaven is unclouded on all sides, does Jupiter never hurl a bolt on the earth or send abroad his claps? Or does he, so soon as clouds have spread under, then go down in person into them, that from them he may aim the strokes of his bolt near at hand? Ay and for what reason does he hurl into the sea? Of what has he to impeach its waters and liquid mass and floating fields? Again if he wills us to avoid the thunderstroke, why fears he to let us see it discharged? Or if he wills to crush us off our guard with his fire, why thunders he from that side, to enable us to shun it? Why stirs he up beforehand darkness and roarings and rumblings? And how can you believe that he hurls at many points at the same time? Or would you venture to maintain that it never has happened that more than one stroke was made at one time? Nay often and often it has happened and must happen that, even as it rains and showers fall in many different quarters, so many thunderings go on at one time. Once more why does he dash down the holy sanctuaries of the gods and his own gorgeous seats with the destroying thunderbolt, and break the finewrought idols of the gods, and spoil his own images of their glory by an overbearing wound? and why does he mostly aim at lofty spots, and why do we see most traces of his fire on the mountain tops?

423] To proceed, it is easy from these facts to understand in what way those things, which the Greeks from their nature have named presteres, come down from above into the sea. For sometimes a pillar so to speak is let down from heaven and descends into the sea, and round about it the surges boil, stirred up by heavy blasts of winds; and all ships caught in that turmoil are dashed about and brought into extreme danger. This takes place when at times the force of the wind put in motion cannot burst the cloud which it essays to burst, but weighs it down, so that it is like a pillar let down from heaven into the sea, yet gradually, just as if a thing were thrust down from above and stretched out to the level of the waters by the fist and push of the arm; and when the force of the wind has rent this cloud, it bursts out from it into the sea and occasions a marvellous boiling in the waters; for the whirling eddy descends and brings down together with it yon cloud of limber body; and as soon as it has forced it down full-charged as it is to the levels of the sea, the eddy in a moment plunges itself entire into the water, and stirs up the whole sea with a prodigious noise and forces it to boil. Sometimes too the eddy of wind wraps itself up in clouds and gathers out of the air seeds of cloud and imitates in a sort the prester let down from heaven. When this prester has let itself down to the land and has burst, it belches forth a whirlwind and storm of enormous violence; but as it seldom takes place at all and as mountains cannot but obstruct it on land, it is seen more frequently on the sea with its wide prospect and unobstructed horizon.

451] Clouds are formed, when in this upper space of heaven many bodies flying about have in some one instant met together, of a rougher sort, such as are able, though they have got the very slightest holds of each other, to catch together and be held in union. These bodies first cause small clouds to form; and these next catch together and collect into masses and increase by joining with each other and are carried on by the winds continually until a fierce storm has gathered. The nearer too the tops of a mountain in each case are to heaven, the more constantly at this elevation they smoke with the thick darkness of a swarthy cloud, because, as soon as clouds form, before the eyes can see them, thin as they are, the winds carry and bring them together to the highest summits of a mountain; and then at last when they have gathered in a greater mass, being now dense they are able to make themselves visible and at the same time they are seen to rise up from the very top of the mountain into the ether: the very fact of the case and our sensations, when we climb high mountains, prove that the regions which stretch up on high are windy. Again clothes hung up on the shore, when they drink in the clinging moisture, prove that nature takes up many bodies over the whole sea as well. This makes it still more plain that many bodies may likewise rise up out of the salt heaving sea to add to the bulk of clouds; for the two liquids are near akin in their nature. Again we see mists and steam rise out of all rivers and at the same time from the earth as well; and they forced out like a breath from these parts are then carried upwards and overcast heaven with their darkness and make up clouds on high as they gradually come together; for the heat of starry ether at the same time presses down too on them and by condensing as it were weaves a web of clouds below the blue. Sometimes there come here into heaven from without those bodies which form clouds and the flying storm-rack; for I have shown that their number passes numbering and that the sum of the deep is infinite; and I have proved with what velocity bodies fly and how in a moment of time they are wont to pass through space unspeakable. It is not therefore strange that a tempest and darkness often in a short time cover over with such great mountains of clouds seas and lands, as they hang down upon them overhead, since on all sides through all the cavities of ether and as it were through the vents of the great world around the power of going out and coming in is accorded to the elements.

495] Now mark and I will explain in what way the rainy moisture is formed in the clouds above and then is sent down and falls to the earth in the shape of rain. And first I will prove that many seeds of water rise up together with the clouds themselves out of all things and that both the clouds and the water which is in the clouds thus increase together; just as our body increases together with the blood, as well as the sweat and all the moisture which is in the frame. The clouds likewise imbibe much sea-water as well, like hanging fleeces of wool, when the winds carry them over the great sea. In like manner moisture is taken up out of all rivers into the clouds; and when the seeds of waters full many in number in many ways have met in them, augmented from all sides, then the close-packed clouds endeavour to discharge their moisture from two causes: the force of the wind drives them together, and likewise the very abundance of the rain-clouds, when a greater mass than usual has been brought together, pushes down, presses from above and forces the rain to stream out. Again when the clouds are also rarefied by the winds, or are dispersed, being smitten at the same time by the heat of the sun, they discharge a rainy moisture and trickle down, just as wax over a hot fire melts away and turns fast into liquid. But a violent rain follows, when the clouds are violently pressed upon by both causes, by their own accumulated weight and by the impetuous assault of the wind. And rains are wont to hold out and to last long, when many seeds of waters are stirred to action, and clouds upon clouds and rack upon rack welling forth from all quarters round about are borne along, and when the reeking earth steams moisture back again from its whole surface. When in such a case the sun has shone with his rays amid the murky tempest right opposite the dripping rain-clouds, then the colour of the rainbow shows itself among the black clouds.

527] As to the other things which grow by themselves and are formed by themselves, as well as the things which are formed within the clouds, all, without exception all, snow, winds, hail, and cloud hoarfrosts and the great force of ice, the great congealing power of waters, and the stop which everywhere curbs running rivers, it is yet most easy to find out and apprehend in mind how all these things take place and in what way they are formed, when you have fully understood the properties assigned to elements.

535] Now mark and learn what the law of earthquakes is. And first of all take for granted that the earth below us as well as above is filled in all parts with windy caverns and bears within its bosom many lakes and many chasms, cliffs and craggy rocks; and you must suppose that many rivers hidden beneath the crust of the earth roll on with violence, waves, and submerged stones; for the very nature of the case requires it to be throughout like to itself. With such things then attached and placed below, the earth quakes above from the shock of great falling masses, when underneath time has undermined vast caverns; whole mountains indeed fall in, and in an instant from the mighty shock tremblings spread themselves far and wide from that centre. And with good cause, since buildings beside a road tremble throughout when shaken by a waggon of not such very great weight; and they rock no less, where any sharp pebble on the road jolts up the iron tires of the wheels on both sides. Sometimes too, when an enormous mass of soil through age rolls down from the land into great and extensive pools of water, the earth rocks and sways with the undulation of the water; just as a vessel at times cannot rest, until the liquid within has ceased to sway about in unsteady undulations.

557] Again when the wind gathering itself together in the hollow places underground bears down on one point and pushing on presses with great violence the deep caverns, the earth leans over on the side to which the headlong violence of the wind presses. Then all buildings which are above ground, and ever the more, the more they tower up towards heaven, lean over and bulge out yielding in the same direction, and the timbers wrenched from their supports hang over ready to give way. And yet men shrink from believing that a time of destruction and ruin awaits the nature of the great world, though they see so great a mass of earth hang ready to fall! And if the winds did not abate their blowing, no force could rein things in or hold them up on their road to destruction. As it is, because by turns they do abate and then increase in violence, and so to speak rally and return to the charge, and then are defeated and retire, for this reason the earth oftener threatens to fall than really falls: it leans over and then sways back again, and after tumbling forward recovers in equal poise its fixed position. For this reason the whole house rocks, the top more than the middle, the middle than the bottom, the bottom in a very very slight degree.

577] The same great quaking likewise arises from this cause, when on a sudden the wind and some enormous force of air gathering either from without or within the earth have flung themselves into the hollows of the earth, and there chafe at first with much uproar among the great caverns and are carried on with a whirling motion, and when their force afterwards stirred and lashed into fury bursts abroad and at the same moment cleaves the deep earth and opens up a great yawning chasm. This fell out in Syrian Sidon and took place at Aegium in the Peloponnese, two towns which an outbreak of wind of this sort and the ensuing earthquake threw down. And many walled places besides fell down by great commotions on land and many towns sank down engulfed in the sea together with their burghers. And if they do not break out, still the impetuous fury of the air and the fierce violence of the wind spread over the numerous passages of the earth like a shivering-fit and thereby cause a trembling; just as cold when it has pierced into our frames to the very marrow, sets them a-shivering in spite of themselves, forcing them to shake and move. Men are therefore disturbed by a twofold terror throughout their cities: they fear the roofs above their heads, they dread lest the nature of the earth in a moment break up her caverns underneath, and rent asunder display her own wide-gaping maw and wildly tumbled together seek to fill it up with her own ruins. Let them then fancy as much as they please that heaven and earth shall be incorruptible and consigned to an everlasting exemption from decay; and yet sometimes the very present force of danger applies on some side or other this goad of fear among others, that the earth shall in an instant be withdrawn from under their feet and carried down into the pit, and that the sum of things shall utterly give way and follow after and a jumbled wreck of world ensue.

608] First of all they wonder that nature does not increase the bulk of the sea, when there is so great a flow of water into it, when all rivers from all quarters fall into it. Add to these passing rains and flying storms, which bespatter every sea and moisten every land; add its own springs; yet all these compared with the sum of the sea will be like an addition of bulk hardly amounting to a single drop; it is therefore the less wonderful that the great sea does not increase. Again the sun absorbs a great deal with his heat: we see him with his burning rays thoroughly dry clothes dripping with wet: but we know seas to be many in number and to stretch over a wide surface. Therefore however small the portion of moisture which the sun draws off the surface from any one spot, it will yet in so vast an expanse take largely from its waters. Then again the winds too may withdraw a great deal of moisture as they sweep over the surface, since we very often see the roads dried by the winds in a single night and the soft mud form into hard crusts. Again I have shown that the clouds take off much moisture too imbibed from the great surface of the sea and scatter it about over the whole earth, when it rains on land and the winds carry on the clouds. Lastly since the earth is of a porous body and is in contact with the sea, girding its shores all round, just as water comes from the earth into the sea, in the same way it must ooze into the land out of the salt sea; for the salt is strained off and the matter of liquid streams back again to the source and all flows together to the river-heads, and then passes anew over the lands in a fresh current, where a channel once scooped out has carried down the waters with liquid foot.

639] And now I will explain why it is that fires breathe forth at times through the gorges of Mount Aetna with such hurricane-like fury; for with a destroying force of no ordinary kind the flame-storm gathered itself up and lording it over the lands of the Sicilians drew on itself the gaze of neighbouring nations, when seeing all the quarters of heaven smoke and sparkle men were filled in heart with awe-struck apprehension, not knowing what strange change nature was travailing to work.

647] In these matters you must look far and deep and make a wide survey in all directions, in order to bear in mind that the sum of things is unfathomable and to perceive how very small, how inconceivably minute a fraction of the whole sum one heaven is, not so large a fraction of it as one man is of the whole earth. If you should clearly comprehend, clearly see this point well put, you would cease to wonder at many things. Does any one among us wonder if he has gotten into his frame a fever that has broken out with burning heat, or into his body the pains of any other disease? The foot suddenly swells, sharp pain often seizes the teeth, or else attacks the eyes; the holy fire breaks out and creeping over the body burns whatever part it has seized upon, and spreads over the frame, because sure enough there are seeds of many things, and this earth and heaven bring to us evil enough to allow of a measureless amount of disease springing up. In this way then we must suppose that all things are supplied out of the infinite to the whole heaven and earth in quantity sufficient to allow the earth in a moment to be shaken and stirred, and a rapid hurricane to scour over sea and land, the fire of Aetna to overflow, the heaven to be in flames; for that too is seen and the heavenly quarters are on fire; and rain-storms gather in a heavier mass, when the seeds of water have haply come together for such an end. "Ay but the stormy rage of the conflagration is too too gigantic." Yes and so any river you like is greatest to him who has never before seen any greater, and thus a tree and a man seem gigantic, and in the case of all things of all kinds the greatest a man has seen he fancies to be gigantic, though yet all things with heaven and earth and sea included are nothing to the whole sum of the universal sum.

680] And now at last I will explain in what ways yon flame roused to fury in a moment blazes forth from the huge furnaces of Aetna. And first the nature of the whole mountain is hollow underneath, under-propped throughout with caverns of basalt rocks. Furthermore in all caves are wind and air; for wind is produced, when the air has been stirred and put in motion. When this air has been thoroughly heated and raging about has imparted its heat to all the rocks round, wherever it comes in contact with them, and to the earth, and has struck out from them fire burning with swift flames, it rises up and then forces itself out on high straight through the gorges; and so carries its heat far and scatters far its ashes and rolls on smoke of a thick pitchy blackness and flings out at the same time stones of prodigious weight; leaving no doubt that this is the stormy force of air. Again the sea to a great extent breaks its waves and sucks back its surf at the roots of that mountain. Caverns reach from this sea as far as the deep gorges of the mountain below. Through these you must admit that air mixed up with water passes; and the nature of the case compels this air to enter in from that open sea and pass right within and then go out in blasts and so lift up flame and throw out stones and raise clouds of sand; for on the summit are craters, as they name them in their own language; what we call gorges and mouths.

703] There are things too not a few for which it is not sufficient to assign one cause; you must give several, one of which at the same time is the real cause. For instance should you see the lifeless body of a man lying at some distance, it would be natural to mention all the different causes of death, in order that the one real cause of that man's death be mentioned among them. Thus you may be able to prove that he has not died by steel or cold or from disease or haply from poison; yet we know that it is something of this kind which has befallen him; and so in many other cases we may make the same remark.

712] The Nile rises every summer and overflows the plains, that one sole river throughout the whole land of Egypt. It waters Egypt often in the middle of the hot season, either because in summer there are north winds opposite its mouths, which at that time of year go by the name of Etesian winds. Blowing up the river they retard it and driving the waters backwards fill its channel full and force the river to stand still; for beyond a doubt these blasts which start from the icy constellations of the pole are carried right up the stream. That river comes from the south out of the heat-fraught country, rising far up from the central region of day among races of men black in their sun-baked complexion. It is quite possible too that the great accumulation of sand may bar up the mouths against the opposing waves, when the sea stirred up by the winds throws up the sand within the channel; whereby the outlet of the river is rendered less free and the current of the waters at the same time less rapid in its downward flow. It may be also that the rains are more frequent at its source in that season, because the Etesian blasts of the north winds drive all the clouds together into those parts at that time. And, you are to know, when they have been driven on to the central region of day and have gathered together, then the clouds jammed close against the high mountains are massed together and violently compressed. Perhaps too it gets its increase high up from the lofty mountains of the Ethiopians, when the all-surveying sun with his thawing rays constrains the white snows to descend into the plains.

738] Now mark, and I will make clear to you what kind of nature the several Avernian places and lakes possess. First of all, as to the name Avernian by which they are called, it has been given to them from their real nature, because they are noxious to all birds; for when they have arrived in flight just opposite those spots, they forget to row with their wings, they drop their sails and fall with soft neck outstretched headlong to the earth, if so be
. that the nature of the ground admit of that, or into the water, if so be that a lake of Avernus spreads below. There is such a spot at Cumae, where the mountains are charged with acrid sulphur, and smoke enriched with hot springs. Such a spot there also is within the Athenian walls, on the very summit of the citadel, beside the temple of bountiful Tritonian Pallas; which croaking crows never come near on the wing; no not when the high altars smoke with offerings: so constantly they fly, not before the sharp wrath of Pallas for the sake of yon vigil kept, as the poets of the Greeks have sung, but the nature of the place suffices by its own proper power. In Syria too as well a spot, we are told, is found to exist of such a sort that as soon as ever even four-footed beasts have entered in, its mere natural power forces them to fall down heavily, just as if they were felled in a moment as sacrifices

to the Manes gods. Now all these things go on by a natural law, and it is quite plain whence spring the causes from which they are produced; that the gate of Orcus be not haply believed to exist in such spots; and next we imagine that the Manes gods from beneath do haply draw souls down from them to the borders of Acheron; as wing-footed stags are supposed often by their scent to draw out from their holes the savage serpent-tribes. How widely opposed to true reason this is, now learn; for now I essay to tell of the real fact.

769] First of all I say, as I have often said before, that in the earth are elements of things of every kind: many, which serve for food, helpful to life; and many whose property it is to cause diseases and hasten death. And we have shown before that one thing is more adapted to one, another thing to another living creature for the purposes of life, because of their natures and their textures and their primary elements being all unlike the one to the other. Many which are noxious pass through the ears, many make their way too through the nostrils, dangerous and harsh when they come in contact; and not a few are to be shunned by the touch, and not a few to be avoided by the sight, and others are nauseous in taste.

781] Again you may see how many things are for man of a virulently noxious sensation and are nauseous and oppressive; to certain trees for instance has been given so very oppressive a shade that they often cause headaches when a man has lain down under them extended on the grass. There is a tree too on the great hills of Helicon which has the property of killing a man by the noisome scent of its flower. All these things you are to know rise up out of the earth, because it contains many seeds of many things in many ways mixed up together and gives them out in a state of separation. Again when a newly extinguished night-light encounters the nostrils with its acrid stench, it sends to sleep then and there a man who from disease is subject to falling down and foaming at the mouth. A woman is put to sleep by oppressive castor and falls back in her seat, and her gay work drops out of her soft hands, if she has smelt it at the time when she has her monthly discharges. And many things besides relax through all the frame the fainting limbs and shake the soul in its seats within. Then too if you linger long in the hot baths when you are somewhat full and do bathe, how liable you are to tumble down in a fit while seated in the midst of the hot water! Again how readily do the oppressive power and fumes of charcoal make their way into the brain, if we have not first taken water! But when burning violently it has filled the chambers of a house, the fumes of the virulent substance act on the nerves like a murderous blow. See you not too that even within the earth sulphur is generated and asphalt forms incrustations of a noisome stench? See you not, when they are following up the veins of silver and gold and searching with the pick quite into the bowels of the earth, what stenches Scaptensula exhales from below? Then what mischief do gold mines exhale! To what state do they reduce men's faces and what a complexion they produce! Know you not by sight or hearsay how they commonly perish in a short time and how all vital power fails those whom the hard compulsion of necessity confines in such an employment? All such exhalations then the earth steams forth and breathes out into the open air and light of heaven.

818] Thus too the Avernian spots must send up some power deadly to birds, which rises up from the earth into the air so as to poison a certain portion of the atmosphere; in such a way that a bird as soon as ever it is borne on its wings into it, is then attacked by the unseen poison and so palsied that it tumbles plump down on the spot where this exhalation has its course. And when it falls into it, then the same power of that exhalation robs all its limbs of the remnants of life: first of all it causes a sort of dizziness; but afterwards, when the birds have tumbled into the very springs of the poison, then life too has to be vomited forth, because all round rises up large store of mischievous matter.

830] Sometimes too this power of exhalation of Avernus dispels whatever air lies between the birds and earth, so that almost a void is left there. And when the birds have arrived in their flight just opposite this spot,

at once the buoyant force of their pinions is crippled and rendered vain and all the sustaining efforts of their wings are lost on both sides. So when they are unable to buoy themselves up and lean upon their wings, nature, you know, compels them by their weight to tumble down to earth, and lying stark through what is now almost a void they disperse their soul through all the openings of their body. Again during summer the water in wells becomes colder, because the earth is rarefied by heat and rapidly sends out into the air whatever seeds of heat it happens to have. The more then the earth is drained of heat, the colder becomes the water which is hidden in the earth. Again when all the earth is compressed by cold and contracts and so to say congeals, then, you are to know, while it contracts, it presses out into the wells whatever heat it contains itself.

848] At the fane of Hammon there is said to be a fountain which is cold in the daylight and hot in the night-time. This fountain men marvel at exceedingly and suppose that it suddenly becomes hot by the influence of the fierce sun below the earth, when night has covered the earth with awful darkness. But this is far far removed from true reason. Why when the sun though in contact with the uncovered body of the water has not been able to make it hot on its upper side, though his light above possesses such great heat, how can he below the earth which is of so dense a body boil the water and glut it with heat? above all when he can scarcely with his burning rays force his heat through the walls of houses. What then is the cause? this sure enough: the earth is more porous and warmer round the fountain than the rest of the earth, and there are many seeds of fire near the body of water. For this reason when night has buried the earth in its dewy shadows, the earth at once becomes quite cold and contracts: in this way just as if it were squeezed by the hand it forces out into the fountain whatever seeds of fire it has; and these make the water hot to the touch and taste. Next when the sun has risen and with his rays has loosened the earth and has rarefied it as his heat waxes stronger, the first-beginnings of fire return back to their ancient seats and all the heat of the water withdraws into the earth: for this reason the fountain becomes cold in the daylight. Again the liquid of water is played upon by the sun's rays and in the daytime is rarefied by his throbbing heat; and therefore it gives up whatever seeds of fire it has; just as it often parts with the frost which it holds in itself, and thaws the ice and loosens its bonds.

879] There is also a cold fountain of such a nature that tow often when held over it imbibes fire forthwith and emits flame; a pine-torch in like manner is lighted and shines among the waters, in whatever direction it swims under the impulse of the winds. Because sure enough there are in the water very many seeds of heat, and from the earth itself at the bottom must rise up bodies of fire throughout the whole fountain and at the same time pass abroad in exhalations and go forth into the air, not in such numbers however that the fountain can become hot, for these reasons a force compels those seeds to burst out through the water and disperse abroad and to unite when they have mounted up. In the sea at Aradus is a fountain of this kind, which wells up with fresh water and keeps off the salt waters all round it; and in many other quarters the sea affords a seasonable help in need to thirsting sailors, vomiting forth fresh waters amid the salt. In this way then those seeds may burst forth through that fountain and well out; and when they are met together in the tow or cohere in the body of the pine-torch, they at once readily take fire, because the tow and pinewood contain in them likewise many seeds of latent fire. See you not too that, when you bring a newly extinguished wick near night-lamps it catches light before it has touched the flame; and the same with the pinewood? And many things beside catch fire at some distance touched merely by the heat, before the fire in actual contact infects them. This therefore you must suppose to take place in that fountain as well.

906] Next in order I will proceed to discuss by what law of nature it comes to pass that iron can be attracted by that stone which the Greeks call the Magnet from the name of its native place, because it has its origin within the bounds of the country of the Magnesians. This stone men wonder at; as it often produces a chain of rings hanging down from it. Thus you may see sometimes five and more suspended in succession and tossing about in the light airs, one always hanging down from one and attached to its lower side, and each in turn one from the other experiencing the binding power of the stone: with such a continued current its force flies through all.

917] In things of this kind many points must be established before you can assign the true law of the thing in question, and it must be approached by a very circuitous road; wherefore all the more I call for an attentive ear and mind.

921] In the first place from all things whatsoever which we see there must incessantly stream and be discharged and scattered abroad such bodies as strike the eyes and provoke vision. Smells too incessantly stream from certain things; as does cold from rivers, heat from the sun, spray from the waves of the sea, that eat into walls near the shore. Various sounds too cease not to stream through the air. Then a moist salt flavour often comes into the mouth, when we are moving about beside the sea; and when we look on at the mixing of a decoction of wormwood, its bitterness affects us. In such a constant stream from all things the several qualities of things are carried and are transmitted in all directions round, and no delay, no respite in the flow is ever granted, since we constantly have feeling, and may at any time see, smell and hear the sound of anything.

936] And now I will state once again how rare a body all things have: a question made clear in the first part of my poem also: although the knowledge of this is of importance in regard to many things, above all in regard to this very question which I am coming to discuss, at the very outset it is necessary to establish that nothing comes under sense save body mixed with void. For instance in caves rocks overhead sweat with moisture and trickle down in oozing drops. Sweat too oozes out from our whole body; the beard grows, and hairs over all our limbs and frame. Food is distributed through all the veins, gives increase and nourishment to the very extremities and nails. We feel, too, cold and heat pass through brass, we feel them pass through gold and silver, when we hold full cups. Again voices fly through the stone partitions of houses; smell passes through and cold, and the heat of fire which is wont ay to pierce even the strength of iron, where the Gaulish cuirass girds the body round. And when a storm has gathered in earth and heaven, and when along with it the influence of disease makes its way in from without, they both withdraw respectively to heaven and earth and there work their wills, since there is nothing at all that is not of a rare texture of body.

959] Furthermore all bodies whatever which are discharged from things are not qualified to excite the same sensations nor are adapted for all things alike. The sun for instance bakes and dries up the earth, but thaws ice, and forces the snows piled up high on the high hills to melt away beneath his rays; wax again turns to liquid when placed within reach of his heat. Fire also melts brass and fuses gold, but shrivels up and draws together hides and flesh. The liquid of water after fire hardens steel, but softens hides and flesh hardened by heat. The wild olive delights the bearded she-goats as much as if the flavour it yielded were of ambrosia and steeped in nectar; but nothing that puts forth leaf is more bitter to man than this food. Again a swine eschews marjoram-oil and dreads all perfumes; for they are rank poison to bristly swine, though they are found at times to give us as it were fresh life. But on the other hand though mire is to us the nastiest filth, it is found to be so welcome to swine that they wallow in it all over with a craving not to be satisfied.

979] There is still one point left which it seems proper to mention, before I come to speak of the matter in hand. Since many pores are assigned to various things, they must possess natures differing the one from the other and must have each its own nature, its own direction: thus there are in living creatures various senses, each of which takes into it in its own peculiar way its own special object; for we see that sounds pass into one thing, taste from different flavours into another thing, smells into another. Again one thing is seen to stream through stones and another thing to pass through woods, another through gold, and another still to go out through silver

and brass; for form is seen to stream through this passage, heat through that, and one thing is seen to pass through by the same way more quickly than other things. The nature of the passages, you are to know, compels it so to be, varying in manifold wise, as we have shown a little above, owing to the unlike nature and textures of things.

998] Therefore now that these points have all been established and arranged for us as premises ready to our hand, for what remains, the law will easily be explained out of them, and the whole cause be laid open which attracts the strength of iron. First of all there must stream from this stone very many seeds or a current if you will which dispels with blows all the air which lies between the stone and iron. When this space is emptied and much room left void between, forthwith the first-beginnings of iron fall headlong forward into the void in one mass, and in consequence the ring itself follows and then goes on with its whole body. And nothing has its primal elements more intricately entangled or coheres in closer connexion than the nature of stubborn iron and its coldness that makes you shiver. Therefore what I say is the less strange, that from among such elements as these bodies cannot gather in large numbers out of the iron and be carried into the void without the whole ring following. This it does do, and follows on until it has quite reached the stone and fastened on it with unseen bonds of connexion. The same thing takes place in all directions: on whatever side a void is formed, whether athwart or from above the first bodies next it are at once carried on into the void; for they are set in motion by blows from another source and cannot by their own free act rise up into the air. Moreover (to render it more feasible, this thing also is helped on by external aid and motion) as soon as the air in front of the ring has been made rarer and the space more empty and void, it follows at once that all the air which lies behind, carries and pushes it on as it were at its back. For the air which lies around them always beats on things; but at such a time as this it is liable to push on the iron, because on one side a space is void and receives the iron into it. This air of which I am speaking to you makes its way with much subtlety through the frequent pores of the iron to its minute parts and then thrusts and pushes it on, as the wind a ship and its sails. Again all things must have air in their body, since they are of a rare body and air surrounds and is in contact with all things. This air therefore which is in the inmost recesses of the iron, is ever stirred in restless motion and therefore beats the ring without a doubt and stirs it within, you know: the ring is carried in the direction in which it has once plunged forward, and into the void part towards which it has made its start.

1042] Sometimes too it happens that the nature of iron is repelled from this stone, being in the habit of flying from and following it in turns. I have seen Samothracian iron rings even jump up, and at the same time filings of iron rave within brass basins, when this Magnet stone had been placed under: such a strong desire the iron seems to have to fly from the stone. So great a disturbance is raised by the interposition of the brass, because sure enough when the current of the brass has first seized on and taken possession of the open passages of the iron, the current of the stone comes after and find all things full in the iron and has no opening to swim through as before. It is forced therefore to dash against and beat with its wave the iron texture; by which means it repels from it and sets in motion through the brass that which without the brass it often draws to itself. And forbear herein to wonder that the current from this stone is not able to set in motion other things as well as iron: some of these stand still by the power of their own weight; for instance gold; and others, because they are of so rare a body that the current flies through them uninterrupted, cannot in any case be set in motion; to which class wood is found to belong. When therefore the nature of iron lying between the two has received into it certain first bodies of brass, then do the Magnet stones set it in motion with their stream.

1065] And yet these cases are not so much at variance with other things, that I have only a scanty store of similar instances to relate of things mutually fitted one for the other and for nothing else: stones for instance you see are cemented by mortar alone; wood is united with wood so firmly by bulls' glue only, that the veins of boards often gape in cracks before the binding power of the glue can be brought to loosen its hold. Vine-born juices venture to mix with streams of water, though heavy pitch and light oil cannot. Again the purple dye of the shellfish so unites with the body of wool alone, that it cannot in any case be severed, not were you to take pains to undo what is done with Neptune's wave, not if the whole sea were willed to wash it out with all its waters. Then too is there not one thing only that fastens gold to gold, and is not brass soldered to brass by tin? and how many other cases of the kind might one find! What then? You have no need whatever of such long circuitous roads, nor is it worth my while to spend so much pains on this, but it is better briefly to comprise many things in few words: things whose textures have such a mutual correspondence, that cavities fit solids, the cavities of the first the solids of the second, the cavities of the second the solids of the first, form the closest union. Again some things may be fastened together and held in union with hooks and eyes as it were; and this seems rather to be the case with this stone and iron.

1090] And now I will explain what the law of diseases is and from what causes the force of disease may suddenly gather itself up and bring death-dealing destruction on the race of man and the troops of brute beasts. And first I have shown above that there are seeds of many things helpful to our life; and on the other hand many must fly about conducing to disease and death. When these by chance have happened to gather together and have disordered the atmosphere, the air becomes distempered. And all that force of disease and that pestilence come either from without down through the atmosphere in the shape of clouds and mists, or else do gather themselves up and rise out of the earth, when soaked with wet it has contracted a taint, being beaten upon by unseasonable rains and suns. See you not too that all who come to a place far away from country and home are affected by the strangeness of climate and water, because there are wide differences in such things? For what a difference may we suppose between the climate of the Briton and that of Egypt where the pole of heaven slants askew, and again between that in Pontus and that of Gades and so on to the races of men black with sun-baked complexion?

1110] Now as we see these four climates under the four opposite winds and quarters of heaven all differing from each other, so also the complexions and faces of the men are seen to differ widely and diseases varying in kind are found to seize upon the different races. There is the elephant disease which is generated beside the streams of Nile in the midst of Egypt and nowhere else. In Attica the feet are attacked and the eyes in Achaean lands. And so different places are hurtful to different parts and members: the variations of air occasion that. Therefore when an atmosphere which happens to put itself in motion unsuited to us and a hurtful air begin to advance, they creep slowly on in the shape of mist and cloud and disorder everything in their line of advance and compel all to change; and when they have at length reached our atmosphere, they corrupt it too and make it like to themselves and unsuited to us. This new destroying power and pestilence therefore all at once either fall upon the waters or else sink deep into the corn-crops or other food of man and provender of beast; or else their force remains suspended within the atmosphere, and when we inhale from it mixed airs, we must absorb at the same time into our body those things as well. In like manner pestilence often falls on kine also and a distemper too on the silly sheep. And it makes no difference whether we travel to places unfavourable to us and change the atmosphere which wraps us round, or whether nature without our choice brings to us a tainted atmosphere or something to the use of which we have not been accustomed, and which is able to attack us on its first arrival.

1138] Such a form of disease and a death-fraught miasm erst within the borders of Cecrops defiled the whole land with dead, and dispeopled the streets, drained the town of burghers.[1] Rising first and starting from the inmost corners of Egypt, after traversing much air and many floating fields, the plague

[1] For the following passage, cf. Thucydides, II. 47.

brooded at last over the whole people of Pandion; and then they were handed over in troops to disease and death. First of all they would have the head seized with burning heat and both eyes blood-shot with a glare diffused over; the livid throat within would exude blood and the passage of the voice be clogged and choked with ulcers, and the mind's interpreter the tongue drip with gore, quite enfeebled with sufferings, heavy in movement, rough to touch. Next when the force of disease passing down the throat had filled the breast and had streamed together even into the sad heart of the sufferers, then would all the barriers of life give away. The breath would pour out at the mouth a noisome stench, even as the stench of rotting carcases thrown out unburied. And then the powers of the entire mind, the whole body would sink utterly, now on the very threshold of death. And a bitter bitter despondency was the constant attendant on insufferable ills and complaining mingled with moaning. An ever-recurring hiccup often the night and day through, forcing on continual spasms in sinews and limbs, would break men quite, forwearying those forspent before. And yet in none could you perceive the skin on the surface of the body burn with any great heat, but the body would rather offer to the hand a lukewarm sensation and at the same time be red all over with ulcers burnt into it so to speak, like unto the holy fire as it spreads over the frame. The inward parts of the men however would burn to the very bones, a flame would burn within the stomach as within furnaces. Nothing was light and thin enough to apply to the relief of the body of any one; ever wind and cold alone. Many would plunge their limbs burning with disease into the cool rivers, throwing their body naked into the water. Many tumbled headforemost deep down into the wells, meeting the water straight with mouth wide-agape. Parching thirst with a craving not to be appeased, drenching their bodies, would make an abundant draught no better than the smallest drop. No respite was there of ill: their bodies would lie quite spent. The healing art would mutter low in voiceless fear, as again and again they rolled about their eyeballs wide open, burning with disease, never visited by sleep.

1182] And many symptoms of death besides would then be given, the mind disordered in sorrow and fear, the clouded brow, the fierce delirious expression, the ears too troubled and filled with ringings, the breathing quick or else strangely loud and slow-recurring, and the sweat glistening wet over the neck, the spittle in thin small flakes, tinged with a saffron-colour, salt, scarce forced up the rough throat by coughing. The tendons of the hands ceased not to contract, the limbs to shiver, a coldness to mount with slow sure pace from the feet upwards. Then at their very last moments they had nostrils pinched, the tip of the nose sharp, eyes deep-sunk, temples hollow, the skin cold and hard, on the grim mouth a grin, the brow tense and swollen; and not long after their limbs would be stretched stiff in death: about the eighth day of bright sunlight or else on the ninth return of his lamp they would yield up life. And if any of them at that time had shunned the doom of death, yet in after time consumption and death would await him from noisome ulcers and the black discharge of the bowels, or else a quantity of purulent blood accompanied by headache would often pass out by the gorged nostrils: into these the whole strength and substance of the man would stream. Then too if any one had escaped the acrid discharge of noisome blood, the disease would yet pass into his sinews and joints and onward even into the sexual organs of the body; and some from excessive dread of the gates of death would live bereaved of these parts by the knife; and some though without hands and feet would continue in life, and some would lose their eyes: with such force had the fear of death come upon them. And some were seized with such utter loss of memory that they did not know themselves.

1215] And though bodies lay in heaps above bodies unburied on the ground, yet would the race of birds and beasts either scour far away, to escape the acrid stench, or where any one had tasted, it drooped in near-following death. Though hardly at all in those days would any bird appear, or the sullen breeds of wild beasts quit the forests. Many would droop with dis-

ease and die: above all faithful dogs would lie stretched in all the streets and yield up breath with a struggle; for the power of disease would wrench life from their frame. Funerals lonely, unattended, would be hurried on with emulous haste. And no sure and general method of cure was found; for that which had given to one man the power to inhale the vital air and to gaze on the quarters of heaven, would be destruction to others and would bring on death. But in such times this was what was deplorable and above all eminently heart-rending: when a man saw himself enmeshed by the disease, as though he were doomed to death, losing all spirit he would lie with sorrow-stricken heart, and with his thoughts turned on death would surrender his life then and there. Ay for at no time did they cease to catch from one another the infection of the devouring plague, like to woolly flocks and horned herds. And this above all heaped death on death: whenever any refused to attend their own sick, killing neglect soon after would punish them for their too great love of life and fear of death by a foul and evil death, abandoned in turn, forlorn of help. But they who had stayed by them, would perish by infection and the labour which shame would then compel them to undergo and the sick man's accents of affection mingled with those of complaining: this kind of death the most virtuous would meet. . . . and different bodies on different piles, struggling as they did to bury the multitude of their dead: then spent with tears and grief they would go home; and in great part they would take to their bed from sorrow. And none could be found whom at so fearful a time neither disease nor death nor mourning assailed.

1252] Then too every shepherd and herdsman, ay and sturdy guider of the bent plough sickened; and their bodies would lie huddled together in the corners of a hut, delivered over to death by poverty and disease. Sometimes you might see lifeless bodies of parents above their lifeless children, and then the reverse of this, children giving up life above their mothers and fathers. And in no small measure that affliction streamed from the land into the town, brought thither by the sickening crowd of peasants meeting plague-stricken from every side. They would fill all places and buildings: wherefore all the more the heat would destroy them and thus close-packed death would pile them up in heaps. Many bodies drawn forth by thirst and tumbled out along the street would lie extended by the fountains of water, the breath of life cut off from their too great delight in water; and over all the open places of the people and the streets you might see many limbs drooping with their half-lifeless body, foul with stench and covered with rags, perish away from filth of body, with nothing but skin on their bones, now nearly buried in noisome sores and dirt. All the holy sanctuaries of the gods too death had filled with lifeless bodies, and all the temples of the heavenly powers in all parts stood burdened with carcases: all which places the wardens had thronged with guests.

For now no longer the worship of the gods or their divinities were greatly regarded: so overmastering was the present affliction. Nor did those rites of sepulture continue in force in the city, with which that pious folk had always been wont to be buried; for the whole of it was in dismay and confusion, and each man would sorrowfully bury as the present moment allowed. And the sudden pressure and poverty prompted to many frightful acts; thus with a loud uproar they would place their own kinsfolk upon the funeral piles of others, and apply torches, quarrelling often with much bloodshed sooner than abandon the bodies.

THE DISCOURSES OF
EPICTETUS

BIOGRAPHICAL NOTE

EPICTETUS, *c.* A.D. 60–*c.* 138

EPICTETUS was born sometime in the reign of Nero and lived through the greater part, if not all, of the reign of Hadrian. He was a native of Phrygia, and his language was Greek. His original name is unknown. The name Epictetus ("acquired") refers to his servitude; as a boy he was a slave in Rome of Epaphroditus, a freedman and courtier of Nero.

While still a slave, Epictetus attended the lectures of the Stoic philosopher, Musonius Rufus, who, he records, "spoke in such fashion that each of us as he sat there thought he was himself accused." The slave apparently came to appreciate Musonius' teaching that "the gifted soul is all the more inclined towards its natural object, the more you try to beat it off." According to Celsus, as quoted by Origen, Epictetus was permanently lamed by his master. "When his master was twisting his leg," it is said, "Epictetus only smiled and noted calmly, 'You will break it,' and when it was broken, 'I told you so.'"

Sometime before the year 89, Epictetus obtained his freedom and became a teacher of philosophy in Rome. But along with other philosophers suspected of republicanism he was expelled from Rome and Italy by Domi-

tian around the year 90. Epictetus withdrew to northern Greece, to the city of Nicopolis, which had been founded by Augustus to celebrate the victory of Actium. There he spent the rest of his long life, expounding Stoic doctrine. He lived in poverty, having only, as he said, earth, sky, and a cloak.

Epictetus wrote nothing, but he acquired renown as a teacher. "When he was speaking, his hearers," we learn from one of them, "were forced to feel just what he would have them feel." Their reverence for him is attested by Lucian's story that after his death an admirer paid three thousand drachmas for an earthenware lamp he had used.

Among his pupils, who came from all parts of the Empire, was a certain Flavius Arrian, later consul under Hadrian and the historian of Alexander. Arrian took careful notes of the lectures and teaching of Epictetus and published them in the eight books of the *Discourses,* of which the first four have survived. Arrian says in his preface that the *Discourses* are "in the very language Epictetus used, so far as possible," and preserve "the directness of his speech." Arrian also compiled out of his lecture notes a compendium of the main tenets of Epictetus, the *Encheiridion,* or *Manual.*

CONTENTS

BIOGRAPHICAL NOTE, p. 101

BOOK I

I Of the things which are in our Power, and not in our Power 105
II How a man on every occasion can maintain his proper character 106
III How a man should proceed from the principle of God being the father of all men to the rest 108
IV Of progress or improvement 108
V Against the academics 110
VI Of providence 110
VII Of the use of sophistical arguments, and hypothetical, and the like 112
VIII That the faculties are not safe to the uninstructed 113
IX How from the fact that we are akin to God a man may proceed to the consequences 114
X Against those who eagerly seek preferment at Rome 116
XI Of natural affection 116
XII Of contentment 118
XIII How everything may be done acceptably to the Gods 120
XIV That the deity oversees all things 120
XV What philosophy promises 121
XVI Of providence 121
XVII That the logical art is necessary 122
XVIII That we ought not to be angry with the errors of others 124
XIX How we should behave to tyrants 125
XX About reason, how it contemplates itself 126
XXI Against those who wish to be admired 127
XXII Of precognitions 127
XXIII Against Epicurus 128
XXIV How we should struggle with circumstances 129
XXV On the same 129
XXVI What is the law of life 131
XXVII In how many ways appearances exist, and what aids we should provide against them 132
XXVIII That we ought not to be angry with men; and what are the small and the great things among men 133

XXIX On constancy 134
XXX What we ought to have ready in difficult circumstances 138

BOOK II

I That confidence is not inconsistent with caution 138
II Of Tranquillity 140
III To those who recommend persons to philosophers 141
IV Against a person who had once been detected in adultery 142
V How magnanimity is consistent with care 142
VI Of indifference 144
VII How we ought to use divination 145
VIII What is the nature of the good 146
IX That when we cannot fulfill that which the character of a man promises, we assume the character of a philosopher 147
X How we may discover the duties of life from names 148
XI What the beginning of philosophy is 150
XII Of disputation or discussion 151
XIII On anxiety 152
XIV To Naso 153
XV To or against those who obstinately persist in what they have determined 155
XVI That we do not strive to use our opinions about good and evil 156
XVII How we must adapt preconceptions to particular cases 158
XVIII How we should struggle against appearances 161
XIX Against those who embrace philosophical opinions only in words 162
XX Against the Epicureans and Academics 164
XXI Of inconsistency 166
XXII On friendship 167
XXIII On the power of speaking 170
XXIV To a person who was one of those who were not valued by him 172
XXV That logic is necessary 174
XXVI What is the property of error 174

CONTENTS

BOOK III

I Of finery in dress 175
II In what a man ought to be exercised who has made proficiency; and that we neglect the chief things 177
III What is the matter on which a good man should be employed, and in what we ought chiefly to practice ourselves 178
IV Against a person who showed his partisanship in an unseemly way in a theatre 180
V Against those who on account of sickness go away home 180
VI Miscellaneous 181
VII To the administrator of the free cities who was an Epicurean 182
VIII How we must exercise ourselves against appearances 184
IX To a certain rhetorician who was going up to Rome on a suit 184
X In what manner we ought to bear sickness 185
XI Certain miscellaneous matters 187
XII About exercise 187
XIII What solitude is, and what kind of person a solitary man is 188
XIV Certain miscellaneous matters 189
XV That we ought to proceed with circumspection to everything 190
XVI That we ought with caution to enter into familiar intercourse with men 191
XVII On providence 191
XVIII That we ought not to be disturbed by any news 192
XIX What is the condition of a common kind of man and of a philosopher 192

XX That we can derive advantage from all external things 192
XXI Against those who readily come to the profession of sophists 193
XXII About cynism 195
XXIII To those who read and discuss for the sake of ostentation 201
XXIV That we ought not to be moved by a desire of those things which are not in our power 203
XXV To those who fall off from their purpose 210
XXVI To those who fear want 210

BOOK IV

I About freedom 213
II On familiar intimacy 223
III What things we should exchange for other things 224
IV To those who are desirous of passing life in tranquility 225
V Against the quarrelsome and ferocious 228
VI Against those who lament over being pitied 230
VII On freedom from fear 232
VIII Against those who hastily rush into the use of the philosophic dress 235
IX To a person who had been changed to a character of shamelessness 237
X What things we ought to despise, and what things we ought to value 238
XI About purity 240
XII On attention 242
XIII Against or to those who readily tell their own affairs 244

THE DISCOURSES OF

EPICTETUS

· BOOK ONE ·

CHAPTER I. *Of the things which are in our Power, and not in our Power*

OF all the faculties, you will find not one which is capable of contemplating itself; and, consequently, not capable either of approving or disapproving. How far does the grammatic art possess the contemplating power? As far as forming a judgment about what is written and spoken. And how far music? As far as judging about melody. Does either of them then contemplate itself? By no means. But when you must write something to your friend, grammar will tell you what words you must write; but whether you should write or not, grammar will not tell you. And so it is with music as to musical sounds; but whether you should sing at the present time and play on the lute, or do neither, music will not tell you. What faculty then will tell you? That which contemplates both itself and all other things. And what is this faculty? The rational faculty;[1] for this is the only faculty that we have received which examines itself, what it is, and what power it has, and what is the value of this gift, and examines all other faculties: for what else is there which tells us that golden things are beautiful, for they do not say so themselves? Evidently it is the faculty which is capable of judging of appearances. What else judges of music, grammar, and the other faculties, proves their uses and points out the occasions for using them? Nothing else.

As then it was fit to be so, that which is best of all and supreme over all is the only thing which the gods have placed in our power, the right use of appearances; but all other things they have not placed in our power. Was it because they did not choose? I indeed think that, if they had been able, they would have put these other things also in our power, but they certainly could not.[2] For as we exist on the earth, and are bound to such a body and to such companions, how was it possible for us not to be hindered as to these things by externals?

But what says Zeus? "Epictetus, if it were possible, I would have made both your little body and your little property free and not exposed to hindrance. But now be not ignorant of this: this body is not yours, but it is clay finely tempered. And since I was not able to do for you what I have mentioned, I have given you a small portion of us, this faculty of pursuing an object and avoiding it, and the faculty of desire and aversion, and, in a word, the faculty of using the appearances of things; and if you will take care of this faculty and consider it your only possession, you will never be hindered, never meet with impediments; you will not lament, you will not blame, you will not flatter any person."

"Well, do these seem to you small matters?" I hope not. "Be content with them then and pray to the gods." But now when it is in our power to look after one thing, and to attach ourselves to it, we prefer to look after many things, and to be bound to many things, to the body and to property, and to brother and to friend, and to child and to slave. Since, then, we are bound to many things, we are depressed by them and dragged down. For this reason, when the weather is not fit for sailing, we sit down and torment ourselves, and continually look out to see what wind is blowing. "It is north." What is that to us? "When will the west wind blow?" When it shall choose, my good man, or when it shall please Æolus; for God has not made you the manager of the

[1] Marcus Aurelius, xi. 1.

[2] Compare Marcus Aurelius, ii. 3.

winds, but Æolus. What then? We must make the best use that we can of the things which are in our power, and use the rest according to their nature. What is their nature then? As God may please.

"Must I, then, alone have my head cut off?" What, would you have all men lose their heads that you may be consoled? Will you not stretch out your neck as Lateranus[1] did at Rome when Nero ordered him to be beheaded? For when he had stretched out his neck, and received a feeble blow, which made him draw it in for a moment, he stretched it out again. And a little before, when he was visited by Epaphroditus, Nero's freedman, who asked him about the cause of offense which he had given, he said, "If I choose to tell anything, I will tell your master."

What then should a man have in readiness in such circumstances? What else than this? "What is mine, and what is not mine; and what is permitted to me, and what is not permitted to me." I must die. Must I then die lamenting? I must be put in chains. Must I then also lament? I must go into exile. Does any man then hinder me from going with smiles and cheerfulness and contentment? "Tell me the secret which you possess." I will not, for this is in my power. "But I will put you in chains."[2] Man, what are you talking about? Me in chains? You may fetter my leg, but my will not even Zeus himself can overpower. "I will throw you into prison." My poor body, you mean. "I will cut your head off." When, then, have I told you that my head alone cannot be cut off? These are the things which philosophers should meditate on, which they should write daily, in which they should exercise themselves.

Thrasea[3] used to say, "I would rather be killed to-day than banished to-morrow." What, then, did Rufus[4] say to him? "If you choose death as the heavier misfortune, how great is the folly of your choice? But if, as the lighter, who has given you the choice? Will you not study to be content with that which has been given to you?"

[1] Tacitus, *Annals*, xv. 49, 60.
[2] Euripides, *Bacchantes,* 492 and following.
[3] Tacitus, *Annals*, xvi. 21-35.
[4] Tacitus, *Histories*, iii. 81.

What, then, did Agrippinus[5] say? He said, "I am not a hindrance to myself." When it was reported to him that his trial was going on in the Senate, he said, "I hope it may turn out well; but it is the fifth hour of the day"—this was the time when he was used to exercise himself and then take the cold bath—"let us go and take our exercise." After he had taken his exercise, one comes and tells him, "You have been condemned." "To banishment," he replies, "or to death?" "To banishment." "What about my property?" "It is not taken from you." "Let us go to Aricia then," he said, "and dine."

This it is to have studied what a man ought to study; to have made desire, aversion, free from hindrance, and free from all that a man would avoid. I must die. If now, I am ready to die. If, after a short time, I now dine because it is the dinner-hour; after this I will then die. How? Like a man who gives up what belongs to another.

CHAPTER 2. *How a Man on every occasion can maintain his Proper Character*

To the rational animal only is the irrational intolerable; but that which is rational is tolerable. Blows are not naturally intolerable. "How is that?" See how the Lacedæmonians endure whipping when they have learned that whipping is consistent with reason. "To hang yourself is not intolerable." When, then, you have the opinion that it is rational, you go and hang yourself. In short, if we observe, we shall find that the animal man is pained by nothing so much as by that which is irrational; and, on the contrary, attracted to nothing so much as to that which is rational.

But the rational and the irrational appear such in a different way to different persons, just as the good and the bad, the profitable and the unprofitable. For this reason, particularly, we need discipline, in order to learn how to adapt the preconception of the rational and the irrational to the several things conformably to nature. But in order to determine the rational and the irrational, we use not only the estimates of external things, but we consider also what is appropriate to each person. For to one man it is consistent with reason to hold a chamber pot

[5] Tacitus, *Annals*, xvi. 28.

for another, and to look to this only, that if he does not hold it, he will receive stripes, and he will not receive his food: but if he shall hold the pot, he will not suffer anything hard or disagreeable. But to another man not only does the holding of a chamber pot appear intolerable for himself, but intolerable also for him to allow another to do this office for him. If, then, you ask me whether you should hold the chamber pot or not, I shall say to you that the receiving of food is worth more than the not receiving of it, and the being scourged is a greater indignity than not being scourged; so that if you measure your interests by these things, go and hold the chamber pot. "But this," you say, "would not be worthy of me." Well, then, it is you who must introduce this consideration into the inquiry, not I; for it is you who know yourself, how much you are worth to yourself, and at what price you sell yourself; for men sell themselves at various prices.

For this reason, when Florus was deliberating whether he should go down to Nero's spectacles [1] and also perform in them himself, Agrippinus said to him, "Go down": and when Florus asked Agrippinus, "Why do not you go down?" Agrippinus replied, "Because I do not even deliberate about the matter." For he who has once brought himself to deliberate about such matters, and to calculate the value of external things, comes very near to those who have forgotten their own character. For why do you ask me the question, whether death is preferable or life? I say "life." "Pain or pleasure?" I say "pleasure." But if I do not take a part in the tragic acting, I shall have my head struck off. Go then and take a part, but I will not. "Why?" Because you consider yourself to be only one thread of those which are in the tunic. Well then it was fitting for you to take care how you should be like the rest of men, just as the thread has no design to be anything superior to the other threads. But I wish to be purple, that small part which is bright, and makes all the rest appear graceful and beautiful. Why then do you tell me to make myself like the many? and if I do, how shall I still be purple?

Priscus Helvidius [2] also saw this, and acted

conformably. For when Vespasian sent and commanded him not to go into the senate, he replied, "It is in your power not to allow me to be a member of the senate, but so long as I am, I must go in." "Well, go in then," says the emperor, "but say nothing." "Do not ask my opinion, and I will be silent." "But I must ask your opinion." "And I must say what I think right." "But if you do, I shall put you to death." "When then did I tell you that I am immortal? You will do your part, and I will do mine: it is your part to kill; it is mine to die, but not in fear: yours to banish me; mine to depart without sorrow."

What good then did Priscus do, who was only a single person? And what good does the purple do for the toga? Why, what else than this, that it is conspicuous in the toga as purple, and is displayed also as a fine example to all other things? But in such circumstances another would have replied to Cæsar who forbade him to enter the senate, "I thank you for sparing me." But such a man Vespasian would not even have forbidden to enter the senate, for he knew that he would either sit there like an earthen vessel, or, if he spoke, he would say what Cæsar wished, and add even more.

In this way an athlete also acted who was in danger of dying unless his private parts were amputated. His brother came to the athlete, who was a philosopher, and said, "Come, brother, what are you going to do? Shall we amputate this member and return to the gymnasium?" But the athlete persisted in his resolution and died. When some one asked Epictetus how he did this, as an athlete or a philosopher, "As a man," Epictetus replied, "and a man who had been proclaimed among the athletes at the Olympic games and had contended in them, a man who had been familiar with such a place, and not merely anointed in Baton's school. Another would have allowed even his head to be cut off, if he could have lived without it. Such is that regard to character which is so strong in those who have been accustomed to introduce it of themselves and conjoined with other things into their deliberations."

"Come, then, Epictetus, shave yourself." "If I am a philosopher," I answer, "I will not shave

---

[1] Tacitus, *Annals*, xiv. 14.
[2] Tacitus, *Histories*, iv. 4, 5.

myself." "But I will take off your head?" If that will do you any good, take it off.

Some person asked, "How then shall every man among us perceive what is suitable to his character?" How, he replied, does the bull alone, when the lion has attacked, discover his own powers and put himself forward in defense of the whole herd? It is plain that with the powers the perception of having them is immediately conjoined; and, therefore, whoever of us has such powers will not be ignorant of them. Now a bull is not made suddenly, nor a brave man; but we must discipline ourselves in the winter for the summer campaign, and not rashly run upon that which does not concern us.

Only consider at what price you sell your own will; if for no other reason, at least for this, that you sell it not for a small sum. But that which is great and superior perhaps belongs to Socrates and such as are like him. "Why then, if we are naturally such, are not a very great number of us like him?" Is it true then that all horses become swift, that all dogs are skilled in tracking footprints? "What, then, since I am naturally dull, shall I, for this reason, take no pains?" I hope not. Epictetus is not superior to Socrates; but if he is not inferior, this is enough for me; for I shall never be a Milo, and yet I do not neglect my body; nor shall I be a Crœsus, and yet I do not neglect my property; nor, in a word, do we neglect looking after anything because we despair of reaching the highest degree.

CHAPTER 3. *How a man should proceed from the principle of God being the father of all men to the rest*

IF a man should be able to assent to this doctrine as he ought, that we are all sprung from God in an especial manner, and that God is the father both of men and of gods, I suppose that he would never have any ignoble or mean thoughts about himself. But if Cæsar should adopt you, no one could endure your arrogance; and if you know that you are the son of Zeus, will you not be elated? Yet we do not so; but since these two things are mingled in the generation of man, body in common with the animals, and reason and intelligence in common with the gods, many incline to this kinship,

which is miserable and mortal; and some few to that which is divine and happy. Since then it is of necessity that every man uses everything according to the opinion which he has about it, those, the few, who think that they are formed for fidelity and modesty and a sure use of appearances have no mean or ignoble thoughts about themselves; but with the many it is quite the contrary. For they say, "What am I? A poor, miserable man, with my wretched bit of flesh." Wretched, indeed; but you possess something better than your "bit of flesh." Why then do you neglect that which is better, and why do you attach yourself to this?

Through this kinship with the flesh, some of us inclining to it become like wolves, faithless and treacherous and mischievous: some become like lions, savage and untamed; but the greater part of us become foxes and other worse animals. For what else is a slanderer and a malignant man than a fox, or some other more wretched and meaner animal? See,[1] then, and take care that you do not become some one of these miserable things.

CHAPTER 4. *Of progress or improvement*

HE who is making progress, having learned from philosophers that desire means the desire of good things, and aversion means aversion from bad things; having learned too that happiness and tranquillity are not attainable by man otherwise than by not failing to obtain what he desires, and not falling into that which he would avoid; such a man takes from himself desire altogether and defers it, but he employs his aversion only on things which are dependent on his will. For if he attempts to avoid anything independent of his will, he knows that sometimes he will fall in with something which he wishes to avoid, and he will be unhappy. Now if virtue promises good fortune and tranquillity and happiness, certainly also the progress toward virtue is progress toward each of these things. For it is always true that to whatever point the perfecting of anything leads us, progress is an approach toward this point.

How then do we admit that virtue is such as I have said, and yet seek progress in other things and make a display of it? What is the product of virtue? Tranquillity. Who then

[1]Matt. 16, 6.

makes improvement? It is he who has read many books of Chrysippus? But does virtue consist in having understood Chrysippus? If this is so, progress is clearly nothing else than knowing a great deal of Chrysippus. But now we admit that virtue produces one thing, and we declare that approaching near to it is another thing, namely, progress or improvement. "Such a person," says one, "is already able to read Chrysippus by himself." Indeed, sir, you are making great progress. What kind of progress? But why do you mock the man? Why do you draw him away from the perception of his own misfortunes? Will you not show him the effect of virtue that he may learn where to look for improvement? Seek it there, wretch, where your work lies. And where is your work? In desire and in aversion, that you may not be disappointed in your desire, and that you may not fall into that which you would avoid; in your pursuit and avoiding, that you commit no error; in assent and suspension of assent, that you be not deceived. The first things, and the most necessary, are those which I have named.[1] But if with trembling and lamentation you seek not to fall into that which you avoid, tell me how you are improving.

Do you then show me your improvement in these things? If I were talking to an athlete, I should say, "Show me your shoulders"; and then he might say, "Here are my halteres." You and your halteres[2] look to that. I should reply, "I wish to see the effect of the halteres." So, when you say: "Take the treatise on the active powers, and see how I have studied it." I reply, "Slave, I am not inquiring about this, but how you exercise pursuit and avoidance, desire and aversion, how your design and purpose and prepare yourself, whether conformably to nature or not. If conformably, give me evidence of it, and I will say that you are making progress: but if not conformably, be gone, and not only expound your books, but write such books yourself; and what will you gain by it? Do you not know that the whole book costs only five denarii? Does then the expounder seem to be worth more than five denarii? Never, then, look for the matter itself in one place, and progress toward it in another."

Where then is progress? If any of you, withdrawing himself from externals, turns to his own will to exercise it and to improve it by labour, so as to make it conformable to nature, elevated, free, unrestrained, unimpeded, faithful, modest; and if he has learned that he who desires or avoids the things which are not in his power can neither be faithful nor free, but of necessity he must change with them and be tossed about with them as in a tempest, and of necessity must subject himself to others who have the power to procure or prevent what he desires or would avoid; finally, when he rises in the morning, if he observes and keeps these rules, bathes as a man of fidelity, eats as a modest man; in like manner, if in every matter that occurs he works out his chief principles as the runner does with reference to running, and the trainer of the voice with reference to the voice —this is the man who truly makes progress, and this is the man who has not traveled in vain. But if he has strained his efforts to the practice of reading books, and labours only at this, and has traveled for this, I tell him to return home immediately, and not to neglect his affairs there; for this for which he has traveled is nothing. But the other thing is something, to study how a man can rid his life of lamentation and groaning, and saying, "Woe to me," and "wretched that I am," and to rid it also of misfortune and disappointment, and to learn what death is, and exile, and prison, and poison, that he may be able to say when he is in fetters, "Dear Crito,[3] if it is the will of the gods that it be so, let it be so"; and not to say, "Wretched am I, an old man; have I kept my gray hairs for this?" Who is it that speaks thus? Do you think that I shall name some man of no repute and of low condition? Does not Priam say this? Does not Œdipus say this? Nay, all kings say it![4] For what else is tragedy than the perturbations of men who value externals exhibited in this kind of poetry? But if a man must learn by fiction that no external things which are independent of the will concern us, for my part I should like this fiction, by the aid of which I should live happily and undisturbed.

[1] Compare iii, 2.
[2] Galen. *De Sanitate tuenda*. *Halteres* were masses of lead, used by the Greeks for exercise and in making jumps.

[3] Compare Plato, *Crito*, 1.
[4] Compare Marcus Aurelius, xi. 6.

But you must consider for yourselves what you wish.

What then does Chrysippus teach us? The reply is, "to know that these things are not false, from which happiness comes and tranquillity arises. Take my books, and you will learn how true and conformable to nature are the things which make me free from perturbations." O great good fortune! O the great benefactor who points out the way! To Triptolemus all men have erected temples and altars, because he gave us food by cultivation; but to him who discovered truth and brought it to light and communicated it to all, not the truth which shows us how to live, but how to live well, who of you for this reason has built an altar, or a temple, or has dedicated a statue, or who worships God for this? Because the gods have given the vine, or wheat, we sacrifice to them: but because they have produced in the human mind that fruit by which they designed to show us the truth which relates to happiness, shall we not thank God for this?

CHAPTER 5. *Against the academics*

IF a man, said Epictetus, opposes evident truths, it is not easy to find arguments by which we shall make him change his opinion. But this does not arise either from the man's strength or the teacher's weakness; for when the man, though he has been confuted, is hardened like a stone, how shall we then be able to deal with him by argument?

Now there are two kinds of hardening, one of the understanding, the other of the sense of shame, when a man is resolved not to assent to what is manifest nor to desist from contradictions. Most of us are afraid of mortification of the body, and would contrive all means to avoid such a thing, but we care not about the soul's mortification. And indeed with regard to the soul, if a man be in such a state as not to apprehend anything, or understand at all, we think that he is in a bad condition: but if the sense of shame and modesty are deadened, this we call even power.

Do you comprehend that you are awake? "I do not," the man replies, "for I do not even comprehend when in my sleep I imagine that I am awake." Does this appearance then not differ from the other? "Not at all," he replies.

Shall I still argue with this man? And what fire or what iron shall I apply to him to make him feel that he is deadened? He does perceive, but he pretends that he does not. He is even worse than a dead man. He does not see the contradiction: he is in a bad condition. Another does see it, but he is not moved, and makes no improvement: he is even in a worse condition. His modesty is extirpated, and his sense of shame; and the rational faculty has not been cut off from him, but it is brutalized. Shall I name this strength of mind? Certainly not, unless we also name it such in catamites, through which they do and say in public whatever comes into their head.

CHAPTER 6. *Of providence*

FROM everything which is or happens in the world, it is easy to praise Providence, if a man possesses these two qualities, the faculty of seeing what belongs and happens to all persons and things, and a grateful disposition. If he does not possess these two qualities, one man will not see the use of things which are and which happen; another will not be thankful for them, even if he does know them. If God had made colours, but had not made the faculty of seeing them, what would have been their use? None at all. On the other hand, if He had made the faculty of vision, but had not made objects such as to fall under the faculty, what in that case also would have been the use of it? None at all. Well, suppose that He had made both, but had not made light? In that case, also, they would have been of no use. Who is it, then, who has fitted this to that and that to this? And who is it that has fitted the knife to the case and the case to the knife? Is it no one? And, indeed, from the very structure of things which have attained their completion, we are accustomed to show that the work is certainly the act of some artificer, and that it has not been constructed without a purpose. Does then each of these things demonstrate the workman, and do not visible things and the faculty of seeing and light demonstrate Him? And the existence of male and female, and the desire of each for conjunction, and the power of using the parts which are constructed, do not even these declare the workman? If they do not, let us consider the constitution of our understanding according to which, when we meet with sensible objects, we do not simply receive impressions from them, but we also select something from them, and subtract something, and add, and compound by means of them these things or those, and, in fact, pass from some to other things which, in a manner, resemble them: is not even this sufficient to move some men, and to induce them not to forget the workman? If not so, let them explain to us what it is that makes each several thing, or how it is possible that things so wonderful and like the contrivances of art should exist by chance and from their own proper motion?

What, then, are these things done in us only. Many, indeed, in us only, of which the rational animal had peculiar need; but you will find many common to us with irrational animals. Do they then understand what is done? By no means. For use is one thing, and understanding is another: God had need of irrational animals to make use of appearances, but of us to understand the use of appearances. It is therefore enough for them to eat and to drink, and to sleep and to copulate, and to do all the other things which they severally do. But for us, to whom He has given also the intellectual faculty, these things are not sufficient; for unless we act in a proper and orderly manner, and conformably to the nature and constitution of each thing, we shall never attain our true end. For where the constitutions of living beings are different, there also the acts and the ends are different. In those animals, then, whose constitution is adapted only to use, use alone is enough: but in an animal which has also the power of understanding the use, unless there be the due exercise of the understanding, he will never attain his proper end. Well then God constitutes every animal, one to be eaten, another to serve for agriculture, another to supply cheese, and another for some like use; for which purposes what need is there to understand appearances and to be able to distinguish them? But God has introduced man to be a spectator of God and of His works; and not only a spectator of them, but an interpreter. For this reason it is shameful for man to begin and to end where irrational animals do, but rather he ought to begin where they begin, and to end where nature ends in us; and nature ends in contemplation and understanding, and in a way of life conformable to nature. Take care then not to die without having been spectators of these things.

But you take a journey to Olympia to see the work of Phidias, and all of you think it a misfortune to die without having seen such things. But when there is no need to take a journey, and where a man is, there he has the works (of God) before him, will you not desire to see and understand them? Will you not perceive either what you are, or what you were born for, or what this is for which you have received the faculty of sight? But you may say, "There are some things disagreeable and troublesome in life." And are there none in Olympia? Are you not scorched? Are you not pressed by a crowd? Are you not without comfortable means of bathing? Are you not wet when it rains? Have you not abundance of noise, clamour, and other disagreeable things? But I suppose that setting all these things off against the magnificence of the spectacle, you bear and endure. Well, then, and have you not received faculties by which you will be able to bear all that happens? Have you not received greatness of soul? Have you not received manliness? Have you not received endurance? And why do I trouble myself about anything that can happen if I possess greatness of soul? What shall distract my mind or disturb me, or appear painful? Shall I not use the power for the purposes for which I received it, and shall I grieve and lament over what happens?

"Yes, but my nose runs."[1] For what purpose then, slave, have you hands? Is it not that you may wipe your nose? "Is it, then, consistent with reason that there should be running of noses in the world?" Nay, how much better it is to wipe your nose than to find fault. What do you think that Hercules would have been if there had not been such a lion, and hydra, and stag, and boar, and certain unjust and bestial men, whom Hercules used to drive away and clear out? And what would he have been doing if there had been nothing of the kind? Is it not plain that he would have wrapped himself up and have slept? In the first place, then, he would not have been a Hercules, when he was dreaming away all his life in such luxury and ease; and even if he had been one what would

[1] Compare ii, 16.

have been the use of him? and what the use of his arms, and of the strength of the other parts of his body, and his endurance and noble spirit, if such circumstances and occasions had not roused and exercised him? "Well, then, must a man provide for himself such means of exercise, and seek to introduce a lion from some place into his country, and a boar and a hydra?" This would be folly and madness: but as they did exist, and were found, they were useful for showing what Hercules was and for exercising him. Come then do you also having observed these things look to the faculties which you have, and when you have looked at them, say: "Bring now, O Zeus, any difficulty that Thou pleasest, for I have means given to me by Thee and powers for honoring myself through the things which happen." You do not so; but you sit still, trembling for fear that some things will happen, and weeping, and lamenting, and groaning for what does happen: and then you blame the gods. For what is the consequence of such meanness of spirit but impiety? And yet God has not only given us these faculties; by which we shall be able to bear everything that happens without being depressed or broken by it; but, like a good king and a true father, He has given us these faculties free from hindrance, subject to no compulsion, unimpeded, and has put them entirely in our own power, without even having reserved to Himself any power of hindering or impeding. You, who have received these powers free and as your own, use them not: you do not even see what you have received, and from whom; some of you being blinded to the giver, and not even acknowledging your benefactor, and others, through meanness of spirit, betaking yourselves to fault-finding and making charges against God. Yet I will show to you that you have powers and means for greatness of soul and manliness: but what powers you have for finding fault and making accusations, do you show me.

CHAPTER 7. *Of the use of sophistical arguments, and hypothetical, and the like*

THE handling of sophistical and hypothetical arguments, and of those which derive their conclusions from questioning, and in a word the handling of all such arguments, relates to the duties of life, though the many do not know this truth. For in every matter we inquire how the wise and good man shall discover the proper path and the proper method of dealing with the matter. Let, then, people either say that the grave man will not descend into the contest of question and answer, or that, if he does descend into the contest, he will take no care about not conducting himself rashly or carelessly in questioning and answering. But if they do not allow either the one or the other of these things, they must admit that some inquiry ought to be made into those topics on which particularly questioning and answering are employed. For what is the end proposed in reasoning? To establish true propositions, to remove the false, to withhold assent from those which are not plain. Is it enough then to have learned only this? "It is enough," a man may reply. Is it, then, also enough for a man, who would not make a mistake in the use of coined money, to have heard this precept, that he should receive the genuine drachmæ and reject the spurious? "It is not enough." What, then, ought to be added to this precept? What else than the faculty which proves and distinguishes the genuine and the spurious drachmæ? Consequently also in reasoning what has been said is not enough; but is it necessary that a man should acquire the faculty of examining and distinguishing the true and the false, and that which is not plain? "It is necessary." Besides this, what is proposed in reasoning? "That you should accept what follows from that which you have properly granted." Well, is it then enough in this case also to know this? It is not enough; but a man must learn how one thing is a consequence of other things, and when one thing follows from one thing, and when it follows from several collectively. Consider, then, if it be not necessary that this power should also be acquired by him who purposes to conduct himself skillfully in reasoning, the power of demonstrating himself the several things which he has proposed, and the power of understanding the demonstrations of others, and of not being deceived by sophists, as if they were demonstrating. Therefore there has arisen among us the practice and exercise of conclusive arguments and figures, and it has been shown to be necessary.

But in fact in some cases we have properly granted the premises or assumptions, and there results from them something; and though it is not true, yet none the less it does result. What then ought I to do? Ought I to admit the falsehood? And how is that possible? Well, should I say that I did not properly grant that which we agreed upon? "But you are not allowed to do even this." Shall I then say that the consequence does not arise through what has been conceded? "But neither is it allowed." What then must be done in this case? Consider if it is not this: as to have borrowed is not enough to make a man still a debtor, but to this must be added the fact that he continues to owe the money and that the debt is not paid, so it is not enough to compel you to admit the inference that you have granted the premises, but you must abide by what you have granted. Indeed, if the premises continue to the end such as they were when they were granted, it is absolutely necessary for us to abide by what we have granted, and we must accept their consequences: but if the premises do not remain such as they were when they were granted, it is absolutely necessary for us also to withdraw from what we granted, and from accepting what does not follow from the words in which our concessions were made. For the inference is now not our inference, nor does it result with our assent, since we have withdrawn from the premises which we granted. We ought then both to examine such kind of premises, and such change and variation of them, by which in the course of questioning or answering, or in making the syllogistic conclusion, or in any other such way, the premises undergo variations, and give occasion to the foolish to be confounded, if they do not see what conclusions are. For what reason ought we to examine? In order that we may not in this matter be employed in an improper manner nor in a confused way.

And the same in hypotheses and hypothetical arguments; for it is necessary sometimes to demand the granting of some hypothesis as a kind of passage to the argument which follows. Must we then allow every hypothesis that is proposed, or not allow every one? And if not every one, which should we allow? And if a man has allowed an hypothesis, must he in every case abide by allowing it? or must he

sometimes withdraw from it, but admit the consequences and not admit contradictions? Yes; but suppose that a man says, "If you admit the hypothesis of a possibility, I will draw you to an impossibility." With such a person shall a man of sense refuse to enter into a contest, and avoid discussion and conversation with him? But what other man than the man of sense can use argumentation and is skillful in questioning and answering, and incapable of being cheated and deceived by false reasoning? And shall he enter into the contest, and yet not take care whether he shall engage in argument not rashly and not carelessly? And if he does not take care, how can he be such a man as we conceive him to be? But without some such exercise and preparation, can he maintain a continuous and consistent argument? Let them show this; and all these speculations become superfluous, and are absurd and inconsistent with our notion of a good and serious man.

Why are we still indolent and negligent and sluggish, and why do we seek pretences for not labouring and not being watchful in cultivating our reason? "If then I shall make a mistake in these matters may I not have killed my father?" Slave, where was there a father in this matter that you could kill him? What, then, have you done? The only fault that was possible here is the fault which you have committed. This is the very remark which I made to Rufus[1] when he blamed me for not having discovered the one thing omitted in a certain syllogism: "I suppose," I said, "that I have burnt the Capitol." "Slave," he replied, "was the thing omitted here the Capitol?" Or are these the only crimes, to burn the Capitol and to kill your father? But for a man to use the appearances presented to him rashly and foolishly and carelessly, and not to understand argument, nor demonstration, nor sophism, nor, in a word, to see in questioning and answering what is consistent with that which we have granted or is not consistent; is there no error in this?

CHAPTER 8. *That the faculties*[2] *are not safe to the uninstructed*

IN as many ways as we can change things which are equivalent to one another, in just so

[1] See i.1; Plutarch *Lives,* Tiberius Gracchus.
[2] See below.

many ways we can change the forms of arguments and enthymemes in argumentation. This is an instance: "If you have borrowed and not repaid, you owe me the money: you have not borrowed and you have not repaid; then you do not owe me the money." To do this skillfully is suitable to no man more than to the philosopher; for if the enthymeme is an imperfect syllogism, it is plain that he who has been exercised in the perfect syllogism must be equally expert in the imperfect also.

"Why then do we not exercise ourselves and one another in this manner?" Because, I reply, at present, though we are not exercised in these things and not distracted from the study of morality, by me at least, still we make no progress in virtue. What then must we expect if we should add this occupation? and particularly as this would not only be an occupation which would withdraw us from more necessary things, but would also be a cause of self-conceit and arrogance, and no small cause. For great is the power of arguing and the faculty of persuasion, and particularly if it should be much exercised, and also receive additional ornament from language: and so universally, every faculty acquired by the uninstructed and weak brings with it the danger of these persons being elated and inflated by it. For by what means could one persuade a young man who excels in these matters that he ought not to become an appendage to them, but to make them an appendage to himself? Does he not trample on all such reasons, and strut before us elated and inflated, not enduring that any man should reprove him and remind him of what he has neglected and to what he has turned aside?

"What, then, was not Plato a philosopher?" I reply, "And was not Hippocrates a physician? but you see how Hippocrates speaks." Does Hippocrates, then, speak thus in respect of being a physician? Why do you mingle things which have been accidentally united in the same men? And if Plato was handsome and strong, ought I also to set to work and endeavor to become handsome or strong, as if this was necessary for philosophy, because a certain philosopher was at the same time handsome and a philosopher? Will you not choose to see and to distinguish in respect to what men become

philosophers, and what things belong to them in other respects? And if I were a philosopher, ought you also to be made lame? What then? Do I take away these faculties which you possess? By no means; for neither do I take away the faculty of seeing. But if you ask me what is the good of man, I cannot mention to you anything else than that it is a certain disposition of the will with respect to appearances.[1]

CHAPTER 9. *How from the fact that we are akin to God a man may proceed to the consequences*

IF the things are true which are said by the philosophers about the kinship between God and man, what else remains for men to do than what Socrates did? Never in reply to the question, to what country you belong, say that you are an Athenian or a Corinthian, but that you are a citizen of the world. For why do you say that you are an Athenian, and why do you not say that you belong to the small nook only into which your poor body was cast at birth? Is it not plain that you call yourself an Athenian or Corinthian from the place which has a greater authority and comprises not only that small nook itself and all your family, but even the whole country from which the stock of your progenitors is derived down to you? He then who has observed with intelligence the administration of the world, and has learned that the greatest and supreme and the most comprehensive community is that which is composed of men and God, and that from God have descended the seeds not only to my father and grandfather, but to all beings which are generated on the earth and are produced, and particularly to rational beings—for these only are by their nature formed to have communion with God, being by means of reason conjoined with Him[2]—why should not such a man call himself a citizen of the world, why not a son of God,[3] and why should he be afraid of anything which happens among men? Is kinship with Cæsar or with any other of the powerful in Rome sufficient to enable us to live in safety, and above contempt and without any fear at all? and to have God for your maker and fa-

[1] See also i. 20; i. 29.
[2] Epictetus, i.14; ii. 8.
[3] Compare Acts, 17. 28.

ther and guardian, shall not this release us from sorrows and fears?

But a man may say, "Whence shall I get bread to eat when I have nothing?"

And how do slaves, and runaways, on what do they rely when they leave their masters? Do they rely on their lands or slaves, or their vessels of silver? They rely on nothing but themselves, and food does not fail them.[1] And shall it be necessary for one among us who is a philosopher to travel into foreign parts, and trust to and rely on others, and not to take care of himself, and shall he be inferior to irrational animals and more cowardly, each of which, being self-sufficient, neither fails to get its proper food, nor to find a suitable way of living, and one conformable to nature?

I indeed think that the old man[2] ought to be sitting here, not to contrive how you may have no mean thoughts nor mean and ignoble talk about yourselves, but to take care that there be not among us any young men of such a mind that, when they have recognized their kinship to God, and that we are fettered by these bonds, the body, I mean, and its possessions, and whatever else on account of them is necessary to us for the economy and commerce of life, they should intend to throw off these things as if they were burdens painful and intolerable, and to depart to their kinsmen. But this is the labour that your teacher and instructor ought to be employed upon, if he really were what he should be. You should come to him and say, "Epictetus, we can no longer endure being bound to this poor body, and feeding it and giving it drink, and rest, and cleaning it, and for the sake of the body complying with the wishes of these and of those. Are not these things indifferent and nothing to us, and is not death no evil? And are we not in a manner kinsmen of God, and did we not come from Him? Allow us to depart to the place from which we came; allow us to be released at last from these bonds by which we are bound and weighed down. Here there are robbers and thieves and courts of justice, and those who are named tyrants, and think that they have some power over us by means of the body and its possessions. Permit us to show them that they have no power over any man." And

I on my part would say, "Friends, wait for God; when He shall give the signal[3] and release you from this service, then go to Him; but for the present endure to dwell in this place where He has put you: short indeed is this time of your dwelling here, and easy to bear for those who are so disposed: for what tyrant or what thief, or what courts of justice, are formidable to those who have thus considered as things of no value the body and the possessions of the body? Wait then, do not depart without a reason."

Something like this ought to be said by the teacher to ingenuous youths. But now what happens? The teacher is a lifeless body, and you are lifeless bodies. When you have been well filled to-day, you sit down and lament about the morrow, how you shall get something to eat. Wretch, if you have it, you will have it; if you have it not, you will depart from life. The door is open.[4] Why do you grieve? where does there remain any room for tears? and where is there occasion for flattery? why shall one man envy another? why should a man admire the rich or the powerful, even if they be both very strong and of violent temper? for what will they do to us? We shall not care for that which they can do; and what we do care for, that they cannot do. How did Socrates behave with respect to these matters? Why, in what other way than a man ought to do who was convinced that he was a kinsman of the gods? "If you say to me now," said Socrates to his judges,[5] " 'We will acquit you on the condition that you no longer discourse in the way in which you have hitherto discoursed, nor trouble either our young or our old men,' I shall answer, 'you make yourselves ridiculous by thinking that, if one of our commanders has appointed me to a certain post, it is my duty to keep and maintain it, and to resolve to die a thousand times rather than desert it; but if God has put us in any place and way of life, we ought to desert it.' " Socrates speaks like a man who is really a kinsman of the gods. But we think about ourselves as if we were only stomachs, and intestines, and shame-

---

[1] Matt. 5. 26; 6. 25-34.   [2] Epictetus.

[3] Cicero, *De Republica*, iv. 15. Marcus Aurelius, ii. 17; iii. 5; v. 33.

[4] Epictetus i. 24; i.25; ii.1. Compare Mat. 6. 31.

[5] Plato, *Apology*, 29.

ful parts; we fear, we desire; we flatter those who are able to help us in these matters, and we fear them also.

A man asked me to write to Rome about him, a man who, as most people thought, had been unfortunate, for formerly he was a man of rank and rich, but had been stripped of all, and was living here. I wrote on his behalf in a submissive manner; but when he had read the letter, he gave it back to me and said, "I wished for your help, not your pity: no evil has happened to me."

Thus also Musonius Rufus, in order to try me, used to say: "This and this will befall you from your master"; and I replied that these were things which happen in the ordinary course of human affairs. "Why, then," said he, "should I ask him for anything when I can obtain it from you?" For, in fact, what a man has from himself, it is superfluous and foolish to receive from another? Shall I, then, who am able to receive from myself greatness of soul and a generous spirit, receive from you land and money or a magisterial office? I hope not: I will not be so ignorant about my own possessions. But when a man is cowardly and mean, what else must be done for him than to write letters as you would about a corpse. "Please to grant us the body of a certain person and a sextarius of poor blood." For such a person is, in fact, a carcass and a sextarius of blood, and nothing more. But if he were anything more, he would know that one man is not miserable through the means of another.

CHAPTER 10. *Against those who eagerly seek preferment at Rome*

IF we applied ourselves as busily to our own work as the old men at Rome do to those matters about which they are employed, perhaps we also might accomplish something. I am acquainted with a man older than myself who is now superintendent of corn at Rome, and I remember the time when he came here on his way back from exile, and what he said as he related the events of his former life, and how he declared that with respect to the future after his return he would look after nothing else than passing the rest of his life in quiet and tranquillity. "For how little of life," he said, "remains for me." I replied, "You will not do

it, but as soon as you smell Rome, you will forget all that you have said; and if admission is allowed even into the imperial palace, you will gladly thrust yourself in and thank God." "If you find me, Epictetus," he answered, "setting even one foot within the palace, think what you please." Well, what then did he do? Before he entered the city he was met by letters from Cæsar, and as soon as he received them he forgot all, and ever after has added one piece of business to another. I wish that I were now by his side to remind him of what he said when he was passing this way and to tell him how much better a seer I am than he is.

Well, then, do I say that man is an animal made for doing nothing?[1] Certainly not. But why are we not active? For example, as to myself, as soon as day comes, in a few words I remind myself of what I must read over to my pupils; then forthwith I say to myself, "But what is it to me how a certain person shall read? the first thing for me is to sleep." And indeed what resemblance is there between what other persons do and what we do? If you observe what they do, you will understand. And what else do they do all day long than make up accounts, inquire among themselves, give and take advice about some small quantity of grain, a bit of land, and such kind of profits? Is it then the same thing to receive a petition and to read in it: "I entreat you to permit me to export a small quantity of corn"; and one to this effect: "I entreat you to learn from Chrysippus what is the administration of the world, and what place in it the rational animal holds; consider also who you are, and what is the nature of your good and bad." Are these things like the other, do they require equal care, and is it equally base to neglect these and those? Well, then, are we the only persons who are lazy and love sleep? No; but much rather you young men are. For we old men, when we see young men amusing themselves, are eager to play with them; and if I saw you active and zealous, much more should I be eager myself to join you in your serious pursuits.

CHAPTER 11. *Of natural affection*

WHEN he was visited by one of the magistrates, Epictetus inquired of him about several partic-

[1] Marcus Aurelius, v. 1; viii, 19.

ulars, and asked if he had children and a wife. The man replied that he had; and Epictetus inquired further, how he felt under the circumstances. "Miserable," the man said. Then Epictetus asked, "In what respect," for men do not marry and beget children in order to be wretched, but rather to be happy. "But I," the man replied, "am so wretched about my children that lately, when my little daughter was sick and was supposed to be in danger, I could not endure to stay with her, but I left home till a person sent me news that she had recovered." Well then, said Epictetus, do you think that you acted right? "I acted naturally," the man replied. But convince me of this that you acted naturally, and I will convince you that everything which takes place according to nature takes place rightly. "This is the case," said the man, "with all or at least most fathers." I do not deny that: but the matter about which we are inquiring is whether such behaviour is right; for in respect to this matter we must say that tumours also come for the good of the body, because they do come; and generally we must say that to do wrong is natural, because nearly all or at least most of us do wrong. Do you show me then how your behaviour is natural. "I cannot," he said; "but do you rather show me how it is not according to nature and is not rightly done."

Well, said Epictetus, if we were inquiring about white and black, what criterion should we employ for distinguishing between them? "The sight," he said. And if about hot and cold, and hard and soft, what criterion? "The touch." Well then, since we are inquiring about things which are according to nature, and those which are done rightly or not rightly, what kind of criterion do you think that we should employ? "I do not know," he said. And yet not to know the criterion of colours and smells, and also of tastes, is perhaps no great harm; but if a man do not know the criterion of good and bad, and of things according to nature and contrary to nature, does this seem to you a small harm? "The greatest harm." Come tell me, do all things which seem to some persons to be good and becoming rightly appear such; and at present as to Jews and Syrians and Egyptians and Romans, is it possible that the opinions of all of them in respect to

food are right? "How is it possible?" he said. Well, I suppose it is absolutely necessary that, if the opinions of the Egyptians are right, the opinions of the rest must be wrong: if the opinions of the Jews are right, those of the rest cannot be right. "Certainly." But where there is ignorance, there also there is want of learning and training in things which are necessary. He assented to this. You then, said Epictetus, since you know this, for the future will employ yourself seriously about nothing else, and will apply your mind to nothing else than to learn the criterion of things which are according to nature, and by using it also to determine each several thing. But in the present matter I have so much as this to aid you toward what you wish. Does affection to those of your family appear to you to be according to nature and to be good? "Certainly." Well, is such affection natural and good, and is a thing consistent with reason not good? "By no means." Is then that which is consistent with reason in contradiction with affection? "I think not." You are right, for if it is otherwise, it is necessary that one of the contradictions being according to nature, the other must be contrary to nature. Is it not so? "It is," he said. Whatever, then, we shall discover to be at the same time affectionate and also consistent with reason, this we confidently declare to be right and good. "Agreed." Well then to leave your sick child and to go away is not reasonable, and I suppose that you will not say that it is; but it remains for us to inquire if it is consistent with affection. "Yes, let us consider." Did you, then, since you had an affectionate disposition to your child, do right when you ran off and left her; and has the mother no affection for the child? "Certainly, she has." Ought, then, the mother also to have left her, or ought she not? "She ought not." And the nurse, does she love her? "She does." Ought, then, she also to have left her? "By no means." And the pedagogue, does he not love her? "He does love her." Ought, then, he also to have deserted her? and so should the child have been left alone and without help on account of the great affection of you, the parents, and of those about her, or should she have died in the hands of those who neither loved her nor cared for her? "Certainly not." Now this is unfair and unreasonable, not to allow those who have equal affection with yourself to do what you think to be proper for yourself to do because you have affection. It is absurd. Come then, if you were sick, would you wish your relations to be so affectionate, and all the rest, children and wife, as to leave you alone and deserted? "By no means." And would you wish to be so loved by your own that through their excessive affection you would always be left alone in sickness? or for this reason would you rather pray, if it were possible, to be loved by your enemies and deserted by them? But if this is so, it results that your behaviour was not at all an affectionate act.

Well then, was it nothing which moved you and induced you to desert your child? and how is that possible? But it might be something of the kind which moved a man at Rome to wrap up his head while a horse was running which he favoured; and when contrary to expectation the horse won, he required sponges to recover from his fainting fit. What then is the thing which moved? The exact discussion of this does not belong to the present occasion perhaps; but it is enough to be convinced of this, if what the philosophers say is true, that we must not look for it anywhere without, but in all cases it is one and the same thing which is the cause of our doing or not doing something, of saying or not saying something, of being elated or depressed, of avoiding anything or pursuing: the very thing which is now the cause to me and to you, to you of coming to me and sitting and hearing, and to me of saying what I do say. And what is this? Is it any other than our will to do so? "No other." But if we had willed otherwise, what else should we have been doing than that which we willed to do? This, then, was the cause of Achilles' lamentation, not the death of Patroclus; for another man does not behave thus on the death of his companion; but it was because he chose to do so. And to you this was the very cause of your then running away, that you chose to do so; and on the other side, if you should stay with her, the reason will be the same. And now you are going to Rome because you choose; and if you should change your mind, you will not go thither. And in a word, neither death nor exile nor pain nor anything of the kind is the cause of our doing anything or not doing; but our own opinions and our wills.

Do I convince you of this or not? "You do convince me." Such, then, as the causes are in each case, such also are the effects. When, then, we are doing anything not rightly, from this day we shall impute it to nothing else than to the will from which we have done it: and it is that which we shall endeavour to take away and to extirpate more than the tumours and abscesses out of the body. And in like manner we shall give the same account of the cause of the things which we do right; and we shall no longer allege as causes of any evil to us, either slave or neighbour, or wife or children, being persuaded that, if we do not think things to be what we do think them to be, we do not the acts which follow from such opinions; and as to thinking or not thinking, that is in our power and not in externals. "It is so," he said. From this day then we shall inquire into and examine nothing else, what its quality is, or its state, neither land nor slaves nor horses nor dogs, nothing else than opinions. "I hope so." You see, then, that you must become a Scholasticus, an animal whom all ridicule, if you really intend to make an examination of your own opinions: and that this is not the work of one hour or day, you know yourself.

CHAPTER 12. *Of contentment*

WITH respect to gods, there are some who say that a divine being does not exist: others say that it exists, but is inactive and careless, and takes no forethought about anything; a third class say that such a being exists and exercises forethought, but only about great things and heavenly things, and about nothing on the earth; a fourth class say that a divine being exercises forethought both about things on the earth and heavenly things, but in a general way only, and not about things severally. There is a fifth class to whom Ulysses and Socrates belong, who say: "I move not without thy knowledge."[1]

Before all other things, then, it is necessary to inquire about each of these opinions, whether it is affirmed truly or not truly. For if there are no gods, how is it our proper end to fol-

[1] Homer, *Iliad*, x. 278.

low them?[1] And if they exist, but take no care of anything, in this case also how will it be right to follow them? But if indeed they do exist and look after things, still if there is nothing communicated from them to men, nor in fact to myself, how even so is it right? The wise and good man, then, after considering all these things, submits his own mind to him who administers the whole, as good citizens do to the law of the state. He who is receiving instruction ought to come to be instructed with this intention: "How shall I follow the gods in all things, how shall I be contented with the divine administration, and how can I become free?" For he is free to whom everything happens according to his will, and whom no man can hinder. "What then, is freedom madness?" Certainly not: for madness and freedom do not consist. "But," you say, "I would have everything result just as I like, and in whatever way I like." You are mad, you are beside yourself. Do you not know that freedom is a noble and valuable thing? But for me inconsiderately to wish for things to happen as I inconsiderately like, this appears to be not only not noble, but even most base. For how do we proceed in the matter of writing? Do I wish to write the name of Dion as I choose? No, but I am taught to choose to write it as it ought to be written. And how with respect to music? In the same manner. And what universally in every art or science? Just the same. If it were not so, it would be of no value to know anything, if knowledge were adapted to every man's whim. Is it, then, in this alone, in this which is the greatest and the chief thing, I mean freedom, that I am permitted to will inconsiderately? By no means; but to be instructed is this, to learn to wish that everything may happen as it does.[2] And how do things happen? As the disposer has disposed them? And he has appointed summer and winter, and abundance and scarcity, and virtue and vice, and all such opposites for the harmony of the whole; and to each of us he has given a body, and parts of the body, and possessions, and companions.

Remembering, then, this disposition of things, we ought to go to be instructed, not that we may change the constitution of things —for we have not the power to do it, nor is it better that we should have the power—but in order that, as the things around us are what they are and by nature exist, we may maintain our minds in harmony with the things which happen. For can we escape from men? and how is it possible? And if we associate with them, can we change them? Who gives us the power? What then remains, or what method is discovered of holding commerce with them? Is there such a method by which they shall do what seems fit to them, and we not the less shall be in a mood which is conformable to nature? But you are unwilling to endure and are discontented: and if you are alone, you call it solitude; and if you are with men, you call them knaves and robbers; and you find fault with your own parents and children, and brothers and neighbours. But you ought when you are alone to call this condition by the name of tranquillity and freedom, and to think yourself like to the gods; and when you are with many, you ought not to call it crowd, nor trouble, nor uneasiness, but festival and assembly, and so accept all contentedly.

What, then, is the punishment of those who do not accept? It is to be what they are. Is any person dissatisfied with being alone? let him be alone. Is a man dissatisfied with his parents? let him be a bad son, and lament. Is he dissatisfied with his children? let him be a bad father. "Cast him into prison." What prison? Where he is already, for he is there against his will; and where a man is against his will, there he is in prison. So Socrates was not in prison, for he was there willingly. "Must my leg then be lamed?" Wretch, do you then on account of one poor leg find fault with the world? Will you not willingly surrender it for the whole? Will you not withdraw from it? Will you not gladly part with it to him who gave it? And will you be vexed and discontented with the things established by Zeus, which he with the Moiræ[3] who were present and spinning the thread of your generation, defined and put in order? Know you not how small a part you are compared with the whole. I mean with respect to the body,

---

[1] Marcus Aurelius, x. 11.
[2] Marcus Aurelius, iv. 23.

[3] Fates.

for as to intelligence you are not inferior to the gods nor less; for the magnitude of intelligence is not measured by length nor yet by height, but by thoughts.

Will you not, then, choose to place your good in that in which you are equal to the gods? "Wretch that I am to have such a father and mother." What, then, was it permitted to you to come forth, and to select, and to say: "Let such a man at this moment unite with such a woman that I may be produced?" It was not permitted, but it was a necessity for your parents to exist first, and then for you to be begotten. Of what kind of parents? Of such as they were. Well then, since they are such as they are, is there no remedy given to you? Now if you did not know for what purpose you possess the faculty of vision, you would be unfortunate and wretched if you closed your eyes when colours were brought before them; but in that you possess greatness of soul and nobility of spirit for every event that may happen, and you know not that you possess them, are you not more unfortunate and wretched? Things are brought close to you which are proportionate to the power which you possess, but you turn away this power most particularly at the very time when you ought to maintain it open and discerning. Do you not rather thank the gods that they have allowed you to be above these things which they have not placed in your power; and have made you accountable only for those which are in your power? As to your parents, the gods have left you free from responsibility; and so with respect to your brothers, and your body, and possessions, and death and life. For what, then, have they made you responsible? For that which alone is in your power, the proper use of appearances. Why then do you draw on yourself the things for which you are not responsible? It is, indeed, a giving of trouble to yourself.

CHAPTER 13. *How everything may be done acceptably to the gods*

WHEN some one asked, how may a man eat acceptably to the gods, he answered: If he can eat justly and contentedly, and with equanimity, and temperately and orderly, will it not be also acceptably to the gods? But when you have asked for warm water and the slave has not heard, or if he did hear has brought only tepid water, or he is not even found to be in the house, then not to be vexed or to burst with passion, is not this acceptable to the gods? "How then shall a man endure such persons as this slave?" Slave yourself, will you not bear with your own brother, who has Zeus for his progenitor, and is like a son from the same seeds and of the same descent from above? But if you have been put in any such higher place, will you immediately make yourself a tyrant? Will you not remember who you are, and whom you rule? that they are kinsmen, that they are brethren by nature, that they are the offspring of Zeus?[1] "But I have purchased them, and they have not purchased me." Do you see in what direction you are looking, that it is toward the earth, toward the pit, that it is toward these wretched laws of dead men? but toward the laws of the gods you are not looking.

CHAPTER 14. *That the deity oversees all things*

WHEN a person asked him how a man could be convinced that all his actions are under the inspection of God, he answered, Do you not think that all things are united in one?[2] "I do," the person replied. Well, do you not think that earthly things have a natural agreement and union with heavenly things? "I do." And how else so regularly as if by God's command, when He bids the plants to flower, do they flower? when He bids them to send forth shoots, do they shoot? when He bids them to produce fruit, how else do they produce fruit? when He bids the fruit to ripen, does it ripen? when again He bids them to cast down the fruits, how else do they cast them down? and when to shed the leaves, do they shed the leaves? and when He bids them to fold themselves up and to remain quiet and rest, how else do they remain quiet and rest? And how else at the growth and the wane of the moon, and at the approach and recession of the sun, are so great an alteration and change to the contrary seen in earthly things? But are plants and our bodies so bound up and united with the whole, and are not our

[1] Compare Job, 31. 15.
[2] Marcus Aurelius, vi. 10; vii. 9.

souls much more? and our souls so bound up and in contact with God as parts of Him and portions of Him; and does not God perceive every motion of these parts as being His own motion connate with Himself? Now are you able to think of the divine administration, and about all things divine, and at the same time also about human affairs, and to be moved by ten thousand things at the same time in your senses and in your understanding, and to assent to some, and to dissent from others, and again as to some things to suspend your judgment; and do you retain in your soul so many impressions from so many and various things, and being moved by them, do you fall upon notions similar to those first impressed, and do you retain numerous arts and the memories of ten thousand things; and is not God able to oversee all things, and to be present with all, and to receive from all a certain communication? And is the sun able to illuminate so large a part of the All, and to leave so little not illuminated, that part only which is occupied by the earth's shadow; and He who made the sun itself and makes it go round, being a small part of Himself compared with the whole, cannot He perceive all things?

"But I cannot," the man may reply, "comprehend all these things at once." But who tells you that you have equal power with Zeus? Nevertheless he has placed by every man a guardian, every man's Demon,[1] to whom he has committed the care of the man, a guardian who never sleeps, is never deceived. For to what better and more careful guardian could He have intrusted each of us? When, then, you have shut the doors and made darkness within, remember never to say that you are alone, for you are not; but God is within, and your Demon is within, and what need have they of light to see what you are doing? To this God you ought to swear an oath just as the soldiers do to Cæsar. But they who are hired for pay swear to regard the safety of Cæsar before all things; and you who have received so many and such great favours, will you not swear, or when you have sworn, will you not abide by your oath? And what shall you swear? Never to be dis-

[1] Marcus Aurelius, iii. 5; v, 27. I Cor. i. 3, 16.

obedient, never to make any charges, never to find fault with anything that he has given, and never unwillingly to do or to suffer anything that is necessary. Is this oath like the soldier's oath? The soldiers swear not to prefer any man to Cæsar: in this oath men swear to honour themselves before all.

CHAPTER 15. *What philosophy promises*
WHEN a man was consulting him how he should persuade his brother to cease being angry with him, Epictetus replied: Philosophy does not propose to secure for a man any external thing. If it did philosophy would be allowing something which is not within its province. For as the carpenter's material is wood, and that of the statuary is copper, so the matter of the art of living is each man's life. "What then is my brother's?" That again belongs to his own art; but with respect to yours, it is one of the external things, like a piece of land, like health, like reputation. But Philosophy promises none of these. "In every circumstance I will maintain," she says, "the governing part conformable to nature." Whose governing part? "His in whom I am," she says.

"How then shall my brother cease to be angry with me?" Bring him to me and I will tell him. But I have nothing to say to you about his anger.

When the man, who was consulting him, said, "I seek to know this—how, even if my brother is not reconciled to me, shall I maintain myself in a state conformable to nature?" Nothing great, said Epictetus, is produced suddenly, since not even the grape or the fig is. If you say to me now that you want a fig, I will answer to you that it requires time: let it flower first, then put forth fruit, and then ripen. Is, then, the fruit of a fig-tree not perfected suddenly and in one hour, and would you possess the fruit of a man's mind in so short a time and so easily? Do not expect it, even if I tell you.

CHAPTER 16. *Of providence*
Do NOT wonder if for other animals than man all things are provided for the body, not only food and drink, but beds also, and they have no need of shoes nor bed materials, nor cloth-

ing; but we require all these additional things. For, animals not being made for themselves, but for service, it was not fit for them to be made so as to need other things. For consider what it would be for us to take care not only of ourselves, but also about cattle and asses, how they should be clothed, and how shod, and how they should eat and drink. Now as soldiers are ready for their commander, shod, clothed and armed: but it would be a hard thing for the chiliarch[1] to go round and shoe or clothe his thousand men; so also nature has formed the animals which are made for service, all ready, prepared, and requiring no further care. So one little boy with only a stick drives the cattle.

But now we, instead of being thankful that we need not take the same care of animals as of ourselves, complain of God on our own account; and yet, in the name of Zeus and the gods, any one thing of those which exist would be enough to make a man perceive the providence of God, at least a man who is modest and grateful. And speak not to me now of the great things, but only of this, that milk is produced from grass, and cheese from milk, and wool from skins. Who made these things or devised them? "No one," you say. Oh, amazing shamelessness and stupidity!

Well, let us omit the works of nature and contemplate her smaller acts. Is there anything less useful than the hair on the chin? What then, has not nature used this hair also in the most suitable manner possible? Has she not by it distinguished the male and the female? does not the nature of every man forthwith proclaim from a distance, "I am a man; as such approach me, as such speak to me; look for nothing else; see the signs"? Again, in the case of women, as she has mingled something softer in the voice, so she has also deprived them of hair (on the chin). You say: "Not so; the human animal ought to have been left without marks of distinction, and each of us should have been obliged to proclaim, 'I am a man.'" But how is not the sign beautiful and becoming and venerable? how much more beautiful than the cock's comb, how much more becoming than the lion's mane? For this reason we ought to pre-

serve the signs which God has given, we ought not to throw them away, nor to confound, as much as we can, the distinctions of the sexes.

Are these the only works of providence in us? And what words are sufficient to praise them and set them forth according to their worth? For if we had understanding, ought we to do anything else both jointly and severally than to sing hymns and bless the deity, and to tell of his benefits? Ought we not when we are digging and ploughing and eating to sing this hymn to God? "Great is God, who has given us such implements with which we shall cultivate the earth: great is God who has given us hands, the power of swallowing, a stomach, imperceptible growth, and the power of breathing while we sleep." This is what we ought to sing on every occasion, and to sing the greatest and most divine hymn for giving us the faculty of comprehending these things and using a proper way. Well then, since most of you have become blind, ought there not to be some man to fill this office, and on behalf of all to sing the hymn to God? For what else can I do, a lame old man, than sing hymns to God? If then I was a nightingale, I would do the part of a nightingale: if I were a swan, I would do like a swan. But now I am a rational creature, and I ought to praise God: this is my work; I do it, nor will I desert this post, so long as I am allowed to keep it; and I exhort you to join in this same song.

CHAPTER 17. *That the logical art is necessary*
SINCE reason is the faculty which analyses and perfects the rest, and it ought itself not to be unanalysed, by what should it be analysed? for it is plain that this should be done either by itself or by another thing. Either, then, this other thing also is reason, or something else superior to reason; which is impossible. But if it is reason, again who shall analyse that reason? For if that reason does this for itself, our reason also can do it. But we shall require something else, the thing will go on to infinity and have no end.[2] Reason therefore is analysed by itself. "Yes: but it is more urgent to cure (our opinions) and the like." Will you then hear about those things? Hear.

[1] Tribune.

[2] Marcus Aurelius, xi. 1.

But if you should say, "I know not whether you are arguing truly or falsely," and if I should express myself in any way ambiguously, and you should say to me, " Distinguish," I will bear with you no longer, and I shall say to you, "It is more urgent." This is the reason, I suppose, why they[1] place the logical art first, as in the measuring of corn we place first the examination of the measure. But if we do not determine first what is a modius, and what is a balance, how shall we be able to measure or weigh anything?

In this case, then, if we have not fully learned and accurately examined the criterion of all other things, by which the other things are learned, shall we be able to examine accurately and to learn fully anything else? "Yes; but the modius is only wood, and a thing which produces no fruit." But it is a thing which can measure corn. "Logic also produces no fruit." As to this indeed we shall see: but then even if a man should grant this, it is enough that logic has the power of distinguishing and examining other things, and, as we may say, of measuring and weighing them. Who says this? Is it only Chrysippus, and Zeno, and Cleanthes? And does not Antisthenes say so? And who is it that has written that the examination of names is the beginning of education? And does not Socrates say so? And of whom does Xenophon write, that he began with the examination of names, what each name signified? Is this then the great and wondrous thing to understand or interpret Chrysippus? Who says this? What then is the wondrous thing? To understand the will of nature. Well then do you apprehend it yourself by your own power? and what more have you need of? For if it is true that all men err involuntarily, and you have learned the truth, of necessity you must act right. "But in truth I do not apprehend the will of nature." Who then tells us what it is? They say that it is Chrysippus. I proceed, and I inquire what this interpreter of nature says. I begin not to understand what he says; I seek an interpreter of Chrysippus. "Well, consider how this is said, just as if it were said in the Roman tongue." What then is this superciliousness of the interpreter? There is no superciliousness which

can justly be charged even to Chrysippus, if he only interprets the will of nature, but does not follow it himself; and much more is this so with his interpreter. For we have no need of Chrysippus for his own sake, but in order that we may understand nature. Nor do we need a diviner on his own account, but because we think that through him we shall know the future and understand the signs given by the gods; nor do we need the viscera of animals for their own sake, but because through them signs are given; nor do we look with wonder on the crow or raven, but on God, who through them gives signs?

I go then to the interpreter of these things and the sacrificer, and I say, "Inspect the viscera for me, and tell me what signs they give." The man takes the viscera, opens them, and interprets them: "Man," he says, "you have a will free by nature from hindrance and compulsion; this is written here in the viscera. I will show you this first in the matter of assent. Can any man hinder you from assenting to the truth? No man can. Can any man compel you to receive what is false? No man can. You see that in this matter you have the faculty of the will free from hindrance, free from compulsion, unimpeded." Well, then, in the matter of desire and pursuit of an object, is it otherwise? And what can overcome pursuit except another pursuit? And what can overcome desire and aversion except another desire and aversion? But, you object: "If you place before me the fear of death, you do compel me." No, it is not what is placed before you that compels, but your opinion that it is better to do so-and-so than to die. In this matter, then, it is your opinion that compelled you: that is, will compelled will.[2] For if God had made that part of Himself, which He took from Himself and gave to us, of such a nature as to be hindered or compelled either by Himself or by another, He would not then be God nor would He be taking care of us as He ought. "This," says the diviner, "I find in the victims: these are the things which are signified to you. If you choose, you are free; if you choose, you will blame no one: you will charge no one. All will be at the same time according to your mind and the mind of God."

For the sake of this divination I go to this diviner and to the philosopher, not admiring him for this interpretation, but admiring the things which he interprets.

CHAPTER 18. *That we ought not to be angry with the errors of others*

IF what philosophers say is true, that all men have one principle, as in the case of assent the persuasion that a thing is so, and in the case of dissent the persuasion that a thing is not so, and in the case of a suspense of judgment the persuasion that a thing is uncertain, so also in the case of a movement toward anything the persuasion that a thing is for a man's advantage, and it is impossible to think that one thing is advantageous and to desire another, and to judge one thing to be proper and to move toward another, why then are we angry with the many? "They are thieves and robbers," you may say. What do you mean by thieves and robbers? "They are mistaken about good and evil." Ought we then to be angry with them, or to pity them? But show them their error, and you will see how they desist from their errors. If they do not see their errors, they have nothing superior to their present opinion.

"Ought not then this robber and this adulterer to be destroyed?" By no means say so, but speak rather in this way: "This man who has been mistaken and deceived about the most important things, and blinded, not in the faculty of vision which distinguishes white and black, but in the faculty which distinguishes good and bad, should we not destroy him?" If you speak thus, you will see how inhuman this is which you say, and that it is just as if you would say, "Ought we not to destroy this blind and deaf man?" But if the greatest harm is the privation of the greatest things, and the greatest thing in every man is the will or choice such as it ought to be, and a man is deprived of this will, why are you also angry with him? Man, you ought not to be affected contrary to nature by the bad things of another. Pity him rather: drop this readiness to be offended and to hate, and these words which the many utter: "These accursed and odious fellows." How have you been made so wise at once? and how are you so

peevish? Why then are we angry? Is it because we value so much the things of which these men rob us? Do not admire your clothes, and then you will not be angry with the thief. Do not admire the beauty of your wife, and you will not be angry with the adulterer. Learn that a thief and an adulterer have no place in the things which are yours, but in those which belong to others and which are not in your power. If you dismiss these things and consider them as nothing, with whom are you still angry? But so long as you value these things, be angry with yourself rather than with the thief and the adulterer. Consider the matter thus: you have fine clothes; your neighbor has not: you have a window; you wish to air the clothes. The thief does not know wherein man's good consists, but he thinks that it consists in having fine clothes, the very thing which you also think. Must he not then come and take them away? When you show a cake to greedy persons, and swallow it all yourself, do you expect them not to snatch it from you? Do not provoke them: do not have a window: do not air your clothes. I also lately had an iron lamp placed by the side of my household gods: hearing a noise at the door, I ran down, and found that the lamp had been carried off. I reflected that he who had taken the lamp had done nothing strange. What then? To-morrow, I said, you will find an earthen lamp: for a man only loses that which he has. "I have lost my garment." The reason is that you had a garment. "I have pain in my head." Have you any pain in your horns? Why then are you troubled? for we only lose those things, we have only pains about those things which we possess.

"But the tyrant will chain." What? the leg. "He will take away." What? the neck. What then will he not chain and not take away? the will. This is why the ancients taught the maxim, "Know thyself." Therefore we ought to exercise ourselves in small things and, beginning with them, to proceed to the greater. "I have pain in the head." Do not say, "Alas!" "I have pain in the ear." Do not say, "Alas!" And I do not say that you are not allowed to groan, but do not groan inwardly; and if your slave is slow in bringing a bandage, do not cry out and torment yourself, and say, "Everybody hates me": for who would not hate such a man? For the future, relying on these opinions, walk about upright, free; not trusting to the size of your body, as an athlete, for a man ought not to be invincible in the way that an ass is.

Who then is the invincible? It is he whom none of the things disturb which are independent of the will. Then examining one circumstance after another I observe, as in the case of an athlete; he has come off victorious in the first contest: well then, as to the second? and what if there should be great heat? and what, if it should be at Olympia? And the same I say in this case: if you should throw money in his way, he will despise it. Well, suppose you put a young girl in his way, what then? and what, if it is in the dark? what if it should be a little reputation, or abuse; and what, if it should be praise; and what if it should be death? He is able to overcome all. What then if it be in heat, and what if it is in the rain, and what if he be in a melancholy mood, and what if he be asleep? He will still conquer. This is my invincible athlete.

CHAPTER 19. *How we should behave to tyrants*
IF a man possesses any superiority, or thinks that he does, when he does not, such a man, if he is uninstructed, will of necessity be puffed up through it. For instance, the tyrant says, "I am master of all." And what can you do for me? Can you give me desire which shall have no hindrance? How can you? Have you the infallible power of avoiding what you would avoid? Have you the power of moving toward an object without error? And how do you possess this power? Come, when you are in a ship, do you trust to yourself or to the helmsman? And when you are in a chariot, to whom do you trust but to the driver? And how is it in all other arts? Just the same. In what then lies your power? "All men pay respect to me." Well, I also pay respect to my platter, and I wash it and wipe it; and for the sake of my oil flask, I drive a peg into the wall. Well then, are these things superior to me? No, but they supply some of my wants, and for this reason I take care of them. Well, do I not attend to my ass? Do I not wash his feet? Do I not clean him? Do you not know

that every man has regard to himself, and to you just the same as he has regard to his ass? For who has regard to you as a man? Show me. Who wishes to become like you? Who imitates you, as he imitates Socrates? "But I can cut off your head." You say right. I had forgotten that I must have regard to you, as I would to a fever and the bile, and raise an altar to you, as there is at Rome an altar to fever.

What is it then that disturbs and terrifies the multitude? is it the tyrant and his guards? I hope that it is not so. It is not possible that what is by nature free can be disturbed by anything else, or hindered by any other thing than by itself. But it is a man's own opinions which disturb him: for when the tyrant says to a man, "I will chain your leg," he who values his leg says, "Do not; have pity": but he who values his own will says, "If it appears more advantageous to you, chain it." "Do you not care?" I do not care. "I will show you that I am master." You cannot do that. Zeus has set me free: do you think that he intended to allow his own son[1] to be enslaved? But you are master of my carcass: take it. "So when you approach me, you have no regard to me?" No, but I have regard to myself; and if you wish me to say that I have regard to you also, I tell you that I have the same regard to you that I have to my pipkin.

This is not a perverse self-regard, for the animal is constituted so as to do all things for itself. For even the sun does all things for itself; nay, even Zeus himself. But when he chooses to be the Giver of rain and the Giver of fruits, and the Father of gods and men, you see that he cannot obtain these functions and these names, if he is not useful to man; and, universally, he has made the nature of the rational animal such that it cannot obtain any one of its own proper interests, if it does not contribute something to the common interest. In this manner and sense it is not unsociable for a man to do everything for the sake of himself. For what do you expect? that a man should neglect himself and his own interest? And how in that case can there be one and the same principle in all animals, the principle of attachment to themselves?

[1] Compare i. 3.

What then? when absurd notions about things independent of our will, as if they were good and bad, lie at the bottom of our opinions, we must of necessity pay regard to tyrants; for I wish that men would pay regard to tyrants only, and not also to the bedchamber men. How is it that the man becomes all at once wise, when Cæsar has made him superintendent of the close stool? How is it that we say immediately, "Felicion spoke sensibly to me." I wish he were ejected from the bedchamber, that he might again appear to you to be a fool.

Epaphroditus[1] had a shoemaker whom he sold because he was good for nothing. This fellow by some good luck was bought by one of Cæsar's men, and became Cæsar's shoemaker. You should have seen what respect Epaphroditus paid to him: "How does the good Felicion do, I pray?" Then if any of us asked, "What is master doing?" the answer was, "He is consulting about something with Felicion." Had he not sold the man as good for nothing? Who then made him wise all at once? This is an instance of valuing something else than the things which depend on the will.

Has a man been exalted to the tribuneship? All who meet him offer their congratulations; one kisses his eyes, another the neck, and the slaves kiss his hands. He goes to his house, he finds torches lighted. He ascends the Capitol: he offers a sacrifice on the occasion. Now who ever sacrificed for having had good desires? for having acted conformably to nature? For in fact we thank the gods for those things in which we place our good.[2]

A person was talking to me to-day about the priesthood of Augustus. I say to him: "Man, let the thing alone: you will spend much for no purpose." But he replies, "Those who draw up agreements will write my name." Do you then stand by those who read them, and say to such persons, "It is I whose name is written there?" And if you can now be present on all such occasions, what will you do when you are dead? "My name will remain." Write it on a stone, and it will remain. But come, what remembrance of you will there be beyond Nicopolis? "But I shall wear

a crown of gold." If you desire a crown at all, take a crown of roses and put it on, for it will be more elegant in appearance.

CHAPTER 20. *About reason, how it contemplates itself*[3]

EVERY art and faculty contemplates certain things especially. When then it is itself of the same kind with the objects which it contemplates, it must of necessity contemplate itself also: but when it is of an unlike kind, it cannot contemplate itself. For instance, the shoemaker's art is employed on skins, but itself is entirely distinct from the material of skins: for this reason it does not contemplate itself. Again, the grammarian's art is employed about articulate speech; is then the art also articulate speech? By no means. For this reason it is not able to contemplate itself. Now reason, for what purpose has it been given by nature? For the right use of appearances. What is it then itself? A system of certain appearances. So by its nature it has the faculty of contemplating itself so. Again, sound sense, for the contemplation of what things does it belong to us? Good and evil, and things which are neither. What is it then itself? Good. And want of sense, what is it? Evil. Do you see then that good sense necessarily contemplates both itself and the opposite? For this reason it is the chief and the first work of a philosopher to examine appearances, and to distinguish them, and to admit none without examination. You see even in the matter of coin, in which our interest appears to be somewhat concerned, how we have invented an art, and how many means the assayer uses to try the value of coin, the sight, the touch, the smell, and lastly the hearing. He throws the coin down, and observes the sound, and he is not content with its sounding once, but through his great attention he becomes a musician. In like manner, where we think that to be mistaken and not to be mistaken make a great difference, there we apply great attention to discovering the things which can deceive. But in the matter of our miserable ruling faculty, yawning and sleeping, we carelessly admit every appearance, for the harm is not noticed.

[1] See i. 1.
[2] Matt. 6. 21.
[3] Compare i. 1 and 17.

When then you would know how careless you are with respect to good and evil, and how active with respect to things which are indifferent, observe how you feel with respect to being deprived of the sight of the eyes, and how with respect to being deceived, and you will discover that you are far from feeling as you ought to do in relation to good and evil. "But this is a matter which requires much preparation, and much labour and study." Well then do you expect to acquire the greatest of arts with small labour? And yet the chief doctrine of philosophers is very brief. If you would know, read Zeno's writings and you will see. For how few words it requires to say that man's end is to follow[1] the gods, and that the nature of good is a proper use of appearances. But if you say, "What is 'God,' what is 'appearance,' and what is 'particular' and what is 'universal[2] nature'?" then indeed many words are necessary. If then Epicurus should come and say that the good must be in the body; in this case also many words become necessary, and we must be taught what is the leading principle in us, and the fundamental and the substantial; and as it is not probable that the good of a snail is in the shell, is it probable that the good of a man is in the body? But you yourself, Epicurus, possess something better than this. What is that in you which deliberates, what is that which examines everything, what is that which forms a judgement about the body itself, that it is the principal part? and why do you light your lamp and labour for us, and write so many books? is it that we may not be ignorant of the truth, who we are, and what we are with respect to you? Thus the discussion requires many words.

CHAPTER 21. *Against those who wish to be admired*

WHEN a man holds his proper station in life, he does not gape after things beyond it. Man, what do you wish to happen to you? "I am satisfied if I desire and avoid conformably to nature, if I employ movements toward and from an object as I am by nature formed to do, and purpose and design and assent." Why

[1] See i. 12.
[2] Marcus Aurelius, v. 25; xi. 5.

then do you strut before us as if you had swallowed a spit? "My wish has always been that those who meet me should admire me, and those who follow me should exclaim, 'Oh, the great philosopher.'" Who are they by whom you wish to be admired? Are they not those of whom you are used to say that they are mad? Well then do you wish to be admired by madmen?

CHAPTER 22. *On precognitions*

PRECOGNITIONS are common to all men, and precognition is not contradictory to precognition. For who of us does not assume that Good is useful and eligible, and in all circumstances that we ought to follow and pursue it? And who of us does not assume that Justice is beautiful and becoming? When, then, does the contradiction arise? It arises in the adaptation of the precognitions to the particular cases. When one man says, "He has done well: he is a brave man," and another says, "Not so; but he has acted foolishly"; then the disputes arise among men. This is the dispute among the Jews and the Syrians and the Egyptians and the Romans; not whether holiness should be preferred to all things and in all cases should be pursued, but whether it is holy to eat pig's flesh or not holy. You will find this dispute also between Agamemnon and Achilles; for call them forth. What do you say, Agamemnon? ought not that to be done which is proper and right? "Certainly." Well, what do you say, Achilles? do you not admit that what is good ought to be done? "I do most certainly." Adapt your precognitions then to the present matter. Here the dispute begins. Agamemnon says, "I ought not to give up Chryseis to her father." Achilles says, "You ought." It is certain that one of the two makes a wrong adaptation of the precognition of "ought" or "duty." Further, Agamemnon says, "Then if I ought to restore Chryseis, it is fit that I take his prize from some of you." Achilles replies, "Would you then take her whom I love?" "Yes, her whom you love." "Must I then be the only man who goes without a prize? and must I be the only man who has no prize?" Thus the dispute begins.

What then is education? Education is the

learning how to adapt the natural precognitions to the particular things conformably to nature; and then to distinguish that of things some are in our power, but others are not; in our power are will and all acts which depend on the will; things not in our power are the body, the parts of the body, possessions, parents, brothers, children, country, and, generally, all with whom we live in society. In what, then, should we place the good? To what kind of things shall we adapt it? "To the things which are in our power?" Is not health then a good thing, and soundness of limb, and life? and are not children and parents and country? Who will tolerate you if you deny this?

Let us then transfer the notion of good to these things. Is it possible, then, when a man sustains damage and does not obtain good things, that he can be happy? "It is not possible." And can he maintain toward society a proper behavior? He cannot. For I am naturally formed to look after my own interest. If it is my interest to have an estate in land, it is my interest also to take it from my neighbor. If it is my interest to have a garment, it is my interest also to steal it from the bath.[1] This is the origin of wars, civil commotions, tyrannies, conspiracies. And how shall I be still able to maintain my duty toward Zeus? for if I sustain damage and am unlucky, he takes no care of me; and what is he to me if he allows me to be in the condition in which I am? I now begin to hate him. Why, then, do we build temples, why set up statues to Zeus, as well as to evil demons, such as to Fever; and how is Zeus the Saviour, and how the Giver of rain, and the Giver of fruits? And in truth if we place the nature of Good in any such things, all this follows.

What should we do then? This is the inquiry of the true philosopher who is in labour.[2] "Now I do not see what the Good is nor the Bad. Am I not mad? Yes." But suppose that I place the good somewhere among the things which depend on the will: all will laugh at me. There will come some grey-head wearing many gold rings on his fingers, and he will shake his head and say, "Hear, my child. It is right that you should philosophize; but you ought to have some brains also: all this that you are doing is silly. You learn the syllogism from philosophers; but you know how to act better than philosophers do." Man, why then do you blame me, if I know? What shall I say to this slave? If I am silent, he will burst. I must speak in this way: "Excuse me, as you would excuse lovers: I am not my own master: I am mad."

CHAPTER 23. *Against Epicurus*

EVEN Epicurus perceives that we are by nature social, but having once placed our good in the husk[3] he is no longer able to say anything else. For on the other hand he strongly maintains this, that we ought not to admire nor to accept anything which is detached from the nature of good; and he is right in maintaining this. How then are we [suspicious],[4] if we have no natural affection to our children? Why do you advise the wise man not to bring up children? Why are you afraid that he may thus fall into trouble? For does he fall into trouble on account of the mouse which is nurtured in the house? What does he care if a little mouse in the house makes lamentation to him? But Epicurus knows that if once a child is born, it is no longer in our power not to love it nor care about it. For this reason, Epicurus says that a man who has any sense also does not engage in political matters; for he knows what a man must do who is engaged in such things; for, indeed, if you intend to behave among men as you do among a swarm of flies, what hinders you? But Epicurus, who knows this, ventures to say that we should not bring up children. But a sheep does not desert its own offspring, nor yet a wolf; and shall a man desert his child? What do you mean? that we should be as silly as sheep? but not even do they desert their offspring: or as savage as wolves, but not even do wolves desert their young. Well, who would follow your advice, if he saw his child weeping after falling on the ground? For my part I think that, even if your mother and your father had been told by an oracle that you would say what you have said, they would not have cast you away.

---

[1] Jam. 4. 1.
[2] Compare Plato, *Theætetus*, 150.

[3] See i. 20. Compare ii. 20.
[4] The word is not intelligible.

CHAPTER 24. *How we should struggle with circumstances*

IT is circumstances which show what men are. Therefore when a difficulty falls upon you, remember that God, like a trainer of wrestlers, has matched you with a rough young man. "For what purpose?" you may say. Why, that you may become an Olympic conqueror; but it is not accomplished without sweat. In my opinion no man has had a more profitable difficulty than you have had, if you choose to make use of it as an athlete would deal with a young antagonist. We are now sending a scout to Rome; but no man sends a cowardly scout, who, if he only hears a noise and sees a shadow anywhere, comes running back in terror and reports that the enemy is close at hand. So now if you should come and tell us, "Fearful is the state of affairs at Rome, terrible is death, terrible is exile; terrible is calumny; terrible is poverty; fly, my friends; the enemy is near"; we shall answer, "Begone, prophesy for yourself; we have committed only one fault, that we sent such a scout."

Diogenes,[1] who was sent as a scout before you, made a different report to us. He says that death is no evil, for neither is it base: he says that fame is the noise of madmen. And what has this spy said about pain, about pleasure, and about poverty? He says that to be naked is better than any purple robe, and to sleep on the bare ground is the softest bed; and he gives as a proof of each thing that he affirms his own courage, his tranquillity, his freedom, and the healthy appearance and compactness of his body. "There is no enemy near," he says; "all is peace." How so, Diogenes? "See," he replies, "if I am struck, if I have been wounded, if I have fled from any man." This is what a scout ought to be. But you come to us and tell us one thing after another. Will you not go back, and you will see clearer when you have laid aside fear?

What then shall I do? What do you do when you leave a ship? Do you take away the helm or the oars? What then do you take away? You take what is your own, your bottle and your wallet; and now if you think of what is your own, you will never claim what belongs to others. The emperor says, "Lay

aside your laticlave."[2] See, I put on the angusticlave. "Lay aside this also." See, I have only my toga. "Lay aside your toga." See, I am now naked. "But you still raise my envy." Take then all my poor body; when, at a man's command, I can throw away my poor body, do I still fear him?

"But a certain person will not leave to me the succession to his estate." What then? had I forgotten that not one of these things was mine. How then do we call them mine? Just as we call the bed in the inn. If, then, the innkeeper at his death leaves you the beds, all well; but if he leaves them to another, he will have them, and you will seek another bed. If then you shall not find one, you will sleep on the ground: only sleep with a good will and snore, and remember that tragedies have their place among the rich and kings and tyrants, but no poor man fills a part in the tragedy, except as one of the chorus. Kings indeed commence with prosperity: "ornament the palaces with garlands," then about the third or fourth act they call out, "O Cithæron, why didst thou receive me?"[3] Slave, where are the crowns, where the diadem? The guards help thee not at all. When then you approach any of these persons, remember this that you are approaching a tragedian, not the actor but Œdipus himself. But you say, "Such a man is happy; for he walks about with many," and I also place myself with the many and walk about with many. In sum remember this: the door is open;[4] be not more timid than little children, but as they say, when the thing does not please them, "I will play no longer," so do you, when things seem to you of such a kind, say I will no longer play, and begone: but if you stay, do not complain.

CHAPTER 25. *On the same*

IF these things are true, and if we are not silly, and are not acting hypocritically when we say that the good of man is in the will, and the evil too, and that everything else does not concern us, why are we still disturbed, why are we still afraid? The things about which we

---

[1] See iii. 22.

[2] Laticlave, the dress of a senator; angusticlave, the dress of the equestrian order.

[3] Sophocles, *Œdipus the King*, 1390.

[4] Compare i. 9.

have been busied are in no man's power: and the things which are in the power of others, we care not for. What kind of trouble have we still?

"But give me directions." Why should I give you directions? has not Zeus given you directions? Has he not given to you what is your own free from hindrance and free from impediment, and what is not your own subject to hindrance and impediment? What directions then, what kind of orders did you bring when you came from him? Keep by every means what is your own; do not desire what belongs to others. Fidelity is your own, virtuous shame is your own; who then can take these things from you? who else than yourself will hinder you from using them? But how do you act? when you seek what is not your own, you lose that which is your own. Having such promptings and commands from Zeus, what kind do you still ask from me? Am I more powerful than he, am I more worthy of confidence? But if you observe these, do you want any others besides? "Well, but he has not given these orders," you will say. Produce your precognitions, produce the proofs of philosophers, produce what you have often heard, and produce what you have said yourself, produce what you have read, produce what you have meditated on (and you will then see that all these things are from God).[1] How long, then, is it fit to observe these precepts from God, and not to break up the play?[2] As long as the play is continued with propriety. In the Saturnalia[3] a king is chosen by lot, for it has been the custom to play at this game. The king commands: "Do you drink," "Do you mix the wine," "Do you sing," "Do you go," "Do you come." I obey that the game may not be broken up through me. But if he says, "Think that you are in evil plight": I answer, "I do not think so"; and who will compel me to think so? Further, we agreed to play Agamemnon and Achilles. He who is appointed to play Agamemnon says to me, "Go to Achilles and tear from him Briseis." I go. He says, "Come," and I come.

For as we behave in the matter of hypothetical arguments, so ought we to do in life. "Suppose it to be night." I suppose that it is night. "Well then; is it day?" No, for I admitted the hypothesis that it was night. "Suppose that you think that it is night?" Suppose that I do. "But also think that it is night." That is not consistent with the hypothesis. So in this case also: "Suppose that you are unfortunate." Well, suppose so. "Are you then unhappy?" Yes. "Well, then, are you troubled with an unfavourable demon?" Yes. "But think also that you are in misery." This is not consistent with the hypothesis; and Another[4] forbids me to think so.

How long then must we obey such orders? As long as it is profitable; and this means as long as I maintain that which is becoming and consistent. Further, some men are sour and of bad temper, and they say, "I cannot sup with this man to be obliged to hear him telling daily how he fought in Mysia: 'I told you, brother, how I ascended the hill: then I began to be besieged again.' " But another says, "I prefer to get my supper and to hear him talk as much as he likes." And do you compare these estimates: only do nothing in a depressed mood, nor as one afflicted, nor as thinking that you are in misery, for no man compels you to that. Has it smoked in the chamber? If the smoke is moderate, I will stay; if it is excessive, I go out: for you must always remember this and hold it fast, that the door is open. Well, but you say to me, "Do not live in Nicopolis." I will not live there. "Nor in Athens." I will not live in Athens. "Nor in Rome." I will not live in Rome. "Live in Gyarus." I will live in Gyarus, but it seems like a great smoke to live in Gyarus; and I depart to the place where no man will hinder me from living, for that dwelling-place is open to all; and as to the last garment, that is the poor body, no one has any power over me beyond this. This was the reason why Demetrius said to Nero, "You threaten me with death, but nature threatens you." If I set my admiration on the poor body, I have given myself up to be a slave: if on my little possessions, I also make myself a slave: for I immediately make it plain with what I may be caught; as

---

[1] The conclusion is not in the text, but it is what Epictetus means.

[2] See the end of the preceding chapter. Compare also Epictetus, ii. 16.

[3] Compare Tacitus, *Annals,* xiii. 15.

[4] Zeus.

if the snake draws in his head, I tell you to strike that part of him which he guards; and do you be assured that whatever part you choose to guard, that part your master will attack. Remembering this, whom will you still flatter or fear?

"But I should like to sit where the Senators sit." Do you see that you are putting yourself in straits, you are squeezing yourself. "How then shall I see well in any other way in the amphitheatre?" Man, do not be a spectator at all; and you will not be squeezed. Why do you give yourself trouble? Or wait a little, and when the spectacle is over, seat yourself in the place reserved for the Senators and sun yourself. For remember this general truth, that it is we who squeeze ourselves, who put ourselves in straits; that is, our opinions squeeze us and put us in straits. For what is it to be reviled? Stand by a stone and revile it; and what will you gain? If, then, a man listens like a stone, what profit is there to the reviler? But if the reviler has as a stepping-stone the weakness of him who is reviled, then he accomplishes something. "Strip him." What do you mean by "him"? Lay hold of his garment, strip it off. "I have insulted you." Much good may it do you.

This was the practice of Socrates: this was the reason why he always had one face. But we choose to practice and study anything rather than the means by which we shall be unimpeded and free. You say, "Philosophers talk paradoxes."[1] But are there no paradoxes in the other arts? and what is more paradoxical than to puncture a man's eye in order that he may see? If any one said this to a man ignorant of the surgical art, would he not ridicule the speaker? Where is the wonder then if in philosophy also many things which are true appear paradoxical to the inexperienced?

CHAPTER 26. *What is the law of life*
WHEN a person was reading hypothetical arguments, Epictetus said: This also is an hypothetical law that we must accept what follows from the hypothesis. But much before this law is the law of life, that we must act conformably to nature. For if in every matter and circumstance we wish to observe what is natural, it

[1] See iv. 1.

is plain that in everything we ought to make it our aim that that which is consequent shall not escape us, and that we do not admit the contradictory. First, then, philosophers exercise us in theory, which is easier; and then next they lead us to the more difficult things; for in theory, there is nothing which draws us away from following what is taught; but in the matters of life, many are the things which distract us. He is ridiculous, then, who says that he wishes to begin with the matters of real life, for it is not easy to begin with the more difficult things; and we ought to employ this fact as an argument to those parents who are vexed at their children learning philosophy: "Am I doing wrong then, my father, and do I not know what is suitable to me and becoming? If indeed this can neither be learned nor taught, why do you blame me? but if it can be taught, teach me; and if you cannot, allow me to learn from those who say that they know how to teach. For what do you think? do you suppose that I voluntarily fall into evil and miss the good? I hope that it may not be so. What is then the cause of my doing wrong? Ignorance. Do you not choose then that I should get rid of my ignorance? Who was ever taught by anger the art of a pilot or music? Do you think then that by means of your anger I shall learn the art of life?" He only is allowed to speak in this way who has shown such an intention. But if a man only intending to make a display at a banquet and to show that he is acquainted with hypothetical arguments reads them and attends the philosophers, what other object has he than that some man of senatorian rank who sits by him may admire? For there[2] are the really great materials, and the riches here[3] appear to be trifles there. This is the reason why it is difficult for a man to be master of the appearances, where the things which disturb the judgement are great. I know a certain person who complained, as he embraced the knees of Epaphroditus, that he had only one hundred and fifty times ten thousand denarii remaining. What then did Epaphroditus do? Did he laugh at him, as we slaves of Epaphroditus did? No, but he cried out with amazement,

[2] Rome.
[3] Nicopolis.

"Poor man, how then did you keep silence, how did you endure it?"

When Epictetus had reproved the person who was reading the hypothetical arguments, and the teacher who had suggested the reading was laughing at the reader, Epictetus said to the teacher: "You are laughing at yourself; you did not prepare the young man nor did you ascertain whether he was able to understand these matters; but perhaps you are only employing him as a reader." Well then, said Epictetus, if a man has not ability enough to understand a complex, do we trust him in giving praise, do we trust him in giving blame, do we allow that he is able to form a judgement about good or bad? and if such a man blames any one, does the man care for the blame? and if he praises any one, is the man elated, when in such small matters as an hypothetical syllogism he who praises cannot see what is consequent on the hypothesis?

This then is the beginning of philosophy,[1] a man's perception of the state of his ruling faculty; for when a man knows that it is weak, then he will not employ it on things of the greatest difficulty. But at present, if men cannot swallow even a morsel, they buy whole volumes and attempt to devour them; and this is the reason why they vomit them up or suffer indigestion: and then come gripings, defluxes, and fevers. Such men ought to consider what their ability is. In theory it is easy to convince an ignorant person; but in the affairs of real life no one offers himself to be convinced, and we hate the man who has convinced us. But Socrates advised us not to live a life which is not subjected to examination.[2]

CHAPTER 27. *In how many ways appearances exist, and what aids we should provide against them*

APPEARANCES are to us in four ways: for either things appear as they are; or they are not, and do not even appear to be; or they are, and do not appear to be; or they are not, and yet appear to be. Further, in all these cases to form a right judgement is the office of an educated man. But whatever it is that annoys us, to that we ought to apply a remedy. If the sophisms

[1] See ii. 11.
[2] See Plato, *Apology,* 38; and Marcus Aurelius, iii. 5.

of Pyrrho and of the Academics are what annoys, we must apply the remedy to them. If it is the persuasion of appearances, by which some things appear to be good, when they are not good, let us seek a remedy for this. If it is habit which annoys us, we must try to seek aid against habit. What aid then can we find against habit? The contrary habit. You hear the ignorant say: "That unfortunate person is dead: his father and mother are overpowered with sorrow; he was cut off by an untimely death and in a foreign land." Here the contrary way of speaking: tear yourself from these expressions: oppose to one habit the contrary habit; to sophistry oppose reason, and the exercise and discipline of reason; against persuasive appearances we ought to have manifest precognitions, cleared of all impurities and ready to hand.

When death appears an evil, we ought to have this rule in readiness, that it is fit to avoid evil things, and that death is a necessary thing. For what shall I do, and where shall I escape it? Suppose that I am not Sarpedon, the son of Zeus, nor able to speak in this noble way: "I will go and I am resolved either to behave bravely myself or to give to another the opportunity of doing so; if I cannot succeed in doing anything myself, I will not grudge another the doing of something noble." Suppose that it is above our power to act thus; is it not in our power to reason thus? Tell me where I can escape death: discover for me the country, show me the men to whom I must go, whom death does not visit. Discover to me a charm against death. If I have not one, what do you wish me to do? I cannot escape from death. Shall I not escape from the fear of death, but shall I die lamenting and trembling? For the origin of perturbation is this, to wish for something, and that this should not happen. Therefore if I am able to change externals according to my wish, I change them; but if I cannot, I am ready to tear out the eyes of him who hinders me. For the nature of man is not to endure to be deprived of the good, and not to endure the falling into the evil. Then, at last, when I am neither able to change circumstances nor to tear out the eyes of him who hinders me, I sit down and groan, and abuse whom I can, Zeus and the rest of the gods. For if they do not care for me, what are they to me? "Yes, but you will be an impious man." In what respect then will it be worse for me than it is now? To sum up, remember this that unless piety and your interest be in the same thing, piety cannot be maintained in any man. Do not these things seem necessary?

Let the followers of Pyrrho and the Academics come and make their objections. For I, as to my part, have no leisure for these disputes, nor am I able to undertake the defense of common consent. If I had a suit even about a bit of land, I would call in another to defend my interests. With what evidence then am I satisfied? With that which belongs to the matter in hand. How indeed perception is effected, whether through the whole body or any part, perhaps I cannot explain: for both opinions perplex me. But that you and I are not the same, I know with perfect certainty. "How do you know it?" When I intend to swallow anything, I never carry it to your mouth, but to my own. When I intend to take bread, I never lay hold of a broom, but I always go to the bread as to a mark. And you yourselves[1] who take away the evidence of the senses, do you act otherwise? Who among you, when he intended to enter a bath, ever went into a mill?

What then? Ought we not with all our power to hold to this also, the maintaining of general opinion, and fortifying ourselves against the arguments which are directed against it? Who denies that we ought to do this? Well, he should do it who is able, who has leisure for it; but as to him who trembles and is perturbed and is inwardly broken in heart, he must employ his time better on something else.

CHAPTER 28. *That we ought not to be angry with men; and what are the small and the great things among men*[2]
WHAT is the cause of assenting to anything? The fact that it appears to be true. It is not possible then to assent to that which appears not to be true. Why? Because this is the nature of the understanding, to incline to the true, to be dissatisfied with the false, and in matters uncertain to withhold assent. What is

the proof of this? "Imagine, if you can, that it is now night." It is not possible. "Take away your persuasion that it is day." It is not possible. "Persuade yourself or take away your persuasion that the stars are even in number." It is impossible. When, then, any man assents to that which is false, be assured that he did not intend to assent to it as false, for every soul is unwillingly deprived of the truth, as Plato says; but the falsity seemed to him to be true. Well, in acts what have we of the like kind as we have here truth or falsehood? We have the fit and the not fit, the profitable and the unprofitable, that which is suitable to a person and that which is not, and whatever is like these. Can, then, a man think that a thing is useful to him and not choose it? He cannot. How says Medea?

" 'Tis true I know what evil I shall do,
But passion overpowers the better counsel."[3]

She thought that to indulge her passion and take vengeance on her husband was more profitable than to spare her children. "It was so; but she was deceived." Show her plainly that she is deceived, and she will not do it; but so long as you do not show it, what can she follow except that which appears to herself? Nothing else. Why, then, are you angry with the unhappy woman that she has been bewildered about the most important things, and is become a viper instead of a human creature? And why not, if it is possible, rather pity, as we pity the blind and the lame, those who are blinded and maimed in the faculties which are supreme?

Whoever, then, clearly remembers this, that to man the measure of every act is the appearance—whether the thing appears good or bad: if good, he is free from blame; if bad, himself suffers the penalty, for it is impossible that he who is deceived can be one person, and he who suffers another person—whoever remembers this will not be angry with any man, will not be vexed at any man, will not revile or blame any man, nor hate nor quarrel with any man.

"So then all these great and dreadful deeds have this origin, in the appearance?" Yes, this origin and no other. The *Iliad* is nothing

---

[1] The Pyrrhonists.   [2] See i. 18.   [3] Euripides, *Medea*, 1079.

else than appearance and the use of appearances. It appeared to Paris to carry off the wife of Menelaus: it appeared to Helen to follow him. If then it had appeared to Menelaus to feel that it was a gain to be deprived of such a wife, what would have happened? Not only would the *Iliad* have been lost, but the *Odyssey* also. "On so small a matter then did such great things depend?" But what do you mean by such great things? Wars and civil commotions, and the destruction of many men and cities. And what great matter is this? "Is it nothing?" But what great matter is the death of many oxen, and many sheep, and many nests of swallows or storks being burnt or destroyed? "Are these things, then, like those?" Very like. Bodies of men are destroyed, and the bodies of oxen and sheep; the dwellings of men are burnt, and the nests of storks. What is there in this great or dreadful? Or show me what is the difference between a man's house and a stork's nest, as far as each is a dwelling; except that man builds his little houses of beams and tiles and bricks, and the stork builds them of sticks and mud. "Are a stork and a man, then, like things?" What say you? In body they are very much alike.

"Does a man then differ in no respect from a stork?" Don't suppose that I say so; but there is no difference in these matters. "In what, then, is the difference?" Seek and you will find that there is a difference in another matter. See whether it is not in a man the understanding of what he does, see if it is not in social community, in fidelity, in modesty, in steadfastness, in intelligence. Where then is the great good and evil in men? It is where the difference is. If the difference is preserved and remains fenced round, and neither modesty is destroyed, nor fidelity, nor intelligence, then the man also is preserved; but if any of these things is destroyed and stormed like a city, then the man too perishes; and in this consist the great things. Paris, you say, sustained great damage, then, when the Hellenes invaded and when they ravaged Troy, and when his brothers perished. By no means; for no man is damaged by an action which is not his own; but what happened at that time was only the destruction of storks' nests: now the ruin of Paris was when he lost the character

of modesty, fidelity, regard to hospitality, and to decency. When was Achilles ruined? Was it when Patroclus died? Not so. But it happened when he began to be angry, when he wept for a girl, when he forgot that he was at Troy not to get mistresses, but to fight. These things are the ruin of men, this is being besieged, this is the destruction of cities, when right opinions are destroyed, when they are corrupted.

"When, then, women are carried off, when children are made captives, and when the men are killed, are these not evils?" How is it then that you add to the facts these opinions? Explain this to me also. "I shall not do that; but how is it that you say that these are not evils?" Let us come to the rules: produce the precognitions: for it is because this is neglected that we cannot sufficiently wonder at what men do. When we intend to judge of weights, we do not judge by guess: where we intend to judge of straight and crooked, we do not judge by guess. In all cases where it is our interest to know what is true in any matter, never will any man among us do anything by guess. But in things which depend on the first and on the only cause of doing right or wrong, of happiness or unhappiness, of being unfortunate or fortunate, there only we are inconsiderate and rash. There is then nothing like scales, nothing like a rule: but some appearance is presented, and straightway I act according to it. Must I then suppose that I am superior to Achilles or Agamemnon, so that they by following appearances do and suffer so many evils: and shall not the appearance be sufficient for me? And what tragedy has any other beginning? The *Atreus* of Euripides, what is it? An appearance. The *Œdipus* of Sophocles, what is it? An appearance. The *Phœnix?* An appearance. The *Hippolytus?* An appearance. What kind of a man then do you suppose him to be who pays no regard to this matter? And what is the name of those who follow every appearance? "They are called madmen." Do we then act at all differently?

CHAPTER 29. *On constancy*

THE being of the Good is a certain Will; the being of the Bad is a certain kind of Will. What then are externals? Materials for the

Will, about which the will being conversant shall obtain its own good or evil. How shall it obtain the good? If it does not admire the materials; for the opinions about the materials, if the opinions are right, make the will good: but perverse and distorted opinions make the will bad. God has fixed this law, and says, "If you would have anything good, receive it from yourself." You say, "No, but I will have it from another." Do not so: but receive it from yourself. Therefore when the tyrant threatens and calls me, I say, "Whom do you threaten?" If he says, "I will put you in chains," I say, "You threaten my hands and my feet." If he says, "I will cut off your head," I reply, "You threaten my head." If he says, "I will throw you into prison," I say, "You threaten the whole of this poor body." If he threatens me with banishment, I say the same. "Does he, then, not threaten you at all?" If I feel that all these things do not concern me, he does not threaten me at all; but if I fear any of them, it is I whom he threatens. Whom then do I fear? the master of what? The master of things which are in my own power? There is no such master. Do I fear the master of things which are not in my power? And what are these things to me?

"Do you philosophers then teach us to despise kings?" I hope not. Who among us teaches to claim against them the power over things which they possess? Take my poor body, take my property, take my reputation, take those who are about me. If I advise any persons to claim these things, they may truly accuse me. "Yes, but I intend to command your opinions also." And who has given you this power? How can you conquer the opinion of another man? "By applying terror to it," he replies, "I will conquer it." Do you not know that opinion conquers itself, and is not conquered by another? But nothing else can conquer Will except the Will itself. For this reason, too, the law of God is most powerful and most just, which is this: "Let the stronger always be superior to the weaker." "Ten are stronger than one." For what? For putting in chains, for killing, for dragging whither they choose, for taking away what a man has. The ten therefore conquer the one in this in which they are stronger. "In what then are the ten

weaker?" If the one possess right opinions and the others do not. "Well then, can the ten conquer in this matter?" How is it possible? If we were placed in the scales, must not the heavier draw down the scale in which it is?

"How strange, then, that Socrates should have been so treated by the Athenians." Slave, why do you say Socrates? Speak of the thing as it is: how strange that the poor body of Socrates should have been carried off and dragged to prison by stronger men, and that any one should have given hemlock to the poor body of Socrates, and that it should breathe out the life. Do these things seem strange, do they seem unjust, do you on account of these things blame God? Had Socrates then no equivalent for these things? Where, then, for him was the nature of good? Whom shall we listen to, you or him? And what does Socrates say? "Anytus and Meletus[1] can kill me, but they cannot hurt me": and further, he says, "If it so pleases God, so let it be."

But show me that he who has the inferior principles overpowers him who is superior in principles. You will never show this, nor come near showing it; for this is the law of nature and of God that the superior shall always overpower the inferior. In what? In that in which it is superior. One body is stronger than another: many are stronger than one: the thief is stronger than he who is not a thief. This is the reason why I also lost my lamp,[2] because in wakefulness the thief was superior to me. But the man bought the lamp at this price: for a lamp he became a thief, a faithless fellow, and like a wild beast. This seemed to him a good bargain. Be it so. But a man has seized me by the cloak, and is drawing me to the public place: then others bawl out, "Philosopher, what has been the use of your opinions? see you are dragged to prison, you are going to be beheaded." And what system of philosophy could I have made so that, if a stronger man should have laid hold of my cloak, I should not be dragged off; that if ten men should have laid hold of me and cast me into prison, I should not be cast in? Have I learned nothing else then? I have learned to

[1] Plato, *Apology*, 30; Epictetus, ii. 2.　　[2] See i. 18.

see that everything which happens, if it be independent of my will, is nothing to me. I may ask if you have not gained by this. Why then do you seek advantage in anything else than in that in which you have learned that advantage is?

Then sitting in prison I say: "The man who cries out in this way neither hears what words mean, nor understands what is said, nor does he care at all to know what philosophers say or what they do. Let him alone."

But now he says to the prisoner, "Come out from your prison." If you have no further need of me in prison, I come out: if you should have need of me again, I will enter the prison. "How long will you act thus?" So long as reason requires me to be with the body: but when reason does not require this, take away the body, and fare you well.[1] Only we must not do it inconsiderately, nor weakly, nor for any slight reason; for, on the other hand, God does not wish it to be done, and he has need of such a world and such inhabitants in it.[2] But if he sounds the signal for retreat, as he did to Socrates, we must obey him who gives the signal, as if he were a general.[3]

"Well, then, ought we to say such things to the many?" Why should we? Is it not enough for a man to be persuaded himself? When children come clapping their hands and crying out, "To-day is the good Saturnalia,"[4] do we say, "The Saturnalia are not good?" By no means, but we clap our hands also. Do you also then, when you are not able to make a man change his mind, be assured that he is a child, and clap your hands with him, and if you do not choose to do this, keep silent.

A man must keep this in mind; and when he is called to any such difficulty, he should know that the time is come for showing if he has been instructed. For he who is come into a difficulty is like a young man from a school who has practiced the resolution of syllogisms; and if any person proposes to him an easy syllogism, he says, "Rather propose to me a syllogism which is skillfully complicated that I may exercise myself on it." Even athletes are

[1] See i. 9.
[2] See i. 6.
[3] Plato, *Apology*, 38-42; Epictetus, i. 9.
[4] See i. 25.

dissatisfied with slight young men, and say, "He cannot lift me." "This is a youth of noble disposition." But when the time of trial is come, one of you must weep and say, "I wish that I had learned more." A little more of what? If you did not learn these things in order to show them in practice, why did you learn them? I think that there is some one among you who are sitting here, who is suffering like a woman in labour, and saying, "Oh, that such a difficulty does not present itself to me as that which has come to this man; oh, that I should be wasting my life in a corner, when I might be crowned at Olympia. When will any one announce to me such a contest?" Such ought to be the disposition of all of you. Even among the gladiators of Cæsar there are some who complain grievously that they are not brought forward and matched, and they offer up prayers to God and address themselves to their superintendents entreating that they might fight. And will no one among you show himself such? I would willingly take a voyage for this purpose and see what my athlete is doing, how he is studying his subject. "I do not choose such a subject," he says. Why, is it in your power to take what subject you choose? There has been given to you such a body as you have, such parents, such brethren, such a country, such a place in your country: then you come to me and say, "Change my subject." Have you not abilities which enable you to manage the subject which has been given to you? "It is your business to propose; it is mine to exercise myself well." However, you do not say so, but you say, "Do not propose to me such a tropic, but such: do not urge against me such an objection, but such." There will be a time, perhaps, when tragic actors will suppose that they are masks and buskins and the long cloak. I say, these things, man, are your material and subject. Utter something that we may know whether you are a tragic actor or a buffoon; for both of you have all the rest in common. If any one then should take away the tragic actor's buskins and his mask, and introduce him on the stage as a phantom, is the tragic actor lost, or does he still remain? If he has voice, he still remains.

An example of another kind. "Assume the

governorship of a province." I assume it, and when I have assumed it, I show how an instructed man behaves. "Lay aside the laticlave and, clothing yourself in rags, come forward in this character." What then have I not the power of displaying a good voice? How, then, do you now appear? As a witness summoned by God. "Come forward, you, and bear testimony for me, for you are worthy to be brought forward as a witness by me: is anything external to the will good or bad? do I hurt any man? have I made every man's interest dependent on any man except himself?" What testimony do you give for God? "I am in a wretched condition, Master, and I am unfortunate; no man cares for me, no man gives me anything; all blame me, all speak ill of me." Is this the evidence that you are going to give, and disgrace his summons, who has conferred so much honour on you, and thought you worthy of being called to bear such testimony?

But suppose that he who has the power has declared, "I judge you to be impious and profane." What has happened to you? "I have been judged to be impious and profane?" Nothing else? "Nothing else." But if the same person had passed judgment on an hypothetical syllogism, and had made a declaration, "the conclusion that, if it is day, it is light, I declare to be false," what has happened to the hypothetical syllogism? who is judged in this case? who has been condemned? the hypothetical syllogism, or the man who has been deceived by it? Does he, then, who has the power of making any declaration about you know what is pious or impious? Has he studied it, and has he learned it? Where? From whom? Then is it the fact that a musician pays no regard to him who declares that the lowest chord in the lyre is the highest; nor yet a geometrician, if he declares that the lines from the centre of a circle to the circumference are not equal; and shall he who is really instructed pay any regard to the uninstructed man when he pronounces judgment on what is pious and what is impious, on what is just and unjust? Oh, the signal wrong done by the instructed. Did they learn this here?

Will you not leave the small arguments about these matters to others, to lazy fellows, that they may sit in a corner and receive their sorry pay, or grumble that no one gives them anything; and will you not come forward and make use of what you have learned? For it is not these small arguments that are wanted now: the writings of the Stoics are full of them. What then is the thing which is wanted? A man who shall apply them, one who by his acts shall bear testimony to his words.[1] Assume, I entreat you, this character, that we may no longer use in the schools the examples of the ancients, but may have some example of our own.

To whom then does the contemplation of these matters belong? To him who has leisure, for man is an animal that loves contemplation. But it is shameful to contemplate these things as runaway slaves do; we should sit, as in a theatre, free from distraction, and listen at one time to the tragic actor, at another time to the lute-player; and not do as slaves do. As soon as the slave has taken his station he praises the actor and at the same time looks round: then if any one calls out his master's name, the slave is immediately frightened and disturbed. It is shameful for philosophers thus to contemplate the works of nature. For what is a master? Man is not the master of man; but death is, and life and pleasure and pain; for if he comes without these things, bring Cæsar to me and you will see how firm I am. But when he shall come with these things, thundering and lightning,[2] and when I am afraid of them, what do I do then except to recognize my master like the runaway slave? But so long as I have any respite from these terrors, as a runaway slave stands in the theatre, so do I: I bathe, I drink, I sing; but all this I do with terror and uneasiness. But if I shall release myself from my masters, that is from those things by means of which masters are formidable, what further trouble have I, what master have I still?

"What then, ought we to publish these things to all men?" No, but we ought to accommodate ourselves to the ignorant and to say: "This man recommends to me that which he thinks good for himself: I excuse him."

---

[1] Jam. 2. 14-18.
[2] Aristophanes, *The Acharnians*, 531.

For Socrates also excused the gaoler, who had the charge of him in prison and was weeping when Socrates was going to drink the poison, and said, "How generously he laments over us."[1] Does he then say to the gaoler that for this reason we have sent away the women? No, but he says it to his friends who were able to hear it; and he treats the gaoler as a child.

CHAPTER 30. *What we ought to have ready in difficult circumstances*

WHEN you are going into any great personage, remember that Another also from above sees what is going on, and that you ought to please Him rather than the other. He, then, who sees from above asks you: "In the schools what used you to say about exile and bonds and death and disgrace?" I used to say that they are things indifferent. "What then do you say of them now? Are they changed at all?" No. "Are you changed then?" No. "Tell me

[1] Plato, *Phædo*, 116.

then what things are indifferent?" The things which are independent of the will. "Tell me, also, what follows from this." The things which are independent of the will are nothing to me. "Tell me also about the Good, what was your opinion?" A will such as we ought to have and also such a use of appearances. "And the end, what is it?" To follow Thee. "Do you say this now also?" I say the same now also.

Then go into the great personage boldly and remember these things; and you will see what a youth is who has studied these things when he is among men who have not studied them. I indeed imagine that you will have such thoughts as these: "Why do we make so great and so many preparations for nothing? Is this the thing which men name power? Is this the antechamber? this the men of the bedchamber? this the armed guards? Is it for this that I listened to so many discourses? All this is nothing: but I have been preparing myself for something great."

· BOOK TWO ·

CHAPTER 1. *That confidence is not inconsistent with caution*

THE opinion of the philosophers, perhaps, seems to some to be a paradox; but still let us examine as well as we can, if it is true that it is possible to do everything both with caution and with confidence. For caution seems to be in a manner contrary to confidence, and contraries are in no way consistent. That which seems to many to be a paradox in the matter under consideration in my opinion is of this kind: if we asserted that we ought to employ caution and confidence in the same things, men might justly accuse us of bringing together things which cannot be united. But now where is the difficulty in what is said? for if these things are true, which have been often said and often proved, that the nature of good is in the use of appearances, and the nature of evil likewise, and that things independent of our will do not admit either the nature of evil nor of good, what paradox do the philosophers assert if they say that where

things are not dependent on the will, there you should employ confidence, but where they are dependent on the will, there you should employ caution? For if the bad consists in a bad exercise of the will, caution ought only to be used where things are dependent on the will. But if things independent of the will and not in our power are nothing to us, with respect to these we must employ confidence; and thus we shall both be cautious and confident, and indeed confident because of our caution. For by employing caution toward things which are really bad, it will result that we shall have confidence with respect to things which are not so.

We are then in the condition of deer;[2] when they flee from the huntsmen's feathers in fright, whither do they turn and in what do they seek refuge as safe? They turn to the nets, and thus they perish by confounding things which are objects of fear with things that they ought not to fear. Thus we also act:

[2] Virgil, *Georgics*, iii. 372.

in what cases do we fear? In things which are independent of the will. In what cases, on the contrary, do we behave with confidence, as if there were no danger? In things dependent on the will. To be deceived then, or to act rashly, or shamelessly or with base desire to seek something, does not concern us at all, if we only hit the mark in things which are independent of our will. But where there is death, or exile or pain or infamy, there we attempt to run away, there we are struck with terror. Therefore, as we may expect it to happen with those who err in the greatest matters, we convert natural confidence into audacity, desperation, rashness, shamelessness; and we convert natural caution and modesty into cowardice and meanness, which are full of fear and confusion. For if a man should transfer caution to those things in which the will may be exercised and the acts of the will, he will immediately, by willing to be cautious, have also the power of avoiding what he chooses: but if he transfer it to the things which are not in his power and will, and attempt to avoid the things which are in the power of others, he will of necessity fear, he will be unstable, he will be disturbed. For death or pain is not formidable, but the fear of pain or death. For this reason we commend the poet who said

Not death is evil, but a shameful death.[1]

Confidence then ought to be employed against death, and caution against the fear of death. But now we do the contrary, and employ against death the attempt to escape; and to our opinion about it we employ carelessness, rashness and indifference. These things Socrates[2] properly used to call "tragic masks"; for as to children masks appear terrible and fearful from inexperience, we also are affected in like manner by events for no other reason than children are by masks. For what is a child? Ignorance. What is a child? Want of knowledge. For when a child knows these things, he is in no way inferior to us. What is death? A "tragic mask." Turn it and examine it. See, it does not bite. The poor body must be separated from the spirit either now or later, as it was separated from it before. Why, then,

are you troubled, if it be separated now? for if it is not separated now, it will be separated afterward. Why? That the period of the universe may be completed,[3] for it has need of the present, and of the future, and of the past. What is pain? A mask. Turn it and examine it. The poor flesh is moved roughly, then, on the contrary, smoothly. If this does not satisfy you, the door is open:[4] if it does, bear. For the door ought to be open for all occasions; and so we have no trouble.

What then is the fruit of these opinions? It is that which ought to be the most noble and the most becoming to those who are really educated, release from perturbation, release from fear, freedom. For in these matters we must not believe the many, who say that free persons only ought to be educated, but we should rather believe the philosophers, who say that the educated only are free. "How is this?" In this manner. Is freedom anything else than the power of living as we choose? "Nothing else." Tell me then, ye men, do you wish to live in error? "We do not." No one then who lives in error is free. Do you wish to live in fear? Do you wish to live in sorrow? Do you wish to live in perturbation? "By no means." No one, then, who is in a state of fear or sorrow or perturbation is free; but whoever is delivered from sorrows and fears and perturbations, he is at the same time also delivered from servitude. How then can we continue to believe you, most dear legislators, when you say, "We only allow free persons to be educated?" For philosophers say we allow none to be free except the educated; that is, God does not allow it. "When then a man has turned[5] round before the prætor his own slave, has he done nothing?" He has done something. "What?" He has turned round his own slave before the prætor. "Has he done nothing more?" Yes: he is also bound to pay for him the tax called the twentieth. "Well then, is not the man who has gone through this ceremony become free?" No more than he is become free from perturbations. Have you who are able to turn round others no master? is not money your master, or a girl or a boy, or some tyrant,

---

[1] Euripides, *Fragments.*
[2] Plato, *Phædo*, 78.

[3] Marcus Aurelius, xi. 1.
[4] See i. 9.
[5] See also iii. 26.

or some friend of the tyrant? why do you tremble then when you are going off to any trial of this kind? It is for this reason that I often say: Study and hold in readiness these principles by which you may determine what those things are with reference to which you ought to have confidence, and those things with reference to which you ought to be cautious: courageous in that which does not depend on your will; cautious in that which does depend on it.

"Well have I not read to you, and do you not know what I was doing?" In what? "In my little dissertations." Show me how you are with respect to desire and aversion; and show me if you do not fail in getting what you wish, and if you do not fall into the things which you would avoid: but as to these long and laboured sentences, you will take them and blot them out.

"What then did not Socrates write?" And who wrote so much? But how? As he could not always have at hand one to argue against his principles or to be argued against in turn, he used to argue with and examine himself, and he was always treating at least some one subject in a practical way. These are the things which a philosopher writes. But little dissertations and that method, which I speak of, he leaves to others, to the stupid, or to those happy men who being free from perturbations have leisure, or to such as are too foolish to reckon consequences.

And will you now, when the opportunity invites, go and display those things which you possess, and recite them, and make an idle show, and say, "See how I make dialogues?" Do not so, my man: but rather say: "See how I am not disappointed of that which I desire. See how I do not fall into that which I would avoid. Set death before me, and you will see. Set before me pain, prison, disgrace and condemnation." This is the proper display of a young man who is come out of the schools. But leave the rest to others, and let no one ever hear you say a word about these things; and if any man commends you for them, do not allow it; but think that you are nobody and know nothing. Only show that you know this, how never to be disappointed in your desire and how never to fall into that which you

would avoid. Let others labour at forensic causes, problems and syllogisms: do you labour at thinking about death, chains, the rack, exile;[1] and do all this with confidence and reliance on him who has called you to these sufferings, who has judged you worthy of the place in which, being stationed, you will show what things the rational governing power can do when it takes its stand against the forces which are not within the power of our will. And thus this paradox will no longer appear either impossible or a paradox, that a man ought to be at the same time cautious and courageous: courageous toward the things which do not depend on the will, and cautious in things which are within the power of the will.

CHAPTER 2. *Of Tranquillity*

CONSIDER, you who are going into court, what you wish to maintain and what you wish to succeed in. For if you wish to maintain a will conformable to nature, you have every security, every facility, you have no troubles. For if you wish to maintain what is in your own power and is naturally free, and if you are content with these, what else do you care for? For who is the master of such things? Who can take them away? If you choose to be modest and faithful, who shall not allow you to be so? If you choose not to be restrained or compelled, who shall compel you to desire what you think that you ought not to desire? who shall compel you to avoid what you do not think fit to avoid? But what do you say? The judge will determine against you something that appears formidable; but that you should also suffer in trying to avoid it, how can he do that? When then the pursuit of objects and the avoiding of them are in your power, what else do you care for? Let this be your preface, this your narrative, this your confirmation, this your victory, this your peroration, this your applause.

Therefore Socrates said to one who was reminding him to prepare for his trial, "Do you not think then that I have been preparing for it all my life?" By what kind of preparation? "I have maintained that which was in my own power." How then? "I have never done any-

[1] See i. 30.

thing unjust either in my private or in my public life."

But if you wish to maintain externals also, your poor body, your little property and your little estimation, I advise you to make from this moment all possible preparation, and then consider both the nature of your judge and your adversary. If it is necessary to embrace his knees, embrace his knees; if to weep, weep; if to groan, groan. For when you have subjected to externals what is your own, then be a slave and do not resist, and do not sometimes choose to be a slave, and sometimes not choose, but with all your mind be one or the other, either free or a slave, either instructed or uninstructed, either a well-bred cock or a mean one, either endure to be beaten until you die or yield at once; and let it not happen to you to receive many stripes and then to yield. But if these things are base, determine immediately: "Where is the nature of evil and good? It is where truth is: where truth is and where nature is, there is caution: where truth is, there is courage where nature is."

For what do you think? do you think that, if Socrates had wished to preserve externals, he would have come forward and said: "Anytus and Meletus can certainly kill me, but to harm me they are not able?" Was he so foolish as not to see that this way leads not to the preservation of life and fortune, but to another end? What is the reason then that he takes no account of his adversaries, and even irritates them? Just in the same way my friend Heraclitus, who had a little suit in Rhodes about a bit of land, and had proved to the judges that his case was just, said, when he had come to the peroration of his speech, "I will neither entreat you nor do I care what judgment you will give, and it is you rather than I who are on your trial." And thus he ended the business. What need was there of this? Only do not entreat; but do not also say, "I do not entreat"; unless there is a fit occasion to irritate purposely the judges, as was the case with Socrates. And you, if you are preparing such a peroration, why do you wait, why do you obey the order to submit to trial? For if you wish to be crucified, wait and the cross will come: but if you choose to submit and to plead your cause as well as you can, you must

do what is consistent with this object, provided you maintain what is your own.

For this reason also it is ridiculous to say, "Suggest something to me." What should I suggest to you? "Well, form my mind so as to accommodate itself to any event." Why that is just the same as if a man who is ignorant of letters should say, "Tell me what to write when any name is proposed to me." For if I should tell him to write Dion, and then another should come and propose to him not the name of Dion but that of Theon, what will be done? what will he write? But if you have practiced writing, you are also prepared to write anything that is required. If you are not, what can I now suggest? For if circumstances require something else, what will you say or what will you do? Remember, then, this general precept and you will need no suggestion. But if you gape after externals, you must of necessity ramble up and down in obedience to the will of your master. And who is the master? He who has the power over the things which you seek to gain or try to avoid.

CHAPTER 3. *To those who recommend persons to philosophers*

DIOGENES said well to one who asked from him letters of recommendation, "That you are a man," he said, "he will know as soon as he sees you; and he will know whether you are good or bad, if he is by experience skillful to distinguish the good and the bad; but if he is without experience, he will never know, if I write to him ten thousand times."[1] For it is just the same as if a drachma asked to be recommended to a person to be tested. If he is skillful in testing silver, he will know what you are, for you will recommend yourself. We ought then in life also to have some skill as in the case of silver coin that a man may be able to say, like the judge of silver, "Bring me any drachma and I will test it." But in the case of syllogisms I would say, "Bring any man that you please, and I will distinguish for you the man who knows how to resolve syllogisms and the man who does not." Why? Because I know how to resolve syllogisms. I have the power, which a man must have who is able to discover those who have the power of resolving syllogisms. But in life how do I act? At

[1] Compare Euripides, *Medea*, 518.

one time I call a thing good, and at another time bad. What is the reason? The contrary to that which is in the case of syllogisms, ignorance and inexperience.

CHAPTER 4. *Against a person who had once been detected in adultery*

As Epictetus was saying that man is formed for fidelity, and that he who subverts fidelity subverts the peculiar characteristic of men, there entered one of those who are considered to be men of letters, who had once been detected in adultery in the city. Then Epictetus continued: But if we lay aside this fidelity for which we are formed and make designs against our neighbor's wife, what are we doing? What else but destroying and overthrowing? Whom? The man of fidelity, the man of modesty, the man of sanctity. Is this all? And are we not overthrowing neighbourhood, and friendship, and the community; and in what place are we putting ourselves? How shall I consider you, man? As a neighbour, as a friend? What kind of one? As a citizen? Wherein shall I trust you? So if you were an utensil so worthless that a man could not use you, you would be pitched out on the dung heaps, and no man would pick you up. But if, being a man, you are unable to fill any place which befits a man, what shall we do with you? For suppose that you cannot hold the place of a friend, can you hold the place of a slave? And who will trust you? Are you not then content that you also should be pitched somewhere on a dung heap, as a useless utensil, and a bit of dung? Then will you say, "No man cares for me, a man of letters"? They do not, because you are bad and useless. It is just as if the wasps complained because no man cares for them, but all fly from them, and if a man can, he strikes them and knocks them down. You have such a sting that you throw into trouble and pain any man that you wound with it. What would you have us do with you? You have no place where you can be put.

"What then, are not women common by nature?" So I say also; for a little pig is common to all the invited guests, but when the portions have been distributed, go, if you think it right, and snatch up the portion of him who reclines next to you, or slyly steal it, or place your hand down by it and lay hold of it, and if you cannot tear away a bit of the meat, grease your fingers and lick them. A fine companion over cups, and Socratic guest indeed! "Well, is not the theatre common to the citizens?" When then they have taken their seats, come, if you think proper, and eject one of them. In this way women also are common by nature. When, then, the legislator, like the master of a feast, has distributed them, will you not also look for your own portion and not filch and handle what belongs to another. "But I am a man of letters and understand Archedemus." Understand Archedemus then, and be an adulterer, and faithless, and instead of a man, be a wolf or an ape: for what is the difference?

CHAPTER 5. *How magnanimity is consistent with care*

THINGS themselves are indifferent; but the use of them is not indifferent. How then shall a man preserve firmness and tranquillity, and at the same time be careful and neither rash nor negligent? If he imitates those who play at dice. The counters are indifferent; the dice are indifferent. How do I know what the cast will be? But to use carefully and dexterously the cast of the dice, this is my business. Thus then in life also the chief business is this: distinguish and separate things, and say, "Externals are not in my power: will is in my power. Where shall I seek the good and the bad? Within, in the things which are my own." But in what does not belong to you call nothing either good or bad, or profit or damage or anything of the kind.

"What then? Should we use such things carelessly?" In no way: for this on the other hand is bad for the faculty of the will, and consequently against nature; but we should act carefully because the use is not indifferent, and we should also act with firmness and freedom from perturbations because the material is indifferent. For where the material is not indifferent, there no man can hinder me nor compel me. Where I can be hindered and compelled, the obtaining of those things is not in my power, nor is it good or bad; but the use is either bad or good, and the use is in my power. But it is difficult to mingle and to bring together these two things, the carefulness of him who is affected by the matter and the firmness of him who has no regard for it; but it is not impossible; and if it is, happiness is impossible. But we should act as we do in the case of a voyage. What can I do? I can choose the master of the ship, the sailors, the day, the opportunity. Then comes a storm. What more have I to care for? for my part is done. The business belongs to another—the master. But the ship is sinking—what then have I to do? I do the only thing that I can, not to be drowned full of fear, nor screaming, nor blaming God, but knowing that what has been produced must also perish: for I am not an immortal being, but a man, a part of the whole, as an hour is a part of the day: I must be present like the hour, and past like the hour. What difference, then, does it make to me how I pass away, whether by being suffocated or by a fever, for I must pass through some such means?

This is just what you will see those doing who play at ball skillfully. No one cares about the ball as being good or bad, but about throwing and catching it. In this therefore is the skill, in this the art, the quickness, the judgement, so that if I spread out my lap I may not be able to catch it, and another, if I throw, may catch the ball. But if with perturbation and fear we receive or throw the ball, what kind of play is it then, and wherein shall a man be steady, and how shall a man see the order in the game? But one will say, "Throw"; or, "Do not throw"; and another will say, "You have thrown once." This is quarreling, not play.

Socrates, then, knew how to play at ball. "How?" By using pleasantry in the court where he was tried. "Tell me," he says, "Anytus, how do you say that I do not believe in God. The Demons, who are they, think you? Are they not sons of Gods, or compounded of gods and men?" When Anytus admitted this, Socrates said, "Who then, think you, can believe that there are mules, but not asses"; and this he said as if he were playing at ball.[1] And what was the ball in that case? Life, chains, banishment, a draught of poison, separation

[1] Plato, *Apology,* 27.

from wife and leaving children orphans. These were the things with which he was playing; but still he did play and threw the ball skillfully. So we should do: we must employ all the care of the players, but show the same indifference about the ball. For we ought by all means to apply our art to some external material, not as valuing the material, but, whatever it may be, showing our art in it. Thus too the weaver does not make wool, but exercises his art upon such as he receives. Another gives you food and property and is able to take them away and your poor body also. When then you have received the material, work on it. If then you come out without having suffered anything, all who meet you will congratulate you on your escape; but he who knows how to look at such things, if he shall see that you have behaved properly in the matter, will commend you and be pleased with you; and if he shall find that you owe your escape to any want of proper behavior, he will do the contrary. For where rejoicing is reasonable, there also is congratulation reasonable.

How then is it said that some external things are according to nature and others contrary to nature? It is said as it might be said if we were separated from union: for to the foot I shall say that it is according to nature for it to be clean; but if you take it as a foot and as a thing not detached, it will befit it both to step into the mud and tread on thorns, and sometimes to be cut off for the benefit of the whole body; otherwise it is no longer a foot. We should think in some way about ourselves also. What are you? A man. If you consider yourself as detached from other men, it is according to nature to live to old age, to be rich, to be healthy. But if you consider yourself as a man and a part of a certain whole, it is for the sake of that whole that at one time you should be sick, at another time take a voyage and run into danger, and at another time be in want, and, in some cases, die prematurely. Why then are you troubled? Do you not know, that as a foot is no longer a foot if it is detached from the body, so you are no longer a man if you are separated from other men. For what is a man? A part of a state, of that first which consists of Gods and of men; then of that which is called next to it, which is a small image of the universal state. "What then must I be brought to trial; must another have a fever, another sail on the sea, another die, and another be condemned?" Yes, for it is impossible in such a body, in such a universe of things, among so many living together, that such things should not happen, some to one and others to others. It is your duty then, since you are come here, to say what you ought, to arrange these things as it is fit. Then some one says, "I shall charge you with doing me wrong." Much good may it do you: I have done my part; but whether you also have done yours, you must look to that; for there is some danger of this too, that it may escape your notice.

Chapter 6. *Of Indifference*

The hypothetical proposition is indifferent: the judgment about it is not indifferent, but it is either knowledge or opinion or error. Thus life is indifferent: the use is not indifferent. When any man then tells you that these things also are indifferent, do not become negligent; and when a man invites you to be careful, do not become abject and struck with admiration of material things. And it is good for you to know your own preparation and power, that in those matters where you have not been prepared, you may keep quiet, and not be vexed, if others have the advantage over you. For you, too, in syllogisms will claim to have the advantage over them; and if others should be vexed at this, you will console them by saying, "I have learned them, and you have not." Thus also where there is need of any practice, seek not that which is required from the need, but yield in that matter to those who have had practice, and be yourself content with firmness of mind.

Go and salute a certain person. "How?" Not meanly. "But I have been shut out, for I have not learned to make my way through the window; and when I have found the door shut, I must either come back or enter through the window." But still speak to him. "In what way?" Not meanly. But suppose that you have not got what you wanted. Was this your business, and not his? Why then do you claim that which belongs to another? Always remember what is your own, and what belongs to another; and you will not be disturbed. Chrysippus therefore said well, "So long as future things are uncertain, I always cling to those which are more adapted to the conservation of that which is according to nature; for God himself has given me the faculty of such choice." But if I knew that it was fated for me to be sick, I would even move toward it; for the foot also, if it had intelligence, would move to go into the mud.[1] For why are ears of corn produced? Is it not that they may become dry? And do they not become dry that they may be reaped?[2] for they are not separated from communion with other things. If then they had perception, ought they to wish never to be reaped? But this is a curse upon ears of corn, never to be reaped. So we must know that in the case of men too it is a curse not to die, just the same as not to be ripened and not to be reaped. But since we must be reaped, and we also know that we are reaped, we are vexed at it; for we neither know what we are nor have we studied what belongs to man, as those who have studied horses know what belongs to horses. But Chrysantas, when he was going to strike the enemy, checked himself when he heard the trumpet sounding a retreat: so it seemed better to him to obey the general's command than to follow his own inclination. But not one of us chooses, even when necessity summons, readily to obey it, but weeping and groaning we suffer what we do suffer, and we call them "circumstances." What kind of circumstances, man? If you give the name of circumstances to the things which are around you, all things are circumstances; but if you call hardships by this name, what hardship is there in the dying of that which has been produced? But that which destroys is either a sword, or a wheel, or the sea, or a tile, or a tyrant. Why do you care about the way of going down to Hades? All ways are equal. But if you will listen to the truth, the way which the tyrant sends you is shorter. A tyrant never killed a man in six months: but a fever is often a year about it. All these things are only sound and the noise of empty names.

"I am in danger of my life from Cæsar."

---

[1] See ii. 5.
[2] Marcus Aurelius, vii. 40

And am not I in danger who dwell in Nicopolis, where there are so many earthquakes: and when you are crossing the Hadriatic, what hazard do you run? Is it not the hazard of your life? "But I am in danger also as to opinion." Do you mean your own? how? For who can compel you to have any opinion which you do not choose? But is it as to another man's opinion? and what kind of danger is yours, if others have false opinions? "But I am in danger of being banished." What is it to be banished? To be somewhere else than at Rome? "Yes: what then if I should be sent to Gyara?" If that suits you, you will go there; but if it does not, you can go to another place instead of Gyara, whither he also will go, who sends you to Gyara, whether he choose or not. Why then do you go up to Rome as if it were something great? It is not worth all this preparation, that an ingenuous youth should say, "It was not worth while to have heard so much and to have written so much and to have sat so long by the side of an old man who is not worth much." Only remember that division by which your own and not your own are distinguished: never claim anything which belongs to others. A tribunal and a prison are each a place, one high and the other low; but the will can be maintained equal, if you choose to maintain it equal in each. And we shall then be imitators of Socrates, when we are able to write pæans in prison. But in our present disposition, consider if we could endure in prison another person saying to us. "Would you like me to read Pæans to you?" "Why do you trouble me? do you not know the evils which hold me? Can I in such circumstances?" What circumstances? "I am going to die." And will other men be immortal?

CHAPTER 7. *How we ought to use divination*
THROUGH an unreasonable regard to divination many of us omit many duties. For what more can the diviner see than death or danger or disease, or generally things of that kind? If then I must expose myself to danger for a friend, and if it is my duty even to die for him, what need have I then for divination? Have I not within me a diviner who has told me the nature of good and of evil, and has explained to me the signs of both? What need

have I then to consult the viscera of victims or the flight of birds, and why do I submit when he says, "It is for your interest"? For does he know what is for my interest, does he know what is good; and as he has learned the signs of the viscera, has he also learned the signs of good and evil? For if he knows the signs of these, he knows the signs both of the beautiful and of the ugly, and of the just and of the unjust. Do you tell me, man, what is the thing which is signified for me: is it life or death, poverty or wealth? But whether these things are for my interest or whether they are not, I do not intend to ask you. Why don't you give your opinion on matters of grammar, and why do you give it here about things on which we are all in error and disputing with one another? The woman, therefore, who intended to send by a vessel a month's provisions to Gratilla in her banishment, made a good answer to him who said that Domitian would seize what she sent. "I would rather," she replied, "that Domitian should seize all than that I should not send it."

What then leads us to frequent use of divination? Cowardice, the dread of what will happen. This is the reason why we flatter the diviners. "Pray, master, shall I succeed to the property of my father?" "Let us see: let us sacrifice on the occasion." "Yes, master, as fortune chooses." When he has said, "You shall succeed to the inheritance," we thank him as if we received the inheritance from him. The consequence is that they play upon us.

What then should we do? We ought to come without desire or aversion, as the wayfarer asks of the man whom he meets which of two roads leads (to his journey's end), without any desire for that which leads to the right rather than to the left, for he has no wish to go by any road except the road which leads (to his end). In the same way ought we to come to God also as a guide; as we use our eyes, not asking them to show us rather such things as we wish, but receiving the appearances of things such as the eyes present them to us. But now we trembling take the augur by the hand, and, while we invoke God, we entreat the augur, and say, "Master have mercy on me; suffer me to come safe out of this difficulty." Wretch, would you have, then, anything other than what is best? Is there then anything better than what pleases God? Why do you, so far as in your power, corrupt your judge and lead astray your adviser?

CHAPTER 8. *What is the nature of the good*

GOD is beneficial. But the Good also is beneficial. It is consistent then that where the nature of God is, there also the nature of the good should be. What then is the nature of God?[1] Flesh? Certainly not. An estate in land? By no means. Fame? No. Is it intelligence, knowledge, right reason? Yes. Herein then simply seek the nature of the good; for I suppose that you do not seek it in a plant. No. Do you seek it in an irrational animal? No. If then you seek it in a rational animal, why do you still seek it anywhere except in the superiority of rational over irrational animals? Now plants have not even the power of using appearances, and for this reason you do not apply the term good to them. The good then requires the use of appearances. Does it require this use only? For if you say that it requires this use only, say that the good, and that happiness and unhappiness are in irrational animals also. But you do not say this, and you do right; for if they possess even in the highest degree the use of appearances, yet they have not the faculty of understanding the use of appearances; and there is good reason for this, for they exist for the purpose of serving others, and they exercise no superiority. For the ass, I suppose, does not exist for any superiority over others. No; but because we had need of a back which is able to bear something; and in truth we had need also of his being able to walk, and for this reason he received also the faculty of making use of appearances, for otherwise he would not have been able to walk. And here then the matter stopped. For if he had also received the faculty of comprehending the use of appearances, it is plain that consistently with reason he would not then have been subjected to us, nor would he have done us these services, but he would have been equal to us and like to us.

Will you not then seek the nature of good in the rational animal? for if it is not there, you will not choose to say that it exists in any

other thing. "What then? are not plants and animals also the works of God?" They are; but they are not superior things, nor yet parts of the Gods. But you are a superior thing; you are a portion separated from the deity; you have in yourself a certain portion of him. Why then are you ignorant of your own noble descent?[2] Why do you not know whence you came? will you not remember when you are eating, who you are who eat and whom you feed? When you are in conjunction with a woman, will you not remember who you are who do this thing? When you are in social intercourse, when you are exercising yourself, when you are engaged in discussion, know you not that you are nourishing a god, that you are exercising a god? Wretch, you are carrying about a god with you, and you know it not.[3] Do you think that I mean some God of silver or of gold, and external? You carry him within yourself, and you perceive not that you are polluting him by impure thoughts and dirty deeds. And if an image of God were present, you would not dare to do any of the things which you are doing: but when God himself is present within and sees all and hears all, you are not ashamed of thinking such things and doing such things, ignorant as you are of your own nature and subject to the anger of God. Then why do we fear when we are sending a young man from the school into active life, lest he should do anything improperly, eat improperly, have improper intercourse with women; and lest the rags in which he is wrapped should debase him, lest fine garments should make him proud? This youth does not know his own God: he knows not with whom he sets out. But can we endure when he says, "I wish I had you with me." Have you not God with you? and do you seek for any other, when you have him? or will God tell you anything else than this? If you were a statue of Phidias, either Athena or Zeus, you would think both of yourself and of the artist, and if you had any understanding you would try to do nothing unworthy of him who made you or of yourself, and try not to appear in an unbecoming dress to those who look on you. But now because

---

[1] See ii. 14.

[2] See i. 9.

[3] I Cor. 6. 19; II Cor. 6. 16.

Zeus has made you, for this reason do you care not how you shall appear? And yet is the artist like the artist in the other? or the work in the one case like the other? And what work of an artist, for instance, has in itself the faculties, which the artist shows in making it? Is it not marble or bronze, or gold or ivory? and the Athena of Phidias when she has once extended the hand and received in it the figure of Victory[1] stands in that attitude forever. But the works of God have power of motion, they breathe, they have the faculty of using the appearances of things, and the power of examining them. Being the work of such an artist, do you dishonor him? And what shall I say, not only that he made you, but also intrusted you to yourself and made you a deposit to yourself? Will you not think of this too, but do you also dishonor your guardianship? But if God had intrusted an orphan to you, would you thus neglect him? He has delivered yourself to your care, and says, "I had no one fitter to intrust him to than yourself: keep him for me such as he is by nature, modest, faithful, erect, unterrified, free from passion and perturbation." And then you do not keep him such.

But some will say, "Whence has this fellow got the arrogance which he displays and these supercilious looks?" I have not yet so much gravity as befits a philosopher; for I do not yet feel confidence in what I have learned and in what I have assented to: I still fear my own weakness. Let me get confidence and then you shall see a countenance such as I ought to have and an attitude such as I ought to have: then I will show to you the statue, when it is perfected, when it is polished. What do you expect? a supercilious countenance? Does the Zeus at Olympia lift up his brow? No, his look is fixed as becomes him who is ready to say

Irrevocable is my word and shall not fail.[2]
Such will I show myself to you, faithful, modest, noble, free from perturbation. "What, and immortal too, exempt from old age, and from sickness?" No, but dying as becomes a god, sickening as becomes a god. This power I possess; this I can do. But the rest I do not

¹ See i. 6.
² Homer, *Iliad*, i. 526.

possess, nor can I do. I will show the nerves of a philosopher. "What nerves[3] are these?" A desire never disappointed, an aversion[4] which never falls on that which it would avoid, a proper pursuit, a diligent purpose, an assent which is not rash. These you shall see.

CHAPTER 9. *That when we cannot fulfill that which the character of a man promises, we assume the character of a philosopher*

IT is no common thing to do this only, to fulfill the promise of a man's nature. For what is a man? The answer is: "A rational and mortal being." Then, by the rational faculty, from whom are we separated?[5] From wild beasts. And from what others? From sheep and like animals. Take care then to do nothing like a wild beast; but if you do, you have lost the character of a man; you have not fulfilled your promise. See that you do nothing like a sheep; but if you do, in this case the man is lost. What then do we do as sheep? When we act gluttonously, when we act lewdly, when we act rashly, filthily, inconsiderately, to what have we declined? To sheep. What have we lost? The rational faculty. When we act contentiously and harmfully and passionately, and violently, to what have we declined? To wild beasts. Consequently some of us are great wild beasts, and others little beasts, of a bad disposition and small, whence we may say, "Let me be eaten by a lion." But in all these ways the promise of a man acting as a man is destroyed. For when is a conjunctive proposition maintained? When it fulfills what its nature promises; so that the preservation of a complex proposition is when it is a conjunction of truths. When is a disjunctive maintained? When it fulfills what it promises. When are flutes, a lyre, a horse, a dog, preserved? What is the wonder then if man also in like manner is preserved, and in like manner is lost? Each man is improved and preserved by corresponding acts, the carpenter by acts of carpentry, the grammarian by acts of grammar. But if a man accustoms himself to write ungrammatically, of necessity his art will be corrupted and destroyed. Thus modest ac-

³ See i. 4; ii. 18; iii. 22.
⁴ See iii. 2.
⁵ See Epictetus, ii. 8.

tions preserve the modest man, and immodest actions destroy him: and actions of fidelity preserve the faithful man, and the contrary actions destroy him. And on the other hand contrary actions strengthen contrary characters: shamelessness strengthens the shameless man, faithlessness the faithless man, abusive words the abusive man, anger the man of an angry temper, and unequal receiving and giving make the avaricious man more avaricious.

For this reason philosophers admonish us not to be satisfied with learning only, but also to add study, and then practice. For we have long been accustomed to do contrary things, and we put in practice opinions which are contrary to true opinions. If then we shall not also put in practice right opinions, we shall be nothing more than the expositors of the opinions of others. For now who among us is not able to discuss according to the rules of art about good and evil things? "That of things some are good, and some are bad, and some are indifferent: the good then are virtues, and the things which participate in virtues; and the bad are the contrary; and the indifferent are wealth, health, reputation." Then, if in the midst of our talk there should happen some greater noise than usual, or some of those who are present should laugh at us, we are disturbed. Philosopher, where are the things which you were talking about? Whence did you produce and utter them? From the lips, and thence only. Why then do you corrupt the aids provided by others? Why do you treat the weightiest matters as if you were playing a game of dice? For it is one thing to lay up bread and wine as in a storehouse, and another thing to eat. That which has been eaten, is digested, distributed, and is become sinews, flesh, bones, blood, healthy colour, healthy breath. Whatever is stored up, when you choose you can readily take and show it; but you have no other advantage from it except so far as to appear to possess it. For what is the difference between explaining these doctrines and those of men who have different opinions? Sit down now and explain according to the rules of art the opinions of Epicurus, and perhaps you will explain his opinions in a more useful manner than Epicurus himself. Why then do you call yourself a Stoic?

Why do you deceive the many? Why do you act the part of a Jew, when you are a Greek? Do you not see how each is called a Jew, or a Syrian or an Egyptian? and when we see a man inclining to two sides, we are accustomed to say, "This man is not a Jew, but he acts as one." But when he has assumed the affects of one who has been imbued with Jewish doctrine and has adopted that sect, then he is in fact and he is named a Jew.[1] Thus we too being falsely imbued, are in name Jews, but in fact we are something else. Our affects are inconsistent with our words; we are far from practicing what we say, and that of which we are proud, as if we knew it. Thus being unable to fulfill even what the character of a man promises, we even add to it the profession of a philosopher, which is as heavy a burden, as if a man who is unable to bear ten pounds should attempt to raise the stone which Ajax[2] lifted.

CHAPTER 10. *How we may discover the duties of life from names*

CONSIDER who you are. In the first place, you are a man; and this is one who has nothing superior to the faculty of the will, but all other things subjected to it; and the faculty itself he possesses unenslaved and free from subjection. Consider then from what things you have been separated by reason. You have been separated from wild beasts: you have been separated from domestic animals. Further, you are a citizen of the world,[3] and a part of it, not one of the subservient, but one of the principal parts, for you are capable of comprehending the divine administration and of considering the connection of things. What then does the character of a citizen promise? To hold nothing as profitable to himself; to deliberate about nothing as if he were detached from the community, but to act as the hand or foot would do, if they had reason and understood the constitution of nature, for they would never put themselves in motion nor desire anything otherwise than with reference to the whole. Therefore the philosophers say well, that if the good man had foreknowl-

[1] See iv. 7; Rom. 2. 17-29.
[2] See ii. 24; Homer, *Iliad*, vii. 264, etc.
[3] See i. 9. Marcus Aurelius, vi. 44.

edge of what would happen, he would co-operate toward his own sickness and death and mutilation, since he knows that these things are assigned to him according to the universal arrangement, and that the whole is superior to the part, and the state to the citizen.[1] But now, because we do not know the future, it is our duty to stick to the things which are in their nature more suitable for our choice, for we were made among other things for this.

After this, remember that you are a son. What does this character promise? To consider that everything which is the son's belongs to the father, to obey him in all things, never to blame him to another, nor to say or do anything which does him injury, to yield to him in all things and give way, co-operating with him as far as you can. After this know that you are a brother also, and that to this character it is due to make concessions; to be easily persuaded, to speak good of your brother, never to claim in opposition to him any of the things which are independent of the will, but readily to give them up, that you may have the larger share in what is dependent on the will. For see what a thing it is, in place of a lettuce, if it should so happen, or a seat, to gain for yourself goodness of disposition. How great is the advantage.

Next to this, if you are senator of any state, remember that you are a senator: if a youth, that you are a youth: if an old man, that you are an old man; for each of such names, if it comes to be examined, marks out the proper duties. But if you go and blame your brother, I say to you, "You have forgotten who you are and what is your name." In the next place, if you were a smith and made a wrong use of the hammer, you would have forgotten the smith; and if you have forgotten the brother and instead of a brother have become an enemy, would you appear not to have changed one thing for another in that case? And if instead of a man, who is a tame animal and social, you are become a mischievous wild beast, treacherous, and biting, have you lost nothing? But, you must lose a bit of money that you may suffer damage? And does the loss of nothing else do a man damage? If you

had lost the art of grammar or music, would you think the loss of it a damage? and if you shall lose modesty, moderation and gentleness, do you think the loss nothing? And yet the things first mentioned are lost by some cause external and independent of the will, and the second by our own fault; and as to the first neither to have them nor to lose them is shameful; but as to the second, not to have them and to lose them is shameful and matter of reproach and a misfortune. What does the pathic lose? He loses the man. What does he lose who makes the pathic what he is? Many other things; and he also loses the man no less than the other. What does he lose who commits adultery? He loses the modest, the temperate, the decent, the citizen, the neighbour. What does he lose who is angry? Something else. What does the coward lose? Something else. No man is bad without suffering some loss and damage. If then you look for the damage in the loss of money only, all these men receive no harm or damage; it may be, they have even profit and gain, when they acquire a bit of money by any of these deeds. But consider that if you refer everything to a small coin, not even he who loses his nose is in your opinion damaged. "Yes," you say, "for he is mutilated in his body." Well; but does he who has lost his smell only lose nothing? Is there, then, no energy of the soul which is an advantage to him who possesses it, and a damage to him who has lost it? "Tell me what sort you mean." Have we not a natural modesty? "We have." Does he who loses this sustain no damage? is he deprived of nothing, does he part with nothing of the things which belong to him? Have we not naturally fidelity? natural affection, a natural disposition to help others, a natural disposition to forbearance? The man then who allows himself to be damaged in these matters, can he be free from harm and uninjured? "What then? shall I not hurt him, who has hurt me?"[2] In the first place consider what hurt is, and remember what you have heard from the philosophers. For if the good consists in the will, and the evil also in the will,[3] see if what you say is not this: "What then, since that man has hurt

[1] Marcus Aurelius, vi. 42.

[2] Plato, *Crito*, 49.
[3] See ii. 16.

himself by doing an unjust act to me, shall I not hurt myself by doing some unjust act to him?" Why do we not imagine to ourselves something of this kind? But where there is any detriment to the body or to our possession, there is harm there; and where the same thing happens to the faculty of the will, there is no harm; for he who has been deceived or he who has done an unjust act neither suffers in the head nor in the eye nor in the hip, nor does he lose his estate; and we wish for nothing else than these things. But whether we shall have the will modest and faithful or shameless and faithless, we care not the least, except only in the school so far as a few words are concerned. Therefore our proficiency is limited to these few words; but beyond them it does not exist even in the slightest degree.

CHAPTER 11. *What the beginning of philosophy is*

THE beginning of philosophy to him at least who enters on it in the right way and by the door, is a consciousness of his own weakness and inability about necessary things. For we come into the world with no natural notion of a right-angled triangle, or of a diesis, or of a half tone; but we learn each of these things by a certain transmission according to art; and for this reason those who do not know them, do not think that they know them. But as to good and evil, and beautiful and ugly, and becoming and unbecoming, and happiness and misfortune, and proper and improper, and what we ought to do and what we ought not to do, whoever came into the world without having an innate idea of them? Wherefore we all use these names, and we endeavor to fit the preconceptions[1] to the several cases thus: "He has done well, he has not done well; he has done as he ought, not as he ought; he has been unfortunate, he has been fortunate; he is unjust, he is just": who does not use these names? who among us defers the use of them till he has learned them, as he defers the use of the words about lines or sounds? And the cause of this is that we come into the world already taught as it were by nature some things on this matter, and proceeding from these we have added to them self-conceit. "For why,"

[1] See i. 2.

a man says, "do I not know the beautiful and the ugly? Have I not the notion of it?" You have. "Do I not adapt it to particulars?" You do. "Do I not then adapt it properly?" In that lies the whole question; and conceit is added here. For, beginning from these things which are admitted, men proceed to that which is matter of dispute by means of unsuitable adaptation; for if they possessed this power of adaptation in addition to those things, what would hinder them from being perfect? But now since you think that you properly adapt the preconceptions to the particulars, tell me whence you derive this. Because I think so. But it does not seem so to another, and he thinks that he also makes a proper adaptation; or does he not think so? He does think so. Is it possible then that both of you can properly apply the preconceptions to things about which you have contrary opinions? It is not possible. Can you then show us anything better toward adapting the preconceptions beyond your thinking that you do? Does the madman do any other things than the things which seem to him right? Is then this criterion sufficient for him also? It is not sufficient. Come then to something which is superior to seeming. What is this?

Observe, this is the beginning of philosophy, a perception of the disagreement of men with one another, and an inquiry into the cause of the disagreement, and a condemnation and distrust of that which only "seems," and a certain investigation of that which "seems" whether it "seems" rightly, and a discovery of some rule, as we have discovered a balance in the determination of weights, and a carpenter's rule in the case of straight and crooked things. This is the beginning of philosophy. "Must we say that all things are right which seem so to all?" And how is it possible that contradictions can be right? "Not all then, but all which seem to us to be right." How more to you than those which seem right to the Syrians? why more than what seem right to the Egyptians? why more than what seems right to me or to any other man? "Not at all more." What then "seems" to every man is not sufficient for determining what "is"; for neither in the case of weights or measures are we satisfied with the bare appearance, but in each case we have discovered a certain rule. In this matter then is there no rule superior to what "seems?" And how is it possible that the most necessary things among men should have no sign, and be incapable of being discovered? There is then some rule. And why then do we not seek the rule and discover it, and afterward use it without varying from it, not even stretching out the finger without it?[1] For this, I think, is that which when it is discovered cures of their madness those who use mere "seeming" as a measure, and misuse it; so that for the future proceeding from certain things known and made clear we may use in the case of particular things the preconceptions which are distinctly fixed.

What is the matter presented to us about which we are inquiring? "Pleasure." Subject it to the rule, throw it into the balance. Ought the good to be such a thing that it is fit that we have confidence in it? "Yes." And in which we ought to confide? "It ought to be." Is it fit to trust to anything which is insecure? "No." Is then pleasure anything secure? "No." Take it then and throw it out of the scale, and drive it far away from the place of good things. But if you are not sharp-sighted, and one balance is not enough for you, bring another. Is it fit to be elated over what is good? "Yes." Is it proper then to be elated over present pleasure? See that you do not say that it is proper; but if you do, I shall then not think you are worthy even of the balance. Thus things are tested and weighed when the rules are ready. And to philosophize is this, to examine and confirm the rules; and then to use them when they are known is the act of a wise and good man.

CHAPTER 12. *Of disputation or discussion*

WHAT things a man must learn in order to be able to apply the art of disputation, has been accurately shown by our philosophers;[2] but with respect to the proper use of the things, we are entirely without practice. Only give to any of us, whom you please, an illiterate man to discuss with, and he cannot discover how to deal with the man. But when he has moved the man a little, if he answers beside the purpose, he does not know how to treat him, but

he then either abuses or ridicules him, and says, "He is an illiterate man; it is not possible to do anything with him." Now a guide, when he has found a man out of the road leads him into the right way: he does not ridicule or abuse him and then leave him. Do you also show this illiterate man the truth, and you will see that he follows. But so long as you do not show him the truth, do not ridicule him, but rather feel your own incapacity.

How then did Socrates act? He used to compel his adversary in disputation to bear testimony to him, and he wanted no other witness.[3] Therefore he could say, "I care not for other witnesses, but I am always satisfied with the evidence of my adversary, and I do not ask the opinion of others, but only the opinion of him who is disputing with me." For he used to make the conclusions drawn from natural notions so plain that every man saw the contradiction and withdrew from it: "Does the envious man rejoice?" "By no means, but he is rather pained." Well, "Do you think that envy is pain over evils? and what envy is there of evils?" Therefore he made his adversary say that envy is pain over good things. "Well then, would any man envy those who are nothing to him?" "By no means." Thus having completed the notion and distinctly fixed it he would go away without saying to his adversary, "Define to me envy"; and if the adversary had defined envy, he did not say, "You have defined it badly, for the terms of the definition do not correspond to the thing defined." These are technical terms, and for this reason disagreeable and hardly intelligible to illiterate men, which terms we cannot lay aside. But that the illiterate man himself, who follows the appearances presented to him, should be able to concede anything or reject it, we can never by the use of these terms move him to do. Accordingly, being conscious of our own inability, we do not attempt the thing; at least such of us as have any caution do not. But the greater part and the rash, when they enter into such disputations, confuse themselves and confuse others; and finally abusing their adversaries and abused by them, they walk away.

[1] Marcus Aurelius, ii. 16.   [2] The Stoics.   [3] Plato, *Gorgias*, 472, 474.

Now this was the first and chief peculiarity of Socrates, never to be irritated in argument, never to utter anything abusive, anything insulting, but to bear with abusive persons and to put an end to the quarrel. If you would know what great power he had in this way, read the *Symposium* of Xenophon,[1] and you will see how many quarrels he put an end to. Hence with good reason in the poets also this power is most highly praised,

Quickly with skill he settles great disputes.

Well then; the matter is not now very safe, and particularly at Rome; for he who attempts to do it, must not do it in a corner, you may be sure, but must go to a man of consular rank, if it so happen, or to a rich man, and ask him, "Can you tell me, Sir, to whose care you have intrusted your horses?" "I can tell you." Have you intrusted them to any person indifferently and to one who has no experience of horses? "By no means." Well then; can you tell me to whom you intrust your gold or silver things or your vestments? "I don't intrust even these to any one indifferently." Well; your own body, have you already considered about intrusting the care of it to any person? "Certainly." To a man of experience, I suppose, and one acquainted with the aliptic, or with the healing art? "Without doubt." Are these the best things that you have, or do you also possess something else which is better than all these? "What kind of a thing do you mean?" That I mean which makes use of these things, and tests each of them, and deliberates. "Is it the soul that you mean?" You think right, for it is the soul that I mean. "In truth I do think that the soul is a much better thing than all the others which I possess." Can you then show us in what way you have taken care of the soul? for it is not likely that you, who are so wise a man and have a reputation in the city, inconsiderately and carelessly allow the most valuable thing that you possess to be neglected and to perish? "Certainly not." But have you taken care of the soul yourself; and have you learned from another to do this, or have you discovered the means yourself? Here comes the danger that in the first place he may say, "What is this to

[1] Compare Epictetus, iii. 16; iv. 5.

you, my good man, who are you?" Next, if you persist in troubling him, there is danger that he may raise his hands and give you blows. I was once myself also an admirer of this mode of instruction until I fell into these dangers.

CHAPTER 13. *On anxiety*

WHEN I see a man anxious, I say, "What does this man want? If he did not want something which is not in his power, how could he be anxious?" For this reason a lute player when he is singing by himself has no anxiety, but when he enters the theatre, he is anxious even if he has a good voice and plays well on the lute; for he not only wishes to sing well, but also to obtain applause: but this is not in his power. Accordingly, where he has skill, there he has confidence. Bring any single person who knows nothing of music, and the musician does not care for him. But in the matter where a man knows nothing and has not been practiced, there he is anxious. What matter is this? He knows not what a crowd is or what the praise of a crowd is. However he has learned to strike the lowest chord and the highest; but what the praise of the many is, and what power it has in life he neither knows nor has he thought about it. Hence he must of necessity tremble and grow pale. I cannot then say that a man is not a lute player when I see him afraid, but I can say something else, and not one thing, but many. And first of all I call him a stranger and say, "This man does not know in what part of the world he is, but though he has been here so long, he is ignorant of the laws of the State and the customs, and what is permitted and what is not; and he has never employed any lawyer to tell him and to explain the laws." But a man does not write a will, if he does not know how it ought to be written, or he employs a person who does know; nor does he rashly seal a bond or write a security. But he uses his desire without a lawyer's advice, and aversion, and pursuit, and attempt and purpose. "How do you mean without a lawyer?" He does not know that he wills what is not allowed, and does not will that which is of necessity; and he does not know either what is his own or what is another man's; but if he did know, he would never be impeded, he would never be hindered, he would not be anxious. "How so?" Is any man then afraid about things which are not evils? "No." Is he afraid about things which are evils, but still so far within his power that they may not happen? "Certainly he is not." If, then, the things which are independent of the will are neither good nor bad, and all things which do depend on the will are within our power, and no man can either take them from us or give them to us, if we do not choose, where is room left for anxiety? But we are anxious about our poor body, our little property, about the will of Cæsar; but not anxious about things internal. Are we anxious about not forming a false opinion? No, for this is in my power. About not exerting our movements contrary to nature? No, not even about this. When then you see a man pale, as the physician says, judging from the complexion, this man's spleen is disordered, that man's liver; so also say, this man's desire and aversion are disordered, he is not in the right way, he is in a fever. For nothing else changes the colour, or causes trembling or chattering of the teeth, or causes a man to

Sink in his knees and shift from foot to foot.[1]
For this reason when Zeno was going to meet Antigonus, he was not anxious, for Antigonus had no power over any of the things which Zeno admired; and Zeno did not care for those things over which Antigonus had power. But Antigonus was anxious when he was going to meet Zeno, for he wished to please Zeno; but this was a thing external. But Zeno did not want to please Antigonus; for no man who is skilled in any art wishes to please one who has no such skill.

Should I try to please you? Why? I suppose, you know the measure by which one man is estimated by another. Have you taken pains to learn what is a good man and what is a bad man, and how a man becomes one or the other? Why, then, are you not good yourself? "How," he replies, "am I not good?" Because no good man laments or groans or weeps, no good man is pale and trembles, or says, "How will he receive me, how will he listen to me?" Slave, just as it pleases him. Why do you care about what belongs to others? Is it now his fault if he receives badly what proceeds from

you? "Certainly." And is it possible that a fault should be one man's, and the evil in another? "No." Why then are you anxious about that which belongs to others? "Your question is reasonable; but I am anxious how I shall speak to him." Cannot you then speak to him as you choose? "But I fear that I may be disconcerted?" If you are going to write the name of Dion, are you afraid that you would be disconcerted? "By no means." Why? is it not because you have practiced writing the name? "Certainly." Well, if you were going to read the name, would you not feel the same? and why? Because every art has a certain strength and confidence in the things which belong to it. Have you then not practiced speaking? and what else did you learn in the school? Syllogisms and sophistical propositions?[2] For what purpose? was it not for the purpose of discoursing skillfully? and is not discoursing skillfully the same as discoursing seasonably and cautiously and with intelligence, and also without making mistakes and without hindrance, and besides all this with confidence? "Yes." When, then, you are mounted on a horse and go into a plain, are you anxious at being matched against a man who is on foot, and anxious in a matter in which you are practiced, and he is not? "Yes, but that person has power to kill me." Speak the truth then, unhappy man, and do not brag, nor claim to be a philosopher, nor refuse to acknowledge your masters, but so long as you present this handle in your body, follow every man who is stronger than yourself. Socrates used to practice speaking, he who talked as he did to the tyrants, to the dicasts, he who talked in his prison. Diogenes had practiced speaking, he who spoke as he did to Alexander, to the pirates, to the person who bought him. These men were confident in the things which they practiced. But do you walk off to your own affairs and never leave them: go and sit in a corner, and weave syllogisms, and propose them to another. There is not in you the man who can rule a state.

CHAPTER 14. *To Naso*
WHEN a certain Roman entered with his son and listened to one reading, Epictetus said,

---

[1] Homer, *Iliad*, xiii. 281.   [2] See i. 7.

"This is the method of instruction"; and he stopped. When the Roman asked him to go on, Epictetus said: Every art, when it is taught, causes labour to him who is unacquainted with it and is unskilled in it, and indeed the things which proceed from the arts immediately show their use in the purpose for which they were made; and most of them contain something attractive and pleasing. For indeed to be present and to observe how a shoemaker learns is not a pleasant thing; but the shoe is useful and also not disagreeable to look at. And the discipline of a smith when he is learning is very disagreeable to one who chances to be present and is a stranger to the art: but the work shows the use of the art. But you will see this much more in music; for if you are present while a person is learning, the discipline will appear most disagreeable; and yet the results of music are pleasing and delightful to those who know nothing of music. And here we conceive the work of a philosopher to be something of this kind: he must adapt his wish to what is going on, so that neither any of the things which are taking place shall take place contrary to our wish, nor any of the things which do not take place shall not take place when we wish that they should. From this the result is to those who have so arranged the work of philosophy, not to fail in the desire, nor to fall in with that which they would avoid; without uneasiness, without fear, without perturbation to pass through life themselves, together with their associates maintaining the relations both natural and acquired,[1] as the relation of son, of father, of brother, of citizen, of man, of wife, of neighbour, of fellow-traveler, of ruler, of ruled. The work of a philosopher we conceive to be something like this. It remains next to inquire how this must be accomplished.

We see then that the carpenter when he has learned certain things becomes a carpenter; the pilot by learning certain things becomes a pilot. May it not, then, in philosophy also not be sufficient to wish to be wise and good, and that there is also a necessity to learn certain things? We inquire then what these things are. The philosophers say that we ought first

to learn that there is a God and that he provides for all things; also that it is not possible to conceal from him our acts, or even our intentions and thoughts.[2] The next thing is to learn what is the nature of the Gods; for such as they are discovered to be, he, who would please and obey them, must try with all his power to be like them. If the divine is faithful, man also must be faithful; if it is free, man also must be free; if beneficent, man also must be beneficent; if magnanimous, man also must be magnanimous; as being then an imitator of God, he must do and say everything consistently with this fact.

"With what then must we begin?" If you will enter on the discussion, I will tell you that you must first understand names.[3] "So, then, you say that I do not now understand names?" You do not understand them. "How, then, do I use them?" Just as the illiterate use written language, as cattle use appearances: for use is one thing, understanding is another. But if you think that you understand them, produce whatever word you please, and let us try whether we understand it. But it is a disagreeable thing for a man to be confuted who is now old and, it may be, has now served his three campaigns. I too know this: for now you are come to me as if you were in want of nothing: and what could you even imagine to be wanting to you? You are rich, you have children, and a wife, perhaps, and many slaves: Cæsar knows you, in Rome you have many friends, you render their dues to all, you know how to requite him who does you a favour, and to repay in the same kind him who does you a wrong. What do you lack? If, then, I shall show you that you lack the things most necessary and the chief things for happiness, and that hitherto you have looked after everything rather than what you ought, and, to crown all, that you neither know what God is nor what man is, nor what is good nor what is bad; and as to what I have said about your ignorance of other matters, that may perhaps be endured, but if I say that you know nothing about yourself, how is it possible that you should endure

---

[1] Compare iii. 2; iv. 8; Marcus Aurelius, viii. 27.

[2] See i. 14; ii. 8. Marcus Aurelius, x. 8. Also Epictetus, i. 16; iii. 17.

[3] See i. 17; ii. 10, 11; Marcus Aurelius, x. 8.

me and bear the proof and stay here? It is not possible; but you immediately go off in bad humour. And yet what harm have I done you? unless the mirror also injures the ugly man because it shows him to himself such as he is; unless the physician also is supposed to insult the sick man, when he says to him, "Man, do you think that you ail nothing? But you have a fever: go without food to-day; drink water." And no one says, "What an insult!" But if you say to a man, "Your desires are inflamed, your aversions are low, your intentions are inconsistent, your pursuits are not conformable to nature, your opinions are rash and false," the man immediately goes away and says, "He has insulted me."

Our way of dealing is like that of a crowded assembly. Beasts are brought to be sold and oxen; and the greater part of the men come to buy and sell, and there are some few who come to look at the market and to inquire how it is carried on, and why, and who fixes the meeting and for what purpose. So it is here also in this assembly: some like cattle trouble themselves about nothing except their fodder. For to all of you who are busy about possessions and lands and slaves and magisterial offices, these are nothing except fodder. But there are a few who attend the assembly, men who love to look on and consider what is the world, who governs it. Has it no governor? And how is it possible that a city or a family cannot continue to exist, not even the shortest time without an administrator and guardian, and that so great and beautiful a system should be administered with such order and yet without a purpose and by chance? There is then an administrator. What kind of administrator and how does he govern? And who are we, who were produced by him, and for what purpose? Have we some connection with him and some relation toward him, or none? This is the way in which these few are affected, and then they apply themselves only to this one thing, to examine the meeting and then to go away. What then? They are ridiculed by the many, as the spectators at the fair are by the traders; and if the beasts had any understanding, they would ridicule those who admired anything else than fodder.

Chapter 15. *To or against those who obstinately persist in what they have determined*

WHEN some persons have heard these words, that a man ought to be constant, and that the will is naturally free and not subject to compulsion, but that all other things are subject to hindrance, to slavery, and are in the power of others, they suppose that they ought without deviation to abide by everything which they have determined. But in the first place that which has been determined ought to be sound. I require tone in the body, but such as exists in a healthy body, in an athletic body; but if it is plain to me that you have the tone of a frenzied man and you boast of it, I shall say to you, "Man, seek the physician": this is not tone, but atony. In a different way something of the same kind is felt by those who listen to these discourses in a wrong manner; which was the case with one of my companions who for no reason resolved to starve himself to death. I heard of it when it was the third day of his abstinence from food and I went to inquire what had happened. "I have resolved," he said. But still tell me what it was which induced you to resolve; for if you have resolved rightly, we shall sit with you and assist you to depart; but if you have made an unreasonable resolution, change your mind. "We ought to keep to our determinations." What are you doing, man? We ought to keep not to all our determinations, but to those which are right; for if you are now persuaded that it is right, do not change your mind, if you think fit, but persist and say, "We ought to abide by our determinations." Will you not make the beginning and lay the foundation in an inquiry whether the determination is sound or not sound, and so then build on it firmness and security? But if you lay a rotten and ruinous foundation, will not your miserable little building fall down the sooner, the more and the stronger are the materials which you shall lay on it? Without any reason would you withdraw from us out of life a man who is a friend, and a companion, a citizen of the same city, both the great and the small city? Then, while you are committing murder and destroying a man who has done no wrong, do you say that you ought to abide by your determinations? And if it ever in any way came into your head to kill me, ought you to abide by your determinations?

Now this man was with difficulty persuaded to change his mind. But it is impossible to convince some persons at present; so that I seem now to know, what I did not know before, the meaning of the common saying, "That you can neither persuade nor break a fool."[1] May it never be my lot to have a wise fool for my friend: nothing is more untractable. "I am determined," the man says. Madmen are also; but the more firmly they form a judgment on things which do not exist, the more ellebore they require. Will you not act like a sick man and call in the physician? "I am sick, master, help me; consider what I must do: it is my duty to obey you." So it is here also: "I know not what I ought to do, but I am come to learn." Not so; but, "Speak to me about other things: upon this I have determined." What other things? for what is greater and more useful than for you to be persuaded that it is not sufficient to have made your determination and not to change it. This is the tone of madness, not of health. "I will die, if you compel me to this." Why, man? What has happened? "I have determined." I have had a lucky escape that you have not determined to kill me. "I take no money." Why? "I have determined." Be assured that with the very tone which you now use in refusing to take, there is nothing to hinder you at some time from inclining without reason to take money and then saying, "I have determined." As in a distempered body, subject to defluxions, the humor inclines sometimes to these parts and then to those, so too a sickly soul knows not which way to incline: but if to this inclination and movement there is added a tone, then the evil becomes past help and cure.

CHAPTER 16. *That we do not strive to use our opinions about good and evil*

WHERE is the good? In the will.[2] Where is the evil? In the will. Where is neither of them? In those things which are independent of the will. Well then? Does any one among us think of these lessons out of the schools? Does any one meditate by himself to give an answer to

[1] Prov. 27. 22.   [2] See ii. 10.

things as in the case of questions? Is it day? "Yes." Is it night? "No." Well, is the number of stars even? "I cannot say." When money is shown to you, have you studied to make the proper answer, that money is not a good thing? Have you practiced yourself in these answers, or only against sophisms? Why do you wonder then if in the cases which you have studied, in those you have improved; but in those which you have not studied, in those you remain the same? When the rhetorician knows that he has written well, that he has committed to memory what he has written, and brings an agreeable voice, why is he still anxious? Because he is not satisfied with having studied. What then does he want? To be praised by the audience? For the purpose, then, of being able to practice declamation, he has been disciplined: but with respect to praise and blame he has not been disciplined. For when did he hear from any one what praise is, what blame is, what the nature of each is, what kind of praise should be sought, or what kind of blame should be shunned? And when did he practice this discipline which follows these words? Why then do you still wonder if, in the matters which a man has learned, there he surpasses others, and in those in which he has not been disciplined, there he is the same with the many. So the lute player knows how to play, sings well, and has a fine dress, and yet he trembles when he enters on the stage; for these matters he understands, but he does not know what a crowd is, nor the shouts of a crowd, nor what ridicule is. Neither does he know what anxiety is, whether it is our work or the work of another, whether it is possible to stop it or not. For this reason, if he has been praised, he leaves the theatre puffed up, but if he has been ridiculed, the swollen bladder has been punctured and subsides.

This is the case also with ourselves. What do we admire? Externals. About what things are we busy? Externals. And have we any doubt then why we fear or why we are anxious? What, then, happens when we think the things which are coming on us to be evils? It is not in our power not to be afraid, it is not in our power not to be anxious. Then we say, "Lord God, how shall I not be anxious?" Fool, have you not hands, did not God make them for you? Sit down now and pray that your nose may not run. Wipe yourself rather and do not blame him. Well then, has he given to you nothing in the present case? Has he not given to you endurance? has he not given to you magnanimity? has he not given to you manliness? When you have such hands, do you still look for one who shall wipe your nose? But we neither study these things nor care for them. Give me a man who cares how he shall do anything, not for the obtaining of a thing, but who cares about his own energy. What man, when he is walking about, cares for his own energy? who, when he is deliberating, cares about his own deliberation, and not about obtaining that about which he deliberates? And if he succeeds, he is elated and says, "How well we have deliberated; did I not tell you, brother, that it is impossible, when we have thought about anything, that it should not turn out thus?" But if the thing should turn out otherwise, the wretched man is humbled; he knows not even what to say about what has taken place. Who among us for the sake of this matter has consulted a seer? Who among us as to his actions has not slept in indifference? Who? Give to me one that I may see the man whom I have long been looking for, who is truly noble and ingenuous, whether young or old; name him.

Why then are we still surprised, if we are well practiced in thinking about matters, but in our acts are low, without decency, worthless, cowardly, impatient of labour, altogether bad? For we do not care about things, nor do we study them. But if we had feared not death or banishment, but fear itself,[1] we should have studied not to fall into those things which appear to us evils. Now in the school we are irritable and wordy; and if any little question arises about any of these things, we are able to examine them fully. But drag us to practice, and you will find us miserably shipwrecked. Let some disturbing appearance come on us, and you will know what we have been studying and in what we have been exercising ourselves. Consequently, through want of discipline, we are always adding something to the appearance and representing things to be greater than what they are. For instance as to

myself, when I am on a voyage and look down on the deep sea, or look round on it and see no land, I am out of my mind and imagine that I must drink up all this water if I am wrecked, and it does not occur to me that three pints are enough. What then disturbs me? The sea? No, but my opinion. Again, when an earthquake shall happen, I imagine that the city is going to fall on me; but is not one little stone enough to knock my brains out?

What then are the things which are heavy on us and disturb us? What else than opinions? What else than opinions lies heavy upon him who goes away and leaves his companions and friends and places and habits of life? Now little children, for instance, when they cry on the nurse leaving them for a short time, forget their sorrow if they receive a small cake. Do you choose then that we should compare you to little children? No, by Zeus, for I do not wish to be pacified by a small cake, but by right opinions. And what are these? Such as a man ought to study all day, and not to be affected by anything that is not his own, neither by companion nor place nor gymnasia, and not even by his own body, but to remember the law and to have it before his eyes. And what is the divine law? To keep a man's own, not to claim that which belongs to others, but to use what is given, and when it is not given, not to desire it; and when a thing is taken away, to give it up readily and immediately, and to be thankful for the time that a man has had the use of it, if you would not cry for your nurse and mamma. For what matter does it make by what thing a man is subdued, and on what he depends? In what respect are you better than he who cries for a girl, if you grieve for a little gymnasium, and little porticoes and young men and such places of amusement? Another comes and laments that he shall no longer drink the water of Dirce. Is the Marcian water worse than that of Dirce? "But I was used to the water of Dirce."[2] And you in turn will be used to the other. Then if you become attached to this also, cry for this too, and try to make a verse like the verse of Euripides,

The hot baths of Nero and the Marcian water.
See how tragedy is made when common things happen to silly men.

---

[1] See ii. 1.

[2] Euripides, *Heracles Mad*, 573.

"When then shall I see Athens again and the Acropolis?" Wretch, are you not content with what you see daily? have you anything better or greater to see than the sun, the moon, the stars, the whole earth, the sea? But if indeed you comprehend him who administers the Whole, and carry him about in yourself, do you still desire small stones, and a beautiful rock? When, then, you are going to leave the sun itself and the moon, what will you do? will you sit and weep like children? Well, what have you been doing in the school? what did you hear, what did you learn? why did you write yourself a philosopher, when you might have written the truth; as, "I made certain introductions, and I read Chrysippus, but I did not even approach the door of a philosopher." For how should I possess anything of the kind which Socrates possessed, who died as he did, who lived as he did, or anything such as Diogenes possessed? Do you think that any one of such men wept or grieved, because he was not going to see a certain man, or a certain woman, nor to be in Athens or in Corinth, but, if it should so happen, in Susa or in Ecbatana? For if a man can quit the banquet when he chooses, and no longer amuse himself, does he still stay and complain, and does he not stay, as at any amusement, only so long as he is pleased? Such a man, I suppose, would endure perpetual exile or to be condemned to death. Will you not be weaned now, like children, and take more solid food, and not cry after mammas and nurses, which are the lamentations of old women? "But if I go away, I shall cause them sorrow." You cause them sorrow? By no means; but that will cause them sorrow which also causes you sorrow, opinion. What have you to do then? Take away your own opinion, and if these women are wise, they will take away their own: if they do not, they will lament through their own fault.

My man, as the proverb says, make a desperate effort on behalf of tranquillity of mind, freedom and magnanimity. Lift up your head at last as released from slavery. Dare to look up to God and say, "Deal with me for the future as thou wilt; I am of the same mind as thou art; I am thine: I refuse nothing that pleases thee: lead me where thou wilt: clothe me in any dress thou choosest: is it thy will

that I should hold the office of a magistrate, that I should be in the condition of a private man, stay here or be an exile, be poor, be rich? I will make thy defense to men in behalf of all these conditions.[1] I will show the nature of each thing what it is." You will not do so; but sit in an ox's belly, and wait for your mamma till she shall feed you. Who would Hercules have been, if he had sat at home? He would have been Eurystheus and not Hercules. Well, and in his travels through the world how many intimates and how many friends had he? But nothing more dear to him than God. For this reason it was believed that he was the son of God, and he was. In obedience to God, then, he went about purging away injustice and lawlessness. But you are not Hercules and you are not able to purge away the wickedness of others; nor yet are you Theseus, able to purge away the evil things of Attica. Clear away your own. From yourself, from your thoughts cast away, instead of Procrustes and Sciron,[2] sadness, fear, desire, envy, malevolence, avarice, effeminacy, intemperance. But it is not possible to eject these things otherwise than by looking to God only, by fixing your affections on him only, by being consecrated to his commands. But if you choose anything else, you will with sighs and groans be compelled to follow[3] what is stronger than yourself, always seeking tranquillity and never able to find it; for you seek tranquillity there where it is not, and you neglect to seek it where it is.

CHAPTER 17. *How we must adapt preconceptions to particular cases*

WHAT is the first business of him who philosophizes? To throw away self-conceit.[4] For it is impossible for a man to begin to learn that which he thinks that he knows. As to things then which ought to be done and ought not to be done, and good and bad, and beautiful and ugly, all of us talking of them at random go to the philosophers; and on these matters we praise, we censure, we accuse, we blame, we judge and determine about principles hon-

[1] See Acts, 20. 23, 24; Rom. 5. 3; 8. 38-39; II Tim. 4. 6.
[2] Plutarch, *Lives*, Theseus.
[3] Marcus Aurelius, x. 28.
[4] See ii. 11, and iii. 14.

ourable and dishonourable. But why do we go to the philosophers? Because we wish to learn what we do not think that we know. And what is this? Theorems. For we wish to learn what philosophers say as being something elegant and acute; and some wish to learn that they may get profit from what they learn. It is ridiculous then to think that a person wishes to learn one thing, and will learn another; or further, that a man will make proficiency in that which he does not learn. But the many are deceived by this which deceived also the rhetorician Theopompus, when he blames even Plato for wishing everything to be defined. For what does he say? "Did none of us before you use the words 'good' or 'just,' or do we utter the sounds in an unmeaning and empty way without understanding what they severally signify?" Now who tells you, Theopompus, that we had not natural notions of each of these things and preconceptions? But it is not possible to adapt preconceptions to their correspondent objects if we have not distinguished them, and inquired what object must be subjected to each preconception. You may make the same charge against physicians also. For who among us did not use the words "healthy" and "unhealthy" before Hippocrates lived, or did we utter these words as empty sounds? For we have also a certain preconception of health, but we are not able to adapt it. For this reason one says, "Abstain from food"; another says, "Give food"; another says, "Bleed"; and another says, "Use cupping." What is the reason? is it any other than that a man cannot properly adapt the preconception of health to particulars?

So it is in this matter also, in the things which concern life. Who among us does not speak of good and bad, of useful and not useful; for who among us has not a preconception of each of these things? Is it then a distinct and perfect preconception? Show this. How shall I show this? Adapt the preconception properly to the particular things. Plato, for instance, subjects definitions to the preconception of the useful, but you to the preconception of the useless. Is it possible then that both of you are right? How is it possible? Does not one man adapt the preconception of good to the matter of wealth, and another not

to wealth, but to the matter of pleasure and to that of health? For, generally, if all of us who use those words know sufficiently each of them, and need no diligence in resolving the notions of the preconceptions, why do we differ, why do we quarrel, why do we blame one another?

And why do I now allege this contention with one another and speak of it? If you yourself properly adapt your preconceptions, why are you unhappy, why are you hindered? Let us omit at present the second topic about the pursuits and the study of the duties which relate to them. Let us omit also the third topic, which relates to the assents: I give up to you these two topics. Let us insist upon the first, which presents an almost obvious demonstration that we do not properly adapt the preconceptions.[1] Do you now desire that which is possible and that which is possible to you? Why then are you hindered? why are you unhappy? Do you not now try to avoid the unavoidable? Why then do you fall in with anything which you would avoid? Why are you unfortunate? Why, when you desire a thing, does it not happen, and, when you do not desire it, does it happen? For this is the greatest proof of unhappiness and misery: "I wish for something, and it does not happen." And what is more wretched than I?[2]

It was because she could not endure this that Medea came to murder her children: an act of a noble spirit in this view at least, for she had a just opinion what it is for a thing not to succeed which a person wishes. Then she says, "Thus I shall be avenged on him who has wronged and insulted me; and what shall I gain if he is punished thus? how then shall it be done? I shall kill my children, but I shall punish myself also: and what do I care?"[3] This is the aberration of soul which possesses great energy. For she did not know wherein lies the doing of that which we wish; that you cannot get this from without, nor yet by the alteration and new adaptation of things. Do not desire the man, and nothing which you desire will fail to happen: do not obstinately desire that he shall live with you: do not desire

[1] See. iii. 2.
[2] Compare i. 27.
[3] Euripides, *Medea*. Epictetus does not give the words of the poet.

to remain in Corinth; and, in a word, desire nothing than that which God wills. And who shall hinder you? who shall compel you? No man shall compel you any more than he shall compel Zeus.

When you have such a guide,[1] and your wishes and desires are the same as his, why do you still fear disappointment? Give up your desire to wealth and your aversion to poverty, and you will be disappointed in the one, you will fall into the other. Well, give them up to health, and you will be unfortunate: give them up to magistracies, honours, country, friends, children, in a word to any of the things which are not in man's power. But give them up to Zeus and to the rest of the gods; surrender them to the gods, let the gods govern, let your desire and aversion be ranged on the side of the gods, and wherein will you be any longer unhappy? But if, lazy wretch, you envy, and complain, and are jealous, and fear, and never cease for a single day complaining both of yourself and of the gods, why do you still speak of being educated? What kind of an education, man? Do you mean that you have been employed about sophistical syllogisms?[2] Will you not, if it is possible, unlearn all these things and begin from the beginning, and see at the same time that hitherto you have not even touched the matter; and then, commencing from this foundation, will you not build up all that comes after, so that nothing may happen which you do not choose, and nothing shall fail to happen which you do choose?

Give me one young man who has come to the school with this intention, who is become a champion for this matter and says, "I give up everything else, and it is enough for me if it shall ever be in my power to pass my life free from hindrance and free from trouble, and to stretch out my neck to all things like a free man, and to look up to heaven as a friend of God, and fear nothing that can happen." Let any of you point out such a man that I may say, "Come, young man, into the possession of that which is your own, for it is your destiny to adorn philosophy: yours are these possessions, yours these books, yours these dis-

courses." Then when he shall have laboured sufficiently and exercised himself in this part of the matter, let him come to me again and say, "I desire to be free from passion and free from perturbation; and I wish as a pious man and a philosopher and a diligent person to know what is my duty to the gods, what to my parents, what to my brothers, what to my country, what to strangers." Come also to the second matter: this also is yours. "But I have now sufficiently studied the second part also, and I would gladly be secure and unshaken, and not only when I am awake, but also when I am asleep, and when I am filled with wine, and when I am melancholy." Man, you are a god, you have great designs.

"No: but I wish to understand what Chrysippus says in his treatise of the *Pseudomenos*." Will you not hang yourself, wretch, with such your intention? And what good will it do you? You will read the whole with sorrow, and you will speak to others trembling. Thus you also do. "Do you wish me, brother, to read to you, and you to me?" "You write excellently, my man; and you also excellently in the style of Xenophon, and you in the style of Plato, and you in the style of Antisthenes." Then, having told your dreams to one another, you return to the same things: your desires are the same, your aversions the same, your pursuits are the same, and your designs and purposes, you wish for the same things and work for the same. In the next place you do not even seek for one to give you advice, but you are vexed if you hear such things. Then you say, "An ill-natured old fellow: when I was going away, he did not weep nor did he say, 'Into what danger you are going: if you come off safe, my child, I will burn lights.'[3] This is what a good-natured man would do." It will be a great thing for you if you do return safe, and it will be worth while to burn lights for such a person: for you ought to be immortal and exempt from disease.

Casting away then, as I say, this conceit of thinking that we know something useful, we must come to philosophy as we apply to geometry, and to music: but if we do not, we shall not even approach to proficiency, though we read all the collections and commentaries of

[1] Compare iv. 7.
[2] See i. 7.
[3] Compare i. 19.

Chrysippus and those of Antipater and Archedemus.[1]

CHAPTER 18. *How we should struggle against appearances*

EVERY habit and faculty[2] is maintained and increased by the corresponding actions: the habit of walking by walking, the habit of running by running. If you would be a good reader, read; if a writer, write. But when you shall not have read for thirty days in succession, but have done something else, you will know the consequence. In the same way, if you shall have lain down ten days, get up and attempt to make a long walk, and you will see how your legs are weakened. Generally, then, if you would make anything a habit, do it; if you would not make it a habit, do not do it, but accustom yourself to do something else in place of it.

So it is with respect to the affections of the soul: when you have been angry, you must know that not only has this evil befallen you, but that you have also increased the habit, and in a manner thrown fuel upon fire. When you have been overcome in sexual intercourse with a person, do not reckon this single defeat only, but reckon that you have also nurtured, increased your incontinence. For it is impossible for habits and faculties, some of them not to be produced, when they did not exist before, and others not be increased and strengthened by corresponding acts.

In this manner certainly, as philosophers say, also diseases of the mind grow up. For when you have once desired money, if reason be applied to lead to a perception of the evil, the desire is stopped, and the ruling faculty of our mind is restored to the original authority. But if you apply no means of cure, it no longer returns to the same state, but, being again excited by the corresponding appearance, it is inflamed to desire quicker than before: and when this takes place continually, it is henceforth hardened, and the disease of the mind confirms the love of money. For he who has had a fever, and has been relieved from it, is not in the same state that he was before, unless he has been completely cured. Something of the kind happens also in diseases of the soul. Certain traces and blisters are left in it, and unless a man shall completely efface them, when he is again lashed on the same places, the lash will produce not blisters but sores. If then you wish not to be of an angry temper, do not feed the habit: throw nothing on it which will increase it: at first keep quiet, and count the days on which you have not been angry. I used to be in passion every day; now every second day; then every third, then every fourth. But if you have intermitted thirty days, make a sacrifice to God. For the habit at first begins to be weakened, and then is completely destroyed. "I have not been vexed to-day, nor the day after, nor yet on any succeeding day during two or three months; but I took care when some exciting things happened." Be assured that you are in a good way. To-day when I saw a handsome person, I did not say to myself, "I wish I could lie with her," and "Happy is her husband"; for he who says this says, "Happy is her adulterer also." Nor do I picture the rest to my mind; the woman present, and stripping herself and lying down by my side. I stroke my head and say, "Well done, Epictetus, you have solved a fine little sophism, much finer than that which is called the master sophism." And if even the woman is willing, and gives signs, and sends messages, and if she also fondle me and come close to me, and I should abstain and be victorious, that would be a sophism beyond that which is named "The Liar," and "The Quiescent." Over such a victory as this a man may justly be proud; not for proposing the master sophism.

How then shall this be done? Be willing at length to be approved by yourself, be willing to appear beautiful to God, desire to be in purity with your own pure self and with God. Then when any such appearance visits you, Plato says, "Have recourse to expiations, go a suppliant to the temples of the averting deities."[3] It is even sufficient if "you resort to the society of noble and just men," and compare yourself with them, whether you find one who is living or dead. Go to Socrates and see him lying down with Alcibiades, and mocking his beauty: consider what a victory he at last found that he had gained over himself; what

---

[1] Archedemus, see ii. 4; Antipater, ii. 19.
[2] See iv. 12.
[3] Plato, *Laws,* ix. 854. Compare Matt. 6. 29.

an Olympian victory; in what number he stood from Hercules; so that, by the Gods, one may justly salute him, "Hail, wondrous man, you who have conquered not less these sorry boxers and pancratiasts, nor yet those who are like them, the gladiators." By placing these objects on the other side you will conquer the appearance: you will not be drawn away by it. But, in the first place, be not hurried away by the rapidity of the appearance, but say, "Appearances, wait for me a little: let me see who you are, and what you are about:[1] let me put you to the test." And then do not allow the appearance to lead you on and draw lively pictures of the things which will follow; for if you do, it will carry you off wherever it pleases. But rather bring in to oppose it some other beautiful and noble appearance and cast out this base appearance. And if you are accustomed to be exercised in this way, you will see what shoulders, what sinews, what strength you have. But now it is only trifling words, and nothing more.

This is the true athlete, the man who exercises himself against such appearances. Stay, wretch, do not be carried away. Great is the combat, divine is the work; it is for kingship, for freedom, for happiness, for freedom from perturbation. Remember God: call on him as a helper and protector, as men at sea call on the Dioscuri in a storm. For what is a greater storm than that which comes from appearances which are violent and drive away the reason? For the storm itself, what else is it but an appearance? For take away the fear of death, and suppose as many thunders and lightnings as you please, and you will know what calm[2] and serenity there is in the ruling faculty. But if you have once been defeated and say that you will conquer hereafter, and then say the same again, be assured that you will at last be in so wretched a condition and so weak that you will not even know afterward that you are doing wrong, but you will even begin to make apologies for your wrongdoing, and then you will confirm the saying of Hesiod to be true,

"*With constant ills the dilatory strives.*"

1 Compare iii. 12.
2 Marcus Aurelius, xii. 22.

CHAPTER 19. *Against those who embrace philosophical opinions only in words*

THE argument called the "ruling argument" appears to have been proposed from such principles as these: there is in fact a common contradiction between one another in these three positions, each two being in contradiction to the third. The propositions are, that everything past must of necessity be true; that an impossibility does not follow a possibility; and that a thing is possible which neither is nor will be true. Diodorus observing this contradiction employed the probative force of the first two for the demonstration of this proposition, "That nothing is possible which is not true and never will be." Now another will hold these two: "That something is possible, which is neither true nor ever will be": and "That an impossibility does not follow a possibility." But he will not allow that everything which is past is necessarily true, as the followers of Cleanthes seem to think, and Antipater copiously defended them. But others maintain the other two propositions, "That a thing is possible which is neither true nor will be true": and "That everything which is past is necessarily true"; but then they will maintain that an impossibility can follow a possibility. But it is impossible to maintain these three propositions, because of their common contradiction.

If then any man should ask me which of these propositions do I maintain? I will answer him that I do not know; but I have received this story, that Diodorus maintained one opinion, the followers of Panthoides, I think, and Cleanthes maintained another opinion, and those of Chrysippus a third. "What then is your opinion?" I was not made for this purpose, to examine the appearances that occur to me and to compare what others say and to form an opinion of my own on the thing. Therefore I differ not at all from the grammarian. "Who was Hector's father?" Priam. "Who were his brothers?" Alexander and Deiphobus. "Who was their mother?" Hecuba. I have heard this story. "From whom?" From Homer. And Hellanicus also, I think, writes about the same things, and perhaps others like him. And what further have I about the ruling argument? Nothing.

But, if I am a vain man, especially at a banquet, I surprise the guests by enumerating those who have written on these matters. Both Chrysippus has written wonderfully in his first book about "Possibilities," and Cleanthes has written specially on the subject, and Archedemus. Antipater also has written not only in his work about "Possibilities," but also separately in his work on the ruling argument. Have you not read the work? "I have not read it." Read. And what profit will a man have from it? he will be more trifling and impertinent than he is now; for what else have you gained by reading it? What opinion have you formed on this subject? none; but you will tell us of Helen and Priam, and the island of Calypso which never was and never will be. And in this matter indeed it is of no great importance if you retain the story, but have formed no opinion of your own. But in matters of morality this happens to us much more than in these things of which we are speaking.

"Speak to me about good and evil." Listen:

> *The wind from Ilium to Ciconian shores*
> *Brought me.*[1]

"Of things some are good, some are bad, and others are indifferent. The good then are the virtues and the things which partake of the virtues; the bad are the vices, and the things which partake of them; and the indifferent are the things which lie between the virtues and the vices, wealth, health, life, death, pleasure, pain." Whence do you know this? "Hellanicus says it in his Egyptian history"; for what difference does it make to say this, or to say that "Diogenes has it in his *Ethic*," or Chrysippus or Cleanthes? Have you then examined any of these things and formed an opinion of your own? Show how you are used to behave in a storm on shipboard? Do you remember this division, when the sail rattles and a man, who knows nothing of times and seasons, stands by you when you are screaming and says, "Tell me, I ask you by the Gods, what you were saying just now. Is it a vice to suffer shipwreck: does it participate in vice?" Will you not take up a stick and lay it on his head? What have we to do with you, man?

[1] Homer, *Odyssey*, ix. 39.

we are perishing and you come to mock us? But if Cæsar sent for you to answer a charge, do you remember the distinction? If, when you are going in, pale and trembling, a person should come up to you and say, "Why do you tremble, man? what is the matter about which you are engaged? Does Cæsar who sits within give virtue and vice to those who go in to him?" You reply, "Why do you also mock me and add to my present sorrows?" Still tell me, philosopher, tell me why you tremble? Is it not death of which you run the risk, or a prison, or pain of the body, or banishment, or disgrace? What else is there? Is there any vice or anything which partakes of vice? What then did you use to say of these things? "What have you to do with me, man? my own evils are enough for me." And you say right. Your own evils are enough for you, your baseness, your cowardice, your boasting which you showed when you sat in the school. Why did you decorate yourself with what belonged to others? Why did you call yourself a Stoic?

Observe yourselves thus in your actions, and you will find to what sect you belong. You will find that most of you are Epicureans, a few Peripatetics, and those feeble. For wherein will you show that you really consider virtue equal to everything else or even superior? But show me a Stoic, if you can. Where or how? But you can show me an endless number who utter small arguments of the Stoics. For do the same persons repeat the Epicurean opinions any worse? And the Peripatetic, do they not handle them also with equal accuracy? who then is a Stoic? As we call a statue *Phidiac,* which is fashioned according to the art of Phidias; so show me a man who is fashioned according to the doctrines which he utters. Show me a man who is sick and happy, in danger and happy, dying and happy, in exile and happy, in disgrace and happy. Show him: I desire, by the gods, to see a Stoic. You cannot show me one fashioned so; but show me at least one who is forming, who has shown a tendency to be a Stoic. Do me this favor: do not grudge an old man seeing a sight which I have not seen yet. Do you think that you must show me the Zeus of Phidias or the Athena, a work of ivory and gold?[1] Let any of you show me a human soul ready to think as God does, and not to blame either God or man, ready not to be disappointed about anything, not to consider himself damaged by anything, not to be angry, not to be envious, not to be jealous; and why should I not say it direct? desirous from a man to become a god, and in this poor mortal body thinking of his fellowship with Zeus.[2] Show me the man. But you cannot. Why then do you delude yourselves and cheat others? and why do you put on a guise which does not belong to you, and walk about being thieves and pilferers of these names and things which do not belong to you?

And now I am your teacher, and you are instructed in my school. And I have this purpose, to make you free from restraint, compulsion, hindrance, to make you free, prosperous, happy, looking to God in everything small and great. And you are here to learn and practice these things. Why, then, do you not finish the work, if you also have such a purpose as you ought to have, and if I, in addition to the purpose, also have such qualification as I ought to have? What is that which is wanting? When I see an artificer and material lying by him, I expect the work. Here, then, is the artificer, here the material; what is it that we want? Is not the thing one that can be taught? It is. Is it not then in our power? The only thing of all that is in our power. Neither wealth is in our power, nor health, nor reputation, nor in a word anything else except the right use of appearances. This is by nature free from restraint, this alone is free from impediment. Why then do you not finish the work? Tell me the reason. For it is either through my fault that you do not finish it, or through your own fault, or through the nature of the thing. The thing itself is possible, and the only thing in our power. It remains then that the fault is either in me or in you, or, what is nearer the truth, in both. Well then, are you willing that we begin at last to bring such a purpose into this school, and to take no notice of the past? Let us only make a beginning. Trust to me, and you will see.

[1] See ii. 8.
[2] I John, i. 3.

CHAPTER 20. *Against the Epicureans and Academics*

THE propositions which are true and evident are of necessity used even by those who contradict them: and a man might perhaps consider it to be the greatest proof of a thing being evident that it is found to be necessary even for him who denies it to make use of it at the same time. For instance, if a man should deny that there is anything universally true, it is plain that he must make the contradictory negation, that nothing is universally true. What, wretch, do you not admit even this? For what else is this than to affirm that whatever is universally affirmed is false? Again if a man should come forward and say: "Know that there is nothing that can be known, but all things are incapable of sure evidence"; or if another say, "Believe me and you will be the better for it, that a man ought not to believe anything"; or again, if another should say, "Learn from me, man, that it is not possible to learn anything; I tell you this and will teach you, if you choose." Now in what respect do these differ from those? Whom shall I name? Those who call themselves Academics? "Men, agree that no man agrees: believe us that no man believes anybody."

Thus Epicurus also, when he designs to destroy the natural fellowship of mankind, at the same time makes use of that which he destroys. For what does he say? "Be not deceived, men, nor be led astray, nor be mistaken: there is no natural fellowship among rational animals; believe me. But those who say otherwise, deceive you and seduce you by false reasons." What is this to you? Permit us to be deceived. Will you fare worse, if all the rest of us are persuaded that there is a natural fellowship among us, and that it ought by all means to be preserved? Nay, it will be much better and safer for you. Man, why do you trouble yourself about us? Why do you keep awake for us? Why do you light your lamp? Why do you rise early? Why do you write so many books, that no one of us may be deceived about the gods and believe that they take care of men; or that no one may suppose the nature of good to be other than pleasure? For if this is so, lie down and sleep, and lead the life of a worm, of which you judged yourself worthy: eat and drink, and enjoy women, and ease yourself, and snore.[1] And what is it to you, how the rest shall think about these things, whether right or wrong? For what have we to do with you? You take care of sheep because they supply us with wool, and milk, and, last of all, with their flesh. Would it not be a desirable thing if men could be lulled and enchanted by the Stoics, and sleep and present themselves to you and to those like you to be shorn and milked? For this you ought to say to your brother Epicureans: but ought you not to conceal it from others, and particularly before everything to persuade them that we are by nature adapted for fellowship, that temperance is a good thing; in order that all things may be secured for you? Or ought we to maintain this fellowship with some and not with others? With whom, then, ought we to maintain it? With such as on their part also maintain it, or with such as violate this fellowship? And who violate it more than you who establish such doctrines?

What then was it that waked Epicurus from his sleepiness, and compelled him to write what he did write? What else was it than that which is the strongest thing in men, nature, which draws a man to her own will though he be unwilling and complaining? "For since," she says, "you think that there is no community among mankind, write this opinion and leave it for others, and break your sleep to do this, and by your own practice condemn your own opinions." Shall we then say that Orestes was agitated by the Erinyes and roused from his deep sleep, and did not more savage Erinyes and Pains rouse Epicurus from his sleep and not allow him to rest, but compelled him to make known his own evils, as madness and wine did the Galli? So strong and invincible is man's nature. For how can a vine be moved not in the manner of a vine, but in the manner of an olive tree? or on the other hand how can an olive tree be moved not in the manner of an olive tree, but in the manner of a vine? It is impossible: it cannot be conceived. Neither then is it possible for a man completely to lose the movements of a man; and even those who are deprived of their genital members are not able to deprive themselves of

[1] I Cor. 15. 32.

man's desires. Thus Epicurus also mutilated all the offices of a man, and of a father of a family, and of a citizen and of a friend, but he did not mutilate human desires, for he could not; not more than the lazy Academics can cast away or blind their own senses, though they have tried with all their might to do it. What a shame is this? when a man has received from nature measures and rules for the knowing of truth, and does not strive to add to these measures and rules and to improve them, but, just the contrary, endeavors to take away and destroy whatever enables us to discern the truth?

What say you philosopher? piety and sanctity, what do you think that they are? "If you like, I will demonstrate that they are good things." Well, demonstrate it, that our citizens may be turned and honor the deity and may no longer be negligent about things of the highest value. "Have you then the demonstrations?" I have, and I am thankful. "Since then you are well pleased with them, hear the contrary: 'That there are no Gods, and, if there are, they take no care of men, nor is there any fellowship between us and them; and that this piety and sanctity which is talked of among most men is the lying of boasters and sophists, or certainly of legislators for the purpose of terrifying and checking wrong-doers.'" Well done, philosopher, you have done something for our citizens, you have brought back all the young men to contempt of things divine. "What then, does not this satisfy you? Learn now, that justice is nothing, that modesty is folly, that a father is nothing, a son nothing." Well done, philosopher, persist, persuade the young men, that we may have more with the same opinions as you and who say the same as you. From such principles as those have grown our well-constituted states; by these was Sparta founded: Lycurgus fixed these opinions in the Spartans by his laws and education, that neither is the servile condition more base than honourable, nor the condition of free men more honourable than base, and that those who died at Thermopylæ died from these opinions; and through what other opinions did the Athenians leave their city? Then those who talk thus, marry and beget children, and employ themselves in public affairs and make themselves priests and interpreters. Of whom? of gods who do not exist: and they consult the Pythian priestess that they may hear lies, and they repeat the oracles to others. Monstrous impudence and imposture.

Man what are you doing? are you refuting yourself every day; and will you not give up these frigid attempts? When you eat, where do you carry your hand to? to your mouth or to your eye? when you wash yourself, what do you go into? do you ever call a pot a dish, or a ladle a spit? If I were a slave of any of these men, even if I must be flayed by him daily, I would rack him. If he said, "Boy, throw some olive-oil into the bath," I would take pickle sauce and pour it down on his head. "What is this?" he would say. An appearance was presented to me, I swear by your genius, which could not be distinguished from oil and was exactly like it. "Here give me the barley drink," he says. I would fill and carry him a dish of sharp sauce. "Did I not ask for the barley drink?" Yes, master; this is the barley drink. "Take it and smell; take it and taste." How do you know then if our senses deceive us? If I had three or four fellow-slaves of the same opinion, I should force him to hang himself through passion or to change his mind. But now they mock us by using all the things which nature gives, and in words destroying them.

Grateful indeed are men and modest, who, if they do nothing else, are daily eating bread and yet are shameless enough to say, we do not know if there is a Demeter or her daughter Persephone or a Pluto; not to mention that they are enjoying the night and the day, the seasons of the year, and the stars, and the sea, and the land, and the co-operation of mankind, and yet they are not moved in any degree by these things to turn their attention to them; but they only seek to belch out their little problem, and when they have exercised their stomach to go off to the bath. But what they shall say, and about what things or to what persons, and what their hearers shall learn from this talk, they care not even in the least degree, nor do they care if any generous youth after hearing such talk should suffer any harm from it, nor after he has suffered harm should lose all the seeds of his generous nature: nor if we should give an adulterer help toward being shameless in his acts; nor if a public peculator should lay hold of some cunning excuse from these doctrines; nor if another who neglects his parents should be confirmed in his audacity by this teaching. What then in your opinion is good or bad? This or that? Why then should a man say any more in reply to such persons as these, or give them any reason or listen to any reasons from them, or try to convince them? By Zeus one might much sooner expect to make catamites change their mind than those who are become so deaf and blind to their own evils.[1]

CHAPTER 21. *Of inconsistency*

SOME things men readily confess, and other things they do not. No one then will confess that he is a fool or without understanding; but, quite the contrary, you will hear all men saying, "I wish that I had fortune equal to my understanding." But men readily confess that they are timid, and they say: "I am rather timid, I confess; but as to other respects you will not find me to be foolish." A man will not readily confess that he is intemperate; and that he is unjust, he will not confess at all. He will by no means confess that he is envious or a busybody. Most men will confess that they are compassionate. What then is the reason? The chief thing is inconsistency and confusion in the things which relate to good and evil. But different men have different reasons; and generally what they imagine to be base, they do not confess at all. But they suppose timidity to be a characteristic of a good disposition, and compassion also; but silliness to be the absolute characteristic of a slave. And they do not at all admit the things which are offenses against society. But in the case of most errors, for this reason chiefly, they are induced to confess them, because they imagine that there is something involuntary in them as in timidity and compassion; and if a man confess that he is in any respect intemperate, he alleges love as an excuse for what is involuntary. But men do not imagine injustice to be at all involuntary. There is also in jealousy, as they suppose, something involuntary;

[1] Compare Matt. 21. 31.

and for this reason they confess to jealousy also.

Living then among such men, who are so confused, so ignorant of what they say, and of evils which they have or have not, and why they have them, or how they shall be relieved of them, I think it is worth the trouble for a man to watch constantly "Whether I also am one of them, what imagination I have about myself, how I conduct myself, whether I conduct myself as a prudent man, whether I conduct myself as a temperate man, whether I ever say this, that I have been taught to be prepared for everything that may happen. Have I the consciousness, which a man who knows nothing ought to have, that I know nothing? Do I go to my teacher as men go to oracles, prepared to obey? or do I like a sniveling boy go to my school to learn history and understand the books which I did not understand before, and, if it should happen so, to explain them also to others?" Man, you have had a fight in the house with a poor slave, you have turned the family upside down, you have frightened the neighbours, and you come to me as if you were a wise man, and you take your seat and judge how I have explained some word, and how I have babbled whatever came into my head. You come full of envy, and humbled, because you bring nothing from home; and you sit during the discussion thinking of nothing else than how your father is disposed toward you and your brother. "What are they saying about me there? now they think that I am improving, and are saying, 'He will return with all knowledge.' I wish I could learn everything before I return: but much labour is necessary, and no one sends me anything, and the baths at Nicopolis are dirty; everything is bad at home, and bad here."

Then they say, "No one gains any profit from the school." Why, who comes to the school? who comes for the purpose of being improved? who comes to present his opinions to be purified? who comes to learn what he is in want of? Why do you wonder then if you carry back from the school the very things which you bring into it? For you come not to lay aside or to correct them or to receive other principles in place of them. By no means, nor anything like it. You rather look to this,

whether you possess already that for which you come. You wish to prattle about theorems? What then? Do you not become greater triflers? Do not your little theorems give you some opportunity of display? You solve sophistical syllogisms.[1] Do you not examine the assumptions of the syllogism named "The Liar"?[2] Do you not examine hypothetical syllogisms? Why, then, are you still vexed if you receive the things for which you come to the school? "Yes; but if my child die or my brother, or if I must die or be racked, what good will these things do me?" Well, did you come for this? for this do you sit by my side? did you ever for this light your lamp or keep awake? or, when you went out to the walking-place, did you ever propose any appearance that had been presented to you instead of a syllogism, and did you and your friends discuss it together? Where and when? Then you say, "Theorems are useless." To whom? To such as make a bad use of them. For eyesalves are not useless to those who use them as they ought and when they ought. Fomentations are not useless. Dumb-bells[3] are not useless; but they are useless to some, useful to others. If you ask me now if syllogisms are useful, I will tell you that they are useful, and if you choose, I will prove it.[4] "How then will they in any way be useful to me?" Man, did you ask if they are useful to you, or did you ask generally? Let him who is suffering from dysentery ask me if vinegar is useful: I will say that it is useful. "Will it then be useful to me?" I will say, "No." Seek first for the discharge to be stopped and the ulcers to be closed. And do you, O men, first cure the ulcers and stop the discharge; be tranquil in your mind, bring it free from distraction into the school, and you will know what power reason has.

CHAPTER 22. *On friendship*

WHAT a man applies himself to earnestly, that he naturally loves. Do men then apply themselves earnestly to the things which are bad? By no means. Well, do they apply themselves to things which in no way concern themselves? Not to these either. It remains, then,

---

[1] See i. 7.   [2] See ii. 17.
[3] See page 109, note on halteres.   [4] See ii. 25.

that they employ themselves earnestly only about things which are good; and if they are earnestly employed about things, they love such things also. Whoever, then, understands what is good, can also know how to love; but he who cannot distinguish good from bad, and things which are neither good nor bad from both, how can he possess the power of loving? To love, then, is only in the power of the wise.

"How is this?" a man may say; "I am foolish, and yet I love my child." I am surprised indeed that you have begun by making the admission that you are foolish. For what are you deficient in? Can you not make use of your senses? do you not distinguish appearances? do you not use food which is suitable for your body, and clothing and habitation? Why then do you admit that you are foolish? It is in truth because you are often disturbed by appearances and perplexed, and their power of persuasion often conquers you; and sometimes you think these things to be good, and then the same things to be bad, and lastly neither good nor bad; and in short you grieve, fear, envy, are disturbed, you are changed. This is the reason why you confess that you are foolish. And are you not changeable in love? But wealth, and pleasure and, in a word, things themselves, do you sometimes think them to be good and sometimes bad? and do you not think the same men at one time to be good, at another time bad? and have you not at one time a friendly feeling toward them and at another time the feeling of an enemy? and do you not at one time praise them and at another time blame them? "Yes; I have these feelings also." Well then, do you think that he who has been deceived about a man is his friend? "Certainly not." And he who has selected a man as his friend and is of a changeable disposition, has he good-will toward him? "He has not." And he who now abuses a man, and afterward admires him? "This man also has no good-will to the other." Well then, did you never see little dogs caressing and playing with one another, so that you might say there is nothing more friendly? but, that you may know what friendship is, throw a bit of flesh among them, and you will learn. Throw between yourself and your son a little estate, and

you will know how soon he will wish to bury you and how soon you wish your son to die. Then you will change your tone and say, "What a son I have brought up! He has long been wishing to bury me." Throw a smart girl between you; and do you, the old man, love her, and the young one will love her too. If a little fame intervene, or dangers, it will be just the same. You will utter the words of the father of Admetus!

Life gives you pleasure: and why not your father.[1]

Do you think that Admetus did not love his own child when he was little? that he was not in agony when the child had a fever? that he did not often say, "I wish I had the fever instead of the child?" then when the test (the thing) came and was near, see what words they utter. Were not Eteocles and Polynices from the same mother and from the same father? Were they not brought up together, had they not lived together, drunk together, slept together, and often kissed one another? So that, if any man, I think, had seen them, he would have ridiculed the philosophers for the paradoxes which they utter about friendship. But when a quarrel rose between them about the royal power, as between dogs about a bit of meat, see what they say

Polynices. Where will you take your station before the towers?
Eteocles. Why do you ask me this?
Pol. I will place myself opposite and try to kill you.
Et. I also wish to do the same.[2]

Such are the wishes that they utter.

For universally, be not deceived, every animal is attached to nothing so much as to its own interest. Whatever then appears to it an impediment to this interest, whether this be a brother, or a father, or a child, or beloved, or lover, it hates, spurns, curses: for its nature is to love nothing so much as its own interest; this is father, and brother and kinsman, and country, and God. When, then, the gods appear to us to be an impediment to this, we abuse them and throw down their statues and burn their temples, as Alexander ordered the temples of Æsculapius to be burned when his dear friend died.

[1] Euripides, *Alcestis,* 691.
[2] Euripides, *Phoenician Maidens,* 623.

For this reason if a man put in the same place his interest, sanctity, goodness, and country, and parents, and friends, all these are secured: but if he puts in one place his interest, in another his friends, and his country and his kinsmen and justice itself, all these give way being borne down by the weight of interest. For where the "I" and the "Mine" are placed, to that place of necessity the animal inclines: if in the flesh, there is the ruling power: if in the will, it is there: and if it is in externals, it is there.[1] If then I am there where my will is, then only shall I be a friend such as I ought to be, and son, and father; for this will be my interest, to maintain the character of fidelity, of modesty, of patience, of abstinence, of active co-operation, of observing my relations. But if I put myself in one place, and honesty in another, then the doctrine of Epicurus becomes strong, which asserts either that there is no honesty or it is that which opinion holds to be honest.[2]

It was through this ignorance that the Athenians and the Lacedæmonians quarreled, and the Thebans with both; and the great king quarreled with Hellas, and the Macedonians with both; and the Romans with the Getæ.[3] And still earlier the Trojan war happened for these reasons. Alexander was the guest of Menelaus; and if any man had seen their friendly disposition, he would not have believed any one who said that they were not friends. But there was cast between them a bit of meat, a handsome woman, and about her war arose. And now when you see brothers to be friends appearing to have one mind, do not conclude from this anything about their friendship, not even if they say it and swear that it is impossible for them to be separated from one another. For the ruling principle of a bad man cannot be trusted, it is insecure, has no certain rule by which it is directed, and is overpowered at different times by different appearances. But examine, not what other men examine, if they are born of the same parents and brought up together, and under the same pedagogue; but examine this only, wherein they place their interest, whether in externals or in the will. If in externals, do not name them friends, no more than name them trustworthy or constant, or brave or free: do not name them even men, if you have any judgment. For that is not a principle of human nature which makes them bite one another, and abuse one another, and occupy deserted places or public places, as if they were mountains, and in the courts of justice display the acts of robbers; nor yet that which makes them intemperate and adulterers and corrupters, nor that which makes them do whatever else men do against one another through this one opinion only, that of placing themselves and their interests in the things which are not within the power of their will. But if you hear that in truth these men think the good to be only there, where will is, and where there is a right use of appearances, no longer trouble yourself whether they are father or son, or brothers, or have associated a long time and are companions, but when you have ascertained this only, confidently declare that they are friends, as you declare that they are faithful, that they are just. For where else is friendship than where there is fidelity, and modesty, where there is a communion of honest things and of nothing else?

"But," you may say, "such a one treated me with regard so long; and did he not love me?" How do you know, slave, if he did not regard you in the same way as he wipes his shoes with a sponge, or as he takes care of his beast? How do you know, when you have ceased to be useful as a vessel, he will not throw you away like a broken platter? "But this woman is my wife, and we have lived together so long." And how long did Eriphyle live with Amphiaraus, and was the mother of children and of many? But a necklace came between them. "And what is a necklace?" It is the opinion about such things. That was the bestial principle, that was the thing which broke asunder the friendship between husband and wife, that which did not allow the woman to be a wife nor the mother to be a mother. And let every man among you who has seriously resolved either to be a friend himself or to have another for his friend, cut out these opinions, hate them, drive them from his soul. And thus, first of all, he will not reproach himself,

[1] Matt. 6. 21.
[2] Compare Eccles. 12. 13.
[3] Thucydides, i. 1. Herodotus, i. 1.

he will not be at variance with himself, he will not change his mind, he will not torture himself. In the next place, to another also, who is like himself, he will be altogether and completely a friend. But he will bear with the man who is unlike himself, he will be kind to him, gentle, ready to pardon on account of his ignorance, on account of his being mistaken in things of the greatest importance; but he will be harsh to no man, being well convinced of Plato's doctrine that every mind is deprived of truth unwillingly. If you cannot do this, yet you can do in all other respects as friends do, drink together, and lodge together, and sail together, and you may be born of the same parents; for snakes also are: but neither will they be friends nor you, so long as you retain these bestial and cursed opinions.

CHAPTER 23. *On the power of speaking*

EVERY man will read a book with more pleasure or even with more ease, if it is written in fairer characters. Therefore every man will also listen more readily to what is spoken, if it is signified by appropriate and becoming words. We must not say, then, that there is no faculty of expression: for this affirmation is the characteristic of an impious and also of a timid man. Of an impious man, because he undervalues the gifts which come from God, just as if he would take away the commodity of the power of vision, or of hearing, or of seeing. Has, then, God given you eyes to no purpose? and to no purpose has he infused into them a spirit so strong and of such skillful contrivance as to reach a long way and to fashion the forms of things which are seen? What messenger is so swift and vigilant? And to no purpose has he made the interjacent atmosphere so efficacious and elastic that the vision penetrates through the atmosphere which is in a manner moved? And to no purpose has he made light, without the presence of which there would be no use in any other thing?

Man, be neither ungrateful for these gifts nor yet forget the things which are superior to them. But indeed for the power of seeing and hearing, and indeed for life itself, and for the things which contribute to support it, for the fruits which are dry, and for wine and oil give thanks to God: but remember that he has given you something else better than all these, I mean the power of using them, proving them and estimating the value of each. For what is that which gives information about each of these powers, what each of them is worth?[1] Is it each faculty itself? Did you ever hear the faculty of vision saying anything about itself? or the faculty of hearing? or wheat, or barley, or a horse or a dog? No; but they are appointed as ministers and slaves to serve the faculty which has the power of making use of the appearances of things. And if you inquire what is the value of each thing, of whom do you inquire? who answers you? How then can any other faculty be more powerful than this, which uses the rest as ministers and itself proves each and pronounces about them? for which of them knows what itself is, and what is its own value? which of them knows when it ought to employ itself and when not? what faculty is it which opens and closes the eyes, and turns them away from objects to which it ought not to apply them and does apply them to other objects? Is it the faculty of vision? No; but it is the faculty of the will. What is that faculty which closes and opens the ears? what is that by which they are curious and inquisitive, or, on the contrary, unmoved by what is said? is it the faculty of hearing? It is no other than the faculty of the will. Will this faculty then, seeing that it is amid all the other faculties which are blind and dumb and unable to see anything else except the very acts for which they are appointed in order to minister to this and serve it, but this faculty alone sees sharp and sees what is the value of each of the rest; will this faculty declare to us that anything else is the best, or that itself is? And what else does the eye do when it is opened than see? But whether we ought to look on the wife of a certain person, and in what manner, who tells us? The faculty of the will. And whether we ought to believe what is said or not to believe it, and if we do believe, whether we ought to be moved by it or not, who tells us? Is it not the faculty of the will? But this faculty of speaking and of ornamenting words, if there is indeed any such peculiar faculty, what else does it do, when there happens to be discourse

[1] See i. 1.

about a thing, than to ornament the words and arrange them as hairdressers do the hair? But whether it is better to speak or to be silent, and better to speak in this way or that way, and whether this is becoming or not becoming, and the season for each and the use, what else tells us than the faculty of the will? Would you have it then to come forward and condemn itself?

"What then?" it says, "if the fact is so, can that which ministers be superior to that to which it ministers, can the horse be superior to the rider, or the dog to the huntsman, or the instrument to the musician, or the servants to the king?" What is that which makes use of the rest? The will. What takes care of all? The will. What destroys the whole man, at one time by hunger, at another time by hanging, and at another time by a precipice? The will. Then is anything stronger in men than this? and how is it possible that the things which are subject to restraint are stronger than that which is not? What things are naturally formed to hinder the faculty of vision? Both will and things which do not depend on the faculty of the will. It is the same with the faculty of hearing, with the faculty of speaking in like manner. But what has a natural power of hindering the will? Nothing which is independent of the will; but only the will itself, when it is perverted. Therefore this is alone vice or alone virtue.

Then being so great a faculty and set over all the rest, let it come forward and tell us that the most excellent of all things is the flesh. Not even if the flesh itself declared that it is the most excellent, would any person bear that it should say this. But what is it, Epicurus, which pronounces this, which wrote about "The End of our Being," which wrote on "The Nature of Things," which wrote about the Canon, which led you to wear a beard, which wrote when it was dying that it was spending the last and a happy day? Was this the flesh or the will? Then do you admit that you possess anything superior to this? and are you not mad? are you in fact so blind and deaf?

What then? Does any man despise the other faculties? I hope not. Does any man say that there is no use or excellence in the speaking faculty? I hope not. That would be foolish, impious, ungrateful toward God. But a man renders to each thing its due value. For there is some use even in an ass, but not so much as in an ox: there is also use in a dog, but not so much as in a slave: there is also some use in a slave, but not so much as in citizens: there is also some use in citizens, but not so much as in magistrates. Not, indeed, because some things are superior, must we undervalue the use which other things have. There is a certain value in the power of speaking, but it is not so great as the power of the will. When, then, I speak thus, let no man think that I ask you to neglect the power of speaking, for neither do I ask you to neglect the eyes, nor the ears nor the hands nor the feet, nor clothing nor shoes. But if you ask me, "What, then, is the most excellent of all things?" what must I say? I cannot say the power of speaking, but the power of the will, when it is right. For it is this which uses the other, and all the other faculties both small and great. For when this faculty of the will is set right, a man who is not good becomes good: but when it fails, a man becomes bad. It is through this that we are unfortunate, that we are fortunate, that we blame one another, are pleased with one another. In a word, it is this which if we neglect it makes unhappiness, and if we carefully look after it makes happiness.

But to take away the faculty of speaking, and to say that there is no such faculty in reality, is the act not only of an ungrateful man toward those who gave it, but also of a cowardly man: for such a person seems to me to fear, if there is any faculty of this kind, that we shall not be able to despise it. Such also are those who say that there is no difference between beauty and ugliness. Then it would happen that a man would be affected in the same way if he saw Thersites and if he saw Achilles; in the same way, if he saw Helen and any other woman. But these are foolish and clownish notions, and the notions of men who know not the nature of each thing, but are afraid, if a man shall see the difference, that he shall immediately be seized and carried off vanquished. But this is the great matter; to leave to each thing the power which it has, and leaving to it this power to see what is the worth of the power, and to learn what is the most excellent of all things, and to pursue this always, to be diligent about this, considering all other things of secondary value compared with this, but yet, as far as we can, not neglecting all those other things. For we must take care of the eyes also, not as if they were the most excellent thing, but we must take care of them on account of the most excellent thing, because it will not be in its true natural condition, if it does not rightly use the other faculties, and prefer some things to others.

What then is usually done? Men generally act as a traveler would do on his way to his own country, when he enters a good inn, and being pleased with it should remain there. Man, you have forgotten your purpose: you were not traveling to this inn, but you were passing through it. "But this is a pleasant inn." And how many other inns are pleasant? and how many meadows are pleasant? yet only for passing through. But your purpose is this, to return to your country, to relieve your kinsmen of anxiety, to discharge the duties of a citizen, to marry, to beget children, to fill the usual magistracies. For you are not come to select more pleasant places, but to live in these where you were born and of which you were made a citizen. Something of the kind takes place in the matter which we are considering. Since, by the aid of speech and such communication as you receive here, you must advance to perfection, and purge your will, and correct the faculty which makes use of the appearances of things; and since it is necessary also for the teaching of theorems to be effected by a certain mode of expression and with a certain variety and sharpness, some persons captivated by these very things abide in them, one captivated by the expression, another by syllogisms, another again by sophisms, and still another by some other inn of the kind; and there they stay and waste away as if they were among Sirens.

Man, your purpose was to make yourself capable of using conformably to nature the appearances presented to you, in your desires not to be frustrated, in your aversion from things not to fall into that which you would avoid, never to have no luck, nor ever to have bad luck, to be free, not hindered, not compelled, conforming yourself to the administration of Zeus, obeying it, well satisfied with this, blaming no one, charging no one with fault, able from your whole soul to utter these verses:

"Lead me, O Zeus, and thou, too, Destiny."

Then having this purpose before you, if some little form of expression pleases you, if some theorems please you, do you abide among them and choose to dwell there, forgetting the things at home, and do you say, "These things are fine"? Who says that they are not fine? but only as being a way home, as inns are. For what hinders you from being an unfortunate man, even if you speak like Demosthenes? and what prevents you, if you can resolve syllogisms like Chrysippus, from being wretched, from sorrowing, from envying, in a word, from being disturbed, from being unhappy? Nothing. You see then that these were inns, worth nothing; and that the purpose before you was something else. When I speak thus to some persons, they think that I am rejecting care about speaking or care about theorems. I am not rejecting this care, but I am rejecting the abiding about these things incessantly and putting our hopes in them. If a man by this teaching does harm to those who listen to him, reckon me too among those who do this harm: for I am not able, when I see one thing which is most excellent and supreme, to say that another is so, in order to please you.

CHAPTER 24. *To a person who was one of those who were not valued by him*

A CERTAIN person said to him: "Frequently I desired to hear you and came to you, and you never gave me any answer: and now, if it is possible, I entreat you to say something to me." Do you think, said Epictetus, that as there is an art in anything else, so there is also an art in speaking, and that he who has the art, will speak skillfully, and he who has not, will speak unskillfully? "I do think so." He, then, who by speaking receives benefit himself, and is able to benefit others, will speak skillfully: but he who is rather damaged by speaking and does damage to others, will he be unskilled in this art of speaking? And you may find that some are damaged and others benefited by speaking. And are all who hear benefited by what they hear? Or will you find that among them also some are benefited and some damaged? "There are both among these also," he said. In this case also, then, those who hear skillfully are benefited, and those who hear unskillfully are damaged? He admitted this. Is there then a skill in hearing also, as there is in speaking? "It seems so." If you choose, consider the matter in this way also. The practice of music, to whom does it belong? "To a musician." And the proper making of a statue, to whom do you think that it belongs? "To a statuary." And the looking at a statue skillfully, does this appear to you to require the aid of no art? "This also requires the aid of art." Then if speaking properly is the business of the skillful man, do you see that to hear also with benefit is the business of the skillful man? Now as to speaking and hearing perfectly, and usefully, let us for the present, if you please, say no more, for both of us are a long way from everything of the kind. But I think that every man will allow this, that he who is going to hear philosophers requires some amount of practice in hearing. Is it not so?

Tell me then about what I should talk to you: about what matter are you able to listen? "About good and evil." Good and evil in what? In a horse? "No." Well, in an ox? "No." What then? In a man? "Yes." Do we know then what a man is, what the notion is that we have of him, or have we our ears in any degree practiced about this matter? But do you understand what nature is? or can you even in any degree understand me when I say, "I shall use demonstration to you?" How? Do you understand this very thing, what demonstration is, or how anything is demonstrated, or by what means; or what things are like demonstration, but are not demonstration? Do you know what is true or what is false? What is consequent on a thing, what is repugnant to a thing, or not consistent, or inconsistent? But must I excite you to philosophy, and how? Shall I show to you the repugnance in the opinions of most men, through which they differ about things good and evil, and about things which are profitable and unprofitable, when you know not this very thing, what

repugnance is? Show me then what I shall accomplish by discoursing with you; excite my inclination to do this. As the grass which is suitable, when it is presented to a sheep, moves its inclination to eat, but if you present to it a stone or bread, it will not be moved to eat; so there are in us certain natural inclinations also to speak, when the hearer shall appear to be somebody, when he himself shall excite us: but when he shall sit by us like a stone or like grass, how can he excite a man's desire? Does the vine say to the husbandman, "Take care of me?" No, but the vine by showing in itself that it will be profitable to the husbandman, if he does take care of it, invites him to exercise care. When children are attractive and lively, whom do they not invite to play with them, and crawl with them, and lisp with them? But who is eager to play with an ass or to bray with it? for though it is small, it is still a little ass.

"Why then do you say nothing to me?" I can only say this to you, that he who knows not who he is, and for what purpose he exists, and what is this world, and with whom he is associated, and what things are the good and the bad, and the beautiful and the ugly, and who neither understands discourse nor demonstration, nor what is true nor what is false, and who is not able to distinguish them, will neither desire according to nature, nor turn away, nor move upward, nor intend, nor assent, nor dissent, nor suspend his judgment: to say all in a few words, he will go about dumb and blind, thinking that he is somebody, but being nobody. Is this so now for the first time? Is it not the fact that, ever since the human race existed, all errors and misfortunes have arisen through this ignorance? Why did Agamemnon and Achilles quarrel with one another? Was it not through not knowing what things are profitable and not profitable? Does not the one say it is profitable to restore Chryseis to her father, and does not the other say that it is not profitable? does not the one say that he ought to take the prize of another, and does not the other say that he ought not? Did they not for these reasons forget both who they were and for what purpose they had come there? Oh, man, for what purpose did you come? to gain mistresses or to fight? "To fight." With whom? the Trojans or the Hellenes? "With the Trojans." Do you then leave Hector alone and draw your sword against your own king? And do you, most excellent Sir, neglect the duties of the king, you who are the people's guardian and have such cares; and are you quarreling about a little girl with the most warlike of your allies, whom you ought by every means to take care of and protect? and do you become worse than a well-behaved priest who treats you these fine gladiators with all respect? Do you see what kind of things ignorance of what is profitable does?

"But I also am rich." Are you then richer than Agamemnon? "But I am also handsome." Are you then more handsome than Achilles? "But I have also beautiful hair." But had not Achilles more beautiful hair and gold-colored? and he did not comb it elegantly nor dress it. "But I am also strong." Can you then lift so great a stone as Hector or Ajax? "But I am also of noble birth." Are you the son of a goddess mother? are you the son of a father sprung from Zeus? What good then do these things do to him, when he sits and weeps for a girl? "But I am an orator." And was he not? Do you not see how he handled the most skillful of the Hellenes in oratory, Odysseus and Phœnix? how he stopped their mouths?[1]

This is all that I have to say to you; and I say even this not willingly. "Why?" Because you have not roused me. For what must I look to in order to be roused, as men who are expert in riding are roused by generous horses? Must I look to your body? You treat it disgracefully. To your dress? That is luxurious. To your behaviour, to your look? That is the same as nothing. When you would listen to a philosopher, do not say to him, "You tell me nothing"; but only show yourself worthy of hearing or fit for hearing; and you will see how you will move the speaker.

CHAPTER 25. *That logic is necessary*[2]

WHEN one of those who were present said, "Persuade me that logic is necessary," he replied: Do you wish me to prove this to you? The answer was, "Yes." Then I must use a demonstrative form of speech. This was granted. How then will you know if I am cheating you by argument? The man was silent. Do you see, said Epictetus, that you yourself are admitting that logic is necessary, if without it you cannot know so much as this, whether logic is necessary or not necessary?

CHAPTER 26. *What is the property of error*

EVERY error comprehends contradiction: for since he who errs does not wish to err, but to be right, it is plain that he does not do what he wishes. For what does the thief wish to do? That which is for his own interest. If, then, the theft is not for his interest, he does not do that which he wishes. But every rational soul is by nature offended at contradiction, and so long as it does not understand this contradiction, it is not hindered from doing contradictory things: but when it does understand the contradiction, it must of necessity avoid the contradiction and avoid it as much as a man must dissent from the false when he sees that a thing is false; but so long as this falsehood does not appear to him, he assents to it as to truth.

He, then, is strong in argument and has the faculty of exhorting and confuting, who is able to show to each man the contradiction through which he errs and clearly to prove how he does not do that which he wishes and does that which he does not wish. For if any one shall show this, a man will himself withdraw from that which he does; but so long as you do not show this, do not be surprised if a man persists in his practice; for having the appearance of doing right, he does what he does. For this reason Socrates, also trusting to this power, used to say, "I am used to call no other witness of what I say, but I am always satisfied with him with whom I am discussing, and I ask him to give his opinion and call him as a witness, and though he is only one, he is sufficient in the place of all." For Socrates knew by what the rational soul is moved, just like a pair of scales, and that it must incline, whether it chooses or not. Show the rational governing faculty a contradiction, and it will withdraw from it; but if you do not show it, rather blame yourself than him who is not persuaded.[3]

[1] Homer, *Iliad*, ix.
[2] See i. 17.
[3] Marcus Aurelius, v. 28; x. 4.

· BOOK THREE ·

CHAPTER I. *Of finery in dress*

A CERTAIN young man a rhetorician came to see Epictetus, with his hair dressed more carefully than was usual and his attire in an ornamental style; whereupon Epictetus said: Tell me if you do not think that some dogs are beautiful and some horses, and so of all other animals. "I do think so," the youth replied. Are not then some men also beautiful and others ugly? "Certainly." Do we, then, for the same reason call each of them in the same kind beautiful, or each beautiful for something peculiar? And you will judge of this matter thus. Since we see a dog naturally formed for one thing, and a horse for another, and for another still, as an example, a nightingale, we may generally and not improperly declare each of them to be beautiful then when it is most excellent according to its nature; but since the nature of each is different, each of them seems to me to be beautiful in a different way. Is it not so? He admitted that it was. That then which makes a dog beautiful, makes a horse ugly; and that which makes a horse beautiful, makes a dog ugly, if it is true that their natures are different. "It seems to be so." For I think that what makes a pancratiast beautiful, makes a wrestler to be not good, and a runner to be most ridiculous; and he who is beautiful for the Pentathlon, is very ugly for wrestling.[1] "It is so," said he. What, then, makes a man beautiful? Is it that which in its kind makes both a dog and a horse beautiful? "It is," he said. What then makes a dog beautiful? The possession of the excellence of a dog. And what makes a horse beautiful? The possession of the excellence of a horse. What then makes a man beautiful? Is it not the possession of the excellence of a man? And do you, then, if you wish to be beautiful, young man, labour at this, the acquisition of human excellence. But what is this? Observe whom you yourself praise, when you praise many persons without partiality: do you praise the just or the unjust? "The just." Whether do you praise the

moderate or the immoderate? "The moderate." And the temperate or the intemperate? "The temperate." If, then, you make yourself such a person, you will know that you will make yourself beautiful: but so long as you neglect these things, you must be ugly, even though you contrive all you can to appear beautiful.

Further I do not know what to say to you: for if I say to you what I think, I shall offend you, and you will perhaps leave the school and not return to it: and if I do not say what I think, see how I shall be acting, if you come to me to be improved, and I shall not improve you at all, and if you come to me as to a philosopher, and I shall say nothing to you as a philosopher. And how cruel it is to you to leave you uncorrected. If at any time afterward you shall acquire sense, you will with good reason blame me and say, "What did Epictetus observe in me that, when he saw me in such a plight coming to him in such a scandalous condition, he neglected me and never said a word? did he so much despair of me? was I not young? was I not able to listen to reason? and how many other young men at this age commit many like errors? I hear that a certain Polemon from being a most dissolute youth underwent such a great change. Well, suppose that he did not think that I should be a Polemon;[2] yet he might have set my hair right, he might have stripped off my decorations, he might have stopped me from plucking the hair out of my body; but when he saw me dressed like—what shall I say?—he kept silent." I do not say like what; but you will say, when you come to your senses and shall know what it is and what persons use such a dress.

If you bring this charge against me hereafter, what defense shall I make? Why, shall I say that the man will not be persuaded by me? Was Laius persuaded by Apollo? Did he not go away and get drunk and show no care for the oracle? Well then, for this reason did

[1] Compare Aristotle, *Rhetoric*, i. 5.

[2] See iv. 11.

Apollo refuse to tell him the truth? I indeed do not know, whether you will be persuaded by me or not; but Apollo knew most certainly that Laius would not be persuaded and yet he spoke. But why did he speak? I say in reply: But why is he Apollo, and why does he deliver oracles, and why has he fixed himself in this place as a prophet and source of truth and for the inhabitants of the world to resort to him? and why are the words "Know yourself" written in front of the temple, though no person takes any notice of them?

Did Socrates persuade all his hearers to take care of themselves? Not the thousandth part. But, however, after he had been placed in this position by the deity, as he himself says, he never left it. But what does he say even to his judges? "If you acquit me on these conditions that I no longer do that which I do now, I will not consent and I will not desist; but I will go up both to young and to old, and, to speak plainly, to every man whom I meet, and I will ask the questions which I ask now; and most particularly will I do this to you my fellow-citizens, because you are more nearly related to me."[1] Are you so curious, Socrates, and such a busybody? and how does it concern you how we act? and what is it that you say? "Being of the same community and of the same kin, you neglect yourself, and show yourself a bad citizen to the state, and a bad kinsman to your kinsmen, and a bad neighbor to your neighbors." "Who, then are you?" Here it is a great thing to say, "I am he whose duty it is to take care of men; for it is not every little heifer which dares to resist a lion; but if the bull comes up and resists him, say to the bull, if you choose, 'And who are you, and what business have you here?'" Man, in every kind there is produced something which excels; in oxen, in dogs, in bees, in horses. Do not then say to that which excels, "Who, then, are you?" If you do, it will find a voice in some way and say, "I am such a thing as the purple in a garment: do not expect me to be like the others, or blame my nature that it has made me different from the rest of men."

What then? am I such a man? Certainly not. And are you such a man as can listen to

[1] Plato, *Apology*, 30.

the truth? I wish you were. But however since in a manner I have been condemned to wear a white beard and a cloak, and you come to me as to a philosopher, I will not treat you in a cruel way nor yet as if I despaired of you, but I will say: Young man, whom do you wish to make beautiful? In the first place, know who you are and then adorn yourself appropriately. You are a human being; and this is a mortal animal which has the power of using appearances rationally. But what is meant by "rationally?" Conformably to nature and completely. What, then, do you possess which is peculiar? Is it the animal part? No. Is it the condition of mortality? No. Is it the power of using appearances? No. You possess the rational faculty as a peculiar thing: adorn and beautify this; but leave your hair to him who made it as he chose. Come, what other appellations have you? Are you man or woman? "Man." Adorn yourself then as man, not as woman. Woman is naturally smooth and delicate; and if she has much hair (on her body), she is a monster and is exhibited at Rome among monsters. And in a man it is monstrous not to have hair; and if he has no hair, he is a monster; but if he cuts off his hairs and plucks them out, what shall we do with him? where shall we exhibit him? and under what name shall we show him? "I will exhibit to you a man who chooses to be a woman rather than a man." What a terrible sight! There is no man who will not wonder at such a notice. Indeed I think that the men who pluck out their hairs do what they do without knowing what they do. Man what fault have you to find with your nature? That it made you a man? What then? was it fit that nature should make all human creatures women? and what advantage in that case would you have had in being adorned? for whom would you have adorned yourself, if all human creatures were women? But you are not pleased with the matter: set to work then upon the whole business. Take away—what is its name?—that which is the cause of the hairs: make yourself a woman in all respects, that we may not be mistaken: do not make one half man, and the other half woman. Whom do you wish to please? The women? Please them as a man. "Well; but they like smooth men." Will you not hang yourself? and if women took delight in cata-mites, would you become one? Is this your business? were you born for this purpose, that dissolute women should delight in you? Shall we make such a one as you a citizen of Cor-inth and perchance a prefect of the city, or chief of the youth, or general or superinten-dent of the games? Well, and when you have taken a wife, do you intend to have your hairs plucked out? To please whom and for what purpose? And when you have begotten chil-dren, will you introduce them also into the state with the habit of plucking their hairs? A beautiful citizen, and senator and rhetorician. We ought to pray that such young men be born among us and brought up.

Do not so, I entreat you by the Gods, young man: but when you have once heard these words, go away and say to yourself, "Epictetus has not said this to me; for how could he? but some propitious God through him: for it would never have come into his thoughts to say this, since he is not accustomed to talk thus with any person. Come then let us obey God, that we may not be subject to his anger." You say, "No." But, if a crow by his croaking sig-nifies anything to you, it is not the crow which signifies, but God through the crow; and if he signifies anything through a human voice, will he not cause the man to say this to you, that you may know the power of the divinity, that he signifies to some in this way, and to others in that way, and concerning the greatest things and the chief he signifies through the noblest messenger? What else is it which the poet says:

For we ourselves have warned him, and have sent
Hermes the careful watcher, Argus' slayer,
The husband not to kill nor wed the wife.[1]

Was Hermes going to descend from heaven to say this to him? And now the Gods say this to you and send the messenger, the slayer of Argus, to warn you not to pervert that which is well arranged, nor to busy yourself about it, but to allow a man to be a man, and a woman to be a woman, a beautiful man to be as a beautiful man, and an ugly man as an ugly man, for you are not flesh and hair, but you are will; and if your will is beautiful, then you will be beautiful. But up to the present time I

[1] Homer, *Odyssey*, i. 37.

dare not tell you that you are ugly, for I think that you are readier to hear anything than this. But see what Socrates says to the most beautiful and blooming of men Alcibiades: "Try, then, to be beautiful." What does he say to him? "Dress your hair and pluck the hairs from your legs." Nothing of that kind. But "Adorn your will, take away bad opinions." "How with the body?" Leave it as it is by na-ture. Another has looked after these things: intrust them to him. "What then, must a man be uncleaned?" Certainly not; but what you are and are made by nature, cleanse this. A man should be cleanly as a man, a woman as a woman, a child as a child. You say no: but let us also pluck out the lion's mane, that he may not be uncleaned, and the cock's comb for he also ought to be cleaned. Granted, but as a cock, and the lion as a lion, and the hunt-ing dog as a hunting dog.

CHAPTER 2. *In what a man ought to be exer-cised who has made proficiency; and that we neglect the chief things*

THERE are three things in which a man ought to exercise himself who would be wise and good. The first concerns the desires and the aversions, that a man may not fail to get what he desires, and that he may not fall into that which he does not desire.[2] The second con-cerns the movements (toward) and the move-ments from an object, and generally in doing what a man ought to do, that he may act ac-cording to order, to reason, and not carelessly. The third thing concerns freedom from decep-tion and rashness in judgement, and generally it concerns the assents. Of these topics the chief and the most urgent is that which relates to the affects; for an affect is produced in no other way than by a failing to obtain that which a man desires or a falling into that which a man would wish to avoid. This is that which brings in perturbations, disorders, bad fortune, misfortunes, sorrows, lamentations and envy; that which makes men envious and jealous; and by these causes we are unable even to listen to the precepts of reason. The second topic concerns the duties of a man; for I ought not to be free from affects like a statue, but I ought to maintain the relations natural and ac-

[2] Marcus Aurelius, xi. 37.

quired, as a pious man, as a son, as a father, as a citizen.

The third topic is that which immediately concerns those who are making proficiency, that which concerns the security of the other two, so that not even in sleep any appearance unexamined may surprise us, nor in intoxication, nor in melancholy. "This," it may be said, "is above our power." But the present philosophers neglecting the first topic and the second, employ themselves on the third, using sophistical arguments, making conclusions from questioning, employing hypotheses, lying. "For a man must," as it is said, "when employed on these matters, take care that he is not deceived." Who must? The wise and good man. This then is all that is wanting to you. Have you successfully worked out the rest? Are you free from deception in the matter of money? If you see a beautiful girl, do you resist the appearance? If your neighbor obtains an estate by will, are you not vexed? Now is there nothing else wanting to you except unchangeable firmness of mind? Wretch, you hear these very things with fear and anxiety that some person may despise you, and with inquiries about what any person may say about you. And if a man come and tell you that in a certain conversation in which the question was, "Who is the best philosopher," a man who was present said that a certain person was the chief philosopher, your little soul which was only a finger's length stretches out to two cubits. But if another who is present says, "You are mistaken; it is not worth while to listen to a certain person, for what does he know? he has only the first principles, and no more?" then you are confounded, you grow pale, you cry out immediately, "I will show him who I am, that I am a great philosopher." It is seen by these very things: why do you wish to show it by others? Do you not know that Diogenes pointed out one of the sophists in this way by stretching out his middle finger? And then when the man was wild with rage, "This," he said, "is the certain person: I have pointed him out to you." For a man is not shown by the finger, as a stone or a piece of wood: but when any person shows the man's principles, then he shows him as a man.

Let us look at your principles also. For is it

not plain that you value not at all your own will, but you look externally to things which are independent of your will? For instance, what will a certain person say? and what will people think of you? will you be considered a man of learning; have you read Chrysippus or Antipater? for if you have read Archedemus[1] also, you have everything. Why are you still uneasy lest you should not show us who you are? Would you let me tell you what manner of man you have shown us that you are? You have exhibited yourself to us as a mean fellow, querulous, passionate, cowardly, finding fault with everything, blaming everybody, never quiet, vain: this is what you have exhibited to us. Go away now and read Archedemus; then, if a mouse should leap down and make a noise, you are a dead man. For such a death awaits you as it did— what was the man's name?—Crinis; and he too was proud, because he understood Archedemus.

Wretch, will you not dismiss these things that do not concern you at all? These things are suitable to those who are able to learn them without perturbation, to those who can say: "I am not subject to anger, to grief, to envy: I am not hindered, I am not restrained. What remains for me? I have leisure, I am tranquil: let us see how we must deal with sophistical arguments; let us see how when a man has accepted an hypothesis he shall not be led away to anything absurd." To them such things belong. To those who are happy it is appropriate to light a fire, to dine; if they choose, both to sing and to dance. But when the vessel is sinking, you come to me and hoist the sails.

CHAPTER 3. *What is the matter on which a good man should be employed, and in what we ought chiefly to practice ourselves*

THE material for the wise and good man is his own ruling faculty: and the body is the material for the physician and the aliptes;[2] the land is the matter for the husbandman. The business of the wise and good man is to use appearances conformably to nature: and as it is the nature of every soul to assent to the

[1] See ii, 4.
[2] The man who oils persons.

truth, to dissent from the false, and to remain in suspense as to that which is uncertain; so it is its nature to be moved toward the desire of the good, and to aversion from the evil; and with respect to that which is neither good nor bad it feels indifferent. For as the money-changer is not allowed to reject Cæsar's coin, nor the seller of herbs, but if you show the coin, whether he chooses or not, he must give up what is sold for the coin; so it is also in the matter of the soul. When the good appears, it immediately attracts to itself; the evil repels from itself. But the soul will never reject the manifest appearance of the good, any more than persons will reject Cæsar's coin. On this principle depends every movement both of man and God.[1]

For this reason the good is preferred to every intimate relationship. There is no intimate relationship between me and my father, but there is between me and the good. "Are you so hard-hearted?" Yes, for such is my nature; and this is the coin which God has given me. For this reason, if the good is something different from the beautiful and the just, both father is gone, and brother and country, and everything. But shall I overlook my own good, in order that you may have it, and shall I give it up to you? Why? "I am your father." But you are not my good. "I am your brother." But you are not my good. But if we place the good in a right determination of the will, the very observance of the relations of life is good, and accordingly he who gives up any external things obtains that which is good. Your father takes away your property. But he does not injure you. Your brother will have the greater part of the estate in land. Let him have as much as he chooses. Will he then have a greater share of modesty, of fidelity, of brotherly affection? For who will eject you from this possession? Not even Zeus, for neither has he chosen to do so; but he has made this in my own power, and he has given it to me just as he possessed it himself, free from hindrance, compulsion, and impediment. When then the coin which another uses is a different coin, if a man presents this coin, he receives that which is sold for it. Suppose that there comes into the province a thievish proconsul, what

coin does he use? Silver coin. Show it to him, and carry off what you please. Suppose one comes who is an adulterer: what coin does he use? Little girls. "Take," a man says, "the coin, and sell me the small thing." "Give," says the seller, "and buy." Another is eager to possess boys. Give him the coin, and receive what you wish. Another is fond of hunting: give him a fine nag or a dog. Though he groans and laments, he will sell for it that which you want. For another compels him from within, he who has fixed this coin.[2]

Against this kind of thing chiefly a man should exercise himself. As soon as you go out in the morning, examine every man whom you see, every man whom you hear; answer as to a question, "What have you seen?" A handsome man or woman? Apply the rule: Is this independent of the will, or dependent? Independent. Take it away. What have you seen? A man lamenting over the death of a child. Apply the rule. Death is a thing independent of the will. Take it away. Has the proconsul met you? Apply the rule. What kind of thing is a proconsul's office? Independent of the will, or dependent on it? Independent. Take this away also: it does not stand examination: cast it away: it is nothing to you.

If we practiced this and exercised ourselves in it daily from morning to night, something indeed would be done. But now we are forthwith caught half-asleep by every appearance, and it is only, if ever, that in the school we are roused a little. Then when we go out, if we see a man lamenting, we say, "He is undone." If we see a consul, we say, "He is happy." If we see an exiled man, we say, "He is miserable." If we see a poor man, we say, "He is wretched: he has nothing to eat."

We ought then to eradicate these bad opinions, and to this end we should direct all our efforts. For what is weeping and lamenting? Opinion. What is bad fortune? Opinion. What is civil sedition, what is divided opinion, what is blame, what is accusation, what is impiety, what is trifling? All these things are opinions, and nothing more, and opinions about things independent of the will, as if they were good and bad. Let a man transfer

[1] Compare i. 19.

[2] Compare Rom. 7. 21-23.

these opinions to things dependent on the will, and I engage for him that he will be firm and constant, whatever may be the state of things around him. Such as is a dish of water, such is the soul. Such as is the ray of light which falls on the water, such are the appearances. When the water is moved, the ray also seems to be moved, yet it is not moved. And when, then, a man is seized with giddiness, it is not the arts and the virtues which are confounded, but the spirit on which they are impressed; but if the spirit be restored to its settled state, those things also are restored.

CHAPTER 4. *Against a person who showed his partisanship in an unseemly way in a theatre*
THE governor of Epirus having shown his favor to an actor in an unseemly way and being publicly blamed on this account, and afterward having reported to Epictetus that he was blamed and that he was vexed at those who blamed him, Epictetus said: What harm have they been doing? These men also were acting as partisans, as you were doing. The governor replied, "Does, then, any person show his partisanship in this way?" When they see you, said Epictetus, who are their governor, a friend of Cæsar and his deputy, showing partisanship in this way, was it not to be expected that they also should show their partisanship in the same way? for if it is not right to show partisanship in this way, do not do so yourself; and if it is right, why are you angry if they followed your example? For whom have the many to imitate except you, who are their superiors? to whose example should they look when they go to the theatre except yours? "See how the deputy of Cæsar looks on: he has cried out, and I too, then, will cry out. He springs up from his seat, and I will spring up. His slaves sit in various parts of the theatre and call out. I have no slaves, but I will myself cry out as much as I can and as loud as all of them together." You ought then to know when you enter the theatre that you enter as a rule and example to the rest how they ought to look at the acting. Why then did they blame you? Because every man hates that which is a hindrance to him. They wished one person to be crowned; you wished another. They were a hindrance to you, and you were a hindrance

to them. You were found to be the stronger; and they did what they could; they blamed that which hindered them. What, then, would you have? That you should do what you please, and they should not even say what they please? And what is the wonder? Do not the husbandmen abuse Zeus when they are hindered by him? do not the sailors abuse him? do they ever cease abusing Cæsar? What then? does not Zeus know? is not what is said reported to Cæsar? What, then, does he do? he knows that, if he punished all who abuse him, he would have nobody to rule over. What then? when you enter the theatre, you ought to say not, "Let Sophron be crowned," but you ought to say this, "Come let me maintain my will in this matter so that it shall be conformable to nature: no man is dearer to me than myself. It would be ridiculous, then, for me to be hurt (injured) in order that another who is an actor may be crowned." Whom then do I wish to gain the prize? Why the actor who does gain the prize; and so he will always gain the prize whom I wish to gain it. "But I wish Sophron to be crowned." Celebrate as many games as you choose in your own house, Nemean, Pythian, Isthmian, Olympian, and proclaim him victor. But in public do not claim more than your due, nor attempt to appropriate to yourself what belongs to all. If you do not consent to this, bear being abused: for when you do the same as the many, you put yourself on the same level with them.

CHAPTER 5. *Against those who on account of sickness go away home*
"I AM sick here," said one of the pupils, "and I wish to return home." At home, I suppose, you were free from sickness. Do you not consider whether you are doing anything here which may be useful to the exercise of your will, that it may be corrected? For if you are doing nothing toward this end, it was to no purpose that you came. Go away. Look after your affairs at home. For if your ruling power cannot be maintained in a state conformable to nature, it is possible that your land can, that you will be able to increase your money, you will take care of your father in his old age, frequent the public place, hold magisterial office: being bad you will do badly anything else

that you have to do. But if you understand yourself, and know that you are casting away certain bad opinions and adopting others in their place, and if you have changed your state of life from things which are not within your will to things which are within your will, and if you ever say, "Alas!" you are not saying what you say on account of your father, or your brother, but on account of yourself, do you still allege your sickness? Do you not know that both disease and death must surprise us while we are doing something? the husbandman while he is tilling the ground, the sailor while he is on his voyage? what would you be doing when death surprises you, for you must be surprised when you are doing something? If you can be doing anything better than this when you are surprised, do it. For I wish to be surprised by disease or death when I am looking after nothing else than my own will, that I may be free from perturbation, that I may be free from hindrance, free from compulsion, and in a state of liberty. I wish to be found practicing these things that I may be able to say to God, "Have I in any respect transgressed thy commands? have I in any respect wrongly used the powers which Thou gavest me? have I misused my perceptions or my preconceptions?[1] have I ever blamed Thee? have I ever found fault with Thy administration? I have been sick, because it was Thy will, and so have others, but I was content to be sick. I have been poor because it was Thy will, but I was content also. I have not filled a magisterial office, because it was not Thy pleasure that I should: I have never desired it. Hast Thou ever seen me for this reason discontented? have I not always approached Thee with a cheerful countenance, ready to do Thy commands and to obey Thy signals? Is it now Thy will that I should depart from the assemblage of men? I depart. I give Thee all thanks that Thou hast allowed me to join in this Thy assemblage of men and to see Thy works, and to comprehend this Thy administration." May death surprise me while I am thinking of these things, while I am thus writing and reading.

"But my mother will not hold my head when I am sick." Go to your mother then; for you are a fit person to have your head held when you are sick. "But at home I used to lie down on a delicious bed." Go away to your bed: indeed you are fit to lie on such a bed even when you are in health: do not, then, lose what you can do there.

But what does Socrates say?[2] "As one man," he says, "is pleased with improving his land, another with improving his horse, so I am daily pleased in observing that I am growing better." "Better in what? in using nice little words?" Man, do not say that. "In little matters of speculation?" What are you saying? "And indeed I do not see what else there is on which philosophers employ their time." Does it seem nothing to you to have never found fault with any person, neither with God nor man? to have blamed nobody? to carry the same face always in going out and coming in? This is what Socrates knew, and yet he never said that he knew anything or taught anything. But if any man asked for nice little words or little speculations, he would carry him to Protagoras or to Hippias; and if any man came to ask for pot-herbs, he would carry him to the gardener. Who then among you has this purpose? for if indeed you had it, you would both be content in sickness, and in hunger, and in death. If any among you has been in love with a charming girl, he knows that I say what is true.

CHAPTER 6. *Miscellaneous*
WHEN some person asked him how it happened that since reason has been more cultivated by the men of the present age, the progress made in former times was greater. In what respect, he answered, has it been more cultivated now, and in what respect was the progress greater then? For in that in which it has now been more cultivated, in that also the progress will now be found. At present it has been cultivated for the purpose of resolving syllogisms, and progress is made. But in former times it was cultivated for the purpose of maintaining the governing faculty in a condition conformable to nature, and progress was made. Do not, then, mix things which are different and do not expect, when you are laboring at one thing, to make progress in another. But

[1] See i. 2.

[2] Marcus Aurelius, viii. 43.

see if any man among us when he is intent upon this, the keeping himself in a state conformable to nature and living so always, does not make progress. For you will not find such a man.

The good man is invincible, for he does not enter the contest where he is not stronger. If you want to have his land and all that is on it, take the land; take his slaves, take his magisterial office, take his poor body. But you will not make his desire fail in that which it seeks, nor his aversion fall into that which he would avoid. The only contest into which he enters is that about things which are within the power of his will; how then will he not be invincible?

Some person having asked him what is Common sense, Epictetus replied: As that may be called a certain Common hearing which only distinguishes vocal sounds, and that which distinguishes musical sounds is not Common, but artificial; so there are certain things which men, who are not altogether perverted, see by the common notions which all possess. Such a constitution of the mind is named Common sense.

It is not easy to exhort weak young men; for neither is it easy to hold cheese with a hook. But those who have a good natural disposition, even if you try to turn them aside, cling still more to reason. Wherefore Rufus generally attempted to discourage, and he used this method as a test of those who had a good natural disposition and those who had not. "For," it was his habit to say, "as a stone, if you cast it upward, will be brought down to the earth by its own nature, so the man whose mind is naturally good, the more you repel him, the more he turns toward that to which he is naturally inclined."

CHAPTER 7. *To the administrator of the free cities who was an Epicurean*

WHEN the administrator came to visit him, and the man was an Epicurean, Epictetus said: It is proper for us who are not philosophers to inquire of you who are philosophers, as those who come to a strange city inquire of the citizens and those who are acquainted with it, what is the best thing in the world, in order that we also, after inquiry, may go in quest of that which is best and look at it, as strangers

do with the things in cities. For that there are three things which relate to man, soul, body, and things external, scarcely any man denies. It remains for you philosophers to answer what is the best. What shall we say to men? Is the flesh the best? and was it for this that Maximus sailed as far as Cassiope in winter with his son, and accompanied him that he might be gratified in the flesh? Then the man said that it was not, and added, "Far be that from him." Is it not fit then, Epictetus said, to be actively employed about the best? "It is certainly of all things the most fit." What, then, do we possess which is better than the flesh? "The soul," he replied. And the good things of the best, are they better, or the good things of the worse? "The good things of the best." And are the good things of the best within the power of the will or not within the power of the will? "They are within the power of the will." Is, then, the pleasure of the soul a thing within the power of the will? "It is," he replied. And on what shall this pleasure depend? On itself? But that cannot be conceived: for there must first exist a certain substance or nature of good, by obtaining which we shall have pleasure in the soul. He assented to this also. On what, then, shall we depend for this pleasure of the soul? for if it shall depend on things of the soul, the substance of the good is discovered; for good cannot be one thing, and that at which we are rationally delighted another thing; nor if that which precedes is not good, can that which comes after be good, for in order that the thing which comes after may be good, that which precedes must be good. But you would not affirm this, if you are in your right mind, for you would then say what is inconsistent both with Epicurus and the rest of your doctrines. It remains, then, that the pleasure of the soul is in the pleasure from things of the body: and again that those bodily things must be the things which precede and the substance of the good.

For this reason Maximus acted foolishly if he made the voyage for any other reason than for the sake of the flesh, that is, for the sake of the best. And also a man acts foolishly if he abstains from that which belongs to others, when he is a judge and able to take it. But, if you please, let us consider this only, how this thing may be done secretly, and safely, and so that no man will know it. For not even does Epicurus himself declare stealing to be bad, but he admits that detection is; and because it is impossible to have security against detection, for this reason he says, "Do not steal." But I say to you that if stealing is done cleverly and cautiously, we shall not be detected: further also we have powerful friends in Rome both men and women, and the Hellenes are weak, and no man will venture to go up to Rome for the purpose. Why do you refrain from your own good? This is senseless, foolish. But even if you tell me that you do refrain, I will not believe you. For as it is impossible to assent to that which appears false, and to turn away from that which is true, so it is impossible to abstain from that which appears good. But wealth is a good thing, and certainly most efficient in producing pleasure. Why will you not acquire wealth? And why should we not corrupt our neighbor's wife, if we can do it without detection? and if the husband foolishly prates about the matter, why not pitch him out of the house? If you would be a philosopher such as you ought to be, if a perfect philosopher, if consistent with your own doctrines. If you would not, you will not differ at all from us who are called Stoics; for we also say one thing, but we do another: we talk of the things which are beautiful, but we do what is base. But you will be perverse in the contrary way, teaching what is bad, practicing what is good.

In the name of God,[1] are you thinking of a city of Epicureans? "I do not marry." "Nor I, for a man ought not to marry; nor ought we to beget children, nor engage in public matters." What then will happen? whence will the citizens come? who will bring them up? who will be governor of the youth, who preside over gymnastic exercises? and in what also will the teacher instruct them? will he teach them what the Lacedæmonians were taught, or what the Athenians were taught? Come take a young man, bring him up according to your doctrines. The doctrines are bad, subversive of a state, pernicious to families, and not becoming to women. Dismiss them, man. You live in a chief city: it is your duty to be

a magistrate, to judge justly, to abstain from that which belongs to others; no woman ought to seem beautiful to you except your own wife, and no youth, no vessel of silver, no vessel of gold. Seek for doctrines which are consistent with what I say, and, by making them your guide, you will with pleasure abstain from things which have such persuasive power to lead us and overpower us. But if to the persuasive power of these things, we also devise such a philosophy as this which helps to push us on toward them and strengthens us to this end, what will be the consequence? In a piece of toreutic art which is the best part? the silver or the workmanship? The substance of the hand is the flesh; but the work of the hand is the principal part. The duties then are also three; those which are directed toward the existence of a thing; those which are directed toward its existence in a particular kind; and third, the chief or leading things themselves. So also in man we ought not to value the material, the poor flesh, but the principal. What are these? Engaging in public business, marrying, begetting children, venerating God, taking care of parents, and, generally, having desires, aversions, pursuits of things and avoidances, in the way in which we ought to do these things, and according to our nature. And how are we constituted by nature? Free, noble, modest: for what other animal blushes? what other is capable of receiving the appearance of shame? and we are so constituted by nature as to subject pleasure to these things, as a minister, a servant, in order that it may call forth our activity, in order that it may keep us constant in acts which are conformable to nature.

"But I am rich and I want nothing." Why, then, do you pretend to be a philosopher? Your golden and your silver vessels are enough for you. What need have you of principles? "But I am also a judge of the Greeks." Do you know how to judge? Who taught you to know? "Cæsar wrote to me a codicil." Let him write and give you a commission to judge of music; and what will be the use of it to you? Still how did you become a judge? whose hand did you kiss? the hand of Symphorus or Numenius? Before whose bedchamber have you slept?[2] To whom have you sent gifts?

[1] Compare Euripides, *Cyclops*, 333; see Epictetus, i. 23.

[2] Compare i. 19.

Then do you not see that to be a judge is just of the same value as Numenius is? "But I can throw into prison any man whom I please." So you can do with a stone. "But I can beat with sticks whom I please." So you may an ass. This is not a governing of men. Govern us as rational animals: show us what is profitable to us, and we will follow it: show us what is un-profitable, and we will turn away from it. Make us imitators of yourself, as Socrates made men imitators of himself. For he was like a governor of men, who made them sub-ject to him their desires, their aversion, their movements toward an object and their turning away from it. "Do this: do not do this: if you do not obey, I will throw you into prison." This is not governing men like rational ani-mals. But I: As Zeus has ordained, so act: if you do not act so, you will feel the penalty, you will be punished. What will be the pun-ishment? Nothing else than not having done your duty: you will lose the character of fidel-ity, modesty, propriety. Do not look for great-er penalties than these.

CHAPTER 8. *How we must exercise ourselves against appearances*

As we exercise ourselves against sophistical questions, so we ought to exercise ourselves daily against appearances; for these appear-ances also propose questions to us. "A certain person's son is dead." Answer: the thing is not within the power of the will: it is not an evil. "A father has disinherited a certain son. What do you think of it?" It is a thing beyond the power of the will, not an evil. "Cæsar has condemned a person." It is a thing beyond the power of the will, not an evil. "The man is afflicted at this." Affliction is a thing which de-pends on the will: it is an evil. "He has borne the condemnation bravely." That is a thing within the power of the will: it is a good. If we train ourselves in this manner, we shall make progress; for we shall never assent to anything of which there is not an appearance capable of being comprehended. Your son is dead. What has happened? Your son is dead. Nothing more? Nothing. Your ship is lost. What has happened? Your ship is lost. A man has been led to prison. What has happened? He has been led to prison. But that herein he

has fared badly, every man adds from his own opinion. "But Zeus," you say, "does not do right in these matters." Why? because he has made you capable of endurance? because he has made you magnanimous? because he has taken from that which befalls you the power of being evil? because it is in your power to be happy while you are suffering what you suf-fer; because he has opened the door to you, when things do not please you? Man, go out and do not complain.

Hear how the Romans feel toward philos-ophers, if you would like to know. Italicus, who was the most in repute of the philos-ophers, once when I was present being vexed with his own friends and as if he was suffering something intolerable said, "I cannot bear it, you are killing me: you will make me such as that man is"; pointing to me.

CHAPTER 9. *To a certain rhetorician who was going up to Rome on a suit*

WHEN a certain person came to him, who was going up to Rome on account of a suit which had regard to his rank, Epictetus inquired the reason of his going to Rome, and the man then asked what he thought about the matter. Epic-tetus replied: If you ask me what you will do in Rome, whether you will succeed or fail, I have no rule about this. But if you ask me how you will fare, I can tell you: if you have right opinions, you will fare well; if they are false, you will fare ill. For to every man the cause of his acting is opinion. For what is the reason why you desired to be elected governor of the Cnossians? Your opinion. What is the reason that you are now going up to Rome? Your opinion. And going in winter, and with danger and expense. "I must go." What tells you this? Your opinion. Then if opinions are the causes of all actions, and a man has bad opinions, such as the cause may be, such also is the effect. Have we then all sound opinions, both you and your adversary? And how do you differ? But have you sounder opinions than your adversary? Why? You think so. And so does he think that his opinions are better; and so do madmen. This is a bad criterion. But show to me that you have made some in-quiry into your opinions and have taken some pains about them. And as now you are sailing to Rome in order to become governor of the Cnossians, and you are not content to stay at home with the honors which you had, but you desire something greater and more conspicuous, so when did you ever make a voyage for the purpose of examining your own opinions, and casting them out, if you have any that are bad? Whom have you approached for this purpose? What time have you fixed for it? What age? Go over the times of your life by yourself, if you are ashamed of me. When you were a boy, did you examine your own opinions? and did you not then, as you do all things now, do as you did do? and when you were become a youth and attended the rhetoricians, and yourself practiced rhetoric, what did you imagine that you were deficient in? And when you were a young man and engaged in public matters, and pleaded causes yourself, and were gaining reputation, who then seemed your equal? And when would you have submitted to any man examining and showing that your opinions are bad? What, then, do you wish me to say to you? "Help me in this matter." I have no theorem (rule) for this. Nor have you, if you came to me for this purpose, come to me as a philosopher, but as to a seller of vegetables or a shoemaker. "For what purpose then have philosophers theorems?" For this purpose, that whatever may happen, our ruling faculty may be and continue to be conformable to nature. Does this seem to you a small thing? "No; but the greatest." What then? does it need only a short time? and is it possible to seize it as you pass by? If you can, seize it.

Then you will say, "I met with Epictetus as I should meet with a stone or a statue": for you saw me, and nothing more. But he meets with a man as a man, who learns his opinions, and in his turn shows his own. Learn my opinions: show me yours; and then say that you have visited me. Let us examine one another: if I have any bad opinion, take it away; if you have any, show it. This is the meaning of meeting with a philosopher. "Not so, but this is only a passing visit, and while we are hiring the vessel, we can also see Epictetus. Let us see what he says." Then you go away and say: "Epictetus was nothing: he used solecisms and spoke in a barbarous way." For

of what else do you come as judges? "Well, but a man may say to me, "if I attend to such matters, I shall have no land, as you have none; I shall have no silver cups as you have none, nor fine beasts as you have none." In answer to this it is perhaps sufficient to say: I have no need of such things: but if you possess many things, you have need of others: whether you choose or not, you are poorer than I am. "What then have I need of?" Of that which you have not: of firmness, of a mind which is conformable to nature, of being free from perturbation. Whether I have a patron or not, what is that to me? but it is something to you. I am richer than you: I am not anxious what Cæsar will think of me: for this reason, I flatter no man. This is what I possess instead of vessels of silver and gold. You have utensils of gold; but your discourse, your opinions, your assents, your movements, your desires are of earthen ware. But when I have these things conformable to nature, why should I not employ my studies also upon reason? for I have leisure: my mind is not distracted. What shall I do, since I have no distraction? What more suitable to a man have I than this? When you have nothing to do, you are disturbed, you go to the theatre or you wander about without a purpose. Why should not the philosopher labour to improve his reason? You employ yourself about crystal vessels: I employ myself about the syllogism named "The Lying":[1] you about myrrhine vessels; I employ myself about the syllogism named "The Denying." To you everything appears small that you possess: to me all that I have appears great. Your desire is insatiable: mine is satisfied. To (children) who put their hand into a narrow-necked earthen vessel and bring out figs and nuts, this happens; if they fill the hand, they cannot take it out, and then they cry. Drop a few of them and you will draw things out. And do you part with your desires: do not desire many things and you will have what you want.

CHAPTER 10. *In what manner we ought to bear sickness*
WHEN the need of each opinion comes, we ought to have it in readiness:[2] on the occasion

---

[1] See Epictetus, ii. 17.   [2] Marcus Aurelius, iii. 13.

of breakfast, such opinions as relate to breakfast; in the bath, those that concern the bath;
in bed, those that concern bed.

Let sleep not come upon thy languid eyes
Before each daily action thou hast scann'd;
What's done amiss, what done, what left undone;
From first to last examine all, and then
Blame what is wrong, in what is right rejoice.[1]

And we ought to retain these verses in such
way that we may use them, not that we may
utter them aloud, as when we exclaim "Pæan
Apollo." Again in fever we should have ready
such opinions as concern a fever; and we
ought not, as soon as the fever begins, to lose
and forget all. (A man who has a fever) may
say: "If I philosophize any longer, may I be
hanged: wherever I go, I must take care of the
poor body, that a fever may not come." But
what is philosophizing? Is it not a preparation
against events which may happen? Do you
not understand that you are saying something
of this kind? "If I shall still prepare myself to
bear with patience what happens, may I be
hanged." But this is just as if a man after receiving blows should give up the Pancratium.
In the Pancratium it is in our power to desist
and not to receive blows. But in the other matter, if we give up philosophy, what shall we
gain? What then should a man say on the occasion of each painful thing? "It was for this
that I exercised myself, for this I disciplined
myself." God says to you, "Give me a proof
that you have duly practiced athletics, that you
have eaten what you ought, that you have
been exercised, that you have obeyed the aliptes." Then do you show yourself weak when
the time for action comes? Now is the time
for the fever. Let it be borne well. Now is the
time for thirst, bear it well; now is the time for
hunger, bear it well. Is it not in your power?
who shall hinder you? The physician will hinder you from drinking; but he cannot prevent
you from bearing thirst well: and he will hinder you from eating; but he cannot prevent
you from bearing hunger well.

"But I cannot attend to my philosophical
studies." And for what purpose do you follow
them? Slave, is it not that you may be happy,
that you may be constant, is it not that you
may be in a state conformable to nature and

live so? What hinders you when you have a
fever from having your ruling faculty conformable to nature? Here is the proof of the
thing, here is the test of the philosopher. For
this also is a part of life, like walking, like
sailing, like journeying by land, so also is
fever. Do you read when you are walking?
No. Nor do you when you have a fever. But
if you walk about well, you have all that belongs to a man who walks. If you bear fever
well, you have all that belongs to a man in a
fever. What is it to bear a fever well? Not to
blame God or man; not to be afflicted at that
which happens, to expect death well and nobly, to do what must be done: when the physician comes in, not to be frightened at what he
says; nor if he says, "You are doing well,"[2] to
be overjoyed. For what good has he told you?
and when you were in health, what good was
that to you? And even if he says, "You are in
a bad way," do not despond. For what is it to
be ill? is it that you are near the severance of
the soul and the body? what harm is there in
this? If you are not near now, will you not
afterward be near? Is the world going to be
turned upside down when you are dead? Why
then do you flatter the physician? Why do you
say, "If you please, master, I shall be well"?[3]
Why do you give him an opportunity of raising his eyebrows? Do you not value a physician, as you do a shoemaker when he is measuring your foot, or a carpenter when he is
building your house, and so treat the physician
as to the body which is not yours, but by nature dead? He who has a fever has an opportunity of doing this: if he does these things, he
has what belongs to him. For it is not the business of a philosopher to look after these externals, neither his wine nor his oil nor his
poor body, but his own ruling power. But as
to externals how must he act? so far as not to
be careless about them. Where then is there
reason for fear? where is there, then, still reason for anger, and of fear about what belongs
to others, about things which are of no value?
For we ought to have these two principles in
readiness: that except the will nothing is good
nor bad; and that we ought not to lead events,
but to follow them.[4] "My brother ought not

[1] See iv. 6.

[2] See ii. 18.
[3] Compare Matt. 8. 2.
[4] See Epictetus, i. 4.

to have behaved thus to me." No; but he will see to that: and, however he may behave, I will conduct myself toward him as I ought. For this is my own business: that belongs to another; no man can prevent this, the other thing can be hindered.

CHAPTER 11. *Certain miscellaneous matters*
THERE are certain penalties fixed as by law for those who disobey the divine administration.[1] Whoever thinks any other thing to be good except those things which depend on the will, let him envy, let him desire, let him flatter, let him be perturbed: whoever considers anything else to be evil, let him grieve, let him lament, let him weep, let him be unhappy. And yet, though so severely punished, we cannot desist.

Remember what the poet[2] says about the stranger:

Stranger, I must not, e'en if a worse man come.

This, then, may be applied even to a father: "I must not, even if a worse man than you should come, treat a father unworthily; for all are from paternal Zeus." And of a brother, "For all are from the Zeus who presides over kindred." And so in the other relations of life we shall find Zeus to be an inspector.

CHAPTER 12. *About exercise*
WE ought not to make our exercises consist in means contrary to nature and adapted to cause admiration, for, if we do so, we, who call ourselves philosophers, shall not differ at all from jugglers. For it is difficult even to walk on a rope; and not only difficult, but it is also dangerous. Ought we for this reason to practice walking on a rope, or setting up a palm tree, or embracing statues? By no means. Everything which is difficult and dangerous is not suitable for practice; but that is suitable which conduces to the working out of that which is proposed to us as a thing to be worked out. To live with desire and aversion, free from restraint. And what is this? Neither to be disappointed in that which you desire, nor to fall into anything which you would avoid. Toward this object, then, exercise ought to tend.

For, since it is not possible to have your desire not disappointed and your aversion free from falling into that which you would avoid, without great and constant practice, you must know that if you allow your desire and aversion to turn to things which are not within the power of the will, you will neither have your desire capable of attaining your object, nor your aversion free from the power of avoiding that which you would avoid. And since strong habit leads, and we are accustomed to employ desire and aversion only to things which are not within the power of our will, we ought to oppose to this habit a contrary habit, and where there is great slipperiness in the appearances, there to oppose the habit of exercise.

I am rather inclined to pleasure: I will incline to the contrary side above measure for the sake of exercise. I am averse to pain: I will rub and exercise against this the appearances which are presented to me for the purpose of withdrawing my aversion from every such thing. For who is a practitioner in exercise? He who practices not using his desire, and applies his aversion only to things which are within the power of his will, and practices most in the things which are difficult to conquer. For this reason one man must practice himself more against one thing and another against another thing. What, then, is it to the purpose to set up a palm tree, or to carry about a tent of skins, or a mortar and a pestle? Practice, man, if you are irritable, to endure if you are abused, not to be vexed if you are treated with dishonour. Then you will make so much progress that, even if a man strikes you, you will say to yourself, "Imagine that you have embraced a statue": then also exercise yourself to use wine properly so as not to drink much, for in this also there are men who foolishly practice themselves; but first of all you should abstain from it, and abstain from a young girl and dainty cakes. Then at last, if occasion presents itself, for the purpose of trying yourself at a proper time, you will descend into the arena to know if appearances overpower you as they did formerly. But at first fly far from that which is stronger than yourself: the contest is unequal between a charming young girl and a beginner in philosophy. "The earthen pitcher," as the saying is, "and the rock do not agree."

[1] See iii. 24.
[2] Homer, *Odyssey*, xiv. 55.

After the desire and the aversion comes the second topic of the movements toward action and the withdrawals from it; that you may be obedient to reason, that you do nothing out of season or place, or contrary to any propriety of the kind. The third topic concerns the assents, which is related to the things which are persuasive and attractive. For as Socrates said, "we ought not to live a life without examination,"[1] so we ought not to accept an appearance without examination, but we should say, "Wait, let me see what you are and whence you come"; like the watch at night, "Show me the pass." "Have you the signal from nature which the appearance that may be accepted ought to have?" And finally whatever means are applied to the body by those who exercise it, if they tend in any way toward desire and aversion, they also may be fit means of exercise; but if they are for display, they are the indications of one who has turned himself toward something external, and who is hunting for something else, and who looks for spectators who will say, "Oh the great man." For this reason, Apollonius said well, "When you intend to exercise yourself for your own advantage, and you are thirsty from heat, take in a mouthful of cold water, and spit it out, and tell nobody."

CHAPTER 13. *What solitude is, and what kind of person a solitary man is*

SOLITUDE is a certain condition of a helpless man. For because a man is alone, he is not for that reason also solitary; just as though a man is among numbers, he is not therefore not solitary. When then we have lost either a brother, or a son, or a friend on whom we were accustomed to repose, we say that we are left solitary, though we are often in Rome, though such a crowd meet us, though so many live in the same place, and sometimes we have a great number of slaves. For the man who is solitary, as it is conceived, is considered to be a helpless person and exposed to those who wish to harm him. For this reason when we travel, then especially do we say that we are lonely when we fall among robbers, for it is not the sight of a human creature which removes us from solitude, but the sight of one

[1] See i. 26, and iii. 2.

who is faithful and modest and helpful to us. For if being alone is enough to make solitude, you may say that even Zeus is solitary in the conflagration and bewails himself saying, "Unhappy that I am who have neither Hera, nor Athena, nor Apollo, nor brother, nor son, nor descendant nor kinsman." This is what some say that he does when he is alone at the conflagration.[2] For they do not understand how a man passes his life when he is alone, because they set out from a certain natural principle, from the natural desire of community and mutual love and from the pleasure of conversation among men. But none the less a man ought to be prepared in a manner for this also, to be able to be sufficient for himself and to be his own companion. For as Zeus dwells with himself, and is tranquil by himself, and thinks of his own administration and of its nature, and is employed in thoughts suitable to himself; so ought we also to be able to talk with ourselves, not to feel the want of others also, not to be unprovided with the means of passing our time; to observe the divine administration, and the relation of ourselves to everything else; to consider how we formerly were affected toward things that happen and how at present; what are still the things which give us pain; how these also can be cured and how removed; if any things require improvement, to improve them according to reason.

For you see that Cæsar appears to furnish us with great peace, that there are no longer enemies nor battles nor great associations of robbers nor of pirates, but we can travel at every hour and sail from east to west. But can Cæsar give us security from fever also, can he from shipwreck, from fire, from earthquake or from lightning? well, I will say, can he give us security against love? He cannot. From sorrow? He cannot. From envy? He cannot. In a word then he cannot protect us from any of these things. But the doctrine of philosophers promises to give us security even against these things. And what does it say? "Men, if you will attend to me, wherever you are, whatever you are doing, you will not feel sorrow, nor anger, nor compulsion, nor hindrance, but you will pass your time without perturbations and

[2] See also Herodotus, ii. 11.

free from everything." When a man has this peace, not proclaimed by Cæsar (for how should he be able to proclaim it?), but by God through reason, is he not content when he is alone? when he sees and reflects, "Now no evil can happen to me; for me there is no robber, no earthquake, everything is full of peace, full of tranquillity: every way, every city, every meeting, neighbor, companion is harmless. One person whose business it is, supplies me with food;[1] another with raiment; another with perceptions, and preconceptions. And if he does not supply what is necessary, He gives the signal for retreat, opens the door, and says to you, 'Go.' Go whither? To nothing terrible, but to the place from which you came, to your friends and kinsmen, to the elements:[2] what there was in you of fire goes to fire; of earth, to earth; of air, to air; of water to water: no Hades, nor Acheron, nor Cocytus, nor Pyriphlegethon, but all is full of Gods and Demons." When a man has such things to think on, and sees the sun, the moon and stars, and enjoys earth and sea, he is not solitary nor even helpless. "Well then, if some man should come upon me when I am alone and murder me?" Fool, not murder you, but your poor body.

What kind of solitude then remains? what want? why do we make ourselves worse than children? and what do children do when they are left alone? They take up shells and ashes, and they build something, then pull it down, and build something else, and so they never want the means of passing the time. Shall I, then, if you sail away, sit down and weep, because I have been left alone and solitary? Shall I then have no shells, no ashes? But children do what they do through want of thought, and we through knowledge are unhappy.

Every great power is dangerous to beginners. You must then bear such things as you are able, but conformably to nature: but not . . . Practice sometimes a way of living like a person out of health that you may at some time live like a man in health. Abstain from food, drink water, abstain sometimes altogether from desire, in order that you may some time

desire consistently with reason; and if consistently with reason, when you have anything good in you, you will desire well. "Not so; but we wish to live like wise men immediately and to be useful to men." Useful how? what are you doing? have you been useful to yourself? "But, I suppose, you wish to exhort them." You exhort them! You wish to be useful to them. Show to them in your own example what kind of men philosophy makes, and don't trifle. When you are eating, do good to those who eat with you; when you are drinking, to those who are drinking with you; by yielding to all, giving way, bearing with them, thus do them good, and do not spit on them your phlegm.

CHAPTER 14. *Certain miscellaneous matters*
As bad tragic actors cannot sing alone, but in company with many: so some persons cannot walk about alone. Man, if you are anything, both walk alone and talk to yourself, and do not hide yourself in the chorus. Examine a little at last, look around, stir yourself up, that you may know who you are.

When a man drinks water, or does anything for the sake of practice, whenever there is an opportunity he tells it to all: "I drink water." Is it for this that you drink water, for the purpose of drinking water? Man, if it is good for you to drink, drink; but if not, you are acting ridiculously. But if it is good for you and you do drink, say nothing about it to those who are displeased with water-drinkers. What then, do you wish to please these very men?

Of things that are done some are done with a final purpose, some according to occasion, others with a certain reference to circumstances, others for the purpose of complying with others, and some according to a fixed scheme of life.

You must root out of men these two things, arrogance and distrust. Arrogance, then, is the opinion that you want nothing: but distrust is the opinion that you cannot be happy when so many circumstances surround you. Arrogance is removed by confutation; and Socrates was the first who practiced this. And, that the thing is not impossible, inquire and seek. This search will do you no harm; and in a manner

[1] See iii. 1, 43.
[2] Compare Eccles. 12. 7; I Thess. 4. 14; John, 6. 39, 40; 11. 25, 26; I Cor. 6. 14; 15. 53; II Cor. 5. 14, etc. See also Epictetus, iii. 24.

this is philosophizing, to seek how it is possible to employ desire and aversion without impediment.

"I am superior to you, for my father is a man of consular rank." Another says, "I have been a tribune, but you have not." If we were horses, would you say, "My father was swifter?" "I have much barley and fodder, or elegant neck ornaments." If, then, while you were saying this, I said, "Be it so: let us run then." Well, is there nothing in a man such as running in a horse, by which it will be known which is superior and inferior? Is there not modesty, fidelity, justice? Show yourself superior in these, that you may be superior as a man. If you tell me that you can kick violently, I also will say to you that you are proud of that which is the act of an ass.

CHAPTER 15. *That we ought to proceed with circumspection to everything*[1]

IN every act consider what precedes and what follows, and then proceed to the act. If you do not consider, you will at first begin with spirit, since you have not thought at all of the things which follow; but afterward, when some consequences have shown themselves, you will basely desist. "I wish to conquer at the Olympic games." "And I too, by the gods: for it is a fine thing." But consider here what precedes and what follows; and then, if it is for your good, undertake the thing. You must act according to rules, follow strict diet, abstain from delicacies, exercise yourself by compulsion at fixed times, in heat, in cold; drink no cold water, nor wine, when there is opportunity of drinking it.[2] In a word you must surrender yourself to the trainer as you do to a physician. Next in the contest, you must be covered with sand, sometimes dislocate a hand, sprain an ankle, swallow a quantity of dust, be scourged with the whip; and after undergoing all this, you must sometimes be conquered. After reckoning all these things, if you have still an inclination, go to the athletic practice. If you do not reckon them, observe you will behave like children who at one time play as wrestlers, then as gladiators, then blow a trumpet, then act a tragedy, when they have

seen and admired such things. So you also do: you are at one time a wrestler, then a gladiator, then a philosopher, then a rhetorician; but with your whole soul you are nothing: like the ape, you imitate all that you see; and always one thing after another pleases you, but that which becomes familiar displeases you. For you have never undertaken anything after consideration, nor after having explored the whole matter and put it to a strict examination; but you have undertaken it at hazard and with a cold desire. Thus some persons having seen a philosopher and having heard one speak like Euphrates[3]—and yet who can speak like him? —wish to be philosophers themselves.

Man, consider first what the matter is, then your own nature also, what it is able to bear. If you are a wrestler, look at your shoulders, your thighs, your loins: for different men are naturally formed for different things. Do you think that, if you do, you can be a philosopher? Do you think that you can eat as you do now, drink as you do now, and in the same way be angry and out of humour? You must watch, labour, conquer certain desires, you must depart from your kinsmen, be despised by your slave, laughed at by those who meet you, in everything you must be in an inferior condition, as to magisterial office, in honours, in courts of justice. When you have considered all these things completely, then, if you think proper, approach to philosophy, if you would gain in exchange for these things freedom from perturbations, liberty, tranquillity. If you have not considered these things, do not approach philosophy: do not act like children, at one time a philosopher, then a tax collector, then a rhetorician, then a procurator of Cæsar. These things are not consistent. You must be one man either good or bad: you must either labour at your own ruling faculty or at external things: you must either labour at things within or at external things: that is, you must either occupy the place of a philosopher or that of one of the vulgar.

A person said to Rufus[4] when Galba was murdered, "Is the world now governed by Providence?" But Rufus replied, "Did I ever

---

[1] Compare Luke, 14. 28-33.
[2] Compare I Cor. 9. 25.
[3] Marcus Aurelius, x. 31.
[4] See i. 1 and 9. This passage is out of place here but perhaps belongs to chapter 11, 14, or 17.

incidentally form an argument from Galba that the world is governed by Providence?"

CHAPTER 16. *That we ought with caution to enter into familiar intercourse with men*

IF a man has frequent intercourse with others, either for talk, or drinking together, or generally for social purposes, he must either become like them, or change them to his own fashion. For if a man places a piece of quenched charcoal close to a piece that is burning, either the quenched charcoal will quench the other, or the burning charcoal will light that which is quenched. Since, then, the danger is so great, we must cautiously enter into such intimacies with those of the common sort, and remember that it is impossible that a man can keep company with one who is covered with soot without being partaker of the soot himself. For what will you do if a man speaks about gladiators, about horses, about athletes, or, what is worse, about men? "Such a person is bad," "Such a person is good": "This was well done," "This was done badly." Further, if he scoff, or ridicule, or show an ill-natured disposition? Is any man among us prepared like a lute-player when he takes a lute, so that as soon as he has touched the strings, he discovers which are discordant, and tunes the instrument? such a power as Socrates had who in all his social intercourse could lead his companions to his own purpose? How should you have this power? It is therefore a necessary consequence that you are carried about by the common kind of people.

Why, then, are they more powerful than you? Because they utter these useless words from their real opinions: but you utter your elegant words only from your lips; for this reason they are without strength and dead, and it is nauseous to listen to your exhortations and your miserable virtue, which is talked of everywhere. In this way the vulgar have the advantage over you: for every opinion is strong and invincible. Until, then, the good sentiments are fixed in you, and you shall have acquired a certain power for your security, I advise you to be careful in your association with common persons: if you are not, every day like wax in the sun there will be melted away whatever you inscribe on your minds in the

school. Withdraw, then, yourselves far from the sun so long as you have these waxen sentiments. For this reason also philosophers advise men to leave their native country, because ancient habits distract them and do not allow a beginning to be made of a different habit; nor can we tolerate those who meet us and say: "See such a one is now a philosopher, who was once so-and-so." Thus also physicians send those who have lingering diseases to a different country and a different air; and they do right. Do you also introduce other habits than those which you have: fix your opinions and exercise yourselves in them. But you do not so: you go hence to a spectacle, to a show of gladiators, to a place of exercise, to a circus; then you come back hither, and again from this place you go to those places, and still the same persons. And there is no pleasing habit, nor attention, nor care about self and observation of this kind, "How shall I use the appearances presented to me? according to nature, or contrary to nature? how do I answer to them? as I ought, or as I ought not? Do I say to those things which are independent of the will, that they do not concern me?" For if you are not yet in this state, fly from your former habits, fly from the common sort, if you intend ever to begin to be something.

CHAPTER 17. *On providence*

WHEN you make any charge against Providence, consider, and you will learn that the thing has happened according to reason. "Yes, but the unjust man has the advantage." In what? "In money." Yes, for he is superior to you in this, that he flatters, is free from shame, and is watchful. What is the wonder? But see if he has the advantage over you in being faithful, in being modest: for you will not find it to be so; but wherein you are superior, there you will find that you have the advantage. And I once said to a man who was vexed because Philostorgus was fortunate: "Would you choose to lie with Sura?" "May it never happen," he replied, "that this day should come?" "Why then are you vexed, if he receives something in return for that which he sells; or how can you consider him happy who acquires those things by such means as you abominate; or what wrong does Providence, if he gives the better things to the better men? Is it not better to be modest than to be rich?" He admitted this. Why are you vexed then, man, when you possess the better thing? Remember, then, always, and have in readiness, the truth that this is a law of nature, that the superior has an advantage over the inferior in that in which he is superior; and you will never be vexed.

"But my wife treats me badly." Well, if any man asks you what this is, say, "My wife treats me badly." "Is there, then, nothing more?" Nothing. "My father gives me nothing." But to say that this is an evil is something which must be added to it externally, and falsely added. For this reason we must not get rid of poverty, but of the opinion about poverty, and then we shall be happy.

CHAPTER 18. *That we ought not to be disturbed by any news*

WHEN anything shall be reported to you which is of a nature to disturb, have this principle in readiness, that the news is about nothing which is within the power of your will. Can any man report to you that you have formed a bad opinion, or had a bad desire? By no means. But perhaps he will report that some person is dead. What then is that to you? He may report that some person speaks ill of you. What then is that to you? Or that your father is planning something or other. Against whom? Against your will? How can he? But is it against your poor body, against your little property? You are quite safe: it is not against you. But the judge declares that you have committed an act of impiety. And did not the judges make the same declaration against Socrates? Does it concern you that the judge has made this declaration? No. Why then do you trouble yourself any longer about it? Your father has a certain duty, and if he shall not fulfill it, he loses the character of a father, of a man of natural affection, of gentleness. Do not wish him to lose anything else on this account. For never does a man do wrong in one thing, and suffer in another. On the other side it is your duty to make your defense firmly, modestly, without anger: but if you do not, you also lose the character of a son, of a man of modest behaviour, of generous character. Well then, is the judge free from danger? No;

but he also is in equal danger. Why then are you still afraid of his decision? What have you to do with that which is another man's evil? It is your own evil to make a bad defense: be on your guard against this only. But to be condemned or not to be condemned, as that is the act of another person, so it is the evil of another person. "A certain person threatens you." Me? No. "He blames you." Let him see how he manages his own affairs. "He is going to condemn you unjustly." He is a wretched man.

CHAPTER 19. *What is the condition of a common kind of man and of a philosopher*

THE first difference between a common person and a philosopher is this: the common person says, "Woe to me for my little child, for my brother, for my father."[1] The philosopher, if he shall ever be compelled to say, "Woe to me," stops and says, "but for myself." For nothing which is independent of the will can hinder or damage the will, and the will can only hinder or damage itself. If, then, we ourselves incline in this direction, so as, when we are unlucky, to blame ourselves and to remember that nothing else is the cause of perturbation or loss of tranquillity except our own opinion, I swear to you by all the gods that we have made progress. But in the present state of affairs we have gone another way from the beginning. For example, while we were still children, the nurse, if we ever stumbled through want of care, did not chide us, but would beat the stone. But what did the stone do? Ought the stone to have moved on account of your child's folly? Again, if we find nothing to eat on coming out of the bath, the pedagogue never checks our appetite, but he flogs the cook. Man, did we make you the pedagogue of the cook and not of the child? Correct the child, improve him. In this way even when we are grown up we are like children. For he who is unmusical is a child in music; he who is without letters is a child in learning: he who is untaught, is a child in life.

CHAPTER 20. *That we can derive advantage from all external things*

IN the case of appearances, which are objects of the vision, nearly all have allowed the good and the evil to be in ourselves, and not in ex-

[1] Compare iii. 5.

ternals. No one gives the name of good to the fact that it is day, nor bad to the fact that it is night, nor the name of the greatest evil to the opinion that three are four. But what do men say? They say that knowledge is good, and that error is bad; so that even in respect to falsehood itself there is a good result, the knowledge that it is falsehood. So it ought to be in life also. "Is health a good thing, and is sickness a bad thing?" No, man. "But what is it?" To be healthy, and healthy in a right way, is good: to be healthy in a bad way is bad; so that it is possible to gain advantage even from sickness, I declare. For is it not possible to gain advantage even from death, and is it not possible to gain advantage from mutilation? Do you think that Menœceus gained little by death?[1] "Could a man who says so, gain so much as Menœceus gained?" Come, man, did he not maintain the character of being a lover of his country, a man of great mind, faithful, generous? And if he had continued to live, would he not have lost all these things? would he not have gained the opposite? would he not have gained the name of coward, ignoble, a hater of his country, a man who feared death? Well, do you think that he gained little by dying? "I suppose not." But did the father of Admetus[2] gain much by prolonging his life so ignobly and miserably? Did he not die afterward? Cease, I adjure you by the gods, to admire material things. Cease to make yourselves slaves, first of things, then on account of things slaves of those who are able to give them or take them away.

"Can advantage then be derived from these things?" From all; and from him who abuses you. Wherein does the man who exercises before the combat profit the athlete? Very greatly. This man becomes my exerciser before the combat: he exercises me in endurance, in keeping my temper, in mildness. You say no: but he, who lays hold of my neck and disciplines my loins and shoulders, does me good; and the exercise master does right when he says: "Raise him up with both hands, and the heavier he is, so much the more is my advantage." But if a man exercises me in keeping my temper, does he not do me good? This is not

[1] Euripides, *Phoenician Maidens*, 913.
[2] Euripides, *Alcestis*.

knowing how to gain an advantage from men. "Is my neighbour bad?" Bad to himself, but good to me: he exercises my good disposition, my moderation. "Is my father bad?" Bad to himself, but to me good. This is the rod of Hermes: "Touch with it what you please," as the saying is, "and it will be of gold." I say not so: but bring what you please, and I will make it good. Bring disease, bring death, bring poverty, bring abuse, bring trial on capital charges: all these things through the rod of Hermes shall be made profitable. "What will you do with death?" Why, what else than that it shall do you honour, or that it shall show you by act through it, what a man is who follows the will of nature? "What will you do with disease?" I will show its nature, I will be conspicuous in it, I will be firm, I will be happy, I will not flatter the physician, I will not wish to die. What else do you seek? Whatever you shall give me, I will make it happy, fortunate, honoured, a thing which a man shall seek.

You say No: but take care that you do not fall sick: it is a bad thing." This is the same as if you should say, "Take care that you never receive the impression that three are four: that is bad." Man, how is it bad? If I think about it as I ought, how shall it, then, do me any damage? and shall it not even do me good? If, then, I think about poverty as I ought to do, about disease, about not having office, is not that enough for me? will it not be an advantage? How, then, ought I any longer to look to seek evil and good in externals? What happens? these doctrines are maintained here, but no man carries them away home; but immediately every one is at war with his slave, with his neighbours, with those who have sneered at him, with those who have ridiculed him. Good luck to Lesbius, who daily proves that I know nothing.

CHAPTER 21. *Against those who readily come to the profession of sophists*

THEY who have taken up bare theorems immediately wish to vomit them forth, as persons whose stomach is diseased do with food. First digest the thing, then do not vomit it up thus: if you do not digest it, the thing become truly an emetic, a crude food and unfit to eat. But after digestion show us some change in your ruling faculty, as athletes show in their shoulders by what they have been exercised and what they have eaten; as those who have taken up certain arts show by what they have learned. The carpenter does not come and say, "Hear me talk about the carpenter's art"; but having undertaken to build a house, he makes it, and proves that he knows the art. You also ought to do something of the kind; eat like a man, drink like a man, dress, marry, beget children, do the office of a citizen, endure abuse, bear with an unreasonable brother, bear with your father, bear with your son, neighbour, companion. Show us these things that we may see that you have in truth learned something from the philosophers. You say, "No; but come and hear me read commentaries." Go away, and seek somebody to vomit them on. "And indeed I will expound to you the writings of Chrysippus as no other man can: I will explain his text most clearly: I will add also, if I can, the vehemence of Antipater and Archedemus."

Is it, then, for this that young men shall leave their country and their parents, that they may come to this place, and hear you explain words? Ought they not to return with a capacity to endure, to be active in association with others, free from passions, free from perturbation, with such a provision for the journey of life with which they shall be able to bear well the things that happen and derive honour from them? And how can you give them any of these things which you do not possess? Have you done from the beginning anything else than employ yourself about the resolution of Syllogisms, of sophistical arguments, and in those which work by questions? "But such a man has a school; why should not I also have a school?" These things are not done, man, in a careless way, nor just as it may happen; but there must be a (fit) age and life and God as a guide. You say, "No." But no man sails from a port without having sacrificed to the Gods and invoked their help; nor do men sow without having called on Demeter; and shall a man who has undertaken so great a work undertake it safely without the Gods? and shall they who undertake this work come to it with success? What else are you doing, man, than divulging the mysteries? You say, "There is a temple at Eleusis, and one here also. There is

an Hierophant at Eleusis, and I also will make an Hierophant: there is a herald, and I will establish a herald; there is a torch-bearer at Eleusis, and I also will establish a torch-bearer; there are torches at Eleusis, and I will have torches here. The words are the same: how do the things done here differ from those done there?" Most impious man, is there no difference? these things are done both in due place and in due time; and when accompanied with sacrifice and prayers, when a man is first purified, and when he is disposed in his mind to the thought that he is going to approach sacred rites and ancient rites. In this way the mysteries are useful, in this way we come to the notion that all these things were established by the ancients for the instruction and correction of life. But you publish and divulge them out of time, out of place, without sacrifices, without purity; you have not the garments which the hierophant ought to have, nor the hair, nor the head-dress, nor the voice, nor the age; nor have you purified yourself as he has: but you have committed to memory the words only, and you say: "Sacred are the words by themselves."

You ought to approach these matters in another way; the thing is great, it is mystical, not a common thing, nor is it given to every man. But not even wisdom perhaps is enough to enable a man to take care of youths: a man must have also a certain readiness and fitness for this purpose, and a certain quality of body, and above all things he must have God to advise him to occupy this office, as God advised Socrates to occupy the place of one who confutes error, Diogenes the office of royalty and reproof, and the office of teaching precepts. But you open a doctor's shop, though you have nothing except physic: but where and how they should be applied, you know not nor have you taken any trouble about it. "See," that man says, "I too have salves for the eyes." Have you also the power of using them? Do you know both when and how they will do good, and to whom they will do good? Why then do you act at hazard in things of the greatest importance? why are you careless? why do you undertake a thing that is in no way fit for you? Leave it to those who are able to do it, and to do it well. Do not yourself bring disgrace on philosophy through your own acts, and be not one of those who load it with a bad reputation. But if theorems please you, sit still and turn them over by yourself; but never say that you are a philosopher, nor allow another to say it; but say: "He is mistaken, for neither are my desires different from what they were before, nor is my activity directed to other objects, nor do I assent to other things, nor in the use of appearances have I altered at all from my former condition." This you must think and say about yourself, if you would think as you ought: if not, act at hazard, and do what you are doing; for it becomes you.

CHAPTER 22. *About cynism*

WHEN one of his pupils inquired of Epictetus, and he was a person who appeared to be inclined to Cynism, what kind of person a Cynic ought to be and what was the notion of the thing, We will inquire, said Epictetus, at leisure: but I have so much to say to you that he who without God attempts so great a matter, is hateful to God, and has no other purpose than to act indecently in public. For in any well-managed house no man comes forward, and says to himself, "I ought to be manager of the house." If he does so, the master turns round and, seeing him insolently giving orders, drags him forth and flogs him. So it is also in this great city; for here also there is a master of the house who orders everything. "You are the sun; you can by going round make the year and seasons, and make the fruits grow and nourish them, and stir the winds and make them remit, and warm the bodies of men properly: go, travel round, and so administer things from the greatest to the least." "You are a calf; when a lion shall appear, do your proper business: if you do not, you will suffer." "You are a bull: advance and fight, for this is your business, and becomes you, and you can do it." "You can lead the army against Ilium; be Agamemnon." "You can fight in single combat against Hector: be Achilles." But if Thersites[1] came forward and claimed the command, he would either not have obtained it; or, if he did obtain it, he would have disgraced himself before many witnesses.

[1] Homer, *Iliad*, ii. 212.

Do you also think about the matter carefully: it is not what it seems to you. "I wear a cloak now and I shall wear it then: I sleep hard now, and I shall sleep hard then: I will take in addition a little bag now and a staff, and I will go about and begin to beg and to abuse those whom I meet; and if I see any man plucking the hair out of his body, I will rebuke him, or if he has dressed his hair, or if he walks about in purple." If you imagine the thing to be such as this, keep far away from it: do not approach it: it is not at all for you. But if you imagine it to be what it is, and do not think yourself to be unfit for it, consider what a great thing you undertake.

In the first place in the things which relate to yourself, you must not be in any respect like what you do now: you must not blame God or man: you must take away desire altogether, you must transfer avoidance only to the things which are within the power of the will: you must not feel anger nor resentment nor envy nor pity; a girl must not appear handsome to you, nor must you love a little reputation, nor be pleased with a boy or a cake. For you ought to know that the rest of men throw walls around them and houses and darkness when they do any such things, and they have many means of concealment. A man shuts the door, he sets somebody before the chamber: if a person comes, say that he is out, he is not at leisure. But the Cynic instead of all these things must use modesty as his protection: if he does not, he will be indecent in his nakedness and under the open sky. This is his house, his door: this is the slave before his bedchamber: this is his darkness. For he ought not to wish to hide anything that he does: and if he does, he is gone, he has lost the character of a Cynic, of a man who lives under the open sky, of a free man: he has begun to fear some external thing, he has begun to have need of concealment, nor can he get concealment when he chooses. For where shall he hide himself and how? And if by chance this public instructor shall be detected, this pedagogue, what kind of things will he be compelled to suffer? when then a man fears these things, is it possible for him to be bold with his whole soul to superintend men? It cannot be: it is impossible.

In the first place, then, you must make your ruling faculty pure, and this mode of life also. "Now, to me the matter to work on is my understanding, as wood is to the carpenter, as hides to the shoemaker; and my business is the right use of appearances. But the body is nothing to me: the parts of it are nothing to me. Death? Let it come when it chooses, either death of the whole or of a part. Fly, you say. And whither; can any man eject me out of the world? He cannot. But wherever I go, there is the sun, there is the moon, there are the stars, dreams, omens, and the conversation with Gods."

Then, if he is thus prepared, the true Cynic cannot be satisfied with this; but he must know that he is sent a messenger from Zeus to men about good and bad things, to show them that they have wandered and are seeking the substance of good and evil where it is not, but where it is, they never think; and that he is a spy, as Diogenes was carried off to Philip after the battle of Chæroneia as a spy. For, in fact, a Cynic is a spy of the things which are good for men and which are evil, and it is his duty to examine carefully and to come and report truly, and not to be struck with terror so as to point out as enemies those who are not enemies, nor in any other way to be perturbed by appearances nor confounded.

It is his duty, then, to be able with a loud voice, if the occasion should arise, and appearing on the tragic stage to say like Socrates: "Men, whither are you hurrying, what are you doing, wretches? like blind people you are wandering up and down: you are going by another road, and have left the true road: you seek for prosperity and happiness where they are not, and if another shows you where they are, you do not believe him." Why do you seek it without? In the body? It is not there. If you doubt, look at Myro, look at Ophellius. In possessions? It is not there. But if you do not believe me, look at Crœsus: look at those who are now rich, with what lamentations their life is filled. In power? It is not there. If it is, those must be happy who have been twice and thrice consuls; but they are not. Whom shall we believe in these matters? You who from without see their affairs and are dazzled by an appearance, or the men themselves? What do they say? Hear them when they groan, when they grieve, when on account of these very consulships and glory and splendour they think that they are more wretched and in greater danger. Is it in royal power? It is not: if it were, Nero would have been happy, and Sardanapalus. But neither was Agamemnon happy, though he was a better man than Sardanapalus and Nero; but while others are snoring what is he doing?

"Much from his head he tore his rooted hair."[1] And what does he say himself?

"I am perplexed," he says, *"and Disturb'd I am,"* and *"my heart out of my bosom Is leaping."*[2]

Wretch, which of your affairs goes badly? Your possessions? No. Your body? No. But you are rich in gold and copper. What then is the matter with you? That part of you, whatever it is, has been neglected by you and is corrupted, the part with which we desire, with which we avoid, with which we move toward and move from things. How neglected? He knows not the nature of good for which he is made by nature and the nature of evil; and what is his own, and what belongs to another; and when anything that belongs to others goes badly, he says, "Woe to me, for the Hellenes are in danger." Wretched is his ruling faculty, and alone neglected and uncared for. "The Hellenes are going to die destroyed by the Trojans." And if the Trojans do not kill them, will they not die? "Yes; but not all at once." What difference, then, does it make? For if death is an evil, whether men die altogether, or if they die singly, it is equally an evil. Is anything else then going to happen than the separation of the soul and the body? Nothing. And if the Hellenes perish, is the door closed, and is it not in your power to die? "It is." Why then do you lament "Oh, you who are a king and have the sceptre of Zeus?" An unhappy king does not exist more than an unhappy god. What then art thou? In truth a shepherd: for you weep as shepherds do, when a wolf has carried off one of their sheep: and these who are governed by you are sheep. And why did you come hither? Was your desire in any danger? was your aversion? was your

[1] Homer, *Iliad*, x. 15.
[2] Homer, *Iliad*, x. 91.

movement? was your avoidance of things? He replies, "No; but the wife of my brother was carried off." Was it not then a great gain to be deprived of an adulterous wife? "Shall we be despised, then, by the Trojans?" What kind of people are the Trojans, wise or foolish? If they are wise, why do you fight with them? If they are fools, why do you care about them.

In what, then, is the good, since it is not in these things? Tell us, you who are lord, messenger and spy. Where you do not think that it is, nor choose to seek it: for if you chose to seek it, you would have found it to be in yourselves; nor would you be wandering out of the way, nor seeking what belongs to others as if it were your own. Turn your thoughts into yourselves: observe the preconceptions which you have. What kind of a thing do you imagine the good to be? "That which flows easily, that which is happy, that which is not impeded." Come, and do you not naturally imagine it to be great, do you not imagine it to be valuable? do you not imagine it to be free from harm? In what material then ought you to seek for that which flows easily, for that which is not impeded? in that which serves or in that which is free? "In that which is free." Do you possess the body, then, free or is it in servile condition? "We do not know." Do you not know that it is the slave of fever, of gout, ophthalmia, dysentery, of a tyrant, of fire, of iron, of everything which is stronger? Yes, it is a slave." How, then, is it possible that anything which belongs to the body can be free from hindrance? and how is a thing great or valuable which is naturally dead, or earth, or mud? Well then, do you possess nothing which is free? "Perhaps nothing." And who is able to compel you to assent to that which appears false? "No man." And who can compel you not to assent to that which appears true? "No man." By this, then, you see that there is something in you naturally free. But to desire or to be averse from, or to move toward an object or to move from it, or to prepare yourself, or to propose to do anything, which of you can do this, unless he has received an impression of the appearance of that which is profitable or a duty? "No man." You have, then, in these things also something which is

not hindered and is free. Wretched men, work out this, take care of this, seek for good here.

"And how is it possible that a man who has nothing, who is naked, houseless, without a hearth, squalid, without a slave, without a city, can pass a life that flows easily?" See, God has sent you a man to show you that it is possible. "Look at me, who am without a city, without a house, without possessions, without a slave; I sleep on the ground; I have no wife, no children; no prætorium, but only the earth and heavens, and one poor cloak. And what do I want? Am I not without sorrow? am I not without fear? Am I not free? When did any of you see me failing in the object of my desire? or ever falling into that which I would avoid? did I ever blame God or man? did I ever accuse any man? did any of you ever see me with sorrowful countenance? And how do I meet with those whom you are afraid of and admire? Do not I treat them like slaves? Who, when he sees me, does not think that he sees his king and master?"

This is the language of the Cynics, this their character, this is their purpose. You say "No": but their characteristic is the little wallet, and staff, and great jaws: the devouring of all that you give them, or storing it up, or the abusing unseasonably all whom they meet, or displaying their shoulder as a fine thing. Do you see how you are going to undertake so great a business? First take a mirror: look at your shoulders; observe your loins, your thighs. You are going, my man, to be enrolled as a combatant in the Olympic games, no frigid and miserable contest. In the Olympic games a man is not permitted to be conquered only and to take his departure; but first he must be disgraced in the sight of all the world, not in the sight of Athenians only, or of Lacedæmonians or of Nicopolitans; next he must be whipped also if he has entered into the contests rashly: and before being whipped, he must suffer thirst and heat, and swallow much dust.

Reflect more carefully, know thyself, consult the divinity, without God attempt nothing; for if he shall advise you, be assured that he intends you to become great or to receive many blows. For this very amusing quality is conjoined to a Cynic: he must be flogged like an ass, and when he is flogged, he must love those who flog him, as if he were the father of all, and the brother of all.[1] You say "No"; but if a man flogs you, stand in the public place and call out, "Cæsar, what do I suffer in this state of peace under thy protection? Let us bring the offender before the proconsul." But what is Cæsar to a Cynic, or what is a proconsul, or what is any other except him who sent the Cynic down hither, and whom he serves, namely Zeus? Does he call upon any other than Zeus? Is he not convinced that, whatever he suffers, it is Zeus who is exercising him? Hercules when he was exercised by Eurystheus did not think that he was wretched, but without hesitation he attempted to execute all that he had in hand. And is he who is trained to the contest and exercised by Zeus going to call out and to be vexed, he who is worthy to bear the sceptre of Diogenes? Hear what Diogenes says to the passers-by when he is in a fever, "Miserable wretches, will you not stay? but are you going so long a journey to Olympia to see the destruction or the fight of athletes; and will you not choose to see the combat between a fever and a man?" Would such a man accuse God who sent him down as if God were treating him unworthily, a man who gloried in his circumstances, and claimed to be an example to those who were passing by? For what shall he accuse him of? because he maintains a decency of behaviour, because he displays his virtue more conspicuously? Well, and what does he say of poverty, about death, about pain? How did he compare his own happiness with that of the Great King? or rather he thought that there was no comparison between them. For where there are perturbations, and griefs, and fears, and desires not satisfied, and aversions of things which you cannot avoid, and envies and jealousies, how is there a road to happiness there? But where there are corrupt principles, there these things must of necessity be.

When the young man asked, if when a Cynic is sick, and a friend asks him to come to his house and be taken care of in his sickness, shall the Cynic accept the invitation, he replied: And where shall you find, I ask, a Cynic's friend? For the man who invites

ought to be such another as the Cynic that he may be worthy of being reckoned the Cynic's friend. He ought to be a partner in the Cynic's sceptre and his royalty, and a worthy minister, if he intends to be considered worthy of a Cynic's friendship, as Diogenes was a friend of Antisthenes, as Crates was a friend of Diogenes. Do you think that, if a man comes to a Cynic and salutes him, he is the Cynic's friend, and that the Cynic will think him worthy of receiving a Cynic into his house? So that, if you please, reflect on this also: rather look round for some convenient dunghill on which you shall bear your fever and which will shelter you from the north wind that you may not be chilled. But you seem to me to wish to go into some man's house and to be well fed there for a time. Why then do you think of attempting so great a thing?

"But," said the young man, "shall marriage and the procreation of children as a chief duty be undertaken by the Cynic?" If you grant me a community of wise men, Epictetus replies, perhaps no man will readily apply himself to the Cynic practice. For on whose account should he undertake this manner of life? However if we suppose that he does, nothing will prevent him from marrying and begetting children; for his wife will be another like himself, and his father-in-law another like himself, and his children will be brought up like himself. But in the present state of things which is like that of an army placed in battle order, is it not fit that the Cynic should without any distraction be employed only on the ministration of God,[2] able to go about among men, not tied down to the common duties of mankind, nor entangled in the ordinary relations of life, which if he neglects, he will not maintain the character of an honourable and good man? and if he observes them he will lose the character of the messenger, and spy and herald of God. For consider that it is his duty to do something toward his father-in-law, something to the other kinsfolk of his wife, something to his wife also. He is also excluded by being a Cynic from looking after the sickness of his own family, and from providing for their support. And, to say nothing of the rest, he must have a vessel for heating

---

[1] Compare Matt. 5. 39-44.

[2] Compare I Cor. 7. 2 and 35.

water for the child that he may wash it in the bath; wool for his wife when she is delivered of a child, oil, a bed, a cup: so the furniture of the house is increased. I say nothing of his other occupations and of his distraction. Where, then, now is that king, he who devotes himself to the public interests,

The people's guardian and so full of cares.[1]

whose duty it is to look after others, the married and those who have children; to see who uses his wife well, who uses her badly; who quarrels; what family is well administered, what is not; going about as a physician does and feels pulses? He says to one, "You have a fever," to another, "You have a headache, or the gout": he says to one, "Abstain from food"; to another he says, "Eat"; or "Do not use the bath"; to another, "You require the knife, or the cautery." How can he have time for this who is tied to the duties of common life? is it not his duty to supply clothing to his children, and to send them to the schoolmaster with writing tablets, and styles. Besides, must he not supply them with beds? for they cannot be genuine Cynics as soon as they are born. If he does not do this, it would be better to expose the children as soon as they are born than to kill them in this way. Consider what we are bringing the Cynic down to, how we are taking his royalty from him. "Yes, but Crates took a wife." You are speaking of a circumstance which arose from love and of a woman who was another Crates. But we are inquiring about ordinary marriages and those which are free from distractions, and making this inquiry we do not find the affair of marriage in this state of the world a thing which is especially suited to the Cynic.

"How, then, shall a man maintain the existence of society?" In the name of God, are those men greater benefactors to society who introduce into the world to occupy their own places two or three grunting children, or those who superintend as far as they can all mankind, and see what they do, how they live, what they attend to, what they neglect contrary to their duty? Did they who left little children to the Thebans do them more good

than Epaminondas who died childless? And did Priamus, who begat fifty worthless sons, or Danaus or Æolus contribute more to the community than Homer? then shall the duty of a general or the business of a writer exclude a man from marriage or the begetting of children, and such a man shall not be judged to have accepted the condition of childlessness for nothing; and shall not the royalty of a Cynic be considered an equivalent for the want of children? Do we not perceive his grandeur and do we not justly contemplate the character of Diogenes; and do we, instead of this, turn our eyes to the present Cynics, who are dogs that wait at tables and in no respect imitate the Cynics of old except perchance in breaking wind, but in nothing else? For such matters would not have moved us at all nor should we have wondered if a Cynic should not marry or beget children. Man, the Cynic is the father of all men; the men are his sons, the women are his daughters: he so carefully visits all, so well does he care for all. Do you think that it is from idle impertinence that he rebukes those whom he meets? He does it as a father, as a brother, and as the minister of the father of all, the minister of Zeus.

If you please, ask me also if a Cynic shall engage in the administration of the state. Fool, do you seek a greater form of administration than that in which he is engaged? Do you ask if he shall appear among the Athenians and say something about the revenues and the supplies, he who must talk with all men, alike with Athenians, alike with Corinthians, alike with Romans, not about supplies, nor yet about revenues, nor about peace or war, but about happiness and unhappiness, about good fortune and bad fortune, about slavery and freedom? When a man has undertaken the administration of such a state, do you ask me if he shall engage in the administration of a state? ask me also if he shall govern: again I will say to you: Fool, what greater government shall he exercise than that which he exercises now?

It is necessary also for such a man to have a certain habit of body: for if he appears to be consumptive, thin and pale, his testimony has not then the same weight. For he must not only by showing the qualities of the soul prove

[1] Homer, *Iliad*, ii. 25.

to the vulgar that it is in his power independent of the things which they admire to be a good man, but he must also show by his body that his simple and frugal way of living in the open air does not injure even the body. "See," he says, "I am a proof of this, and my own body also is." So Diogenes used to do, for he used to go about fresh-looking, and he attracted the notice of the many by his personal appearance. But if a Cynic is an object of compassion, he seems to be a beggar: all persons turn away from him, all are offended with him; for neither ought he to appear dirty so that he shall not also in this respect drive away men; but his very roughness ought to be clean and attractive.

There ought also to belong to the Cynic much natural grace and sharpness; and if this is not so, he is a stupid fellow, and nothing else; and he must have these qualities that he may be able readily and fitly to be a match for all circumstances that may happen. So Diogenes replied to one who said, "Are you the Diogenes who does not believe that there are gods?" "And, how," replied Diogenes, "can this be when I think that you are odious to the gods?" On another occasion in reply to Alexander, who stood by him when he was sleeping, and quoted Homer's line

A man a councilor should not sleep all night,[1]

he answered, when he was half-asleep,

The people's guardian and so full of cares.

But before all the Cynic's ruling faculty must be purer than the sun; and, if it is not, he must necessarily be a cunning knave and a fellow of no principle, since while he himself is entangled in some vice he will reprove others. For see how the matter stands: to these kings and tyrants their guards and arms give the power of reproving some persons, and of being able even to punish those who do wrong though they are themselves bad; but to a Cynic instead of arms and guards it is conscience which gives this power. When he knows that he has watched and labored for mankind, and has slept pure, and sleep has left him still purer, and that he thought whatever he has thought as a friend of the gods, as a minister,

[1] *Iliad*, ii. 24.

as a participator of the power of Zeus, and that on all occasions he is ready to say

Lead me, O Zeus, and thou, O Destiny;

and also, "If so it pleases the gods, so let it be"; why should he not have confidence to speak freely to his own brothers, to his children, in a word to his kinsmen? For this reason he is neither overcurious nor a busybody when he is in this state of mind: for he is not a meddler with the affairs of others when he is superintending human affairs, but he is looking after his own affairs. If that is not so, you may also say that the general is a busybody, when he inspects his soldiers, and examines them, and watches them, and punishes the disorderly. But if, while you have a cake under your arm, you rebuke others, I will say to you: "Will you not rather go away into a corner and eat that which you have stolen"; what have you to do with the affairs of others? For who are you? are you the bull of the herd, or the queen of the bees? Show me the tokens of your supremacy, such as they have from nature. But if you are a drone claiming the sovereignty over the bees, do you not suppose that your fellow-citizens will put you down as the bees do the drones?

The Cynic also ought to have such power of endurance as to seem insensible to the common sort and a stone: no man reviles him, no man strikes him, no man insults him, but he gives his body that any man who chooses may do with it what he likes. For he bears in mind that the inferior must be overpowered by the superior in that in which it is inferior; and the body is inferior to the many, the weaker to the stronger. He never then descends into such a contest in which he can be overpowered; but he immediately withdraws from things which belong to others, he claims not the things which are servile. But where there is will and the use of appearances, there you will see how many eyes he has so that you may say, "Argus was blind compared with him." Is his assent ever hasty, his movement rash, does his desire ever fail in its object, does that which he would avoid befall him, is his purpose unaccomplished, does he ever find fault, is he ever humiliated, is he ever envious? To these he directs all his attention and energy; but as to everything else he snores supine. All is peace; there is no robber who takes away his will, no tyrant. But what say you as to his body? I say there is. And as to magistracies and honours? What does he care for them? When then any person would frighten him through them, he says to him, "Begone, look for children: masks are formidable to them; but I know that they are made of shell, and they have nothing inside."

About such a matter as this you are deliberating. Therefore, if you please, I urge you in God's name, defer the matter, and first consider your preparation for it. For see what Hector says to Andromache, "Retire rather," he says, "into the house and weave":

> War is the work of men
> Of all indeed, but specially 'tis mine.[1]

So he was conscious of his own qualification, and knew her weakness.

CHAPTER 23. *To those who read and discuss for the sake of ostentation*

FIRST say to yourself, who you wish to be: then do accordingly what you are doing; for in nearly all other things we see this to be so. Those who follow athletic exercises first determine what they wish to be, then do accordingly what follows. If a man is a runner in the long course, there is a certain kind of diet, of walking, rubbing and exercise: if a man is a runner in the stadium, all these things are different; if he is a Pentathlete, they are still more different. So you will find it also in the arts. If you are a carpenter, you will have such and such things: if a worker in metal, such things. For everything that we do, if we refer it to no end, we shall do it to no purpose; and if we refer it to the wrong end, we shall miss the mark. Further, there is a general end or purpose, and a particular purpose. First of all, we must act as a man. What is comprehended in this? We must not be like a sheep, though gentle; nor mischievous, like a wild beast. But the particular end has reference to each person's mode of life and his will. The lute-player acts as a lute-player, the carpenter as a carpenter, the philosopher as a philosopher, the rhetorician as a rhetorician. When then you say, "Come and hear me read to you": take care first of all that

[1]Homer, *Iliad*, vi. 490.

you are not doing this without a purpose; then, if you have discovered that you are doing this with reference to a purpose, consider if it is the right purpose. Do you wish to do good or to be praised? Immediately you hear him saying, "To me what is the value of praise from the many?" and he says well, for it is of no value to a musician, so far as he is a musician, nor to a geometrician. Do you then wish to be useful? in what? tell us that we may run to your audience-room. Now can a man do anything useful to others, who has not received something useful himself? No, for neither can a man do anything useful in the carpenter's art, unless he is a carpenter; nor in the shoemaker's art, unless he is a shoemaker.

Do you wish to know then if you have received any advantage? Produce your opinions, philosopher. What is the thing which desire promises? Not to fail in the object. What does aversion promise? Not to fall into that which you would avoid. Well; do we fulfill their promise? Tell me the truth; but if you lie, I will tell you. Lately when your hearers came together rather coldly, and did not give you applause, you went away humbled. Lately again when you had been praised, you went about and said to all, "What did you think of me?" "Wonderful, master, I swear by all that is dear to me." "But how did I treat of that particular matter?" "Which?" "The passage in which I described Pan and the nymphs?" "Excellently." Then do you tell me that in desire and in aversion you are acting according to nature? Begone; try to persuade somebody else. Did you not praise a certain person contrary to your opinion? and did you not flatter a certain person who was the son of a senator? Would you wish your own children to be such persons? "I hope not." Why then did you praise and flatter him? "He is an ingenuous youth and listens well to discourses." How is this? "He admires me." You have stated your proof. Then what do you think? do not these very people secretly despise you? When, then, a man who is conscious that he has neither done any good nor ever thinks of it, finds a philosopher who says, "You have a great natural talent, and you have a candid and good disposition," what else do you think that he says except this, "This man has some need of me?" Or tell me what act that indicates a great mind has he shown? Observe; he has been in your company a long time; he has listened to your discourses, he has heard you reading; has he become more modest? has he been turned to reflect on himself? has he perceived in what a bad state he is? has he cast away self-conceit? does he look for a person to teach him? "He does." A man who will teach him to live? No, fool, but how to talk; for it is for this that he admires you also. Listen and hear what he says: "This man writes with perfect art, much better than Dion." This is altogether another thing. Does he say, "This man is modest, faithful, free from perturbations?" and even if he did say it, I should say to him, "Since this man is faithful, tell me what this faithful man is." And if he could not tell me, I should add this, "First understand what you say, then speak."

You, then, who are in a wretched plight and gaping after applause and counting your auditors, do you intend to be useful to others? "To-day many more attended my discourse." "Yes, many; we suppose five hundred." "That is nothing; suppose that there were a thousand." "Dion never had so many hearers." "How could he?" "And they understand what is said beautifully." "What is fine, master, can move even a stone." See, these are the words of a philosopher. This is the disposition of a man who will do good to others; here is a man who has listened to discourses, who has read what is written about Socrates as Socratic, not as the compositions of Lysias and Isocrates. "I have often wondered by what arguments." Not so, but "by what argument": this is more exact than that. What, have you read the words at all in a different way from that in which you read little odes? For if you read them as you ought, you would not have been attending to such matters, but you would rather have been looking to these words: "Anytus and Melitus are able to kill me, but they cannot harm me": and "I am always of such a disposition as to pay regard to nothing of my own except to the reason which on inquiry seems to me the best."[1] Hence whoever heard Socrates say, "I know something and I teach"; but he used to send different

[1] Plato *Crito,* 46.

people to different teachers. Therefore they used to come to him and ask to be introduced to philosophers by him; and he would take them and recommend them. Not so; but as he accompanied them he would say, "Hear me to-day discoursing in the house of Quadratus." Why should I hear you? Do you wish to show me that you put words together cleverly? You put them together, man; and what good will it do you? "But only praise me." What do you mean by praising? "Say to me, "Admirable, wonderful." Well, I say so. But if that is praise whatever it is which philosophers mean by the name of good, what have I to praise in you? If it is good to speak well, teach me, and I will praise you. "What then? ought a man to listen to such things without pleasure?" I hope not. For my part I do not listen even to a lute-player without pleasure. Must I then for this reason stand and play the lute? Hear what Socrates says, "Nor would it be seemly for a man of my age, like a young man composing addresses, to appear before you."[2] "Like a young man," he says. For in truth this small art is an elegant thing, to select words, and to put them together, and to come forward and gracefully to read them or to speak, and while he is reading to say, "There are not many who can do these things, I swear by all that you value."

Does a philosopher invite people to hear him? As the sun himself draws men to him, or as food does, does not the philosopher also draw to him those who will receive benefit? What physician invites a man to be treated by him? Indeed I now hear that even the physicians in Rome do invite patients, but when I lived there, the physicians were invited. "I invite you to come and hear that things are in a bad way for you, and that you are taking care of everything except that of which you ought to take care, and that you are ignorant of the good and the bad and are unfortunate and unhappy." A fine kind of invitation: and yet if the words of the philosopher do not produce this effect on you, he is dead, and so is the speaker. Rufus was used to say: "If you have leisure to praise me, I am speaking to no purpose." Accordingly he used to speak in such a way that every one of us who were sit-

[2] Plato *Apology.*

ting there supposed that some one had accused him before Rufus: he so touched on
what was doing, he so placed before the eyes
every man's faults.

The philosopher's school, ye men, is a sur-
gery: you ought not to go out of it with pleasure, but with pain. For you are not in sound
health when you enter: one has dislocated his
shoulder, another has an abscess, a third a
fistula, and a fourth a headache. Then do I sit
and utter to you little thoughts and exclama-
tions that you may praise me and go away, one
with his shoulder in the same condition in
which he entered, another with his head still
aching, and a third with his fistula or his abscess just as they were? Is it for this then that
young men shall quit home, and leave their
parents and their friends and kinsmen and
property, that they may say to you, "Wonderful!" when you are uttering your exclama-
tions. Did Socrates do this, or Zeno, or Cleanthes?

What then? is there not the hortatory style?
Who denies it? as there is the style of refutation, and the didactic style. Who, then, ever
reckoned a fourth style with these, the style of
display? What is the hortatory style? To be
able to show both to one person and to many
the struggle in which they are engaged, and
that they think more about anything than
about what they really wish. For they wish the
things which lead to happiness, but they look
for them in the wrong place. In order that this
may be done, a thousand seats must be placed
and men must be invited to listen, and you
must ascend the pulpit in a fine robe or cloak
and describe the death of Achilles. Cease, I entreat you by the gods, to spoil good words and
good acts as much as you can. Nothing can
have more power in exhortation than when
the speaker shows to the hearers that he has
need of them. But tell me who when he hears
you reading or discoursing is anxious about
himself or turns to reflect on himself? or when
he has gone out says, "The philosopher hit me
well: I must no longer do these things." But
does he not, even if you have a great reputation, say to some person, "He spoke finely
about Xerxes"; and another says, "No, but
about the battle of Thermopylæ"? Is this listening to a philosopher?

CHAPTER 24. *That we ought not to be moved
by a desire of those things which are not in
our power*

LET not that which in another is contrary to
nature be an evil to you: for you are not
formed by nature to be depressed with others
nor to be unhappy with others, but to be happy with them. If a man is unhappy, remember
that his unhappiness is his own fault: for God
has made all men to be happy, to be free from
perturbations. For this purpose he has given
means to them, some things to each person as
his own, and other things not as his own: some
things subject to hindrance and compulsion
and deprivation; and these things are not a
man's own: but the things which are not subject to hindrances are his own; and the nature
of good and evil, as it was fit to be done by him
who takes care of us and protects us like a
father, he has made our own. "But," you say,
"I have parted from a certain person, and he
is grieved." Why did he consider as his own
that which belongs to another? why, when he
looked on you and was rejoiced, did he not
also reckon that you are mortal, that it is natural for you to part from him for a foreign
country? Therefore he suffers the consequences of his own folly. But why do you or
for what purpose bewail yourself? Is it that
you also have not thought of these things? but
like poor women who are good for nothing,
you have enjoyed all things in which you took
pleasure, as if you would always enjoy them,
both places and men and conversation; and
now you sit and weep because you do not see
the same persons and do not live in the same
places. Indeed you deserve this, to be more
wretched than crows and ravens who have the
power of flying where they please and changing their nests for others, and crossing the seas
without lamenting or regretting their former
condition. "Yes, but this happens to them because they are irrational creatures." Was reason, then, given to us by the gods for the purpose of unhappiness and misery, that we may
pass our lives in wretchedness and lamentation? Must all persons be immortal and must
no man go abroad, and must we ourselves not
go abroad, but remain rooted like plants; and,
if any of our familiar friends go abroad, must
we sit and weep; and, on the contrary, when

he returns, must we dance and clap our hands like children?

Shall we not now wean ourselves and remember what we have heard from the philosophers? if we did not listen to them as if they were jugglers: they tell us that this world is one city,[1] and the substance out of which it has been formed is one, and that there must be a certain period, and that some things must give way to others, that some must be dissolved, and others come in their place; some to remain in the same place, and others to be moved; and that all things are full of friendship, first of the gods,[2] and then of men who by nature are made to be of one family; and some must be with one another, and others must be separated, rejoicing in those who are with them, and not grieving for those who are removed from them; and man in addition to being by nature of a noble temper and having a contempt of all things which are not in the power of his will, also possesses this property, not to be rooted nor to be naturally fixed to the earth, but to go at different times to different places, sometimes from the urgency of certain occasions, and at others merely for the sake of seeing. So it was with Ulysses, who saw

Of many men the states, and learned their ways.[3]
And still earlier it was the fortune of Hercules to visit all the inhabited world
Seeing men's lawless deeds and their good rules of law:[4]
casting out and clearing away their lawlessness and introducing in their place good rules of law. And yet how many friends do you think that he had in Thebes, how many in Argos, how many in Athens? and how many do you think that he gained by going about? And he married also, when it seemed to him a proper occasion, and begot children, and left them without lamenting or regretting or leaving them as orphans; for he knew that no man is an orphan; but it is the father who takes care of all men always and continuously. For it was not as mere report that he had heard that Zeus is the father of men, for he thought that Zeus was his own father, and he called

him so, and to him he looked when he was doing what he did. Therefore he was enabled to live happily in all places. And it is never possible for happiness and desire of what is not present to come together. For that which is happy must have all[5] that it desires, must resemble a person who is filled with food, and must have neither thirst nor hunger. "But Ulysses felt a desire for his wife and wept as he sat on a rock." Do you attend to Homer and his stories in everything? Or if Ulysses really wept, what was he else than an unhappy man? and what good man is unhappy? In truth, the whole is badly administered, if Zeus does not take care of his own citizens that they may be happy like himself. But these things are not lawful nor right to think of: and if Ulysses did weep and lament, he was not a good man. For who is good if he knows not who he is? and who knows what he is, if he forgets that things which have been made are perishable, and that it is not possible for one human being to be with another always? To desire, then, things which are impossible is to have a slavish character and is foolish: it is the part of a stranger, of a man who fights against God in the only way that he can, by his opinions.

"But my mother laments when she does not see me." Why has she not learned these principles? and I do not say this, that we should not take care that she may not lament, but I say that we ought not to desire in every way what is not our own. And the sorrow of another is another's sorrow: but my sorrow is my own. I, then, will stop my own sorrow by every means, for it is in my power: and the sorrow of another I will endeavor to stop as far as I can; but I will not attempt to do it by every means; for if I do, I shall be fighting against God, I shall be opposing Zeus and shall be placing myself against him in the administration of the universe; and the reward of this fighting against God and of this disobedience not only will the children of my children pay, but I also shall myself, both by day and by night, startled by dreams, perturbed, trembling at every piece of news, and having my tranquillity depending on the letters of others. Some person has arrived from Rome. "I only

[1] See ii. 5.
[2] See iii. 13.
[3] Homer, *Odyssey*, i. 3
[4] Homer, *Odyssey*, xvii. 487.
[5] See iii. 2; Phil. 4. 18.

hope that there is no harm." But what harm can happen to you, where you are not? From Hellas some one is come: "I hope that there is no harm." In this way every place may be the cause of misfortune to you. Is it not enough for you to be unfortunate there where you are, and must you be so even beyond sea, and by the report of letters? Is this the way in which your affairs are in a state of security? "Well, then, suppose that my friends have died in the places which are far from me." What else have they suffered than that which is the condition of mortals? Or how are you desirous at the same time to live to old age, and at the same time not to see the death of any person whom you love? Know you not that in the course of a long time many and various kinds of things must happen; that a fever shall overpower one, a robber another, and a third a tyrant? Such is the condition of things around us, such are those who live with us in the world: cold and heat, and unsuitable ways of living, and journeys by land, and voyages by sea, and winds, and various circumstances which surround us, destroy one man, and banish another, and throw one upon an embassy and another into an army. Sit down, then, in a flutter at all these things, lamenting, unhappy, unfortunate, dependent on another, and dependent not on one or two, but on ten thousands upon ten thousands.

Did you hear this when you were with the philosophers? did you learn this? do you not know that human life is a warfare? that one man must keep watch, another must go out as a spy, and a third must fight? and it is not possible that all should be in one place, nor is it better that it should be so. But you, neglecting to do the commands of the general, complain when anything more hard than usual is imposed on you, and you do not observe what you make the army become as far as it is in your power; that if all imitate you, no man will dig a trench, no man will put a rampart round, nor keep watch, nor expose himself to danger, but will appear to be useless for the purposes of an army. Again, in a vessel if you go as a sailor, keep to one place and stick to it. And if you are ordered to climb the mast, refuse; if to run to the head of the ship, refuse; and what master of a ship will endure you?

and will he not pitch you overboard as a useless thing, an impediment only and bad example to the other sailors? And so it is here also: every man's life is a kind of warfare, and it is long and diversified. You must observe the duty of a soldier and do everything at the nod of the general; if it is possible, divining what his wishes are: for there is no resemblance between that general and this, neither in strength nor in superiority of character. You are placed in a great office of command and not in any mean place; but you are always a senator. Do you not know that such a man must give little time to the affairs of his household, but be often away from home, either as a governor or one who is governed, or discharging some office, or serving in war or acting as a judge? Then do you tell me that you wish, as a plant, to be fixed to the same places and to be rooted? "Yes, for it is pleasant." Who says that it is not? but a soup is pleasant, and a handsome woman is pleasant. What else do those say who make pleasure their end? Do you not see of what men you have uttered the language? that it is the language of Epicureans and catamites? Next while you are doing what they do and holding their opinions, do you speak to us the words of Zeno and of Socrates? Will you not throw away as far as you can the things belonging to others with which you decorate yourself, though they do not fit you at all? For what else do they desire than to sleep without hindrance and free from compulsion, and when they have risen to yawn at their leisure, and to wash the face, then write and read what they choose, and then talk about some trifling matter being praised by their friends whatever they may say, then to go forth for a walk, and having walked about a little to bathe, and then eat and sleep, such sleep as is the fashion of such men? why need we say how? for one can easily conjecture. Come, do you also tell your own way of passing the time which you desire, you who are an admirer of truth and of Socrates and Diogenes. What do you wish to do in Athens? the same, or something else? Why then do you call yourself a Stoic? Well, but they who falsely call themselves Roman citizens, are severely punished; and should those, who falsely claim so great and reverend a thing and name, get off unpunished? or is this not possible, but the law divine and strong and inevitable is this, which exacts the severest punishments from those who commit the greatest crimes? For what does this law say? "Let him who pretends to things which do not belong to him be a boaster, a vainglorious man: let him who disobeys the divine administration be base, and a slave; let him suffer grief, let him be envious, let him pity; and in a word let him be unhappy and lament."

"Well then; do you wish me to pay court to a certain person? to go to his doors?" If reason requires this to be done for the sake of country, for the sake of kinsmen, for the sake of mankind, why should you not go? You are not ashamed to go to the doors of a shoemaker, when you are in want of shoes, nor to the door of a gardener, when you want lettuces; and are you ashamed to go to the doors of the rich when you want anything? "Yes, for I have no awe of a shoemaker." Don't feel any awe of the rich. "Nor will I flatter the gardener." And do not flatter the rich. "How, then, shall I get what I want?" Do I say to you, "Go as if you were certain to get what you want"? And do not I only tell you that you may do what is becoming to yourself? "Why, then, should I still go?" That you may have gone, that you may have discharged the duty of a citizen, of a brother, of a friend. And further remember that you have gone to the shoemaker, to the seller of vegetables, who have no power in anything great or noble, though he may sell dear. You go to buy lettuces: they cost an obolus, but not a talent. So it is here also. The matter is worth going for to the rich man's door. Well, I will go. It is worth talking about. Let it be so; I will talk with him. But you must also kiss his hand and flatter him with praise. Away with that, it is a talent's worth: it is not profitable to me, nor to the state nor to my friends, to have done that which spoils a good citizen and a friend. "But you will seem not to have been eager about the matter, if you do not succeed." Have you again forgotten why you went? Know you not that a good man does nothing for the sake of appearance, but for the sake of doing right? "What advantage is it, then, to him to have done right?" And what advantage is it to a man who writes the name of Dion to write it as he ought? The advantage is to have written it. "Is there no reward then?"[1] Do you seek a reward for a good man greater than doing what is good and just? At Olympia you wish for nothing more, but it seems to you enough to be crowned at the games. Does it seem to you so small and worthless a thing to be good and happy? For these purposes being introduced by the gods into this city, and it being now your duty to undertake the work of a man, do you still want nurses also and a mamma, and do foolish women by their weeping move you and make you effeminate? Will you thus never cease to be a foolish child? know you not that he who does the acts of a child, the older he is, the more ridiculous he is?

In Athens did you see no one by going to his house? "I visited any man that I pleased." Here also be ready to see, and you will see whom you please: only let it be without meanness, neither with desire nor with aversion, and your affairs will be well managed. But this result does not depend on going nor on standing at the doors, but it depends on what is within, on your opinions. When you have learned not to value things which are external, and not dependent on the will, and to consider that not one of them is your own, but that these things only are your own, to exercise the judgment well, to form opinions, to move toward an object, to desire, to turn from a thing, where is there any longer room for flattery, where for meanness? why do you still long for the quiet there, and for the places to which you are accustomed? Wait a little and you will again find these places familiar: then, if you are of so ignoble a nature, again if you leave these also, weep and lament.

"How then shall I become of an affectionate temper?" By being of a noble disposition, and happy. For it is not reasonable to be mean-spirited nor to lament yourself, nor to depend on another, nor even to blame God or man. I entreat you, become an affectionate person in this way, by observing these rules. But if through this affection, as you name it, you are going to be a slave and wretched, there is no profit in being affectionate. And what prevents you from loving another as a person sub-

[1] Marcus Aurelius, ix. 42.

ject to mortality, as one who may go away from you. Did not Socrates love his own children? He did; but it was as a free man, as one who remembered that he must first be a friend to the gods. For this reason he violated nothing which was becoming to a good man, neither in making his defense nor by fixing a penalty on himself,[1] nor even in the former part of his life when he was a senator or when he was a soldier. But we are fully supplied with every pretext for being of ignoble temper, some for the sake of a child, some for a mother, and others for brethren's sake. But it is not fit for us to be unhappy on account of any person, but to be happy on account of all, but chiefly on account of God who has made us for this end. Well, did Diogenes love nobody, who was so kind and so much a lover of all that for mankind in general he willingly undertook so much labour and bodily sufferings? He did love mankind, but how? As became a minister of God, at the same time caring for men, and being also subject to God. For this reason all the earth was his country, and no particular place; and when he was taken prisoner he did not regret Athens nor his associates and friends there, but even he became familiar with the pirates and tried to improve them; and being sold afterward he lived in Corinth as before at Athens; and he would have behaved the same, if he had gone to the country of the Perrhæbi. Thus is freedom acquired. For this reason he used to say, "Ever since Antisthenes made me free, I have not been a slave." How did Antisthenes make him free? Hear what he says: "Antisthenes taught me what is my own, and what is not my own; possessions are not my own, nor kinsmen, domestics, friends, nor reputation, nor places familiar, nor mode of life; all these belong to others." What then is your own? "The use of appearances. This he showed to me, that I possess it free from hindrance, and from compulsion, no person can put an obstacle in my way, no person can force me to use appearances otherwise than I wish." Who then has any power over me? Philip or Alexander, or Perdiccas or the Great King? How have they this power? For if a man is going to be overpowered by a man, he must long before be

[1] Plato *Apology*, 36.

overpowered by things. If, then, pleasure is not able to subdue a man, nor pain, nor fame, nor wealth, but he is able, when he chooses, to spit out all his poor body in a man's face and depart from life, whose slave can he still be? But if he dwelt with pleasure in Athens, and was overpowered by this manner of life, his affairs would have been at every man's command; the stronger would have had the power of grieving him. How do you think that Diogenes would have flattered the pirates that they might sell him to some Athenian, that some time he might see that beautiful Piræus, and the Long Walls and the Acropolis? In what condition would you see them? As a captive, a slave and mean: and what would be the use of it for you? "Not so: but I should see them as a free man." Show me, how you would be free. Observe, some person has caught you, who leads you away from your accustomed place of abode and says, "You are my slave, for it is in my power to hinder you from living as you please, it is in my power to treat you gently, and to humble you: when I choose, on the contrary you are cheerful and go elated to Athens." What do you say to him who treats you as a slave? What means have you of finding one who will rescue you from slavery? Or cannot you even look him in the face, but without saying more do you entreat to be set free? Man, you ought to go gladly to prison, hastening, going before those who lead you there. Then, I ask you, are you unwilling to live in Rome and desire to live in Hellas? And when you must die, will you then also fill us with your lamentations, because you will not see Athens nor walk about in the Lyceion? Have you gone abroad for this? was it for this reason you have sought to find some person from whom you might receive benefit? What benefit? That you may solve syllogisms more readily, or handle hypothetical arguments? and for this reason did you leave brother, country, friends, your family, that you might return when you had learned these things? So you did not go abroad to obtain constancy of mind, nor freedom from perturbation, nor in order that, being secure from harm, you may never complain of any person, accuse no person, and no man may wrong you, and thus you may maintain your relative position without impediment? This is a fine traffic that you have gone abroad for in syllogisms and sophistical arguments and hypothetical: if you like, take your place in the agora and proclaim them for sale like dealers in physic. Will you not deny even all that you have learned that you may not bring a bad name on your theorems as useless? What harm has philosophy done you? Wherein has Chrysippus injured you that you should prove by your acts that his labours are useless? Were the evils that you had there not enough, those which were the cause of your pain and lamentation, even if you had not gone abroad? Have you added more to the list? And if you again have other acquaintances and friends, you will have more causes for lamentation; and the same also if you take an affection for another country. Why, then, do you live to surround yourself with other sorrows upon sorrows through which you are unhappy? Then, I ask you, do you call this affection? What affection, man! If it is a good thing, it is the cause of no evil: if it is bad, I have nothing to do with it. I am formed by nature for my own good: I am not formed for my own evil.

What then is the discipline for this purpose? First of all the highest and the principal, and that which stands as it were at the entrance, is this; when you are delighted with anything, be delighted as with a thing which is not one of those which cannot be taken away, but as with something of such a kind, as an earthen pot is, or a glass cup, that, when it has been broken, you may remember what it was and may not be troubled. So in this matter also: if you kiss your own child, or your brother or friend, never give full license to the appearance, and allow not your pleasure to go as far as it chooses; but check it, and curb it as those who stand behind men in their triumphs and remind them that they are mortal. Do you also remind yourself in like manner, that he whom you love is mortal, and that what you love is nothing of your own: it has been given to you for the present, not that it should not be taken from you, nor has it been given to you for all time, but as a fig is given to you or a bunch of grapes at the appointed season of the year. But if you wish for these things in winter, you are a fool. So if you wish for your son or friend

when it is not allowed to you, you must know that you are wishing for a fig in winter. For such as winter is to a fig, such is every event which happens from the universe to the things which are taken away according to its nature. And further, at the times when you are delighted with a thing, place before yourself the contrary appearances. What harm is it while you are kissing your child to say with a lisping voice, "To-morrow you will die"; and to a friend also, "To-morrow you will go away or I shall, and never shall we see one another again"? "But these are words of bad omen." And some incantations also are of bad omen; but because they are useful, I don't care for this; only let them be useful. "But do you call things to be of bad omen except those which are significant of some evil?" Cowardice is a word of bad omen, and meanness of spirit, and sorrow, and grief and shamelessness. These words are of bad omen: and yet we ought not to hesitate to utter them in order to protect ourselves against the things. Do you tell me that a name which is significant of any natural thing is of evil omen? say that even for the ears of corn to be reaped is of bad omen, for it signifies the destruction of the ears, but not of the world. Say that the falling of the leaves also is of bad omen, and for the dried fig to take the place of the green fig, and for raisins to be made from the grapes. For all these things are changes from a former state into other states; not a destruction, but a certain fixed economy and administration. Such is going away from home and a small change: such is death, a greater change, not from the state which now is to that which is not, but to that which is not now.[1] "Shall I then no longer exist?" You will not exist, but you will be something else, of which the world now has need: for you also came into existence not when you chose, but when the world had need of you.[2]

Wherefore the wise and good man, remembering who he is and whence he came, and by whom he was produced, is attentive only to this, how he may fill his place with due regularity and obediently to God. "Dost Thou still

[1] Marcus Aurelius, xi. 35. Compare Epictetus, iii. 13, and iv. 7.
[2] Compare Marcus Aurelius, iv. 14, 21; and I Cor. 15. 13, 19, 20, 32, 35, 36, 50, and 16. 8.

wish me to exist? I will continue to exist as free, as noble in nature, as Thou hast wished me to exist: for Thou hast made me free from hindrance in that which is my own. But hast Thou no further need of me? I thank Thee; and so far I have remained for Thy sake, and for the sake of no other person, and now in obedience to Thee I depart." "How dost thou depart?" Again, I say, as Thou hast pleased, as free, as Thy servant, as one who has known Thy commands and Thy prohibitions. And so long as I shall stay in Thy service, whom dost Thou will me to be? A prince or a private man, a senator or a common person, a soldier or a general, a teacher or a master of a family? whatever place and position Thou mayest assign to me, as Socrates says, "I will die ten thousand times rather than desert them." And where dost Thou will me to be? in Rome or Athens, or Thebes or Gyara. Only remember me there where I am. If Thou sendest me to a place where there are no means for men living according to nature, I shall not depart in disobedience to Thee, but as if Thou wast giving me the signal to retreat: I do not leave Thee, let this be far from my intention, but I perceive that Thou hast no need of me. If means of living according to nature be allowed me, I will seek no other place than that in which I am, or other men than those among whom I am.

Let these thoughts be ready to hand by night and by day: these you should write, these you should read: about these you should talk to yourself, and to others. Ask a man, "Can you help me at all for this purpose?" and further, go to another and to another. Then if anything that is said be contrary to your wish, this reflection first will immediately relieve you, that it is not unexpected. For it is a great thing in all cases to say, "I knew that I begot a son who is mortal." For so you also will say, "I knew that I am mortal, I knew that I may leave my home, I knew that I may be ejected from it, I knew that I may be led to prison." Then if you turn round, and look to yourself, and seek the place from which comes that which has happened, you will forthwith recollect that it comes from the place of things which are out of the power of the will, and of things which are not my own. "What then is

it to me?" Then, you will ask, and this is the chief thing: "And who is it that sent it?" The leader, or the general, the state, the law of the state. Give it me then, for I must always obey the law in everything. Then, when the appearance pains you, for it is not in your power to prevent this, contend against it by the aid of reason, conquer it: do not allow it to gain strength nor to lead you to the consequences by raising images such as it pleases and as it pleases. If you be in Gyara, do not imagine the mode of living at Rome, and how many pleasures there were for him who lived there and how many there would be for him who returned to Rome: but fix your mind on this matter, how a man who lives in Gyara ought to live in Gyara like a man of courage. And if you be in Rome, do not imagine what the life in Athens is, but think only of the life in Rome.

Then in the place of all other delights substitute this, that of being conscious that you are obeying God, that, not in word but in deed, you are performing the acts of a wise and good man. For what a thing it is for a man to be able to say to himself, "Now, whatever the rest may say in solemn manner in the schools and may be judged to be saying in a way contrary to common opinion, this I am doing; and they are sitting and are discoursing of my virtues and inquiring about me and praising me; and of this Zeus has willed that I shall receive from myself a demonstration, and shall myself know if He has a soldier such as He ought to have, a citizen such as He ought to have, and if He has chosen to produce me to the rest of mankind as a witness of the things which are independent of the will: 'See that you fear without reason, that you foolishly desire what you do desire: seek not the good in things external; seek it in yourselves: if you do not, you will not find it.' For this purpose He leads me at one time hither, at another time sends me thither, shows me to men as poor, without authority, and sick; sends me to Gyara, leads me into prison, not because He hates me, far from him be such a meaning, for who hates the best of his servants? nor yet because He cares not for me, for He does not neglect any even of the smallest things;[1] but He does this

[1] Compare i. 12, ii. 14, iii. 26; and Matt. 10. 29, 30.

for the purpose of exercising me and making use of me as a witness to others. Being appointed to such a service, do I still care about the place in which I am, or with whom I am, or what men say about me? and do I not entirely direct my thoughts to God and to His instructions and commands?"

Having these things always in hand, and exercising them by yourself, and keeping them in readiness, you will never be in want of one to comfort you and strengthen you. For it is not shameful to be without something to eat, but not to have reason sufficient for keeping away fear and sorrow. But if once you have gained exemption from sorrow and fear, will there any longer be a tyrant for you, or a tyrant's guard, or attendants on Cæsar?[1] Or shall any appointment to offices at court cause you pain, or shall those who sacrifice in the Capitol, on the occasion of being named to certain functions, cause pain to you who have received so great authority from Zeus? Only do not make a proud display of it, nor boast of it; but show it by your acts; and if no man perceives it, be satisfied that you are yourself in a healthy state and happy.

CHAPTER 25. *To those who fall off from their purpose*

CONSIDER as to the things which you proposed to yourself at first, which you have secured and which you have not; and how you are pleased when you recall to memory the one and are pained about the other; and if it is possible, recover the things wherein you failed. For we must not shrink when we are engaged in the greatest combat, but we must even take blows.[2] For the combat before us is not in wrestling and the Pancration, in which both the successful and the unsuccessful may have the greatest merit, or may have little, and in truth may be very fortunate or very unfortunate; but the combat is for good fortune and happiness themselves. Well then, even if we have renounced the contest in this matter, no man hinders us from renewing the combat again, and we are not compelled to wait for another four years that the games at Olympia may come again; but as soon as you have re-

covered and restored yourself, and employ the same zeal, you may renew the combat again; and if again you renounce it, you may again renew it; and if you once gain the victory, you are like him who has never renounced the combat. Only do not, through a habit of doing the same thing, begin to do it with pleasure, and then like a bad athlete go about after being conquered in all the circuit of the games like quails who have run away.

"The sight of a beautiful young girl overpowers me. Well, have I not been overpowered before? An inclination arises in me to find fault with a person; for have I not found fault with him before?" You speak to us as if you had come off free from harm, just as if a man should say to his physician who forbids him to bathe, "Have I not bathed before?" If, then, the physician can say to him, "Well, and what, then, happened to you after the bath? Had you not a fever, had you not a headache?" And when you found fault with a person lately, did you not do the act of a malignant person, of a trifling babbler; did you not cherish this habit in you by adding to it the corresponding acts? And when you were overpowered by the young girl, did you come off unharmed? Why, then, do you talk of what you did before? You ought, I think, remembering what you did, as slaves remember the blows which they have received, to abstain from the same faults. But the one case is not like the other; for in the case of slaves the pain causes the remembrance: but in the case of your faults, what is the pain, what is the punishment; for when have you been accustomed to fly from evil acts? Sufferings, then, of the trying character are useful to us, whether we choose or not.

CHAPTER 26. *To those who fear want*[3]

ARE you not ashamed at being more cowardly and more mean than fugitive slaves? How do they when they run away leave their masters? on what estates do they depend, and what domestics do they rely on? Do they not, after stealing a little which is enough for the first days, then afterward move on through land or through sea, contriving one method after another for maintaining their lives? And what

[1] See i. 19.
[2] Compare iii. 15.
[3] Compare Matt. 6. 25-34; Luke 12. 22-30.

fugitive slave ever died of hunger? But you are afraid lest necessary things should fail you, and are sleepless by night. Wretch, are you so blind, and don't you see the road to which the want of necessaries leads? "Well, where does it lead?" To the same place to which a fever leads, or a stone that falls on you, to death. Have you not often said this yourself to your companions? have you not read much of this kind, and written much? and how often have you boasted that you were easy as to death?

"Yes: but my wife and children also suffer hunger." Well then, does their hunger lead to any other place? Is there not the same descent to some place for them also? Is not there the same state below for them? Do you not choose, then, to look to that place full of boldness against every want and deficiency, to that place to which both the richest and those who have held the highest offices, and kings themselves and tyrants must descend? or to which you will descend hungry, if it should so happen, but they burst by indigestion and drunkenness. What beggar did you hardly ever see who was not an old man, and even of extreme old age? But chilled with cold day and night, and lying on the ground, and eating only what is absolutely necessary they approach near to the impossibility of dying. Cannot you write? Cannot you teach children? Cannot you be a watchman at another person's door? "But it is shameful to come to such necessity." Learn, then, first what are the things which are shameful, and then tell us that you are a philosopher: but at present do not, even if any other man call you so, allow it.

Is that shameful to you which is not your own act, that of which you are not the cause, that which has come to you by accident, as a headache, as a fever? If your parents were poor, and left their property to others, and if while they live, they do not help you at all, is this shameful to you? Is this what you learned with the philosophers? Did you never hear that the thing which is shameful ought to be blamed, and that which is blamable is worthy of blame? Whom do you blame for an act which is not his own, which he did not do himself? Did you, then, make your father such as he is, or is it in your power to improve him? Is this power given to you? Well then, ought

you to wish the things which are not given to you, or to be ashamed if you do not obtain them? And have you also been accustomed while you were studying philosophy to look to others and to hope for nothing from yourself? Lament then and groan and eat with fear that you may not have food to-morrow. Tremble about your poor slaves lest they steal, lest they run away, lest they die. So live, and continue to live, you who in name only have approached philosophy and have disgraced its theorems as far as you can by showing them to be useless and unprofitable to those who take them up; you who have never sought constancy, freedom from perturbation, and from passions: you who have not sought any person for the sake of this object, but many for the sake of syllogisms; you who have never thoroughly examined any of these appearances by yourself, "Am I able to bear, or am I not able to bear? What remains for me to do?" But as if all your affairs were well and secure, you have been resting on the third topic,[1] that of things being unchanged, in order that you may possess unchanged—what? cowardice, mean spirit, the admiration of the rich, desire without attaining any end, and avoidance which fails in the attempt? About security in these things you have been anxious.

Ought you not to have gained something in addition from reason and, then, to have protected this with security? And whom did you ever see building a battlement all round and not encircling it with a wall? And what doorkeeper is placed with no door to watch? But you practise in order to be able to prove—what? You practise that you may not be tossed as on the sea through sophisms, and tossed about from what? Show me first what you hold, what you measure, or what you weigh; and show me the scales or the medimnus; or how long will you go on measuring the dust? Ought you not to demonstrate those things which make men happy, which make things go on for them in the way as they wish, and why we ought to blame no man, accuse no man, and acquiesce in the administration of the universe? Show me these. "See, I show them: I will resolve syllogisms for you." This is the measure, slave; but it is not the thing

[1] See iii. 2.

measured. Therefore you are now paying the penalty for what you neglected, philosophy: you tremble, you lie awake, you advise with all persons; and if your deliberations are not likely to please all, you think that you have deliberated ill. Then you fear hunger, as you suppose: but it is not hunger that you fear, but you are afraid that you will not have a cook, that you will not have another to purchase provisions for the table, a third to take off your shoes, a fourth to dress you, others to rub you, and to follow you, in order that in the bath, when you have taken off your clothes and stretched yourself out like those who are crucified you may be rubbed on this side and on that, and then the aliptes may say, "Change his position, present the side, take hold of his head, show the shoulder"; and then when you have left the bath and gone home, you may call out, "Does no one bring something to eat?" And then, "Take away the tables, sponge them": you are afraid of this, that you may not be able to lead the life of a sick man. But learn the life of those who are in health, how slaves live, how labourers, how those live who are genuine philosophers; how Socrates lived, who had a wife and children; how Diogenes lived, and how Cleanthes, who attended to the school and drew water. If you choose to have these things, you will have them everywhere, and you will live in full confidence. Confiding in what? In that alone in which a man can confide, in that which is secure, in that which is not subject to hindrance, in that which cannot be taken away, that is, in your own will. And why have you made yourself so useless and good for nothing that no man will choose to receive you into his house, no man to take care of you? but if a utensil entire and useful were cast abroad, every man who found it would take it up and think it a gain; but no man will take you up, and every man will consider you a loss. So cannot you discharge the office of a dog, or of a cock? Why then do you choose to live any longer, when you are what you are?

Does any good man fear that he shall fail to have food? To the blind it does not fail, to the lame it does not: shall it fail to a good man? And to a good soldier there does not fail to be one who gives him pay, nor to a labourer, nor to a shoemaker: and to the good man shall there be wanting such a person? Does God thus neglect the things that He has established, His ministers, His witnesses, whom alone He employs as examples to the uninstructed, both that He exists, and administers well the whole, and does not neglect human affairs, and that to a good man there is no evil either when he is living or when he is dead? What, then, when He does not supply him with food? What else does He do than[1] like a good general He has given me the signal to retreat? I obey, I follow, assenting to the words of the Commander, praising His acts: for I came when it pleased Him, and I will also go away when it pleases Him; and while I lived, it was my duty to praise God both by myself, and to each person severally and to many.[2] He does not supply me with many things, nor with abundance, He does not will me to live luxuriously; for neither did He supply Hercules who was his own son; but another was king of Argos and Mycenæ, and Hercules obeyed orders, and laboured, and was exercised. And Eurystheus was what he was, neither king of Argos nor of Mycenæ, for he was not even king of himself; but Hercules was ruler and leader of the whole earth and sea, who purged away lawlessness, and introduced justice and holiness;[3] and he did these things both naked and alone. And when Ulysses was cast out shipwrecked, did want humiliate him, did it break his spirit? but how did he go off to the virgins to ask for necessaries, to beg which is considered most shameful?[4]

As a lion bred in the mountains trusting in his strength.[5]

Relying on what? Not on reputation nor on wealth nor on the power of a magistrate, but on his own strength, that is, on his opinions about the things which are in our power and those which are not. For these are the only things which make men free, which make them escape from hindrance, which raise the head of those who are depressed, which make them look with steady eyes on the rich and on

[1] See i. 29.   [2] See i. 16.
[3] Compare Heb. 11. and 12.
[4] Homer, *Odyssey*, vi. 127.
[5] *Ibid*, vi. 130.

tyrants. And this was the gift given to the philosopher. But you will not come forth bold, but trembling about your trifling garments and silver vessels. Unhappy man, have you thus wasted your time till now?

"What, then, if I shall be sick?" You will be sick in such a way as you ought to be. "Who will take care of me?" God; your friends. "I shall lie down on a hard bed." But you will lie down like a man. "I shall not have a convenient chamber." You will be sick in an inconvenient chamber. "Who will provide for me the necessary food?" Those who provide for others also. You will be sick like Manes. "And what, also, will be the end of the sickness? Any other than death?" Do you then consider that this the chief of all evils to man and the chief mark of mean spirit and of cowardice is not death, but rather the fear of death? Against this fear then I advise you to exercise yourself: to this let all your reasoning tend, your exercises, and reading; and you will know that thus only are men made free.

· BOOK FOUR ·

CHAPTER 1. *About freedom*

HE is free who lives as he wishes to live; who is neither subject to compulsion nor to hindrance, nor to force; whose movements to action are not impeded, whose desires attain their purpose, and who does not fall into that which he would avoid. Who, then, chooses to live in error? No man. Who chooses to live deceived, liable to mistake, unjust, unrestrained, discontented, mean? No man. Not one then of the bad lives as he wishes; nor is he, then, free. And who chooses to live in sorrow, fear, envy, pity, desiring and failing in his desires, attempting to avoid something and falling into it? Not one. Do we then find any of the bad free from sorrow, free from fear, who does not fall into that which he would avoid, and does not obtain that which he wishes? Not one; nor then do we find any bad man free.[1]

If, then, a man who has been twice consul should hear this, if you add, "But you are a wise man; this is nothing to you": he will pardon you. But if you tell him the truth, and say, "You differ not at all from those who have been thrice sold as to being yourself not a slave," what else ought you to expect than blows? For he says, "What, I a slave, I whose father was free, whose mother was free, I whom no man can purchase: I am also of senatorial rank, and a friend of Cæsar, and I have been a consul, and I own many slaves." In the first place, most excellent senatorial man, perhaps your father also was a slave in the same kind of servitude, and your mother, and your grandfather and all your ancestors in an ascending series. But even if they were as free as it is possible, what is this to you? What if they were of a noble nature, and you of a mean nature; if they were fearless, and you a coward; if they had the power of self-restraint, and you are not able to exercise it.

"And what," you may say, "has this to do with being a slave?" Does it seem to you to be nothing to do a thing unwillingly, with compulsion, with groans, has this nothing to do with being a slave? "It is something," you say: "but who is able to compel me, except the lord of all, Cæsar?" Then even you yourself have admitted that you have one master. But that he is the common master of all, as you say, let not this console you at all: but know that you are a slave in a great family. So also the people of Nicopolis are used to exclaim, "By the fortune of Cæsar,[2] we are free."

However, if you please, let us not speak of Cæsar at present. But tell me this: did you never love any person, a young girl, or slave, or free? What then is this with respect to being a slave or free? Were you never commanded by the person beloved to do something which you did not wish to do? have you never flattered your little slave? have you never kissed her feet? And yet if any man compelled you to kiss Cæsar's feet, you would think it an insult and excessive tyranny. What else, then, is slavery? Did you never go out by

[1] John 8. 34.

[2] See ii. 20.

night to some place whither you did not wish to go, did you not expend what you did not wish to expend, did you not utter words with sighs and groans, did you not submit to abuse and to be excluded?[1] But if you are ashamed to confess your own acts, see what Thrasonides says and does, who having seen so much military service as perhaps not even you have, first of all went out by night, when Geta does not venture out, but if he were compelled by his master, would have cried out much and would have gone out lamenting his bitter slavery. Next, what does Thrasonides say? "A worthless girl has enslaved me, me whom no enemy ever did." Unhappy man, who are the slave even of a girl, and a worthless girl. Why then do you still call yourself free? and why do you talk of your service in the army? Then he calls for a sword and is angry with him who out of kindness refuses it; and he sends presents to her who hates him, and entreats and weeps, and on the other hand, having had a little success, he is elated. But even then how? was he free enough neither to desire nor to fear?

Now consider in the case of animals, how we employ the notion of liberty. Men keep tame lions shut up, and feed them, and some take them about; and who will say that this lion is free? Is it not the fact that the more he lives at his ease, so much the more he is in a slavish condition? and who if he had perception and reason would wish to be one of these lions? Well, these birds when they are caught and are kept shut up, how much do they suffer in their attempts to escape? and some of them die of hunger rather than submit to such a kind of life. And as many of them as live, hardly live and with suffering pine away; and if they ever find any opening, they make their escape. So much do they desire their natural liberty, and to be independent and free from hindrance. And what harm is there to you in this? "What do you say? I am formed by nature to fly where I choose, to live in the open air, to sing when I choose: you deprive me of all this, and say, 'What harm is it to you?'" For this reason we shall say that those animals only are free which cannot endure capture, but, as soon as they are caught, escape from

[1] Lucretius, iv. 1172.

captivity by death. So Diogenes also somewhere says that there is one way to freedom, and that is to die content: and he writes to the Persian king, "You cannot enslave the Athenian state any more than you can enslave fishes." "How is that? cannot I catch them?" "If you catch them," says Diogenes, "they will immediately leave you, as fishes do; for if you catch a fish, it dies; and if these men that are caught shall die, of what use to you is the preparation for war?" These are the words of a free man who had carefully examined the thing and, as was natural, had discovered it. But if you look for it in a different place from where it is, what wonder if you never find it?

The slave wishes to be set free immediately. Why? Do you think that he wishes to pay money to the collectors of twentieths?[2] No; but because he imagines that hitherto through not having obtained this, he is hindered and unfortunate. "If I shall be set free, immediately it is all happiness, I care for no man, I speak to all as an equal and, like to them, I go where I choose, I come from any place I choose, and go where I choose." Then he is set free; and forthwith having no place where he can eat, he looks for some man to flatter, some one with whom he shall sup: then he either works with his body and endures the most dreadful things; and if he can obtain a manger, he falls into a slavery much worse than his former slavery; or even if he is become rich, being a man without any knowledge of what is good, he loves some little girl, and in his happiness laments and desires to be a slave again. He says, "what evil did I suffer in my state of slavery? Another clothed me, another supplied me with shoes, another fed me, another looked after me in sickness; and I did only a few services for him. But now a wretched man, what things I suffer, being a slave of many instead of to one. But however," he says, "if I shall acquire rings, then I shall live most prosperously and happily." First, in order to acquire these rings, he submits to that which he is worthy of; then, when he has acquired them, it is again all the same. Then he says, "if I shall be engaged in military service, I am free from all evils." He obtains military service. He suffers as much as a flogged slave,

[2] See ii. 1.

and nevertheless he asks for a second service and a third. After this, when he has put the finishing stroke to his career and is become a senator, then he becomes a slave by entering into the assembly, then he serves the finer and most splendid slavery—not to be a fool, but to learn what Socrates taught, what is the nature of each thing that exists, and that a man should not rashly adapt preconceptions to the several things which are.[1] For this is the cause to men of all their evils, the not being able to adapt the general preconceptions to the several things. But we have different opinions. One man thinks that he is sick: not so however, but the fact is that he does not adapt his preconceptions right. Another thinks that he is poor; another that he has a severe father or mother; and another, again, that Cæsar is not favourable to him. But all this is one and only one thing, the not knowing how to adapt the preconceptions. For who has not a preconception of that which is bad, that it is hurtful, that it ought to be avoided, that it ought in every way to be guarded against? One preconception is not repugnant to another,[2] only where it comes to the matter of adaptation. What then is this evil, which is both hurtful, and a thing to be avoided? He answers, "Not to be Cæsar's friend." He is gone far from the mark, he has missed the adaptation, he is embarrassed, he seeks the things which are not at all pertinent to the matter; for when he has succeeded in being Cæsar's friend, nevertheless he has failed in finding what he sought. For what is that which every man seeks? To live secure, to be happy, to do everything as he wishes, not to be hindered, nor compelled. When then he is become the friend of Cæsar, is he free from hindrance? free from compulsion, is he tranquil, is he happy? Of whom shall we inquire? What more trustworthy witness have we than this very man who is become Cæsar's friend? Come forward and tell us when did you sleep more quietly, now or before you became Cæsar's friend? Immediately you hear the answer, "Stop, I entreat you, and do not mock me: you know not what miseries I suffer, and sleep does not come to me; but one comes and says, 'Cæsar is already

awake, he is now going forth': then come troubles and cares." Well, when did you sup with more pleasure, now or before? Hear what he says about this also. He says that if he is not invited, he is pained: and if he is invited, he sups like a slave with his master, all the while being anxious that he does not say or do anything foolish. And what do you suppose that he is afraid of; lest he should be lashed like a slave? How can he expect anything so good? No, but as befits so great a man, Cæsar's friend, he is afraid that he may lose his head. And when did you bathe more free from trouble, and take your gymnastic exercise more quietly? In fine, which kind of life did you prefer? your present or your former life? I can swear that no man is so stupid or so ignorant of truth as not to bewail his own misfortunes the nearer he is in friendship to Cæsar.

Since, then, neither those who are called kings live as they choose, nor the friends of kings, who finally are those who are free? Seek, and you will find; for you have aids from nature for the discovery of truth. But if you are not able yourself by going along these ways only to discover that which follows, listen to those who have made the inquiry. What do they say? Does freedom seem to you a good thing? "The greatest good." Is it possible, then, that he who obtains the greatest good can be unhappy or fare badly? "No." Whomsoever, then, you shall see unhappy, unfortunate, lamenting, confidently declare that they are not free. "I do declare it." We have now, then, got away from buying and selling and from such arrangements about matters of property; for if you have rightly assented to these matters, if the Great King is unhappy, he cannot be free, nor can a little king, nor a man of consular rank, nor one who has been twice consul. "Be it so."

Further, then, answer me this question also: Does freedom seem to you to be something great and noble and valuable? "How should it not seem so?" Is it possible, then, when a man obtains anything so great and valuable and noble to be mean? "It is not possible." When, then, you see any man subject to another, or flattering him contrary to his own opinion, confidently affirm that this man also is not

[1] Compare i. 2.
[2] Compare i. 22.

free; and not only if he do this for a bit of supper, but also if he does it for a government or a consulship: and call these men "little slaves" who for the sake of little matters do these things, and those who do so for the sake of great things call "great slaves," as they deserve to be. "This is admitted also." Do you think that freedom is a thing independent and self-governing? "Certainly." Whomsoever, then, it is in the power of another to hinder and compel, declare that he is not free. And do not look, I entreat you, after his grandfathers and great-grandfathers, or inquire about his being bought or sold; but if you hear him saying from his heart and with feeling, "Master," even if the twelve fasces precede him, call him a slave. And if you hear him say, "Wretch that I am, how much I suffer," call him a slave. If, finally, you see him lamenting, complaining, unhappy, call him a slave though he wears a prætexta. If, then, he is doing nothing of this kind, do not yet say that he is free, but learn his opinions, whether they are subject to compulsion, or may produce hindrance, or to bad fortune; and if you find him such, call him a slave who has a holiday in the Saturnalia: say that his master is from home: he will return soon, and you will know what he suffers. "Who will return?" Whoever has in himself the power over anything which is desired by the man, either to give it to him or to take it away? "Thus, then, have we many masters?" We have: for we have circumstances as masters prior to our present masters; and these circumstances are many. Therefore it must of necessity be that those who have the power over any of these circumstances must be our masters. For no man fears Cæsar himself, but he fears death, banishment, deprivation of his property, prison, and disgrace. Nor does any man love Cæsar, unless Cæsar is a person of great merit, but he loves wealth, the office of tribune, prætor or consul. When we love, and hate, and fear these things, it must be that those who have the power over them must be our masters. Therefore we adore them even as gods; for we think that what possesses the power of conferring the greatest advantage on us is divine. Then we wrongly assume that a certain person has the power of conferring the greatest advantages; therefore he is something divine. For if we wrongly assume that a certain person has the power of conferring the greatest advantages, it is a necessary consequence that the conclusion from these premises must be false.

What, then, is that which makes a man free from hindrance and makes him his own master? For wealth does not do it, nor consulship, nor provincial government, nor royal power; but something else must be discovered. What then is that which, when we write, makes us free from hindrance and unimpeded? "The knowledge of the art of writing." What, then, is it in playing the lute? "The science of playing the lute." Therefore in life also it is the science of life. You have, then, heard in a general way: but examine the thing also in the several parts. Is it possible that he who desires any of the things which depend on others can be free from hindrance? "No." Is it possible for him to be unimpeded? "No." Therefore he cannot be free. Consider then: whether we have nothing which is in our own power only, or whether we have all things, or whether some things are in our own power, and others in the power of others. "What do you mean?" When you wish the body to be entire, is it in your power or not? "It is not in my power." When you wish it to be healthy? "Neither is this in my power." When you wish it to be handsome? "Nor is this." Life or death? "Neither is this in my power." Your body, then, is another's, subject to every man who is stronger than yourself? "It is." But your estate, is it in your power to have it when you please, and as long as you please, and such as you please? "No." And your slaves? "No." And your clothes? "No." And your house? "No." And your horses? "Not one of these things." And if you wish by all means your children to live, or your wife, or your brother, or your friends, is it in your power? "This also is not in my power."

Whether, then, have you nothing which is in your own power, which depends on yourself only and cannot be taken from you, or have you anything of the kind? "I know not." Look at the thing, then, thus, and examine it. Is any man able to make you assent to that which is false?[1] "No man." In the matter of

____
[1] See iii. 22.

assent, then, you are free from hindrance and obstruction. "Granted." Well; and can a man force you to desire to move toward that to which you do not choose? "He can, for when he threatens me with death or bonds, he compels me to desire to move toward it." If, then, you despise death and bonds, do you still pay any regard to him? "No." Is, then, the despising of death an act of your own, or is it not yours? "It is my act." It is your own act, then, also to desire to move toward a thing: or is it not so? "It is my own act." But to desire to move away from a thing, whose act is that? This also is your act. "What, then, if I have attempted to walk, suppose another should hinder me." What part of you does he hinder? does he hinder the faculty of assent? "No: but my poor body." Yes, as he would do with a stone. "Granted; but I no longer walk." And who told you that walking is your act free from hindrance? for I said that this only was free from hindrance, to desire to move: but where there is need of body and its co-operation, you have heard long ago that nothing is your own. "Granted this also." And who can compel you to desire what you do not wish? "No man." And to propose, or intend, or in short to make use of the appearances which present themselves, can any man compel you? "He cannot do this: but he will hinder me when I desire from obtaining what I desire." If you desire anything which is your own, and one of the things which cannot be hindered, how will he hinder you? "He cannot in any way." Who, then, tells you that he who desires the things that belong to another is free from hindrance?

"Must I, then, not desire health?" By no means, nor anything else that belongs to another: for what is not in your power to acquire or to keep when you please, this belongs to another. Keep, then, far from it not only your hands but, more than that, even your desires. If you do not, you have surrendered yourself as a slave; you have subjected your neck, if you admire anything not your own, to everything that is dependent on the power of others and perishable, to which you have conceived a liking. "Is not my hand my own?" It is a part of your own body; but it is by nature earth, subject to hindrance, compulsion, and

the slave of everything which is stronger. And why do I say your hand? You ought to possess your whole body as a poor ass loaded, as long as it is possible, as long as you are allowed. But if there be a press,[1] and a soldier should lay hold of it, let it go, do not resist, nor murmur; if you do, you will receive blows, and nevertheless you will also lose the ass. But when you ought to feel thus with respect to the body, consider what remains to be done about all the rest, which is provided for the sake of the body. When the body is an ass, all the other things are bits belonging to the ass, pack-saddles, shoes, barley, fodder. Let these also go: get rid of them quicker and more readily than of the ass.

When you have made this preparation, and have practised this discipline, to distinguish that which belongs to another from that which is your own, the things which are subject to hindrance from those which are not, to consider the things free from hindrance to concern yourself, and those which are not free not to concern yourself, to keep your desire steadily fixed to the things which do concern yourself, and turned from the things which do not concern yourself; do you still fear any man? "No one." For about what will you be afraid? about the things which are your own, in which consists the nature of good and evil? and who has power over these things? who can take them away? who can impede them? No man can, no more than he can impede God. But will you be afraid about your body and your possessions, about things which are not yours, about things which in no way concern you? and what else have you been studying from the beginning than to distinguish between your own and not your own, the things which are in your power and not in your power, the things subject to hindrance and not subject? and why have you come to the philosophers? was it that you may nevertheless be unfortunate and unhappy? You will then in this way, as I have supposed you to have done, be without fear and disturbance. And what is grief to you? for fear comes from what you expect, but grief from that which is present. But what further will you desire? For of the things which are within the power of the will, as be-

[1] Herodotus, viii. 98.

ing good and present, you have a proper and regulated desire: but of the things which are not in the power of the will you do not desire any one, and so you do not allow any place to that which is irrational, and impatient, and above measure hasty.

When, then, you are thus affected toward things, what man can any longer be formidable to you? For what has a man which is formidable to another, either when you see him or speak to him or, finally, are conversant with him? Not more than one horse has with respect to another, or one dog to another, or one bee to another bee. Things, indeed, are formidable to every man; and when any man is able to confer these things on another or to take them away, then he too becomes formidable. How then is an acropolis demolished? Not by the sword, not by fire, but by opinion. For if we abolish the acropolis which is in the city, can we abolish also that of fever, and that of beautiful women? Can we, in a word, abolish the acropolis which is in us and cast out the tyrants within us, whom we have daily over us, sometimes the same tyrants, at other times different tyrants? But with this we must begin, and with this we must demolish the acropolis and eject the tyrants, by giving up the body, the parts of it, the faculties of it, the possessions, the reputation, magisterial offices, honours, children, brothers, friends, by considering all these things as belonging to others. And if tyrants have been ejected from us, why do I still shut in the acropolis by a wall of circumvallation, at least on my account; for if it still stands, what does it do to me? why do I still eject guards? For where do I perceive them? against others they have their fasces, and their spears, and their swords. But I have never been hindered in my will, nor compelled when I did not will. And how is this possible? I have placed my movements toward action in obedience to God. Is it His will that I shall have fever? It is my will also. Is it His will that I should move toward anything? It is my will also. Is it His will that I should obtain anything? It is my wish also. Does He not will? I do not wish. Is it His will that I die, is it His will that I be put to the rack? It is my will then to die: it is my will then to be put to the rack. Who, then, is still able to hinder me

contrary to my own judgment, or to compel me? No more than he can hinder or compel Zeus.

Thus the more cautious of travelers also act. A traveler has heard that the road is infested by robbers; he does not venture to enter on it alone, but he waits for the companionship on the road either of an ambassador, or of a quæstor, or of a proconsul, and when he has attached himself to such persons he goes along the road safely. So in the world the wise man acts. There are many companies of robbers, tyrants, storms, difficulties, losses of that which is dearest. "Where is there any place of refuge? how shall he pass along without being attacked by robbers? what company shall he wait for that he may pass along in safety? to whom shall he attach himself? To what person generally? to the rich man, to the man of consular rank? and what is the use of that to me? Such a man is stripped himself, groans and laments. But what if the fellow-companion himself turns against me and becomes my robber, what shall I do? I will be 'a friend of Cæsar': when I am Cæsar's companion no man will wrong me. In the first place, that I may become illustrious, what things must I endure and suffer? how often and by how many must I be robbed? Then, if I become Cæsar's friend, he also is mortal. And if Cæsar from any circumstance becomes my enemy, where is it best for me to retire? Into a desert? Well, does fever not come there? What shall be done then? Is it not possible to find a safe fellow-traveler, a faithful one, strong, secure against all surprises?" Thus he considers and perceives that if he attaches himself to God, he will make his journey in safety.

"How do you understand 'attaching yourself to God'?" In this sense, that whatever God wills, a man also shall will; and what God does not will, a man shall not will. How, then, shall this be done? In what other way than by examining the movements of God and his administration? What has He given to me as my own and in my own power? what has He reserved to Himself? He has given to me the things which are in the power of the will: He has put them in my power free from impediment and hindrance. How was He able to make the earthly body free from hindrance?

And accordingly He has subjected to the revolution of the whole, possessions, household things, house, children, wife. Why, then, do I fight against God? why do I will what does not depend on the will? why do I will to have absolutely what is not granted to me? But how ought I to will to have things? In the way in which they are given and as long as they are given. But He who has given takes away.[1] Why then do I resist? I do not say that I shall be a fool if I use force to one who is stronger, but I shall first be unjust. For whence had I things when I came into the world? My father gave them to me. And who gave them to him? and who made the sun? and who made the fruits of the earth? and who the seasons? and who made the connection of men with one another and their fellowship?

Then after receiving everything from another and even yourself, are you angry and do you blame the Giver if he takes anything from you? Who are you, and for what purpose did you come into the world? Did not He introduce you here, did He not show you the light, did he not give you fellow-workers, and perception, and reason? and as whom did He introduce you here? did He not introduce you as subject to death, and as one to live on the earth with a little flesh, and to observe His administration, and to join with Him in the spectacle and the festival for a short time? Will you not, then, as long as you have been permitted, after seeing the spectacle and the solemnity, when He leads you out, go with adoration of Him and thanks for what you have seen and heard? "No; but I would still enjoy the feast." The initiated, too, would wish to be longer in the initiation: and perhaps also those at Olympia to see other athletes; but the solemnity is ended: go away like a grateful and modest man; make room for others: others also must be born, as you were, and being born they must have a place, and houses and necessary things. And if the first do not retire, what remains? Why are you insatiable? Why are you not content? why do you contract the world? "Yes, but I would have my little children with me and my wife." What, are they yours? do they not belong to the Giver, and to Him who made you? then will you not give

up what belongs to others? will you not give way to Him who is superior? "Why, then, did He introduce me into the world on these conditions?" And if the conditions do not suit you, depart. He has no need of a spectator who is not satisfied. He wants those who join in the festival, those who take part in the chorus, that they may rather applaud, admire, and celebrate with hymns the solemnity. But those who can bear no trouble, and the cowardly He will not unwillingly see absent from the great assembly; for they did not when they were present behave as they ought to do at a festival nor fill up their place properly, but they lamented, found fault with the deity, fortune, their companions; not seeing both what they had, and their own powers, which they received for contrary purposes, the powers of magnanimity, of a generous mind, manly spirit, and what we are now inquiring about, freedom. "For what purpose, then, have I received these things?" To use them. "How long?" So long as He who has lent them chooses. "What if they are necessary to me?" Do not attach yourself to them and they will not be necessary: do not say to yourself that they are necessary, and then they are not necessary.

This study you ought to practise from morning to evening, beginning with the smallest things and those most liable to damage, with an earthen pot, with a cup. Then proceed in this way to a tunic, to a little dog, to a horse, to a small estate in land: then to yourself, to your body, to the parts of your body, to your children, to your wife, to your brothers. Look all round and throw these things from you. Purge your opinions, so that nothing cleave to you of the things which are not your own, that nothing grow to you, that nothing give you pain when it is torn from you; and say, while you are daily exercising yourself as you do there, not that you are philosophizing, for this is an arrogant expression, but that you are presenting an asserter of freedom: for this is really freedom. To this freedom Diogenes was called by Antisthenes, and he said that he could no longer be enslaved by any man. For this reason when he was taken prisoner,[2] how did he behave to the pirates? Did he call any of them

---

[1] Job i. 21.

[2] See iii. 24; ii. 13.

master? and I do not speak of the name, for I am not afraid of the word, but of the state of mind by which the word is produced. How did he reprove them for feeding badly their captives? How was he sold? Did he seek a master? no; but a slave, And, when he was sold, how did he behave to his master? Immediately he disputed with him and said to his master that he ought not to be dressed as he was, nor shaved in such a manner; and about the children he told them how he ought to bring them up. And what was strange in this? for if his master had bought an exercise master, would he have employed him in the exercises of the palæstra as a servant or as a master? and so if he had bought a physician or an architect. And so, in every matter, it is absolutely necessary that he who has skill must be the superior of him who has not. Whoever, then, generally possesses the science of life, what else must he be than master? For who is master of a ship? "The man who governs the helm." Why? Because he who will not obey him suffers for it. "But a master can give me stripes." Can he do it, then, without suffering for it? "So I also used to think." But because he cannot do it without suffering for it, for this reason it is not in his power: and no man can do what is unjust without suffering for it. "And what is the penalty for him who puts his own slave in chains, what do you think that is?" The fact of putting the slave in chains: and you also will admit this, if you choose to maintain the truth, that man is not a wild beast, but a tame animal. For when is a vine doing badly? When it is in a condition contrary to its nature. When is a cock? Just the same. Therefore a man also is so. What then is a man's nature? To bite, to kick, and to throw into prison and to behead? No; but to do good, to co-operate with others, to wish them well. At that time, then, he is in a bad condition, whether you choose to admit it or not, when he is acting foolishly.

"Socrates, then, did not fare badly?" No; but his judges and his accusers did. "Nor did Helvidius at Rome fare badly?" No; but his murderer did. "How do you mean?" The same as you do when you say that a cock has not fared badly when he has gained the victory and been severely wounded; but that the cock

has fared badly when he has been defeated and is unhurt: nor do you call a dog fortunate who neither pursues game nor labors, but when you see him sweating, when you see him in pain and panting violently after running. What paradox do we utter if we say that the evil in everything is that which is contrary to the nature of the thing? Is that a paradox? for do you not say this in the case of all other things? Why then in the case of man only do you think differently? But because we say that the nature of man is tame and social and faithful, you will not say that this is a paradox? "It is not." What then is it a paradox to say that a man is not hurt when he is whipped, or put in chains, or beheaded? does he not, if he suffers nobly, come off even with increased advantage and profit? But is he not hurt, who suffers in a most pitiful and disgraceful way, who in place of a man becomes a wolf, or viper or wasp?

Well then let us recapitulate the things which have been agreed on. The man who is not under restraint is free, to whom things are exactly in that state in which he wishes them to be; but he who can be restrained or compelled or hindered, or thrown into any circumstances against his will, is a slave. But who is free from restraint? He who desires nothing that belongs to others. And what are the things which belong to others? Those which are not in our power either to have or not to have, or to have of a certain kind or in a certain manner. Therefore the body belongs to another, the parts of the body belong to another, possession belongs to another. If, then, you are attached to any of these things as your own, you will pay the penalty which it is proper for him to pay who desires what belongs to another. This road leads to freedom, that is the only way of escaping from slavery, to be able to say at last with all your soul

> Lead me, O Zeus, and thou O destiny,
> The way that I am bid by you to go.[1]

But what do you say, philosopher? The tyrant summons you to say something which does not become you. Do you say it or do you not? Answer me. "Let me consider." Will you consider now? But when you were in the school, what was it which you used to consider? Did

[1] Epictetus, *Encheiridion*, 53.

you not study what are the things that are good and what are bad, and what things are neither one nor the other? "I did." What then was our opinion? "That just and honourable acts were good; and that unjust and disgraceful acts were bad." Is life a good thing? "No." Is death a bad thing? "No." Is prison? "No." But what did we think about mean and faithless words and betrayal of a friend and flattery of a tyrant? "That they are bad." Well then, you are not considering, nor have you considered nor deliberated. For what is the matter for consideration: is it whether it is becoming for me, when I have it in my power, to secure for myself the greatest of good things, and not to secure for myself the greatest evils? A fine inquiry indeed, and necessary, and one that demands much deliberation. Man, why do you mock us? Such an inquiry is never made. If you really imagined that base things were bad and honourable things were good, and that all other things were neither good nor bad, you would not even have approached this inquiry, nor have come near it; but immediately you would have been able to distinguish them by the understanding as you would do by the vision. For when do you inquire if black things are white, if heavy things are light, and do not comprehend the manifest evidence of the senses? How, then, do you now say that you are considering whether things which are neither good nor bad ought to be avoided more than things which are bad? But you do not possess these opinions; and neither do these things seem to you to be neither good nor bad, but you think that they are the greatest evils; nor do you think those other things to be evils, but matters which do not concern us at all. For thus from the beginning you have accustomed yourself. "Where am I? In the schools: and are any listening to me? I am discoursing among philosophers. But I have gone out of the school. Away with this talk of scholars and fools." Thus a friend is overpowered by the testimony of a philosopher:[1] thus a philosopher becomes a parasite; thus he lets himself for hire for money: thus in the senate a man does not say what he thinks; in private he proclaims his opinions. You are a cold and miserable little opinion, suspended from idle

words as from a hair. But keep yourself strong and fit for the uses of life and initiated by being exercised in action. How do you hear? I do not say that your child is dead—for how could you bear that?—but that your oil is spilled, your wine drunk up. Do you act in such a way that one standing by you while you are making a great noise, may say this only, "Philosopher, you say something different in the school. Why do you deceive us? Why, when you are only a worm, do you say that you are a man?" I should like to be present when one of the philosophers is lying with a woman, that I might see how he is exerting himself, and what words he is uttering, and whether he remembers his title of philosopher, and the words which he hears or says or reads.

"And what is this to liberty?" Nothing else than this, whether you who are rich choose or not. "And who is your evidence for this?" who else than yourselves? who have a powerful master, and who live in obedience to his nod and motion, and who faint if he only looks at you with a scowling countenance; you who court old women and old men, and say, "I cannot do this: it is not in my power." Why is it not in your power? Did you not lately contend with me and say that you are free? "But Aprulla[2] has hindered me." Tell the truth, then, slave, and do not run away from your masters, nor deny, nor venture to produce any one to assert your freedom, when you have so many evidences of your slavery. And indeed when a man is compelled by love to do something contrary to his opinion, and at the same time sees the better but has not the strength to follow it, one might consider him still more worthy of excuse as being held by a certain violent and, in a manner, a divine power.[3] But who could endure you who are in love with old women and old men, and wipe the old women's noses, and wash them and give them presents, and also wait on them like a slave when they are sick, and at the same time wish them dead, and question the physicians whether they are sick unto death? And again, when in order to obtain these great and much-admired magistracies and honours, you kiss the hands of these slaves of others, and so you

[1] Tacitus, *Annals*, xvi. 32.

[2] Some old woman who is courted for her money.
[3] Compare Plato *Symposium*, 206; I Cor. 7.

are not the slave even of free men. Then you walk about before me in stately fashion, a prætor or a consul. Do I not know how you became a prætor, by what means you got your consulship, who gave it to you? I would not even choose to live, if I must live by help of Felicion[1] and endure his arrogance and servile insolence: for I know what a slave is, who is fortunate, as he thinks, and puffed up by pride.

"You then," a man may say, "are you free?" I wish, by the Gods, and pray to be free; but I am not yet able to face my masters, I still value my poor body, I value greatly the preservation of it entire, though I do not possess it entire.[2] But I can point out to you a free man, that you may no longer seek an example. Diogenes was free. How was he free?—not because he was born of free parents, but because he was himself free, because he had cast off all the handles of slavery, and it was not possible for any man to approach him, nor had any man the means of laying hold of him to enslave him. He had everything easily loosed, everything only hanging to him. If you laid hold of his property, he would rather have let it go and be yours than he would have followed you for it: if you had laid hold of his leg, he would have let go his leg; if of all his body, all his poor body; his intimates, friends, country, just the same. For he knew from whence he had them, and from whom, and on what conditions. His true parents indeed, the Gods, and his real country he would never have deserted, nor would he have yielded to any man in obedience to them or to their orders, nor would any man have died for his country more readily. For he was not used to inquire when he should be considered to have done anything on behalf of the whole of things, but he remembered that everything which is done comes from thence and is done on behalf of that country and is commanded by him who administers it. Therefore see what Diogenes himself says and writes: "For this reason," he says, "Diogenes, it is in your power to speak both with the King of the Persians and with Archidamus the king of the Lacedæmonians, as you please." Was it because he was born of free parents? I suppose all the Athenians and all the Lacedæmonians, because they were born of slaves, could not talk with them as they wished, but feared and paid court to them. Why then does he say that it is in his power? "Because I do not consider the poor body to be my own, because I want nothing, because law[3] is everything to me, and nothing else is." These were the things which permitted him to be free.

And that you may not think that I show you the example of a man who is a solitary person, who has neither wife nor children, nor country, nor friends nor kinsmen, by whom he could be bent and drawn in various directions, take Socrates and observe that he had a wife and children, but he did not consider them as his own; that he had a country, so long as it was fit to have one, and in such a manner as was fit; friends and kinsmen also, but he held all in subjection to law and to the obedience due to it. For this reason he was the first to go out as a soldier, when it was necessary; and in war he exposed himself to danger most unsparingly,[4] and when he was sent by the tyrants to seize Leon, he did not even deliberate about the matter, because he thought that it was a base action, and he knew that he must die, if it so happened.[5] And what difference did that make to him? for he intended to preserve something else, not his poor flesh, but his fidelity, his honourable character. These are things which could not be assailed nor brought into subjection. Then, when he was obliged to speak in defense of his life, did he behave like a man who had children, who had a wife? No, but he behaved like a man who has neither. And what did he do when he was to drink the poison, and when he had the power of escaping from prison, and when Crito said to him, "Escape for the sake of your children," what did Socrates say?[6] Did he consider the power of escape as an unexpected gain? By no means: he considered what was fit and proper; but the rest he did not even look at or take into the reckoning. For he did not choose, he said, to save his poor body, but to save that which is increased and saved by doing what is just, and is impaired and de-

[1] See i. 19.   [2] Compare i. 8; i. 16.
[3] Compare Plato, *Crito,* 50.
[4] Plato, *Apology.*
[5] Plato, *Apology;* Marcus Aurelius, vii. 66.
[6] Plato, *Crito.*

stroyed by doing what is unjust. Socrates will not save his life by a base act; he who would not put the Athenians to the vote when they clamoured that he should do so,[1] he who refused to obey the tyrants, he who discoursed in such a manner about virtue and right behaviour. It is not possible to save such a man's life by base acts, but he is saved by dying, not by running away. For the good actor also preserves his character by stopping when he ought to stop, better than when he goes on acting beyond the proper time. What then shall the children of Socrates do? "If," said Socrates, "I had gone off to Thessaly, would you have taken care of them; and if I depart to the world below, will there be no man to take care of them?" See how he gives to death a gentle name and mocks it. But if you and I had been in his place, we should have immediately answered as philosophers that those who act unjustly must be repaid in the same way, and we should have added, "I shall be useful to many, if my life is saved, and if I die, I shall be useful to no man." For, if it had been necessary, we should have made our escape by slipping through a small hole. And how in that case should we have been useful to any man? for where would they have been then staying? or if we were useful to men while we were alive, should we not have been much more useful to them by dying when we ought to die, and as we ought? And now, Socrates being dead, no less useful to men, and even more useful, is the remembrance of that which he did or said when he was alive.

Think of these things, these opinions, these words: look to these examples, if you would be free, if you desire the thing according to its worth. And what is the wonder if you buy so great a thing at the price of things so many and so great? For the sake of this which is called "liberty," some hang themselves, others throw themselves down precipices, and sometimes even whole cities have perished: and will you not for the sake of the true and unassailable and secure liberty give back to God when He demands them the things which He has given? Will you not, as Plato says, study not to die only, but also to endure torture, and exile, and scourging, and, in a word, to give up

[1] Plato *Apology*.

all which is not your own? If you will not, you will be a slave among slaves, even if you be ten thousand times a consul; and if you make your way up to the Palace, you will no less be a slave; and you will feel, that perhaps philosophers utter words which are contrary to common opinion, as Cleanthes also said, but not words contrary to reason. For you will know by experience that the words are true, and that there is no profit from the things which are valued and eagerly sought to those who have obtained them; and to those who have not yet obtained them there is an imagination that when these things are come, all that is good will come with them; then, when they are come, the feverish feeling is the same, the tossing to and fro is the same, the satiety, the desire of things which are not present; for freedom is acquired not by the full possession of the things which are desired, but by removing the desire. And that you may know that this is true, as you have laboured for those things, so transfer your labour to these; be vigilant for the purpose of acquiring an opinion which will make you free; pay court to a philosopher instead of to a rich old man: be seen about a philosopher's doors: you will not disgrace yourself by being seen; you will not go away empty nor without profit, if you go to the philosopher as you ought, and if not, try at least: the trial is not disgraceful.

CHAPTER 2. *On familiar intimacy*

To THIS matter before all you must attend: that you be never so closely connected with any of your former intimates or friends as to come down to the same acts as he does. If you do not observe this rule, you will ruin yourself. But if the thought arises in your mind. "I shall seem disobliging to him, and he will not have the same feeling toward me," remember that nothing is done without cost, nor is it possible for a man if he does not do the same things to be the same man that he was. Choose, then, which of the two you will have, to be equally loved by those by whom you were formerly loved, being the same with your former self; or, being superior, not to obtain from your friends the same that you did before. For if this is better, immediately turn away to it, and let not other considerations draw you in a different direction. For no man is able to make progress, when he is wavering between opposite things; but if you have preferred this to all things, if you choose to attend to this only, to work out this only, give up everything else. But if you will not do this, your wavering will produce both these results: you will neither improve as you ought, nor will you obtain what you formerly obtained. For before, by plainly desiring the things which were worth nothing, you pleased your associates. But you cannot excel in both kinds, and it is necessary that so far as you share in the one, you must fall short in the other. You cannot, when you do not drink with those with whom you used to drink, be agreeable to them as you were before. Choose, then, whether you will be a hard drinker and pleasant to your former associates or a sober man and disagreeable to them. You cannot, when you do not sing with those with whom you used to sing, be equally loved by them. Choose, then, in this matter also which of the two you will have. For if it is better to be modest and orderly than for a man to say, "He is a jolly fellow," give up the rest, renounce it, turn away from it, have nothing to do with such men. But if this behaviour shall not please you, turn altogether to the opposite: become a catamite, an adulterer, and act accordingly, and you will get what you wish. And jump up in the theatre and bawl out in praise of the dancer. But characters so different cannot be mingled: you cannot act both Thersites and Agamemnon. If you intend to be Thersites,[1] you must be humpbacked and bald: if Agamemnon, you must be tall and handsome, and love those who are placed in obedience to you.

CHAPTER 3. *What things we should exchange for other things*

KEEP this thought in readiness, when you lose anything external, what you acquire in place of it; and if it be worth more, never say, "I have had a loss"; neither if you have got a horse in place of an ass, or an ox in place of a sheep, nor a good action in place of a bit of money, nor in place of idle talk such tranquillity as befits a man, nor in place of lewd talk if you have acquired modesty. If you remember this, you will always maintain your character such as it ought to be. But if you do not, consider that the times of opportunity are perishing, and that whatever pains you take about yourself, you are going to waste them all and overturn them. And it needs only a few things for the loss and overturning of all, namely a small deviation from reason. For the steerer of a ship to upset it, he has no need of the same means as he has need of for saving it: but if he turns it a little to the wind, it is lost; and if he does not do this purposely, but has been neglecting his duty a little, the ship is lost. Something of the kind happens in this case also: if you only fall to nodding a little, all that you have up to this time collected is gone. Attend therefore to the appearances of things, and watch over them; for that which you have to preserve is no small matter, but it is modesty and fidelity and constancy, freedom from the affects, a state of mind undisturbed, freedom from fear, tranquillity, in a word, "liberty." For what will you sell these things? See what is the value of the things which you will obtain in exchange for these. "But shall I not obtain any such thing for it?" See, and if you do in return get that, see what you receive in place of it. "I possess decency, he possesses a tribuneship: he possesses a prætorship, I possess modesty. But I do not make acclamations where it is not becoming: I will not stand up where I ought not;[2] for I am free, and a friend of God, and so I obey Him willingly. But I must not claim anything else, neither body nor possession, nor magistracy, nor good report, nor in fact anything. For He does not allow me to claim them: for if He had chosen, He would have made them good for me; but He has not done so, and for this reason I cannot transgress his commands."[3] Preserve that which is your own good in everything; and as to every other thing, as it is permitted, and so far as to behave consistently with reason in respect to them, content with this only. If you do not, you will be unfortunate, you will fail in all things, you will be hindered, you will be impeded. These are the laws which have been sent from thence; these are the orders. Of these laws a man ought to be an expositor, to these he ought to submit, not to those of Masurius and Cassius.

[1] See Homer, *Iliad*, ii. 216; iii. 167.

[2] See iii. 4; iv. 2-9.   [3] See i. 25; iv. 7.

CHAPTER 4. *To those who are desirous of passing life in tranquillity*

REMEMBER that not only the desire of power and of riches makes us mean and subject to others, but even the desire of tranquillity, and of leisure, and of traveling abroad, and of learning. For, to speak plainly, whatever the external thing may be, the value which we set upon it places us in subjection to others. What, then, is the difference between desiring to be a senator or not desiring to be one; what is the difference between desiring power or being content with a private station; what is the difference between saying, "I am unhappy, I have nothing to do, but I am bound to my books as a corpse"; or saying, "I am unhappy, I have no leisure for reading"? For as salutations and power are things external and independent of the will, so is a book. For what purpose do you choose to read? Tell me. For if you only direct your purpose to being amused or learning something, you are a silly fellow and incapable of enduring labour. But if you refer reading to the proper end, what else is this than a tranquil and happy life? But if reading does not secure for you a happy and tranquil life, what is the use of it? "But it does secure this," the man replies, "and for this reason I am vexed that I am deprived of it." And what is this tranquil and happy life, which any man can impede; I do not say Cæsar or Cæsar's friend, but a crow, a piper, a fever, and thirty thousand other things? But a tranquil and happy life contains nothing so sure as continuity and freedom from obstacle. Now I am called to do something: I will go, then, with the purpose of observing the measures which I must keep,[1] of acting with modesty, steadiness, without desire and aversion to things external; and then that I may attend to men, what they say, how they are moved; and this not with any bad disposition, or that I may have something to blame or to ridicule; but I turn to myself, and ask if I also commit the same faults. "How then shall I cease to commit them?" Formerly I also acted wrong, but now I do not: thanks to God.

Come, when you have done these things and have attended to them, have you done a worse act than when you have read a thousand

verses or written as many? For when you eat, are you grieved because you are not reading? are you not satisfied with eating according to what you have learned by reading, and so with bathing and with exercise? Why, then, do you not act consistently in all things, both when you approach Cæsar and when you approach any person? If you maintain yourself free from perturbation, free from alarm, and steady; if you look rather at the things which are done and happen than are looked at yourself; if you do not envy those who are preferred before you; if surrounding circumstances do not strike you with fear or admiration, what do you want? Books? How or for what purpose? for is not this a preparation for life? and is not life itself made up of certain other things than this? This is just as if an athlete should weep when he enters the stadium, because he is not being exercised outside of it. It was for this purpose that you used to practise exercise; for this purpose were used the halteres,[2] the dust, the young men as antagonists; and do you seek for those things now when it is the time of action? This is just as if in the topic of assent when appearances present themselves, some of which can be comprehended, and some cannot be comprehended, we should not choose to distinguish them but should choose to read what has been written about comprehension.

What then is the reason of this? The reason is that we have never read for this purpose, we have never written for this purpose, so that we may in our actions use in a way conformable to nature the appearances presented to us; but we terminate in this, in learning what is said, and in being able to expound it to another, in resolving a syllogism,[3] and in handling the hypothetical syllogism. For this reason where our study is, there alone is the impediment. Would you have by all means the things which are not in your power? Be prevented then, be hindered, fail in your purpose. But if we read what is written about action, not that we may see what is said about action, but that we may act well: if we read what is said about desire and aversion, in order that we may neither fail in our desires, nor

[1] Marcus Aurelius, iii. 1.

[2] See i. 4, iii.15; and i. 24; i. 29.

[3] Marcus Aurelius, i. 17.

fall into that which we try to avoid: if we read what is said about duty, in order that, remembering the relations, we may do nothing irrationally nor contrary to these relations; we should not be vexed in being hindered as to our readings, but we should be satisfied with doing the acts which are conformable, and we should be reckoning not what so far we have been accustomed to reckon; "To-day I have read so many verses, I have written so many"; but, "To-day I have employed my action as it is taught by the philosophers; I have not employed my desire; I have used avoidance only with respect to things which are within the power of my will; I have not been afraid of such a person, I have not been prevailed upon by the entreaties of another; I have exercised my patience, my abstinence, my co-operation with others"; and so we should thank God for what we ought to thank Him.

But now we do not know that we also in another way are like the many. Another man is afraid that he shall not have power: you are afraid that you will. Do not do so, my man; but as you ridicule him who is afraid that he shall not have power, so ridicule yourself also. For it makes no difference whether you are thirsty like a man who has a fever, or have a dread of water like a man who is mad. Or how will you still be able to say as Socrates did, "If so it pleases God, so let it be"? Do you think that Socrates, if he had been eager to pass his leisure in the Lyceum or in the Academy and to discourse daily with the young men, would have readily served in military expeditions so often as he did; and would he not have lamented and groaned, "Wretch that I am; I must now be miserable here, when I might be sunning myself in the Lyceum"? Why, was this your business, to sun yourself? And is it not your business to be happy, to be free from hindrance, free from impediment? And could he still have been Socrates, if he had lamented in this way: how would he still have been able to write Pæans in his prison?[1]

In short, remember this, that what you shall prize which is beyond your will, so far you have destroyed your will. But these things are out of the power of the will, not only power, but also a private condition: not only occupa-

[1] Plato, *Phædo*, 61.

tion, but also leisure. "Now, then, must I live in this tumult?" Why do you say "tumult"? "I mean among many men." Well what is the hardship? Suppose that you are at Olympia: imagine it to be a panegyris, where one is calling out one thing, another is doing another thing, and a third is pushing another person: in the baths there is a crowd: and who of us is not pleased with this assembly and leaves it unwillingly? Be not difficult to please nor fastidious about what happens. "Vinegar is disagreeable, for it is sharp; honey is disagreeable, for it disturbs my habit of body. I do not like vegetables." So also, "I do not like leisure; it is a desert: I do not like a crowd; it is confusion." But if circumstances make it necessary for you to live alone or with a few, call it quiet and use the thing as you ought: talk with yourself, exercise the appearances, work up your preconceptions. If you fall into a crowd, call it a celebration of games, a panegyris, a festival: try to enjoy the festival with other men. For what is a more pleasant sight to him who loves mankind than a number of men? We see with pleasure herds of horses or oxen: we are delighted when we see many ships: who is pained when he sees many men? "But they deafen me with their cries." Then your hearing is impeded. What, then, is this to you? Is, then, the power of making use of appearances hindered? And who prevents you from using, according to nature, inclination to a thing and aversion from it; and movement toward a thing and movement from it? What tumult is able to do this?

Do you only bear in mind the general rules: "What is mine, what is not mine; what is given to me; what does God will that I should do now? what does He not will?" A little before he willed you to be at leisure, to talk with yourself, to write about these things, to read, to hear, to prepare yourself. You had sufficient time for this. Now He says to you: "Come now to the contest; show us what you have learned, how you have practised the athletic art. How long will you be exercised alone? Now is the opportunity for you to learn whether you are an athlete worthy of victory, or one of those who go about the world and are defeated." Why, then, are you vexed? No contest is without confusion. There must be many who exercise themselves for the contests, many who call out to those who exercise themselves, many masters, many spectators. "But my wish is to live quietly." Lament, then, and groan as you deserve to do. For what other is a greater punishment than this to the untaught man and to him who disobeys the divine commands: to be grieved, to lament, to envy, in a word, to be disappointed and to be unhappy? Would you not release yourself from these things? "And how shall I release myself?" Have you not often heard that you ought to remove entirely desire, apply aversion to those things only which are within your power, that you ought to give up everything, body, property, fame, books, tumult, power, private station? for whatever way you turn, you are a slave, you are subjected, you are hindered, you are compelled, you are entirely in the power of others. But keep the words of Cleanthes in readiness.

Lead me, O Zeus, and thou necessity.

Is it your will that I should go to Rome? I will go to Rome. To Gyara? I will go to Gyara. To Athens? I will go to Athens. To prison? I will go to prison. If you should once say, "When shall a man go to Athens?" you are undone. It is a necessary consequence that this desire, if it is not accomplished, must make you unhappy; and if it is accomplished, it must make you vain, since you are elated at things at which you ought not to be elated; and on the other hand, if you are impeded, it must make you wretched because you fall into that which you would not fall into. Give up then all these things. "Athens is a good place." But happiness is much better; and to be free from passions, free from disturbance, for your affairs not to depend on any man. "There is tumult at Rome and visits of salutation."[1] But happiness is an equivalent for all troublesome things. If, then, the time comes for these things, why do you not take away the wish to avoid them? what necessity is there to carry a burden like an ass, and to be beaten with a stick? But if you do not so, consider that you must always be a slave to him who has it in his power to effect your release, and also to impede you, and you must serve him as an evil genius.[2]

[1] Virgil, *Georgics*, ii. 461.
[2] Compare i. 19.

There is only one way to happiness, and let this rule be ready both in the morning and during the day and by night; the rule is not to look toward things which are out of the power of our will, to think that nothing is our own, to give up all things to the Divinity, to Fortune; to make them the superintendents of these things, whom Zeus also has made so; for a man to observe that only which is his own, that which cannot be hindered; and when we read, to refer our reading to this only, and our writing and our listening. For this reason, I cannot call the man industrious, if I hear this only, that he reads and writes; and even if a man adds that he reads all night, I cannot say so, if he knows not to what he should refer his reading. For neither do you say that a man is industrious if he keeps awake for a girl; nor do I. But if he does it for reputation, I say that he is a lover of reputation. And if he does it for money, I say that he is a lover of money, not a lover of labour; and if he does it through love of learning, I say that he is a lover of learning. But if he refers his labour to his own ruling power, that he may keep it in a state conformable to nature and pass his life in that state, then only do I say that he is industrious. For never commend a man on account of these things which are common to all, but on account of his opinions; for these are the things which belong to each man, which make his actions bad or good. Remembering these rules, rejoice in that which is present, and be content with the things which come in season.[3] If you see anything which you have learned and inquired about occurring to you in your course of life, be delighted at it. If you have laid aside or have lessened bad disposition and a habit of reviling; if you have done so with rash temper, obscene words, hastiness, sluggishness; if you are not moved by what you formerly were, and not in the same way as you once were, you can celebrate a festival daily, to-day because you have behaved well in one act, and tomorrow because you have behaved well in another. How much greater is this a reason for making sacrifices than a consulship or the government of a province? These things come to you from yourself and from the gods. Remem-

[3] See Marcus Aurelius, vi. 2; ix. 6.

ber this, Who gives these things and to whom, and for what purpose. If you cherish yourself in these thoughts, do you still think that it makes any difference where you shall be happy, where you shall please God? Are not the gods equally distant from all places? Do they not see from all places alike that which is going on?

CHAPTER 5. *Against the quarrelsome and ferocious*

THE wise and good man neither himself fights with any person, nor does he allow another, so far as he can prevent it. And an example of this as well as of all other things is proposed to us in the life of Socrates, who not only himself on all occasions avoided fights, but would not allow even others to quarrel. See in Xenophon's *Symposium*[1] how many quarrels he settled; how further he endured Thrasymachus and Polus and Callicles; how he tolerated his wife, and how he tolerated his son who attempted to confute him and to cavil with him. For he remembered well that no man has in his power another man's ruling principle. He wished, therefore, for nothing else than that which was his own. And what is this? Not that this or that man may act according to nature; for that is a thing which belongs to another; but that while others are doing their own acts, as they choose, he may never the less be in a condition conformable to nature and live in it, only doing what is his own to the end that others also may be in a state conformable to nature. For this is the object always set before him by the wise and good man. Is it to be commander of an army? No: but if it is permitted him, his object is in this matter to maintain his own ruling principle. Is it to marry? No; but if marriage is allowed to him, in this matter his object is to maintain himself in a condition conformable to nature. But if he would have his son not to do wrong, or his wife, he would have what belongs to another not to belong to another; and to be instructed is this: to learn what things are a man's own and what belongs to another.

How, then, is there left any place for fighting to a man who has this opinion? Is he surprised at anything which happens, and does it

[1] See ii. 12.

appear new to him? Does he not expect that which comes from the bad to be worse and more grievous than what actually befalls him? And does he not reckon as pure gain whatever they may do which falls short of extreme wickedness? "Such a person has reviled you." Great thanks to him for not having struck you. "But he has struck me also." Great thanks that he did not wound you. "But he wounded me also." Great thanks that he did not kill you. For when did he learn or in what school that man is a tame[2] animal, that men love one another, that an act of injustice is a great harm to him who does it. Since then he has not learned this and is not convinced of it, why shall he not follow that which seems to be for his own interest? "Your neighbour has thrown stones." Have you then done anything wrong? "But the things in the house have been broken." Are you then a utensil? No; but a free power of will.[3] What, then, is given to you in answer to this? If you are like a wolf, you must bite in return, and throw more stones. But if you consider what is proper for a man, examine your store-house, see with what faculties you came into the world. Have you the disposition of a wild beast, have you the disposition of revenge for an injury? When is a horse wretched? When he is deprived of his natural faculties; not when he cannot crow like a cock, but when he cannot run. When is a dog wretched? Not when he cannot fly, but when he cannot track his game. Is, then, a man also unhappy in this way, not because he cannot strangle lions or embrace statues,[4] for he did not come into the world in the possession of certain powers from nature for this purpose, but because he has lost his probity and his fidelity? People ought to meet and lament such a man for the misfortunes into which he has fallen; not indeed to lament because a man has been born or has died,[5] but because it has happened to him in his lifetime to have lost the things which are his own, not that which he received from his father, not his land and house, and his inn, and his slaves; for not one of these things is a man's own, but

[2] See ii. 10; iv, 1; Plato, *Laws*, vi.
[3] See iii. 1.
[4] See iii. 12.
[5] Compare Herodotus, v. 4, on the Trausi.

all belong to others, are servile and subject to account, at different times given to different persons by those who have them in their power: but I mean the things which belong to him as a man, the marks in his mind with which he came into the world, such as we seek also on coins, and if we find them, we approve of the coins, and if we do not find the marks, we reject them. What is the stamp on this Sestertius? "The stamp of Trajan." Present it. "It is the stamp of Nero." Throw it away: it cannot be accepted, it is counterfeit. So also in this case. What is the stamp of his opinions? "It is gentleness, a sociable disposition, a tolerant temper, a disposition to mutual affection." Produce these qualities. I accept them: I consider this man a citizen, I accept him as a neighbour, a companion in my voyages. Only see that he has not Nero's stamp. Is he passionate, is he full of resentment, is he fault-finding? If the whim seizes him, does he break the heads of those who come in his way? Why, then, did you say that he is a man? Is everything judged by the bare form? If that is so, say that the form in wax is an apple and has the smell and the taste of an apple. But the external figure is not enough: neither then is the nose enough and the eyes to make the man, but he must have the opinions of a man. Here is a man who does not listen to reason, who does not know when he is refuted: he is an ass: in another man the sense of shame is become dead: he is good for nothing, he is anything rather than a man. This man seeks whom he may meet and kick or bite, so that he is not even a sheep or an ass, but a kind of wild beast.

"What then? would you have me to be despised?" By whom? by those who know you? and how shall those who know you despise a man who is gentle and modest? Perhaps you mean by those who do not know you? What is that to you? For no other artisan cares for the opinion of those who know not his art. "But they will be more hostile to me for this reason." Why do you say "me"? Can any man injure your will, or prevent you from using in a natural way the appearances which are presented to you? "In no way can he." Why, then, are you still disturbed and why do you choose to show yourself afraid? And why do you not

come forth and proclaim that you are at peace with all men whatever they may do, and laugh at those chiefly who think that they can harm you? "These slaves," you can say, "know not either who I am nor where lies my good or my evil, because they have no access to the things which are mine."

In this way, also, those who occupy a strong city mock the besiegers: "What trouble these men are now taking for nothing: our wall is secure, we have food for a very long time, and all other resources." These are the things which make a city strong and impregnable: but nothing else than his opinions makes a man's soul impregnable. For what wall is so strong, or what body is so hard, or what possession is so safe, or what honour so free from assault? All things everywhere are perishable, easily taken by assault, and, if any man in any way is attached to them, he must be disturbed, expect what is bad, he must fear, lament, find his desires disappointed, and fall into things which he would avoid. Then do we not choose to make secure the only means of safety which are offered to us, and do we not choose to withdraw ourselves from that which is perishable and servile and to labour at the things which are imperishable and by nature free; and do we not remember that no man either hurts another or does good to another, but that a man's opinion about each thing is that which hurts him, is that which overturns him; this is fighting, this is civil discord, this is war? That which made Eteocles and Polynices[1] enemies was nothing else than this opinion which they had about royal power, their opinion about exile, that the one is the extreme of evils, the other the greatest good. Now this is the nature of every man to seek the good, to avoid the bad; to consider him who deprives us of the one and involves us in the other an enemy and treacherous, even if he be a brother, or a son or a father. For nothing is more akin to us than the good: therefore if these things are good and evil, neither is a father a friend to sons, nor a brother to a brother, but all the world is everywhere full of enemies, treacherous men, and sycophants. But if the will, being what it ought to be, is the only good; and if the will,

[1] Aeschylus, *Seven Against Thebes;* Euripides, *Phoenician Maidens.*

being such as it ought not to be, is the only evil, where is there any strife, where is there reviling? about what? about the things which do not concern us? and strife with whom? with the ignorant, the unhappy, with those who are deceived about the chief things?

Remembering this Socrates managed his own house and endured a very ill-tempered wife and a foolish son. For in what did she show her bad temper? In pouring water on his head as much as she liked, and in trampling on the cake. And what is this to me, if I think that these things are nothing to me? But this is my business; and neither tyrant shall check my will nor a master; nor shall the many check me who am only one, nor shall the stronger check me who am the weaker; for this power of being free from check is given by God to every man. For these opinions make love in a house, concord in a state, among nations peace, and gratitude to God; they make a man in all things cheerful in externals as about things which belong to others, as about things which are of no value. We indeed are able to write and to read these things, and to praise them when they are read, but we do not even come near to being convinced of them. Therefore what is said of the Lacedæmonians, "Lions at home, but in Ephesus foxes," will fit in our case also, "Lions in the school, but out of it foxes."

CHAPTER 6. *Against those who lament over being pitied*

"I AM grieved," a man says, "at being pitied." Whether, then, is the fact of your being pitied a thing which concerns you or those who pity you? Well, is it in your power to stop this pity? "It is in my power, if I show them that I do not require pity." And whether, then, are you in the condition of not deserving pity, or are you not in that condition? "I think I am not: but these persons do not pity me for the things for which, if they ought to pity me, it would be proper, I mean, for my faults; but they pity me for my poverty, for not possessing honourable offices, for diseases and deaths and other such things." Whether, then, are you prepared to convince the many that not one of these things is an evil, but that it is possible for a man who is poor and has no office and enjoys

no honour to be happy; or to show yourself to them as rich and in power? For the second of these things belong to a man who is boastful, silly and good for nothing. And consider by what means the pretense must be supported. It will be necessary for you to hire slaves and to possess a few silver vessels, and to exhibit them in public, if it is possible, though they are often the same, and to attempt to conceal the fact that they are the same, and to have splendid garments, and all other things for display, and to show that you are a man honoured by the great, and to try to sup at their houses, or to be supposed to sup there, and as to your person to employ some mean arts, that you may appear to be more handsome and nobler than you are. These things you must contrive, if you choose to go by the second path in order not to be pitied. But the first way is both impracticable and long, to attempt the very thing which Zeus has not been able to do, to convince all men what things are good and bad. Is this power given to you? This only is given to you, to convince yourself; and you have not convinced yourself. Then I ask you, do you attempt to persuade other men? and who has lived so long with you as you with yourself? and who has so much power of convincing you as you have of convincing yourself; and who is better disposed and nearer to you than you are to yourself? How, then, have you not convinced yourself in order to learn? At present are not things upside down? Is this what you have been earnest about doing, to learn to be free from grief and free from disturbance, and not to be humbled, and to be free? Have you not heard, then, that there is only one way which leads to this end, to give up the things which do not depend on the will, to withdraw from them, and to admit that they belong to others? For another man, then, to have an opinion about you, of what kind is it? "It is a thing independent of the will." Then is it nothing to you? "It is nothing." When, then, you are still vexed at this and disturbed, do you think that you are convinced about good and evil?

Will you not, then, letting others alone, be to yourself both scholar and teacher? "The rest of mankind will look after this, whether it is to their interest to be and to pass their lives in a state contrary to nature: but to me no man is nearer than myself. What, then, is the meaning of this, that I have listened to the words of the philosophers and I assent to them, but in fact I am no way made easier? Am I so stupid? And yet, in all other things such as I have chosen, I have not been found very stupid; but I learned letters quickly, and to wrestle, and geometry, and to resolve syllogisms. Has not, then, reason convinced me? and indeed no other things have I from the beginning so approved and chosen: and now I read about these things, hear about them, write about them; I have so far discovered no reason stronger than this. In what, then, am I deficient? Have the contrary opinions not been eradicated from me? Have the notions themselves not been exercised nor used to be applied to action, but as armour are laid aside and rusted and cannot fit me? And yet neither in the exercises of the palæstra, nor in writing or reading am I satisfied with learning, but I turn up and down the syllogisms which are proposed, and I make others, and sophistical syllogisms also. But the necessary theorems, by proceeding from which a man can become free from grief, fear, passions, hindrance, and a free man, these I do not exercise myself in nor do I practise in these the proper practice. Then I care about what others will say of me, whether I shall appear to them worth notice, whether I shall appear happy."

Wretched man, will you not see what you are saying about yourself? What do you appear to yourself to be? in your opinions, in your desires, in your aversions from things, in your movements, in your preparation, in your designs, and in other acts suitable to a man? But do you trouble yourself about this, whether others pity you? "Yes, but I am pitied not as I ought to be." Are you then pained at this? and is he who is pained, an object of pity? "Yes." How, then, are you pitied not as you ought to be? For by the very act that you feel about being pitied, you make yourself deserving of pity. What then says Antisthenes? Have you not heard? "It is a royal thing, O Cyrus, to do right and to be ill-spoken of."[1] My head is sound, and all think that I have the headache. What do I care for that? I am free from fever, and people sympathize with

[1] Marcus Aurelius, vii. 36.

me as if I had a fever: "Poor man, for so long a time you have not ceased to have fever." I also say with a sorrowful countenance: "In truth it is now a long time that I have been ill." "What will happen then?" "As God may please": and at the same time I secretly laugh at those who are pitying me. What, then, hinders the same being done in this case also? I am poor, but I have a right opinion about poverty. Why, then, do I care if they pity me for my poverty? I am not in power; but others are: and I have the opinion which I ought to have about having and not having power. Let them look to it who pity me; but I am neither hungry nor thirsty nor do I suffer cold; but because they are hungry or thirsty they think that I too am. What, then, shall I do for them? Shall I go about and proclaim and say: "Be not mistaken, men, I am very well, I do not trouble myself about poverty, nor want of power, nor in a word about anything else than right opinions. These I have free from restraint, I care for nothing at all." What foolish talk is this? How do I possess right opinions when I am not content with being what I am, but am uneasy about what I am supposed to be?

"But," you say, "others will get more and be preferred to me." What, then, is more reasonable than for those who have laboured about anything to have more in that thing in which they have laboured? They have laboured for power, you have laboured about opinions; and they have laboured for wealth, you for the proper use of appearances. See if they have more than you in this about which you have laboured, and which they neglect; if they assent better than you with respect to the natural rules of things; if they are less disappointed than you in their desires; if they fall less into things which they would avoid than you do; if in their intentions, if in the things which they propose to themselves, if in their purposes, if in their motions toward an object they take a better aim; if they better observe a proper behaviour, as men, as sons, as parents, and so on as to the other names by which we express the relations of life. But if they exercise power, and you do not, will you not choose to tell yourself the truth, that you do nothing for the sake of this, and they do all?

But it is most unreasonable that he who looks after anything should obtain less than he who does not look after it.

"Not so: but since I care about right opinions, it is more reasonable for me to have power." Yes in the matter about which you do care, in opinions. But in a matter in which they have cared more than you, give way to them. The case is just the same as if, because you have right opinions, you thought that in using the bow you should hit the mark better than an archer, and in working in metal you should succeed better than a smith. Give up, then, your earnestness about opinions and employ yourself about the things which you wish to acquire; and then lament, if you do not succeed; for you deserve to lament. But now you say that you are occupied with other things, that you are looking after other things; but the many say this truly, that one act has no community with another. He who has risen in the morning seeks whom he shall salute, to whom he shall say something agreeable, to whom he shall send a present, how he shall please the dancing man, how by bad behaviour to one he may please another. When he prays, he prays about these things; when he sacrifices, he sacrifices for these things: the saying of Pythagoras

Let sleep not come upon thy languid eyes
he transfers to these things. "Where have I failed in the matters pertaining to flattery?" "What have I done?" Anything like a free man, anything like a noble-minded man? And if he finds anything of the kind, he blames and accuses himself: "Why did you say this? Was it not in your power to lie? Even the philosophers say that nothing hinders us from telling a lie." But do you, if indeed you have cared about nothing else except the proper use of appearances, as soon as you have risen in the morning reflect, "What do I want in order to be free from passion, and free from perturbation? What am I? Am I a poor body, a piece of property, a thing of which something is said? I am none of these. But what am I? I am a rational animal. What then is required of me?" Reflect on your acts. "Where have I omitted the things which conduce to happiness? What have I done which is either unfriendly or unsocial? what have I not done as

to these things which I ought to have done?"

So great, then, being the difference in desires, actions, wishes, would you still have the same share with others in those things about which you have not laboured, and they have laboured? Then are you surprised if they pity you, and are you vexed? But they are not vexed if you pity them. Why? Because they are convinced that they have that which is good, and you are not convinced. For this reason you are not satisfied with your own, but you desire that which they have: but they are satisfied with their own, and do not desire what you have: since, if you were really convinced that with respect to what is good, it is you who are the possessor of it and that they have missed it, you would not even have thought of what they say about you.

CHAPTER 7. *On freedom from fear*
WHAT makes the tyrant formidable? "The guards," you say, "and their swords, and the men of the bedchamber and those who exclude them who would enter." Why, then, if you bring a boy to the tyrant when he is with his guards, is he not afraid; or is it because the child does not understand these things? If, then, any man does understand what guards are and that they have swords, and comes to the tyrant for this very purpose because he wishes to die on account of some circumstance and seeks to die easily by the hand of another, is he afraid of the guards? "No, for he wishes for the thing which makes the guards formidable." If, then, neither any man wishing to die nor to live by all means, but only as it may be permitted, approaches the tyrant, what hinders him from approaching the tyrant without fear? "Nothing." If, then, a man has the same opinion about his property as the man whom I have instanced has about his body; and also about his children and his wife, and in a word is so affected by some madness or despair that he cares not whether he possesses them or not, but like children who are playing with shells care about the play, but do not trouble themselves about the shells, so he too has set no value on the materials, but values the pleasure that he has with them and the occupation, what tyrant is then formidable to him or what guards or what swords?

Then through madness is it possible for a man to be so disposed toward these things, and the Galilæans through habit,[1] and is it possible that no man can learn from reason and from demonstration that God has made all the things in the universe and the universe itself completely free from hindrance and perfect, and the parts of it for the use of the whole? All other animals indeed are incapable of comprehending the administration of it; but the rational animal, man, has faculties for the consideration of all these things, and for understanding that it is a part, and what kind of a part it is, and that it is right for the parts to be subordinate to the whole. And besides this being naturally noble, magnanimous and free, man sees that of the things which surround him some are free from hindrance and in his power, and the other things are subject to hindrance and in the power of others; that the things which are free from hindrance are in the power of the will; and those which are subject to hindrance are the things which are not in the power of the will. And, for this reason, if he thinks that his good and his interest be in these things only which are free from hindrance and in his own power, he will be free, prosperous, happy, free from harm, magnanimous, pious, thankful to God[2] for all things; in no matter finding fault with any of the things which have not been put in his power, nor blaming any of them. But if he thinks that his good and his interest are in externals and in things which are not in the power of his will, he must of necessity be hindered, be impeded, be a slave to those who have the power over things which he admires and fears; and he must of necessity be impious because he thinks that he is harmed by God, and he must be unjust because he always claims more than belongs to him; and he must of necessity be abject and mean.

What hinders a man, who has clearly separated these things, from living with a light heart and bearing easily the reins, quietly expecting everything which can happen, and enduring that which has already happened? "Would you have me to bear poverty?" Come and you will know what poverty is when it has

found one who can act well the part of a poor man. "Would you have me to possess power?" Let me have power, and also the trouble of it. "Well, banishment?" Wherever I shall go, there it will be well with me; for here also where I am, it was not because of the place that it was well with me, but because of my opinions which I shall carry off with me: for neither can any man deprive me of them; but my opinions alone are mine and they cannot be taken from me, and I am satisfied while I have them, wherever I may be and whatever I am doing. "But now it is time to die." Why do you say "to die"? Make no tragedy show of the thing, but speak of it as it is: it is now time for the matter to be resolved into the things out of which it was composed. And what is the formidable thing here? what is going to perish of the things which are in the universe? what new thing or wondrous is going to happen? Is it for this reason that a tyrant is formidable? Is it for this reason that the guards appear to have swords which are large and sharp? Say this to others; but I have considered about all these things; no man has power over me. I have been made free; I know His commands, no man can now lead me as a slave. I have a proper person to assert my freedom; I have proper judges. Are you not the master of my body? What, then, is that to me? Are you not the master of my property? What, then, is that to me? Are you not the master of my exile or of my chains? Well, from all these things and all the poor body itself I depart at your bidding, when you please. Make trial of your power, and you will know how far it reaches.

Whom then can I still fear? Those who are over the bedchamber? Lest they should do, what? Shut me out? If they find that I wish to enter, let them shut me out. "Why, then, do you go to the doors?" Because I think it befits me, while the play lasts, to join in it. "How, then, are you not shut out?" Because, unless some one allows me to go in, I do not choose to go in, but am always content with that which happens; for I think that what God chooses is better than what I choose.[3] I will attach myself as a minister and follower to Him; I have the same movements as He has, I have

[1] The Christians. See Marcus Aurelius, xi. 3.
[2] Eph. 5. 20.
[3] Matt. 26. 39.

the same desires; in a word, I have the same will. There is no shutting out for me, but for those who would force their way in. Why, then, do not I force my way in? Because I know that nothing good is distributed within to those who enter. But when I hear any man called fortunate because he is honoured by Cæsar, I say, "What does he happen to get?" A province. Does he also obtain an opinion such as he ought? The office of a Prefect. Does he also obtain the power of using his office well? Why do I still strive to enter? A man scatters dried figs and nuts: the children seize them and fight with one another; men do not, for they think them to be a small matter. But if a man should throw about shells, even the children do not seize them. Provinces are distributed: let children look to that. Money is distributed: let children look to that. Prætorships, consulships are distributed: let children scramble for them, let them be shut out, beaten, kiss the hands of the giver, of the slaves: but to me these are only dried figs and nuts. What then? If you fail to get them, while Cæsar is scattering them about, do not be troubled: if a dried fig come into your lap, take it and eat it; for so far you may value even a fig. But if I shall stoop down and turn another over, or be turned over by another, and shall flatter those who have got into chamber, neither is a dried fig worth the trouble, nor anything else of the things which are not good, which the philosophers have persuaded me not to think good.

Show me the swords of the guards. "See how big they are, and how sharp." What, then, do these big and sharp swords do? "They kill." And what does a fever do? "Nothing else." And what else a tile? "Nothing else." Would you then have me to wonder at these things and worship them, and go about as the slave of all of them? I hope that this will not happen: but when I have once learned that everything which has come into existence must also go out of it, that the universe may not stand still nor be impeded, I no longer consider it any difference whether a fever shall do it, or a tile, or a soldier. But if a man must make a comparison between these things, I know that the soldier will do it with less trouble, and quicker. When, then, I neither

fear anything which a tyrant can do to me, nor desire anything which he can give, why do I still look on with wonder? Why am I still confounded? Why do I fear the guards? Why am I pleased if he speaks to me in a friendly way, and receives me, and why do I tell others how he spoke to me? Is he a Socrates, is he a Diogenes that his praise should be a proof of what I am? Have I been eager to imitate his morals? But I keep up the play and go to him, and serve him so long as he does not bid me to do anything foolish or unreasonable. But if he says to me, "Go and bring Leon[1] of Salamis," I say to him, "Seek another, for I am no longer playing." "Lead him away." I follow; that is part of the play. "But your head will be taken off." Does the tyrant's head always remain where it is, and the heads of you who obey him? "But you will be cast out unburied." If the corpse is I, I shall be cast out; but if I am different from the corpse, speak more properly according as the fact is, and do not think of frightening me. These things are formidable to children and fools. But if any man has once entered a philosopher's school and knows not what he is, he deserves to be full of fear and to flatter those whom afterward he used to flatter; if he has not yet learned that he is not flesh nor bones nor sinews, but he is that which makes use of these parts of the body and governs them and follows the appearances of things.

"Yes, but this talk makes us despise the laws." And what kind of talk makes men more obedient to the laws who employ such talk? And the things which are in the power of a fool are not law. And yet see how this talk makes us disposed as we ought to be even to these men; since it teaches us to claim in opposition to them none of the things in which they are able to surpass us. This talk teaches us, as to the body, to give it up, as to property, to give that up also, as to children, parents, brothers, to retire from these, to give up all; it only makes an exception of the opinions, which even Zeus has willed to be the select property of every man. What transgression of the laws is there here, what folly? Where you are superior and stronger, there I give way to you: on the other hand, where I

[1] See iv. i.

am superior, do you yield to me; for I have studied this, and you have not. It is your study to live in houses with floors formed of various stones, how your slaves and dependents shall serve you, how you shall wear fine clothing, have many hunting men, lute players, and tragic actors. Do I claim any of these? have you made any study of opinions and of your own rational faculty? Do you know of what parts it is composed, how they are brought together, how they are connected, what powers it has, and of what kind? Why then are you vexed, if another, who has made it his study, has the advantage over you in these things? "But these things are the greatest." And who hinders you from being employed about these things and looking after them? And who has a better stock of books, of leisure, of persons to aid you? Only turn your mind at last to these things, attend, if it be only a short time, to your own ruling faculty:[1] consider what this is that you possess, and whence it came, this which uses all others, and tries them, and selects and rejects. But so long as you employ yourself about externals you will possess them as no man else does; but you will have this such as you choose to have it, sordid and neglected.

CHAPTER 8. *Against those who hastily rush into the use of the philosophic dress*

NEVER praise nor blame a man because of the things which are common,[2] and do not ascribe to him any skill or want of skill; and thus you will be free from rashness and from malevolence. "This man bathes very quickly." Does he then do wrong? Certainly not. But what does he do? He bathes very quickly. Are all things then done well? By no means: but the acts which proceed from right opinions are done well; and those which proceed from bad opinions are done ill. But do you, until you know the opinion from which a man does each thing, neither praise nor blame the act. But the opinion is not easily discovered from the external things. "This man is a carpenter." Why? "Because he uses an ax." What, then, is this to the matter? "This man is a musician because he sings." And what does that sig-

nify?"This man is a philosopher. Because he wears a cloak and long hair." And what does a juggler wear? For this reason if a man sees any philosopher acting indecently, immediately he says, "See what the philosopher is doing"; but he ought because of the man's indecent behaviour rather to say that he is not a philosopher. For if this is the preconceived notion of a philosopher and what he professes, to wear a cloak and long hair, men would say well; but if what he professes is this rather, to keep himself free from faults, why do we not rather, because he does not make good his professions, take from him the name of philosopher? For so we do in the case of all other arts. When a man sees another handling an ax badly, he does not say, "What is the use of the carpenter's art? See how badly carpenters do their work"; but he says just the contrary, "This man is not a carpenter, for he uses an ax badly." In the same way if a man hears another singing badly, he does not say, "See how musicians sing"; but rather, "This man is not a musician." But it is in the matter of philosophy only that people do this. When they see a man acting contrary to the profession of a philosopher, they do not take away his title, but they assume him to be a philosopher, and from his acts deriving the fact that he is behaving indecently they conclude that there is no use in philosophy.

What, then, is the reason of this? Because we attach value to the notion of a carpenter, and to that of a musician, and to the notion of other artisans in like manner, but not to that of a philosopher, and we judge from externals only that it is a thing confused and ill defined. And what other kind of art has a name from the dress and the hair; and has not theorems and a material and an end? What, then, is the material of the philosopher? Is it a cloak? No, but reason. What is his end? is it to wear a cloak? No, but to possess the reason in a right state. Of what kind are his theorems? Are they those about the way in which the beard becomes great or the hair long? No, but rather what Zeno says, to know the elements of reason, what kind of a thing each of them is, and how they are fitted to one another, and what things are consequent upon them. Will you not, then, see first if he does what he professes

---

[1] See i. 26, etc.
[2] See iv. 4.

when he acts in an unbecoming manner, and then blame his study? But now when you yourself are acting in a sober way, you say in consequence of what he seems to you to be doing wrong, "Look at the philosopher," as if it were proper to call by the name of philosopher one who does these things; and further, "This is the conduct of a philosopher." But you do not say, "Look at the carpenter," when you know that a carpenter is an adulterer or you see him to be a glutton; nor do you say, "See the musician." Thus to a certain degree even you perceive the profession of a philosopher, but you fall away from the notion, and you are confused through want of care.

But even the philosophers themselves as they are called pursue the thing by beginning with things which are common to them and others: as soon as they have assumed a cloak and grown a beard, they say, "I am a philosopher." But no man will say, "I am a musician," if he has bought a plectrum and a lute: nor will he say, "I am a smith," if he has put on a cap and apron. But the dress is fitted to the art; and they take their name from the art, and not from the dress. For this reason Euphrates[1] used to say well, "A long time I strove to be a philosopher without people knowing it; and this," he said, "was useful to me: for first I knew that when I did anything well, I did not do it for the sake of the spectators, but for the sake of myself: I ate well for the sake of myself; I had my countenance well composed and my walk: all for myself and for God. Then, as I struggled alone, so I alone also was in danger: in no respect through me, if I did anything base or unbecoming, was philosophy endangered; nor did I injure the many by doing anything wrong as a philosopher. For this reason those who did not know my purpose used to wonder how it was that, while I conversed and lived altogether with all philosophers, I was not a philosopher myself. And what was the harm for me to be known to be a philosopher by my acts and not by outward marks?"[2] See how I eat, how I drink, how I sleep, how I bear and forbear, how I co-operate, how I employ desire, how I employ aversion, how I maintain the relations, those which

[1] See iii. 15.
[2] Compare Jas. 2. 18.

are natural or those which are acquired, how free from confusion, how free from hindrance. Judge of me from this, if you can. But if you are so deaf and blind that you cannot conceive even Hephæstus to be a good smith, unless you see the cap on his head, what is the harm in not being recognized by so foolish a judge?

So Socrates was not known to be a philosopher by most persons; and they used to come to him and ask to be introduced to philosophers. Was he vexed then as we are, and did he say, "And do you not think that I am a philosopher?" No, but he would take them and introduce them, being satisfied with one thing, with being a philosopher; and being pleased also with not being thought to be a philosopher, he was not annoyed: for he thought of his own occupation. What is the work of an honourable and good man? To have many pupils? By no means. They will look to this matter who are earnest about it. But was it his business to examine carefully difficult theorems? Others will look after these matters also. In what, then, was he, and who was he and whom did he wish to be? He was in that wherein there was hurt and advantage. "If any man can damage me," he says, "I am doing nothing: if I am waiting for another man to do me good, I am nothing. If I wish for anything, and it does not happen, I am unfortunate." To such a contest he invited every man, and I do not think that he would have declined the contest with any one. What do you suppose? was it by proclaiming and saying, "I am such a man?" Far from it, but by being such a man. For further, this is the character of a fool and a boaster to say, "I am free from passions and disturbance: do not be ignorant, my friends, that while you are uneasy and disturbed about things of no value, I alone am free from all perturbation." So is it not enough for you to feel no pain, unless you make this proclamation: "Come together all who are suffering gout, pains in the head, fever, ye who are lame, blind, and observe that I am sound from every ailment." This is empty and disagreeable to hear, unless like Æsculapius you are able to show immediately by what kind of treatment they also shall be immediately free from disease, and unless you show your own health as an example.

For such is the Cynic who is honoured with the sceptre and the diadem of Zeus, and says, "That you may see, O men, that you seek happiness and tranquillity not where it is, but where it is not, behold I am sent to you by God as an example.[1] I who have neither property nor house, nor wife nor children, nor even a bed, nor coat nor household utensil; and see how healthy I am: try me, and if you see that I am free from perturbations, hear the remedies and how I have been cured." This is both philanthropic and noble. But see whose work it is, the work of Zeus, or of him whom He may judge worthy of this service, that he may never exhibit anything to the many, by which he shall make of no effect his own testimony, whereby he gives testimony to virtue, and bears evidence against external things:

His beauteous face pales not, nor from his cheeks He wipes a tear.[2]

And not this only, but he neither desires nor seeks anything, nor man nor place nor amusement, as children seek the vintage or holidays; always fortified by modesty as others are fortified by walls and doors and doorkeepers.

But now, being only moved to philosophy, as those who have a bad stomach are moved to some kinds of food which they soon loathe, straightway toward the sceptre and to the royal power. They let the hair grow, they assume the cloak, they show the shoulder bare, they quarrel with those whom they meet; and if they see a man in a thick winter coat, they quarrel with him. Man, first exercise yourself in winter weather: see your movements that they are not those of a man with a bad stomach or those of a longing woman. First strive that it be not known what you are: be a philosopher to yourself a short time. Fruit grows thus: the seed must be buried for some time, hid, grow slowly in order that it may come to perfection. But if it produces the ear before the jointed stem, it is imperfect, a produce of the garden of Adonis.[3] Such a poor plant are you also: you have blossomed too soon; the cold weather will scorch you up. See what the husbandmen say about seeds when there is warm weather too early. They are afraid lest the seeds should be too luxuriant, and then a single frost should lay hold of them and show that they are too forward. Do you also consider, my man: you have shot out too soon, you have hurried toward a little fame before the proper season: you think that you are something, a fool among fools: you will be caught by the frost, and rather you have been frost-bitten in the root below, but your upper parts still blossom a little, and for this reason you think that you are still alive and flourishing. Allow us to ripen in the natural way: why do you bare us? why do you force us? we are not yet able to bear the air. Let the root grow, then acquire the first joint, then the second, and then the third: in this way, then, the fruit will naturally force itself out, even if I do not choose. For who that is pregnant and filled with such great principles does not also perceive his own powers and move toward the corresponding acts? A bull is not ignorant of his own nature and his powers, when a wild beast shows itself, nor does he wait for one to urge him on; nor a dog when he sees a wild animal. But if I have the powers of a good man, shall I wait for you to prepare me for my own acts? At present I have them not, believe me. Why then do you wish me to be withered up before the time, as you have been withered up?

CHAPTER 9. *To a person who had been changed to a character of shamelessness*

WHEN you see another man in the possession of power, set against this the fact that you have not the want of power; when you see another rich, see what you possess in place of riches: for if you possess nothing in place of them, you are miserable; but if you have not the want of riches, know that you possess more than this man possesses and what is worth much more. Another man possesses a handsome woman: you have the satisfaction of not desiring a handsome wife. Do these things appear to you to be small? And how much would these persons give, these very men who are rich and in possession of power, and live with handsome women, to be able to despise riches and power and these very women whom they love and enjoy? Do you not know, then, what

[1] Compare iii. 22.
[2] Homer, *Odyssey*, xi. 528.
[3] Things growing in earthen vessels, carried about for show only.

is the thirst of a man who has a fever? He possesses that which is in no degree like the thirst of a man who is in health: for the man who is in health ceases to be thirsty after he has drunk; but the sick man, being pleased for a short time, has a nausea; he converts the drink into bile, vomits, is griped, and more thirsty. It is such a thing to have desire of riches and to possess riches, desire of power and to possess power, desire of a beautiful woman and to sleep with her: to this is added jealousy, fear of being deprived of the thing which you love, indecent words, indecent thoughts, unseemly acts.

"And what do I lose?" you will say. My man, you were modest, and you are so no longer. Have you lost nothing? In place of Chrysippus and Zeno you read Aristides and Evenus;[1] have you lost nothing? In place of Socrates and Diogenes, you admire him who is able to corrupt and seduce most women. You wish to appear handsome and try to make yourself so, though you are not. You like to display splendid clothes that you may attract women; and if you find any fine oil, you imagine that you are happy. But formerly you did not think of any such thing, but only where there should be decent talk, a worthy man, and a generous conception. Therefore you slept like a man, walked forth like a man, wore a manly dress, and used to talk in a way becoming a good man; then do you say to me, "I have lost nothing?" So do men lose nothing more than coin? Is not modesty lost? Is not decent behaviour lost? is it that he who has lost these things has sustained no loss? Perhaps you think that not one of these things is a loss. But there was a time when you reckoned this the only loss and damage, and you were anxious that no man should disturb you from these words and actions.

Observe, you are disturbed from these good words and actions by nobody but by yourself. Fight with yourself, restore yourself to decency, to modesty, to liberty. If any man ever told you this about me, that a person forces me to be an adulterer, to wear such a dress as yours, to perfume myself with oils, would you not have gone and with your own hand have killed the man who thus calumniated me?

[1] Plutarch, *Lives*, Crassus.

Now will you not help yourself? and how much easier is this help? There is no need to kill any man, nor to put him in chains, nor to treat him with contumely, nor to enter the Forum, but it is only necessary for you to speak to yourself who will be the most easily persuaded, with whom no man has more power of persuasion than yourself. First of all, condemn what you are doing, and then, when you have condemned it, do not despair of yourself, and be not in the condition of those men of mean spirit, who, when they have once given in, surrender themselves completely and are carried away as if by a torrent. But see what the trainers of boys do. Has the boy fallen? "Rise," they say, "wrestle again till you are made strong." Do you also do something of the same kind: for be well assured that nothing is more tractable than the human soul. You must exercise the will, and the thing is done, it is set right: as on the other hand, only fall a-nodding, and the thing is lost: for from within comes ruin and from within comes help. "Then what good do I gain?" And what greater good do you seek than this? From a shameless man you will become a modest man, from a disorderly you will become an orderly man, from a faithless you will become a faithful man, from a man of unbridled habits a sober man. If you seek anything more than this, go on doing what you are doing: not even a God can now help you.

CHAPTER 10. *What things we ought to despise, and what things we ought to value*

THE difficulties of all men are about external things, their helplessness is about externals. "What shall I do, how will it be, how will it turn out, will this happen, will that?" All these are the words of those who are turning themselves to things which are not within the power of the will. For who says, "How shall I not assent to that which is false? how shall I not turn away from the truth?" If a man be of such a good disposition as to be anxious about these things, I will remind him of this: "Why are you anxious? The thing is in your own power: be assured: do not be precipitate in assenting before you apply the natural rule." On the other side, if a man is anxious about desire, lest it fail in its purpose and miss its end, and with respect to the avoidance of things, lest he should fall into that which he would avoid, I will first kiss him, because he throws away the things about which others are in a flutter, and their fears, and employs his thoughts about his own affairs and his own condition. Then I shall say to him: "If you do not choose to desire that which you will fail to obtain nor to attempt to avoid that into which you will fall, desire nothing which belongs to others, nor try to avoid any of the things which are not in your power. If you do not observe this rule, you must of necessity fail in your desires and fall into that which you would avoid. What is the difficulty here? where is there room for the words, 'How will it be?' and 'How will it turn out?' and, 'Will this happen or that?'"

Now is not that which will happen independent of the will? "Yes." And the nature of good and of evil, is it not in the things which are within the power of the will? "Yes." Is it in your power, then, to treat according to nature everything which happens? Can any person hinder you? "No man." No longer then say to me, "How will it be?" For however it may be, you will dispose of it well, and the result to you will be a fortunate one. What would Hercules have been if he had said, "How shall a great lion not appear to me, or a great boar, or savage men?" And what do you care for that? If a great boar appear, you will fight a greater fight: if bad men appear, you will relieve the earth of the bad. "Suppose, then, that I may lose my life in this way." You will die a good man, doing a noble act. For since we must certainly die, of necessity a man must be found doing something, either following the employment of a husbandman, or digging, or trading, or serving in a consulship or suffering from indigestion or from diarrhœa. What then do you wish to be doing when you are found by death? I for my part would wish to be found doing something which belongs to a man, beneficent, suitable to the general interest, noble. But if I cannot be found doing things so great, I would be found doing at least that which I cannot be hindered from doing, that which is permitted me to do, correcting myself, cultivating the faculty which makes use of appearances, labouring at free-

dom from the affects, rendering to the relations of life their due; if I succeed so far, also touching on the third topic, safety in the forming judgements about things.[1] If death surprises me when I am busy about these things, it is enough for me if I can stretch out my hands to God and say:

"The means which I have received from Thee for seeing Thy administration and following it, I have not neglected: I have not dishonoured Thee by my acts: see how I have used my perceptions, see how I have used my preconceptions: have I ever blamed Thee? have I been discontented with anything that happens, or wished it to be otherwise? have I wished to transgress the relations? That Thou hast given me life, I thank Thee for what Thou has given me: so long as I have used the things which are Thine, I am content; take them back and place them wherever Thou mayest choose; for Thine were all things, Thou gavest them to me."[2] Is it not enough to depart in this state of mind, and what life is better and more becoming than that of a man who is in this state of mind? and what end is more happy?

But that this may be done, a man must receive no small things, nor are the things small which he must lose. You cannot both wish to be a consul and to have these things, and to be eager to have lands and these things also; and to be solicitous about slaves and about yourself. But if you wish for anything which belongs to another, that which is your own is lost. This is the nature of the thing: nothing is given or had for nothing.[3] And where is the wonder? If you wish to be a consul, you must keep awake, run about, kiss hands, waste yourself with exhaustion at other men's doors, say and do many things unworthy of a free man, send gifts to many, daily presents to some. And what is the thing that is got? Twelve bundles of rods, to sit three or four times on the tribunal, to exhibit the games in the Circus and to give suppers in small baskets. Or, if you do not agree about this, let some one show me what there is besides these things. In order, then, to secure freedom from passions, tranquillity, to sleep well when you do sleep, to be

[1] See iii. 2. [3] See iv. 2.
[2] John, 17. 6.

really awake when you are awake, to fear nothing, to be anxious about nothing, will you spend nothing and give no labour? But if anything belonging to you be lost while you are thus busied, or be wasted badly, or another obtains what you ought to have obtained, will you immediately be vexed at what has happened? Will you not take into the account on the other side what you receive and for what, how much for how much? Do you expect to have for nothing things so great? And how can you? One work has no community with another. You cannot have both external things after bestowing care on them and your own ruling faculty:[1] but if you would have those, give up this. If you do not, you will have neither this nor that, while you are drawn in different ways to both.[2] The oil will be spilled, the household vessels will perish: but I shall be free from passions. There will be a fire when I am not present, and the books will be destroyed: but I shall treat appearances according to nature. "Well; but I shall have nothing to eat." If I am so unlucky, death is a harbour; and death is the harbour for all; this is the place of refuge; and for this reason not one of the things in life is difficult: as soon as you choose, you are out of the house, and are smoked no more.[3] Why, then, are you anxious, why do you lose your sleep, why do you not straightway, after considering wherein your good is and your evil, say, "Both of them are in my power? Neither can any man deprive me of the good, nor involve me in the bad against my will. Why do I not throw myself down and snore? for all that I have is safe. As to the things which belong to others, he will look to them who gets them, as they may be given by Him who has the power. Who am I who wish to have them in this way or in that? is a power of selecting them given to me? has any person made me the dispenser of them? Those things are enough for me over which I have power: I ought to manage them as well as I can: and all the rest, as the Master of them may choose."

When a man has these things before his eyes, does he keep awake and turn hither and thither? What would he have, or what does he regret, Patroclus or Antilochus or Menelaus?[4] For when did he suppose that any of his friends was immortal, and when had he not before his eyes that on the morrow or the day after he or his friend must die? "Yes," he says, "but I thought that he would survive me and bring up my son." You were a fool for that reason, and you were thinking of what was uncertain. Why, then, do you not blame yourself, and sit crying like girls? "But he used to set my food before me." Because he was alive, you fool, but now he cannot: but Automedon will set it before you, and if Automedon also dies, you will find another. But if the pot, in which your meat was cooked, should be broken, must you die of hunger, because you have not the pot which you are accustomed to? Do you not send and buy a new pot? He says:

"No greater ill than this could fall on me."[5]

Why is this your ill? Do you, then, instead of removing it, blame your mother for not foretelling it to you that you might continue grieving from that time? What do you think? do you not suppose that Homer wrote this that we may learn that those of noblest birth, the strongest and the richest, the most handsome, when they have not the opinions which they ought to have, are not prevented from being most wretched and unfortunate?

CHAPTER 11. *About Purity*
SOME persons raise a question whether the social feeling[6] is contained in the nature of man; and yet I think that these same persons would have no doubt that love of purity is certainly contained in it, and that, if man is distinguished from other animals by anything, he is distinguished by this. When, then, we see any other animal cleaning itself, we are accustomed to speak of the act with surprise, and to add that the animal is acting like a man: and, on the other hand, if a man blames an animal for being dirty, straightway as if we were making an excuse for it, we say that of course the animal is not a human creature. So we suppose that there is something superior in

[1] Matt. 6. 24.
[2] See iv. 2.
[3] Compare i. 9 and 25.

[4] Homer, *Iliad*, xxiv. 5.
[5] Homer, *Iliad*, xix. 321.
[6] Compare i. 23, ii. 10 and 20.

man, and that we first receive it from the Gods. For since the Gods by their nature are pure and free from corruption, so far as men approach them by reason, so far do they cling to purity and to a love of purity. But since it is impossible that man's nature can be altogether pure being mixed of such materials, reason is applied, as far as it is possible, and reason endeavours to make human nature love purity.

The first, then, and highest purity is that which is in the soul; and we say the same of impurity. Now you could not discover the impurity of the soul as you could discover that of the body: but as to the soul, what else could you find in it than that which makes it filthy in respect to the acts which are her own? Now the acts of the soul are movement toward an object or movement from it, desire, aversion, preparation, design, assent. What, then, is it which in these acts makes the soul filthy and impure? Nothing else than her own bad judgements. Consequently, the impurity of the soul is the soul's bad opinions; and the purification of the soul is the planting in it of proper opinions; and the soul is pure which has proper opinions, for the soul alone in her own acts is free from perturbation and pollution.

Now we ought to work at something like this in the body also, as far as we can. It was impossible for the defluxions of the nose not to run when man has such a mixture in his body. For this reason, nature has made hands and the nostrils themselves as channels for carrying off the humours. If, then, a man sucks up the defluxions, I say that he is not doing the act of a man. It was impossible for a man's feet not to be made muddy and not be soiled at all when he passes through dirty places. For this reason, nature has made water and hands. It was impossible that some impurity should not remain in the teeth from eating: for this reason, she says, wash the teeth. Why? In order that you may be a man and not a wild beast or a hog. It was impossible that from the sweat and the pressing of the clothes there should not remain some impurity about the body which requires to be cleaned away. For this reason water, oil, hands, towels, scrapers, nitre, sometimes all other kinds of means are necessary for cleaning the body.

You do not act so: but the smith will take off the rust from the iron, and he will have tools prepared for this purpose, and you yourself wash the platter when you are going to eat, if you are not completely impure and dirty: but will you not wash the body nor make it clean? "Why?" he replies. I will tell you again; in the first place, that you may do the acts of a man; then, that you may not be disagreeable to those with whom you associate. You do something of this kind even in this matter, and you do not perceive it: you think that you deserve to stink. Let it be so: deserve to stink. Do you think that also those who sit by you, those who recline at table with you, that those who kiss you deserve the same? Either go into a desert, where you deserve to go, or live by yourself, and smell yourself. For it is just that you alone should enjoy your own impurity. But when you are in a city, to behave so inconsiderately and foolishly, to what character do you think that it belongs? If nature had intrusted to you a horse, would you have overlooked and neglected him? And now think that you have been intrusted with your own body as with a horse; wash it, wipe it, take care that no man turns away from it, that no one gets out of the way for it. But who does not get out of the way of a dirty man, of a stinking man, of a man whose skin is foul, more than he does out of the way of a man who is daubed with muck? That smell is from without, it is put upon him; but the other smell is from want of care, from within, and in a manner from a body in putrefaction.

"But Socrates washed himself seldom." Yes, but his body was clean and fair: and it was so agreeable and sweet that the most beautiful and the most noble loved him, and desired to sit by him rather than by the side of those who had the handsomest forms. It was in his power neither to use the bath nor to wash himself, if he chose; and yet the rare use of water had an effect. If you do not choose to wash with warm water, wash with cold. But Aristophanes says: *Those who are pale, unshod, 'tis those I mean.*[1] For Aristophanes says of Socrates that he also walked the air and stole clothes from the palæstra.[2] But all who have written about

[1] Aristophanes, *Clouds*, 102.
[2] *Ibid.* 225 and 179.

Socrates bear exactly the contrary evidence in his favour; they say that he was pleasant not only to hear, but also to see. On the other hand they write the same about Diogenes.[1] For we ought not even by the appearance of the body to deter the multitude from philosophy; but as in other things, a philosopher should show himself cheerful and tranquil, so also he should in the things that relate to the body: "See, ye men, that I have nothing, that I want nothing: see how I am without a house, and without a city, and an exile, if it happens to be so, and without a hearth I live more free from trouble and more happily than all of noble birth and than the rich. But look at my poor body also and observe that it is not injured by my hard way of living." But if a man says this to me, who has the appearance and face of a condemned man, what God shall persuade me to approach philosophy, if it makes men such persons? Far from it; I would not choose to do so, even if I were going to become a wise man. I indeed would rather that a young man, who is making his first movements toward philosophy, should come to me with his hair carefully trimmed than with it dirty and rough, for there is seen in him a certain notion of beauty and a desire of that which is becoming; and where he supposes it to be, there also he strives that it shall be. It is only necessary to show him, and to say: "Young man, you seek beauty, and you do well: you must know then that it grows in that part of you where you have the rational faculty: seek it there where you have the movements toward and the movements from things, where you have the desire toward, and the aversion from things: for this is what you have in yourself of a superior kind; but the poor body is naturally only earth: why do you labour about it to no purpose? if you shall learn nothing else, you will learn from time that the body is nothing." But if a man comes to me daubed with filth, dirty, with a mustache down to his knees, what can I say to him, by what kind of resemblance can I lead him on? For about what has he busied himself which resembles beauty, that I may be able to change him and say, "Beauty is not in this, but in that?" Would you have me to tell him, that beauty consists

[1] See iii, 22.

not in being daubed with muck, but that it lies in the rational part? Has he any desire of beauty? has he any form of it in his mind? Go and talk to a hog, and tell him not to roll in the mud.

For this reason the words of Xenocrates touched Polemon also; since he was a lover of beauty, for he entered, having in him certain incitements to love of beauty, but he looked for it in the wrong place.[2] For nature has not made even the animals dirty which live with man. Does a horse ever wallow in the mud, or a well-bred dog? But the hog, and the dirty geese, and worms and spiders do, which are banished furthest from human intercourse. Do you, then, being a man, choose to be not as one of the animals which live with man, but rather a worm, or a spider? Will you not wash yourself somewhere some time in such manner as you choose? Will you not wash off the dirt from your body? Will you not come clean that those with whom you keep company may have pleasure in being with you? But do you go with us even into the temples in such a state, where it is not permitted to spit or blow the nose, being a heap of spittle and of snot?

When then? does any man require you to ornament yourself? Far from it; except to ornament that which we really are by nature, the rational faculty, the opinions, the actions; but as to the body only so far as purity, only so far as not to give offense. But if you are told that you ought not to wear garments dyed with purple, go and daub your cloak with muck or tear it. "But how shall I have a neat cloak?" Man, you have water; wash it. Here is a youth worthy of being loved, here is an old man worthy of loving and being loved in return, a fit person for a man to intrust to him a son's instruction, to whom daughters and young men shall come, if opportunity shall so happen, that the teacher shall deliver his lessons to them on a dunghill. Let this not be so: every deviation comes from something which is in man's nature; but this is near being something not in man's nature.

CHAPTER 12. *On attention*

WHEN you have remitted your attention for a short time, do not imagine this, that you

[2] See iii, 1.

will recover it when you choose; but let this thought be present to you, that in consequence of the fault committed to-day your affairs must be in a worse condition for all that follows. For first, and what causes most trouble, a habit of not attending is formed in you; then a habit of deferring your attention. And continually from time to time you drive away, by deferring it, the happiness of life, proper behaviour, the being and living conformably to nature. If, then, the procrastination of attention is profitable, the complete omission of attention is more profitable; but if it is not profitable, why do you not maintain your attention constant? "To-day I choose to play." Well then, ought you not to play with attention? "I choose to sing." What, then, hinders you from doing so with attention? Is there any part of life excepted, to which attention does not extend? For will you do it worse by using attention, and better by not attending at all? And what else of things in life is done better by those who do not use attention? Does he who works in wood work better by not attending to it? Does the captain of a ship manage it better by not attending? and is any of the smaller acts done better by inattention? Do you not see that, when you have let your mind loose, it is no longer in your power to recall it, either to propriety, or to modesty, or to moderation: but you do everything that comes into your mind in obedience to your inclinations?

To what things then ought I to attend? First to those general (principles) and to have them in readiness, and without them not to sleep, not to rise, not to drink, not to eat, not to converse with men; that no man is master of another man's will, but that in the will alone is the good and the bad. No man, then, has the power either to procure for me any good or to involve me in any evil, but I alone myself over myself have power in these things. When, then, these things are secured to me, why need I be disturbed about external things? What tyrant is formidable, what disease, what poverty, what offense? "Well, I have not pleased a certain person." Is he then my work, my judgement? "No." Why then should I trouble myself about him? "But he is supposed to be some one." He will look to that himself; and

those who think so will also. But I have One Whom I ought to please, to Whom I ought to subject myself, Whom I ought to obey, God and those who are next to Him.[1] He has placed me with myself, and has put my will in obedience to myself alone, and has given me rules for the right use of it; and when I follow these rules in syllogisms, I do not care for any man who says anything else: in sophistical argument, I care for no man. Why then in greater matters do those annoy me who blame me? What is the cause of this perturbation? Nothing else than because in this matter I am not disciplined. For all knowledge despises ignorance and the ignorant; and not only the sciences, but even the arts. Produce any shoemaker that you please, and he ridicules the many in respect to his own work.[2] Produce any carpenter.

First, then, we ought to have these in readiness, and to do nothing without them, and we ought to keep the soul directed to this mark, to pursue nothing external, and nothing which belongs to others, but to do as He has appointed Who has the power; we ought to pursue altogether the things which are in the power of the will, and all other things as it is permitted. Next to this we ought to remember who we are, and what is our name, and to endeavour to direct our duties toward the character of our several relations in this manner: what is the season for singing, what is the season for play, and in whose presence; what will be the consequence of the act; whether our associates will despise us, whether we shall despise them; when to jeer, and whom to ridicule; and on what occasion to comply and with whom; and finally, in complying how to maintain our own character.[3] But wherever you have deviated from any of these rules, there is damage immediately, not from anything external, but from the action itself.

What then? is it possible to be free from faults? It is not possible; but this is possible, to direct your efforts incessantly to being faultless. For we must be content if by never remitting this attention we shall escape at least a few errors. But now when you have said, "To-

[1] Compare iv. 4; i. 14.
[2] Compare ii. 13; Marcus Aurelius, vi. 35.
[3] See i. 29; iii. 14.

morrow I will begin to attend," you must be told that you are saying this, "To-day I will be shameless, disregardful of time and place, mean; it will be in the power of others to give me pain; to-day I will be passionate and envious." See how many evil things you are permitting yourself to do. If it is good to use attention to-morrow, how much better is it to do so to-day? if to-morrow it is in your interest to attend, much more is it to-day, that you may be able to do so to-morrow also, and may not defer it again to the third day.[1]

Chapter 13. *Against or to those who readily tell their own affairs*

When a man has seemed to us to have talked with simplicity about his own affairs, how is it that at last we are ourselves also induced to discover to him our own secrets and we think this to be candid behaviour? In the first place, because it seems unfair for a man to have listened to the affairs of his neighbour, and not to communicate to him also in turn our own affairs: next, because we think that we shall not present to them the appearance of candid men when we are silent about our own affairs. Indeed men are often accustomed to say, "I have told you all my affairs, will you tell me nothing of your own? where is this done?" Besides, we have also this opinion that we can safely trust him who has already told us his own affairs; for the notion rises in our mind that this man could never divulge our affairs because he would be cautious that we also should not divulge his. In this way also the incautious are caught by the soldiers at Rome. A soldier sits by you in a common dress and begins to speak ill of Cæsar; then you, as if you had received a pledge of his fidelity by his having begun the abuse, utter yourself also what you think, and then you are carried off in chains.

Something of this kind happens to us generally. Now as this man has confidently intrusted his affairs to me, shall I also do so to any man whom I meet? For when I have heard, I keep silence, if I am of such a disposition; but he goes forth and tells all men what he has heard. Then if I hear what has been done, if I be a man like him, I resolve to be re-

[1] Compare Marcus Aurelius, viii. 22.

venged, I divulge what he has told me; I both disturb others and am disturbed myself. But if I remember that one man does not injure another, and that every man's acts injure and profit him, I secure this, that I do not anything like him, but still I suffer what I do suffer through my own silly talk.

"True: but it is unfair when you have heard the secrets of your neighbour for you in turn to communicate nothing to him." Did I ask you for your secrets, my man? did you communicate your affairs on certain terms, that you should in return hear mine also? If you are a babbler and think that all who meet you are friends, do you wish me also to be like you? But why, if you did well in intrusting your affairs to me, and it is not well for me to intrust mine to you, do you wish me to be so rash? It is just the same as if I had a cask which is water-tight, and you one with a hole in it, and you should come and deposit with me your wine that I might put it into my cask, and then should complain that I also did not intrust my wine to you, for you have a cask with a hole in it. How then is there any equality here? You intrusted your affairs to a man who is faithful and modest, to a man who thinks that his own actions alone are injurious and useful, and that nothing external is. Would you have me intrust mine to you, a man who has dishonoured his own faculty of will, and who wishes to gain some small bit of money or some office or promotion in the court, even if you should be going to murder your own children, like Medea? Where is this equality? But show yourself to me to be faithful, modest, and steady: show me that you have friendly opinions; show that your cask has no hole in it; and you will see how I shall not wait for you to trust me with your affairs, but I myself shall come to you and ask you to hear mine. For who does not choose to make use of a good vessel? Who does not value a benevolent and faithful adviser? who will not willingly receive a man who is ready to bear a share, as we may say, of the difficulty of his circumstances, and by this very act to ease the burden, by taking a part of it.

"True: but I trust you; you do not trust me." In the first place, not even do you trust me, but you are a babbler, and for this reason you cannot hold anything; for indeed, if it is true that you trust me, trust your affairs to me only; but now, whenever you see a man at leisure, you seat yourself by him and say: "Brother, I have no friend more benevolent than you nor dearer; I request you to listen to my affairs." And you do this even to those who are not known to you at all. But if you really trust me, it is plain that you trust me because I am faithful and modest, not because I have told my affairs to you. Allow me, then, to have the same opinion about you. Show me that, if one man tells his affairs to another, he who tells them is faithful and modest. For if this were so, I would go about and tell my affairs to every man, if that would make me faithful and modest. But the thing is not so, and it requires no common opinions. If, then, you see a man who is busy about things not dependent on his will and subjecting his will to them, you must know that this man has ten thousand persons to compel and hinder him. He has no need of pitch or the wheel to compel him to declare what he knows:[1] but a little girl's nod, if it should so happen, will move him, the blandishment of one who belongs to Cæsar's court, desire of a magistracy or of an inheritance, and things without end of that sort. You must remember, then, among general principles that secret discourses require fidelity and corresponding opinions. But where can we now find these easily? Or if you cannot answer that question, let some one point out to me a man who can say: "I care only about the things which are my own, the things which are not subject to hindrance, the things which are by nature free." This I hold to be the nature of the good: but let all other things be as they are allowed; I do not concern myself.

[1] See ii. 6.

THE MEDITATIONS OF
MARCUS AURELIUS

BIOGRAPHICAL NOTE
MARCUS AURELIUS, A.D. 121–180

MARCUS ANNIUS VERUS, known to history as the Emperor Marcus Aurelius, was born at Rome in the year 121. His father's family, like that of Trajan, was Spanish, but had been resident in Rome for many years and had received patrician rank from Vespasian. He lost his father in infancy and was brought up by his mother and his paternal grandfather, who not only gave him the example of their own virtue and piety, but secured for him the best of teachers in Greek and Latin literature, rhetoric, philosophy, law, and even painting. In the first book of his *Meditations* Marcus Aurelius makes grateful and precise acknowledgment of what he learned from the members of his family and from his teachers. "To the gods I am indebted for having good grandfathers, good parents, a good sister, good teachers, good associates, good kinsmen and friends, nearly everything good."

Among the teachers of Marcus Aurelius were Sextus of Chaeronea, a grandson of Plutarch, Junius Rusticus, to whom he owed his acquaintance with the discourses of Epictetus, and the rhetorician Marcus Cornelius Fronto, with whom between the years 143 and 161 he carried on a correspondence. From Diognetus the Stoic he learned what it meant "to have become intimate with philosophy . . . and to have desired a plank bed and skin and whatever else of the kind belongs to the Grecian discipline." For a time he assumed the dress of the Stoic sect and lived so abstemious and laborious a life that he injured his health.

As a child Marcus Aurelius had gained the favor of Hadrian by the frankness of his character. Hadrian called him *Verissimus* (most true or sincere) from his family name Verus, gave him equestrian honors at the age of six, and made him a priest of the Salian brotherhood at the age of eight. After the death of Aelius Caesar, Hadrian adopted as his heir Marcus Antoninus Pius, the uncle of Marcus, on condition that he in turn adopt Marcus Aurelius and Lucius Ceionius Commodus, son of Aelius Caesar.

Hadrian died in 138. In 139 the title of Caesar was conferred upon Marcus Aurelius; in 140 he was consul and from 147, when he was invested with the tribunician power, to the death of Antoninus Pius in 161, Marcus Aurelius shared the burdens, if not the honors, of imperial rule. At the age of fifteen he had been betrothed to a daughter of Aelius Caesar, but after his adoption this engagement was broken and he married Faustina, the daughter of Antoninus Pius.

When the Emperor Antoninus was dying he had the Statue of Victory carried into the rooms of Marcus Aurelius as the material sign of the transfer of imperial power, and he recommended Marcus Aurelius to the senate as his successor without any mention of Commodus. Marcus Aurelius, however, at once conferred upon his adoptive brother the tribunician and proconsular powers and the titles of Caesar and Augustus. For the first time Rome had two emperors. But Lucius Verus, as Commodus was henceforth known, was more interested in his pleasures than in his imperial duties. He deferred to Marcus Aurelius and was content to play the second role until his death in 169.

The reign of Antoninus Pius had been a time of peace and prosperity; that of Marcus Aurelius was filled with every kind of calamity. The wisdom and firmness of the emperor could not prevent the beginning of decline. In the first year of his reign there were floods and famine in Italy, earthquakes in Asia, eruptions of barbarians across the northern frontier, riots and seditions of the legionaries in Britain. But there were even more serious preoccupations for Marcus Aurelius. Hadrian and Antoninus had kept the kingdom of Armenia under Roman influence, but as soon as Antoninus died the Parthians drove out the Armenian king, friendly to Rome, and put in a king of their own choice. The province of Syria was at once attacked. At the same time the Goths, coming down from the Baltic, were driving other German tribes before them, some of whom overflowed into the Roman provinces on the right bank of the Danube. Marcus Aurelius spent most of his reign fighting the Parthians in the East and the Quadi, the Marcomanni, and other barbarian nations in the North. The last ten years of his life he was almost continuously absent from Rome. The *Meditations,* "Thoughts addressed to himself" and not, presumably, intended for publication, were written down, in part at least, during the time Marcus Aurelius was campaigning against the Germans.

In 175, after a series of victories, Marcus Aurelius left the Danube to restore order in Syria, where the brilliant general, Avidius Cassius, had revolted and declared himself emperor. Before the arrival of Marcus Aurelius, Cassius was assassinated by one of his officers, thereby depriving the emperor "of the pleasure of pardoning him." Marcus Aurelius showed remarkable clemency toward the family and friends of Cassius and is said to have burned his correspondence without reading it.

While he was returning from the pacifica-

tion of the East, Marcus Aurelius lost his wife, who died in a village of Asia Minor. Faustina's name has become a symbol for infidelity and debauchery, though all that is known of her is that she bore eleven children, that her husband trusted her and mourned her death. On his way home Marcus Aurelius visited Athens where he endowed chairs of philosophy and rhetoric and was initiated into the Eleusinian mysteries. In 176 he entered Rome with his son, Commodus, and celebrated a triumph for his German victories, after which he took the title of Germanicus Maximus.

The role played by Marcus Aurelius in the persecution of the Christians in 177 has been the subject of much controversy. He was undoubtedly unsympathetic to Christianity as he knew it. His attitude as emperor was perhaps the same as that of Trajan, that the Christians should not be "pursued," but if, when asked to sacrifice to the gods, they refused, they should be punished on the ground that they were opposing the order and authority of the state.

The German war soon broke out again and Marcus Aurelius had to return to the Danube, where he died, probably from natural causes, on the 17th of March, 180, toward the close of his fifty-ninth year. His ensuing deification met with wide-spread response, and for a long time his statue held a prominent place among the penates of the Romans.

CONTENTS

Biographical Note, p. 249

Book I, p. 253   Book II, p. 256   Book III, p. 259

Book IV, p. 263   Book V, p. 268   Book VI, p. 274

Book VII, p. 279   Book VIII, p. 285   Book IX, p. 291

Book X, p. 296   Book XI, p. 302   Book XII, p. 307

THE MEDITATIONS OF
MARCUS AURELIUS ANTONINUS

· BOOK ONE ·

FROM my grandfather Verus I learned good morals and the government of my temper.

2. From the reputation and remembrance of my father,[1] modesty and a manly character.

3. From my mother, piety and beneficence, and abstinence, not only from evil deeds, but even from evil thoughts; and further, simplicity in my way of living, far removed from the habits of the rich.

4. From my great-grandfather, not to have frequented public schools, and to have had good teachers at home, and to know that on such things a man should spend liberally.

5. From my governor, to be neither of the green nor of the blue party at the games in the Circus, nor a partizan either of the Parmularius or the Scutarius at the gladiators' fights; from him too I learned endurance of labour, and to want little, and to work with my own hands, and not to meddle with other people's affairs, and not to be ready to listen to slander.

6. From Diognetus, not to busy myself about trifling things, and not to give credit to what was said by miracle-workers and jugglers about incantations and the driving away of daemons and such things; and not to breed quails for fighting, nor to give myself up passionately to such things; and to endure freedom of speech; and to have become intimate with philosophy; and to have been a hearer, first of Bacchius, then of Tandasis and Marcianus; and to have written dialogues in my youth; and to have desired a plank bed and skin, and whatever else of the kind belongs to the Grecian discipline.

7. From Rusticus I received the impression that my character required improvement and discipline; and from him I learned not to be

[1] His real father, Annius Verus.

led astray to sophistic emulation, nor to writing on speculative matters, nor to delivering little hortatory orations, nor to showing myself off as a man who practises much discipline, or does benevolent acts in order to make a display; and to abstain from rhetoric, and poetry, and fine writing; and not to walk about in the house in my outdoor dress, nor to do other things of the kind; and to write my letters with simplicity, like the letter which Rusticus wrote from Sinuessa to my mother; and with respect to those who have offended me by words, or done me wrong, to be easily disposed to be pacified and reconciled, as soon as they have shown a readiness to be reconciled; and to read carefully, and not to be satisfied with a superficial understanding of a book; nor hastily to give my assent to those who talk overmuch; and I am indebted to him for being acquainted with the discourses of Epictetus, which he communicated to me out of his own collection.

8. From Apollonius I learned freedom of will and undeviating steadiness of purpose; and to look to nothing else, not even for a moment, except to reason; and to be always the same, in sharp pains, on the occasion of the loss of a child, and in long illness; and to see clearly in a living example that the same man can be both most resolute and yielding, and not peevish in giving his instruction; and to have had before my eyes a man who clearly considered his experience and his skill in expounding philosophical principles as the smallest of his merits; and from him I learned how to receive from friends what are esteemed favours, without being either humbled by them or letting them pass unnoticed.

9. From Sextus, a benevolent disposition, and the example of a family governed in a

fatherly manner, and the idea of living conformably to nature; and gravity without affectation, and to look carefully after the interests of friends, and to tolerate ignorant persons, and those who form opinions without consideration: he had the power of readily accommodating himself to all, so that intercourse with him was more agreeable than any flattery; and at the same time he was most highly venerated by those who associated with him: and he had the faculty both of discovering and ordering, in an intelligent and methodical way, the principles necessary for life; and he never showed anger or any other passion, but was entirely free from passion, and also most affectionate; and he could express approbation without noisy display, and he possessed much knowledge without ostentation.

10. From Alexander the grammarian, to refrain from fault-finding, and not in a reproachful way to chide those who uttered any barbarous or solecistic or strange-sounding expression; but dexterously to introduce the very expression which ought to have been used, and in the way of answer or giving confirmation, or joining in an inquiry about the thing itself, not about the word, or by some other fit suggestion.

11. From Fronto I learned to observe what envy, and duplicity, and hypocrisy are in a tyrant, and that generally those among us who are called Patricians are rather deficient in paternal affection.

12. From Alexander the Platonic, not frequently nor without necessity to say to any one, or to write in a letter, that I have no leisure; nor continually to excuse the neglect of duties required by our relation to those with whom we live, by alleging urgent occupations.

13. From Catulus, not to be indifferent when a friend finds fault, even if he should find fault without reason, but to try to restore him to his usual disposition; and to be ready to speak well of teachers, as it is reported of Domitius and Athenodotus; and to love my children truly.

14. From my brother Severus, to love my kin, and to love truth, and to love justice; and through him I learned to know Thrasea, Helvidius, Cato, Dion, Brutus; and from him I received the idea of a polity in which there is the same law for all, a polity administered with regard to equal rights and equal freedom of speech, and the idea of a kingly government which respects most of all the freedom of the governed; I learned from him also consistency and undeviating steadiness in my regard for philosophy; and a disposition to do good, and to give to others readily, and to cherish good hopes, and to believe that I am loved by my friends; and in him I observed no concealment of his opinions with respect to those whom he condemned, and that his friends had no need to conjecture what he wished or did not wish, but it was quite plain.

15. From Maximus I learned self-government, and not to be led aside by anything; and cheerfulness in all circumstances, as well as in illness; and a just admixture in the moral character of sweetness and dignity, and to do what was set before me without complaining. I observed that everybody believed that he thought as he spoke, and that in all that he did he never had any bad intention; and he never showed amazement and surprise, and was never in a hurry, and never put off doing a thing, nor was perplexed nor dejected, nor did he ever laugh to disguise his vexation, nor, on the other hand, was he ever passionate or suspicious. He was accustomed to do acts of beneficence, and was ready to forgive, and was free from all falsehood; and he presented the appearance of a man who could not be diverted from right rather than of a man who had been improved. I observed, too, that no man could ever think that he was despised by Maximus, or ever venture to think himself a better man. He had also the art of being humorous in an agreeable way.

16. In my father[1] I observed mildness of temper, and unchangeable resolution in the things which he had determined after due deliberation; and no vainglory in those things which men call honours; and a love of labour and perseverance; and a readiness to listen to those who had anything to propose for the common weal; and undeviating firmness in giving to every man according to his deserts; and a knowledge derived from experience of the occasions for vigorous action and for remission. And I observed that he had overcome all passion for boys; and he considered himself no more than any other citizen; and he re-

[1] His adoptive father, the Emperor Antoninus Pius.

leased his friends from all obligation to sup with him or to attend him of necessity when he went abroad, and those who had failed to accompany him, by reason of any urgent circumstances, always found him the same. I observed too his habit of careful inquiry in all matters of deliberation, and his persistency, and that he never stopped his investigation through being satisfied with appearances which first present themselves; and that his disposition was to keep his friends, and not to be soon tired of them, nor yet to be extravagant in his affection; and to be satisfied on all occasions, and cheerful; and to foresee things a long way off, and to provide for the smallest without display; and to check immediately popular applause and all flattery; and to be ever watchful over the things which were necessary for the administration of the empire, and to be a good manager of the expenditure, and patiently to endure the blame which he got for such conduct; and he was neither superstitious with respect to the gods, nor did he court men by gifts or by trying to please them, or by flattering the populace; but he showed sobriety in all things and firmness, and never any mean thoughts or action, nor love of novelty. And the things which conduce in any way to the commodity of life, and of which fortune gives an abundant supply, he used without arrogance and without excusing himself; so that when he had them, he enjoyed them without affectation, and when he had them not, he did not want them. No one could ever say of him that he was either a sophist or a home-bred flippant slave or a pedant; but every one acknowledged him to be a man ripe, perfect, above flattery, able to manage his own and other men's affairs. Besides this, he honoured those who were true philosophers, and he did not reproach those who pretended to be philosophers, nor yet was he easily led by them. He was also easy in conversation, and he made himself agreeable without any offensive affectation. He took a reasonable care of his body's health, not as one who was greatly attached to life, nor out of regard to personal appearance, nor yet in a careless way, but so that, through his own attention, he very seldom stood in need of the physician's art or of medicine or external applications. He was most ready to give way without envy to those who possessed any particular faculty, such as that of eloquence or knowledge of the law or of morals, or of anything else; and he gave them his help, that each might enjoy reputation according to his deserts; and he always acted conformably to the institutions of his country, without showing any affectation of doing so. Further, he was not fond of change nor unsteady, but he loved to stay in the same places, and to employ himself about the same things; and after his paroxysms of headache he came immediately fresh and vigorous to his usual occupations. His secrets were not many, but very few and very rare, and these only about public matters; and he showed prudence and economy in the exhibition of the public spectacles and the construction of public buildings, his donations to the people, and in such things, for he was a man who looked to what ought to be done, not to the reputation which is got by a man's acts. He did not take the bath at unseasonable hours; he was not fond of building houses, nor curious about what he ate, nor about the texture and colour of his clothes, nor about the beauty of his slaves. His dress came from Lorium, his villa on the coast, and from Lanuvium generally. We know how he behaved to the toll-collector at Tusculum who asked his pardon; and such was all his behaviour. There was in him nothing harsh, nor implacable, nor violent, nor, as one may say, anything carried to the sweating point; but he examined all things severally, as if he had abundance of time, and without confusion, in an orderly way, vigorously and consistently. And that might be applied to him which is recorded of Socrates, that he was able both to abstain from, and to enjoy, those things which many are too weak to abstain from, and cannot enjoy without excess. But to be strong enough both to bear the one and to be sober in the other is the mark of a man who has a perfect and invincible soul, such as he showed in the illness of Maximus.

17. To the gods I am indebted for having good grandfathers, good parents, a good sister, good teachers, good associates, good kinsmen and friends, nearly everything good. Further, I owe it to the gods that I was not hurried into any offence against any of them, though I had a disposition which, if opportunity had offered,

might have led me to do something of this kind; but, through their favour, there never was such a concurrence of circumstances as put me to the trial. Further, I am thankful to the gods that I was not longer brought up with my grandfather's concubine, and that I preserved the flower of my youth, and that I did not make proof of my virility before the proper season, but even deferred the time; that I was subjected to a ruler and a father who was able to take away all pride from me, and to bring me to the knowledge that it is possible for a man to live in a palace without wanting either guards or embroidered dresses, or torches and statues, and such-like show; but that it is in such a man's power to bring himself very near to the fashion of a private person, without being for this reason either meaner in thought, or more remiss in action, with respect to the things which must be done for the public interest in a manner that befits a ruler. I thank the gods for giving me such a brother,[1] who was able by his moral character to rouse me to vigilance over myself, and who, at the same time, pleased me by his respect and affection; that my children have not been stupid nor deformed in body; that I did not make more proficiency in rhetoric, poetry, and the other studies, in which I should perhaps have been completely engaged, if I had seen that I was making progress in them; that I made haste to place those who brought me up in the station of honour, which they seemed to desire, without putting them off with hope of my doing it some time after, because they were then still young; that I knew Apollonius, Rusticus, Maximus; that I received clear and frequent impressions about living according to nature, and what kind of a life that is, so that, so far as depended on the gods, and their gifts, and help, and inspirations, nothing hindered me from forthwith living according to nature, though I still fall short of it through my own fault, and through not observing the admonitions of the gods, and, I may almost say, their direct instructions; that my body has held out so long in such a kind of life; that I never touched either Benedicta or Theodotus, and that, after having fallen into amatory passions, I was cured; and, though I was often out of humour with Rusticus, I never did anything of which I had occasion to repent; that, though it was my mother's fate to die young, she spent the last years of her life with me; that, whenever I wished to help any man in his need, or on any other occasion, I was never told that I had not the means of doing it; and that to myself the same necessity never happened, to receive anything from another; that I have such a wife, so obedient, and so affectionate, and so simple; that I had abundance of good masters for my children; and that remedies have been shown to me by dreams, both others, and against bloodspitting and giddiness . . . ; and that, when I had an inclination to philosophy, I did not fall into the hands of any sophist, and that I did not waste my time on writers of histories, or in the resolution of syllogisms, or occupy myself about the investigation of appearances in the heavens; for all these things require the help of the gods and fortune.

Among the Quadi at the Granua.

· BOOK TWO ·

BEGIN the morning by saying to thyself, I shall meet with the busy-body, the ungrateful, arrogant, deceitful, envious, unsocial. All these things happen to them by reason of their ignorance of what is good and evil. But I who have seen the nature of the good that it is beautiful, and of the bad that it is ugly, and the nature of him who does wrong, that it is akin to me, not only of the same blood or seed, but that it participates in the same intelligence and the same portion of the divinity, I can neither be injured by any of them, for no one can fix on me what is ugly, nor can I be angry with my kinsman, nor hate him. For we are made for co-operation, like feet, like hands, like eyelids, like the rows of the upper and lower teeth. To act against one another then is contrary to nature; and it is acting against one another to be vexed and to turn away.

[1] Probably his adoptive brother, L. Verus.

2. Whatever this is that I am, it is a little flesh and breath, and the ruling part. Throw away thy books; no longer distract thyself: it is not allowed; but as if thou wast now dying, despise the flesh; it is blood and bones and a network, a contexture of nerves, veins, and arteries. See the breath also, what kind of a thing it is, air, and not always the same, but every moment sent out and again sucked in. The third then is the ruling part: consider thus: Thou art an old man; no longer let this be a slave, no longer be pulled by the strings like a puppet to unsocial movements, no longer be either dissatisfied with thy present lot, or shrink from the future.

3. All that is from the gods is full of Providence. That which is from fortune is not separated from nature or without an interweaving and involution with the things which are ordered by Providence. From thence all things flow; and there is besides necessity, and that which is for the advantage of the whole universe, of which thou art a part. But that is good for every part of nature which the nature of the whole brings, and what serves to maintain this nature. Now the universe is preserved, as by the changes of the elements so by the changes of things compounded of the elements. Let these principles be enough for thee, let them always be fixed opinions. But cast away the thirst after books, that thou mayest not die murmuring, but cheerfully, truly, and from thy heart thankful to the gods.

4. Remember how long thou hast been putting off these things, and how often thou hast received an opportunity from the gods, and yet dost not use it. Thou must now at last perceive of what universe thou art a part, and of what administrator of the universe thy existence is an efflux, and that a limit of time is fixed for thee, which if thou dost not use for clearing away the clouds from thy mind, it will go and thou wilt go, and it will never return.

5. Every moment think steadily as a Roman and a man to do what thou hast in hand with perfect and simple dignity, and feeling of affection, and freedom, and justice; and to give thyself relief from all other thoughts. And thou wilt give thyself relief, if thou doest every act of thy life as if it were the last, laying aside all carelessness and passionate aversion from the commands of reason, and all hypocrisy, and self-love, and discontent with the portion which has been given to thee. Thou seest how few the things are, the which if a man lays hold of, he is able to live a life which flows in quiet, and is like the existence of the gods; for the gods on their part will require nothing more from him who observes these things.

6. Do wrong to thyself, do wrong to thyself, my soul; but thou wilt no longer have the opportunity of honouring thyself. Every man's life is sufficient. But thine is nearly finished, though thy soul reverences not itself, but places thy felicity in the souls of others.

7. Do the things external which fall upon thee distract thee? Give thyself time to learn something new and good, and cease to be whirled around. But then thou must also avoid being carried about the other way. For those too are triflers who have wearied themselves in life by their activity, and yet have no object to which to direct every movement, and, in a word, all their thoughts.

8. Through not observing what is in the mind of another a man has seldom been seen to be unhappy; but those who do not observe the movements of their own minds must of necessity be unhappy.

9. This thou must always bear in mind, what is the nature of the whole, and what is my nature, and how this is related to that, and what kind of a part it is of what kind of a whole; and that there is no one who hinders thee from always doing and saying the things which are according to the nature of which thou art a part.

10. Theophrastus, in his comparison of bad acts—such a comparison as one would make in accordance with the common notions of mankind—says, like a true philosopher, that the offences which are committed through desire are more blameable than those which are committed through anger. For he who is excited by anger seems to turn away from reason with a certain pain and unconscious contraction; but he who offends through desire, being overpowered by pleasure, seems to be in a manner more intemperate and more womanish in his offences. Rightly then, and in a way worthy of philosophy, he said that the offence which is committed with pleasure is more blameable

than that which is committed with pain; and on the whole the one is more like a person who has been first wronged and through pain is compelled to be angry; but the other is moved by his own impulse to do wrong, being carried towards doing something by desire.

11. Since it is possible that thou mayest depart from life this very moment, regulate every act and thought accordingly. But to go away from among men, if there are gods, is not a thing to be afraid of, for the gods will not involve thee in evil; but if indeed they do not exist, or if they have no concern about human affairs, what is it to me to live in a universe devoid of gods or devoid of Providence? But in truth they do exist, and they do care for human things, and they have put all the means in man's power to enable him not to fall into real evils. And as to the rest, if there was anything evil, they would have provided for this also, that it should be altogether in a man's power not to fall into it. Now that which does not make a man worse, how can it make a man's life worse? But neither through ignorance, nor having the knowledge, but not the power to guard against or correct these things, is it possible that the nature of the universe has overlooked them; nor is it possible that it has made so great a mistake, either through want of power or want of skill, that good and evil should happen indiscriminately to the good and the bad. But death certainly, and life, honour and dishonour, pain and pleasure, all these things equally happen to good men and bad, being things which make us neither better nor worse. Therefore they are neither good nor evil.

12. How quickly all things disappear, in the universe the bodies themselves, but in time the remembrance of them; what is the nature of all sensible things, and particularly those which attract with the bait of pleasure or terrify by pain, or are noised abroad by vapoury fame; how worthless, and contemptible, and sordid, and perishable, and dead they are—all this it is the part of the intellectual faculty to observe. To observe too who these are whose opinions and voices give reputation; what death is, and the fact that, if a man looks at it in itself, and by the abstractive power of reflection resolves into their parts all the things which present themselves to the imagination in it, he will

then consider it to be nothing else than an operation of nature; and if any one is afraid of an operation of nature, he is a child. This, however, is not only an operation of nature, but it is also a thing which conduces to the purposes of nature. To observe too how man comes near to the deity, and by what part of him, and when this part of man is so disposed.

13. Nothing is more wretched than a man who traverses everything in a round, and pries into the things beneath the earth, as the poet [1] says, and seeks by conjecture what is in the minds of his neighbours, without perceiving that it is sufficient to attend to the daemon within him, and to reverence it sincerely. And reverence of the daemon consists in keeping it pure from passion and thoughtlessness, and dissatisfaction with what comes from gods and men. For the things from the gods merit veneration for their excellence; and the things from men should be dear to us by reason of kinship; and sometimes even, in a manner, they move our pity by reason of men's ignorance of good and bad; this defect being not less than that which deprives us of the power of distinguishing things that are white and black.

14. Though thou shouldst be going to live three thousand years, and as many times ten thousand years, still remember that no man loses any other life than this which he now lives, nor lives any other than this which he now loses. The longest and shortest are thus brought to the same. For the present is the same to all, though that which perishes is not the same; and so that which is lost appears to be a mere moment. For a man cannot lose either the past or the future: for what a man has not, how can any one take this from him? These two things then thou must bear in mind; the one, that all things from eternity are of like forms and come round in a circle, and that it makes no difference whether a man shall see the same things during a hundred years or two hundred, or an infinite time; and the second, that the longest liver and he who will die soonest lose just the same. For the present is the only thing of which a man can be deprived, if it is true that this is the only thing which he has, and that a man cannot lose a thing if he has it not.

[1] Cf. Plato, *Theætetus*, 173.

15. Remember that all is opinion. For what was said by the Cynic Monimus is manifest: and manifest too is the use of what was said, if a man receives what may be got out of it as far as it is true.

16. The soul of man does violence to itself, first of all, when it becomes an abscess and, as it were, a tumour on the universe, so far as it can. For to be vexed at anything which happens is a separation of ourselves from nature, in some part of which the natures of all other things are contained. In the next place, the soul does violence to itself when it turns away from any man, or even moves towards him with the intention of injuring, such as are the souls of those who are angry. In the third place, the soul does violence to itself when it is overpowered by pleasure or by pain. Fourthly, when it plays a part, and does or says anything insincerely and untruly. Fifthly, when it allows any act of its own and any movement to be without an aim, and does anything thoughtlessly and without considering what it is, it being right that even the smallest things be done with reference to an end; and the end of rational animals is to follow the reason and the law of the most ancient city and polity.

17. Of human life the time is a point, and the substance is in a flux, and the perception dull, and the composition of the whole body subject to putrefaction, and the soul a whirl, and fortune hard to divine, and fame a thing devoid of judgement. And, to say all in a word, everything which belongs to the body is a stream, and what belongs to the soul is a dream and vapour, and life is a warfare and a stranger's sojourn, and after-fame is oblivion. What then is that which is able to conduct a man? One thing and only one, philosophy. But this consists in keeping the daemon within a man free from violence and unharmed, superior to pains and pleasures, doing nothing without a purpose, nor yet falsely and with hypocrisy, not feeling the need of another man's doing or not doing anything; and besides, accepting all that happens, and all that is allotted, as coming from thence, wherever it is, from whence he himself came; and, finally, waiting for death with a cheerful mind, as being nothing else than a dissolution of the elements of which every living being is compounded. But if there is no harm to the elements themselves in each continually changing into another, why should a man have any apprehension about the change and dissolution of all the elements? For it is according to nature, and nothing is evil which is according to nature.

This in Carnuntum.

: BOOK THREE :

WE OUGHT to consider not only that our life is daily wasting away and a smaller part of it is left, but another thing also must be taken into the account, that if a man should live longer, it is quite uncertain whether the understanding will still continue sufficient for the comprehension of things, and retain the power of contemplation which strives to acquire the knowledge of the divine and the human. For if he shall begin to fall into dotage, perspiration and nutrition and imagination and appetite, and whatever else there is of the kind, will not fail; but the power of making use of ourselves, and filling up the measure of our duty, and clearly separating all appearances, and considering whether a man should now depart from life, and whatever else of the kind absolutely requires a disciplined reason, all this is already extinguished. We must make haste then, not only because we are daily nearer to death, but also because the conception of things and the understanding of them cease first.

2. We ought to observe also that even the things which follow after the things which are produced according to nature contain something pleasing and attractive. For instance, when bread is baked some parts are split at the surface, and these parts which thus open, and have a certain fashion contrary to the purpose of the baker's art, are beautiful in a manner, and in a peculiar way excite a desire for eating. And again, figs, when they are quite ripe, gape open; and in the ripe olives the very circumstance of their being near to rottenness adds a

peculiar beauty to the fruit. And the ears of corn bending down, and the lion's eyebrows, and the foam which flows from the mouth of wild boars, and many other things—though they are far from being beautiful, if a man should examine them severally—still, because they are consequent upon the things which are formed by nature, help to adorn them, and they please the mind; so that if a man should have a feeling and deeper insight with respect to the things which are produced in the universe, there is hardly one of those which follow by way of consequence which will not seem to him to be in a manner disposed so as to give pleasure. And so he will see even the real gaping jaws of wild beasts with no less pleasure than those which painters and sculptors show by imitation; and in an old woman and an old man he will be able to see a certain maturity and comeliness; and the attractive loveliness of young persons he will be able to look on with chaste eyes; and many such things will present themselves, not pleasing to every man, but to him only who has become truly familiar with nature and her works.

3. Hippocrates after curing many diseases himself fell sick and died. The Chaldaei foretold the deaths of many, and then fate caught them too. Alexander, and Pompeius, and Caius Caesar, after so often completely destroying whole cities, and in battle cutting to pieces many ten thousands of cavalry and infantry, themselves too at last departed from life. Heraclitus, after so many speculations on the conflagration of the universe, was filled with water internally and died smeared all over with mud. And lice destroyed Democritus; and other lice killed Socrates. What means all this? Thou hast embarked, thou hast made the voyage, thou art come to shore; get out. If indeed to another life, there is no want of gods, not even there. But if to a state without sensation, thou wilt cease to be held by pains and pleasures, and to be a slave to the vessel, which is as much inferior as that which serves it is superior: for the one is intelligence and deity; the other is earth and corruption.

4. Do not waste the remainder of thy life in thoughts about others, when thou dost not refer thy thoughts to some object of common utility. For thou losest the opportunity of doing something else when thou hast such thoughts as these, What is such a person doing, and why, and what is he saying, and what is he thinking of, and what is he contriving, and whatever else of the kind makes us wander away from the observation of our own ruling power. We ought then to check in the series of our thoughts everything that is without a purpose and useless, but most of all the over-curious feeling and the malignant; and a man should use himself to think of those things only about which if one should suddenly ask, What hast thou now in thy thoughts? With perfect openness thou mightest, immediately answer, This or That; so that from thy words it should be plain that everything in thee is simple and benevolent, and such as befits a social animal, and one that cares not for thoughts about pleasure or sensual enjoyments at all, nor has any rivalry or envy and suspicion, or anything else for which thou wouldst blush if thou shouldst say that thou hadst it in thy mind. For the man who is such and no longer delays being among the number of the best, is like a priest and minister of the gods, using too the deity which is planted within him, which makes the man uncontaminated by pleasure, unharmed by any pain, untouched by any insult, feeling no wrong, a fighter in the noblest fight, one who cannot be overpowered by any passion, dyed deep with justice, accepting with all his soul everything which happens and is assigned to him as his portion; and not often, nor yet without great necessity and for the general interest, imagining what another says, or does, or thinks. For it is only what belongs to himself that he makes the matter for his activity; and he constantly thinks of that which is allotted to himself out of the sum total of things, and he makes his own acts fair, and he is persuaded that his own portion is good. For the lot which is assigned to each man is carried along with him and carries him along with it. And he remembers also that every rational animal is his kinsman, and that to care for all men is according to man's nature; and a man should hold on to the opinion not of all, but of those only who confessedly live according to nature. But as to those who live not so, he always bears in mind what kind of men they are both at home and from home, both by night and by day, and what

they are, and with what men they live an impure life. Accordingly, he does not value at all the praise which comes from such men, since they are not even satisfied with themselves.

5. Labour not unwillingly, nor without regard to the common interest, nor without due consideration, nor with distraction; nor let studied ornament set off thy thoughts, and be not either a man of many words, or busy about too many things. And further, let the deity which is in thee be the guardian of a living being, manly and of ripe age, and engaged in matter political, and a Roman, and a ruler, who has taken his post like a man waiting for the signal which summons him from life, and ready to go, having need neither of oath nor of any man's testimony. Be cheerful also, and seek not external help nor the tranquillity which others give. A man then must stand erect, not be kept erect by others.

6. If thou findest in human life anything better than justice, truth, temperance, fortitude, and, in a word, anything better than thy own mind's self-satisfaction in the things which it enables thee to do according to right reason, and in the condition that is assigned to thee without thy own choice; if, I say, thou seest anything better than this, turn to it with all thy soul, and enjoy that which thou hast found to be the best. But if nothing appears to be better than the deity which is planted in thee, which has subjected to itself all thy appetites, and carefully examines all the impressions, and, as Socrates said, has detached itself from the persuasions of sense, and has submitted itself to the gods, and cares for mankind; if thou findest everything else smaller and of less value than this, give place to nothing else, for if thou dost once diverge and incline to it, thou wilt no longer without distraction be able to give the preference to that good thing which is thy proper possession and thy own; for it is not right that anything of any other kind, such as praise from the many, or power, or enjoyment of pleasure, should come into competition with that which is rationally and politically or practically good. All these things, even though they may seem to adapt themselves to the better things in a small degree, obtain the superiority all at once, and carry us away. But do thou, I say, simply and freely choose the better, and

hold to it.—But that which is useful is the better.—Well then, if it is useful to thee as a rational being, keep to it; but if it is only useful to thee as an animal, say so, and maintain thy judgement without arrogance: only take care that thou makest the inquiry by a sure method.

7. Never value anything as profitable to thyself which shall compel thee to break thy promise, to lose thy self-respect, to hate any man, to suspect, to curse, to act the hypocrite, to desire anything which needs walls and curtains: for he who has preferred to everything else his own intelligence and daemon and the worship of its excellence, acts no tragic part, does not groan, will not need either solitude or much company; and, what is chief of all, he will live without either pursuing or flying from death; but whether for a longer or a shorter time he shall have the soul inclosed in the body, he cares not at all: for even if he must depart immediately, he will go as readily as if he were going to do anything else which can be done with decency and order; taking care of this only all through life, that his thoughts turn not away from anything which belongs to an intelligent animal and a member of a civil community.

8. In the mind of one who is chastened and purified thou wilt find no corrupt matter, nor impurity, nor any sore skinned over. Nor is his life incomplete when fate overtakes him, as one may say of an actor who leaves the stage before ending and finishing the play. Besides, there is in him nothing servile, nor affected, nor too closely bound to other things, nor yet detached from other things, nothing worthy of blame, nothing which seeks a hiding-place.

9. Reverence the faculty which produces opinion. On this faculty it entirely depends whether there shall exist in thy ruling part any opinion inconsistent with nature and the constitution of the rational animal. And this faculty promises freedom from hasty judgement, and friendship towards men, and obedience to the gods.

10. Throwing away then all things, hold to these only which are few; and besides bear in mind that every man lives only this present time, which is an indivisible point, and that all the rest of his life is either past or it is uncer-

tain. Short then is the time which every man lives, and small the nook of the earth where he lives; and short too the longest posthumous fame, and even this only continued by a succession of poor human beings, who will very soon die, and who know not even themselves, much less him who died long ago.

11. To the aids which have been mentioned let this one still be added:—Make for thyself a definition or description of the thing which is presented to thee, so as to see distinctly what kind of a thing it is in its substance, in its nudity, in its complete entirety, and tell thyself its proper name, and the names of the things of which it has been compounded, and into which it will be resolved. For nothing is so productive of elevation of mind as to be able to examine methodically and truly every object which is presented to thee in life, and always to look at things so as to see at the same time what kind of universe this is, and what kind of use everything performs in it, and what value everything has with reference to the whole, and what with reference to man, who is a citizen of the highest city, of which all other cities are like families; what each thing is, and of what it is composed, and how long it is the nature of this thing to endure which now makes an impression on me, and what virtue I have need of with respect to it, such as gentleness, manliness, truth, fidelity, simplicity, contentment, and the rest. Wherefore, on every occasion a man should say: this comes from God; and this is according to the apportionment and spinning of the thread of destiny, and such-like coincidence and chance; and this is from one of the same stock, and a kinsman and partner, one who knows not however what is according to his nature. But I know; for this reason I behave towards him according to the natural law of fellowship with benevolence and justice. At the same time however in things indifferent I attempt to ascertain the value of each.

12. If thou workest at that which is before thee, following right reason seriously, vigorously, calmly, without allowing anything else to distract thee, but keeping thy divine part pure, as if thou shouldst be bound to give it back immediately; if thou holdest to this, expecting nothing, fearing nothing, but satisfied with thy present activity according to nature, and with heroic truth in every word and sound which thou utterest, thou wilt live happy. And there is no man who is able to prevent this.

13. As physicians have always their instruments and knives ready for cases which suddenly require their skill, so do thou have principles ready for the understanding of things divine and human, and for doing everything, even the smallest, with a recollection of the bond which unites the divine and human to one another. For neither wilt thou do anything well which pertains to man without at the same time having a reference to things divine; nor the contrary.

14. No longer wander at hazard; for neither wilt thou read thy own memoirs, nor the acts of the ancient Romans and Hellenes, and the selections from books which thou wast reserving for thy old age. Hasten then to the end which thou hast before thee, and throwing away idle hopes, come to thy own aid, if thou carest at all for thyself, while it is in thy power.

15. They know not how many things are signified by the words stealing, sowing, buying, keeping quiet, seeing what ought to be done; for this is not effected by the eyes, but by another kind of vision.

16. Body, soul, intelligence: to the body belong sensations, to the soul appetites, to the intelligence principles. To receive the impressions of forms by means of appearances belongs even to animals; to be pulled by the strings of desire belongs both to wild beasts and to men who have made themselves into women, and to a Phalaris and a Nero: and to have the intelligence that guides to the things which appear suitable belongs also to those who do not believe in the gods, and who betray their country, and do their impure deeds when they have shut the doors. If then everything else is common to all that I have mentioned, there remains that which is peculiar to the good man, to be pleased and content with what happens, and with the thread which is spun for him; and not to defile the divinity which is planted in his breast, nor disturb it by a crowd of images, but to preserve it tranquil, following it obediently as a god, neither saying anything contrary to the truth, nor doing any-

thing contrary to justice. And if all men refuse to believe that he lives a simple, modest, and contented life, he is neither angry with any of them, nor does he deviate from the way which leads to the end of life, to which a man ought to come pure, tranquil, ready to depart, and without any compulsion perfectly reconciled to his lot.

· BOOK FOUR :

THAT which rules within, when it is according to nature, is so affected with respect to the events which happen, that it always easily adapts itself to that which is possible and is presented to it. For it requires no definite material, but it moves towards its purpose, under certain conditions however; and it makes a material for itself out of that which opposes it, as fire lays hold of what falls into it, by which a small light would have been extinguished: but when the fire is strong, it soon appropriates to itself the matter which is heaped on it, and consumes it, and rises higher by means of this very material.

2. Let no act be done without a purpose, nor otherwise than according to the perfect principles of art.

3. Men seek retreats for themselves, houses in the country, sea-shores, and mountains; and thou too art wont to desire such things very much. But this is altogether a mark of the most common sort of men, for it is in thy power whenever thou shalt choose to retire into thyself. For nowhere either with more quiet or more freedom from trouble does a man retire than into his own soul, particularly when he has within him such thoughts that by looking into them he is immediately in perfect tranquillity; and I affirm that tranquillity is nothing else than the good ordering of the mind. Constantly then give to thyself this retreat, and renew thyself; and let thy principles be brief and fundamental, which, as soon as thou shalt recur to them, will be sufficient to cleanse the soul completely, and to send thee back free from all discontent with the things to which thou returnest. For with what art thou discontented? With the badness of men? Recall to thy mind this conclusion, that rational animals exist for one another, and that to endure is a part of justice, and that men do wrong involuntarily; and consider how many

already, after mutual enmity, suspicion, hatred, and fighting, have been stretched dead, reduced to ashes; and be quiet at last.—But perhaps thou art dissatisfied with that which is assigned to thee out of the universe.—Recall to thy recollection this alternative; either there is providence or atoms, fortuitous concurrence of things; or remember the arguments by which it has been proved that the world is a kind of political community, and be quiet at last.—But perhaps corporeal things will still fasten upon thee.—Consider then further that the mind mingles not with the breath, whether moving gently or violently, when it has once drawn itself apart and discovered its own power, and think also of all that thou hast heard and assented to about pain and pleasure, and be quiet at last.—But perhaps the desire of the thing called fame will torment thee.— See how soon everything is forgotten, and look at the chaos of infinite time on each side of the present, and the emptiness of applause, and the changeableness and want of judgement in those who pretend to give praise, and the narrowness of the space within which it is circumscribed, and be quiet at last. For the whole earth is a point, and how small a nook in it is this thy dwelling, and how few are there in it, and what kind of people are they who will praise thee.

This then remains: Remember to retire into this little territory of thy own, and above all do not distract or strain thyself, but be free, and look at things as a man, as a human being, as a citizen, as a mortal. But among the things readiest to thy hand to which thou shalt turn, let there be these, which are two. One is that things do not touch the soul, for they are external and remain immovable; but our perturbations come only from the opinion which is within. The other is that all these things, which thou seest, change immediately and will no longer be; and constantly bear in mind how many of these changes thou hast already witnessed. The universe is transformation: life is opinion.

4. If our intellectual part is common, the reason also, in respect of which we are rational beings, is common: if this is so, common also is the reason which commands us what to do, and what not to do; if this is so, there is a common law also; if this is so, we are fellow-citizens; if this is so, we are members of some political community; if this is so, the world is in a manner a state. For of what other common political community will any one say that the whole human race are members? And from thence, from this common political community comes also our very intellectual faculty and reasoning faculty and our capacity for law; or whence do they come? For as my earthly part is a portion given to me from certain earth, and that which is watery from another element, and that which is hot and fiery from some peculiar source (for nothing comes out of that which is nothing, as nothing also returns to non-existence), so also the intellectual part comes from some source.

5. Death is such as generation is, a mystery of nature; a composition out of the same elements, and a decomposition into the same; and altogether not a thing of which any man should be ashamed, for it is not contrary to the nature of a reasonable animal, and not contrary to the reason of our constitution.

6. It is natural that these things should be done by such persons, it is a matter of necessity; and if a man will not have it so, he will not allow the fig-tree to have juice. But by all means bear this in mind, that within a very short time both thou and he will be dead; and soon not even your names will be left behind.

7. Take away thy opinion, and then there is taken away the complaint, "I have been harmed." Take away the complaint, "I have been harmed," and the harm is taken away.

8. That which does not make a man worse than he was, also does not make his life worse, nor does it harm him either from without or from within.

9. The nature of that which is universally useful has been compelled to do this.

10. Consider that everything which happens, happens justly, and if thou observest carefully, thou wilt find it to be so. I do not say only with respect to the continuity of the series of things, but with respect to what is just, and as if it were done by one who assigns to each thing its value. Observe then as thou hast begun; and whatever thou doest, do it in conjunction with this, the being good, and in the sense in which a man is properly understood to be good. Keep to this in every action.

11. Do not have such an opinion of things as he has who does thee wrong, or such as he wishes thee to have, but look at them as they are in truth.

12. A man should always have these two rules in readiness; the one, to do only whatever the reason of the ruling and legislating faculty may suggest for the use of men; the other, to change thy opinion, if there is any one at hand who sets thee right and moves thee from any opinion. But this change of opinion must proceed only from a certain persuasion, as of what is just or of common advantage, and the like, not because it appears pleasant or brings reputation.

13. Hast thou reason? I have.—Why then dost not thou use it? For if this does its own work, what else dost thou wish?

14. Thou hast existed as a part. Thou shalt disappear in that which produced thee; but rather thou shalt be received back into its seminal principle by transmutation.

15. Many grains of frankincense on the same altar: one falls before, another falls after; but it makes no difference.

16. Within ten days thou wilt seem a god to those to whom thou art now a beast and an ape, if thou wilt return to thy principles and the worship of reason.

17. Do not act as if thou wert going to live ten thousand years. Death hangs over thee. While thou livest, while it is in thy power, be good.

18. How much trouble he avoids who does not look to see what his neighbour says or does or thinks, but only to what he does himself, that it may be just and pure; or as Agathon says, look not round at the depraved morals of others, but run straight along the line without deviating from it.

19. He who has a vehement desire for post-humous fame does not consider that every one of those who remember him will himself also die very soon; then again also they who have succeeded them, until the whole remembrance shall have been extinguished as it is transmitted through men who foolishly admire and perish. But suppose that those who will remember are even immortal, and that the remembrance will be immortal, what then is this to thee? And I say not what is it to the dead, but what is it to the living? What is praise except indeed so far as it has a certain utility? For thou now rejectest unseasonably the gift of nature, clinging to something else . . .

20. Everything which is in any way beautiful is beautiful in itself, and terminates in itself, not having praise as part of itself. Neither worse then nor better is a thing made by being praised. I affirm this also of the things which are called beautiful by the vulgar, for example, material things and works of art. That which is really beautiful has no need of anything; not more than law, not more than truth, not more than benevolence or modesty. Which of these things is beautiful because it is praised, or spoiled by being blamed? Is such a thing as an emerald made worse than it was, if it is not praised? Or gold, ivory, purple, a lyre, a little knife, a flower, a shrub?

21. If souls continue to exist, how does the air contain them from eternity?—But how does the earth contain the bodies of those who have been buried from time so remote? For as here the mutation of these bodies after a certain continuance, whatever it may be, and their dissolution make room for other dead bodies; so the souls which are removed into the air after subsisting for some time are transmuted and diffused, and assume a fiery nature by being received into the seminal intelligence of the universe, and in this way make room for the fresh souls which come to dwell there. And this is the answer which a man might give on the hypothesis of souls continuing to exist. But we must not only think of the number of bodies which are thus buried, but also of the number of animals which are daily eaten by us and the other animals. For what a number is consumed, and thus in a manner buried in the bodies of those who feed on them! And never-

theless this earth receives them by reason of the changes of these bodies into blood, and the transformations into the aërial or the fiery element.

What is the investigation into the truth in this matter? The division into that which is material and that which is the cause of form, the formal.

22. Do not be whirled about, but in every movement have respect to justice, and on the occasion of every impression maintain the faculty of comprehension or understanding.

23. Everything harmonizes with me, which is harmonious to thee, O Universe. Nothing for me is too early nor too late, which is in due time for thee. Everything is fruit to me which thy seasons bring, O Nature: from thee are all things, in thee are all things, to thee all things return. The poet says, Dear city of Cecrops; and wilt not thou say, Dear city of Zeus?

24. Occupy thyself with few things, says the philosopher, if thou wouldst be tranquil.—But consider if it would not be better to say, Do what is necessary, and whatever the reason of the animal which is naturally social requires, and as it requires. For this brings not only the tranquillity which comes from doing well, but also that which comes from doing few things. For the greatest part of what we say and do being unnecessary, if a man takes this away, he will have more leisure and less uneasiness. Accordingly on every occasion a man should ask himself, Is this one of the unnecessary things? Now a man should take away not only unnecessary acts, but also, unnecessary thoughts, for thus superfluous acts will not follow after.

25. Try how the life of the good man suits thee, the life of him who is satisfied with his portion out of the whole, and satisfied with his own just acts and benevolent disposition.

26. Hast thou seen those things? Look also at these. Do not disturb thyself. Make thyself all simplicity. Does any one do wrong? It is to himself that he does the wrong. Has anything happened to thee? Well; out of the universe from the beginning everything which happens has been apportioned and spun out to thee. In a word, thy life is short. Thou must turn to profit the present by the aid of reason and justice. Be sober in thy relaxation.

27. Either it is a well-arranged universe or a chaos huddled together, but still a universe. But can a certain order subsist in thee, and disorder in the All? And this too when all things are so separated and diffused and sympathetic.

28. A black character, a womanish character, a stubborn character, bestial, childish, animal, stupid, counterfeit, scurrilous, fraudulent, tyrannical.

29. If he is a stranger to the universe who does not know what is in it, no less is he a stranger who does not know what is going on in it. He is a runaway, who flies from social reason; he is blind, who shuts the eyes of the understanding; he is poor, who has need of another, and has not from himself all things which are useful for life. He is an abscess on the universe who withdraws and separates himself from the reason of our common nature through being displeased with the things which happen, for the same nature produces this, and has produced thee too: he is a piece rent asunder from the state, who tears his own soul from that of reasonable animals, which is one.

30. The one is a philosopher without a tunic, and the other without a book: here is another half naked: Bread I have not, he says, and I abide by reason.—And I do not get the means of living out of my learning, and I abide by my reason.

31. Love the art, poor as it may be, which thou hast learned, and be content with it; and pass through the rest of life like one who has intrusted to the gods with his whole soul all that he has, making thyself neither the tyrant nor the slave of any man.

32. Consider, for example, the times of Vespasian. Thou wilt see all these things, people marrying, bringing up children, sick, dying, warring, feasting, trafficking, cultivating the ground, flattering, obstinately arrogant, suspecting, plotting, wishing for some to die, grumbling about the present, loving, heaping up treasure, desiring counsulship, kingly power. Well then, that life of these people no longer exists at all. Again, remove to the times of Trajan. Again, all is the same. Their life too is gone. In like manner view also the other epochs of time and of whole nations, and see how many after great efforts soon fell and were resolved into the elements. But chiefly thou shouldst think of those whom thou hast thyself known distracting themselves about idle things, neglecting to do what was in accordance with their proper constitution, and to hold firmly to this and to be content with it. And herein it is necessary to remember that the attention given to everything has its proper value and proportion. For thus thou wilt not be dissatisfied, if thou appliest thyself to smaller matters no further than is fit.

33. The words which were formerly familiar are now antiquated: so also the names of those who were famed of old, are now in a manner antiquated, Camillus, Caeso, Volesus, Leonnatus, and a little after also Scipio and Cato, then Augustus, then also Hadrian and Antoninus. For all things soon pass away and become a mere tale, and complete oblivion soon buries them. And I say this of those who have shone in a wondrous way. For the rest, as soon as they have breathed out their breath, they are gone, and no man speaks of them. And, to conclude the matter, what is even an eternal remembrance? A mere nothing. What then is that about which we ought to employ our serious pains? This one thing, thoughts just, and acts social, and words which never lie, and a disposition which gladly accepts all that happens, as necessary, as usual, as flowing from a principle and source of the same kind.

34. Willingly give thyself up to Clotho, one of the Fates, allowing her to spin thy thread into whatever things she pleases.

35. Everything is only for a day, both that which remembers and that which is remembered.

36. Observe constantly that all things take place by change, and accustom thyself to consider that the nature of the Universe loves nothing so much as to change the things which are and to make new things like them. For everything that exists is in a manner the seed of that which will be. But thou art thinking only of seeds which are cast into the earth or into a womb: but this is a very vulgar notion.

37. Thou wilt soon die, and thou art not yet simple, not free from perturbations, nor without suspicion of being hurt by external things,

nor kindly disposed towards all; nor dost thou yet place wisdom only in acting justly.

38. Examine men's ruling principles, even those of the wise, what kind of things they avoid, and what kind they pursue.

39. What is evil to thee does not subsist in the ruling principle of another; nor yet in any turning and mutation of thy corporeal covering. Where is it then? It is in that part of thee in which subsists the power of forming opinions about evils. Let this power then not form such opinions, and all is well. And if that which is nearest to it, the poor body, is cut, burnt, filled with matter and rottenness, nevertheless let the part which forms opinions about these things be quiet, that is, let it judge that nothing is either bad or good which can happen equally to the bad man and the good. For that which happens equally to him who lives contrary to nature and to him who lives according to nature, is neither according to nature nor contrary to nature.

40. Constantly regard the universe as one living being, having one substance and one soul; and observe how all things have reference to one perception, the perception of this one living being; and how all things act with one movement; and how all things are the co-operating causes of all things which exist; observe too the continuous spinning of the thread and the contexture of the web.

41. Thou art a little soul bearing about a corpse, as Epictetus used to say.

42. It is no evil for things to undergo change, and no good for things to subsist in consequence of change.

43. Time is like a river made up of the events which happen, and a violent stream; for as soon as a thing has been seen, it is carried away, and another comes in its place, and this will be carried away too.

44. Everything which happens is as familiar and well known as the rose in spring and the fruit in summer; for such is disease, and death, and calumny, and treachery, and whatever else delights fools or vexes them.

45. In the series of things those which follow are always aptly fitted to those which have gone before; for this series is not like a mere enumeration of disjointed things, which has only a necessary sequence, but it is a rational

connection: and as all existing things are arranged together harmoniously, so the things which come into existence exhibit no mere succession, but a certain wonderful relationship.

46. Always remember the saying of Heraclitus, that the death of earth is to become water, and the death of water is to become air, and the death of air is to become fire, and reversely. And think too of him who forgets whither the way leads, and that men quarrel with that with which they are most constantly in communion, the reason which governs the universe; and the things which they daily meet with seem to them strange: and consider that we ought not to act and speak as if we were asleep, for even in sleep we seem to act and speak; and that we ought not, like children who learn from their parents, simply to act and speak as we have been taught.

47. If any god told thee that thou shalt die to-morrow, or certainly on the day after to-morrow, thou wouldst not care much whether it was on the third day or on the morrow, unless thou wast in the highest degree mean-spirited—for how small is the difference?—so think it no great thing to die after as many years as thou canst name rather than to-morrow.

48. Think continually how many physicians are dead after often contracting their eyebrows over the sick; and how many astrologers after predicting with great pretensions the deaths of others; and how many philosophers after endless discourses on death or immortality; how many heroes after killing thousands; and how many tyrants who have used their power over men's lives with terrible insolence as if they were immortal; and how many cities are entirely dead, so to speak, Helice and Pompeii and Herculaneum, and others innumerable. Add to the reckoning all whom thou hast known, one after another. One man after burying another has been laid out dead, and another buries him: and all this in a short time. To conclude, always observe how ephemeral and worthless human things are, and what was yesterday a little mucus to-morrow will be a mummy or ashes. Pass then through this little space of time conformably to nature, and end thy journey in content, just as an olive falls off when it is ripe, blessing nature

who produced it, and thanking the tree on which it grew.

49. Be like the promontory against which the waves continually break, but it stands firm and tames the fury of the water around it.

Unhappy am I, because this has happened to me.—Not so, but happy am I, though this has happened to me, because I continue free from pain, neither crushed by the present nor fearing the future. For such a thing as this might have happened to every man; but every man would not have continued free from pain on such an occasion. Why then is that rather a misfortune than this a good fortune? And dost thou in all cases call that a man's misfortune, which is not a deviation from man's nature? And does a thing seem to thee to be a deviation from man's nature, when it is not contrary to the will of man's nature? Well, thou knowest the will of nature. Will then this which has happened prevent thee from being just, magnanimous, temperate, prudent, secure against inconsiderate opinions and falsehood; will it prevent thee from having modesty, freedom, and everything else, by the presence of which man's nature obtains all that is its own? Remember too on every occasion which leads thee to vexation to apply this principle: not that this is a misfortune, but that to bear it nobly is good fortune.

50. It is a vulgar, but still a useful help towards contempt of death, to pass in review those who have tenaciously stuck to life. What more then have they gained than those who have died early? Certainly they lie in their tombs somewhere at last, Cadicianus, Fabius, Julianus, Lepidus, or any one else like them, who have carried out many to be buried, and then were carried out themselves. Altogether the interval is small between birth and death; and consider with how much trouble, and in company with what sort of people and in what a feeble body this interval is laboriously passed. Do not then consider life a thing of any value. For look to the immensity of time behind thee, and to the time which is before thee, another boundless space. In this infinity then what is the difference between him who lives three days and him who lives three generations?

51. Always run to the short way; and the short way is the natural: accordingly say and do everything in conformity with the soundest reason. For such a purpose frees a man from trouble, and warfare, and all artifice and ostentatious display.

· BOOK FIVE ·

IN THE morning when thou risest unwillingly, let this thought be present—I am rising to the work of a human being. Why then am I dissatisfied if I am going to do the things for which I exist and for which I was brought into the world? Or have I been made for this, to lie in the bed-clothes and keep myself warm?—But this is more pleasant.—Dost thou exist then to take thy pleasure, and not at all for action or exertion? Dost thou not see the little plants, the little birds, the ants, the spiders, the bees working together to put in order their several parts of the universe? And art thou unwilling to do the work of a human being, and dost thou not make haste to do that which is according to thy nature?—But it is necessary to take rest also.—It is necessary: however nature has fixed bounds to this too: she has fixed bounds both to eating and drinking, and yet thou goest beyond these bounds, beyond what is sufficient; yet in thy acts it is not so, but thou stoppest short of what thou canst do. So thou lovest not thyself, for if thou didst, thou wouldst love thy nature and her will. But those who love their several arts exhaust themselves in working at them unwashed and without food; but thou valuest thy own nature less than the turner values the turning art, or the dancer the dancing art, or the lover of money values his money, or the vainglorious man his little glory. And such men, when they have a violent affection to a thing, choose neither to eat nor to sleep rather than to perfect the things which they care for. But are the acts which concern society more vile in thy eyes and less worthy of thy labour?

2. How easy it is to repel and to wipe away every impression which is troublesome or unsuitable, and immediately to be in all tranquillity.

3. Judge every word and deed which are according to nature to be fit for thee; and be not diverted by the blame which follows from any people nor by their words, but if a thing is good to be done or said, do not consider it unworthy of thee. For those persons have their peculiar leading principle and follow their peculiar movement; which things do not thou regard, but go straight on, following thy own nature and the common nature; and the way of both is one.

4. I go through the things which happen according to nature until I shall fall and rest, breathing out my breath into that element out of which I daily draw it in, and falling upon that earth out of which my father collected the seed, and my mother the blood, and my nurse the milk; out of which during so many years I have been supplied with food and drink; which bears me when I tread on it and abuse it for so many purposes.

5. Thou sayest, Men cannot admire the sharpness of thy wits.—Be it so: but there are many other things of which thou canst not say, I am not formed for them by nature. Show those qualities then which are altogether in thy power, sincerity, gravity, endurance of labour, aversion to pleasure, contentment with thy portion and with few things, benevolence, frankness, no love of superfluity, freedom from trifling magnanimity. Dost thou not see how many qualities thou art immediately able to exhibit, in which there is no excuse of natural incapacity and unfitness, and yet thou still remainest voluntarily below the mark? Or art thou compelled through being defectively furnished by nature to murmur, and to be stingy, and to flatter, and to find fault with thy poor body, and to try to please men, and to make great display, and to be so restless in thy mind? No, by the gods: but thou mightest have been delivered from these things long ago. Only if in truth thou canst be charged with being rather slow and dull of comprehension, thou must exert thyself about this also, not neglecting it nor yet taking pleasure in thy dulness.

6. One man, when he has done a service to another, is ready to set it down to his account as a favour conferred. Another is not ready to do this, but still in his own mind he thinks of the man as his debtor, and he knows what he has done. A third in a manner does not even know what he has done, but he is like a vine which has produced grapes, and seeks for nothing more after it has once produced its proper fruit. As a horse when he has run, a dog when he has tracked the game, a bee when it has made the honey, so a man when he has done a good act, does not call out for others to come and see, but he goes on to another act, as a vine goes on to produce again the grapes in season.—Must a man then be one of these, who in a manner act thus without observing it?—Yes.—But this very thing is necessary, the observation of what a man is doing: for, it may be said, it is characteristic of the social animal to perceive that he is working in a social manner, and indeed to wish that his social partner also should perceive it.—It is true what thou sayest, but thou dost not rightly understand what is now said: and for this reason thou wilt become one of those of whom I spoke before, for even they are misled by a certain show of reason. But if thou wilt choose to understand the meaning of what is said, do not fear that for this reason thou wilt omit any social act.

7. A prayer of the Athenians: Rain, rain, O dear Zeus, down on the ploughed fields of the Athenians and on the plains.—In truth we ought not to pray at all, or we ought to pray in this simple and noble fashion.

8. Just as we must understand when it is said, That Aesculapius prescribed to this man horse-exercise, or bathing in cold water or going without shoes; so we must understand it when it is said, That the nature of the universe prescribed to this man disease or mutilation or loss or anything else of the kind. For in the first case Prescribed means something like this: he prescribed this for this man as a thing adapted to procure health; and in the second case it means: That which happens to (or, suits) every man is fixed in a manner for him suitably to his destiny. For this is what we mean when we say that things are suitable to us, as the workmen say of squared stones in walls or the pyramids, that they are suitable, when they fit them to one another in some

kind of connexion. For there is altogether one fitness, harmony. And as the universe is made up out of all bodies to be such a body as it is, so out of all existing causes necessity (destiny) is made up to be such a cause as it is. And even those who are completely ignorant understand what I mean, for they say, It (necessity, destiny) brought this to such a person.—This then was brought and this was precribed to him. Let us then receive these things, as well as those which Aesculapius prescribes. Many as a matter of course even among his prescriptions are disagreeable, but we accept them in the hope of health. Let the perfecting and accomplishment of the things, which the common nature judges to be good, be judged by thee to be of the same kind as thy health. And so accept everything which happens, even if it seem disagreeable, because it leads to this, to the health of the universe and to the prosperity and felicity of Zeus (the universe). For he would not have brought on any man what he has brought, if it were not useful for the whole. Neither does the nature of anything, whatever it may be, cause anything which is not suitable to that which is directed by it. For two reasons then it is right to be content with that which happens to thee; the one, because it was done for thee and prescribed for thee, and in a manner had reference to thee, originally from the most ancient causes spun with thy destiny; and the other, because even that which comes severally to every man is to the power which administers the universe a cause of felicity and perfection, nay even of its very continuance. For the integrity of the whole is mutilated, if thou cuttest off anything whatever from the conjunction and the continuity either of the parts or of the causes. And thou dost cut off, as far as it is in thy power, when thou art dissatisfied, and in a manner triest to put anything out of the way.

9. Be not disgusted, nor discouraged, nor dissatisfied, if thou dost not succeed in doing everything according to right principles; but when thou hast failed, return back again, and be content if the greater part of what thou doest is consistent with man's nature, and love this to which thou returnest; and do not return to philosophy as if she were a master, but act like those who have sore eyes and apply a bit of sponge and egg, or as another applies a plaster, or drenching with water. For thus thou wilt not fail to obey reason, and thou wilt repose in it. And remember that philosophy requires only the things which thy nature requires; but thou wouldst have something else which is not according to nature.—It may be objected, Why what is more agreeable than this which I am doing?—But is not this the very reason why pleasure deceives us? And consider if magnanimity, freedom, simplicity, equanimity, piety, are not more agreeable. For what is more agreeable than wisdom itself, when thou thinkest of the security and the happy course of all things which depend on the faculty of understanding and knowledge?

10. Things are in such a kind of envelopment that they have seemed to philosophers, not a few nor those common philosophers, altogether unintelligible; nay even to the Stoics themselves they seem difficult to understand. And all our assent is changeable; for where is the man who never changes? Carry thy thoughts then to the objects themselves, and consider how short-lived they are and worthless, and that they may be in the possession of a filthy wretch or a whore or a robber. Then turn to the morals of those who live with thee, and it is hardly possible to endure even the most agreeable of them, to say nothing of a man being hardly able to endure himself. In such darkness then and dirt and in so constant a flux both of substance and of time, and of motion and of things moved, what there is worth being highly prized or even an object of serious pursuit, I cannot imagine. But on the contrary it is a man's duty to comfort himself, and to wait for the natural dissolution and not to be vexed at the delay, but to rest in these principles only: the one, that nothing will happen to me which is not conformable to the nature of the universe; and the other, that it is in my power never to act contrary to my god and daemon: for there is no man who will compel me to this.

11. About what am I now employing my own soul? On every occasion I must ask myself this question, and inquire, what have I now in this part of me which they call the ruling principle? And whose soul have I now? That of a child, or of a young man, or of a

feeble woman, or of a tyrant, or of a domestic animal, or of a wild beast?

12. What kind of things those are which appear good to the many, we may learn even from this. For if any man should conceive certain things as being really good, such as prudence, temperance, justice, fortitude, he would not after having first conceived these endure to listen to anything which should not be in harmony with what is really good. But if a man has first conceived as good the things which appear to the many to be good, he will listen and readily receive as very applicable that which was said by the comic writer. Thus even the many perceive the difference. For were it not so, this saying would not offend and would not be rejected in the first case, while we receive it when it is said of wealth, and of the means which further luxury and fame, as said fitly and wittily. Go on then and ask if we should value and think those things to be good, to which after their first conception in the mind the words of the comic writer might be aptly applied—that he who has them, through pure abundance has not a place to ease himself in.[1]

13. I am composed of the formal and the material; and neither of them will perish into non-existence, as neither of them came into existence out of non-existence. Every part of me then will be reduced by change into some part of the universe, and that again will change into another part of the universe, and so on for ever. And by consequence of such a change I too exist, and those who begot me, and so on for ever in the other direction. For nothing hinders us from saying so, even if the universe is administered according to definite periods of revolution.

14. Reason and the reasoning art (philosophy) are powers which are sufficient for themselves and for their own works. They move then from a first principle which is their own, and they make their way to the end which is proposed to them; and this is the reason why such acts are named *catorthóseis* or right acts, which word signifies that they proceed by the right road.

15. None of these things ought to be called a man's, which do not belong to a man, as man. They are not required of a man, nor does man's nature promise them, nor are they the means of man's nature attaining its end. Neither then does the end of man lie in these things, nor yet that which aids to the accomplishment of this end, and that which aids towards this end is that which is good. Besides, if any of these things did belong to man, it would not be right for a man to despise them and to set himself against them; nor would a man be worthy of praise who showed that he did not want these things, nor would he who stinted himself in any of them be good, if indeed these things were good. But now the more of these things a man deprives himself of, or of other things like them, or even when he is deprived of any of them, the more patiently he endures the loss, just in the same degree he is a better man.

16. Such as are thy habitual thoughts, such also will be the character of thy mind; for the soul is dyed by the thoughts. Dye it then with a continuous series of such thoughts as these: for instance, that where a man can live, there he can also live well. But he must live in a palace;—well then, he can also live well in a palace. And again, consider that for whatever purpose each thing has been constituted, for this it has been constituted, and towards this it is carried; and its end is in that towards which it is carried; and where the end is, there also is the advantage and the good of each thing. Now the good for the reasonable animal is society; for that we are made for society has been shown above.[2] Is it not plain that the inferior exist for the sake of the superior? But the things which have life are superior to those which have not life, and of those which have life the superior are those which have reason.

17. To seek what is impossible is madness: and it is impossible that the bad should not do something of this kind.

18. Nothing happens to any man which he is not formed by nature to bear. The same things happen to another, and either because he does not see that they have happened or because he would show a great spirit he is firm and remains unharmed. It is a shame then that ignorance and conceit should be stronger than wisdom.

[1] Menander.

[2] Cf. Book II, section 1.

19. Things themselves touch not the soul, not in the least degree; nor have they admission to the soul, nor can they turn or move the soul: but the soul turns and moves itself alone, and whatever judgements it may think proper to make, such it makes for itself the things which present themselves to it.

20. In one respect man is the nearest thing to me, so far as I must do good to men and endure them. But so far as some men make themselves obstacles to my proper acts, man becomes to me one of the things which are indifferent, no less than the sun or wind or a wild beast. Now it is true that these may impede my action, but they are no impediments to my affects and disposition, which have the power of acting conditionally and changing: for the mind converts and changes every hindrance to its activity into an aid; and so that which is a hindrance is made a furtherance to an act; and that which is an obstacle on the road helps us on this road.

21. Reverence that which is best in the universe; and this is that which makes use of all things and directs all things. And in like manner also reverence that which is best in thyself; and this is of the same kind as that. For in thyself also, that which makes use of everything else, is this, and thy life is directed by this.

22. That which does no harm to the state, does no harm to the citizen. In the case of every appearance of harm apply this rule: if the state is not harmed by this, neither am I harmed. But if the state is harmed, thou must not be angry with him who does harm to the state. Show him where his error is.

23. Often think of the rapidity with which things pass by and disappear, both the things which are and the things which are produced. For substance is like a river in a continual flow, and the activities of things are in constant change, and the causes work in infinite varieties; and there is hardly anything which stands still. And consider this which is near to thee, this boundless abyss of the past and of the future in which all things disappear. How then is he not a fool who is puffed up with such things or plagued about them and makes himself miserable? for they vex him only for a time, and a short time.

24. Think of the universal substance, of which thou hast a very small portion; and of universal time, of which a short and indivisible interval has been assigned to thee; and of that which is fixed by destiny, and how small a part of it thou art.

25. Does another do me wrong? Let him look to it. He has his own disposition, his own activity. I now have what the universal nature wills me to have; and I do what my nature now wills me to do.

26. Let the part of thy soul which leads and governs be undisturbed by the movements in the flesh, whether of pleasure or of pain; and let it not unite with them, but let it circumscribe itself and limit those affects to their parts. But when these affects rise up to the mind by virtue of that other sympathy that naturally exists in a body which is all one, then thou must not strive to resist the sensation, for it is natural: but let not the ruling part of itself add to the sensation the opinion that it is either good or bad.

27. Live with the gods. And he does live with the gods who constantly shows to them that his own soul is satisfied with that which is assigned to him, and that it does all that the daemon wishes, which Zeus hath given to every man for his guardian and guide, a portion of himself. And this is every man's understanding and reason.

28. Art thou angry with him whose armpits stink? Art thou angry with him whose mouth smells foul? What good will this danger do thee? He has such a mouth, he has such arm-pits: it is necessary that such an emanation must come from such things—but the man has reason, it will be said, and he is able, if he takes pain, to discover wherein he offends—I wish thee well of thy discovery. Well then, and thou hast reason: by thy rational faculty stir up his rational faculty; show him his error, admonish him. For if he listens, thou wilt cure him, and there is no need of anger. Neither tragic actor nor whore . . .

29. As thou intendest to live when thou art gone out, . . . so it is in thy power to live here. But if men do not permit thee, then get away out of life, yet so as if thou wert suffering no harm. The house is smoky, and I quit it. Why dost thou think that this is any trouble? But

so long as nothing of the kind drives me out, I remain, am free, and no man shall hinder me from doing what I choose; and I choose to do what is according to the nature of the rational and social animal.

30. The intelligence of the universe is social. Accordingly it has made the inferior things for the sake of the superior, and it has fitted the superior to one another. Thou seest how it has subordinated, co-ordinated and assigned to everything its proper portion, and has brought together into concord with one another the things which are the best.

31. How hast thou behaved hitherto to the gods, thy parents, brethren, children, teachers, to those who looked after thy infancy, to thy friends, kinsfolk, to thy slaves? Consider if thou hast hitherto behaved to all in such a way that this may be said of thee:

Never has wronged a man in deed or word.[1]

And call to recollection both how many things thou hast passed through, and how many things thou hast been able to endure: and that the history of thy life is now complete and thy service is ended: and how many beautiful things thou hast seen: and how many pleasures and pains thou hast despised; and how many things called honourable thou hast spurned; and to how many ill-minded folks thou hast shown a kind disposition.

32. Why do unskilled and ignorant souls disturb him who has skill and knowledge? What soul then has skill and knowledge? That which knows beginning and end, and knows the reason which pervades all substance and through all time by fixed periods (revolutions) administers the universe.

33. Soon, very soon, thou wilt be ashes, or a skeleton, and either a name or not even a name; but name is sound and echo. And the things which are much valued in life are empty and rotten and trifling, and like little dogs biting one another, and little children quarrelling, laughing, and then straightway weeping. But fidelity and modesty and justice and truth are fled

Up to Olympus from the wide-spread earth.[2]

[1] Homer, *Odyssey*, iv. 690.
[2] Hesiod, *Works and Days*, 197.

What then is there which still detains thee here? If the objects of sense are easily changed and never stand still, and the organs of perception are dull and easily receive false impressions; and the poor soul itself is an exhalation from blood. But to have good repute amidst such a world as this is an empty thing. Why then dost thou not wait in tranquillity for thy end, whether it is extinction or removal to another state? And until that time comes, what is sufficient? Why, what else than to venerate the gods and bless them, and to do good to men, and to practise tolerance and self-restraint; but as to everything which is beyond the limits of the poor flesh and breath, to remember that this is neither thine nor in thy power.

34. Thou canst pass thy life in an equable flow of happiness, if thou canst go by the right way, and think and act in the right way. These two things are common both to the soul of God and to the soul of man, and to the soul of every rational being, not to be hindered by another; and to hold good to consist in the disposition to justice and the practice of it, and in this to let thy desire find its termination.

35. If this is neither my own badness, nor an effect of my own badness, and the common weal is not injured, why am I troubled about it? And what is the harm to the common weal?

36. Do not be carried along inconsiderately by the appearance of things, but give help to all according to thy ability and their fitness; and if they should have sustained loss in matters which are indifferent, do not imagine this to be a damage. For it is a bad habit. But as the old man, when he went away, asked back his foster-child's top, remembering that it was a top, so do thou in this case also.

When thou art calling out on the Rostra, hast thou forgotten, man, what these things are?—Yes; but they are objects of great concern to these people—wilt thou too then be made a fool for these things?—I was once a fortunate man, but I lost it, I know not how.—But fortunate means that a man has assigned to himself a good fortune: and a good fortune is good disposition of the soul, good emotions, good actions.

· BOOK SIX ·

THE substance of the universe is obedient and compliant; and the reason which governs it has in itself no cause for doing evil, for it has no malice, nor does it do evil to anything, nor is anything harmed by it. But all things are made and perfected according to this reason.

2. Let it make no difference to thee whether thou art cold or warm, if thou art doing thy duty; and whether thou art drowsy or satisfied with sleep; and whether ill-spoken of or praised; and whether dying or doing something else. For it is one of the acts of life, this act by which we die: it is sufficient then in this act also to do well what we have in hand.

3. Look within. Let neither the peculiar quality of anything nor its value escape thee.

4. All existing things soon change, and they will either be reduced to vapour, if indeed all substance is one, or they will be dispersed.

5. The reason which governs knows what its own disposition is, and what it does, and on what material it works.

6. The best way of avenging thyself is not to become like the wrong doer.

7. Take pleasure in one thing and rest in it, in passing from one social act to another social act, thinking of God.

8. The ruling principle is that which rouses and turns itself, and while it makes itself such as it is and such as it wills to be, it also makes everything which happens appear to itself to be such as it wills.

9. In conformity to the nature of the universe every single thing is accomplished, for certainly it is not in conformity to any other nature that each thing is accomplished, either a nature which externally comprehends this, or a nature which is comprehended within this nature, or a nature external and independent of this.

10. The universe is either a confusion, and a mutual involution of things, and a dispersion; or it is unity and order and providence. If then it is the former, why do I desire to tarry in a fortuitous combination of things and

such a disorder? And why do I care about anything else than how I shall at last become earth? And why am I disturbed, for the dispersion of my elements will happen whatever I do. But if the other supposition is true, I venerate, and I am firm, and I trust in him who governs.

11. When thou hast been compelled by circumstances to be disturbed in a manner, quickly return to thyself and do not continue out of tune longer than the compulsion lasts; for thou wilt have more mastery over the harmony by continually recurring to it.

12. If thou hadst a step-mother and a mother at the same time, thou wouldst be dutiful to thy step-mother, but still thou wouldst constantly return to thy mother. Let the court and philosophy now be to thee step-mother and mother: return to philosophy frequently and repose in her, through whom what thou meetest with in the court appears to thee tolerable, and thou appearest tolerable in the court.

13. When we have meat before us and such eatables, we receive the impression, that this is the dead body of a fish, and this is the dead body of a bird or of a pig; and again, that this Falernian is only a little grape juice, and this purple robe some sheep's wool dyed with the blood of a shell-fish: such then are these impressions, and they reach the things themselves and penetrate them, and so we see what kind of things they are. Just in the same way ought we to act all through life, and where there are things which appear most worthy of our approbation, we ought to lay them bare and look at their worthlessness and strip them of all the words by which they are exalted. For outward show is a wonderful perverter of the reason, and when thou art most sure that thou art employed about things worth thy pains, it is then that it cheats thee most. Consider then what Crates says of Xenocrates himself.

14. Most of the things which the multitude admire are referred to objects of the most general kind, those which are held together by co-

hesion or natural organization, such as stones, wood, fig-trees, vines, olives. But those which are admired by men who are a little more reasonable are referred to the things which are held together by a living principle, as flocks, herds. Those which are admired by men who are still more instructed are the things which are held together by a rational soul, not however a universal soul, but rational so far as it is a soul skilled in some art, or expert in some other way, or simply rational so far as it possesses a number of slaves. But he who values a rational soul, a soul universal and fitted for political life, regards nothing else except this; and above all things he keeps his soul in a condition and in an activity conformable to reason and social life, and he co-operates to this end with those who are of the same kind as himself.

15. Some things are hurrying into existence, and others are hurrying out of it; and of that which is coming into existence part is already extinguished. Motions and changes are continually renewing the world, just as the uninterrupted course of time is always renewing the infinite duration of ages. In this flowing stream then, on which there is no abiding, what is there of the things which hurry by on which a man would set a high price? It would be just as if a man should fall in love with one of the sparrows which fly by, but it has already passed out of sight. Something of this kind is the very life of every man, like the exhalation of the blood and the respiration of the air. For such as it is to have once drawn in the air and to have given it back, which we do every moment, just the same is it with the whole respiratory power, which thou didst receive at thy birth yesterday and the day before, to give it back to the element from which thou didst first draw it.

16. Neither is transpiration, as in plants, a thing to be valued, nor respiration, as in domesticated animals and wild beasts, nor the receiving of impressions by the appearances of things, nor being moved by desires as puppets by strings, nor assembling in herds, nor being nourished by food; for this is just like the act of separating and parting with the useless part of our food. What then is worth being valued? To be received with clapping of hands? No.

Neither must we value the clapping of tongues, for the praise which comes from the many is a clapping of tongues. Suppose then that thou hast given up this worthless thing called fame, what remains that is worth valuing? This in my opinion, to move thyself and to restrain thyself in conformity to thy proper constitution, to which end both all employments and arts lead. For every art aims at this, that the thing which has been made should be adapted to the work for which it has been made; and both the vine-planter who looks after the vine, and the horse-breaker, and he who trains the dog, seek this end. But the education and the teaching of youth aim at something. In this then is the value of the education and the teaching. And if this is well, thou wilt not seek anything else. Wilt thou not cease to value many other things too? Then thou wilt be neither free, nor sufficient for thy own happiness, nor without passion. For of necessity thou must be envious, jealous, and suspicious of those who can take away those things, and plot against those who have that which is valued by thee. Of necessity a man must be altogether in a state of perturbation who wants any of these things; and besides, he must often find fault with the gods. But to reverence and honour thy own mind will make thee content with thyself, and in harmony with society, and in agreement with the gods, that is, praising all that they give and have ordered.

17. Above, below, all around are the movements of the elements. But the motion of virtue is in none of these: it is something more divine, and advancing by a way hardly observed it goes happily on its road.

18. How strangely men act. They will not praise those who are living at the same time and living with themselves; but to be themselves praised by posterity, by those whom they have never seen or ever will see, this they set much value on. But this is very much the same as if thou shouldst be grieved because those who have lived before thee did not praise thee.

19. If a thing is difficult to be accomplished by thyself, do not think that it is impossible for man: but if anything is possible for man and conformable to his nature, think that this can be attained by thyself too.

20. In the gymnastic exercises suppose that a man has torn thee with his nails, and by dashing against thy head has inflicted a wound. Well, we neither show any signs of vexation, nor are we offended, nor do we suspect him afterwards as a treacherous fellow; and yet we are on our guard against him, not however as an enemy, nor yet with suspicion, but we quietly get out of his way. Something like this let thy behaviour be in all the other parts of life; let us overlook many things in those who are like antagonists in the gymnasium. For it is in our power, as I said, to get out of the way, and to have no suspicion nor hatred.

21. If any man is able to convince me and show me that I do not think or act right, I will gladly change; for I seek the truth by which no man was ever injured. But he is injured who abides in his error and ignorance.

22. I do my duty: other things trouble me not; for they are either things without life, or things without reason, or things that have rambled and know not the way.

23. As to the animals which have no reason and generally all things and objects, do thou, since thou hast reason and they have none, make use of them with a generous and liberal spirit. But towards human beings, as they have reason, behave in a social spirit. And on all occasions call on the gods, and do not perplex thyself about the length of time in which thou shalt do this; for even three hours so spent are sufficient.

24. Alexander the Macedonian and his groom by death were brought to the same state; for either they were received among the same seminal principles of the universe, or they were alike dispersed among the atoms.

25. Consider how many things in the same indivisible time take place in each of us, things which concern the body and things which concern the soul: and so thou wilt not wonder if many more things, or rather all things which come into existence in that which is the one and all, which we call Cosmos, exist in it at the same time.

26. If any man should propose to thee the question, how the name Antoninus is written, wouldst thou with a straining of the voice utter each letter? What then if they grow angry, wilt thou be angry too? Wilt thou not go on with composure and number every letter? Just so then in this life also remember that every duty is made up of certain parts. These it is thy duty to observe and without being disturbed or showing anger towards those who are angry with thee to go on thy way and finish that which is set before thee.

27. How cruel it is not to allow men to strive after the things which appear to them to be suitable to their nature and profitable! And yet in a manner thou dost not allow them to do this, when thou art vexed because they do wrong. For they are certainly moved towards things because they suppose them to be suitable to their nature and profitable to them.—But it is not so.—Teach them then, and show them without being angry.

28. Death is a cessation of the impressions through the senses, and of the pulling of the strings which move the appetites, and of the discursive movements of the thoughts, and of the service to the flesh.

29. It is a shame for the soul to be first to give way in this life, when thy body does not give way.

30. Take care that thou art not made into a Cæsar, that thou art not dyed with this dye; for such things happen. Keep thyself then simple, good, pure, serious, free from affectation, a friend of justice, a worshipper of the gods, kind, affectionate, strenuous in all proper acts. Strive to continue to be such as philosophy wished to make thee. Reverence the gods, and help men. Short is life. There is only one fruit of this terrene life, a pious disposition and social acts. Do everything as a disciple of Antoninus. Remember his constancy in every act which was conformable to reason, and his evenness in all things, and his piety, and the serenity of his countenance, and his sweetness, and his disregard of empty fame, and his efforts to understand things; and how he would never let anything pass without having first most carefully examined it and clearly understood it; and how he bore with those who blamed him unjustly without blaming them in return; how he did nothing in a hurry; and how he listened not to calumnies, and how exact an examiner of manners and actions he was; and not given to reproach people, nor tim-

id, nor suspicious, nor a sophist; and with how little he was satisfied, such as lodging, bed, dress, food, servants; and how laborious and patient; and how he was able on account of his sparing diet to hold out to the evening, not even requiring to relieve himself by any evacuations except at the usual hour; and his firmness and uniformity in his friendships; and how he tolerated freedom of speech in those who opposed his opinions; and the pleasure that he had when any man showed him anything better; and how religious he was without superstition. Imitate all this that thou mayest have as good a conscience, when thy last hour comes, as he had.

31. Return to thy sober senses and call thyself back; and when thou hast roused thyself from sleep and hast perceived that they were only dreams which troubled thee, now in thy waking hours look at these (the things about thee) as thou didst look at those (the dreams).

32. I consist of a little body and a soul. Now to this little body all things are indifferent, for it is not able to perceive differences. But to the understanding those things only are indifferent, which are not the works of its own activity. But whatever things are the works of its own activity, all these are in its power. And of these however only those which are done with reference to the present; for as to the future and the past activities of the mind, even these are for the present indifferent.

33. Neither the labour which the hand does nor that of the foot is contrary to nature, so long as the foot does the foot's work and the hand the hand's. So then neither to a man as a man is his labour contrary to nature, so long as it does the things of a man. But if the labour is not contrary to his nature, neither is it an evil to him.

34. How many pleasures have been enjoyed by robbers, patricides, tyrants.

35. Dost thou not see how the handicraftsmen accommodate themselves up to a certain point to those who are not skilled in their craft—nevertheless they cling to the reason (the principles) of their art and do not endure to depart from it? Is it not strange if the architect and the physician shall have more respect to the reason (the principles) of their own arts than man to his own reason, which is common to him and the gods?

36. Asia, Europe are corners of the universe: all the sea a drop in the universe; Athos a little clod of the universe: all the present time is a point in eternity. All things are little, changeable, perishable. All things come from thence, from that universal ruling power either directly proceeding or by way of sequence. And accordingly the lion's gaping jaws, and that which is poisonous, and every harmful thing, as a thorn, as mud, are after-products of the grand and beautiful. Do not then imagine that they are of another kind from that which thou dost venerate, but form a just opinion of the source of all.

37. He who has seen present things has seen all, both everything which has taken place from all eternity and everything which will be for time without end; for all things are of one kin and of one form.

38. Frequently consider the connexion of all things in the universe and their relation to one another. For in a manner all things are implicated with one another, and all in this way are friendly to one another; for one thing comes in order after another, and this is by virtue of the active movement and mutual conspiration and the unity of the substance.

39. Adapt thyself to the things with which thy lot has been cast: and the men among whom thou hast received thy portion, love them, but do it truly, sincerely.

40. Every instrument, tool, vessel, if it does that for which it has been made, is well, and yet he who made it is not there. But in the things which are held together by nature there is within and there abides in them the power which made them; wherefore the more is it fit to reverence this power, and to think, that, if thou dost live and act according to its will, everything in thee is in conformity to intelligence. And thus also in the universe the things which belong to it are in conformity to intelligence.

41. Whatever of the things which are not within thy power thou shalt suppose to be good for thee or evil, it must of necessity be that, if such a bad thing befall thee or the loss of such a good thing, thou wilt blame the gods, and hate men too, those who are the cause of

the misfortune or the loss, or those who are suspected of being likely to be the cause; and indeed we do much injustice, because we make a difference between these things. But if we judge only those things which are in our power to be good or bad, there remains no reason either for finding fault with God or standing in a hostile attitude to man.

42. We are all working together to one end, some with knowledge and design, and others without knowing what they do; as men also when they are asleep, of whom it is Heraclitus, I think, who says that they are labourers and co-operators in the things which take place in the universe. But men co-operate after different fashions: and even those co-operate abundantly, who find fault with what happens and those who try to oppose it and to hinder it; for the universe had need even of such men as these. It remains then for thee to understand among what kind of workmen thou placest thyself; for he who rules all things will certainly make a right use of thee, and he will receive thee among some part of the co-operators and of those whose labours conduce to one end. But be not thou such a part as the mean and ridiculous verse in the play, which Chrysippus speaks of.[1]

43. Does the sun undertake to do the work of the rain, or Aesculapius the work of the Fruit-bearer (the earth)? And how is it with respect to each of the stars, are they not different and yet they work together to the same end?

44. If the gods have determined about me and about the things which must happen to me, they have determined well, for it is not easy even to imagine a deity without forethought; and as to doing me harm, why should they have any desire towards that? For what advantage would result to them from this or to the whole, which is the special object of their providence? But if they have not determined about me individually, they have certainly determined about the whole at least, and the things which happen by way of sequence in this general arrangement I ought to accept with pleasure and to be content with them. But if they determine about nothing—which it is wicked to believe, or if we do believe it, let us neither sacrifice nor pray nor swear by them nor do anything else which we do as if the gods were present and lived with us—but if however the gods determine about none of the things which concern us, I am able to determine about myself, and I can inquire about that which is useful; and that is useful to every man which is conformable to his own constitution and nature. But my nature is rational and social; and my city and country, so far as I am Antoninus, is Rome, but so far as I am a man, it is the world. The things then which are useful to these cities are alone useful to me.

45. Whatever happens to every man, this is for the interest of the universal: this might be sufficient. But further thou wilt observe this also as a general truth, if thou dost observe, that whatever is profitable to any man is profitable also to other men. But let the word profitable be taken here in the common sense as said of things of the middle kind, neither good nor bad.

46. As it happens to thee in the amphitheatre and such places, that the continual sight of the same things and the uniformity make the spectacle wearisome, so it is in the whole of life; for all things above, below, are the same and from the same. How long then?

47. Think continually that all kinds of men and of all kinds of pursuits and of all nations are dead, so that thy thoughts come down even to Philistion and Phoebus and Origanion. Now turn thy thoughts to the other kinds of men. To that place then we must remove, where there are so many great orators, and so many noble philosophers, Heraclitus, Pythagoras, Socrates; so many heroes of former days, and so many generals after them, and tyrants; besides these, Eudoxus, Hipparchus, Archimedes, and other men of acute natural talents, great minds, lovers of labour, versatile, confident, mockers even of the perishable and ephemeral life of man, as Menippus and such as are like him. As to all these consider that they have long been in the dust. What harm then is this to them; and what to those whose names are altogether unknown? One thing here is worth a great deal, to pass thy life in truth and justice, with a benevolent disposition even to liars and unjust men.

[1] Cf. Plutarch, *adversus Stoicos*, 13-14.

48. When thou wishest to delight thyself, think of the virtues of those who live with thee; for instance, the activity of one, and the modesty of another, and the liberality of a third, and some other good quality of a fourth. For nothing delights so much as the examples of the virtues, when they are exhibited in the morals of those who live with us and present themselves in abundance, as far as is possible. Wherefore we must keep them before us.

49. Thou art not dissatisfied, I suppose, because thou weighest only so many litrae and not three hundred. Be not dissatisfied then that thou must live only so many years and not more; for as thou art satisfied with the amount of substance which has been assigned to thee, so be content with the time.

50. Let us try to persuade them (men). But act even against their will, when the principles of justice lead that way. If however any man by using force stands in thy way, betake thyself to contentment and tranquillity, and at the same time employ the hindrance towards the exercise of some other virtue; and remember that thy attempt was with a reservation, that thou didst not desire to do impossibilities. What then didst thou desire?—Some such effort as this.—But thou attainest thy object, if the things to which thou wast moved are accomplished.

51. He who loves fame considers another man's activity to be his own good; and he who loves pleasure, his own sensations; but he who has understanding, considers his own acts to be his own good.

52. It is in our power to have no opinion about a thing, and not to be disturbed in our soul; for things themselves have no natural power to form our judgements.

53. Accustom thyself to attend carefully to what is said by another, and as much as it is possible, be in the speaker's mind.

54. That which is not good for the swarm, neither is it good for the bee.

55. If sailors abused the helmsman or the sick the doctor, would they listen to anybody else; or how could the helmsman secure the safety of those in the ship or the doctor the health of those whom he attends?

56. How many together with whom I came into the world are already gone out of it.

57. To the jaundiced honey tastes bitter, and to those bitten by mad dogs water causes fear; and to little children the ball is a fine thing. Why then am I angry? Dost thou think that a false opinion has less power than the bile in the jaundiced or the poison in him who is bitten by a mad dog?

58. No man will hinder thee from living according to the reason of thy own nature: nothing will happen to thee contrary to the reason of the universal nature.

59. What kind of people are those whom men wish to please, and for what objects, and by what kind of acts? How soon will time cover all things, and how many it has covered already.

· BOOK SEVEN ·

WHAT is badness? It is that which thou hast often seen. And on the occasion of everything which happens keep this in mind, that it is that which thou hast often seen. Everywhere up and down thou wilt find the same things, with which the old histories are filled, those of the middle ages and those of our own day; with which cities and houses are filled now. There is nothing new: all things are both familiar and short-lived.

2. How can our principles become dead, unless the impressions (thoughts) which correspond to them are extinguished? But it is in thy power continuously to fan these thoughts into a flame. I can have that opinion about anything, which I ought to have. If I can, why am I disturbed? The things which are external to my mind have no relation at all to my mind.—Let this be the state of thy affects, and thou standest erect. To recover thy life is in thy power. Look at things again as thou didst use to look at them; for in this consists the recovery of thy life.

3. The idle business of show, plays on the

stage, flocks of sheep, herds, exercises with spears, a bone cast to little dogs, a bit of bread into fish-ponds, labourings of ants and bur-den-carrying, runnings about of frightened little mice, puppets pulled by strings—all alike. It is thy duty then in the midst of such things to show good humour and not a proud air; to understand however that every man is worth just so much as the things are worth about which he busies himself.

4. In discourse thou must attend to what is said, and in every movement thou must ob-serve what is doing. And in the one thou shouldst see immediately to what end it refers, but in the other watch carefully what is the thing signified.

5. Is my understanding sufficient for this or not? If it is sufficient, I use it for the work as an instrument given by the universal nature. But if it is not sufficient, then either I retire from the work and give way to him who is able to do it better, unless there be some reason why I ought not to do so; or I do it as well as I can, taking to help me the man who with the aid of my ruling principle can do what is now fit and useful for the general good. For what-soever either by myself or with another I can do, ought to be directed to this only, to that which is useful and well suited to society.

6. How many after being celebrated by fame have been given up to oblivion; and how many who have celebrated the fame of others have long been dead.

7. Be not ashamed to be helped; for it is thy business to do thy duty like a soldier in the as-sault on a town. How then, if being lame thou canst not mount up on the battlements alone, but with the help of another it is possible?

8. Let not future things disturb thee, for thou wilt come to them, if it shall be necessary, having with thee the same reason which now thou usest for present things.

9. All things are implicated with one an-other, and the bond is holy; and there is hard-ly anything unconnected with any other thing. For things have been co-ordinated, and they combine to form the same universe (order). For there is one universe made up of all things, and one God who pervades all things, and one substance, and one law, one common reason in all intelligent animals, and one truth; if indeed

there is also one perfection for all animals which are of the same stock and participate in the same reason.

10. Everything material soon disappears in the substance of the whole; and everything formal (causal) is very soon taken back into the universal reason; and the memory of every-thing is very soon overwhelmed in time.

11. To the rational animal the same act is according to nature and according to reason.

12. Be thou erect, or be made erect.

13. Just as it is with the members in those bodies which are united in one, so it is with rational beings which exist separate, for they have been constituted for one co-operation. And the perception of this will be more ap-parent to thee, if thou often sayest to thyself that I am a member (μέλος) of the system of rational beings. But if (using the letter *r*) thou sayest that thou art a part (μέρος) thou dost not yet love men from thy heart; beneficence does not yet delight thee for its own sake; thou still doest it barely as a thing of propriety, and not yet as doing good to thyself.

14. Let there fall externally what will on the parts which can feel the effects of this fall. For those parts which have felt will complain, if they choose. But I, unless I think that what has happened is an evil, am not injured. And it is in my power not to think so.

15. Whatever any one does or says, I must be good, just as if the gold, or the emerald, or the purple were always saying this, Whatever any one does or says, I must be emerald and keep my colour.

16. The ruling faculty does not disturb it-self; I mean, does not frighten itself or cause itself pain. But if any one else can frighten or pain it, let him do so. For the faculty itself will not by its own opinion turn itself into such ways. Let the body itself take care, if it can, that is suffer nothing, and let it speak, if it suffers. But the soul itself, that which is sub-ject to fear, to pain, which has completely the power of forming an opinion about these things, will suffer nothing, for it will never deviate into such a judgement. The leading principle in itself wants nothing, unless it makes a want for itself; and therefore it is both free from perturbation and unimpeded, if it does not disturb and impede itself.

17. Eudaemonia (happiness) is a good daemon, or a good thing. What then art thou doing here, O imagination? Go away, I entreat thee by the gods, as thou didst come, for I want thee not. But thou art come according to thy old fashion. I am not angry with thee: only go away.

18. Is any man afraid of change? Why what can take place without change? What then is more pleasing or more suitable to the universal nature? And canst thou take a bath unless the wood undergoes a change? And canst thou be nourished, unless the food undergoes a change? And can anything else that is useful be accomplished without change? Dost thou not see then that for thyself also to change is just the same, and equally necessary for the universal nature?

19. Through the universal substance as through a furious torrent all bodies are carried, being by their nature united with and co-operating with the whole, as the parts of our body with one another. How many a Chrysippus, how many a Socrates, how many an Epictetus has time already swallowed up? And let the same thought occur to thee with reference to every man and thing.

20. One thing only troubles me, lest I should do something which the constitution of man does not allow, or in the way which it does not allow, or what it does not allow now.

21. Near is thy forgetfulness of all things; and near the forgetfulness of thee by all.

22. It is peculiar to man to love even those who do wrong. And this happens, if when they do wrong it occurs to thee that they are kinsmen, and that they do wrong through ignorance and unintentionally, and that soon both of you will die; and above all, that the wrong-doer has done thee no harm, for he has not made thy ruling faculty worse than it was before.

23. The universal nature out of the universal substance, as if it were wax, now moulds a horse, and when it has broken this up, it uses the material for a tree, then for a man, then for something else; and each of these things subsists for a very short time. But it is no hardship for the vessel to be broken up, just as there was none in its being fastened together.

24. A scowling look is altogether unnatural; when it is often assumed, the result is that all comeliness dies away, and at last is so completely extinguished that it cannot be again lighted up at all. Try to conclude from this very fact that it is contrary to reason. For if even the perception of doing wrong shall depart, what reason is there for living any longer?

25. Nature which governs the whole will soon change all things which thou seest, and out of their substance will make other things, and again other things from the substance of them, in order that the world may be ever new.

26. When a man has done thee any wrong, immediately consider with what opinion about good or evil he has done wrong. For when thou hast seen this, thou wilt pity him, and wilt neither wonder nor be angry. For either thou thyself thinkest the same thing to be good that he does or another thing of the same kind. It is thy duty then to pardon him. But if thou dost not think such things to be good or evil, thou wilt more readily be well disposed to him who is in error.

27. Think not so much of what thou hast not as of what thou hast: but of the things which thou hast select the best, and then reflect how eagerly they would have been sought, if thou hadst them not. At the same time however take care that thou dost not through being so pleased with them accustom thyself to overvalue them, so as to be disturbed if ever thou shouldst not have them.

28. Retire into thyself. The rational principle which rules has this nature, that it is content with itself when it does what is just, and so secures tranquillity.

29. Wipe out the imagination. Stop the pulling of the strings. Confine thyself to the present. Understand well what happens either to thee or to another. Divide and distribute every object into the causal (formal) and the material. Think of thy last hour. Let the wrong which is done by a man stay there where the wrong was done.

30. Direct thy attention to what is said. Let thy understanding enter into the things that are doing and the things which do them.

31. Adorn thyself with simplicity and modesty and with indifference towards the things which lie between virtue and vice. Love mankind. Follow God. The poet says that Law

rules all.—And it is enough to remember that Law rules all.

32. About death: Whether it is a dispersion, or a resolution into atoms, or annihilation, it is either extinction or change.

33. About pain: The pain which is intolerable carries us off; but that which lasts a long time is tolerable; and the mind maintains its own tranquillity by retiring into itself, and the ruling faculty is not made worse. But the parts which are harmed by pain, let them, if they can, give their opinion about it.

34. About fame: Look at the minds of those who seek fame, observe what they are, and what kind of things they avoid, and what kind of things they pursue. And consider that as the heaps of sand piled on one another hide the former sands, so in life the events which go before are soon covered by those which come after.

35. From Plato: The man who has an elevated mind and takes a view of all time and of all substance, dost thou suppose it possible for him to think that human life is anything great? it is not possible, he said.—Such a man then will think that death also is no evil.—Certainly not.[1]

36. From Antisthenes: It is royal to do good and to be abused.

37. It is a base thing for the countenance to be obedient and to regulate and compose itself as the mind commands, and for the mind not to be regulated and composed by itself.

38. It is not right to vex ourselves at things,
For they care nought about it.[2]

39. To the immortal gods and us give joy.

40. Life must be reaped like the ripe ears of corn:
One man is born; another dies.[2]

41. If gods care not for me and for my children,
There is a reason for it.[2]

42. For the good is with me, and the just.[2]

43. No joining others in their wailing, no violent emotion.

44. From Plato: But I would make this man a sufficient answer, which is this: Thou sayest not well, if thou thinkest that a man who is good for anything at all ought to compute the hazard of life or death, and should not rather look to this only in all that he does, whether he is doing what is just or unjust, and the works of a good or a bad man.[3]

45. For thus it is, men of Athens, in truth: wherever a man has placed himself thinking it the best place for him, or has been placed by a commander, there in my opinion he ought to stay and to abide the hazard, taking nothing into the reckoning, either death or anything else, before the baseness of deserting his post.[4]

46. But, my good friend, reflect whether that which is noble and good is not something different from saving and being saved; for as to a man living such or such a time, at least one who is really a man, consider if this is not a thing to be dismissed from the thoughts: and there must be no love of life: but as to these matters a man must intrust them to the deity and believe what the women say, that no man can escape his destiny, the next inquiry being how he may best live the time that he has to live.[5]

47. Look round at the courses of the stars, as if thou wert going along with them; and constantly consider the changes of the elements into one another; for such thoughts purge away the filth of the terrene life.

48. This is a fine saying of Plato: That he who is discoursing about men should look also at earthly things as if he viewed them from some higher place; should look at them in their assemblies, armies, agricultural labours, marriages, treaties, births, deaths, noise of the courts of justice, desert places, various nations of barbarians, feasts, lamentations, markets, a mixture of all things and an orderly combination of contraries.

49. Consider the past; such great changes of political supremacies. Thou mayest foresee also the things which will be. For they will certainly be of like form, and it is not possible that they should deviate from the order of the things which take place now: accordingly to have contemplated human life for forty years is the same as to have contemplated it for ten thousand years. For what more wilt thou see?

---

[1] *Republic*, 486.
[2] These are fragments of Euripidean plays.
[3] *Apology*, 28.
[4] *Apology*, 28.
[5] Plato, *Gorgias*, 512.

50. That which has grown from the earth to
the earth,
But that which has sprung from heavenly seed,
Back to the heavenly realms returns.[1]

This is either a dissolution of the mutual involution of the atoms, or a similar dispersion
of the unsentient elements.

51. With food and drinks and cunning mag-
ic arts
Turning the channel's course to 'scape
from death.[2]
The breeze which heaven has sent
We must endure, and toil without complaining.

52. Another may be more expert in casting
his opponent; but he is not more social, nor
more modest, nor better disciplined to meet
all that happens, nor more considerate with respect to the faults of his neighbours.

53. Where any work can be done conformably to the reason which is common to gods
and men, there we have nothing to fear: for
where we are able to get profit by means of the
activity which is successful and proceeds according to our constitution, there no harm is to
be suspected.

54. Everywhere and at all times it is in thy
power piously to acquiesce in thy present condition, and to behave justly to those who are
about thee, and to exert thy skill upon thy
present thoughts, that nothing shall steal into
them without being well examined.

55. Do not look around thee to discover
other men's ruling principles, but look straight
to this, to what nature leads thee, both the universal nature through the things which happen to thee, and thy own nature through the
acts which must be done by thee. But every being ought to do that which is according to its
constitution; and all other things have been
constituted for the sake of rational beings, just
as among irrational things the inferior for the
sake of the superior, but the rational for the
sake of one another.

The prime principle then in man's constitution is the social. And the second is not to
yield to the persuasions of the body, for it is
the peculiar office of the rational and intel-

ligent motion to circumscribe itself, and never
to be overpowered either by the motion of the
senses or of the appetites, for both are animal;
but the intelligent motion claims superiority
and does not permit itself to be overpowered
by the others. And with good reason, for it is
formed by nature to use all of them. The
third thing in the rational constitution is freedom from error and from deception. Let then
the ruling principle holding fast to these
things go straight on, and it has what is its
own.

56. Consider thyself to be dead, and to have
completed thy life up to the present time; and
live according to nature the remainder which
is allowed thee.

57. Love that only which happens to thee
and is spun with the thread of thy destiny.
For what is more suitable?

58. In everything which happens keep before thy eyes those to whom the same things
happened, and how they were vexed, and
treated them as strange things, and found
fault with them: and now where are they?
Nowhere. Why then dost thou too choose to
act in the same way? And why dost thou not
leave these agitations which are foreign to
nature, to those who cause them and those
who are moved by them? And why art thou
not altogether intent upon the right way of
making use of the things which happen to
thee? For then thou wilt use them well, and
they will be a material for thee to work on.
Only attend to thyself, and resolve to be a good
man in every act which thou doest: and remember . . .

59. Look within. Within is the fountain of
good, and it will ever bubble up, if thou wilt
ever dig.

60. The body ought to be compact, and to
show no irregularity either in motion or attitude. For what the mind shows in the face by
maintaining in it the expression of intelligence
and propriety, that ought to be required also
in the whole body. But all of these things
should be observed without affectation.

61. The art of life is more like the wrestler's
art than the dancer's, in respect of this, that it
should stand ready and firm to meet onsets
which are sudden and unexpected.

62. Constantly observe who those are whose

[1] Euripides, fragment.
[2] Euripides, *Suppliants*, 1110.

approbation thou wishest to have, and what ruling principles they possess. For then thou wilt neither blame those who offend involuntarily, nor wilt thou want their approbation, if thou lookest to the sources of their opinions and appetites.

63. Every soul, the philosopher says, is involuntarily deprived of truth; consequently in the same way it is deprived of justice and temperance and benevolence and everything of the kind. It is most necessary to bear this constantly in mind, for thus thou wilt be more gentle towards all.

64. In every pain let this thought be present, that there is no dishonour in it, nor does it make the governing intelligence worse, for it does not damage the intelligence either so far as the intelligence is rational or so far as it is social. Indeed in the case of most pains let this remark of Epicurus aid thee, that pain is neither intolerable nor everlasting, if thou bearest in mind that it has its limits, and if thou addest nothing to it in imagination: and remember this too, that we do not perceive that many things which are disagreeable to us are the same as pain, such as excessive drowsiness, and the being scorched by heat, and the having no appetite. When then thou art discontented about any of these things, say to thyself, that thou art yielding to pain.

65. Take care not to feel towards the inhuman, as they feel towards men.

66. How do we know if Telauges was not superior in character to Socrates? For it is not enough that Socrates died a more noble death, and disputed more skilfully with the sophists, and passed the night in the cold with more endurance, and that when he was bid to arrest Leon of Salamis, he considered it more noble to refuse, and that he walked in a swaggering way in the streets[1]—though as to this fact one may have great doubts if it was true. But we ought to inquire, what kind of a soul it was that Socrates possessed, and if he was able to be content with being just towards men and pious towards the gods, neither idly vexed on account of men's villainy, nor yet making himself a slave to any man's ignorance, nor receiving as strange anything that fell to his

[1] Cf. Aristophanes, *Clouds*, 363.

share out of the universal, nor enduring it as intolerable, nor allowing his understanding to sympathize with the affects of the miserable flesh.

67. Nature has not so mingled the intelligence with the composition of the body, as not to have allowed thee the power of circumscribing thyself and of bringing under subjection to thyself all that is thy own; for it is very possible to be a divine man and to be recognised as such by no one. Always bear this in mind; and another thing too, that very little indeed is necessary for living a happy life. And because thou hast despaired of becoming a dialectician and skilled in the knowledge of nature, do not for this reason renounce the hope of being both free and modest and social and obedient to God.

68. It is in thy power to live free from all compulsion in the greatest tranquillity of mind, even if all the world cry out against thee as much as they choose, and even if wild beasts tear in pieces the members of this kneaded matter which has grown around thee. For what hinders the mind in the midst of all this from maintaining itself in tranquillity and in a just judgement of all surrounding things and in a ready use of the objects which are presented to it, so that the judgement may say to the thing which falls under its observation: This thou art in substance (reality), though in men's opinion thou mayest appear to be of a different kind; and the use shall say to that which falls under the hand: Thou art the thing that I was seeking; for to me that which presents itself is always a material for virtue both rational and political, and in a word, for the exercise of art, which belongs to man or God. For everything which happens has a relationship either to God or man, and is neither new nor difficult to handle, but usual and apt matter to work on.

69. The perfection of moral character consists in this, in passing every day as the last, and in being neither violently excited nor torpid nor playing the hypocrite.

70. The gods who are immortal are not vexed because during so long a time they must tolerate continually men such as they are and so many of them bad; and besides this, they also take care of them in all ways. But thou,

who art destined to end so soon, art thou wearied of enduring the bad, and this too when thou art one of them?

71. It is a ridiculous thing for a man not to fly from his own badness, which is indeed possible, but to fly from other men's badness, which is impossible.

72. Whatever the rational and political (social) faculty finds to be neither intelligent nor social, it properly judges to be inferior to itself.

73. When thou hast done a good act and another has received it, why dost thou look for a third thing besides these, as fools do, either to have the reputation of having done a good act or to obtain a return?

74. No man is tired of receiving what is useful. But it is useful to act according to nature. Do not then be tired of receiving what is useful by doing it to others.

75. The nature of the All moved to make the universe. But now either everything that takes place comes by way of consequence or continuity; or even the chief things towards which the ruling power of the universe directs its own movement are governed by no rational principle. If this is remembered it will make thee more tranquil in many things.

· BOOK EIGHT ·

THIS reflection also tends to the removal of the desire of empty fame, that it is no longer in thy power to have lived the whole of thy life, or at least thy life from thy youth upwards, like a philosopher; but both to many others and to thyself it is plain that thou art far from philosophy. Thou hast fallen into disorder then, so that it is no longer easy for thee to get the reputation of a philosopher; and thy plan of life also opposes it. If then thou hast truly seen where the matter lies, throw away the thought, How thou shalt seem to others, and be content if thou shalt live the rest of thy life in such wise as thy nature wills. Observe then what it wills, and let nothing else distract thee; for thou hast had experience of many wanderings without having found happiness anywhere, not in syllogisms, nor in wealth, nor in reputation, nor in enjoyment, nor anywhere. Where is it then? In doing what man's nature requires. How then shall a man do this? If he has principles from which come his affects and his acts. What principles? Those which relate to good and bad: the belief that there is nothing good for man, which does not make him just, temperate, manly, free; and that there is nothing bad, which does not do the contrary to what has been mentioned.

2. On the occasion of every act ask thyself, How is this with respect to me? Shall I repent of it? A little time and I am dead, and all is gone. What more do I seek, if what I am now doing is work of an intelligent living being, and a social being, and one who is under the same law with God?

3. Alexander and Gaius[1] and Pompeius, what are they in comparison with Diogenes and Heraclitus and Socrates? For they were acquainted with things, and their causes (forms), and their matter, and the ruling principles of these men were the same. But as to the others, how many things had they to care for, and to how many things were they slaves?

4. Consider that men will do the same things nevertheless, even though thou shouldst burst.

5. This is the chief thing: Be not perturbed, for all things are according to the nature of the universal; and in a little time thou wilt be nobody and nowhere, like Hadrian and Augustus. In the next place having fixed thy eyes steadily on thy business look at it, and at the same time remembering that it is thy duty to be a good man, and what man's nature demands, do that without turning aside; and speak as it seems to thee most just, only let it be with a good disposition and with modesty and without hypocrisy.

6. The nature of the universal has this work to do, to remove to that place the things which are in this, to change them, to take them away hence, and to carry them there. All things are change, yet we need not fear anything new.

[1] I.e., Julius Cæsar.

All things are familiar to us; but the distribution of them still remains the same.

7. Every nature is contented with itself when it goes on its way well; and a rational nature goes on its way well, when in its thoughts it assents to nothing false or uncertain, and when it directs its movements to social acts only, and when it confines its desires and aversions to the things which are in its power, and when it is satisfied with everything that is assigned to it by the common nature. For of this common nature every particular nature is a part, as the nature of the leaf is a part of the nature of the plant; except that in the plant the nature of the leaf is part of a nature which has not perception or reason, and is subject to be impeded; but the nature of man is part of a nature which is not subject to impediments, and is intelligent and just, since it gives to everything in equal portions and according to its worth, times, substance, cause (form), activity, and incident. But examine, not to discover that any one thing compared with any other single thing is equal in all respects, but by taking all the parts together of one thing and comparing them with all the parts together of another.

8. Thou hast not leisure or ability to read. But thou hast leisure or ability to check arrogance: thou hast leisure to be superior to pleasure and pain: thou hast leisure to be superior to love of fame, and not to be vexed at stupid and ungrateful people, nay even to care for them.

9. Let no man any longer hear thee finding fault with the court life or with thy own.

10. Repentance is a kind of self-reproof for having neglected something useful; but that which is good must be something useful, and the perfect good man should look after it. But no such man would ever repent of having refused any sensual pleasure. Pleasure then is neither good nor useful.

11. This thing, what is it in itself, in its own constitution? What is its substance and material? And what its causal nature (or form)? And what is it doing in the world? And how long does it subsist?

12. When thou risest from sleep with reluctance, remember that it is according to thy constitution and according to human nature

to perform social acts, but sleeping is common also to irrational animals. But that which is according to each individual's nature is also more peculiarly its own, and more suitable to its nature, and indeed also more agreeable.

13. Constantly and, if it be possible, on the occasion of every impression on the soul, apply to it the principles of Physic, of Ethic, and of Dialectic.

14. Whatever man thou meetest with, immediately say to thyself: What opinions has this man about good and bad? For if with respect to pleasure and pain and the causes of each, and with respect to fame and ignominy, death and life, he has such and such opinions, it will seem nothing wonderful or strange to me, if he does such and such things; and I shall bear in mind that he is compelled to do so.

15. Remember that as it is a shame to be surprised if the fig-tree produces figs, so it is to be surprised if the world produces such and such things of which it is productive; and for the physician and the helmsman it is a shame to be surprised, if a man has a fever, or if the wind is unfavourable.

16. Remember that to change thy opinion and to follow him who corrects thy error is as consistent with freedom as it is to persist in thy error. For it is thy own, the activity which is exerted according to thy own movement and judgement, and indeed according to thy own understanding too.

17. If a thing is in thy own power, why dost thou do it? But if it is in the power of another, whom dost thou blame? The atoms (chance) or the gods? Both are foolish. Thou must blame nobody. For if thou canst, correct that which is the cause; but if thou canst not do this, correct at least the thing itself; but if thou canst not do even this, of what use is it to thee to find fault? For nothing should be done without a purpose.

18. That which has died falls not out of the universe. If it stays here, it also changes here, and is dissolved into its proper parts, which are elements of the universe and of thyself. And these too change, and they murmur not.

19. Everything exists for some end, a horse, a vine. Why dost thou wonder? Even the sun will say, I am for some purpose, and the rest

of the gods will say the same. For what purpose then art thou? to enjoy pleasure? See if common sense allows this.

20. Nature has had regard in everything no less to the end than to the beginning and the continuance, just like the man who throws up a ball. What good is it then for the ball to be thrown up, or harm for it to come down, or even to have fallen? And what good is it to the bubble while it holds together, or what harm when it is burst? The same may be said of a light also.

21. Turn it (the body) inside out, and see what kind of thing it is; and when it has grown old, what kind of thing it becomes, and when it is diseased.

Short-lived are both the praiser and the praised, and the rememberer and the remembered: and all this in a nook of this part of the world; and not even here do all agree, no, not any one with himself: and the whole earth too is a point.

22. Attend to the matter which is before thee, whether it is an opinion or an act or a word.

Thou sufferest this justly: for thou choosest rather to become good to-morrow than to be good to-day.

23. Am I doing anything? I do it with reference to the good of mankind. Does anything happen to me? I receive it and refer it to the gods, and the source of all things, from which all that happens is derived.

24. Such as bathing appears to thee—oil, sweat, dirt, filthy water, all things disgusting—so is every part of life and everything.

25. Lucilla saw Verus die, and then Lucilla died. Secunda saw Maximus die, and then Secunda died. Epitynchanus saw Diotimus die, and Epitynchanus died. Antoninus saw Faustina die, and then Antoninus died. Such is everything. Celer saw Hadrian die, and then Celer died. And those sharp-witted men, either seers or men inflated with pride, where are they? For instance the sharp-witted men, Charax and Demetrius the Platonist and Eudaemon, and any one else like them. All ephemeral, dead long ago. Some indeed have not been remembered even for a short time, and others have become the heroes of fables, and again others have disappeared even from fables. Remember this then, that this little compound, thyself, must either be dissolved, or thy poor breath must be extinguished, or be removed and placed elsewhere.

26. It is satisfaction to a man to do the proper works of a man. Now it is a proper work of a man to be benevolent to his own kind, to despise the movements of the senses, to form a just judgement of plausible appearances, and to take a survey of the nature of the universe and of the things which happen in it.

27. There are three relations between thee and other things: the one to the body which surrounds thee; the second to the divine cause from which all things come to all; and the third to those who live with thee.

28. Pain is either an evil to the body—then let the body say what it thinks of it—or to the soul; but it is in the power of the soul to maintain its own serenity and tranquillity, and not to think that pain is an evil. For every judgement and movement and desire and aversion is within, and no evil ascends so high.

29. Wipe out thy imaginations by often saying to thyself: now it is in my power to let no badness be in this soul, nor desire nor any perturbation at all; but looking at all things I see what is their nature, and I use each according to its value.—Remember this power which thou hast from nature.

30. Speak both in the senate and to every man, whoever he may be, appropriately, not with any affectation: use plain discourse.

31. Augustus' court, wife, daughter, descendants, ancestors, sister, Agrippa, kinsmen, intimates, friends, Areius, Maecenas, physicians and sacrificing priests—the whole court is dead. Then turn to the rest, not considering the death of a single man, but of a whole race, as of the Pompeii; and that which is inscribed on the tombs—The last of his race. Then consider what trouble those before them have had that they might leave a successor; and then, that of necessity some one must be the last. Again here consider the death of a whole race.

32. It is thy duty to order thy life well in every single act; and if every act does its duty, as far as is possible, be content; and no one is able to hinder thee so that each act shall not do its duty.—But something external will stand in the way.—Nothing will stand in the

way of thy acting justly and soberly and considerately.—But perhaps some other active power will be hindered.—Well, but by acquiescing in the hindrance and by being content to transfer thy efforts to that which is allowed, another opportunity of action is immediately put before thee in place of that which was hindered, and one which will adapt itself to this ordering of which we are speaking.

33. Receive wealth or prosperity without arrogance; and be ready to let it go.

34. If thou didst ever see a hand cut off, or a foot, or a head, lying anywhere apart from the rest of the body, such does a man make himself, as far as he can, who is not content with what happens, and separates himself from others, or does anything unsocial. Suppose that thou hast detached thyself from the natural unity—for thou wast made by nature a part, but now thou hast cut thyself off—yet here there is this beautiful provision, that it is in thy power again to unite thyself. God has allowed this to no other part, after it has been separated and cut asunder, to come together again. But consider the kindness by which he has distinguished man, for he has put it in his power not to be separated at all from the universal; and when he has been separated, he has allowed him to return and to be united and to resume his place as a part.

35. As the nature of the universal has given to every rational being all the other powers that it has, so we have received from it this power also. For as the universal nature converts and fixes in its predestined place everything which stands in the way and opposes it, and makes such things a part of itself, so also the rational animal is able to make every hindrance its own material, and to use it for such purposes as it may have designed.

36. Do not disturb thyself by thinking of the whole of thy life. Let not thy thoughts at once embrace all the various troubles which thou mayest expect to befall thee: but on every occasion ask thyself, What is there in this which is intolerable and past bearing? For thou wilt be ashamed to confess. In the next place remember that neither the future nor the past pains thee, but only the present. But this is reduced to a very little, if thou only circumscrib-

est it, and chidest thy mind, if it is unable to hold out against even this.

37. Does Panthea or Pergamus now sit by the tomb of Verus? Does Chaurias or Diotimus sit by the tomb of Hadrian? That would be ridiculous. Well, suppose they did sit there, would the dead be conscious of it? And if the dead were conscious, would they be pleased? And if they were pleased, would that make them immortal? Was it not in the order of destiny that these persons too should first become old women and old men and then die? What then would those do after these were dead? All this is foul smell and blood in a bag.

38. If thou canst see sharp, look and judge wisely, says the philosopher.

39. In the constitution of the rational animal I see no virtue which is opposed to justice; but I see a virtue which is opposed to love of pleasure, and that is temperance.

40. If thou takest away thy opinion about that which appears to give thee pain, thou thyself standest in perfect security.—Who is this self?—The reason.—But I am not reason.—Be it so. Let then the reason itself not trouble itself. But if any other part of thee suffers, let it have its own opinion about itself.

41. Hindrance to the perceptions of sense is an evil to the animal nature. Hindrance to the movements (desires) is equally an evil to the animal nature. And something else also is equally an impediment and an evil to the constitution of plants. So then that which is a hindrance to the intelligence is an evil to the intelligent nature. Apply all these things then to thyself. Does pain or sensuous pleasure affect thee? The senses will look to that.—Has any obstacle opposed thee in thy efforts towards an object? if indeed thou wast making this effort absolutely (unconditionally, or without any reservation), certainly this obstacle is an evil to thee considered as a rational animal. But if thou takest into consideration the usual course of things, thou hast not yet been injured nor even impeded. The things however which are proper to the understanding no other man is used to impede, for neither fire, nor iron, nor tyrant, nor abuse, touches it in any way. When it has been made a sphere, it continues a sphere.

42. It is not fit that I should give myself pain, for I have never intentionally given pain even to another.

43. Different things delight different people. But it is my delight to keep the ruling faculty sound without turning away either from any man or from any of the things which happen to men, but looking at and receiving all with welcome eyes and using everything according to its value.

44. See that thou secure this present time to thyself: for those who rather pursue posthumous fame do not consider that the men of after time will be exactly such as these whom they cannot bear now; and both are mortal. And what is it in any way to thee if these men of after time utter this or that sound, or have this or that opinion about thee?

45. Take me and cast me where thou wilt; for there I shall keep my divine part tranquil, that is, content, if it can feel and act conformably to its proper constitution. Is this change of place sufficient reason why my soul should be unhappy and worse than it was, depressed, expanded, shrinking, affrighted? And what wilt thou find which is sufficient reason for this?

46. Nothing can happen to any man which is not a human accident, nor to an ox which is not according to the nature of an ox, nor to a vine which is not according to the nature of a vine, nor to a stone which is not proper to a stone. If then there happens to each thing both what is usual and natural, why shouldst thou complain? For the common nature brings nothing which may not be borne by thee.

47. If thou art pained by any external thing, it is not this thing that disturbs thee, but thy own judgement about it. And it is in thy power to wipe out this judgement now. But if anything in thy own disposition gives thee pain, who hinders thee from correcting thy opinion? And even if thou art pained because thou art not doing some particular thing which seems to thee to be right, why dost thou not rather act than complain?—But some insuperable obstacle is in the way?—Do not be grieved then, for the cause of its not being done depends not on thee.—But it is not worth while to live, if this cannot be done.—Take thy departure then from life contentedly, just as

he dies who is in full activity, and well pleased too with the things which are obstacles.

48. Remember that the ruling faculty is invincible, when self-collected it is satisfied with itself, if it does nothing which it does not choose to do, even if it resist from mere obstinacy. What then will it be when it forms a judgement about anything aided by reason and deliberately? Therefore the mind which is free from passions is a citadel, for man has nothing more secure to which he can fly for refuge and for the future be inexpugnable. He then who has not seen this is an ignorant man; but he who has seen it and does not fly to this refuge is unhappy.

49. Say nothing more to thyself than what the first appearances report. Suppose that it has been reported to thee that a certain person speaks ill of thee. This has been reported; but that thou hast been injured, that has not been reported. I see that my child is sick. I do see; but that he is in danger, I do not see. Thus then always abide by the first appearances, and add nothing thyself from within, and then nothing happens to thee. Or rather add something, like a man who knows everything that happens in the world.

50. A cucumber is bitter.—Throw it away. —There are briars in the road.—Turn aside from them.—This is enough. Do not add, And why were such things made in the world? For thou wilt be ridiculed by a man who is acquainted with nature, as thou wouldst be ridiculed by a carpenter and shoemaker if thou didst find fault because thou seest in their workshop shavings and cuttings from the things which they make. And yet they have places into which they can throw these shavings and cuttings, and the universal nature has no external space; but the wondrous part of her art is that though she has circumscribed herself, everything within her which appears to decay and to grow old and to be useless she changes into herself, and again makes other new things from these very same, so that she requires neither substance from without nor wants a place into which she may cast that which decays. She is content then with her own space, and her own matter and her own art.

51. Neither in thy actions be sluggish nor in

thy conversation without method, nor wandering in thy thoughts, nor let there be in thy soul inward contention nor external effusion, nor in life be so busy as to have no leisure.

Suppose that men kill thee, cut thee in pieces, curse thee. What then can these things do to prevent thy mind from remaining pure, wise, sober, just? For instance, if a man should stand by a limpid pure spring, and curse it, the spring never ceases sending up potable water; and if he should cast clay into it or filth, it will speedily disperse them and wash them out, and will not be at all polluted. How then shalt thou possess a perpetual fountain and not a mere well? By forming thyself hourly to freedom conjoined with contentment, simplicity and modesty.

52. He who does not know what the world is, does not know where he is. And he who does not know for what purpose the world exists, does not know who he is, nor what the world is. But he who has failed in any one of these things could not even say for what purpose he exists himself. What then dost thou think of him who avoids or seeks the praise of those who applaud, of men who know not either where they are or who they are?

53. Dost thou wish to be praised by a man who curses himself thrice every hour? Wouldst thou wish to please a man who does not please himself? Does a man please himself who repents of nearly everything that he does?

54. No longer let thy breathing only act in concert with the air which surrounds thee, but let thy intelligence also now be in harmony with the intelligence which embraces all things. For the intelligent power is no less diffused in all parts and pervades all things for him who is willing to draw it to him than the aërial power for him who is able to respire it.

55. Generally, wickedness does no harm at all to the universe; and particularly, the wickedness of one man does no harm to another. It is only harmful to him who has it in his power to be released from it, as soon as he shall choose.

56. To my own free will the free will of my neighbour is just as indifferent as his poor breath and flesh. For though we are made especially for the sake of one another, still the ruling power of each of us has its own office, for otherwise my neighbour's wickedness would be my harm, which God has not willed in order that my unhappiness may not depend on another.

57. The sun appears to be poured down, and in all directions indeed it is diffused, yet it is not effused. For this diffusion is extension: Accordingly its rays are called Extensions [ἀκτῖνες] because they are extended [ἀπὸ τοῦ ἐκτείνεσθαι]. But one may judge what kind of a thing a ray is, if he looks at the sun's light passing through a narrow opening into a darkened room, for it is extended in a right line, and as it were is divided when it meets with any solid body which stands in the way and intercepts the air beyond; but there the light remains fixed and does not glide or fall off. Such then ought to be the out-pouring and diffusion of the understanding, and it should in no way be an effusion, but an extension, and it should make no violent or impetuous collision with the obstacles which are in its way; nor yet fall down, but be fixed and enlighten that which receives it. For a body will deprive itself of the illumination, if it does not admit it.

58. He who fears death either fears the loss of sensation or a different kind of sensation. But if thou shalt have no sensation, neither wilt thou feel any harm; and if thou shalt acquire another kind of sensation, thou wilt be a different kind of living being and thou wilt not cease to live.

59. Men exist for the sake of one another. Teach them then or bear with them.

60. In one way an arrow moves, in another way the mind. The mind indeed, both when it exercises caution and when it is employed about inquiry, moves straight onward not the less, and to its object.

61. Enter into every man's ruling faculty; and also let every other man enter into thine.

· BOOK NINE ·

He who acts unjustly acts impiously. For since the universal nature has made rational animals for the sake of one another to help one another according to their deserts, but in no way to injure one another, he who transgresses her will, is clearly guilty of impiety towards the highest divinity. And he too who lies is guilty of impiety to the same divinity; for the universal nature is the nature of things that are; and things that are have a relation to all things that come into existence. And further, this universal nature is named truth, and is the prime cause of all things that are true. He then who lies intentionally is guilty of impiety inasmuch as he acts unjustly by deceiving; and he also who lies unintentionally, inasmuch as he is at variance with the universal nature, and inasmuch as he disturbs the order by fighting against the nature of the world; for he fights against it, who is moved of himself to that which is contrary to truth, for he had received powers from nature through the neglect of which he is not able now to distinguish falsehood from truth. And indeed he who pursues pleasure as good, and avoids pain as evil, is guilty of impiety. For of necessity such a man must often find fault with the universal nature, alleging that it assigns things to the bad and the good contrary to their deserts, because frequently the bad are in the enjoyment of pleasure and possess the things which procure pleasure, but the good have pain for their share and the things which cause pain. And further, he who is afraid of pain will sometimes also be afraid of some of the things which will happen in the world, and even this is impiety. And he who pursues pleasure will not abstain from injustice, and this is plainly impiety. Now with respect to the things towards which the universal nature is equally affected—for it would not have made both, unless it was equally affected towards both—towards these they who wish to follow nature should be of the same mind with it, and equally affected. With respect to pain, then, and pleasure, or death and life, or honour and dishonour, which the universal nature employs equally, whoever is not equally affected is manifestly acting impiously. And I say that the universal nature employs them equally, instead of saying that they happen alike to those who are produced in continuous series and to those who come after them by virtue of a certain original movement of Providence, according to which it moved from a certain beginning to this ordering of things, having conceived certain principles of the things which were to be, and having determined powers productive of beings and of changes and of such like successions.

2. It would be a man's happiest lot to depart from mankind without having had any taste of lying and hypocrisy and luxury and pride. However to breathe out one's life when a man has had enough of these things is the next best voyage, as the saying is. Hast thou determined to abide with vice, and has not experience yet induced thee to fly from this pestilence? For the destruction of the understanding is a pestilence, much more indeed than any such corruption and change of this atmosphere which surrounds us. For this corruption is a pestilence of animals so far as they are animals; but the other is a pestilence of men so far as they are men.

3. Do not despise death, but be well content with it, since this too is one of those things which nature wills. For such as it is to be young and to grow old, and to increase and to reach maturity, and to have teeth and beard and grey hairs, and to beget, and to be pregnant and to bring forth, and all the other natural operations which the seasons of thy life bring, such also is dissolution. This, then, is consistent with the character of a reflecting man, to be neither careless nor impatient nor contemptuous with respect to death, but to wait for it as one of the operations of nature. As thou now waitest for the time when the child shall come out of thy wife's womb, so be ready for the time when thy soul shall fall out of this envelope. But if thou requirest also a vulgar kind of comfort which shall reach thy

heart, thou wilt be made best reconciled to death by observing the objects from which thou art going to be removed, and the morals of those with whom thy soul will no longer be mingled. For it is no way right to be offended with men, but it is thy duty to care for them and to bear with them gently; and yet to remember that thy departure will be not from men who have the same principles as thyself. For this is the only thing, if there be any, which could draw us the contrary way and attach us to life, to be permitted to live with those who have the same principles as ourselves. But now thou seest how great is the trouble arising from the discordance of those who live together, so that thou mayest say, Come quick, O death, lest perchance I, too, should forget myself.

4. He who does wrong does wrong against himself. He who acts unjustly acts unjustly to himself, because he makes himself bad.

5. He often acts unjustly who does not do a certain thing; not only he who does a certain thing.

6. Thy present opinion founded on understanding, and thy present conduct directed to social good, and thy present disposition of contentment with everything which happens— that is enough.

7. Wipe out imagination: check desire: extinguish appetite: keep the ruling faculty in its own power.

8. Among the animals which have not reason one life is distributed; but among reasonable animals one intelligent soul is distributed: just as there is one earth of all things which are of an earthy nature, and we see by one light, and breathe one air, all of us that have the faculty of vision and all that have life.

9. All things which participate in anything which is common to them all move towards that which is of the same kind with themselves. Everything which is earthy turns towards the earth, everything which is liquid flows together, and everything which is of an aërial kind does the same, so that they require something to keep them asunder, and the application of force. Fire indeed moves upwards on account of the elemental fire, but it is so ready to be kindled together with all the fire which is here, that even every substance which

is somewhat dry, is easily ignited, because there is less mingled with it of that which is a hindrance to ignition. Accordingly then everything also which participates in the common intelligent nature moves in like manner towards that which is of the same kind with itself, or moves even more. For so much as it is superior in comparison with all other things, in the same degree also is it more ready to mingle with and to be fused with that which is akin to it. Accordingly among animals devoid of reason we find swarms of bees, and herds of cattle, and the nurture of young birds, and in a manner, loves; for even in animals there are souls, and that power which brings them together is seen to exert itself in the superior degree, and in such a way as never has been observed in plants nor in stones nor in trees. But in rational animals there are political communities and friendships, and families and meetings of people; and in wars, treaties and armistices. But in the things which are still superior, even though they are separated from one another, unity in a manner exists, as in the stars. Thus the ascent to the higher degree is able to produce a sympathy even in things which are separated. See, then, what now takes place. For only intelligent animals have now forgotten this mutual desire and inclination, and in them alone the property of flowing together is not seen. But still though men strive to avoid this union, they are caught and held by it, for their nature is too strong for them; and thou wilt see what I say, if thou only observest. Sooner, then, will one find anything earthy which comes in contact with no earthy thing than a man altogether separated from other men.

10. Both man and God and the universe produce fruit; at the proper seasons each produces it. But if usage has especially fixed these terms to the vine and like things, this is nothing. Reason produces fruit both for all and for itself, and there are produced from it other things of the same kind as reason itself.

11. If thou art able, correct by teaching those who do wrong; but if thou canst not, remember that indulgence is given to thee for this purpose. And the gods, too, are indulgent to such persons; and for some purposes they even help them to get health, wealth, reputation; so

kind they are. And it is in thy power also; or say, who hinders thee?

12. Labour not as one who is wretched, nor yet as one who would be pitied or admired: but direct thy will to one thing only, to put thyself in motion and to check thyself, as the social reason requires.

13. To-day I have got out of all trouble, or rather I have cast out all trouble, for it was not outside, but within and in my opinions.

14. All things are the same, familiar in experience, and ephemeral in time, and worthless in the matter. Everything now is just as it was in the time of those whom we have buried.

15. Things stand outside of us, themselves by themselves, neither knowing aught of themselves, nor expressing any judgement. What is it, then, which does judge about them? The ruling faculty.

16. Not in passivity, but in activity lie the evil and the good of the rational social animal, just as his virtue and his vice lie not in passivity, but in activity.

17. For the stone which has been thrown up it is no evil to come down, nor indeed any good to have been carried up.

18. Penetrate inwards into men's leading principles, and thou wilt see what judges thou art afraid of, and what kind of judges they are of themselves.

19. All things are changing: and thou thyself art in continuous mutation and in a manner in continuous destruction, and the whole universe too.

20. It is thy duty to leave another man's wrongful act there where it is.

21. Termination of activity, cessation from movement and opinion, and in a sense their death, is no evil. Turn thy thoughts now to the consideration of thy life, thy life as a child, as a youth, thy manhood, thy old age, for in these also every change was a death. Is this anything to fear? Turn thy thoughts now to thy life under thy grandfather, then to thy life under thy mother, then to thy life under thy father; and as thou findest many other differences and changes and terminations, ask thyself, Is this anything to fear? In like manner, then, neither are the termination and cessation and change of thy whole life a thing to be afraid of.

22. Hasten to examine thy own ruling faculty and that of the universe and that of thy neighbour: thy own that thou mayest make it just: and that of the universe, that thou mayest remember of what thou art a part; and that of thy neighbour, that thou mayest know whether he has acted ignorantly or with knowledge, and that thou mayest also consider that his ruling faculty is akin to thine.

23. As thou thyself art a component part of a social system, so let every act of thine be a component part of social life. Whatever act of thine then has no reference either immediately or remotely to a social end, this tears asunder thy life, and does not allow it to be one, and it is of the nature of a mutiny, just as when in a popular assembly a man acting by himself stands apart from the general agreement.

24. Quarrels of little children and their sports, and poor spirits carrying about dead bodies, such is everything; and so what is exhibited in the representation of the mansions of the dead strikes our eyes more clearly.

25. Examine into the quality of the form of an object, and detach it altogether from its material part, and then contemplate it; then determine the time, the longest which a thing of this peculiar form is naturally made to endure.

26. Thou hast endured infinite troubles through not being contented with thy ruling faculty, when it does the things which it is constituted by nature to do. But enough of this.

27. When another blames thee or hates thee, or when men say about thee anything injurious, approach their poor souls, penetrate within, and see what kind of men they are. Thou wilt discover that there is no reason to take any trouble that these men may have this or that opinion about thee. However thou must be well disposed towards them, for by nature they are friends. And the gods too aid them in all ways, by dreams, by signs, towards the attainment of those things on which they set a value.

28. The periodic movements of the universe are the same, up and down from age to age. And either the universal intelligence puts itself in motion for every separate effect, and if this

is so, be thou content with that which is the result of its activity; or it puts itself in motion once, and everything else comes by way of sequence in a manner; or indivisible elements are the origin of all things.—In a word, if there is a god, all is well; and if chance rules, do not thou also be governed by it.

Soon will the earth cover us all: then the earth, too, will change, and the things also which result from change will continue to change for ever, and these again for ever. For if a man reflects on the changes and transformations which follow one another like wave after wave and their rapidity, he will despise everything which is perishable.

29. The universal cause is like a winter torrent: it carries everything along with it. But how worthless are all these poor people who are engaged in matters political, and, as they suppose, are playing the philosopher! All drivellers. Well then, man: do what nature now requires. Set thyself in motion, if it is in thy power, and do not look about thee to see if any one will observe it; nor yet expect Plato's *Republic:* but be content if the smallest thing goes on well, and consider such an event to be no small matter. For who can change men's opinions? And without a change of opinions what else is there than the slavery of men who groan while they pretend to obey? Come now and tell me of Alexander and Philip and Demetrius of Phalerum. They themselves shall judge whether they discovered what the common nature required, and trained themselves accordingly. But if they acted like tragedy heroes, no one has condemned me to imitate them. Simple and modest is the work of philosophy. Draw me not aside to indolence and pride.

30. Look down from above on the countless herds of men and their countless solemnities, and the infinitely varied voyagings in storms and calms, and the differences among those who are born, who live together, and die. And consider, too, the life lived by others in olden time, and the life of those who will live after thee, and the life now lived among barbarous nations, and how many know not even thy name, and how many will soon forget it, and how they who perhaps now are praising thee will very soon blame thee, and that neither a posthumous name is of any value, nor reputation, nor anything else.

31. Let there be freedom from perturbations with respect to the things which come from the external cause; and let there be justice in the things done by virtue of the internal cause, that is, let there be movement and action terminating in this, in social acts, for this is according to thy nature.

32. Thou canst remove out of the way many useless things among those which disturb thee, for they lie entirely in thy opinion; and thou wilt then gain for thyself ample space by comprehending the whole universe in thy mind, and by contemplating the eternity of time, and observing the rapid change of every several thing, how short is the time from birth to dissolution, and the illimitable time before birth as well as the equally boundless time after dissolution.

33. All that thou seest will quickly perish, and those who have been spectators of its dissolution will very soon perish too. And he who dies at the extremest old age will be brought into the same condition with him who died prematurely.

34. What are these men's leading principles, and about what kind of things are they busy, and for what kind of reasons do they love and honour? Imagine that thou seest their poor souls laid bare. When they think that they do harm by their blame or good by their praise, what an idea!

35. Loss is nothing else than change. But the universal nature delights in change, and in obedience to her all things are now done well, and from eternity have been done in like form, and will be such to time without end. What, then, dost thou say? That all things have been and all things always will be bad, and that no power has ever been found in so many gods to rectify these things, but the world has been condemned to be found in never ceasing evil?

36. The rottenness of the matter which is the foundation of everything! Water, dust, bones, filth: or again, marble rocks, the callosities of the earth; and gold and silver, the sediments; and garments, only bits of hair; and purple dye, blood; and everything else is of the same kind. And that which is of the nature of breath

is also another thing of the same kind, changing from this to that.

37. Enough of this wretched life and murmuring and apish tricks. Why art thou disturbed? What is there new in this? What unsettles thee? Is it the form of the thing? Look at it. Or is it the matter? Look at it. But besides these there is nothing. Towards the gods, then, now become at last more simple and better. It is the same whether we examine these things for a hundred years or three.

38. If any man has done wrong, the harm is his own. But perhaps he has not done wrong.

39. Either all things proceed from one intelligent source and come together as in one body, and the part ought not to find fault with what is done for the benefit of the whole; or there are only atoms, and nothing else than mixture and dispersion. Why, then, art thou disturbed? Say to the ruling faculty, Art thou dead, art thou corrupted, art thou playing the hypocrite, art thou become a beast, dost thou herd and feed with the rest?

40. Either the gods have no power or they have power. If, then, they have no power, why dost thou pray to them? But if they have power, why dost thou not pray for them to give thee the faculty of not fearing any of the things which thou fearest, or of not desiring any of the things which thou desirest, or not being pained at anything, rather than pray that any of these things should not happen or happen? for certainly if they can co-operate with men, they can co-operate for these purposes. But perhaps thou wilt say, the gods have placed them in thy power. Well, then, is it not better to use what is in thy power like a free man than to desire in a slavish and abject way what is not in thy power? And who has told thee that the gods do not aid us even in the things which are in our power? Begin, then, to pray for such things, and thou wilt see. One man prays thus: How shall I be able to lie with that woman? Do thou pray thus: How shall I not desire to lie with her? Another prays thus: How shall I be released from this? Another prays: How shall I not desire to be released? Another thus: How shall I not lose my little son? Thou thus: How shall I not be afraid to lose him? In fine, turn thy prayers this way, and see what comes.

41. Epicurus says, In my sickness my conversation was not about my bodily sufferings, nor, says he, did I talk on such subjects to those who visited me; but I continued to discourse on the nature of things as before, keeping to this main point, how the mind, while participating in such movements as go on in the poor flesh, shall be free from perturbations and maintain its proper good. Nor did I, he says, give the physicians an opportunity of putting on solemn looks, as if they were doing something great, but my life went on well and happily. Do, then, the same that he did both in sickness, if thou art sick, and in any other circumstances; for never to desert philosophy in any events that may befall us, nor to hold trifling talk either with an ignorant man or with one unacquainted with nature, is a principle of all schools of philosophy; but to be intent only on that which thou art now doing and on the instrument by which thou doest it.

42. When thou art offended with any man's shameless conduct, immediately ask thyself, Is it possible, then, that shameless men should not be in the world? It is not possible. Do not, then, require what is impossible. For this man also is one of those shameless men who must of necessity be in the world. Let the same considerations be present to thy mind in the case of the knave, and the faithless man, and of every man who does wrong in any way. For at the same time that thou dost remind thyself that it is impossible that such kind of men should not exist, thou wilt become more kindly disposed towards every one individually. It is useful to perceive this, too, immediately when the occasion arises, what virtue nature has given to man to oppose to every wrongful act. For she has given to man, as an antidote against the stupid man, mildness, and against another kind of man some other power. And in all cases it is possible for thee to correct by teaching the man who is gone astray; for every man who errs misses his object and is gone astray. Besides wherein hast thou been injured? For thou wilt find that no one among those against whom thou art irritated has done anything by which thy mind could be made worse; but that which is evil to thee and harmful has its foundation only in the mind. And what harm is done or what is there strange, if

the man who has not been instructed does the acts of an uninstructed man? Consider whether thou shouldst not rather blame thyself, because thou didst not expect such a man to err in such a way. For thou hadst means given thee by thy reason to suppose that it was likely that he would commit this error, and yet thou hast forgotten and art amazed that he has erred. But most of all when thou blamest a man as faithless or ungrateful, turn to thyself. For the fault is manifestly thy own, whether thou didst trust that a man who had such a disposition would keep his promise, or when conferring thy kindness thou didst not confer it absolutely, nor yet in such way as to have received from thy very act all the profit. For what more dost thou want when thou hast done a man a service? Art thou not content that thou hast done something conformable to thy nature, and dost thou seek to be paid for it? Just as if the eye demanded a recompense for seeing, or the feet for walking. For as these members are formed for a particular purpose, and by working according to their several constitutions obtain what is their own; so also as man is formed by nature to acts of benevolence, when he has done anything benevolent or in any other way conducive to the common interest, he has acted conformably to his constitution, and he gets what is his own.

·BOOK TEN·

WILT thou, then, my soul, never be good and simple and one and naked, more manifest than the body which surrounds thee? Wilt thou never enjoy an affectionate and contented disposition? Wilt thou never be full and without a want of any kind, longing for nothing more, nor desiring anything, either animate or inanimate, for the enjoyment of pleasures? Nor yet desiring time wherein thou shalt have longer enjoyment, or place, or pleasant climate, or society of men with whom thou mayest live in harmony? But wilt thou be satisfied with thy present condition, and pleased with all that is about thee, and wilt thou convince thyself that thou hast everything and that it comes from the gods, that everything is well for thee, and will be well whatever shall please them, and whatever they shall give for the conservation of the perfect living being, the good and just and beautiful, which generates and holds together all things, and contains and embraces all things which are dissolved for the production of other like things? Wilt thou never be such that thou shalt so dwell in community with gods and men as neither to find fault with them at all, nor to be condemned by them?

2. Observe what thy nature requires, so far as thou art governed by nature only: then do it and accept it, if thy nature, so far as thou art a living being, shall not be made worse by it. And next thou must observe what thy nature requires so far as thou art a living being. And all this thou mayest allow thyself, if thy nature, so far as thou art a rational animal, shall not be made worse by it. But the rational animal is consequently also a political (social) animal. Use these rules, then, and trouble thyself about nothing else.

3. Everything which happens either happens in such wise as thou art formed by nature to bear it, or as thou art not formed by nature to bear it. If, then, it happens to thee in such way as thou art formed by nature to bear it, do not complain, but bear it as thou art formed by nature to bear it. But if it happens in such wise as thou art not formed by nature to bear it, do not complain, for it will perish after it has consumed thee. Remember, however, that thou art formed by nature to bear everything, with respect to which it depends on thy own opinion to make it endurable and tolerable, by thinking that it is either thy interest or thy duty to do this.

4. If a man is mistaken, instruct him kindly and show him his error. But if thou art not able, blame thyself, or blame not even thyself.

5. Whatever may happen to thee, it was prepared for thee from all eternity; and the implication of causes was from eternity spinning the thread of thy being, and of that which is incident to it.

6. Whether the universe is a concourse of atoms, or nature is a system, let this first be established, that I am a part of the whole which is governed by nature; next, I am in a manner intimately related to the parts which are of the same kind with myself. For remembering this, inasmuch as I am a part, I shall be discontented with none of the things which are assigned to me out of the whole; for nothing is injurious to the part, if it is for the advantage of the whole. For the whole contains nothing which is not for its advantage; and all natures indeed have this common principle, but the nature of the universe has this principle besides, that it cannot be compelled even by any external cause to generate anything harmful to itself. By remembering, then, that I am a part of such a whole, I shall be content with everything that happens. And inasmuch as I am in a manner intimately related to the parts which are of the same kind with myself, I shall do nothing unsocial, but I shall rather direct myself to the things which are of the same kind with myself, and I shall turn all my efforts to the common interest, and divert them from the contrary. Now, if these things are done so, life must flow on happily, just as thou mayest observe that the life of a citizen is happy, who continues a course of action which is advantageous to his fellow-citizens, and is content with whatever the state may assign to him.

7. The parts of the whole, everything, I mean, which is naturally comprehended in the universe, must of necessity perish; but let this be understood in this sense, that they must undergo change. But if this is naturally both an evil and a necessity for the parts, the whole would not continue to exist in a good condition, the parts being subject to change and constituted so as to perish in various ways. For whether did nature herself design to do evil to the things which are parts of herself, and to make them subject to evil and of necessity fall into evil, or have such results happened without her knowing it? Both these suppositions, indeed, are incredible. But if a man should even drop the term Nature (as an efficient power), and should speak of these things as natural, even then it would be ridiculous to affirm at the same time that the parts of the whole are in their nature subject to change, and at the same time to be surprised or vexed as if something were happening contrary to nature, particularly as the dissolution of things is into those things of which each thing is composed. For there is either a dispersion of the elements out of which everything has been compounded, or a change from the solid to the earthy and from the airy to the aërial, so that these parts are taken back into the universal reason, whether this at certain periods is consumed by fire or renewed by eternal changes. And do not imagine that the solid and the airy part belong to thee from the time of generation. For all this received its accretion only yesterday and the day before, as one may say, from the food and the air which is inspired. This, then, which has received the accretion, changes, not that which thy mother brought forth. But suppose that this which thy mother brought forth implicates thee very much with that other part, which has the peculiar quality of change, this is nothing in fact in the way of objection to what is said.

8. When thou hast assumed these names, good, modest, true, rational, a man of equanimity, and magnanimous, take care that thou dost not change these names; and if thou shouldst lose them, quickly return to them. And remember that the term Rational was intended to signify a discriminating attention to every several thing and freedom from negligence; and that Equanimity is the voluntary acceptance of the things which are assigned to thee by the common nature; and that Magnanimity is the elevation of the intelligent part above the pleasurable or painful sensations of the flesh, and above that poor thing called fame, and death, and all such things. If, then, thou maintainest thyself in the possession of these names, without desiring to be called by these names by others, thou wilt be another person and wilt enter on another life. For to continue to be such as thou hast hitherto been, and to be torn in pieces and defiled in such a life, is the character of a very stupid man and one overfond of his life, and like those half-devoured fighters with wild beasts, who though covered with wounds and gore, still intreat to be kept to the following day, though they will be exposed in the same state to the

same claws and bites. Therefore fix thyself in the possession of these few names: and if thou art able to abide in them, abide as if thou wast removed to certain islands of the Happy. But if thou shalt perceive that thou fallest out of them and dost not maintain thy hold, go courageously into some nook where thou shalt maintain them, or even depart at once from life, not in passion, but with simplicity and freedom and modesty, after doing this one laudable thing at least in thy life, to have gone out of it thus. In order, however, to the remembrance of these names, it will greatly help thee, if thou rememberest the gods, and that they wish not to be flattered, but wish all reasonable beings to be made like themselves; and if thou rememberest that what does the work of a fig-tree is a fig-tree, and that what does the work of a dog is a dog, and that what does the work of a bee is a bee, and that what does the work of a man is a man.

9. Mimi,[1] war, astonishment, torpor, slavery, will daily wipe out those holy principles of thine. How many things without studying nature dost thou imagine, and how many dost thou neglect? But it is thy duty so to look on and so to do everything, that at the same time the power of dealing with circumstances is perfected, and the contemplative faculty is exercised, and the confidence which comes from the knowledge of each several thing is maintained without showing it, but yet not concealed. For when wilt thou enjoy simplicity, when gravity, and when the knowledge of every several thing, both what it is in substance, and what place it has in the universe, and how long it is formed to exist and of what things it is compounded, and to whom it can belong, and who are able both to give it and take it away?

10. A spider is proud when it has caught a fly, and another when he has caught a poor hare, and another when he has taken a little fish in a net, and another when he has taken wild boars, and another when he has taken bears, and another when he has taken Sarmatians. Are not these robbers, if thou examinest their opinions?

11. Acquire the contemplative way of seeing how all things change into one another, and

[1] A kind of Roman stage play.

constantly attend to it, and exercise thyself about this part of philosophy. For nothing is so much adapted to produce magnanimity. Such a man has put off the body, and as he sees that he must, no one knows how soon, go away from among men and leave everything here, he gives himself up entirely to just doing in all his actions, and in everything else that happens he resigns himself to the universal nature. But as to what any man shall say or think about him or do against him, he never even thinks of it, being himself contented with these two things, with acting justly in what he now does, and being satisfied with what is now assigned to him; and he lays aside all distracting and busy pursuits, and desires nothing else than to accomplish the straight course through the law, and by accomplishing the straight course to follow God.

12. What need is there of suspicious fear, since it is in thy power to inquire what ought to be done? And if thou seest clear, go by this way content, without turning back: but if thou dost not see clear, stop and take the best advisers. But if any other things oppose thee, go on according to thy powers with due consideration, keeping to that which appears to be just. For it is best to reach this object, and if thou dost fail, let thy failure be in attempting this. He who follows reason in all things is both tranquil and active at the same time, and also cheerful and collected.

13. Inquire of thyself as soon as thou wakest from sleep, whether it will make any difference to thee, if another does what is just and right. It will make no difference.

Thou hast not forgotten, I suppose, that those who assume arrogant airs in bestowing their praise or blame on others, are such as they are at bed and at board, and thou hast not forgotten what they do, and what they avoid and what they pursue, and how they steal and how they rob, not with hands and feet, but with their most valuable part, by means of which there is produced, when a man chooses, fidelity, modesty, truth, law, a good daemon (happiness)?

14. To her who gives and takes back all, to nature, the man who is instructed and modest says, Give what thou wilt; take back what

thou wilt. And he says this not proudly, but obediently and well pleased with her.

15. Short is the little which remains to thee of life. Live as on a mountain. For it makes no difference whether a man lives there or here, if he lives everywhere in the world as in a state (political community). Let men see, let them know a real man who lives according to nature. If they cannot endure him, let them kill him. For that is better than to live thus as men do.

16. No longer talk at all about the kind of man that a good man ought to be, but be such.

17. Constantly contemplate the whole of time and the whole of substance, and consider that all individual things as to substance are a grain of a fig, and as to time, the turning of a gimlet.

18. Look at everything that exists, and observe that it is already in dissolution and in change, and as it were putrefaction or dispersion, or that everything is so constituted by nature as to die.

19. Consider what men are when they are eating, sleeping, generating, easing themselves and so forth. Then what kind of men they are when they are imperious and arrogant, or angry and scolding from their elevated place. But a short time ago to how many they were slaves and for what things; and after a little time consider in what a condition they will be.

20. That is for the good of each thing, which the universal nature brings to each. And it is for its good at the time when nature brings it.

21. "The earth loves the shower"; and "the solemn aether loves"[1]: and the universe loves to make whatever is about to be. I say then to the universe, that I love as thou lovest. And is not this too said, that "this or that loves (is wont) to be produced"?

22. Either thou livest here and hast already accustomed thyself to it, or thou art going away, and this was thy own will; or thou art dying and hast discharged thy duty. But besides these things there is nothing. Be of good cheer, then.

23. Let this always be plain to thee, that this piece of land is like any other; and that all things here are the same with things on the top of a mountain, or on the sea-shore, or wherever thou choosest to be. For thou wilt find just what Plato says, Dwelling within the walls of a city as in a shepherd's fold on a mountain.[2]

24. What is my ruling faculty now to me? And of what nature am I now making it? And for what purpose am I now using it? Is it void of understanding? Is it loosed and rent asunder from social life? Is it melted into and mixed with the poor flesh so as to move together with it?

25. He who flies from his master is a runaway; but the law is master, and he who breaks the law is a runaway. And he also who is grieved or angry or afraid, is dissatisfied because something has been or is or shall be of the things which are appointed by him who rules all things, and he is Law, and assigns to every man what is fit. He then who fears or is grieved or is angry is a runaway.

26. A man deposits seed in a womb and goes away, and then another cause takes it, and labours on it and makes a child. What a thing from such a material! Again, the child passes food down through the throat, and then another cause takes it and makes perception and motion, and in fine life and strength and other things; how many and how strange! Observe then the things which are produced in such a hidden way, and see the power just as we see the power which carries things downwards and upwards, not with the eyes, but still no less plainly.

27. Constantly consider how all things such as they now are, in time past also were; and consider that they will be the same again. And place before thy eyes entire dramas and stages of the same form, whatever thou hast learned from thy experience or from older history; for example, the whole court of Hadrian, and the whole court of Antoninus, and the whole court of Philip, Alexander, Croesus; for all those were such dramas as we see now, only with different actors.

28. Imagine every man who is grieved at anything or discontented to be like a pig which is sacrificed and kicks and screams.

Like this pig also is he who on his bed in silence laments the bonds in which we are

[1] Euripides, fragment.

[2] Cf. *Theaetetus*, 174.

held. And consider that only to the rational animal is it given to follow voluntarily what happens; but simply to follow is a necessity imposed on all.

29. Severally on the occasion of everything that thou doest, pause and ask thyself, if death is a dreadful thing because it deprives thee of this.

30. When thou art offended at any man's fault, forthwith turn to thyself and reflect in what like manner thou dost err thyself; for example, in thinking that money is a good thing, or pleasure, or a bit of reputation, and the like. For by attending to this thou wilt quickly forget thy anger, if this consideration also is added, that the man is compelled: for what else could he do? or, if thou art able, take away from him the compulsion.

31. When thou hast seen Satyron the Socratic, think of either Eutyches or Hymen, and when thou hast seen Euphrates, think of Eutychion or Silvanus, and when thou hast seen Alciphron think of Tropaeophorus, and when thou hast seen Xenophon think of Crito or Severus, and when thou hast looked on thyself, think of any other Cæsar, and in the case of every one do in like manner. Then let this thought be in thy mind, Where then are those men? Nowhere, or nobody knows where. For thus continuously thou wilt look at human things as smoke and nothing at all; especially if thou reflectest at the same time that what has once changed will never exist again in the infinite duration of time. But thou, in what a brief space of time is thy existence? And why art thou not content to pass through this short time in an orderly way? What matter and opportunity for thy activity art thou avoiding? For what else are all these things, except exercises for the reason, when it has viewed carefully and by examination into their nature the things which happen in life? Persevere then until thou shalt have made these things thy own, as the stomach which is strengthened makes all things its own, as the blazing fire makes flame and brightness out of everything that is thrown into it.

32. Let it not be in any man's power to say truly of thee that thou art not simple or that thou are not good; but let him be a liar whoever shall think anything of this kind about thee; and this is altogether in thy power. For who is he that shall hinder thee from being good and simple? Do thou only determine to live no longer, unless thou shalt be such. For neither does reason allow thee to live, if thou art not such.

33. What is that which as to this material (our life) can be done or said in the way most conformable to reason. For whatever this may be, it is in thy power to do it or to say it, and do not make excuses that thou art hindered. Thou wilt not cease to lament till thy mind is in such a condition that, what luxury is to those who enjoy pleasure, such shall be to thee, in the matter which is subjected and presented to thee, the doing of the things which are conformable to man's constitution; for a man ought to consider as an enjoyment everything which it is in his power to do according to his own nature. And it is in his power everywhere. Now, it is not given to a cylinder to move everywhere by its own motion, nor yet to water nor to fire, nor to anything else which is governed by nature or an irrational soul, for the things which check them and stand in the way are many. But intelligence and reason are able to go through everything that opposes them, and in such manner as they are formed by nature and as they choose. Place before thy eyes this facility with which the reason will be carried through all things, as fire upwards, as a stone downwards, as a cylinder down an inclined surface, and seek for nothing further. For all other obstacles either affect the body only which is a dead thing; or, except through opinion and the yielding of the reason itself, they do not crush nor do any harm of any kind; for if they did, he who felt it would immediately become bad. Now, in the case of all things which have a certain constitution, whatever harm may happen to any of them, that which is so affected becomes consequently worse; but in the like case, a man becomes both better, if one may say so, and more worthy of praise by making a right use of these accidents. And finally remember that nothing harms him who is really a citizen, which does not harm the state; nor yet does anything harm the state, which does not harm law (order); and of these things which are called misfortunes not one harms

law. What then does not harm law does not harm either state or citizen.

34. To him who is penetrated by true principles even the briefest precept is sufficient, and any common precept, to remind him that he should be free from grief and fear. For example—

Leaves, some the wind scatters on the ground—
So is the race of men.[1]

Leaves, also, are thy children; and leaves, too, are they who cry out as if they were worthy of credit and bestow their praise, or on the contrary curse, or secretly blame and sneer; and leaves, in like manner, are those who shall receive and transmit a man's fame to aftertimes. For all such things as these "are produced in the season of spring," as the poet says; then the wind casts them down; then the forest produces other leaves in their places. But a brief existence is common to all things, and yet thou avoidest and pursuest all things as if they would be eternal. A little time, and thou shalt close thy eyes; and him who has attended thee to thy grave another soon will lament.

35. The healthy eye ought to see all visible things and not to say, I wish for green things; for this is the condition of a diseased eye. And the healthy hearing and smelling ought to be ready to perceive all that can be heard and smelled. And the healthy stomach ought to be with respect to all food just as the mill with respect to all things which it is formed to grind. And accordingly the healthy understanding ought to be prepared for everything which happens; but that which says, Let my dear children live, and let all men praise whatever I may do, is an eye which seeks for green things, or teeth which seek for soft things.

36. There is no man so fortunate that there shall not be by him when he is dying some who are pleased with what is going to happen. Suppose that he was a good and wise man, will there not be at last some one to say

[1] Homer, *Iliad*, vi. 147.

to himself, Let us at last breathe freely being relieved from this schoolmaster? It is true that he was harsh to none of us, but I perceived that he tacitly condemns us.—This is what is said of a good man. But in our own case how many other things are there for which there are many who wish to get rid of us. Thou wilt consider this then when thou art dying, and thou wilt depart more contentedly by reflecting thus: I am going away from such a life, in which even my associates in behalf of whom I have striven so much, prayed, and cared, themselves wish me to depart, hoping perchance to get some little advantage by it. Why then should a man cling to a longer stay here? Do not however for this reason go away less kindly disposed to them, but preserving thy own character, and friendly and benevolent and mild, and on the other hand not as if thou wast torn away; but as when a man dies a quiet death, the poor soul is easily separated from the body, such also ought thy departure from men to be, for nature united thee to them and associated thee. But does she now dissolve the union? Well, I am separated as from kinsmen, not however dragged resisting, but without compulsion; for this too is one of the things according to nature.

37. Accustom thyself as much as possible on the occasion of anything being done by any person to inquire with thyself, For what object is this man doing this? But begin with thyself, and examine thyself first.

38. Remember that this which pulls the strings is the thing which is hidden within: this is the power of persuasion, this is life, this, if one may so say, is man. In contemplating thyself never include the vessel which surrounds thee and these instruments which are attached about it. For they are like to an axe, differing only in this that they grow to the body. For indeed there is no more use in these parts without the cause which moves and checks them than in the weaver's shuttle, and the writer's pen and the driver's whip.

· BOOK ELEVEN ·

THESE are the properties of the rational soul: it sees itself, analyses itself, and makes itself such as it chooses; the fruit which it bears itself enjoys—for the fruits of plants and that in animals which corresponds to fruits others enjoy—it obtains its own end, wherever the limit of life may be fixed. Not as in a dance and in a play and in such like things, where the whole action is incomplete, if anything cuts it short; but in every part and wherever it may be stopped, it makes what has been set before it full and complete, so that it can say, I have what is my own. And further it traverses the whole universe, and the surrounding vacuum, and surveys its form, and it extends itself into the infinity of time, and embraces and comprehends the periodical renovation of all things, and it comprehends that those who come after us will see nothing new, nor have those before us seen anything more, but in a manner he who is forty years old, if he has any understanding at all, has seen by virtue of the uniformity that prevails all things which have been and all that will be. This too is a property of the rational soul, love of one's neighbour, and truth and modesty, and to value nothing more than itself, which is also the property of Law. Thus then right reason differs not at all from the reason of justice.

2. Thou wilt set little value on pleasing song and dancing and the pancratium, if thou wilt distribute the melody of the voice into its several sounds, and ask thyself as to each, if thou art mastered by this; for thou wilt be prevented by shame from confessing it: and in the matter of dancing, if at each movement and attitude thou wilt do the same; and the like also in the matter of the pancratium. In all things, then, except virtue and the acts of virtue, remember to apply thyself to their several parts, and by this division to come to value them little: and apply this rule also to thy whole life.

3. What a soul that is which is ready, if at any moment it must be separated from the body, and ready either to be extinguished or dispersed or continue to exist; but so that this readiness comes from a man's own judgement, not from mere obstinacy, as with the Christians,[1] but considerately and with dignity and in a way to persuade another, without tragic show.

4. Have I done something for the general interest? Well then I have had my reward. Let this always be present to thy mind, and never stop doing such good.

5. What is thy art? To be good. And how is this accomplished well except by general principles, some about the nature of the universe, and others about the proper constitution of man?

6. At first tragedies were brought on the stage as means of reminding men of the things which happen to them, and that it is according to nature for things to happen so, and that, if you are delighted with what is shown on the stage, you should not be troubled with that which takes place on the larger stage. For you see that these things must be accomplished thus, and that even they bear them who cry out "O Cithaeron."[2] And, indeed, some things are said well by the dramatic writers, of which kind is the following especially:—

> *Me and my children if the gods neglect,*
> *This has its reason too.*[3]

And again—
> *We must not chafe and fret at that which happens.*

And—
> *Life's harvest reap like the wheat's fruitful ear.*

And other things of the same kind.

After tragedy the old comedy was introduced, which had a magisterial freedom of speech, and by its very plainness of speaking was useful in reminding men to beware of insolence; and for this purpose too Diogenes used to take from these writers.

But as to the middle comedy which came next, observe what it was, and again, for what object the new comedy was introduced, which

---

[1] Reference to Christians is possibly a later gloss.
[2] Sophocles, *Oedipus the King*, 1391.
[3] Euripides, fragments.

gradually sunk down into a mere mimic artifice. That some good things are said even by these writers, everybody knows: but the whole plan of such poetry and dramaturgy, to what end does it look!

7. How plain does it appear that there is not another condition of life so well suited for philosophising as this in which thou now happenest to be.

8. A branch cut off from the adjacent branch must of necessity be cut off from the whole tree also. So too a man when he is separated from another man has fallen off from the whole social community. Now as to a branch, another cuts it off, but a man by his own act separates himself from his neighbour when he hates him and turns away from him, and he does not know that he has at the same time cut himself off from the whole social system. Yet he has this privilege certainly from Zeus who framed society, for it is in our power to grow again to that which is near to us, and again to become a part which helps to make up the whole. However, if it often happens, this kind of separation, it makes it difficult for that which detaches itself to be brought to unity and to be restored to its former condition. Finally, the branch, which from the first grew together with the tree, and has continued to have one life with it, is not like that which after being cut off is then ingrafted, for this is something like what the gardeners mean when they say that it grows with the rest of the tree, but that it has not the same mind with it.

9. As those who try to stand in thy way when thou art proceeding according to right reason, will not be able to turn thee aside from thy proper action, so neither let them drive thee from thy benevolent feelings towards them, but be on thy guard equally in both matters, not only in the matter of steady judgement and action, but also in the matter of gentleness towards those who try to hinder or otherwise trouble thee. For this also is a weakness, to be vexed at them, as well as to be diverted from thy course of action and to give way through fear; for both are equally deserters from their post, the man who does it through fear, and the man who is alienated from him who is by nature a kinsman and a friend.

10. There is no nature which is inferior to art, for the arts imitate the nature of things. But if this is so, that nature which is the most perfect and the most comprehensive of all natures, cannot fall short of the skill of art. Now all arts do the inferior things for the sake of the superior; therefore the universal nature does so too. And, indeed, hence is the origin of justice, and in justice the other virtues have their foundation: for justice will not be observed, if we either care for middle things (things indifferent), or are easily deceived and careless and changeable.

11. If the things do not come to thee, the pursuits and avoidances of which disturb thee, still in a manner thou goest to them. Let then thy judgement about them be at rest, and they will remain quiet, and thou wilt not be seen either pursuing or avoiding.

12. The spherical form of the soul maintains its figure, when it is neither extended towards any object, nor contracted inwards, nor dispersed nor sinks down, but is illuminated by light, by which it sees the truth, the truth of all things and the truth that is in itself.

13. Suppose any man shall despise me. Let him look to that himself. But I will look to this, that I be not discovered doing or saying anything deserving of contempt. Shall any man hate me? Let him look to it. But I will be mild and benevolent towards every man, and ready to show even him his mistake, not reproachfully, nor yet as making a display of my endurance, but nobly and honestly, like the great Phocion, unless indeed he only assumed it. For the interior parts ought to be such, and a man ought to be seen by the gods neither dissatisfied with anything nor complaining. For what evil is it to thee, if thou art now doing what is agreeable to thy own nature, and art satisfied with that which at this moment is suitable to the nature of the universe, since thou art a human being placed at thy post in order that what is for the common advantage may be done in some way?

14. Men despise one another and flatter one another; and men wish to raise themselves above one another, and crouch before one another.

15. How unsound and insincere is he who says, I have determined to deal with thee in a fair way.—What art thou doing, man? There

is no occasion to give this notice. It will soon show itself by acts. The voice ought to be plainly written on the forehead. Such as a man's character is, he immediately shows it in his eyes, just as he who is beloved forthwith reads everything in the eyes of lovers. The man who is honest and good ought to be exactly like a man who smells strong, so that the by-stander as soon as he comes near him must smell whether he choose or not. But the affec-tation of simplicity is like a crooked stick. Nothing is more disgraceful than a wolfish friendship (false friendship). Avoid this most of all. The good and simple and benevolent show all these things in the eyes, and there is no mistaking.

16. As to living in the best way, this power is in the soul, if it be indifferent to things which are indifferent. And it will be indiffer-ent, if it looks on each of these things sepa-rately and all together, and if it remembers that not one of them produces in us an opin-ion about itself, nor comes to us; but these things remain immovable, and it is we our-selves who produce the judgements about them, and, as we may say, write them in our-selves, it being in our power not to write them, and it being in our power, if perchance these judgements have imperceptibly got admission to our minds, to wipe them out; and if we re-member also that such attention will only be for a short time, and then life will be at an end. Besides, what trouble is there at all in do-ing this? For if these things are according to nature, rejoice in them, and they will be easy to thee: but if contrary to nature, seek what is conformable to thy own nature, and strive to-wards this, even if it bring no reputation; for every man is allowed to seek his own good.

17. Consider whence each thing is come, and of what it consists, and into what it changes, and what kind of a thing it will be when it has changed, and that it will sustain no harm.

18. If any have offended against thee, con-sider first: What is my relation to men, and that we are made for one another; and in an-other respect, I was made to be set over them, as a ram over the flock or a bull over the herd. But examine the matter from first principles, from this: If all things are not mere atoms, it

is nature which orders all things: if this is so, the inferior things exist for the sake of the superior, and these for the sake of one another.

Second, consider what kind of men they are at table, in bed, and so forth: and particularly, under what compulsions in respect of opinions they are; and as to their acts, consider with what pride they do what they do.

Third, that if men do rightly what they do, we ought not to be displeased; but if they do not right, it is plain that they do so involun-tarily and in ignorance. For as every soul is un-willingly deprived of the truth, so also is it unwillingly deprived of the power of behaving to each man according to his deserts. Accord-ingly men are pained when they are called un-just, ungrateful, and greedy, and in a word wrong-doers to their neighbours.

Fourth, consider that thou also doest many things wrong, and that thou art a man like others; and even if thou dost abstain from cer-tain faults, still thou hast the disposition to commit them, though either through coward-ice, or concern about reputation, or some such mean motive, thou dost abstain from such faults.

Fifth, consider that thou dost not even un-derstand whether men are doing wrong or not, for many things are done with a certain ref-erence to circumstances. And in short, a man must learn a great deal to enable him to pass a correct judgement on another man's acts.

Sixth, consider when thou art much vexed or grieved, that man's life is only a moment, and after a short time we are all laid out dead.

Seventh, that it is not men's acts which dis-turb us, for those acts have their foundation in men's ruling principles, but it is our own opin-ions which disturb us. Take away these opin-ions then, and resolve to dismiss thy judge-ment about an act as if it were something grievous, and thy anger is gone. How then shall I take away these opinions? By reflecting that no wrongful act of another brings shame on thee: for unless that which is shameful is alone bad, thou also must of necessity do many things wrong, and become a robber and every-thing else.

Eighth, consider how much more pain is brought on us by the anger and vexation caused by such acts than by the acts themselves, at which we are angry and vexed.

Ninth, consider that a good disposition is invincible, if it be genuine, and not an affected smile and acting a part. For what will the most violent man do to thee, if thou continuest to be of a kind disposition towards him, and if, as opportunity offers, thou gently admonishest him and calmly correctest his errors at the very time when he is trying to do thee harm, saying, Not so, my child: we are constituted by nature for something else: I shall certainly not be injured, but thou art injuring thyself, my child.—And show him with gentle tact and by general principles that this is so, and that even bees do not do as he does, nor any animals which are formed by nature to be gregarious. And thou must do this neither with any double meaning nor in the way of reproach, but affectionately and without any rancour in thy soul; and not as if thou wert lecturing him, nor yet that any bystander may admire, but either when he is alone, and if others are present . . .

Remember these nine rules, as if thou hadst received them as a gift from the Muses, and begin at last to be a man while thou livest. But thou must equally avoid flattering men and being vexed at them, for both are unsocial and lead to harm. And let this truth be present to thee in the excitement of anger, that to be moved by passion is not manly, but that mildness and gentleness, as they are more agreeable to human nature, so also are they more manly; and he who possesses these qualities possesses strength, nerves and courage, and not the man who is subject to fits of passion and discontent. For in the same degree in which a man's mind is nearer to freedom from all passion, in the same degree also is it nearer to strength: and as the sense of pain is a characteristic of weakness, so also is anger. For he who yields to pain and he who yields to anger, both are wounded and both submit.

But if thou wilt, receive also a tenth present from the leader of the Muses (Apollo), and it is this—that to expect bad men not to do wrong is madness, for he who expects this desires an impossibility. But to allow men to behave so to others, and to expect them not to do thee any wrong, is irrational and tyrannical.

19. There are four principal aberrations of the superior faculty against which thou shouldst be constantly on thy guard, and when thou hast detected them, thou shouldst wipe them out and say on each occasion thus: this thought is not necessary: this tends to destroy social union: this which thou art going to say comes not from the real thoughts; for thou shouldst consider it among the most absurd of things for a man not to speak from his real thoughts. But the fourth is when thou shalt reproach thyself for anything, for this is an evidence of the diviner part within thee being overpowered and yielding to the less honourable and to the perishable part, the body, and to its gross pleasures.

20. Thy aërial part and all the fiery parts which are mingled in thee, though by nature they have an upward tendency, still in obedience to the disposition of the universe they are overpowered here in the compound mass (the body). And also the whole of the earthy part in thee and the watery, though their tendency is downward, still are raised up and occupy a position which is not their natural one. In this manner then the elemental parts obey the universal, for when they have been fixed in any place perforce they remain there until again the universal shall sound the signal for dissolution. Is it not then strange that thy intelligent part only should be disobedient and discontented with its own place? And yet no force is imposed on it, but only those things which are conformable to its nature: still it does not submit, but is carried in the opposite direction. For the movement towards injustice and intemperance and to anger and grief and fear is nothing else than the act of one who deviates from nature. And also when the ruling faculty is discontented with anything that happens, then too it deserts its post: for it is constituted for piety and reverence towards the gods no less than for justice. For these qualities also are comprehended under the generic term of contentment with the constitution of things, and indeed they are prior to acts of justice.

21. He who has not one and always the same object in life, cannot be one and the same all through his life. But what I have said is not enough, unless this also is added, what this ob-

ject ought to be. For as there is not the same opinion about all the things which in some way or other are considered by the majority to be good, but only about some certain things, that is, things which concern the common interest; so also ought we to propose to ourselves an object which shall be of a common kind (social) and political. For he who directs all his own efforts to this object, will make all his acts alike, and thus will always be the same.

22. Think of the country mouse and of the town mouse, and of the alarm and trepidation of the town mouse.[1]

23. Socrates used to call the opinions of the many by the name of Lamiae, bugbears to frighten children.

24. The Lacedaemonians at their public spectacles used to set seats in the shade for strangers, but themselves sat down anywhere.

25. Socrates excused himself to Perdiccas for not going to him, saying, It is because I would not perish by the worst of all ends, that is, I would not receive a favour and then be unable to return it.

26. In the writings of the Ephesians there was this precept, constantly to think of some one of the men of former times who practised virtue.

27. The Pythagoreans bid us in the morning look to the heavens that we may be reminded of those bodies which continually do the same things and in the same manner perform their work, and also be reminded of their purity and nudity. For there is no veil over a star.

28. Consider what a man Socrates was when he dressed himself in a skin, after Xanthippe had taken his cloak and gone out, and what Socrates said to his friends who were ashamed of him and drew back from him when they saw him dressed thus.

29. Neither in writing nor in reading wilt thou be able to lay down rules for others before thou shalt have first learned to obey rules thyself. Much more is this so in life.

[1] Cf. Horace, *Sermones* ii. 6.

30. A slave thou art: free speech is not for thee.

31. ——And my heart laughed within.[2]

32. And virtue they will curse, speaking harsh words.[3]

33. To look for the fig in winter is a madman's act: such is he who looks for his child when it is no longer allowed.[4]

34. When a man kisses his child, said Epictetus, he should whisper to himself, "To-morrow perchance thou wilt die."—But those are words of bad omen.—"No word is a word of bad omen," said Epictetus, "which expresses any work of nature; or if it is so, it is also a word of bad omen to speak of the ears of corn being reaped."[5]

35. The unripe grape, the ripe bunch, the dried grape, all are changes, not into nothing, but into something which exists not yet.[6]

36. No man can rob us of our free will.[7]

37. Epictetus also said, A man must discover an art (or rules) with respect to giving his assent; and in respect to his movements he must be careful that they be made with regard to circumstances, that they be consistent with social interests, that they have regard to the value of the object; and as to sensual desire, he should altogether keep away from it; and as to avoidance (aversion) he should not show it with respect to any of the things which are not in our power.

38. The dispute then, he said, is not about any common matter, but about being mad or not.

39. Socrates used to say, What do you want? Souls of rational men or irrational?—Souls of rational men.—Of what rational men? Sound or unsound?—Sound.—Why then do you not seek for them?—Because we have them.—Why then do you fight and quarrel?

[2] Homer, *Odyssey*, ix. 413.
[3] Hesiod, *Works and Days*, 185.
[4] Epictetus, iii. 24.
[5] *Ibid.*
[6] *Ibid.*
[7] *Ibid.*

· BOOK TWELVE ·

ALL those things at which thou wishest to arrive by a circuitous road, thou canst have now, if thou dost not refuse them to thyself. And this means, if thou wilt take no notice of all the past, and trust the future to providence, and direct the present only conformably to piety and justice. Conformably to piety, that thou mayest be content with the lot which is assigned to thee, for nature designed it for thee and thee for it. Conformably to justice, that thou mayest always speak the truth freely and without disguise, and do the things which are agreeable to law and according to the worth of each. And let neither another man's wickedness hinder thee, nor opinion nor voice, nor yet the sensations of the poor flesh which has grown about thee; for the passive part will look to this. If then, whatever the time may be when thou shalt be near to thy departure, neglecting everything else thou shalt respect only thy ruling faculty and the divinity within thee, and if thou shalt be afraid not because thou must some time cease to live, but if thou shalt fear never to have begun to live according to nature—then thou wilt be a man worthy of the universe which has produced thee, and thou wilt cease to be a stranger in thy native land, and to wonder at things which happen daily as if they were something unexpected, and to be dependent on this or that.

2. God sees the minds (ruling principles) of all men bared of the material vesture and rind and impurities. For with his intellectual part alone he touches the intelligence only which has flowed and been derived from himself into these bodies. And if thou also usest thyself to do this, thou wilt rid thyself of thy much trouble. For he who regards not the poor flesh which envelops him, surely will not trouble himself by looking after raiment and dwelling and fame and such like externals and show.

3. The things are three of which thou art composed, a little body, a little breath (life), intelligence. Of these the first two are thine, so far as it is thy duty to take care of them; but the third alone is properly thine. Therefore if thou shalt separate from thyself, that is, from thy understanding, whatever others do or say, and whatever thou hast done or said thyself, and whatever future things trouble thee because they may happen, and whatever in the body which envelops thee or in the breath (life), which is by nature associated with the body, is attached to thee independent of thy will, and whatever the external circumfluent vortex whirls round, so that the intellectual power exempt from the things of fate can live pure and free by itself, doing what is just and accepting what happens and saying the truth: if thou wilt separate, I say, from this ruling faculty the things which are attached to it by the impressions of sense, and the things of time to come and of time that is past, and wilt make thyself like Empedocles' sphere,

All round, and in its joyous rest reposing;

and if thou shalt strive to live only what is really thy life, that is, the present—then thou wilt be able to pass that portion of life which remains for thee up to the time of thy death, free from perturbations, nobly, and obedient to thy own daemon (to the god that is within thee).

4. I have often wondered how it is that every man loves himself more than all the rest of men, but yet sets less value on his own opinion of himself than on the opinion of others. If then a god or a wise teacher should present himself to a man and bid him to think of nothing and to design nothing which he would not express as soon as he conceived it, he could not endure it even for a single day. So much more respect have we to what our neighbours shall think of us than to what we shall think of ourselves.

5. How can it be that the gods after having arranged all things well and benevolently for mankind, have overlooked this alone, that some men and very good men, and men who, as we may say, have had most communion with the divinity, and through pious acts and

religious observances have been most intimate with the divinity, when they have once died should never exist again, but should be completely extinguished?

But if this is so, be assured that if it ought to have been otherwise, the gods would have done it. For if it were just, it would also be possible; and if it were according to nature, nature would have had it so. But because it is not so, if in fact it is not so, be thou convinced that it ought not to have been so:—for thou seest even of thyself that in this inquiry thou art disputing with the deity; and we should not thus dispute with the gods, unless they were most excellent and most just;—but if this is so, they would not have allowed anything in the ordering of the universe to be neglected unjustly and irrationally.

6. Practise thyself even in the things which thou despairest of accomplishing. For even the left hand, which is ineffectual for all other things for want of practice, holds the bridle more vigorously than the right hand; for it has been practised in this.

7. Consider in what condition both in body and soul a man should be when he is overtaken by death; and consider the shortness of life, the boundless abyss of time past and future, the feebleness of all matter.

8. Contemplate the formative principles (forms) of things bare of their coverings; the purposes of actions; consider what pain is, what pleasure is, and death, and fame; who is to himself the cause of his uneasiness; how no man is hindered by another; that everything is opinion.

9. In the application of thy principles thou must be like the pancratiast, not like the gladiator; for the gladiator lets fall the sword which he uses and is killed; but the other always has his hand, and needs to do nothing else than use it.

10. See what things are in themselves, dividing them into matter, form and purpose.

11. What a power man has to do nothing except what God will approve, and to accept all that God may give him.

12. With respect to that which happens conformably to nature, we ought to blame neither gods, for they do nothing wrong either voluntarily or involuntarily, nor men, for they do nothing wrong except involuntarily. Consequently we should blame nobody.

13. How ridiculous and what a stranger he is who is surprised at anything which happens in life.

14. Either there is a fatal necessity and invincible order, or a kind Providence, or a confusion without a purpose and without a director (iv. 27). If then there is an invincible necessity, why dost thou resist? But if there is a Providence which allows itself to be propitiated, make thyself worthy of the help of the divinity. But if there is a confusion without a governor, be content that in such a tempest thou hast in thyself a certain ruling intelligence. And even if the tempest carry thee away, let it carry away the poor flesh, the poor breath, everything else; for the intelligence at least it will not carry away.

15. Does the light of the lamp shine without losing its splendour until it is extinguished; and shall the truth which is in thee and justice and temperance be extinguished before thy death?

16. When a man has presented the appearance of having done wrong, say, How then do I know if this is a wrongful act? And even if he has done wrong, how do I know that he has not condemned himself? and so this is like tearing his own face. Consider that he, who would not have the bad man do wrong, is like the man who would not have the fig-tree to bear juice in the figs and infants to cry and the horse to neigh, and whatever else must of necessity be. For what must a man do who has such a character? If then thou art irritable, cure this man's disposition.

17. If it is not right, do not do it: if it is not true, do not say it. For let thy efforts be—

18. In everything always observe what the thing is which produces for thee an appearance, and resolve it by dividing it into the formal, the material, the purpose, and the time within which it must end.

19. Perceive at last that thou hast in thee something better and more divine than the things which cause the various affects, and as it were pull thee by the strings. What is there now in my mind? Is it fear, or suspicion, or desire, or anything of the kind?

20. First, do nothing inconsiderately, nor

without a purpose. Second, make thy acts refer to nothing else than to a social end.

21. Consider that before long thou wilt be nobody and nowhere, nor will any of the things exist which thou now seest, nor any of those who are now living. For all things are formed by nature to change and be turned and to perish in order that other things in continuous succession may exist.

22. Consider that everything is opinion, and opinion is in thy power. Take away then, when thou choosest, thy opinion, and like a mariner, who has doubled the promontory, thou wilt find calm, everything stable, and a waveless bay.

23. Any one activity whatever it may be, when it has ceased at its proper time, suffers no evil because it has ceased; nor he who has done this act, does he suffer any evil for this reason that the act has ceased. In like manner then the whole which consists of all the acts, which is our life, if it cease at its proper time, suffers no evil for this reason that it has ceased; nor he who has terminated this series at the proper time, has he been ill dealt with. But the proper time and the limit nature fixes, sometimes as in old age the peculiar nature of man, but always the universal nature, by the change of whose parts the whole universe continues ever young and perfect. And everything which is useful to the universal is always good and in season. Therefore the termination of life for every man is no evil, because neither is it shameful, since it is both independent of the will and not opposed to the general interest, but it is good, since it is seasonable and profitable to and congruent with the universal. For thus too he is moved by the deity who is moved in the same manner with the deity and moved towards the same things in his mind.

24. These three principles thou must have in readiness. In the things which thou doest do nothing either inconsiderately or otherwise than as justice herself would act; but with respect to what may happen to thee from without, consider that it happens either by chance or according to Providence, and thou must neither blame chance nor accuse Providence. Second, consider what every being is from the seed to the time of its receiving a soul, and from the reception of a soul to the giving back of the same, and of what things every being is compounded and into what things it is resolved. Third, if thou shouldst suddenly be raised up above the earth, and shouldst look down on human things, and observe the variety of them how great it is, and at the same time also shouldst see at a glance how great is the number of beings who dwell all around in the air and the aether, consider that as often as thou shouldst be raised up, thou wouldst see the same things, sameness of form and shortness of duration. Are these things to be proud of?

25. Cast away opinion: thou art saved. Who then hinders thee from casting it away?

26. When thou art troubled about anything, thou hast forgotten this, that all things happen according to the universal nature; and forgotten this, that a man's wrongful act is nothing to thee; and further thou hast forgotten this, that everything which happens, always happened so and will happen so, and now happens so everywhere; forgotten this too, how close is the kinship between a man and the whole human race, for it is a community, not of a little blood or seed, but of intelligence. And thou hast forgotten this too, that every man's intelligence is a god, and is an efflux of the deity; and forgotten this, that nothing is a man's own, but that his child and his body and his very soul came from the deity; forgotten this, that everything is opinion; and lastly thou hast forgotten that every man lives the present time only, and loses only this.

27. Constantly bring to thy recollection those who have complained greatly about anything, those who have been most conspicuous by the greatest fame or misfortunes or enmities or fortunes of any kind: then think where are they all now? Smoke and ash and a tale, or not even a tale. And let there be present to thy mind also everything of this sort, how Fabius Catullinus lived in the country, and Lucius Lupus in his gardens, and Stertinius at Baiae, and Tiberius at Capreae and Velius Rufus (or Rufus at Velia); and in fine think of the eager pursuit of anything conjoined with pride; and how worthless everything is after which men violently strain; and how much more philosophical it is for a man in the opportunities

presented to him to show himself just, temperate, obedient to the gods, and to do this with all simplicity: for the pride which is proud of its want of pride is the most intolerable of all.

28. To those who ask, Where hast thou seen the gods or how dost thou comprehend that they exist and so worshipest them, I answer, in the first place, they may be seen even with the eyes;[1] in the second place neither have I seen even my own soul and yet I honour it. Thus then with respect to the gods, from what I constantly experience of their power, from this I comprehend that they exist and I venerate them.

29. The safety of life is this, to examine everything all through, what it is itself, what is its material, what the formal part; with all thy soul to do justice and to say the truth. What remains except to enjoy life by joining one good thing to another so as not to leave even the smallest intervals between?

30. There is one light of the sun, though it is interrupted by walls, mountains, and other things infinite. There is one common substance, though it is distributed among countless bodies which have their several qualities. There is one soul, though it is distributed among infinite natures and individual circumscriptions (or individuals). There is one intelligent soul, though it seems to be divided. Now in the things which have been mentioned all the other parts, such as those which are air and matter, are without sensation and have no fellowship: and yet even these parts the intelligent principle holds together and the gravitation towards the same. But intellect in a peculiar manner tends to that which is of the same kin, and combines with it, and the feeling for communion is not interrupted.

31. What dost thou wish? To continue to exist? Well, dost thou wish to have sensation? Movement? Growth? And then again to cease to grow? To use thy speech? To think? What is there of all these things which seems to thee worth desiring? But if it is easy to set little

value on all these things, turn to that which remains, which is to follow reason and God. But it is inconsistent with honouring reason and God to be troubled because by death a man will be deprived of the other things.

32. How small a part of the boundless and unfathomable time is assigned to every man? For it is very soon swallowed up in the eternal. And how small a part of the whole substance? And how small a part of the universal soul? And on what a small clod of the whole earth thou creepest? Reflecting on all this consider nothing to be great, except to act as thy nature leads thee, and to endure that which the common nature brings.

33. How does the ruling faculty make use of itself? For all lies in this. But everything else, whether it is in the power of thy will or not, is only lifeless ashes and smoke.

34. This reflection is most adapted to move us to contempt of death, that even those who think pleasure to be a good and pain an evil still have despised it.

35. The man to whom that only is good which comes in due season, and to whom it is the same thing whether he has done more or fewer acts conformable to right reason, and to whom it makes no difference whether he contemplates the world for a longer or a shorter time—for this man neither is death a terrible thing.

36. Man, thou hast been a citizen in this great state (the world): what difference does it make to thee whether for five years (or three)? For that which is comformable to the laws is just for all. Where is the hardship then, if no tyrant nor yet an unjust judge sends thee away from the state, but nature who brought thee into it? The same as if a praetor who has employed an actor dismisses him from the stage.—"But I have not finished the five acts, but only three of them."—Thou sayest well, but in life the three acts are the whole drama; for what shall be a complete drama is determined by him who was once the cause of its composition, and now of its dissolution: but thou art the cause of neither. Depart then satisfied, for he also who releases thee is satisfied.

[1] This probably refers to the Stoic belief that the celestial bodies were divine.

THE GREAT IDEAS, *Volumes 2 and 3*

<table>
<tr><td>••••••••••••••••••••••••••••••••••</td><td>FAMILY</td></tr>
<tr><td>ANGEL</td><td>FATE</td></tr>
<tr><td>ANIMAL</td><td>FORM</td></tr>
<tr><td>ARISTOCRACY</td><td>GOD</td></tr>
<tr><td>ART</td><td>GOOD AND EVIL</td></tr>
<tr><td>ASTRONOMY</td><td>GOVERNMENT</td></tr>
<tr><td>BEAUTY</td><td>HABIT</td></tr>
<tr><td>BEING</td><td>HAPPINESS</td></tr>
<tr><td>CAUSE</td><td>HISTORY</td></tr>
<tr><td>CHANCE</td><td>HONOR</td></tr>
<tr><td>CHANGE</td><td>HYPOTHESIS</td></tr>
<tr><td>CITIZEN</td><td>IDEA</td></tr>
<tr><td>CONSTITUTION</td><td>IMMORTALITY</td></tr>
<tr><td>COURAGE</td><td>INDUCTION</td></tr>
<tr><td>CUSTOM AND</td><td>INFINITY</td></tr>
<tr><td> CONVENTION</td><td>JUDGMENT</td></tr>
<tr><td>DEFINITION</td><td>JUSTICE</td></tr>
<tr><td>DEMOCRACY</td><td>KNOWLEDGE</td></tr>
<tr><td>DESIRE</td><td>LABOR</td></tr>
<tr><td>DIALECTIC</td><td>LANGUAGE</td></tr>
<tr><td>DUTY</td><td>LAW</td></tr>
<tr><td>EDUCATION</td><td>LIBERTY</td></tr>
<tr><td>ELEMENT</td><td>LIFE AND DEATH</td></tr>
<tr><td>EMOTION</td><td>LOGIC</td></tr>
<tr><td>ETERNITY</td><td>LOVE</td></tr>
<tr><td>EVOLUTION</td><td>MAN</td></tr>
<tr><td>EXPERIENCE</td><td>MATHEMATICS</td></tr>
</table>